Liberty, Order, and Justice

JUL   2006

James McClellan

Liberty, Order, and Justice

*An Introduction to the
Constitutional Principles of
American Government*

⊷⇒ THIRD EDITION ⇐⊷

James McClellan

LIBERTY FUND

Indianapolis

Third edition copyright © 2000 by Liberty Fund, Inc.
First and second editions (1989, 1991) published by James River Press
for the Center for Judicial Studies

Cover art courtesy of the Library of Congress

04	03	02	01	00	C	5	4	3	2	1
04					P	5	4	3	2	

Library of Congress Cataloging-in-Publication Data

McClellan, James, 1937–
Liberty, order, and justice: an introduction to the constitutional
principles of American government/James McClellan.
p. cm.
Originally published: Cumberland, Va.: James River Press, c1989.
Includes bibliographical references and index.
ISBN 0-86597-255-9 (hc: alk. paper)—ISBN 0-86597-256-7 (pb. alk. paper)
1. United States—Politics and government.
2. Constitutional history—United States.
I. Title.

JK274.M513 2000
342.73'029—dc21   99-046334

LIBERTY FUND, INC.
8335 Allison Pointe Trail, Suite 300
Indianapolis, Indiana 46250-1684

"Miracles do not cluster. Hold on to the Constitution of the United States of America and the republic for which it stands. — What has happened once in six thousand years may never happen again. Hold on to your Constitution, for if the American Constitution shall fail there will be anarchy throughout the world."

Daniel Webster

TO MY CHILDREN,
Graham, Susannah, Margaret, Duncan,
Angus, Douglas, and Darby,
and to the rising generation of American youth
in the hope that they too will enjoy the fruits
of limited constitutional government
bequeathed by our ancestors.

ABOUT THE AUTHOR

Prior to his appointment in 1999 as James Bryce Visiting Fellow in American Studies at the Institute of United States Studies of the University of London, James McClellan was Senior Resident Scholar at Liberty Fund, Inc. He holds a Ph.D. in Political Science from the University of Virginia and a J.D. from the University of Virginia School of Law. Dr. McClellan has served as the President of the Center for Judicial Studies and as John M. Olin Professor of Government at Claremont McKenna College. He has taught American Government and Constitutional Law at the University of Alabama, Emory University, and Hampden-Sydney College in Virginia. Dr. McClellan has also served as a member of the U.S. Senate staff, and from 1981 to 1983 was Chief Counsel and Staff Director of the Subcommittee on Separation of Powers of the Senate Committee on the Judiciary. His publications include *The Political Principles of Robert A. Taft* (co-author, 1967), *Joseph Story and the American Constitution* (1971, 1990), *The Federalist: A Student Edition* (co-editor, 1990), and *Debates in the Federal Convention of 1787 as Reported by James Madison* (co-editor, 1989).

Contents

Preface

Liberty, Order, and Justice represents a new and unique approach to the study of American government. It is based on the premise that in order to understand the dynamics of the American political system, the inquiring reader must first become familiar with the constitutional framework that shapes and controls the political process. In other words, the student of politics cannot fully understand what we call "the game of politics" unless that student first knows the rules of the game. This book, then, deals with the enduring principles and characteristics of the American political system, which serve as a guide for studying and understanding both the development of the American regime and its current operations.

The structure and behavior of our political parties provide a case in point. "Probably the most striking single characteristic of the Democratic and Republican parties," observed Austin Ranney and Willmoore Kendall in their classic work on *Democracy and the American Party System* (1956), "is their decentralization." This is what renders the American party system unique and distinguishes it from most parliamentary party organizations in the Western democracies. Except when they come together in a national convention every four years to nominate candidates for the offices of President and Vice President, neither the Democrat nor the Republican Party is in any meaningful way a national party. Each is really a coalition of State parties, and each State party is actually a confederation of semi-autonomous county and municipal parties, all having their own leadership, workers, and supporters. National conventions have little or no power, formal or actual, over State and local parties; and the numerous committees, caucuses, and officers that provide the formal structure of the Democrat and Republican parties are not, either in theory or practice, organized in a hierarchical or pyramidal arrangement with centripetal power flowing downward. No president or presidential candidate or central authority of any kind dictates policy or determines the makeup of the party's leadership in the American political system.

It is little wonder, therefore, that both of our major political parties are also factionalized, often lacking any unity of thought or direction. They both have their liberal and conservative wings, and to the consternation of many seem unable much of the time to agree among themselves on policies or candidates, or to present a united front to the electorate. Ideological purity is surely not one of the chief attributes of American political parties. The same, of course, cannot be said of the highly disciplined parties of the parliamentary democracies, whose elected officials invariably follow "the party line" and rarely cross over to vote with the opposition.

What explains these peculiarities of the American party system? The answer, in large part, lies in the Constitution—a constitution that does not even mention political parties or acknowledge their existence. Yet it is the case that our political parties often look and behave as they do because of our constitutional system. More specifically, the peculiar structural and behavioral pattern of party politics in the United States may be traced directly to the ubiquitous principle of limited government that shapes, permeates, and protects every article of the Constitution. It was fear of power, especially concentrated power, that motivated the Framers to draft a constitution that limits power by fragmenting, dispersing, and counterbalancing it. One of the first foreign observers to understand all of this was James Bryce, a Scottish diplomat and scholar, who noted in his famous commentaries, *The American Commonwealth* (1888), that "the want of concentration of power in the legal government is reflected in the structure of the party system."

At a more fundamental level, the Constitution reflects the intent of the Framers to make it difficult, if not impossible, for any single interest group, including one representing a popular majority, to gain absolute power over the whole nation and impose its will at the expense of other interests or groups. The political regime established by the Constitution is therefore decentralized, and nowhere in the system is there a single locus of concentrated power. Hence it is the federal structure of our Constitution, which divides power between the national and State governments, that best explains why each party is a loose confederation of State and local parties rather than a unitary organization of one central party. Federalism produces a highly decentralized political system encompassing a broad range of sectional, cultural, and economic differences. Our political parties, built upon a federal structure, are a reflection of that diversity.

A knowledge of the federal features of the Constitution, in other words, and an appreciation of how the federal principle influences the political process, give us greater insight into the programs and policies of our parties, while at the same time providing a standard by which to judge their compatibility with the constitutional design. Simply put, the enterprising student who wishes to acquire a solid understanding of the American party system is sure to fall woefully short of expectation if the student disregards or ignores the constitutional environment in which the parties function.

Liberty, Order, and Justice, it may thus be seen, attempts to prepare the reader for the study of American politics by focusing attention on the constitutional superstructure. In this regard, it is quite unlike other introductory texts. The book introduces not only the general design of the system but, more important, seeks to explain how and why it functions as it does. It deals with timeless principles that have shaped our political institutions and procedures—and will continue to do so as long as we live under the Constitution of 1787. The book does not attempt to cover the entire field of American political activity. There is little or no discussion of politics, parties, and pressure groups, current civil rights disputes, foreign or domestic policy, or State and local government. Nor is a considerable amount of attention given to the organization of the legislative, executive, and judicial branches and their special powers and procedures. The reader will not find in these pages, for example, the steps of the lawmaking process showing how a bill becomes a law. All of this is important to know in due course, but it is beyond the scope and purpose of this book.

The book's purpose, rather, is to deepen our understanding and appreciation of the basic principles of the American political system. In particular, this book seeks to explain how and why the Constitution limits power, particularly through the uniquely American doctrines of federalism and separation of powers. The reader will also learn here the meaning and importance of constitutionalism and rule of law, and the general principles of constitutional interpretation that guide, or should guide, governmental officials when they examine and apply the law in the light of the Constitution.

Moreover, this book emphasizes the importance of knowing the origin and development of these basic principles. The American Constitution is original in many respects, but it is also a product of Western man's endless quest for liberty, order, and justice. The founders of the American republic did not suddenly invent the American Constitution overnight. Learning from the mistakes of the past, they revised and applied constitutional concepts deeply rooted in America's colonial past, the history of Great Britain, and the chronicles of the ancient world. By understanding the mistakes of the past, of course, we improve our chances of not repeating them in the future. There is no doubt that many of the changes that have been proposed over the years to amend or "reform" the American political system would never have been seriously considered had the reformers been aware that their "improvement" undermined the genius of the Constitution or had been tried before and had proved to be a failure. The inclusion in this book of numerous legal and historical documents will, it is hoped, help the reader comprehend the evolution of the American republic and the political experiences of our ancestors that ultimately produced the Constitution.

Above all, *Liberty, Order, and Justice,* as the subtitle suggests, stresses the value and importance of *constitutional* government. It rests on the age-old assumption that in order to achieve liberty, order, and justice, we must first establish limited constitutional government. The Framers of our Constitution understood well enough that political power can be a destructive as well as a creative force, and that our safety and welfare depend upon our ability to check and balance power. Too much political power can be as dangerous as too little, no matter how well intentioned the claim to power may be. Good government is not feeble government, but neither is it unlimited government. These distinctions are sometimes lost or forgotten by those who put their favorite political programs and policies ahead of the Constitution, and act as though the end justifies the means. These lessons and more, it is hoped, greet the reader who ventures forth to read this primer.

James McClellan
Goshen Farm
Cumberland, Virginia

Liberty, Order, and Justice

PART 1

The Constitution's Deep Roots

1. The American Constitution is an *evolutionary* rather than a revolutionary document. Though written in a revolutionary age, it embraces ideas and principles developed through trial and error that grew out of our colonial experience. Constitutional and legal development in England and the political history of the Greek and Roman republics also influenced the thinking of the Framers.

2. Three important political concepts drawn by the Americans from the Roman experience were the doctrines of republicanism, political virtue, and checks and balances. But it is the English Constitution, including the English charters of liberty and the English legal system, that had the greatest impact on American constitutional development. Representative government, a tradition of well-established civil liberties, and the heritage of the common law are three important political and legal institutions of England that Americans adopted in framing their own constitutions. Certain features of the English Constitution were rejected by the Americans, however, including the monarchy and the principle of legislative supremacy. The American Constitution therefore represents a blending of English and American constitutional traditions.

3. The Framers of the American Constitution had learned from ancient and from British history that republics, like other forms of government, are vulnerable to corruption, and that legislative bodies as well as courts of law can be just as much a threat to liberty as all-powerful monarchs. For this reason they did not place all their trust in any one branch of government, and they established checks on the powers of each.

1

The Meaning of Constitutional Government

Two CENTURIES AGO, fifty-five men met at Philadelphia to draw up a constitution for the United States of America. The thirteen States that once had been British colonies urgently needed a more reliable general government, a better common defense against foreign powers, a sounder currency, and other advantages that might be gained through establishing "a more perfect union" founded on a solemn agreement, or fundamental law, called a constitution.

Today, the fundamental law of the United States of America still is that Constitution of 1787, a written document which is respected and obeyed almost as if it were a living thing. This book examines that Constitution, inquiring how it was developed, what its provisions mean, why it has functioned so well, and how it affects everybody's life in America today.

What do we mean by this word *constitution*? As a term of politics, *constitution* signifies a system of fundamental principles—a body of basic laws—for governing a state or country. A constitution is *a design for a permanent political order.*

A constitution does its work through what is known as the rule of law: that is, people respect and obey laws, rather than follow their own whims or yield to the force of somebody else. Every country develops a constitution of some sort, because without a regular pattern of basic law, a people could not live together in peace. Lacking a tolerable constitution, they never would know personal safety, or protection of their property, or any reasonable freedom. Even savage tribes may be said to be governed by "constitutional" customs of a simple nature.

The most widely admired of all constitutions is the United States Constitution. It was written in 1787 and took effect in 1789. It was, and is, rooted in the experience and the thought of many generations of people. This is a major reason why the American Constitution still flourishes in our day. Like some great tree, the Constitution of the United States is anchored and nurtured by roots that run deep into the soil of human experience. Those constitutional roots are the political institutions, the laws, the social customs, and the political and moral beliefs of earlier ages and other lands.

Nowadays we tend to think of a constitution as a written document, but actually constitutions may be partly or even wholly unwritten. These unwritten constitutions are not based on a single document but are made up of old customs, conventions, statutes, charters, and habits in public affairs. The British Constitution is an example of this sort of basic body of laws. Until the Constitution of the United States was agreed upon in Philadelphia, all national constitutions were "unwritten" and informal. A few years after the American Constitution was drawn up, written constitutions were adopted in Poland and France. Even the American Constitution is not entirely set down upon paper, however.

For it has been said that every country possesses two distinct constitutions that exist side by side. One of these is the formal written constitution of modern times; the other is the old "unwritten" one of political conventions, habits, and ways of living together in the civil social order that have developed among a people over many centuries. Thus, for instance, certain important features of America's political structure are not even mentioned in the written Constitution of 1787. For example, what does the written Constitution of the United States say about political parties? The answer is—nothing. Yet political parties direct the course of our national affairs. What does our written Constitution say about the President's cabinet, with its secretaries of state, of the treasury, agriculture, defense, education, and the like? The answer again is nothing; yet the President could not function without a cabinet.

So it is possible to speak of a "visible" and an "invisible" constitution, and of a "written" and an "unwritten" constitution. In this book we are concerned principally with the written Constitution of the United States, although from time to time we will refer also to aspects of our basic political system that have not been set down in writing.

A constitution is an effort to impose order for the achievement of certain ends. Those ends are often set forth in a preamble to the document, as in the American Constitution, which states that the "People of the United States" have established the Constitution "to form a more perfect union, establish justice, ensure domestic Tranquility, provide for the common defense, promote the general Welfare, and secure the Blessings of Liberty to ourselves and our Posterity."

Liberty, order, and justice, it may thus be seen, are the primary objectives of the American political system. They are probably the most important and all-embracing of the many goals we pursue as a nation. The significance of liberty, order, and justice is reflected in other constitutions as well. Thus the constitution of the Republic of Korea (1980) asserts that its purpose is "to consolidate national unity with justice," "destroy all social vices and injustice," "afford equal opportunities," and "strengthen the basic free and democratic order." Portugal's constitution (1974) seeks to "safeguard the fundamental rights of citizens," "secure the primacy of rule of law," and build a "freer, more just" country. The constitution of Venezuela (1972) states that its purpose is to ensure "the freedom, peace, and stability of its institutions," and to provide for "social justice" and support of "the democratic order." Inspired by the nobility of purpose stated in the American Constitution, the preamble to Argentina's constitution of 1853 claims that the fundamental law of this South American republic aims toward "ensuring justice, preserving the domestic peace, providing for the common defense, promoting the general welfare, [and] securing the blessings of liberty to ourselves, to our posterity. . . ."

Liberty, order, and justice are all made possible by sound constitutions; but a constitution is only a "parchment barrier," and even a well-conceived constitution will fall short of its goals if the people fail to support it. Many of the Framers of the American Constitution were of the opinion that constitutional government requires, above all, a "virtuous" citizenry if it is to endure. Certainly a constitution cannot last if it is willfully ignored, or if there is no common understanding among the citizens and their elected leaders as to what the achievement of liberty, order, and justice requires.

What did the Framers mean, then, when they dedicated themselves and their fellow countrymen to the pursuit of these ideals? Let us briefly define these important terms as they have been traditionally understood: *liberty* (or freedom) means the absence of coercion or force, or the ability of an individual to be a thinking and valuing person and to carry out his own plans instead of being subject to the arbitrary will of another. *Order* means the arrangement of duties and rights in a society so that people may live together in peace and harmony. By ordered freedom we mean individual freedom that recognizes the need to limit freedom in some respects and rejects the notion that the individual should have absolute freedom to do as he or she pleases irrespective of the rights of others. Without the restraint of law and order, freedom cannot exist. *Justice* means the securing to persons of the things that rightfully belong to them, and the rewarding of persons according to what they have earned or deserve. Equality of opportunity and equality before the law are normally regarded as attributes of justice in a free society, as distinguished from equality of result or condition, which must be imposed by coercion.

To understand liberty, order, and justice, think of their opposites: slavery, disorder, and injustice. The aim of a good constitution is to enable a society to have a high degree of liberty, order, and justice. No country has ever attained *perfect* freedom, order, and justice for everyone, and presumably no country ever will. This is because human beings and human societies are both very imperfect. The Framers of the Constitution of the United States did not expect to achieve perfection of either human nature or government. What they did expect was "to form a more perfect union" and to surpass the other nations of their era, and of earlier eras, in establishing a good political order.

Over the centuries, constitutions have come into existence in a variety of ways. They have been decreed by a king; they have been proclaimed by conquerors and tyrants; they have been given to a people by religious prophets such as Moses, who gave the Ten Commandments and laws to the Israelites; they have been designed by a single wise man such as Solon, who gave a new constitution to the people of Athens in ancient Greece six centuries before Christ. Other constitutions have grown out of the decisions of judges and popular custom, such as the English "common law." Or, constitutions can be agreed upon by a gathering called a *convention*. The constitutions that have been accepted willingly by the large majority of a people have generally been the constitutions which have endured the longest.

But because people are restless and quarrelsome, few constitutions have lasted for very long. Nearly all of those that were adopted in Europe after the First World War had collapsed by the end of the Second World War a quarter of a century later; many of the newer constitutions proclaimed in Europe, Asia, and Africa not long after the Second World War ended in 1945 have already have been tossed aside or else do not really function anymore. There are today more than one hundred national constitutions in force throughout the world. Nearly all of them were written and adopted after the Second World War. The oldest and most respected constitution is the Constitution of England. It dates back to the beginning of the thirteenth century.

Much of the written Constitution of the United States is derived from the "unwritten" English Constitution—or, to be more precise, from the English Constitution as it stood during the latter half of the eighteenth century. For England's constitution developed and changed over the centuries. By 1774, when the American struggle for independence began, the fundamental laws of England were very different from what they had been in 1215, the year when King John accepted the constitutional document known as the Magna Charta. All good constitutions change over the years because the circumstances of a nation change. As the great parliamentary leader Edmund Burke put this in the eighteenth century, "Change is the means of our preservation." But good constitutions also contain many provisions that are permanent. These are principles and rules of law that help prevent rash or hasty changes which might work mischief. Unlike the English Constitution, which can be changed by a mere statute of Parliament, the American Constitution can be formally changed only when a large majority of the people, through their States, approve an "amendment."

The American Constitution is like the English Constitution in another way. Both are based on the principle that liberty, order, and justice are difficult to achieve and must be preserved through fundamental laws that should be respected and not easily cast aside to serve a temporary expedient or to satisfy the whims of a transient majority that is here today and gone tomorrow.

What is a good constitution supposed to accomplish besides protecting liberty, order, and justice? We may set down below four primary characteristics of a good constitution.

First, a good constitution should provide for stability and continuity in the governing of a country. The subjects or citizens of a political state should be assured by their constitution that the administering of the laws and of major public policies will not change continuously from one day or year to another day or year. What was lawful yesterday must not suddenly be declared unlawful tomorrow unless through a formal amendment to the Constitution. People must be able to live their lives according to certain well-known rules. A good constitution also helps a country to achieve economic prosperity. When a country's constitution does not guarantee stability and continuity, no man or woman can plan for the future. When we make decisions, it is important that we know with reasonable certainty what the consequences will be.

Second, a constitution should restrain government from assuming powers that rightfully belong to other political entities or to families or individuals. This can be accomplished by limiting and dividing power. A wise constitution may allocate certain powers to a central government and other powers to regional or local governments; or it may assign certain functions and prerogatives to each of the major branches of government—the executive, the legislative, the judicial. Certainly a prudent constitution will provide safeguards against arbitrary and unjust actions by persons who hold power.

Third, a constitution should establish a permanent arrangement that enables public officials and others with political authority to represent the people they govern. To put this another way, with a good constitutional order the people ought not to be ruled by a group or class of persons quite different from themselves who do not have at heart the best interests of the majority of the people. This does not necessarily mean that a constitutional government has to be totally democratic. It also does not mean that a good constitution must necessarily provide for "one man, one vote." There have been decent constitutional systems that were monarchical, or aristocratic, or under which the right to vote was limited.

Fourth, a good constitution holds public officials directly accountable to the people. This means that the governing class or public officials must be held responsible—under the constitution—for the actions they take while in public office. Under a truly constitutional government, no man or woman can be permitted to exercise arbitrary power—that is, to disregard laws or popular rights whenever it is thought convenient to do so. All officials must be held accountable to established authorities such as the courts of law, to the legislature, and to the voting public, and should not be allowed to exempt themselves from the laws they enact. Public officials should also be held accountable to fiscal inspectors, and should be subject to removal from office through impeachment for "high crimes or misdemeanors," such as the abuse of power or the misuse of public funds.

Various other characteristics of a sound constitutional system might be named. The four above are particularly important, however, and are now found in one form or another in the constitution of every country that enjoys a high degree of liberty, order, and justice.

These characteristics of a good constitution help us to recognize what can and cannot be achieved through constitutions.

A good constitution, in the first place, ought not to incorporate detailed regulations to cover every contingency. On the contrary, the constitution should be concerned with first principles of government; it should not be an endeavor to provide rules of administration for a multitude of concerns. The longer a constitution is, the fewer people will read it, and the harder it will become to distinguish its major provisions from details of relatively small importance. Respect for a constitution will be diminished if it becomes an entire code of laws dealing with every conceivable subject.

Second, a written constitution ought not to conflict with the "invisible constitution" or long-established patterns of institutions, customs, and beliefs that have strongly influenced a country's politics for many generations. A constitution invented by radicals, one deliberately designed to break down a people's traditional ways, must meet with strong resistance or evasion. The framers of a constitution ought to understand the political traditions of their time and country. A good constitution, in other words, should conform to the character, habits, and mores of the people who will live under it. Because civilizations differ, a constitution that is suitable for one country may be unsuitable for another. It would be unrealistic, for example, to suppose that the entire American Constitution can be exported to foreign nations. A country without a strong democratic tradition of self-government and a well-educated population may also have difficulty preserving a constitution, particularly if that constitution presupposes a level of political understanding and maturity to which the people have not risen. For merely creating an idealistic paper constitution will not bring about substantial improvement in liberty, order, or justice. The "paper constitutions" of many new African states that were proclaimed during the 1950s and 1960s collapsed altogether within a very few years.

Third, a good constitution should be neither easy to alter nor impossible to amend. This is because, on the one hand, a constitution is meant to be permanent and to assure a people that the political pattern of their country will not drastically change. On the other hand, the word *permanent* does not mean *eternal*. It is simply not possible for people who are living near the end of the twentieth century to draft an unalterable constitution for their great-grandchildren who will be living in a century to come.

This is true because, in the course of a century or two centuries, there may occur significant political, economic, technological, military, or even physical changes in the circumstances of a nation. Therefore a good constitution must be elastic enough to allow for modification of certain of its provisions without the need to abolish the whole constitution.

This understanding of what a constitution should do and cannot do is derived chiefly from the success of the Constitution of the United States. "The American Constitution is the most wonderful work ever struck off at a given time by the brain and purpose of man," wrote William Gladstone, an English statesman, in 1878. That may seem to be extravagant praise. But surely no body of men has ever achieved a political result more ennobling and more enduring than that which the Framers of the Constitution produced in the summer of 1787.

The following sections of this book explain the historic roots of the American Constitution, the events of the "Great Convention" of 1787, the major political principles of the Constitution, why the Bill of Rights was added to the original articles of the Constitution, the process of ratification, the meaning of the document's important provisions, how they are to be interpreted, and how they may be changed.

Presumably, nearly all the people who read this book will continue to live under the protection of the Constitution of the United States, so they may find it worthwhile to understand just what the Constitution does, and how it influences their lives, their family, their community, and their nation.

The Lamp of Experience

The Articles of Confederation, America's first national constitution, were hastily drafted in 1776 amidst the turmoil of the American Revolution. Because of disagreements among the States, ratification was slow in coming. In fact, the Articles did not actually go into effect until 1781. By 1787 there was widespread agreement throughout the country that the Articles had proved to be unsatisfactory and that it was therefore necessary to change them substantially, or possibly to abandon them altogether and write a new constitution. In the end, as we shall see, the latter view prevailed. The members of the Federal (or "Philadelphia") Convention who met in Philadelphia in 1787 to "revise" the Articles soon came to the conclusion that the defects were so fundamental that a mere revision would not be practical.

One delegate to the Federal Convention who argued strenuously for a new constitution, and then later led the fight for ratification of the one that was finally drafted, was Alexander Hamilton of New York. After the Convention completed its work on September 17, 1787, Hamilton, joined by John Jay of New York and James Madison of Virginia, wrote a series of essays called *The Federalist.* Written for New York newspapers, and later distributed in other States, the essays in *The Federalist* urged the people to support the new Constitution and attempted to explain why it was preferable to the Articles of Confederation. Seeking to present themselves as neutral observers, the authors of *The Federalist* concealed their identity and wrote under the name of "Publius." Most other writers, whether favoring or opposing the Constitution, did the same. In New York, for example, one of the most effective critics of the new Constitution was an anonymous writer named "Brutus." From New Hampshire to Georgia a great "war of pamphlets" erupted in the struggle over ratification of the Constitution. Those favoring adoption called themselves "Federalists," and those opposing ratification were dubbed "Anti-Federalists." From their very inception, the 85 essays in *The Federalist,* or what are commonly known as *The Federalist Papers,* were immediately recognized as superior to other writings on the Constitution produced during the ratification struggle. Taken together, they constituted a brilliant exposition of the entire Constitution—profound, insightful, and instructive. To this day, *The*

THE

FEDERALIST;

A COLLECTION

O F

ESSAYS,

WRITTEN IN FAVOUR OF THE

NEW CONSTITUTION,

AS AGREED UPON BY THE FEDERAL CONVENTION,
SEPTEMBER 17, 1787.

IN TWO VOLUMES.

VOL. I.

NEW-YORK:

PRINTED AND SOLD BY J. AND A. M'LEAN,
No. 41, HANOVER-SQUARE.
M,DCC,LXXXVIII.

The Federalist.

The first printing of *The Federalist* in book form in 1788. The essays originally appeared in four New York City newspapers and were later carried in a few newspapers and periodicals in Pennsylvania, Virginia (owing to the efforts of George Washington), and some of the New England States. The *New-York Journal*, an anti-Federalist newspaper, ceased publication of the essays after readers complained that the publisher was "cramming us with the voluminous PUBLIUS," which has "become nauseous." Madison later recalled "the haste with which many of the papers were penned"—four numbers every week—"in order to get thro the subject whilst the Constitution was before the public." (Courtesy of Corbis-Bettmann.)

Federalist is universally acknowledged as an American classic, as an indispensable source for an understanding and appreciation of the original meaning and purpose of almost every provision of the Constitution. To his lasting fame and credit, it was Alexander Hamilton who organized the collective effort to publish *The Federalist* and wrote most of the essays.

Speaking for most of the delegates who attended the Philadelphia Convention, and certainly for many of his countrymen as well, Hamilton confronted the basic dilemma Americans faced in 1787. The Articles of Confederation, he wrote in *Federalist* No. 15, were an invitation to disaster. "We may indeed with propriety be said to have reached almost the last stage of national humiliation," wrote Hamilton. Something must be done, he said, "to rescue us from impending anarchy." The nation was steeped in debt to foreigners and its own citizens; valuable American territories were still in the possession of Great Britain; there were no troops or funds to repel invaders; access to the Mississippi River was impeded by Spain; commerce had declined to its lowest point. So great was "the imbecility of our government," he complained, that foreign governments would not even deal with it. "The evils we experience," Hamilton concluded, "do not proceed from minute or partial imperfections, but from fundamental errors in the structure of the building, which cannot be amended otherwise than by an alteration in the first principles and main pillars of the fabric."

It was on this basis that the Framers proceeded to construct a new framework of government, casting aside the Articles of Confederation and building a new edifice, from the ground up, on "first principles." But they did not have to begin from scratch. Before we explore the meaning and substance of those "first principles," and seek to discover how and why they were incorporated into the Constitution, it is essential that we first examine their origin and historical development. "Not to know what happened before one was born," as we were reminded long ago by Cicero, the great Roman statesman, "is always to be a child." American political leaders were hardly ignorant or contemptuous of the past. The Framers respected the wisdom of their ancestors, especially their religious learning. They had been reared on the King James version of the Bible, and at least half of them—being Episcopalians—were well acquainted with the Book of Common Prayer. They also respected the lessons of history and were strongly influenced by historical, legal, and constitutional precedents, both foreign and domestic. They had read a good deal of law and history. They knew something of political philosophy, that great body of learning that seeks to know and understand the first principles of government, and what it takes to establish good government and promote the common good or "general welfare."

But they were not alienated closet-philosophers trying to found a perfect society or utopian paradise, for they were keenly aware of man's imperfections as well as his strengths. Almost to a man, the Framers were aware of the intricate process by which human beings had learned to live together, at least in some places and at certain times, in freedom, order, and justice. Those who forget the mistakes of the past, it has been said, are bound to repeat them. The Framers knew of the many mistakes that had been made in the governing of great nations. Above all, they knew the benefits enjoyed in a society in which the claims of authority and the claims of freedom were maintained in a healthy balance. "Power corrupts," said Lord Acton, the nineteenth-century British political thinker, "and absolute power corrupts absolutely." The men who wrote the American Constitution would have agreed, but they would have also added: "Yes, but absolute liberty can also corrupt a nation. There is no freedom in anarchy."

"I have but one lamp by which my feet are guided," the fiery patriot leader Patrick Henry told his fellow planters of Virginia in 1775, "and that is the lamp of experience. I know of no way of judging the future but by the past." The confidence and trust expressed by American political leaders in the political principles they applied in making the Constitution and evaluating its merits stemmed not from rootless theories and ideals divorced from experience and reality, but from the conviction that these principles were tried and true—the result of trial and error spanning centuries of political conflict. This was true of both Patrick Henry, the Anti-Federalist leader who opposed the Constitution, and Alexander Hamilton, the Federalist leader who favored it. What divided these gentlemen in 1787, as we shall later learn, was not so much a disagreement over first principles as a difference of opinion over whether those principles had been given proper weight and correctly adapted to the American situation.

Patrick Henry (1736–1799).

Engraving, 1896. (Courtesy of Corbis-Bettmann.)

The Constitutions of Antiquity

What had the Framers learned about the art of government in 1787? In the first place, it must be kept in mind that the leaders of the founding generation were steeped in classical learning. The study of Greek and

Latin literature, and of the ancient world's history and politics, loomed much larger in American education during the latter half of the eighteenth century than it does in American education today. Indeed, the classical past was a dynamic force in American public life well into the nineteenth century. The last President of the United States with a truly classical education was probably John Quincy Adams, the son of the second President, John Adams. John Quincy Adams even taught the classics at Harvard as a Professor of Rhetoric and Oratory and in 1810 published his lectures on this subject. His administration (1825–1829) marks a turning point respecting the classical influence, however, and after the Jacksonian era few Presidents have been well read in the classics. None was a classicist in the sense that the Adamses and Jefferson were, and certainly none was portrayed, like George Washington in a famous statue by Horateo Greenough, in the character of a Roman senator—nude to the waist, with uplifted arm, draped by a toga, pointing to the heavens. Few statesmen understood, as the Revolutionary and Federal generations had, that classical history had much to teach the nation. Perhaps the last conspicuous surviving remnants of America's classical tradition in the first half of the nineteenth century were in architecture, which experienced a Greek revival, as seen in the construction and design of great plantation houses in the South; and in oratory, as witnessed in the great senatorial debates and public addresses by John Randolph of Roanoke, John C. Calhoun, Henry Clay, and the most celebrated Ciceronian orator Daniel Webster.

Most of the Framers had read, in translation or in the original Greek and Latin, such ancient authors as Herodotus, Thucydides, Plato, Aristotle, Polybius, Cicero, Livy, and Plutarch—philosophers and historians who described the constitutions of the Greek and Roman civilizations. From their study, the American leaders of the War of Independence and the constitution-making era learned, by their own account, what political blunders of ancient times ought to be avoided by the republic of the United States. "History," Thomas Jefferson wrote, "informs us what bad government is." Perhaps he had the ancient republics in mind when he wrote those words.

The Greek city-states of the sixth and fifth and fourth centuries before Christ never succeeded in developing enduring constitutions that would give them liberty, order, and justice. Civil war within those city-states was the rule rather than the exception, pitting class against class, family against family, faction against faction. And when half of those cities went to war against the other half, in the ruinous Peloponnesian struggle— during the last three decades of the fifth century—Greek civilization never wholly recovered from the disaster.

Leading Americans carefully studied the old Greek constitutions. In his *Defence of the Constitutions of Government of the United States* (published in 1787, on the eve of America's Great Convention), John Adams, for example, critically examined twelve ancient democratic republics, three ancient aristocratic republics, and three ancient monarchical republics. He found them all inferior to the political system of the new American republics in the several States that were formed after 1776. James Monroe, a hero of the American Revolution, a member of the Virginia Ratifying Convention of 1788, and later the fifth President of the United States, wrote descriptions of the ancient constitutions of Athens, Sparta, and Carthage—finding all of them seriously flawed and therefore not to be trusted by Americans. The authors of *The Federalist,* in their defense of the Constitution, often referred to "the turbulent democracies of ancient Greece" (Madison's phrase) and to other ancient constitutions. In general, Hamilton, Madison, and Jay found the political systems of Greece and Rome, as Madison put it, "as unfit for the imitation, as they are repugnant to the genius of America."

Eighteenth-century Americans did respect Solon, the lawgiver of Athens in the sixth century B.C. But Solon's good constitution for his native city had lasted only some thirty years before a tyrant seized power in Athens. Few American leaders were much influenced by Greek political thought; John Adams wrote that he had learned from Plato two things only, that husbandmen and artisans should not be exempted from military service, and that hiccoughing may cure sneezing. It is true that ancient Greek culture helped to shape education in America, but Greek constitutions had almost no influence in the shaping of the Constitution of the United States—except so far as Greek constitutional flaws suggested what the Framers at Philadelphia ought not to adopt.

There is, nevertheless, much to learn about constitutions from reading Plato and Aristotle. Both of these ancient Greek philosophers wrote about monarchical, aristocratic, and democratic constitutions, about oligarchies and democracies, about tyrannies and kingships, about the origin and nature of government, and about the *polity*—that regime described by Aristotle as essentially a limited democracy blending the monarchical, aristocratic, and democratic elements of government, in which the greatest political power is exercised by landholders. This was the dream of Greek democracy, but it was not exactly the model the Americans wished to apply to the infant Republic of the United States. This was because Greek politics in ancient times was the politics primarily of "city-states"— compact in territory, very limited in population, and quite unlike the thirteen original States that formed the United States. Also, in the Greek democracies the entire body of male citizens was able to assemble in a forum to make public decisions of the gravest sort—sometimes foolish decisions with ghastly consequences. The United States in 1787, by comparison, was a vast expanse of territory in which there were few cities. Direct democracy of the Greek sort, where the people gathered to represent themselves, would not have been practical, or even possible, in the American republic. Indeed, the sheer size of the United States was almost overwhelming. From north to south the new nation spanned almost twelve hundred miles, and to the west—from the Atlantic Ocean to the Mississippi River—the distance was about six hundred miles. The Greek city-states were mere specks on the map in comparison with almost any of the American states, and England itself could have just about fit within the State of New York. Although there were fewer than four million inhabitants in the thirteen States, the United States in 1787 was already one of the largest nations in the Western world.

The Roman Republic was taken much more seriously by leading Americans in the 1780s. American boys at any decent school in the eighteenth century studied the orations and the life of Marcus Tullius Cicero, the defender of the Roman Republic in its last years. And they read Plutarch's *Lives of the Most Noble Grecians and Romans*, which taught them the characteristics and qualities of great statesmen. A classical education was considered essential for all young men, and the better academies for young women also provided classical learning.

The vocabulary of American political culture also reflected the influence of America's classical heritage. The English word *constitution* is derived from the Latin *constitutio,* meaning a collection of laws or ordinances made by a Roman emperor. Among other terms, *president* and *federalism* have roots in Roman history; and the Roman term *Senate* was applied by the Framers of the American Constitution to the more select house of the legislative branch of their federal government, although the method of selecting senators in America was to be very different from what it had been in Rome. Hamilton, Jay, and Madison, the authors of *The Federalist,* wrote in the name of *Publius,* a reference to Publius Valerius Publicola, the ancient Roman famous for his defense of the Roman Republic.

Three important political concepts drawn by the Americans from the Roman experience were the doctrines of republicanism, political virtue, and checks and balances. Though theoretically a republic would be any form of government other than a monarchy, it was generally understood by Americans to mean a government in which the people were sovereign. In a small New England town they might rule directly, but on a larger scale the people would have to rule indirectly, through their freely chosen representatives. Advocacy of this form of government in the eighteenth century was a radical idea, and many European thinkers, having grown accustomed to monarchy, looked upon republicanism as a foolish and unworkable relic of the past. Republics might be suitable for a Greek city-state or Swiss canton, but they were too unstable for governing anything larger. The internal collapse of the Roman Republic under the weight of corruption and disorder, resulting in tyranny and the eventual destruction of the nation, seemed to prove the point. In fact, corruption had subverted and toppled almost every republic that had ever existed.

American leaders nevertheless believed that republicanism offered the only hope for preserving liberty, and that republicanism could successfully be revived if the mistakes of the past were understood and not repeated. This goal was within reach, they thought, if a republic could be designed which encouraged public virtue, the animating principle of republican government, and discouraged corruption, the characteristic republican disease. Many of the books that Americans read—Charles Montesquieu's *Considerations on the Grandeur of the Romans and Their Decline,* James Harrington's *Oceana* (an imaginary commonwealth), the writings of Algernon Sidney, Thomas Gordon's *Cato's Letters* and his translations of Roman historians—emphasized the threat of corruption and provided object lessons on how it might be avoided.

Above all, the Americans valued republican virtue, and the American leader who prized it the most was George Washington. In his own lifetime, Washington came to symbolize republican virtue. The story popularized by Parson Weems that Washington could not "tell a lie" when he was once accused of chopping down a cherry tree was a myth; and yet there was an element of truth in it, for Washington was a true public servant whose honesty and integrity were above reproach. Had he been a lesser man, hungry for power and glory, he might have exploited his enormous popularity among the American people to crown himself king or establish a military dictatorship, as Napoleon Bonaparte did in France. But Washington patterned his conduct in war and politics on that of Cincinnatus, the great Roman patriot and statesman who never sought power for himself, who answered Rome's call when he was needed and returned to the plow when the crisis had passed. After the Revolution, Washington's example, the general appeal of Cincinnatus, and the patriotic zeal of American revolutionary war leaders inspired the creation of the Society of the Cincinnati, an organization for officers of the Continental Army. Some politicians expressed concern when the Society first came into existence that it might be part of a military conspiracy to overthrow the government, but Washington's well-known hostility toward such ideas soon put these fears to rest. The Society still exists as a living memorial to the patriotism of the American revolutionary soldier and as a continuing reminder that the spirit of republican virtue, as represented by the life and career of Cincinnatus, guided Washington and other American leaders in their struggle for freedom.

For the delegates at Philadelphia, the most interesting feature of the Roman Republican constitution was its system of checks upon the power of men in public authority, and its balancing of power among different public offices. The Americans learned of these devices from the *History* by Polybius, a Greek statesman compelled to live long in Rome. The two Roman consuls, or executive; the Roman Senate, made up of rich and powerful men who had served in several important offices before being made senators; the Roman assembly, or gathering of the common people—these three bodies exercised separate powers. And the Roman con-

Apotheosis of Washington, 1802

The central figure in this allegory is George Washington, whose virtues, accomplishments, and immortality were thought to be those of America. Assisted by Father Time, the spiritual and temporal Genius, and by Immortality, he rises from the tomb. At his feet is America, holding a staff supporting the Cap of Liberty and weeping over his armor. An Indian is crouched in sorrow. The Christian symbols of Faith, Hope, and Charity appear in the background. In addition to national, classical, and Christian references are two personal items relating to Washington's life—medals of the Order of Freemasons and the Society of the Cincinnati.

This engraving by James John Barralet was the culmination of the eighteenth-century image of Washington. Beloved, if not worshipped, by his countrymen, George Washington is universally regarded as one of the greatest men who ever lived. (Courtesy of the Library of Congress.)

stitution (an "unwritten" one) included other provisions for preventing any one class from putting down other classes, and for preserving the republican form of government. Praised by Polybius as the best constitution of his age, this Roman constitutional system was bound up with a beneficial body of civil law, and with "the high old Roman virtue"—the traditional Roman morality, calling for duty and courage.

The actual forms of checks and balances that the Americans incorporated into their Constitution in 1787, however, were derived from English precedent and from American colonial experience, rather than directly from the Roman model. Instances from the history of the Roman Republic, nevertheless, were cited by the Framers and by other leading Americans of that time as reinforcement for the American concept of political checks and balances.

The Americans' vision of a great and growing republic, it may thus be seen, owed much to the annals of the Roman Republic. The Roman Republic failed because of long civil wars in the first century B.C., and it was supplanted by the Roman Empire. This Roman experience, and the decadence that fell upon Roman civilization as the centuries passed, were much in the minds of American leaders near the end of the eighteenth century. The grim consequences of political centralization under the Roman Empire convinced many Framers that an American government should be federal rather than central—just as some delegates pointed to the Greeks' disunity as a warning against leaving the American Republic a weak confederation. Besides, Roman struggles of class against class reminded Americans that they must seek to reconcile different classes and interests through their own constitutional structure.

Thus Rome's political and moral example was a cautionary lesson to Americans of the early Republic. Edward Gibbon's great history *The Decline and Fall of the Roman Empire* had been published between 1776 and 1783, the period of the American Revolution, and its details were vivid in the minds of the delegates at Philadelphia.

Yet it will not do to make too much of the influence of the Roman constitution upon the Constitution of the United States, two thousand years after Polybius wrote in praise of Roman character and institutions. The more immediate and practical examples of constitutional success were the British and the colonial political structures. The American Republic was joined with England and with her own colonial past by a continuity of culture that much exceeded the Americans' link with old Rome, so distant and so remote in time.

It was the aspiration of the delegates at Philadelphia in 1787 to reconcile the need for a strong federal government with the demand for State sovereignty, local autonomy, and personal liberty. They could not find in the history of the ancient world any model constitution that might achieve this purpose. In 1865, nine decades after the Great Convention at Philadelphia, Orestes Brownson—one of the more interesting of America's political thinkers—would write in his book *The American Republic* that America's mission under God was to realize the true idea of the political state or nation. America's mission, Brownson believed, was to give flesh to that concept of the commonwealth "which secures at once the authority of the public and the freedom of the individual—the sovereignty of the people without social despotism, and individual freedom without anarchy. . . . The Greek and Roman republics asserted the state to the detriment of individual freedom; modern republics either do the same, or assert individual freedom to the detriment of the state. The American republic has been instituted by Providence to realize the freedom of each with advantage to the other."

Certainly such a high ambition, surpassing the political achievements of the ancient world, was the spirit of 1787 at Philadelphia.

English Origins of America's Constitution

"The American Constitution is distinctively English," wrote Sir Henry Maine in his book *Popular Government* (1885). Why should the Americans of 1787, so recently at war with Britain, have drawn up a constitution incorporating among its principal features institutions and principles long established in England? Because they, like their ancestors, were familiar with those British constitutional features and found them desirable; also because colonial charters and the constitutions of the Thirteen States had been framed on the British model, for the most part, and Americans had grown accustomed to their operation. Besides, the great majority of American citizens were British citizens who spoke English, read English books, enjoyed "the rights of Englishmen," and participated in a culture basically English.

There are, of course, a number of important differences between the English and American constitutions that should be understood. As we noted earlier, the English Constitution is not a "written" constitution. That is, it is not contained in any single document like the American Constitution of 1787. It consists, rather, of (1) certain charters and statutes that are regarded as part of the fundamental law, (2) principles derived from the common law, and (3) a great variety of political and legal customs and traditions. Statutes that enjoy a constitutional status are those which deal with the distribution and exercise of power, and those which guarantee certain freedoms. Three great political documents which are essentially compacts or agreements between the Crown and the Nation (the people and their representatives) stand out as prominent landmarks in English constitutional history. These are Magna Charta (1215), the Petition of Right (1628), and the Bill of Rights (1689), which constitute, in the words of the great parliamentary leader Lord Chatham, "the Bible of the English Constitution." Many of the individual rights guaranteed in these documents, as we shall later observe, reappear in our first State constitutions, in our Federal Constitution, and in our Bill of Rights. The "law of the land" clause in Magna Charta, for example, which later came to be known as "due process of law," will be found in the Fifth and Fourteenth amendments of the United States Constitution. Magna Charta is often regarded as the foundation of Anglo-American liberties, because it established the principle that all Englishmen, not just the Lords, are entitled to personal liberty, and that no man, including the King himself, is above the law.

Another and actually more fundamental difference between the English and American constitutions concerns the question of sovereignty. Sovereignty signifies the highest governmental or legal authority. Under the English Constitution, legal sovereignty resides in Parliament. Parliament, in other words, is supreme, and its authority cannot be challenged by the Crown or the judiciary. There is no supreme court, as in the United States, which has the right to declare an act of Parliament unconstitutional. Parliament decides for itself whether its laws are constitutional.

Throughout British history, and particularly during the American revolutionary period, certain statutes were challenged on the ground that they were "unconstitutional." American political leaders, for example, claimed that the Stamp Act, imposing a tax, was "unconstitutional." By this they meant that in their judgment the statute conflicted with basic English liberties and should be repealed. Their appeal was to Parliament, because the English courts did not have jurisdiction over such a claim. By contrast, sovereignty in the American constitutional system is in the Constitution itself, which is declared to be the supreme law of the land. If a party claims that a certain act of Congress is "unconstitutional," not only may he seek to persuade Congress to repeal the statute, but also he may be able under certain conditions to take his case to court and obtain a judicial ruling on the question.

The English and American political systems are also distinguishable on the basis of separation of powers. The English have a *parliamentary* system of government, whereas the Americans have a *presidential* system. Under both systems, the functions of government are separated into legislative, executive, and judicial branches, but there is no clear separation of personnel under a parliamentary system. The real executive in the English system is not the King but the cabinet, which is made up of the King's ministers. Members of the Cabinet, however, also hold a seat in Parliament. The Prime Minister, for example, actually holds a seat in the House of Commons (the lower house) and is the leader of the majority party of that body. The President of the United States, on the other hand, is more independent of the legislature. He is elected by the nation at large, not by the members of Congress. He may actually be a member of a political party that is in opposition to the majority party in control of one or both houses of Congress. Unlike in the English system, members of the House of Representatives and Senate are forbidden by the Constitution from serving in the executive branch. How and why the Americans departed from the English example of separation of powers will be the subject of later discussion.

In many other ways, however, the two constitutions are quite similar, and the British influence may readily be discerned. Congress and Parliament are bicameral legislatures, consisting of two houses. Members of the House of Commons, like those of the House of Representatives, are elected from single-member districts for relatively brief terms. A speaker presides over both chambers, though the speaker of the House of Commons is a neutral figure who does not vote or participate in the proceedings. Both houses are regarded as the "lower" houses and have many more members than the "upper" houses. Because they are subject to more frequent elections and represent a smaller constituency, the members of the House of Commons and the House of Representatives are also commonly regarded as "closer to the people." The House of Lords has ceased to function as an independent body equal to the House of Commons, and nowadays is quite unlike the powerful United States Senate. In 1787, however, there were some similarities. Although the Senate was established to represent the several States rather than an American "nobility," both the Senate and the House of Lords were regarded as smaller, more exclusive bodies that would serve as a moderating influence on the more populous lower houses. Both were free of direct popular control; many (but not all) members of the House of Lords held their seats by inheritance, and Senators were elected by the State legislatures rather than by the people. Bicameralism was thus favored in both England and America as a device for restraining the legislature. By representing different constituencies, with different interests, in two chambers instead of one, no single interest or single class, it was argued, would dominate the entire legislative branch.

Likewise, the Federal judicial system adopted by the Framers in 1787 bore the stamp of the English Constitution. Under both constitutions, the judiciary has been established as an independent branch, largely though not completely free of legislative and executive control. The judges are appointed by the executive for unspecified terms, remain on the bench as long as they exercise "good behavior," and may not be removed from office except by impeachment. Their salaries may not be reduced by the legislature while they serve. This strengthens their independence by preventing an angry legislature from attempting to influence the judicial process through manipulation of judicial salaries.

In many other ways, American constitutionalism, written or unwritten, is rooted in British practices and customs. Almost without exception, all of the individual liberties, including political liberty and the right of property, that are guaranteed in the Federal and State constitutions may be traced to English precedents. Representative government, or what we call the republican tradition, is the bedrock of American constitutionalism. But it is a tradition inherited from Great Britain, and American revolutionary leaders generally regarded the right of representation as the most fundamental right they possessed. To be sure, a principal constitutional grievance of the colonists was the lack of American representation in Parliament—"taxation without representation."

The Growth of Parliament

In contrast to the democracies of the ancient world or of the medieval and renaissance city-states of Italy, there arose in England, by stages, what we now call representative government, through the summoning of an assembly called Parliament. Various forms of representative government had developed in western Europe late in the Middle Ages and down to the late eighteenth century; but of these the English form, with its House of Lords and House of Commons that made up the Parliament, was the most successful and powerful. The origin of Parliament may be traced back to the King's councils (Witans) under the Anglo-Saxons, who ruled England before the Norman invasion in 1066, but some historians prefer to mark the beginning in 1215. This was the year when the English barons compelled King John to grant them a great charter (Magna Charta), which bound the King to extend certain basic liberties to all "freemen." A more precise point of origin, however, is the year 1295. On that date, King Edward I summoned what became known as the "Model Parliament" because it served as the model for all succeeding Parliaments. Here, for the first time, the right of all classes to be represented in Parliament was permanently established. The barons (the English nobility) and the Bishops and other high ranking members of the clergy joined together as the "Lords Temporal and Spiritual" to form the House of Lords. Two knights from every shire (county) and two burgesses from every town or borough were also summoned, and these freemen or "commoners" joined together to form the House of Commons. "What concerns all, should be approved by all." These words appeared in the writs (written orders in the form of letters) sent out by Edward when he summoned the Model Parliament. Edward wanted to raise taxes, and taxation to support Edward's wars concerned all. The Model Parliament granted him that monetary aid, and from this time forward it was understood that the King could not levy a tax without the approval of Parliament. Here too was the birth of the constitutional principle around which the Americans rallied five centuries later: "No Taxation Without Representation." Gradually this "power of the purse" passed into the hands of members of the House of Commons. Under the American Constitution, as the English, the power to initiate tax revenue measures is considered to be so important that only the lower houses may propose money bills. "All bills for raising Revenue," states Article I, Section 7 of the Constitution, "shall originate in the House of Representatives."

By the middle of the fifteenth century, something like real representative government had taken shape in England. In theory, at least, the law was supreme. The King was bound by oath to respect the laws; he could not change the laws or impose new taxes without Parliament's consent. Through elections held in county courts and boroughs, the people of England chose individuals from their own number to represent them in the House of Commons, whose members were privileged against interference or even ordinary arrest. The power of impeachment prevented, or at least curbed, arbitrary acts or corrupt practices among the King's servants. About the middle of the fifteenth century there was no real hostility between the House of Lords and the House of Commons. As the end of medieval times approached, England knew more of liberty, order, and justice than did any other country.

The coming of the strong-willed Tudor sovereigns of England during the sixteenth century delayed for more than a hundred years the growth of Parliament's powers. By manipulating elections or by threatening to use force, the Tudor kings and queens dominated their Parliaments, even if they respected the outward form of England's Constitution. After James I became England's first Stuart king at the beginning of the seventeenth century, the contest between kings and Parliament was resumed.

This struggle led to civil war during the reign of Charles I (James's son), and to the execution of the King himself by the triumphant forces of Parliament and the Puritan faction in the Church (1649). When the monarchy was restored under Charles II, an uneasy compromise was reached between the Royalists and the champions of Parliament.

The accession to the throne of James II, a Catholic, brought on the opposition of the great landed proprietors of England and of most of the English people, who were overwhelmingly Protestant. In 1688 James was forced to flee abroad. He was succeeded as sovereign by the Protestant William III, from the Netherlands, the husband of James's daughter, Mary.

To secure the throne, William III was compelled to recognize the supremacy of Parliament. From 1689 forward, the royal influence over government in England tended to diminish, and the power of Parliament—that is, of the English form of representative government—tended to increase.

In 1714, George, King of Hanover, came over from Germany to be enthroned as George I of England. Throughout the eighteenth century Britain was ruled by three Georges, of whom the first two were unfamiliar with English ways, so that political power inclined toward Parliament and parliamentary political parties. George III, hoping to rule as a "Patriot King," tried to restore much of the royal authority, and in doing so he helped to bring on the American Revolution.

The Challenge of Parliamentary Supremacy

Though not always clearly perceived in England or in the colonies, the English Constitution, it may thus be seen, had changed much since the time of Charles I, and there were often conflicting precedents. The constitutional conflicts of the early seventeenth century centered around a struggle for power between the King and Parliament, whereas the American revolutionary struggle pitted the American colonists and their provincial assemblies against Parliament. The supremacy of the King had been displaced by the supremacy of Parliament, and it was a complicated and confusing task to sort out the arguments against one form of supremacy and apply them to the other. This much the colonists did know: that a legislature could be just as tyrannical as a king, and that in fact it was often more difficult to deal with an entire assembly of tyrants than with one. The reign of Oliver Cromwell following the execution of Charles I in 1649 plunged England into a state of despotic rule that far surpassed the excesses of the Stuart kings and taught the Anglo-Americans the hard lesson that unchecked power can lead to tyranny no matter who wields it.

Trial of Charles I in Westminster Hall, 1649.

(Courtesy of the Library of Congress.)

As we noted earlier, the Glorious Revolution of 1688–89 was an important turning point in English constitutional history. As a result of this bloodless revolt against the monarchy, Parliament became the real sovereign of Great Britain, and parliamentary supremacy became a permanent fixture of the English Constitution. The system adopted was, in effect, a limited or constitutional monarchy. England would thereafter be governed by Parliament and its leaders, or what the English call "the King-in-Parliament" in recognition of the monarch's titular sovereignty. Parliamentary sovereignty was formally established in the famous Act of Settlement of 1701, which confirmed the right of Parliament to determine the line of succession to the throne. The English Constitution, it must be kept in mind, clings to the legal fiction that it is the "King (or Queen)-in-Parliament" that rules the nation, when in reality the monarch is little more than a figurehead. American revolutionary leaders understood this; and although the grievances against Great Britain enumerated in the American Declaration of Independence in 1776 are directed against King George III, almost everyone on both sides of the Atlantic understood that it was the supremacy of Parliament, speaking through its leaders (the "King's Ministers"), that was actually being challenged. King George was no innocent bystander, to be sure, but the man in charge was Lord North, the Tory leader of the majority party in Parliament.

During the eighteenth century, it should be noted, there were two political parties competing for power in Parliament, the Whigs and the Tories. These parties came into existence as a result of the constitutional and religious struggles of the seventeenth century, and by 1680 the names Whig and Tory were commonly used to designate respectively those members who opposed the Stuart claim that sovereignty resided exclusively in the Crown and those who supported it. The Whigs found support for their constitutional theories advocating a limited or constitutional monarchy in the writings of John Locke, whereas the Tories tended to rely on the works of Sir Robert Filmer, Thomas Hobbes, and the proponents of royal absolutism to support a doctrine of non-resistance that favored a strong monarchy. The Whigs emerged victorious in the Revolution of 1688 and were able to dominate Parliament until 1760.

In 1763, a new Tory government began enacting "tax reform" legislation designed to tighten the control of the mother country over the

American colonies and to increase revenue. These reforms, altering the constitutional relationship between Great Britain and the colonies and weakening the political rights of the colonists, led directly to the American Revolution. The King, the King's friends, and some Whigs must share the blame with the Tories, however, in causing the colonial rebellion.

There were many British who joined with the Americans and agreed with colonial leaders that Parliament had overstepped its bounds. Though a monarchist, the great English jurist and legal scholar Sir William Blackstone sided with the Americans in the great constitutional debate between the mother country and the colonies. So too did a number of Whigs in the House of Commons, especially the Irish statesman Edmund Burke, who became the most ardent champion of the American cause. Burke's eloquent speeches were widely read in the American colonies, and his constitutional views had a powerful impact on the American mind. So popular was Burke in America that in 1771 the New York Assembly hired him to represent the colony and defend its interests as its London agent. As a result of his leadership in opposing the doctrines of the French Revolution, Burke would later become the principal architect of the conservative political tradition that came into being in the next century, and the founder of a political movement in Great Britain that led eventually to a major party realignment in which the Whigs and Tories were supplanted by the Liberal and Conservative parties.

In his celebrated *Speech on American Taxation* (1774), Burke assailed the repressive tax measures enacted by Parliament in retaliation for the Boston Tea Party. The King's ministers, he charged, had taken the principle of legislative supremacy beyond its constitutional limits. "Revert to your old principles," he said, and seek peace with the Americans. "Leave America, if she has taxable matter in her, to tax herself." If parliamentary sovereignty is not reconciled with freedom, he warned, the Americans "will cast your sovereignty in your face. Nobody will be argued into slavery."

More powerful yet was Burke's *Speech on Conciliation with the Colonies* (1775), in which he pleaded for moderation and restraint and warned his colleagues that they had seriously underestimated the Americans' love of liberty. "This fierce spirit of liberty," he observed, "is stronger in the English colonies . . . than in any other people of the earth. . . . They are therefore not only devoted to liberty, but to liberty according to English ideas and on English principles." They will not rest until they are given an "interest in the Constitution" and representation in Parliament on an equal basis with other British subjects. Equal representation, he reminded the House, is "the ancient constitutional policy of this kingdom," and without it there can be no equity or justice in taxing the colonies. Blinded by power, believing they could crush the American insurgents, Lord North and his ministers, as well as most members of Parliament, ignored Burke and his small circle of Whig supporters. Within weeks, the first shots of the war were fired at Lexington and Concord. History, of course, proved Burke right, and as a piece of political and constitutional wisdom his famous *Speech on Conciliation* has endured down to our time.

The Common Law Tradition

Most of the delegates to the Philadelphia Convention, active in colonial affairs before the Revolution, understood not only the British government of the North American colonies, but also the British legal system; some had occupied public office before the Americans declared their independence. With few exceptions, the fifty-five delegates had paid close attention to the eighteenth-century Constitution of Britain and to English law; and about half of them had been judges or lawyers who were deeply read in Sir William Blackstone's monumental treatise *Commentaries on the Laws of England*. A great compendium of learning on constitutional principles, the rights of Englishmen, and the laws of property, the *Commentaries* were based on Blackstone's lectures at Oxford University. They soon became the bible of the legal profession. First published in 1765, the work was enormously popular among American lawyers, so much so that as many copies were sold in the colonies as in the mother country. American colonial leaders repeatedly drew from this timely and authoritative source in challenging the policies of the English government and drafting their own fundamental laws. The indictment of George III in the Declaration of Independence is amply supported by Blackstone's description of the rights of Englishmen, and it was for these rights, among others, that the patriots were contending. Such terms in the American Constitution as "crimes and misdemeanors," "ex post facto laws," "judicial power," "due process," and "levying war" were used in the same sense in which Blackstone had employed them. In like manner, most of the early State constitutions drafted in 1776 were influenced by the *Commentaries,* and these in turn were copied in part by the newer States joining the Union. Thus the language of both the Federal and State constitutions in the United States cannot fully be understood without reference to the English common law. And Blackstone's classic, which is still being reprinted today, has generally been accepted as the best exposition of that law.

Prominent American lawyers such as James Iredell of North Carolina, who later served on the Supreme Court of the United States, and John Dickinson of Pennsylvania (and later Delaware), who received his legal training in England and was a delegate to the Federal Convention, were also acquainted with the judicial opinions and legal writings of Blackstone's predecessor—the great Sir Edward Coke (pronounced Cook). Before Blackstone's *Commentaries* appeared, English and American lawyers relied heavily upon Coke's *Reports* and his four-volume *Institutes of the Laws of England* to learn the principles of the common law; and even after the *Commentaries* came into use, Coke's writings were still thought necessary for a complete mastery of property law. What particularly interested American lawyers in the eighteenth century were Coke's judicial opinions of the early seventeenth century, which supported the supremacy of the law, and his opposition to the King's interference in judicial affairs in defense of the principle of an independent judiciary. Coke had challenged the claims and pretensions of the Stuart kings and had helped to prepare the way for the independence of both Parliament and the English courts. More than a century later, the Americans found Coke's arguments useful in challenging the doctrines of legislative supremacy and the claims of Parliament respecting control and domination of colonial affairs. In *Dr. Bonham's Case* (1610), for example, Coke asserted that the common law controlled even acts of Parliament—a dictum that would prove useful to James Otis of Massachusetts when he argued in the famous *Writs of Assistance Case* of 1761 that Parliament had no right to authorize British customs officials to issue general search warrants (without naming any persons). "An Act against the Constitution is void," declared Otis. "An Act against natural equity is void. . . . [and the] Courts must pass such Acts into disuse." Otis repeated this argument in his formal treatise *Rights of the British Colonists Asserted and Proved* (1764), which contended that parliamentary supremacy was limited by the English Constitution and "the laws of God," and that taxation without representation was therefore unconstitutional.

"There is no jewel in the world comparable to learning," wrote Coke, and "no learning so excellent both for prince and subject as knowledge of laws; and no knowledge of any laws (I speak of human) so necessary for all [social classes] and for all causes concerning goods, lands, or life, as the common laws of England." The common law that Coke so greatly admired had evolved over the centuries as a body of legal principles for determining the rights and duties of individuals respecting their personal security and property. It was judge-made law, developed not by parliamentary statutes or royal edicts of the King but by the King's judges, through the accumulation of judicial decisions. The American system of property and contract law, to cite just two examples, may be traced back to general rules based on common sense, habit, and custom that gradually evolved in the English courts. Sir Matthew Hale, an eminent English judge of the seventeenth century, boasted that the common law was superior to other legal systems because it is "not the product of the wisdom of some one man, or society of men, in any one age; but of the wisdom, counsel, experience, and observation, of many ages of wise and observing men."

The different system of jurisprudence called civil law (or Roman law), on the other hand, is derived from legislative enactment. It was based originally upon the system of laws administered in the Roman Empire, particularly as set forth in the compilation of the Emperor Justinian A.D. 529. The jurisprudence of continental Europe, Latin America, and many other parts of the free world is based upon the civil law. The ecclesiastical and administrative courts of England, including the infamous Court of Star Chamber, also applied the civil law, which relied upon different rules of evidence and tried cases before a judge without a jury. The legal system of the State of Louisiana is also based in part on the civil law because of the influence of the French in that region before Louisiana became a part of the United States. In 1804 Napoleon Bonaparte, Emperor of France and military dictator over much of Europe, reduced the enormously complex and disorganized body of ancient civil law to a single written code. The Code Napoleon was widely copied or utilized and soon displaced the Justinian Code and other earlier codifications. It serves today as the modern expression of the civil law.

The English common law runs all the way back to Anglo-Saxon days in England, but it did not begin to take shape until late in the twelfth century during the reign of Henry II. It passed into North America with the coming of the first English settlers to the New World, and over the centuries was incorporated into the American system of laws by legislation and judicial decisions.

In England, the common law is an essential part of the English Constitution. In America, the common law is not mentioned in the written Constitution of 1787, but common law principles underlie much of our "invisible" or "unwritten" constitution. Some provisions of the Constitution, such as the one referring to "contract" in Article 1, Section 10, presume the existence of the common law and cannot be understood properly without reference to it. Although most of Anglo-American common law has been superseded by State constitutions and laws, it is still recognized in courts of law and may even serve as a rule of decision.

This is more true in State courts than in those at the Federal level, because Federal courts are not courts of general or common law jurisdiction. At the time of the Constitutional Convention in Philadelphia, and for some forty years later, Americans debated whether England's common law should remain effective in the United States. Opponents of the common law argued that the Revolution had terminated application of English legal concepts to America. In the period immediately following the American Revolution, there was much opposition to everything English, including the common law; and in the early nineteenth century some American lawyers favored legislative codification of the common law along the French model. Much of this opposition stemmed from the fact that American law reports and legal treatises were scarce, and it was difficult even for lawyers to know what the law was and what features of the English common law had been adapted to American circumstances. The impetus to abandon the common law collapsed in the early nineteenth century, however, when great American legal scholars and jurists such as Joseph Story and James Kent began publishing books on American law.

Sir Francis Bacon, Coke's great political rival, was another important English jurist and legal writer who had a great following in the American colonies. In addition to his famous *Essays* and philosophical works, Bacon published a number of books on the law, including *Elements of the Common Law* and *Maxims of the Law.* Among lawyers, Bacon was probably best known for his genius at stating the principles and philosophy of the law in concise, memorable, and quotable aphorisms, and for his efforts as Lord Chancellor to strengthen equity jurisprudence and check the power of the common law judges. Equity, or chancery as it is sometimes called, denotes fairness, and consists of a body of rules outside of the common law that are intended to produce justice. It begins where the law ends; it supplements the common law. Under the common law, for example, there could be no relief in the way of compensation for a wrong committed against an individual until the injury had actually occurred. This worked a hardship in some cases, however, if an individual was permitted to engage in dangerous activity or was in possession of hazardous property or material likely to produce injury. Equity courts in England, like ecclesiastical and administrative courts, were separate from the common law courts, and were empowered to grant relief where the courts of law were unable to give it or had made the law so technical that it failed to promote the "King's justice." Equity courts thus had the power to issue injunctions (orders forbidding a party to do some act) in order to prevent an injury from occurring. In some instances they were allowed, in effect, to circumvent rulings of the common law courts by providing remedies that the common law courts could not give. As Lord Chancellor under James I, Sir Francis Bacon presided over the equity courts as the "Keeper of the King's Conscience." In this role he frequently came into conflict with Sir Edward Coke, who headed up the common law courts.

After the American colonies gained independence, most of the States, with the notable exception of New York, combined law and equity in one court, abolished separate courts of chancery, and extended the judicial power to both law and equity. The Framers modeled the Constitution along the same lines. Since 1789, when the first Judiciary Act was passed

Edmund Burke (1729–1797). British Statesman and Political Writer.

This bronze statue, located in Washington, D.C. at 11th and Massachusetts Avenue, N.W., is a replica of the one erected in Bristol, England, the city which Burke represented in Parliament. It was presented to the American people in 1922 by Sir Charles Wakefield, former Mayor of London, on behalf of the Sulgrave Institution, an organization which promotes Anglo-American understanding. The Sulgrave Institution has also restored Sulgrave Manor, once the English estate of Lawrence Washington, of whom George Washington is a lineal descendant.

In his celebrated Speech to the Electors of Bristol, November 3, 1774, concerning the duties of a representative to his constituents, Burke rejected the radical doctrine that the people have a right to instruct their representatives on how to vote. Insisting that a member of Parliament should exercise independent judgment, Burke asserted that his primary responsibility was to represent the best interests of his constituents, and not simply their immediate demands. As a result of Burke's influence, the Whig party adopted his principle and the practice of sending instructions soon fell out of use. (Photo courtesy of Dr. and Mrs. Bruce Frohnen.)

by Congress, Federal judges have thus been required to have some knowledge of Anglo-American equity law in order to carry out their duties. Because the equity power is not defined in the Constitution and tends to expand the power and jurisdiction of the Federal courts, it has played a significant role in the growth of judicial power, especially in recent times. Indeed, some Anti-Federalists warned that the fusion of law and equity in the Supreme Court might degenerate into arbitrary judicial discretion, allowing the judges to exceed their powers and ignore the law in the name of "justice." The equity jurisprudence we inherited from England is limited by general rules, however, and it does not authorize the judges to rule as they please. Its proper application thus requires judicial self-restraint.

It is noteworthy that the first great constitutional quarrel between the English and the Americans, prompted by the Stamp Act of 1765, was based on a claim that the statute violated both constitutional and common law rights. The Act provided a stamp tax on the issuance of college diplomas, licenses, commercial paper, deeds of property, leases, and land grants, and on sales of newspapers, pamphlets, and printed advertisements. Even sales of playing cards and dice were subjected to the tax. The Act further stipulated that prosecutions for violations of the law would be tried not at common law, as constitutional custom dictated, but in vice-admiralty courts. These were administrative courts which relied on the civil law and did not use juries. Lord North's administration was persuaded that the Act would not be enforced in the regular courts of law because local juries would sympathize with colonial defendants.

The Stamp Act was repealed before it could be enforced, but not before Americans loudly protested. Among the most cherished common law rights in both England and America was the right of trial by jury, which had traditionally provided an essential check on government and protected the rights of property and individual liberty. Trial without jury, Maryland legislators argued during the Stamp Act crisis, "renders the Subject insecure in his Liberty and Property." The New York assembly asserted that trial by jury was "essential to the Safety" of the "Lives, Liberty, and Property" of British subjects, and the Virginia House of Burgesses echoed these sentiments, insisting that it was "the surest Support of Property." Speaking for the citizens of Braintree, Massachusetts, John

Adams declared that the Stamp Act was "unconstitutional" because "we have always understood it to be a grand and fundamental principle of the Constitution that no freeman should be subject to any tax to which he has not given his own consent, either in person or by proxy." But, said Adams, "the most grievous innovation of all is the alarming extension of the power of courts of admiralty. In these courts, one judge presides alone. No juries have any concern there." The denial of jury trials, he concluded, "is directly repugnant to the Great Charter itself; for, by that charter, 'no freeman shall be taken, or imprisoned, or disseized of his freehold . . . but by the lawful judgment of his peers, or by the law of the land.' "

Thus the Stamp Act, here at the outset of the constitutional struggle that led to the American Revolution and the Philadelphia Convention, threatened two basic constitutional rights—the right to be taxed only by consent and the right to trial by jury. More than any other law of Parliament, this Act eroded the colonists' faith in British rule, and from this point on relations between the mother country and her rebellious colonies steadily deteriorated; and with each new statutory effort by Parliament to discipline and subdue the colonies came another assault on the common law and the constitution. Seeking not new rights but merely the preservation of those threatened or denied by a headstrong Parliament, the Americans slowly and reluctantly came to the conclusion that only by declaring their independence and establishing their own constitutions, laws, and bills of rights could they enjoy the constitutional and common law "rights of Englishmen."

The Republican Tradition and the Struggle for Constitutional Liberty

In responding to the radical policies and innovative constitutional doctrines of King George and his Tory ministers, the Americans were also much attracted to John Hampden and Algernon Sidney, whose names were virtually synonymous with constitutional liberty. Hampden was the leader of a local tax revolt that shook the foundations of royal absolutism in seventeenth-century England. In the Petition of Right of 1628, the King had bound himself never again to imprison any person except

John Hampden (1594–1643).

From a print by J. Houbraken, 1740. (Courtesy of Hampden-Sydney College.)

by due process of law, never again to circumvent the regular courts through court martial trials by commissions, never again to quarter soldiers in private homes without the consent of the householder, and never again to raise money without the consent of Parliament.

There was, however, a potential loophole concerning the limitations imposed on the King's power to levy a tax by virtue of a longstanding practice which permitted the throne to issue special writs calling for a tax in time of emergency. These writs, however, had been imposed only on the port towns of England because their purpose was to raise money for ships of the Royal Navy. Charles I, anxious to build more ships, issued a writ in 1636, clearly in violation of the spirit of the Petition of Right, extending the system inland—to all of the counties. There was no national emergency, but Charles declared the existence of one anyway, and argued that the inland counties should pay because they too enjoyed the protection of His Majesty's Navy.

Many declined to pay, declaring that the King's writ was a tax levied without parliamentary authority. A member of the House of Commons, John Hampden had vigorously opposed the arbitrary rule of the crown for many years. In the famous *Ship Money Case* of 1637, he was tried for refusing to pay the small sum of twenty shillings assessed upon his land, claiming that Charles had no authority to declare a national emergency on his own, and that the writ itself violated his property rights. Although Hampden lost his case, the judges' decision was later stricken from the rolls. Hampden became a popular hero in both England and the American colonies, and a symbol of resistance to oppressive taxation and arbitrary government. A monument memorializing Hampden's courageous stand against the ship money tax remains to this day in his native village of Great Kimble: "Would 20s. Have Ruined Mr. Hampden's Fortune? No, But The Payment of Half 20s. *On the Principle it was Demanded* Would Have Made Him a Slave."

The *Ship Money Case* was cited by American lawyers in their battle with Parliament over the latter's taxing powers, and the constitutional doctrine that the executive has a special prerogative, or reserved power, to rule by decree in times of crises was rejected by the Framers. The American constitutional tradition has never embraced the doctrine of royal absolutism that emergencies create power. Unfortunately, not all nations of the world have learned the lessons of history as well as the Americans. Invoking so-called "emergency powers" has been a favorite executive device for seizing "temporary"—and then permanent—dictatorial control of government in modern democracies, and to this day there are foreign constitutions which confer this dangerous power on the chief executive.

Algernon Sidney, beheaded on a London scaffold in 1683 for the crime of treason, left a different mark on the American mind. Falsely accused of participating in a plot to murder the King, he was arrested and brought to trial by his political opponents before the infamous Chief Justice George Jeffreys, whose cruelty and misconduct on the bench were a disgrace to the English judiciary. Throughout much of the seventeenth century, the courts of England were subjected to political manipulation and control. The Stuart kings had begun the policy of removing judges who disagreed with them, but the Puritans under Cromwell went further by filling the bench with subservient judges, Jeffreys being the worst of the lot.

The Puritans treated Magna Charta, parliamentary government, and the rule of law with contempt, acting in a far more arbitrary fashion than any English king had ever dared to attempt. In the trial of Sidney, principles of due process and established rules of criminal procedure were deliberately violated by the court. The indictment charging Sidney with treason was issued without a grand jury proceeding. He was refused a copy of the indictment. The jury was handpicked to exclude jurors who might declare him innocent. Perjured testimony and hearsay (secondhand) evidence were introduced against him. Sidney had committed no overt act against Charles II, but the court devised a farfetched interpretation of the treason statute to gain a conviction. An unpublished manuscript found among Sidney's personal papers was then produced in court as proof of his treasonous behavior. This was the *Discourses Concerning Government*, a treatise on liberty which praised limited and "mixed" government, denied the divine right of kings, and asserted that "power is originally in the people" and that "the king is subject to the law of God." These and similar non-treasonous statements were interpreted by the court as proof that Sidney was involved in a plot against the King's life, and he was convicted on that fraudulent basis.

The *Discourses* were later published in 1698 and again in 1763 and 1772. The work was hailed in America by Jefferson and other colonial

Trial of Algernon Sidney, 1683.

(Courtesy of the Library of Congress.)

leaders. The two-volume book, though less coherent or profound than John Locke's political writings on the same subjects, served along with Locke's *Two Treatises of Government* as an inspiration to Whigs in the colonies and as one of the main arsenals from which the American revolutionary writers drew their arguments. But Sidney's life, trial, and martyrdom probably had greater influence on American thinking, and many a patriot who had never even read the *Discourses* appealed to Sidney's memory as a symbol of defiance to tyrants. Sidney's trial in particular served as a glowing reminder to American constitution-makers of the need for an independent judiciary that respected rule of law and judicial restraint. Both Hampden and Sidney were held in such high esteem that in 1776, under the leadership of Patrick Henry, James Madison, and other prominent figures, a school was founded in Virginia bearing the name Hampden-Sydney College.

It should be borne in mind, however, that not all of the American colonists were persuaded that a monarchy was necessarily a bad form of government, or that Sidney's *Discourses* were politically or philosophically sound. It has been estimated that at least one-third of the Americans were Tories or Loyalists, who opposed independence. Many believed that a limited constitutional monarchy was preferable to a republican form of government, or what was then often called a commonwealth. Their position was not wholly untenable, or so absurd as Thomas Paine made it appear in his famous tract *Common Sense.* King George III was no Henry VIII or Charles I. In 1776, royal absolutism was a thing of the past, and the English Constitution had changed much since the days of Hampden and Sidney. Besides, the English experiment with republicanism, when Cromwell and the Puritans tyrannized Britain, had been a catastrophic failure. Why blame the King, they asked, when it was the leaders of Parliament who were really at fault for the deprivation of American rights. Parliamentary sovereignty, not the monarchy, was the problem. The French Revolution that began in 1789, far exceeding the crimes and human atrocities of Cromwellian England, would later show that radical republicanism, if unrestrained, might degenerate into anarchy and mob rule. Under the rule of Robespierre, the French actually lapsed into a period of totalitarian democracy, the first the world had ever seen, followed by the rise of a young army captain named Napoleon Bonaparte, who became the first modern dictator, crowned himself Emperor, and plunged all of Europe into nearly two decades of war, death, and destruction. In retrospect, then, it may be seen that the case for a limited constitutional monarchy was not as weak as some maintained. Even today we are struck by the fact that Great Britain, the Netherlands, Sweden, and other regimes that have kept the throne and have evolved into a limited constitutional monarchy have been among the freest and most stable democracies of modern Europe.

A few Americans entertained the notion that perhaps George Washington should be crowned the American king; and there were rumors that John Adams and Alexander Hamilton harbored monarchist sentiments. But Washington never took it seriously, and the charges against Adams and Hamilton were false. Many American political leaders, especially Hamilton, did greatly admire the English Constitution, however, even though they agreed with the great majority of their countrymen that American society, lacking a permanent aristocracy or class system like that of England, was not suited for a monarchy. No proposal to establish such a system was ever made at the Philadelphia Convention, the Framers being unanimously agreed that a republican form of government, though difficult to maintain, was the best system for the people of the United States.

The extent to which the writings of Sidney and Locke contributed to the increasing disenchantment with monarchy and the growing popularity of republicanism among the American people cannot easily be measured. Among the educated class, however, their works were read widely and often discussed. Although James I had published a defense of monarchical government early in the seventeenth century, the principal book was Sir Robert Filmer's *Patriarcha* (1680), a learned treatise which argued nevertheless that the King ruled by divine right and could trace his line of authority back to Holy Scripture. Sidney denied the validity of the theory in his *Discourses*, and Locke repudiated it in his *First Treatise of Civil Government*. With the notable exception of Jonathan Boucher, a Tory preacher from Maryland who published a defense of Filmer and ridiculed the doctrines of Locke, few Americans seem to have been much persuaded by Filmer. With many other Loyalists, Boucher eventually fled the colonies, never to return. What sentiment there was for monar-

Ranking of Political Thinkers by Frequency of Citation

1. Montesquieu	8.3	19. Shakespeare	0.8
2. Blackstone	7.9	20. Livy	0.8
3. Locke	2.9	21. Pope	0.7
4. Hume	2.7	22. Milton	0.7
5. Plutarch	1.5	23. Tacitus	0.6
6. Beccaria	1.5	24. Coxe	0.6
7. Trenchard and		25. Plato	0.5
Gordon (Cato)	1.4	26. Raynal	0.5
8. Delolme	1.4	27. Mably	0.5
9. Pufendorf	1.3	28. Machiavelli	0.5
10. Coke	1.3	29. Vattel	0.5
11. Cicero	1.2	30. Petyt	0.5
12. Hobbes	1.0	31. Voltaire	0.5
13. Robertson	0.9	32. Robinson	0.5
14. Grotius	0.9	33. Sidney	0.5
15. Rousseau	0.9	34. Somers	0.5
16. Bolingbroke	0.9	35. Harrington	0.5
17. Bacon	0.8	36. Rapin-Thoyras	0.5
18. Price	0.8	Other	52.2

This table is based on 3,154 references to 224 European thinkers found in 916 pamphlets, books, and essays. *Source:* Donald Lutz, *A Preface to American Political Theory* (Lawrence: Kansas University Press, 1992), 136.

chical government effectively vanished with the massive emigration of the Loyalists to Canada and the mother country during the Revolution.

Far more influential than any of these writings, however, was Locke's *Second Treatise of Civil Government*, which sought to provide a theoretical justification for the Glorious Revolution, and presented a view of government based on the theory that all men possess certain "natural rights" which government has a duty to protect. Though Locke's understanding of the origin and purpose of civil society was unhistorical and logically unsound, as Boucher and the Scottish philosopher and historian David Hume were quick to point out, his natural rights philosophy was sometimes invoked by American revolutionary leaders to buttress their arguments against the legitimacy of British colonial policies. Americans were entitled not only to the rights of Englishmen, some maintained, but to the "natural rights of life, liberty and estate" (Locke's phrase) common to all mankind.

The Influence of Continental Thinkers

It should come as no surprise that only a handful of contemporary European thinkers on the continent had much influence in the colonies. Most European states were governed by powerful monarchs who were strangers to constitutional government. Germany and Italy, divided into principalities, did not even exist as sovereign nations. Although the Europeans had experimented with confederation government, political power was almost everywhere centralized, and there was no tradition, as in the American colonies, of local self-government to serve as a model for building a modern federal system with two levels of government. The predominant view in Europe, as expressed by Jean Bodin in his *De Republica* (1576), was that national sovereignty could not be divided and was "unrestrained by laws." The European legal system, based on the civil law of ancient Rome, but differing from one nation to the next because of the infusion of local customs and practices, differed substantially from Anglo-American common law. It was far less hospitable to the kinds of civil liberties that the English-speaking peoples had come to expect, and as we have already seen did not even allow for jury trials.

A few educated Americans were familiar with the works of some of the great international law jurists—Jean Jacques Burlamaqui, Emmerich Vattel, Samuel Pufendorf, and Hugo Grotius—who wrote on the law of nations and had much to say about the meaning of justice and ethical practices in international relations; but probably the bulk of their influence in America came later, after the United States had become an independent country, adopted the Constitution, and entered into diplomatic relations with foreign governments.

There was considerable intellectual activity in France, which in the eighteenth century had become the center of radical political theory; but the Americans showed little interest, and when they did, as in the case of John Adams, they often expressed profound disagreement. Few American leaders embraced the wild and visionary doctrines of Jean Jacques

Ranking of Political Thinkers by Frequency of Citation and by Decade

	1760s	1770s	1780s	1790s	1800–1805	Total
Montesquieu	8	7	14	4	1	8.3
Blackstone	1	3	7	11	15	7.9
Locke	11	7	1	1	1	2.9
Hume	1	1	1	6	5	2.7
Plutarch	1	3	1	2	0	1.5
Beccaria	0	1	3	0	0	1.5
Cato	1	1	3	0	0	1.4
Delolme	0	0	3	1	0	1.4
Pufendorf	4	0	1	0	5	1.3
Coke	5	0	1	2	4	1.3
Cicero	1	1	1	2	1	1.2
Hobbes	0	1	1	0	0	1.0
SUBTOTAL	33	25	37	29	32	32.4
Others	67	75	63	71	68	67.6
TOTAL	100	100	100	100	100	100.0
TOTAL CITATIONS EXAMINED	216	544	1306	674	414	3154

All numbers except those in the last column are rounded to the nearest whole. *Source:* Donald Lutz, *A Preface to American Political Theory* (Lawrence: Kansas University Press, 1992), 138.

Rousseau (the patron saint of French revolutionaries), or subscribed to the views of Helvetius, Turgot, or Condorcet. Holbach's *System of Nature* (1773), an attack on religion and government anticipating in many respects the ideas of Karl Marx, seems to have had few if any followers in the American colonies. Many of the French works, in fact, had not been translated into English.

The single great exception was Charles Montesquieu's *Spirit of the Laws* (1748), one of the most widely read and frequently cited authorities relied upon by the Americans in framing a new system of government. Montesquieu did not advocate utopian solutions to the problem of despotism in his age. He favored constitutional reform. His practical aim was to analyze the constitutional conditions upon which freedom depends, in the hope of restoring the ancient liberties of Frenchmen. The *Spirit of the Laws* provided a learned, though not always correct, analysis of governments of all ages and nations. Montesquieu admired the English Constitution in particular, and argued convincingly that the preservation of liberty required a separation of powers.

American constitution-makers were much attracted to his separation of powers doctrine but had difficulty applying it. It was based, in part, on an erroneous interpretation of the English Constitution, and Montesquieu's treatment of the subject lacked clarity and precision. The separation of powers system that he advocated only vaguely acknowledged the need for an accompanying check and balance system, and there was some doubt whether the system could be implemented in America, because Montesquieu believed that a republican form of government could work only in a small territory. The Anti-Federalists were therefore critical of the proposed Constitution of 1787 because it departed from Montesquieu's ideas. Ingenious at adapting Old World ideas to the American situation and revising them to suit their needs, the Framers argued on practical and theoretical grounds that Montesquieu's principles, though basically sound, required some modification. The State constitutions written between 1776 and 1780, particularly the Massachusetts Constitution, showed that a system of checks and balances actually strengthened the separation of powers. Montesquieu's assumption that only small territories were suited for republican government was brilliantly challenged by James Madison in *Federalist* No. 10. Montesquieu's ideas, while serving as an inspiration and catalyst for constitutional change before the Revolution, thus lost some of their purity when the Framers got down to the business of putting them into practice.

The Education of the Founders

American political leaders, it may be seen, drew upon a wide range of philosophers, historians, lawyers, and political thinkers in formulating their constitutional principles. This body of knowledge, combined with their solid grasp of British institutions, their experiences under colonial government and the new State constitutions, to say nothing of American writings on the subject of government, provided a wealth of information for drafting a new constitution. Indeed, the men of the founding generation seemed to love books as much as they loved liberty. We get a glimpse of these American values from the last will and testament of Josiah Quincy, a brilliant Boston lawyer who fought at the side of John Adams against British tyranny: "I leave to my son, when he shall have reached the age of fifteen, the works of Algernon Sidney, John Locke, Francis Bacon, Gordon's *Tacitus* and Cato's Letters. May the spirit of liberty rest upon him."

A letter written by Thomas Jefferson in 1771, when he was twenty-eight years old, gives us yet a better insight into the kinds of books the educated class of Americans read and valued. Robert Skipwith, a friend of Jefferson's, asked Jefferson to draw up a list of the books that a Virginia gentleman should have in his personal library. Jefferson obliged his friend with a lengthy list divided into numerous sections, including "Fine Arts" (including poetry, drama, art, and gardening), "Politics and Trade," "Religion" (which included what we would call philosophy today), "Law," "History," and "Natural Philosophy and Natural History" (what we now call the sciences). Works on poetry and fiction, such as those of John Dryden, Alexander Pope, and Jonathan Swift, were included, he said, because "every thing is useful which contributes to fix us in the principles and practice of virtue." Most of the basic works on Greek and Roman history—Tacitus, Livy, Sallust, and Plutarch—gave detailed accounts of the corruption in Roman politics. Works on English politics and political history focused on the constitutional conflicts of the seventeenth century, but included later works too—Locke, Sidney, Montesquieu, and Bolingbroke. Under religion Jefferson included the writings of Cicero, Seneca, Xenophon, Epictetus, and Hume. Blackstone's *Commentaries,* Lord Kames's *Principles of Equity,* and a law dictionary were the only entries under the heading "Law." The Bible also appeared on the list, as did Samuel Johnson's *Dictionary* and some of the writings of Edmund Burke and the Scottish economists Adam Smith and Sir James Steuart. Almost all of these works, in one degree or another, were read widely by the educated class of Americans who directed the affairs of the American Republic in the formative years. They provided American political leaders with a deep sense of history, an understanding of liberty and constitutional government, and a system of values, both personal

Marcus Tullius Cicero (106–43 B.C.).

Roman Orator and Statesman. Marble bust from Museo Capitoleno in Rome. (Courtesy of Corbis-Bettmann.)

and political, that are reflected in their political behavior and in the constitutions they drafted for their countrymen. No generation of political leaders has been better prepared or better educated for writing a constitution and assuming the reins of government than the Framers of the American Constitution.

The French and American
Revolutions Compared

Representative government, a tradition of well-established civil and political liberties, and the heritage of the common law are only three of the more important examples of English political and legal institutions that passed into the civil social order of the United States. The Congress, the Bill of Rights, and the American system of law and justice today are all the products of British experience and political thought going back more than seven centuries.

Although the Framers of the American Constitution declared that they were creating a new political order for a new age, they never thought of repudiating their American past, their British past, or their classical past. On the floor of the Federal Convention, and in the State ratifying conventions, the leading men repeatedly appealed to examples from ancient times and from English history, and a few even relied upon philosophers of earlier centuries to support their views. They were seeking to preserve their ancestral America.

The wisdom of the Framers and their attachment to the political and moral heritage of Hebraic, classical, and British cultures, combined with the American experience, prevented them from falling into the ruinous political errors that, only two years after the Constitution was written, French reformers would begin to commit. Initially, the French Revolution that began in 1789 with the storming of the Bastille (a prison in Paris that had come to symbolize the oppression of the "ancient regime") was hailed by many in Europe and America as the dawn of a new era and the triumph of liberty over tyranny and injustice. Not a few, including many Frenchmen, likened it to the American Revolution, which was said to have set the example and provided the inspiration. But as time passed and political developments in France indicated that limited constitutional government was not the aim of the Jacobin revolutionaries, public opinion began to turn against the French. As early as 1790, Edmund Burke warned in his famous *Reflections on the Revolution in France* that the revolution was doomed to failure because its leaders sought a radical break with the past and were attempting to create a whole new society based on visionary theories of government. The French, he asserted, were attempting not to restore their ancient liberties, but to set up a new order for all mankind based on what the French called the Rights of Man. Unfamiliar with constitutional government, lacking experience in parliamentary institutions and practices, having no solid grasp of the meaning and substance of the rights the English and Americans had come to know, the French naively believed they could leap over centuries of historical development and instantaneously create an enlightened political system never before experienced by any civilization. The whole scheme of things, thought Burke, was hopelessly idealistic and dangerous.

Not the least of his concerns was the Declaration of the Rights of Man, which lacked any constitutional base of support and therefore amounted to little more than words on paper. As interpreted by revolutionary leaders, the rights themselves—*"liberté, egalité et fraternité"*—called for a complete leveling of society, the abolition of all social classes and distinctions, including the elimination of the clergy, and a redistribution of the wealth. In pursuit of these goals, the Jacobins plunged the nation into what came to be called the Reign of Terror. Death stalked the countryside. Mass executions, murder, cruelty, and human atrocities of every description became the order of the day. France, once the pride of Europe and the hallmark of Western civilization, plummeted into a state of barbarism—on a scale never before thought possible. Thus was born the first modern revolution, the dress rehearsal, it is sometimes said, for the Russian Revolution of 1917.

During the Reign of Terror, Gouverneur Morris of Pennsylvania, who had been a leading member of the Constitutional Convention of 1787, was the American Minister to France. Shocked by what he saw, he began sending home reports to American political leaders. Writing in 1792 to Robert Morris, another Pennsylvania delegate to the Convention, he related on one occasion that the owner of a French quarry had demanded damages because so many corpses had been dumped into his quarry that they "choked it up so he could not get men to work in it." These victims, he continued, were "the best people," killed "without form of trial, and their bodies thrown like dead dogs into the first hole that offered." Other accounts of the Revolution by Gouverneur Morris were equally alarming: "(September 2, 1792) the murder of the priests . . . murder of prisoners. . . . (September 3) The murdering continues all day. . . . (September 4) And still the murders continue."

Eyewitness accounts such as these, and tales of unspeakable horror and brutality told by other foreign visitors to France, confirmed the darkest suspicions of Edmund Burke, and as news about the fate of the French Revolution spread across Europe and North America, so also did Burke's fame and influence. That Burke, who had defended the claims of the American colonists and steadfastly opposed all policies calculated to reduce private liberties or centralize the authority of the crown, should turn against the French Revolution puzzled many of his contemporaries when his *Reflections* first appeared. Had he not sided with American revolutionaries and argued that Americans were entitled to the rights of Englishmen? How, then, could he oppose the French claim for liberty? There seemed to be an inconsistency. Those who thought so misunderstood Burke, however, and, unlike Burke, also misunderstood the French and American revolutions.

Much of this confusion over the similarities and differences between the two revolutions was laid to rest by Friedrich Gentz, a German diplomat who served as an advisor to Clemens von Metternich, the great chancellor of the Hapsburg Empire. It was Metternich who presided over the Congress of Vienna, the famous international peace conference of 1815 that succeeded in restoring lasting peace in Europe after the Napoleonic wars. Gentz was one of Burke's most ardent admirers on the continent, and in 1794 translated Burke's *Reflections* into German. In 1800, Gentz published an important essay of his own, *The French and American Revolutions*. That same year, John Quincy Adams translated this work into English and arranged for its publication in Philadelphia.

Picking up where Burke had finished, Gentz defended the American Revolution as a constitutional struggle for political independence, the restoration of the rights of Englishmen, and the establishment of self-government. The American Revolution, he observed, was not an internal

The Guillotine.

Dr. Guillotin's machine in use during the French Revolution. Though he did not invent the machine, he proposed its use, and so it took his name. (Courtesy of Corbis-Bettmann.)

conflict, pitting Americans against Americans, but a military effort to throw off the yoke of foreign oppression. "The American revolution," he concluded, "had more the appearance of a foreign than a civil war," or what we would today call a rebellion. Moreover, the war was limited primarily to military engagements between British and American militia. There was no war against the general population, although many Americans lost their lives and property; and neither British nor American forces engaged in wholesale acts of savage brutality, mayhem, and murder. "If in America," said Gentz, "single families and districts felt the heavy hand of the revolution and of war, never at least, as in France, were confiscations, banishments, imprisonments, and death decreed in a mass." Having driven the British from American soil, "the country proceeded with rapid steps to a new, a happy, and a flourishing constitution" that enjoyed popular support throughout the country. In retrospect, it could

Legacy of the French Revolution.

This photograph, obtained under great difficulty, was taken in 1929. As was customary before France finally abolished the guillotine, the execution took place in an open
street at 5 A.M. This particular criminal was beheaded for a murder committed under
extremely cruel circumstances. (Courtesy of UPI/Corbis-Bettmann.)

be seen that "the revolution altered little in the internal organization of
the colonies, as it only dissolved the external connection, which the Americans must always have considered rather as a burden."

In contrast, the French Revolution was a true civil war. Its goal was not
to expel a foreign enemy, but to overthrow the government of France and
establish a new political order for all of Europe. As the Revolution progressed, its Jacobin rulers thought it necessary to erase all vestiges of the
past and abolish the ancient institutions of France without any clear understanding of what would replace them. They even abolished the cal-
endar and renamed the days of the week. Professing equality and fraternity, they addressed each other as "citizen." In a mad frenzy, they set out

to destroy the entire social fabric of France, including all traces of the Christian religion. Following the execution of King Louis XVI and Marie Antoinette in 1793, they turned on the aristocracy and the clergy. Those who escaped capture fled the country. The rest were marched to the guillotine, a new and efficient decapitating device first conceived by a French doctor to reduce extended suffering and speed up mass executions. Eventually all classes, including the peasants, fell victim to the Revolution. During the Reign of Terror in 1793, when Maximillian Robespierre was in charge of the Committee of Public Safety, it is estimated that 4,554 persons were put to death by revolutionary courts. In 1794, Robespierre himself felt the executioner's blade. In this bloody revolution, it has been said, France was at war not only with itself but with Western civilization. "With regard to the lawfulness of the origin, character of the conduct, quality of the object, and compass of resistance," Gentz concluded, "every parallel" drawn between the French and American revolutions "will serve much more to display the *contrast* than the resemblance between them."

What is the significance of these distinctions in understanding the origin and nature of the American Constitution? Above all, they help us put in proper perspective the political values and aspirations of American revolutionary leaders. This is important to know, because the men who led the "revolution" also wrote the Constitution, with George Washington at the helm not only as the Commander-in-Chief of the Continental Army but also as President of the Constitutional Convention. The American Constitution was, in effect, the culmination of the American Revolution, and it is through the Constitution that the goals of the revolution were finally achieved.

The American Revolution, viewed in historical perspective, was a constitutional revolt in the English tradition. From virtually every standpoint, the American republic founded in 1787 was really more like the constitutional monarchy of Great Britain than any of the early republics of France. And the French have attempted five since 1789, as well as virtually every other form of government—the Fifth Republic, founded by Charles De Gaulle in 1958 being the first to establish stable government and show real promise, and that because it incorporates some key features of the American Constitution, including judicial review. But in the eighteenth century the French and the Americans had very different ideas about the role and limits of government, about democracy and republicanism, and especially about constitutionalism.

Probably the widest gulf between them, however, concerned the question of individual rights. The Americans fought for and secured the common law rights of Englishmen, whereas the French, much influenced by Jean Jacques Rousseau and other radical French philosophers of the Enlightenment, dreamed of the Rights of Man. Deemed to be the natural rights of all mankind but having no practical base in human experience, let alone that of France, they were reduced by the French revolutionaries to the political slogan of *"liberté, egalité et fraternité."* Assuming that all individuals are "by nature" good but have been "corrupted" by man's institutions, the French believed that by eradicating the monarchy, the aristocracy, and the church, and by erasing the past, this natural goodness would surface and everyone would enjoy a perfect state of strifeless equality. There would then be no need for limited government, or as some believed, for any government at all, because there would be no need to be protected against naturally virtuous citizens. Nor would there be rich and poor, or social classes based on economic distinctions, because all property would be held in common once man reverted to a natural state of equality—"natural," they said, because the state of nature, antedating the first government in prehistorical times, was thought to be the original and true condition of mankind.

The system thus envisioned by French revolutionary leaders approximated a form of philosophical anarchy and glorified a communal system of collective living in a "classless society," a theory that later achieved a more sophisticated expression in the writings of Karl Marx and the Russian revolutionaries of the twentieth century. This utopian scheme never came to fruition, of course, because it was wholly at odds with the true nature of man. The French Revolution, lacking any sensible direction, rapidly degenerated into chaos. A national madness gripped the country, which eventually gave rise to totalitarianism and military dictatorship. With the French Revolution of 1789 we enter upon modern European history. To understand that revolution is to understand the history of the modern world. To understand the American Revolution is to understand why the American Constitution has survived and so many others, much influenced by the ideas and events of Jacobin France, have failed.

The American revolutionaries suffered none of the delusions of their unfortunate counterparts in France. There were a few Americans and British, notably Thomas Paine and the English Unitarian minister Dr. Richard Price, who championed the French Revolution, but they were part of a small and shrinking minority. Seeking to refute Burke, Paine published *The Rights of Man* in 1791, insisting that Burke's view of rights was contrary to reason and that his misgivings were unfounded. "Notwithstanding Mr. Burke's horrid paintings," said Paine, "when the French Revolution is compared with that of other countries, the astonishment will be that it is marked by so few sacrifices." Traveling to Paris to join the Revolution, Paine was at first honored by the revolutionists as "Citizen Tom Paine," only to be thrown into prison, barely escaping France with his life.

The French Revolution left the nation bitter and divided for more than a century. The American people, however, emerged from their struggle united and free. Thus from the beginning American Constitution-makers had the general support of their countrymen. The principles of government they espoused during the Revolution and implemented after the British surrender at Yorktown were widely shared in every town and village. It was on the basis of this remarkable consensus, this serene moment of creation, this fertile ground of American political experience, that the new Constitution was established. Had the Americans fought their revolution a decade later and followed the French rather than the English example, it may be doubted whether the American Constitution, or any other, would have long endured. But history smiled upon the American people. Time and circumstance and the political wisdom of the Founders combined fortuitously to rescue them from the fate of the French republic. No tree of liberty has ever enjoyed a greater chance of survival than the Constitution that germinated in Philadelphia in the summer of 1787. This is because it was deeply rooted in a constitutional tradition favorable to liberty, order, and justice more than five hundred years in the making.

SUGGESTED READING

George Burton Adams, *Constitutional History of England* (New York: Henry Holt & Co., 1921).

A. J. Beitzinger, *A History of American Political Thought* (New York: Dodd, Mead & Co., 1972).

Richard Bernstein, *Are We a Nation? The Making of the American Constitution* (Cambridge: Harvard University Press, 1987).

Trevor Colbourn, *The Lamp of Experience* (Indianapolis: Liberty Fund, 1997).

A. V. Dicey, *Introduction to the Study of the Law of the Constitution* (Indianapolis: Liberty Fund, 1982).

J. C. Holt, *Magna Carta* (Cambridge: Cambridge University Press, 1965).

A. E. Dick Howard, *The Road from Runnymeade: Magna Carta and Constitutionalism in America* (Charlottesville: University of Virginia Press, 1968).

Alfred Kelly, Winfred Harbison, and Herman Belz, *The American Constitution: Its Origins and Development*. 7th ed., 2 vols. (New York: W. W. Norton, 1991).

Russell Kirk, *America's British Culture* (New Brunswick, N.J.: Transaction Publishers, 1993).

Russell Kirk, *The Roots of American Order* (Washington, D.C.: Regnery Gateway, 1991).

David A. Lockmiller, *Sir William Blackstone* (Chapel Hill: University of North Carolina Press, 1938).

Donald S. Lutz, *Origins of American Constitutionalism* (Baton Rouge: Louisiana State University Press, 1988).

Donald S. Lutz, *A Preface to American Political Theory* (Lawrence: University Press of Kansas, 1992).

Sir Henry Maine, *Popular Government* (Indianapolis: Liberty Fund, 1976).

Forrest McDonald, *Novus Ordo Seclorum* (Lawrence: University Press of Kansas, 1985).

William Sharp McKechnie, *Magna Carta: A Commentary on the Great Charter of King John*. 2nd ed. (Glasgow: James Maclehose and Sons, 1914).

Roscoe Pound, *The Development of Constitutional Guarantees of Liberty* (New Haven: Yale University Press, 1957).

Meyer Reinhold, *Classica Americana: The Greek and Roman Heritage of the United States* (Detroit: Wayne State University Press, 1984).

Carl J. Richard, *The Founders and the Classics: Greece, Rome and the American Enlightenment* (Cambridge: Harvard University Press, 1994).

Caroline Robbins, *The Eighteenth Century Commonwealthman* (Cambridge: Harvard University Press, 1959).

Ellis Sandoz, ed., *The Roots of Liberty: Magna Carta, Ancient Constitution, and the Anglo-American Tradition of Rule of Law* (Columbia: University of Missouri Press, 1993).

Barry Alan Shain, *The Myth of American Individualism* (Princeton: Princeton University Press, 1994).

Paul Merrill Spurlin, *Montesquieu in America, 1760–1801.* (Baton Rouge: Louisiana State University Press, 1940).

Arthur E. Sutherland, *Constitutionalism in America* (New York: Blaisdell Publishing Co., 1965).

Richard Vetterli and Gary Bryner, *In Search of the Republic: Public Virtue and the Roots of American Government* (Savage, Md.: Rowman & Littlefield Publishers, 1987).

Stephen D. White, *Sir Edward Coke and "The Grievances of the Commonwealth, 1621–1628"* (Chapel Hill: University of North Carolina Press, 1979).

Francis G. Wilson, *The American Political Mind* (New York: McGraw-Hill, 1949).

John M. Zane, *The Story of Law* (Indianapolis: Liberty Fund, 1998).

Relevant Chapters of Magna Charta (1215)

THE GREAT CHARTER OF KING JOHN, GRANTED JUNE 15, A.D. 1215. John, by the Grace of God, King of England, Lord of Ireland, Duke of Normandy, Aquitaine, and Count of Anjou, to his Archbishops, Bishops, Abbots, Earls, Barons, Justiciaries, Foresters, Sheriffs, Governors, Officers, and to all Bailiffs, and his faithful subjects, greeting. Know ye, that we, in the presence of God, and for the salvation of our soul, and the souls of all our ancestors and heirs, and unto the honour of God and the advancement of Holy Church, and amendment of our Realm, by advice of our venerable Fathers, Stephen, Archbishop of Canterbury, Primate of all England and Cardinal of the Holy Roman Church; Henry, Archbishop of Dublin; William, of London; Peter, of Winchester; Jocelin, of Bath and Glastonbury; Hugh, of Lincoln; Walter, of Worcester; William, of Coventry; Benedict, of Rochester—Bishops: of Master Pandulph, Sub-Deacon and Familiar of our Lord the Pope; Brother Aymeric, Master of the Knights-Templar in England; and the noble Persons, William Marescall, Earl of Pembroke; William, Earl of Salisbury; William, Earl of Warren; William, Earl of Arundel; Alan de Galloway, Constable of Scotland; Warin Fitz-Gerald, Peter FitzHerbert, and Hubert de Burgh, Seneschal of Poitou; Hugh de Neville, Matthew FitzHerbert, Thomas Basset, Alan Basset, Philip of Albiney, Robert de Roppell, John Mareschal, John FitzHugh, and others, our liegemen, have, in the first place, granted to God, and by this our present Charter confirmed, for us and our heirs for ever:

1. RIGHTS OF THE CHURCH

That the Church of England shall be free, and have her whole rights, and her liberties inviolable; and we will have them so observed that it may appear thence that the freedom of elections, which is reckoned chief and indispensable to the English Church, and which we granted and con-

firmed by our Charter, and obtained the confirmation of the same from
our Lord and Pope Innocent III, before the discord between us and our
barons, was granted of mere free will; which Charter we shall observe,
and we do will it to be faithfully observed by our heirs for ever.

2. GRANT OF LIBERTY TO FREEMEN

We also have granted to all the freemen of our kingdom, for us and for
our heirs for ever, all the underwritten liberties, to be had and holden by
them and their heirs, of us and our heirs for ever: If any of our earls, or
barons, or others, who hold of us in chief by military service, shall die,
and at the time of his death his heir shall be of full age, and owe a relief,
he shall have his inheritance by the ancient relief—that is to say, the heir
or heirs of an earl, for a whole earldom, by a hundred pounds; the heir or
heirs of a baron, for a whole barony, by a hundred pounds; their heir or
heirs of a knight, for a whole knight's fee, by a hundred shillings at
most; and whoever oweth less shall give less according to the ancient
custom of fees.

*   *   *   *   *

12. NO TAX (SCUTAGE) EXCEPT BY THE GENERAL COUNCIL

No scutage or aid shall be imposed in our kingdom, unless by the general
council of our kingdom; except for ransoming our person, making our
eldest son a knight, and once for marrying our eldest daughter; and for
these there shall be paid no more than a reasonable aid. In like manner it
shall be concerning the aids of the City of London.

13. LIBERTIES OF LONDON AND OTHER TOWNS

And the City of London shall have all its ancient liberties and free customs, as well by land as by water; furthermore, we will and grant that all
other cities and boroughs, and towns and ports, shall have all their liberties and free customs.

14. GENERAL COUNCIL SHALL CONSENT TO ASSESSMENT OF TAXES

And for holding the general council of the kingdom concerning the assessment of aids, except in the three cases aforesaid, and for the assessing

of scutages, we shall cause to be summoned the archbishops, bishops, abbots, earls, and greater barons of the realm, singly by our letters, and furthermore, we shall cause to be summoned generally, by our sheriffs and
baliffs, all others who hold of us in chief, for a certain day, that is to say,
forty days before their meeting at least, and to a certain place; and in all
letters of such summons we will declare the cause of such summons, and,
summons being thus made the business shall proceed on the day appointed, according to the advice of such as shall be present, although all
that were summoned come not.

*   *   *   *   *

17. COURTS SHALL ADMINISTER JUSTICE IN A FIXED PLACE
Common pleas shall not follow our court, but shall be holden in some
place certain.

18. LAND DISPUTES SHALL BE TRIED IN THEIR
PROPER COUNTIES
Trials upon the Writs of Novel Disseisin, and of Mort d'ancestor, and of
Darrein Presentment, shall not be taken but in their proper counties,
and after this manner: We, or if we should be out of the realm, our chief
justiciary, will send two justiciaries through every county four times a
year, who, with four knights of each county, chosen by the county, shall
hold the said assizes in the county, on the day, and at the place appointed.

19. KEEPING THE ASSIZE COURTS OPEN
And if any matters cannot be determined on the day appointed for holding the assizes in each county, so many of the knights and freeholders as
have been at the assizes aforesaid shall stay to decide them as is necessary, according as there is more or less business.

20. FINES AGAINST FREEMEN TO BE MEASURED BY THE OFFENSE
A freeman shall not be amerced for a small offence, but only according to
the degree of the offence; and for a great crime according to the heinousness of it, saving to him his contentment; and after the same manner a
merchant, saving to him his merchandise. And a villein shall be amerced

after the same manner, saving to him his wainage, if he falls under our mercy; and none of the aforesaid amerciaments shall be assessed but by the oath of honest men in the neighbourhood.

21. SAME FOR NOBLES

Earls and barons shall not be amerced but by their peers, and after the degree of the offence.

22. SAME FOR CLERGYMEN

No ecclesiastical person shall be amerced for his tenement, but according to the proportion of the others aforesaid, and not according to the value of his ecclesiastical benefice.

23. Neither a town nor any tenant shall be distrained to make bridges or embankments, unless that anciently and of right they are bound to do it.

24. No sheriff, constable, coroner, or other our bailiffs, shall hold "Pleas of the Crown."

25. All counties, hundreds, wapentakes, and trethings, shall stand at the old rents, without any increase, except in our demesne manors.

26. If any one holding of us a lay fee die, and the sheriff, or our bailiffs, show our letters patent of summons for debt which the dead man did owe to us, it shall be lawful for the sheriff or our bailiff to attach and register the chattels of the dead, found upon his lay fee, to the amount of the debt, by the view of lawful men, so as nothing be removed until our whole clear debt be paid; and the rest shall be left to the executors to fulfil the testament of the dead; and if there be nothing due from him to us, all the chattels shall go to the use of the dead, saving to his wife and children their reasonable shares.

27. If any freeman shall die intestate, his chattels shall be distributed by the hands of his nearest relations and friends, by view of the Church, saving to every one his debts which the deceased owed to him.

28. COMPENSATION FOR THE TAKING OF PRIVATE PROPERTY
No constable or bailiff of ours shall take corn or other chattels of any man unless he presently give him money for it, or hath respite of payment by the good-will of the seller.

29. No constable shall distrain any knight to give money for castle-guard, if he himself will do it in his person, or by another able man, in case he cannot do it through any reasonable cause. And if we have carried or sent him into the army, he shall be free from such guard for the time he shall be in the army by our command.

30. NO TAKING OF HORSES OR CARTS WITHOUT CONSENT
No sheriff or bailiff of ours, or any other, shall take horses or carts of any freeman for carriage, without the assent of the said freeman.

31. NO TAKING OF TREES FOR TIMBER WITHOUT CONSENT
Neither shall we nor our bailiffs take any man's timber for our castles or other uses, unless by the consent of the owner of the timber.

32. We will retain the lands of those convicted of felony only one year and a day, and then they shall be delivered to the lord of the fee.

33. All kydells (wears) for the time to come shall be put down in the rivers of Thames and Medway, and throughout all England, except upon the sea-coast.

34. The writ which is called *præcipe*, for the future, shall not be made out to any one, of any tenement, whereby a freeman may lose his court.

35. UNIFORM WEIGHTS AND MEASURES
There shall be one measure of wine and one of ale through our whole realm; and one measure of corn, that is to say, the London quarter; and one breadth of dyed cloth, and russets, and haberjects, that is to say, two ells within the lists; and it shall be of weights as it is of measures.

36. NOTHING FROM HENCEFORTH SHALL BE GIVEN OR TAKEN
FOR A WRIT OF INQUISITION OF LIFE OR LIMB, BUT IT SHALL BE
GRANTED FREELY, AND NOT DENIED.

37. If any do hold of us by fee-farm, or by socage, or by burgage, and he
hold also lands of any other by knight's service, we will have the custody
of the heir or land, which is holden of another man's fee by reason of that
fee-farm, socage, or burgage; neither will we have the custody of the fee-
farm, or socage, or burgage, unless knight's service was due to us out of
the same fee-farm. We will not have the custody of an heir, nor of any
land which he holds of another by knight's service, by reason of any
petty serjeanty by which he holds of us, by the service of paying a knife,
an arrow, or the like.

38. No bailiff from henceforth shall put any man to his law upon his own
bare saying, without credible witnesses to prove it.

39. GUARANTEE OF JUDGMENT BY ONE'S PEERS AND OF
PROCEEDINGS ACCORDING TO THE "LAW OF THE LAND."
No freeman shall be taken or imprisoned, or disseised, or outlawed, or
banished, or any ways destroyed, nor will we pass upon him, nor will we
send upon him, unless by the lawful judgment of his peers, or by the law
of the land.

40. GUARANTEE OF EQUAL JUSTICE (EQUALITY BEFORE
THE LAW)
We will sell to no man, we will not deny or delay to any man, either jus-
tice or right.

41. FREEDOM OF MOVEMENT FOR MERCHANTS
All merchants shall have safe and secure conduct, to go out of, and to
come into England, and to stay there and to pass as well by land as by
water, for buying and selling by the ancient and allowed customs, without any unjust tolls; except in time of war, or when they are of any nation
at war with us. And if there be found any such in our land, in the beginning of the war, they shall be attached, without damage to their bodies
or goods, until it be known unto us, or our chief justiciary, how our mer-

chants be treated in the nation at war with us; and if ours be safe there, the others shall be safe in our dominions.

42. FREEDOM TO LEAVE AND REENTER THE KINGDOM
It shall be lawful, for the time to come, for any one to go out of our kingdom, and return safely and securely by land or by water, saving his allegiance to us; unless in time of war, by some short space, for the common benefit of the realm, except prisoners and outlaws, according to the law of the land, and people in war with us, and merchants who shall be treated as is above mentioned.

43. If any man hold of any escheat as of the honour of Wallingford, Nottingham, Boulogne, Lancaster, or of other escheats which be in our hands, and are baronies, and die, his heir shall give no other relief, and perform no other service to us than he would to the baron, if it were in the baron's hand; and we will hold it after the same manner as the baron held it.

44. Those men who dwell without the forest from henceforth shall not come before our justiciaries of the forest, upon common summons, but such as are impleaded, or as sureties for any that are attached for something concerning the forest.

45. APPOINTMENT OF THOSE WHO KNOW THE LAW
We will not make any justices, constables, sheriffs, or bailiffs, but of such as know the law of the realm and mean duly to observe it.

46. All barons who have founded abbeys, which they hold by charter from the kings of England, or by ancient tenure, shall have the keeping of them, when vacant, as they ought to have.

47. All forests that have been made forests in our time shall forthwith be disforested; and the same shall be done with the water-banks that have been fenced in by us in our time.

48. All evil customs concerning forests, warrens, foresters, and warreners, sheriffs and their officers, water-banks and their keeper, shall forth-

with be inquired into in each county, by twelve sworn knights of the same county chosen by creditable persons of the same county; and within forty days after the said inquest be utterly abolished, so as never to be restored: so as we are first acquainted therewith, or our justiciary, if we should not be in England.

49. We will immediately give up all hostages and charters delivered unto us by our English subjects, as securities for their keeping the peace, and yielding us faithful service.

50. We will entirely remove from their bailiwicks the relations of Gerard de Atheyes, so that for the future they shall have no bailiwick in England; we will also remove from their bailiwicks the relations of Gerard de Atheyes, so that for the future they shall have no bailiwick in England; we will also remove Engelard de Cygony, Andrew, Peter, and Gyon, from the Chancery; Gyon de Cygony, Geoffrey de Martyn, and his brothers; Philip Mark, and his brothers, and his nephew, Geoffrey, and their whole retinue.

51. As soon as peace is restored, we will send out of the kingdom all foreign knights, cross-bowmen, and stipendiaries, who are come with horses and arms to the molestation of our people.

52. If any one has been dispossessed or deprived by us, without the lawful judgment of his peers, of his lands, castles, liberties, or rights, we will forthwith restore them to him; and if any dispute arise upon this head, let the matter be decided by the five-and-twenty barons hereafter mentioned, for the preservation of the peace. And for all those things of which any person has, without the lawful judgment of his peers, been dispossessed or deprived, either by our father King Henry, or our brother King Richard, and which we have in our hands, or are possessed by others, and we are bound to warrant and make good, we shall have a respite till the term usually allowed the crusaders; excepting those things about which there is a plea depending, or whereof an inquest hath been made, by our order before we undertook the crusade; but as soon as we return

from our expedition, or if perchance we tarry at home and do not make our expedition, we will immediately cause full justice to be administered therein.

53. The same respite we shall have, and in the same manner, about administering justice, disafforesting or letting continue the forests, which Henry our father, and our brother Richard, have afforested; and the same concerning the wardship of the lands which are in another's fee, but the wardship of which we have hitherto had, by reason of a fee held of us by knight's service; and for the abbeys founded in other fee than our own, in which the lord of the fee says he has a right; and when we return from our expedition, or if we tarry at home, and do not make our expedition, we will immediately do full justice to all the complainants in this behalf.

54. No man shall be taken or imprisoned upon the appeal of a woman, for the death of any other than her husband.

55. All unjust and illegal fines made by us, and all amerciaments imposed unjustly and contrary to the law of the land, shall be entirely given up, or else be left to the decision of the five-and-twenty barons hereafter mentioned for the preservation of the peace, or of the major part of them, together with the foresaid Stephen, Archbishop of Canterbury, if he can be present, and others whom he shall think fit to invite; and if he cannot be present, the business shall notwithstanding go on without him; but so that if one or more of the aforesaid five-and-twenty barons be plaintiffs in the same cause, they shall be set aside as to what concerns this particular affair, and others be chosen in their room, out of the said five-and-twenty, and sworn by the rest to decide the matter.

56. If we have disseised or dispossessed the Welsh of any lands, liberties, or other things, without the legal judgment of their peers, either in England or in Wales, they shall be immediately restored to them; and if any dispute arise upon this head, the matter shall be determined in the Marches by the judgment of their peers; for tenements in England according to the law of England, for tenements in Wales according to the

law of Wales, for tenements of the Marches according to the law of the Marches: the same shall the Welsh do to us and our subjects.

57. As for all those things of which a Welshman hath, without the lawful judgment of his peers, been disseised or deprived of by King Henry our father, or our brother King Richard, and which we either have in our hands or others are possessed of, and we are obliged to warrant it, we shall have a respite till the time generally allowed the crusaders; excepting those things about which a suit is depending, or whereof an inquest has been made by our order, before we undertook the crusade: but when we return, or if we stay at home without performing our expedition, we will immediately do them full justice, according to the laws of the Welsh and of the parts before mentioned.

58. We will without delay dismiss the son of Llewellin, and all the Welsh hostages, and release them from the engagements they have entered into with us for the preservation of the peace.

59. We will treat with Alexander, King of Scots, concerning the restoring of his sisters and hostages, and his right and liberties, in the same form and manner as we shall do to the rest of our barons of England; unless by the charters which we have from his father, William, late King of Scots, it ought to be otherwise; and this shall be left to the determination of his peers in our court.

60. LIBERTIES TO BE GRANTED TO ALL SUBJECTS
All the foresaid customs and liberties, which we have granted to be holden in our kingdom, as much as it belongs to us, all people of our kingdom, as well clergy as laity, shall observe, as far as they are concerned, towards their dependents.

61. OATH TO OBSERVE RIGHTS OF THE CHURCH AND THE PEOPLE
And whereas, for the honour of God and the amendment of our kingdom, and for the better quieting the discord that has arisen between us and our barons, we have granted all these things aforesaid; willing to render them firm and lasting, we do give and grant our subjects the un-

derwritten security, namely, that the barons may choose five-and-twenty barons of the kingdom, whom they think convenient; who shall take care, with all their might, to hold and observe, and cause to be observed, the peace and liberties we have granted them, and by this our present Charter confirmed in this manner; that is to say, that if we, our justiciary, our bailiffs, or any of our officers, shall in any circumstance have failed in the performance of them towards any person, or shall have broken through any of these articles of peace and security, and the offence be notified to four barons chosen out of the five-and-twenty before mentioned, the said four barons shall repair to us, or our justiciary, if we are out of the realm, and, laying open the grievance, shall petition to have it redressed without delay: and if it be not redressed by us, or if we should chance to be out of the realm, if it should not be redressed by our justiciary within forty days, reckoning from the time it been notified to us, or to our justiciary (if we should be out of the realm), the four barons aforesaid shall lay the cause before the rest of the five-and-twenty barons; and the said five-and-twenty barons, together with the community of the whole kingdom, shall distrain and distress us in all the ways in which they shall be able, by seizing our castles, lands, possessions, and in any other manner they can, till the grievance is redressed, according to their pleasure; saving harmless our own person, and the persons of our Queen and children; and when it is redressed, they shall behave to us as before. And any person whatsoever in the kingdom may swear that he will obey the orders of the five-and-twenty barons aforesaid in the execution of the premises, and will distress us, jointly with them, to the utmost of his power; and we give public and free liberty to any one that shall please to swear to this, and never will hinder any person from taking the same oath.

62. As for all those of our subjects who will not, of their own accord, swear to join the five-and-twenty barons in distraining and distressing us, we will issue orders to make them take the same oath as aforesaid. And if any one of the five-and-twenty barons dies, or goes out of the kingdom, or is hindered any other way from carrying the things aforesaid into execution, the rest of the said five-and-twenty barons may choose

another in his room, at their discretion, who shall be sworn in like manner as the rest. In all things that are committed to the execution of these five-and-twenty barons, if, when they are all assembled about any matter, and some of them, when summoned, will not or cannot come, whatever is agreed upon, or enjoined, by the major part of those that are present shall be reputed as firm and valid as if all the five-and-twenty had given their consent; and the aforesaid five-and-twenty shall swear that all the premises they shall faithfully observe, and cause with all their power to be observed. And we will procure nothing from any one, by ourselves nor by another, whereby any of these concessions and liberties may be revoked or lessened; and if any such thing shall have been obtained, let it be null and void; neither will we ever make use of it either by ourselves or any other. And all the ill-will, indignations, and rancours that have arisen between us and our subjects, of the clergy and laity, from the first breaking out of the dissensions between us, we do fully remit and forgive: moreover, all trespasses occasioned by the said dissensions, from Easter in the sixteenth year of our reign till the restoration of peace and tranquility, we hereby entirely remit to all, both clergy and laity, and as far as in us lies do fully forgive. We have, moreover, caused to be made for them the letters patent testimonial of Stephen, Lord Archbishop of Canterbury, Henry, Lord Archbishop of Dublin, and the bishops aforesaid, as also of Master Pandulph, for the security and concessions aforesaid.

63. Wherefore we will and firmly enjoin, that the Church of England be free, and that all men in our kingdom have and hold all the aforesaid liberties, rights, and concessions, truly and peaceably, freely and quietly, fully and wholly to themselves and their heirs, of us and our heirs, in all things and places, for ever, as is aforesaid. It is also sworn, as well on our part as on the part of the barons, that all the things aforesaid shall be observed in good faith, and without evil subtilty. Given under our hand, in the presence of the witnesses above named, and many others, in the meadow called Runingmede, between Windsor and Staines, the 15th day of June, in the 17th year of the reign.

Petition of Right (1628)

The Petition exhibited to his Majesty by the Lords Spiritual and Temporal, and Commons, in this present Parliament assembled, concerning divers Rights and Liberties of the Subjects, with the King's Majesty's royal answer thereunto in full Parliament.

TO THE KING'S MOST EXCELLENT MAJESTY,

Humbly show unto our Sovereign Lord the King, the Lords Spiritual and Temporal, and Commons in Parliament assembled, that whereas it is declared and enacted by a statute made in the time of the reign of King Edward I., commonly called *Statutum de Tallagio non concedendo,* that no tallage or aid shall be laid or levied by the king or his heirs in this realm, without the good will and assent of the archbishops, bishops, earls, barons, knights, burgesses, and other the freemen of the commonalty of this realm; and by authority of Parliament holden in the five-and-twentieth year of the reign of King Edward III., it is declared and enacted, that from thenceforth no person shall be compelled to make any loans to the king against his will, because such loans were against reason and the franchise of the land; and by other laws of this realm it is provided, that none should be charged by any charge or imposition, called a benevolence, nor by such like charge; by which the statutes before mentioned, and other the good laws and statutes of this realm, your subjects have inherited this freedom, that they should not be compelled to contribute to any tax, tallage, aid, or other like charge not set by common consent, in Parliament:

II. Yet nevertheless of late divers commissions directed to sundry commissioners in several counties, with instructions, have issued; by means whereof your people have been in divers places assembled, and required to lend certain sums of money unto your Majesty, and many of them, upon their refusal so to do, have had an oath administered unto them not warrantable by the laws or statutes of this realm, and have been constrained to become bound and make appearance and give utterance before your Privy Council, and in other places, and others of them have been therefore imprisoned, confined, and sundry other ways molested and disquieted; and divers other charges have been laid and levied upon your people in several counties by lord lieutenants, deputy lieutenants, commissioners for musters, justices of peace and others, by command or direction from your Majesty or your Privy Council, against the laws and free customs of the realm.

III. And whereas also by the statute called "The Great Charter of the liberties of England," it is declared and enacted that no freeman may be taken or imprisoned or be disseised of his freeholds or liberties, or his free customs, or be outlawed or exiled, or in any manner destroyed, but by the lawful judgment of his peers, or by the law of the land.

IV. And in the eight-and-twentieth year of the reign of King Edward III., it was declared and enacted by authority of Parliament, that no man, of what estate or condition that he be, should be put out of his lands or tenements, nor taken, nor imprisoned, nor disherited, nor put to death without being brought to answer by due process of law.

V. Nevertheless, against the tenor of the said statutes, and other the good laws and statutes of your realm to that end provided, divers of your subjects have of late been imprisoned without any cause showed; and when for their deliverance they were brought before your justices, by your Majesty's writs of *habeas corpus,* there to undergo and receive as the court should order, and their keepers commanded to certify the causes of their detainer, no cause was certified, but that they were detained by your Majesty's special command, signified by the lords of your Privy Council, and yet were returned back to several prisons, without being charged with anything to which they might make answer according to the law.

VI. And whereas of late great companies of soldiers and mariners have been dispersed into divers counties of the realm, and the inhabitants against their wills have been compelled to receive them into their houses, and there to suffer them to sojourn against the laws and customs of this realm, and to the great grievance and vexation of the people.

VII. And whereas also by authority of Parliament, in the five-and-twentieth year of the reign of King Edward III., it is declared and enacted, that no man shall be forejudged of life or limb against the form of the Great Charter and the law of the land; and by the said Great Charter, and other the laws and statutes of this your realm, no man ought to be adjudged to death but by the laws established in this your realm, either by the customs of the same realm or by acts of Parliament: and whereas no offender of what kind soever is exempted from the proceedings to be used, and punishments to be inflicted by the laws and statutes of this your realm; nevertheless of late time divers commissions under your Majesty's great seal have issued forth, by which certain persons have been assigned and appointed commissioners with power and authority to proceed within the land, according to the justice of martial law, against such soldiers or mariners, or other dissolute persons joining with them, as should commit any murder, robbery, felony, mutiny, or other outrage or misdemeanour whatsoever, and by such summary course and order as is agreeable to martial law, and as is used in armies in time of war, to proceed to the trial and condemnation of such offenders, and them to cause to be executed and put to death according to the law martial.

VIII. By pretext whereof some of your Majesty's subjects have been by some of the said commissioners put to death, when and where, if by the laws and statutes of the land they had deserved death, by the same laws and statutes also they might, and by no other ought to have been, judged and executed.

IX. And also sundry grievous offenders, by colour thereof claiming an exemption, have escaped the punishments due to them by the laws and statutes of this your realm, by reason that divers of your officers and ministers of justice have unjustly refused or forborne to proceed against such offenders according to the same laws and statutes, upon pretence that the said offenders were punishable only by martial law, and by authority of such commissions as aforesaid; which commissioners, and all other of like nature, are wholly and directly contrary to the said laws and statutes of this your realm.

X. They do therefore humbly pray your most excellent Majesty, that no man hereafter be compelled to make or yield any gift, loan, benevolence, tax, or such like charge, without common consent by act of Parliament; and that none be called to make, answer, or take such oath, or to give attendance, or be confined, or otherwise molested or disquieted concerning the same or for refusal thereof; and that no freeman, in any such manner as is before mentioned, be imprisoned or detained; and that your Majesty would be pleased to remove the said soldiers and mariners, and that your people may not be so burdened in time to come; and that the foresaid commissions, for proceeding by martial law, may be revoked and annulled; and that hereafter no commissions of like nature may issue forth to any person or persons whatsoever to be executed as aforesaid, lest by colour of them any of your Majesty's subjects be destroyed or put to death contrary to the laws and franchise of the land.

XI. All which they most humbly pray of your most excellent Majesty as their rights and liberties, according to the laws and statutes of this realm; and that your Majesty would also vouchsafe to declare, that the awards, doings, and proceedings, to the prejudice of your people in any of the premises, shall not be drawn hereafter into consequence or example; and that your Majesty would be also graciously pleased, for the further comfort and safety of your people, to declare your royal will and pleasure, that in the things aforesaid all your officers and ministers shall serve you according to the laws and statutes of this realm, as they tender the honour of your Majesty, and the prosperity of this kingdom.

[Which Petition being read the 2nd of June, 1628, the King's answer was thus delivered unto it.

The King willeth that right be done according to the laws and customs of the realm; and that the statutes be put in due execution, that his subjects may have no cause to complain of any wrong or oppressions, contrary to their just rights and liberties, to the preservation whereof he holds himself as well obliged as of his prerogative.

This form was unusual and was therefore thought to be an evasion; therefore on June 7 the King gave a second answer in the formula usual for approving bills: *Soit droit fait comme il est desire.*]

The English Bill of Rights (1689)

AN ACT FOR DECLARING THE RIGHTS AND LIBERTIES OF THE SUBJECT, AND SETTLING THE SUCCESSION OF THE CROWN.

Whereas the Lords Spiritual and Temporal, and Commons, assembled at Westminster, lawfully, fully, and freely representing all the estates of the people of this realm, did upon the Thirteenth day of February, in the year of our Lord One Thousand Six Hundred Eighty-eight, present unto their Majesties, then called and known by the names and style of William and Mary, Prince and Princess of Orange, being present in their proper persons, a certain Declaration in writing, made by the said Lords and Commons, in the words following, viz.:—

"Whereas the late King James II., by the assistance of divers evil counsellors, judges, and ministers employed by him, did endeavour to subvert and extirpate the Protestant religion, and the laws and liberties of this kingdom:—

(1.) By assuming and exercising a power of dispensing with and suspending of laws, and the execution of laws, without consent of Parliament.

(2.) By committing and prosecuting divers worthy prelates, for humbly petitioning to be excused from concurring to the said assumed power.

(3.) By issuing and causing to be executed a commission under the Great Seal for erecting a court, called the Court of Commissioners for Ecclesiastical Causes.

(4.) By levying money for and to the use of the Crown by pretence of prerogative, for other time and in other manner than the same was granted by Parliament.

(5.) By raising and keeping a standing army within this kingdom in time of peace, without consent of Parliament, and quartering soldiers contrary to law.

(6.) By causing several good subjects, being Protestants, to be disarmed, at the same time when Papists were both armed and employed contrary to law.

(7.) By violating the freedom of election of members to serve in Parliament.

(8.) By prosecutions in the Court of King's Bench for matters and causes cognizable only in Parliament; and by divers other arbitrary and illegal causes.

(9.) And whereas of late years, partial, corrupt, and unqualified persons have been returned, and served on juries in trials, and particularly diverse jurors in trials for high treason, which were not freeholders.

(10.) And excessive bail hath been required of persons committed in criminal cases, to elude the benefit of the laws made for the liberty of the subjects.

(11.) And excessive fines have been imposed; and illegal and cruel punishments inflicted.

(12.) And several grants and promises made of fines and forfeitures, before any conviction or judgment against the persons upon whom the same were to be levied.

All which are utterly and directly contrary to the known laws and statutes, and freedom of this realm.

And whereas the said late King James II, having abdicated the government, and the throne being thereby vacant, his Highness the Prince of Orange (whom it hath pleased Almighty God to make the glorious instrument of delivering this kingdom from Popery and arbitrary power) did (by the advice of the Lords Spiritual and Temporal, and diverse principal persons of the Commons) cause letters to be written to the Lords Spiritual and Temporal, being Protestants, and other letters to the several counties, cities, universities, boroughs, and cinque ports, for the choosing of such persons to represent them, as were of right to be sent to Parliament, to meet and sit at Westminster upon the two-and-twentieth day of January, in this year one thousand six hundred eighty and eight, in order to such an establishment, as that their religion, laws, and liberties might not again be in danger of being subverted; upon which letters elections have been accordingly made.

And thereupon the said Lords Spiritual and Temporal, and Commons, pursuant to their respective letters and elections, being now assembled in a full and free representation of this nation, taking into their most serious consideration the best means for attaining the ends aforesaid, do in the first place (as their ancestors in like case have usually done), for the vindicating and asserting their ancient rights and liberties, declare:—

(1.) That the pretended power of suspending of laws, or the execution of laws, by regal authority, without consent of Parliament, is illegal.

(2.) That the pretended power of dispensing with laws, or the execution of laws by regal authority, as it hath assumed and exercised of late, is illegal.

(3.) That the commission for erecting the late Court of Commissioners for Ecclesiastical causes, and all other commissions and courts of like nature, are illegal and pernicious.

(4.) That levying money for or to the use of the Crown by pretence of prerogative, without grant of Parliament, for longer time or in other manner than the same is or shall be granted, is illegal.

(5.) That it is the right of the subjects to petition the King, and all commitments and prosecutions for such petitioning are illegal.

(6.) That the raising or keeping a standing army within the kingdom in time of peace, unless it be with consent of Parliament, is against law.

(7.) That the subjects which are Protestants may have arms for their defence suitable to their conditions, and as allowed by law.

(8.) That election of members of Parliament ought to be free.

(9.) That the freedom of speech, and debates or proceedings in Parliament, ought not to be impeached or questioned in any court or place out of Parliament.

(10.) That excessive bail ought not to be required, nor excessive fines imposed; nor cruel and unusual punishments inflicted.

(11.) That jurors ought to be duly impanelled and returned, and jurors which pass upon men in trials for high treason ought to be freeholders.

(12.) That all grants and promises of fines and forfeitures of particular persons before conviction are illegal and void.

(13.) And that for redress of all grievances, and for the amending, strengthening, and preserving of the laws, Parliament ought to be held frequently.

And they do claim, demand, and insist upon all and singular the premises, as their undoubted rights and liberties; and that no declarations, judgments, doings or proceedings, to the prejudice of the people in any of the said premises, ought in any wise to be drawn hereafter into consequence or example.

To which demand of their rights they are particularly encouraged by the declaration of his Highness the Prince of Orange, as being the only means for obtaining a full redress and remedy therein.

Having therefore an entire confidence that his said Highness the Prince of Orange will perfect the deliverance so far advanced by him, and will still preserve them from the violation of their rights, which they have here asserted, and from all other attempts upon their religion, rights, and liberties,

II. The said Lords Spiritual and Temporal, and Commons, assembled at Westminster, do resolve, that William and Mary, Prince and Princess of Orange, be, and be declared, King and Queen of England, France, and Ireland, and the dominions thereunto belonging, to hold the crown and royal dignity of the said kingdoms and dominions to them the said Prince and Princess during their lives, and the life of the survivor of them; and that the sole and full exercise of the regal power be only in, and executed by, the said Crown and royal dignity of the said kingdoms and dominions to be to the heirs of the body of the said Princess; and for default of such issue to the Princess Anne of Denmark, and the heirs of her body; and for default of such issue to the heirs of the body of the said Prince of Orange. And the Lords Spiritual and Temporal, and Commons, do pray the said Prince and Princess to accept the same accordingly.

III. And that the oaths hereafter mentioned be taken by all persons of whom the oaths of allegiance and supremacy might be required by law, instead of them; and that the said oaths of allegiance and supremacy be abrogated.

"I, A. B., do sincerely promise and swear, That I will be faithful and bear true allegiance to their Majesties King William and Queen Mary:

"So help me God."

"I, A. B., do swear, That I do from my heart abhor, detest, and abjure as impious and heretical that damnable doctrine and position, that Princes excommunicated or deprived by the Pope, or any authority of the See of Rome, may be deposed or murdered by their subjects, or any other whatsoever. And I do declare, that no foreign prince, person, prelate, state, or potentate hath, or ought to have, any jurisdiction, power, superiority, preeminence, or authority, ecclesiastical or spiritual, within this realm:

"So help me God!"

IV. Upon which their said Majesties did accept the Crown and royal dignity of the kingdoms of England, France, and Ireland, and the dominions thereunto belonging, according to the resolution and desire of the said Lords and Commons contained in the said declaration.

V. And thereupon their Majesties were pleased, that the said Lords Spiritual and Temporal, and Commons, being the two Houses of Parliament, should continue to sit, and with their Majesties' royal concurrence make effectual provision for the settlement of the religion, laws and liberties of this kingdom, so that the same for the future might not be in danger again of being subverted, to which the said Lords Spiritual and Temporal, and Commons, did agree and proceed to act accordingly.

VI. Now in pursuance of the premises, the said Lords Spiritual and Temporal, and Commons, in Parliament assembled, for the ratifying, confirming, and establishing the said declaration, and the articles, clauses, matters, and things therein contained, by the force of a law made in due form by authority of Parliament, do pray that it may be declared and enacted, That all and singular the rights and liberties asserted and claimed in the said declaration are the true, ancient, and indubitable rights and liberties of the people of this kingdom, and so shall be esteemed, allowed, adjudged, deemed, and taken to be, and that all and every of the particulars aforesaid shall be firmly and strictly holden and observed, as they are expressed in the said declaration; and all officers and ministers whatsoever shall serve their Majesties and their successors according to the same in all times to come.

VII. And the said Lords Spiritual and Temporal, and Commons, seriously considering how it hath pleased Almighty God, in his marvellous providence, and merciful goodness to this nation, to provide and preserve their said Majesties' royal persons most happily to reign over us upon the throne of their ancestors, for which they render unto Him from the bottom of their hearts their humblest thanks and praises, do truly, firmly, assuredly, and in the sincerity of their hearts, think, and do hereby recognize, acknowledge, and declare, that King James II, having abdicated the Government, and their Majesties having accepted the Crown and royal dignity aforesaid, their said Majesties did become, were, are, and of right ought to be, by the laws of this realm, our sovereign liege Lord and Lady, King and Queen of England, France, and Ireland, and the dominions thereunto belonging, in and to whose princely persons the royal state, crown, and dignity of the same realms, with all honours, styles, titles, regalties, prerogatives, powers, jurisdictions, and authorities to the same belonging and appertaining, are most fully, rightfully, and entirely invested and incorporated, united, and annexed.

VIII. And for preventing all questions and divisions in this realm, by reason of any pretended titles to the Crown, and for preserving a certainty in the succession thereof, in and upon which the unity, peace, tranquility, and safety of this nation doth, under God, wholly consist and depend, the said Lords Spiritual and Temporal, and Commons, do beseech their Majesties that it may be enacted, established, and declared, that the Crown and regal government of the said kingdoms and dominions, with all and singular the premises thereunto belonging and appertaining, shall be and continue to their said Majesties, and the survivor of them, during their lives, and the life of the survivor of them. And that the entire, perfect, and full exercise of the regal power and government be only in, and executed by, his Majesty, in the names of both their Majesties, during their joint lives; and after their deceases the said Crown and premises shall be and remain to the heirs of the body of her Majesty: and for default of such issue, to her Royal Highness the Princess Anne of Denmark, and the heirs of her body; and for default of such issue, to the heirs of the body of his said Majesty: And thereunto the said Lords Spiritual and Temporal, and Commons, do, in the name of all the people aforesaid, most humbly and faithfully submit themselves, their heirs and posterities, forever: and do faithfully promise, that they will stand to, maintain, and defend their said Majesties, and also the limitation and succession of the Crown herein specified and contained, to the utmost of their powers, with their lives and estates, against all persons whatsoever that shall attempt anything to the contrary.

IX. And whereas it hath been found by experience, that it is inconsistent with the safety and welfare of this Protestant kingdom, to be governed by a Popish prince, or by any king or queen marrying a Papist, the said Lords Spiritual and Temporal, and Commons, do further pray that it may be enacted, That all and every person and persons that is, are, or shall be reconciled to, or shall hold communion with, the See or Church of Rome, or shall profess the Popish religion, or shall marry a Papist, shall be excluded, and be for ever incapable to inherit, possess, or enjoy the Crown and Government of this realm, and Ireland, and the dominions thereunto belonging, or any part of the same, or to have, use, or exercise any regal power, authority, or jurisdiction within the same; and in all and every such case or cases the people of these realms shall be and are hereby absolved of their allegiance; and the said Crown and Government shall from time to time descend to, and be enjoyed by, such person or persons, being Protestants, as should have inherited and enjoyed the same, in case the said person or persons so reconciled, holding communion, or professing, or marrying, as aforesaid, were naturally dead.

X. And that every King and Queen of this realm, who at any time hereafter shall come to and succeed in the Imperial Crown of this kingdom, shall, on the first day of the meeting of the first Parliament, next after his or her coming to the Crown, sitting in his or her throne in the House of Peers, in the presence of the Lords and Commons therein assembled, or at his or her coronation, before such person or persons who shall administer the coronation oath to him or her, at the time of his or her taking the said oath (which shall first happen), make, subscribe, and audibly repeat the declaration mentioned in the statute made in the thirteenth year of the reign of King Charles II., intituled "An act for the more effectual preserving the King's person and Government, by disabling Papists from sitting in either House of Parliament." But if it shall happen, that such King or Queen, upon his or her succession to the Crown of this realm, shall be under the age of twelve years, then every such King or Queen shall make, subscribe, and audibly repeat the said declaration at his or her coronation, or the first day of meeting of the first Parliament as aforesaid, which shall first happen after such King or Queen shall have attained the said age of twelve years.

XI. All which their Majesties are contented and pleased shall be declared, enacted, and established by authority of this present Parliament, and shall stand, remain, and be the law of this realm for ever; and the same are by their said Majesties, by and with the advice and consent of the Lords Spiritual and Temporal, and Commons, in Parliament assembled, and by the authority of the same, declared, enacted, or established accordingly.

XII. And be it further declared and enacted by the authority aforesaid, that from and after this present session of Parliament, no dispensation by *non obstante* of or to any statute, or any part thereof, shall be allowed, but that the same shall be held void and of no effect, except a dispensation be allowed of in such statute, and except in such cases as shall be specially provided for by one or more bill or bills to be passed during this present session of Parliament.

XIII. Provided that no charter, or grant, or pardon granted before the three-and-twentieth day of October, in the year of our Lord One thousand six hundred eighty-nine, shall be any ways impeached or invalidated by this Act, by that the same shall be and remain of the same force and effect in law, and no other, than as if this Act had never been made.

The institutions of America, which were a subject only of curiosity to monarchical France, ought to be a subject of study for republican France. Though it is no longer a question whether we shall have a monarchy or a republic in France, we are yet to learn . . . whether it shall be . . . pacific or warlike, liberal or oppressive, a republic that menaces the sacred rights of property and family, or one that honors and protects them both. . . . Let us look to America . . . less to find examples than instruction; let us borrow from her principles, rather than the details, of her laws. The laws of the French republic may be, and ought to be in many cases, different from those which govern the United States; but the principles on which the American constitutions rest, those principles of order, of the balance of powers, of true liberty, of deep and sincere respect for right, are indispensable to all republics.

Alexis de Tocqueville, *Democracy in America* (12th ed., 1848)

PART 2

America's First Constitutions and Declarations of Rights

⟿ POINTS TO REMEMBER ⟸

1. Beginning with the founding of Jamestown in 1607, Englishmen in the American colonies were entitled to the same rights as their countrymen at home. Not all inhabitants, including indentured servants and slaves, enjoyed these rights, however. As in England, there were also property qualifications for voting. The principles of republicanism and representative government were introduced into the colonies with the establishment of the Virginia House of Burgesses in 1619.

2. The Pilgrims who landed at Plymouth Rock in 1620, by virtue of their Mayflower Compact, brought a contractual theory of government to the colonies. This later served as the basis for popularly based constitutions. All of the colonies, however, carried on the constitutional and legal customs of Great Britain. The American colonists were familiar with the idea of a written constitution as a result of their experience with colonial charters, the Fundamental Orders of Connecticut (1639) being the most famous.

3. The colonists adopted the English theory of representation, which included the principle of geographical representation, or the representation of localities as well as people. The Americans modified the English system of representation, however, by introducing a residency requirement for elected representatives. The most significant colonial departure from the English system was the absence of an aristocratically based upper chamber.

4. Colonial assemblies enjoyed considerable but not complete independence. Their most important and decisive victory was their control of the purse strings. This gave them financial independence and eventually undermined British control of the colonies.

5. Local self-government, based on counties or townships, became

firmly established in the colonial period, and helped to prepare the nation for the concept of federalism that triumphed in the Constitutional Convention of 1787.

6. In general, most American colonists enjoyed a great deal of religious liberty. There was some religious intolerance, however, even though colonial governments were more tolerant of dissenting or minority sects than were European governments. Freedom of speech was protected by British statutes and the common law, and the American press was also much freer than that of most of Europe.

7. The important turning point in Anglo-American relations was 1763, when the British adopted a bold new policy that sought to establish a new economic relationship between the colonies and the mother country. The Stamp Act, passed in 1763 for the purpose of raising revenue, met with the cry: "No taxation without representation." It was the first in a series of parliamentary laws that led eventually to the American Revolution.

8. In the Declaration and Resolves of the First Continental Congress (1774), the colonists declared that, "by the immutable laws of nature, the principles of the English Constitution, and the several [colonial] charters," they were "entitled to life, liberty and property [and] all the rights, liberties, and immunities of free and natural born subjects within the realm of England [and] to the common law of England." Rejecting legislative supremacy, they asserted that the legislative authority of Parliament was limited by the higher law of the Constitution. In their Declaration of the Causes and Necessity of Taking up Arms (1775), the colonists listed their grievances against Parliament, declaring they were "resolved to die freemen rather than to live slaves."

9. The Preamble of the Declaration of Independence is based on the theory that the American people are entitled to certain natural rights, including life, liberty, and the pursuit of happiness, and that all men are created equal. The main text of the document, on the other hand, asserts that the inhabitants of the colonies are entitled to various constitutional, common law, and charter rights. The claim that "all men are created equal" has received different interpretations, one being that the colonists were simply contending that the American people, as a nation, were entitled to the same rights as Englishmen. Later generations interpreted the equality language of the Declaration of Independence more broadly as a prohibition against slavery.

10. The most comprehensive statement of colonial rights and privileges made during the revolutionary period appeared in the Declaration of Rights of 1774, wherein the colonists identified nine different rights. In essence, however, the quarrel between Parliament and the Ameri-

can assemblies over rights was symptomatic of a more fundamental disagreement: the meaning of the English Constitution and of constitutional government.

11. The year 1776 marks the birth of constitutional government in the United States and in the world at large. This was the first time in the world's history that a large group of communities—now independent and sovereign States—had begun the formation of their own governments under written constitutions. This was also the year in which the Articles of Confederation, our first national constitution, was written.

12. The principal figure in the drafting of the new State constitutions was John Adams, "the father of American constitutionalism." His pamphlet, "Thoughts on Government," was widely used as a source of understanding, and Adams was the chief architect of the Massachusetts Constitution of 1780. This was the best of the early State constitutions and the first to employ a check and balance system.

13. The first State constitutions contained a variety of flaws requiring subsequent correction. None was written by a constitutional convention or submitted to the people for approval. The first State constitution resting on a thoroughly republican base was the Massachusetts Constitution of 1780, which set the standard for the United States Constitution. It is still in force today and is the oldest constitution in the country.

14. In general, our first State constitutions contained three basic weaknesses: (a) They failed to provide for an adequate system of separation of powers; (b) all but the Constitution of New York failed to establish an independent executive; (c) all lacked a provision establishing the constitution as the supreme law. In addition, a number of State constitutions neglected to provide for their amendment. Nor did all of the early State constitutions contain a bill of rights.

15. The first draft of the Articles of Confederation was made in the summer of 1776. But the document was not submitted to the States for approval until the fall of 1777 and did not take effect until 1781. The three major sources of contention among the States were: (a) the western land claim of Virginia and other States; (b) the system of representation in Congress; and (c) the basis for determining how much each State should contribute to the national treasury. The most important issue in the writing of the Articles was the question of State sovereignty. This was resolved in favor of the States, Article II declaring that "Each State retains its sovereignty, freedom, and independence."

16. The Articles of Confederation were little more than a treaty among sovereign States. The States granted certain of the same basic rights and privileges to citizens of other States as they granted to their own citi-

zens. The government was exceedingly weak, however, consisting of a unicameral Congress that lacked the power even to regulate commerce or levy a tax. No provision was made for an executive or judiciary and the Confederation government was forced to rely upon the States for the enforcement of its laws. Because the unanimous vote of all of the States was required to amend the Articles, it was virtually impossible to change the document even when its faults were generally acknowledged. Only by circumventing Congress were the nation's leaders able to reform the system and establish a new Constitution.

Colonial Governments

THE SEEDS OF LIBERTY were planted on American soil in 1607, when the first English settlers landed in Virginia and founded Jamestown. They were not the first Englishmen to attempt to establish a colony in Virginia, but they were the first to win a permanent foothold. Lured by tales of great wealth, they were destined to suffer months and even years of hunger, fever, and death in a hostile wilderness. It was the destiny of their children and succeeding generations to develop the richest and most powerful colony in British America.

The plan to colonize Virginia was not a part of any government scheme but an effort by London merchants to discover gold and silver, as the Spanish had done a century before in Mexico and farther south, and to explore for a northwest passage. The Virginia colony was thus established under the auspices of a private corporation known as the London Company, by virtue of a charter granted by James I. In the charter the King guaranteed that the colonists and any children born to them "shall have and enjoy all Liberties, Franchises, and Immunities . . . as if they had been abiding and born within this, our Realm of England." In other words, Englishmen in the colonies were to enjoy the same rights granted to Englishmen at home—such as trial by jury and the right to be taxed by representatives of their own choosing. Freedom was actually planted in Virginia, then, even before the forebears of today's Virginians first saw their land. Before long Virginians were not only defending their freedom but enlarging it to the point that they actually enjoyed more liberty than their British cousins in the mother country.

Despite the hardships of the early years, Virginia became increasingly attractive to Englishmen at home because of the opportunities it presented for private ownership of land. Corporate ownership gave way to individual ownerships in the colony after 1618, when the London Company began paying dividends and increasing incentives by giving away land to its stockholders, to colonists who had served the company, and to individuals who would pay for an immigrant's fare across the Atlantic. Even the poverty-stricken immigrants, who often came as indentured servants, had a powerful incentive to come to Virginia. An indentured servant was a person who signed an indenture, or contract, by which he agreed to sell his services in the colony for three to five years as a way of paying for the voyage from Europe. Having satisfied the terms of the agreement, he was then free to strike out on his own and become an independent landowner himself.

During the years 1634–1704, about 1,500 to 2,000 indentured servants arrived annually. Governor William Berkeley reported in 1671 that there were some 13,000 in the colony, about thirteen percent of the population. Many became great landholders and leaders in Virginia government. Seven of the forty-four members of the colonial legislature in 1629 had been indentured servants just five years earlier. To a great extent, the aristocracy of colonial Virginia was composed of self-made men. Thomas Jefferson would later boast that Virginia had a "natural" aristocracy, which he viewed as superior to an aristocracy based on hereditary entitlement and special privilege. But Virginia denied no Englishman the opportunity to acquire property—and with it a substantial degree of individual freedom. In sharp contrast to Great Britain, landowners constituted the large majority of Virginia's colonial population—eighty percent or more.

The first Negroes—about twenty in number—came to Virginia in 1619 aboard a Dutch warship. They had been captured in a raid in the West Indies and were traded to the Virginians in exchange for supplies. They came not as slaves, however, but as indentured servants. By 1650, there were only 300 Negroes in Virginia, and most of these were freemen who had completed their periods of indentured service. One of the first to gain his freedom was Anthony Johnson, who ironically also became the first man in the colony to own slaves. It was not unusual, even as late as 1865, for free Negroes in Virginia to own Negro slaves, employing them often in places of business. The institution of slavery was not established in Virginia until 1662, when the legislature enacted a law requiring that all servants who were non-Christians should be held as slaves for life. By means of this statute, Virginia accepted slavery and made it legal. It was a fateful step that marked the introduction of slavery into the Southern colonies. Like a blight, it spread to the North as well, and soon became an accepted practice throughout the American colonies. The first slave-trading port on the continent was actually Boston.

Two hundred years would pass before slavery was abolished in North America. The Negro was thus the last of the founding generation of Americans—our first immigrants—to taste the fruits of liberty that were originally cultivated in Tidewater Virginia.

Slavery, of course, had existed since ancient times and was not limited to the American colonies or to the black race. It flourished in Greece and Rome and throughout medieval Europe and the Middle East. The Spanish introduced human bondage into the West Indies in 1502. The discovery of the New World created a heavy demand for labor, stimulating the slave trade. European traders and African chieftains developed a vast commercial system for the capture, sale, and transportation of slaves, and it is estimated that during the sixteenth, seventeenth, and eighteenth centuries at least fifteen million Africans were brought to the New World by the maritime powers of Europe. Although slavery was eradicated in the United States more than a century ago, it persists today, in other parts of the world—but in a far more brutal form and on an even larger scale. This is the system of forced labor that is characteristic of the modern totalitarian state. It consists not of individual ownership of human beings as a species of private property, but of government ownership by the state, usually in the form of the slave labor camp—what Alexander Solzhenitsyn, the Russian writer, has described as the Gulag Archipelago. It is estimated that during the reign of Joseph Stalin (1929–1956) there were twelve to twenty million people housed in Soviet camps during any one year.

At about the same time the first Negroes were brought to the Virginia colony, there were two other important events that would later have an enormous impact on American political and constitutional development. In 1619, the House of Burgesses convened in a small church in James-

"The Slave" by Michelangelo (1495–1564).

(Courtesy of the Library of Congress.)

town. This was the first representative assembly in the Western Hemisphere. It gave Virginians some measure of self-government almost from the outset and established the principle of republicanism not only for Virginia but also for her future sister colonies along the Atlantic Coast. One of the first steps taken by the assembly was to enact legislation prohibiting gambling, drunkenness, swearing, and idleness, and also requiring every colonist to attend church regularly.

The second important event of this period was the landing of the Pilgrims at Plymouth, Massachusetts, in 1620. Almost all of the New England colonists were Puritans who had a religious as well as an economic interest in coming to the New World. They differed in outlook and behavior from their more orthodox Anglican neighbors situated in Jamestown, and brought with them a set of religious doctrines that anticipated the founding of what John Eliot called the Christian Commonwealth, or a blend of theocracy and pure democracy. Like the Jamestown colonists, they came to the rocky shores of New England under the auspices of the Virginia Company. The first inhabitants of Massachusetts were not simply Puritan Nonconformists but radical Separatists. Whereas the Nonconformists aimed to purify the Anglican church from within, the Separatists were determined to break away and worship as they pleased in their own congregations. Before leaving Europe, they had tried and failed to secure a guarantee of religious freedom from James I; but they learned "that he would . . . not molest them, provided they carried themselves peaceably." By virtue of this historic concession on the part of the monarch, British America was opened to settlement by all dissenting Protestants.

Before leaving ship, they entered into a solemn agreement for the formation of a government upon reaching land. This became the famous Mayflower Compact, by which "in the presence of God and one another" they agreed to "covenant and combine ourselves together into a civil Body Politick, for our better Ordering and Preservation" and to "enact, constitute, and frame such just and equal Laws, Ordinances, Acts, Constitutions, and Offices, from time to time, as shall be thought most meet and convenient for the general Good of the Colony; into which we promise all due Submission and Obedience." What the founders of the Massachusetts Bay Colony agreed to, in other words, was to form a government for self-rule based on popular consent and rule of law. The Mayflower Compact was like the church covenant by which Separatists formed congregations, except that it bound its signers to observe the ordinances of a civil rather than a religious society, and professed allegiance to the King as well as God. It marks the introduction into the American colonies of a compact theory of government which would later serve as the basis for both popularly based State constitutions and the United States Constitution, the latter being viewed as a compact among the States as well as the people in the States.

Generally speaking, the Puritans subscribed to the view that a covenant was the necessary basis for both the church and the state. These two classes of covenants were known respectively as the "church covenant" and the "plantation covenant"—and there was a close relation between the democratic method of forming a congregation or church and the democratic method of forming a state, both emphasizing the importance of the individual. In time, the early tendencies in New England toward aristocracy and theocracy disappeared and there was a democratization of its social and political institutions. Perhaps the most significant aspect of this democratic spirit was the emphasis on local self-government, which found expression in the New England town meeting. Puritan democracy, however, was reserved primarily for church members. The Puritans readily embraced English common law and the English constitutional tradition; and they accepted in principle equality of civil rights. But they did not endorse the idea of political equality, and they did not believe that all members of society should participate in the political process. In these respects the New England and Southern colonists shared similar political views.

Although the Catholics in Maryland, the Quakers in Delaware and Pennsylvania, and the Dutch Reformed in New York and New Jersey introduced even more religious diversity into North America, they nevertheless followed the same path of political development as the New England and Southern Colonies. The middle colonies were more of a melting pot of religious and national groups than any other part of America. From the standpoint of their evolving political institutions in the colonial era, however, all of the colonies, despite their ethnic and religious and socioeconomic differences, tended to carry on the constitutional and legal customs of Great Britain, the absence of an hereditary aristocracy being one of the few conspicuous departures from the British model.

In all of the colonies, whether royal, proprietary, or corporate, the colonial governments exhibited the same general pattern. In each colony there was eventually a governor and a bicameral legislature, as in England there was a king and a two-house Parliament. In all of the colonies except Rhode Island and Connecticut, the governor was appointed rather than elected. The upper chamber of the legislature consisted of the Governor's Council, whose members, except in Massachusetts, Rhode Island, and Connecticut, were also appointed; and in the lower chamber the members were elected by the people. As in England, executive, legislative, and judicial functions were somewhat mixed, mainly because the Governor and his Council sat as the Supreme Court. There was nevertheless a rudimentary separation of powers between the governor and the assembly. The American colonists were familiar with the idea of a written constitution as a result of their experience with colonial charters, the Fundamental Orders of Connecticut (1639) being the most famous. Though the Mayflower Compact was the first political covenant, the Fundamental Orders were for all practical purposes the first modern written constitution.

Until the time of the American Revolution, the colonists enjoyed the same civil liberties as native Englishmen. Like their English cousins, however, they did not have equal political rights, and the franchise was generally restricted throughout the colonies. The right to vote or hold office was limited by religious qualifications in some colonies, and by property qualifications everywhere.

One important departure from the English theory of representation was the evolution during the colonial era of the principle of legislative residency. Whereas members of the House of Commons have traditionally been permitted to represent any constituency in the country, no matter where they happened to live, the colonists adopted the distinctively American custom of requiring assemblymen to be residents of the district they represented. This custom was not written into the Constitution, which provides merely that members of the House and Senate must be inhabitants of the *State* in which they are elected, but it has continued to be a part of the American political tradition at both the Federal and State levels down to the present.

The idea behind this principle of representation is the belief that a local resident or "home town boy," as the Americans say, is more likely to have a sympathetic understanding of the wants, needs, and interests of the people in a given community than an outsider. In sharp contrast to England, where the population is homogeneous and concentrated, the United States has always been more culturally diverse, even within a single State, with a population that is partly urban but is also significantly rural, scattered across vast expanses of territory that dwarf the British Isles. In such a society, the residency requirement helps to satisfy the need for familiarity and shared values between the representative and his constituents.

An important feature of the English theory of representation that was continued in the colonies and in the Constitution of 1787 was the principle of geographical representation, which asserts the view that a legislator does not represent just people as such, but people in a broader cultural sense, including their localities and their way of life. It is reflected not only in the residency requirement that grew out of our colonial experience but also in the representational basis of Congress designed by the Framers. Thus the theory of representation embodied in the Constitution rejects absolute political equality and seeks instead to balance the population and geographical principles. The system of representation in the Senate, for example, gives each State the same number of Senators, irrespective of the size of the State's population. Likewise, the House of Representatives, though apportioned on the basis of population, includes at least one Congressman from each State, irrespective of population.

The principle of geographical representation has also served over the years as a check on overbearing majorities. It protects the minority rural population from the multitudes of city dwellers; it gives the small town or village a voice in the formulation of public policy; and it encourages a broad representation of different points of view. In recent years, however, the Supreme Court has taken a different view. In *Gray v. Sanders* (1963), the Court ruled that "The conception of political equality from the Declaration of Independence, to Lincoln's Gettysburg Address, to the Fifteenth, Seventeenth, and Nineteenth Amendments, can mean only one thing—one person, one vote." The Court has been divided on this issue, however, and the dissenters have contended that there is no evidence to support the Court's new philosophy of political equality. According to Justice Frankfurter, it was "the basic English principle of apportioning representatives among the local governmental entities, towns or counties, rather than among units of approximately equal population," that took root in the colonies; and Justice Harlan argued that the principle of "one person, one vote" has "never been the universally accepted political philosophy in England, the American colonies, or in the United States." Although the deeply rooted tradition of geographical representation seemed to refute the historical accuracy of the Court's assertion that the American political tradition of political equality meant absolute equality based on numbers alone, Chief Justice Warren insisted nevertheless in *Reynolds v. Sims* (1964) that "Citizens, not history or economic interests, cast votes. Considerations of area alone provide an insufficient justification for deviations from the equal-population principle. . . . [P]eople, not land or trees or pastures, vote." The question, however, is not who votes, but who and what interests legislators are supposed to represent.

Whatever the merits of the Supreme Court's view of the matter, it seems clear that the principle of republicanism which the English settlers brought with them to North America was only modestly changed during the next century and a half of colonial government. In every colony, local units of government, whether townships and villages or cities and counties, were accorded representation, thereby perpetuating the English system of geographical representation. The only deviation was the addition of the residency requirement, which actually strengthened and reaffirmed the principle of geographical representation. The "one person, one vote" principle is of recent origin, and there is no evidence that it was adopted in any of the colonies—or indeed in any of the States that joined the Union after the Constitution was adopted.

The most significant departure from the British example was the democratic class structure of colonial society, which gave rise to a new form of representative government in America and, as we shall later see, laid the foundation for a system of separation of powers that was radically different from that which existed in Great Britain. In no colony did a landed aristocracy, based on hereditary privilege, gain a foothold. Hence there were no upper chambers comparable to the House of Lords in any of the colonial assemblies. The system of representation adopted made no allowance for the representation of classes or political privilege, and in this sense rested on the principle of political equality. But it was not a complete equality, for the right to vote, as in England, was conditioned, as we noted earlier, on property ownership—and in some colonies on religious belief as well. Catholics, for example, were often excluded from the franchise; Anglicans were at a disadvantage in New England but dominated the southern colonies. These restrictions also applied in a number of colonies to individuals seeking public office.

Political power thus rested in all of the colonies in the hands of the "freemen" or "freeholders," that is, adult white males of some means. Because of the ready availability of cheap land everywhere, the suffrage was actually much broader than one might think, and it would be erroneous to assume that a small elite governed the colonies to the exclusion of the general population. Thus, the landed gentry of Virginia dominated public affairs, but it was open to any enterprising young man of diligence, ability, and good character. Men of education and wealth naturally played a leading role, however, as they do today. In the early period the great landowners and members of the clergy tended to be the leaders of colonial society and government; but as we approach the American Revolution, members of the legal profession, physicians, educators, merchants, and military leaders became increasingly conspicuous in representative assemblies.

The members of the Federal Convention of 1787 resisted attempts to write property or religious qualifications for voting or holding office into the Constitution. Members of Congress, the President, the Judiciary, and presidential electors were not required to meet a property qualification, and religious tests were banned. In deference to States' Rights, the States were left free to maintain property qualifications for the suffrage as they saw fit, and so the colonial practice of limiting the franchise to freeholders was continued into the nineteenth century. As the century progressed, however, pressure for universal suffrage increased and property qualifications were gradually eliminated in all of the States. With the adoption of the Fifteenth Amendment (1870), which extended the right to vote to

Negroes, the exclusive power of the States to determine voter qualifications began to fade. This amendment was followed by the Nineteenth Amendment (1920) granting women the right to vote, and more recently by the Twenty-Fourth (1964) and Twenty-Sixth (1971) amendments eliminating the poll tax and extending the franchise to persons eighteen years of age.

As a result of these amendments and various decisions of the Supreme Court, the principle of republicanism that originated in England and was carried across the Atlantic to the American colonies has changed substantially over the years, and representative government today is considerably different from what it was two hundred years ago. The basis of representation in State and Federal legislative assemblies has changed as a result of the "one person, one vote" decisions of the Supreme Court, and the main standards for voter qualification in elections, whether Federal, State, or local, are now set by the Federal government instead of the States.

The degree to which these changes have contributed to the growth of liberty, order, and justice is a complex question. Although there is more political freedom in the United States than possibly any other country in the world, at least a third of the American electorate—and often as much as half—refuses to participate in the political process or exercise the right to vote. Ironically, political apathy seems to have increased with the expansion of the suffrage.

The price of liberty, it has been said, is eternal vigilance. Can democratic government promote and protect liberty, order, and justice if half the population is failing to hold public officials accountable for their actions? Is there a lesson to be learned from the history of ancient Rome? Once a thriving republic, it fell to tyranny because the people had become more interested in "bread and circuses" than in safeguarding their political institutions. And how informed is the American electorate? Polls taken in recent years reveal an alarming degree of ignorance among the American people about the Constitution, national and international affairs, the record and achievements of their representatives, and of the political and economic forces that are actually controlling their lives and the destiny of the country. The greatest threat to liberty may well be when the people take liberty for granted and allow others to do their thinking and make their decisions for them. There are some who seem to prefer security to liberty. What is the solution? The establishment of voter qualification tests to determine an individual's knowledge of the system, in the hope of encouraging a better informed electorate? Improved teaching of civics in the schools?

These are difficult questions that offer no easy solutions. Yet it behooves us as a free people to reexamine and continually reinvigorate our political institutions; to be alert to the first transgressions before dangerous precedents are set; to jealously protect the fundamental principles which support our form of government and not to compromise them for the sake of convenience. It was this intense love of liberty that compelled the American patriots, pledging their lives, their personal freedom, and their fortunes, to take up arms against the British. Would the American people today make the same personal sacrifices as their forebears for the causes that led to the American Revolution?

Relations with Great Britain

In retrospect, it would seem that the American colonies were destined to gain independence at some point in time; and in many ways they were already independent before the Revolution. From the day the first settlers landed, the colonies governed themselves in most matters. They had their own charters of government, which served as written constitutions of a sort, and their own provincial assemblies, which exercised a considerable degree of autonomy.

The colonies were part of Britain's vastly expanding empire, but the British empire was commercial in nature, not imperial. The King's ministers were not interested in political control of the colonies for its own sake, for military purposes, or as a tax base. They viewed the colonies instead as a great commercial reservoir that contributed to the economic prosperity of the mother country by supplying England with raw materials and by providing markets for the sale of English-made goods. Consequently, neither Parliament nor the King's ministers troubled themselves much with American affairs. They were content if the Thirteen Colonies continued to ship to Britain their tobacco, furs, dried fish, grain, and lumber, and the colonies were content to be ruled from Westminster so long as British regiments and British fleets defended America when wars arose with the French or the Spaniards, and so long as the colonies held the real political power in provincial assemblies. Thus the colonies enjoyed what Edmund Burke called the "salutary neglect" of London officialdom. The more the colonies were neglected politically by England, the more the colonists prospered.

Because England had no real political interest in the colonies, especially in the seventeenth and early eighteenth centuries, colonial administration of the colonies was unplanned and haphazard. No single agency was ever given primary responsibility for the colonies until the very eve of the Revolution. By the early 1700s, there were six agencies of the British government, all located in London and out of touch with America, sharing responsibility for administering the colonies: the Board of Trade, The Privy Council, the Treasury and Customs Office, the Admiralty, the Secretary of State for the Southern Department, and, of course, Parliament. But the colonies were never overrun with meddlesome bureaucrats. Even though the Americans were subjects of George III in 1776, few of them saw many outward signs of British sovereignty. Only nine of the colonies had royal governors, and these grand figures stayed close to the colonial capitals, or else spent much of their time in England. Judges, though appointed by the Crown, were usually American-born. Uniformed British troops were at the frontiers, but not regularly in the settlements. The only fairly numerous body of officials of the British government were the revenue officers who collected port duties under the Navigation Acts, and they too were mostly American-born.

In the eyes of the English, the colonies were technically mere corporations—subordinate to Parliament and without any inherent sovereignty. Colonial legislatures possessed only such privileges as the King chose to grant to them. British officials also insisted that the rights and powers won by Parliament in the Glorious Revolution of 1688 did not automatically extend to the colonial assemblies, and that the royal prerogative (inherent powers reserved by the Crown that were not surrendered to Parliament) was therefore more extensive over the American legislatures than over Parliament.

Acting upon these assumptions, British officials repeatedly rejected requests from the colonies to create new legislative districts or to pass "triennial acts" providing for automatic meetings of the legislatures at regular intervals. They also refused to accept speakers chosen by the assemblies on an automatic basis. These were rights that Parliament had long enjoyed. The principal check on the colonial assemblies was the Board of Trade, which instructed the royal governors, controlled colonial patronage, assisted the Privy Council in appeals from the colonial courts, advised Parliament and the Crown on matters of colonial policy, and, most significantly, had the power to recommend approval or disallowance of colonial legislation, much like a court exercising judicial review. Between 1696 and 1774, some 400 acts of colonial legislatures were recommended for disallowance by the Board. Although this led to disputes from time to time, the colonists cheerfully acknowledged the right of the Board, as an agency of the King-in-Parliament, to carry out its advisory functions, and its legitimacy was never seriously questioned. Nor, for that matter, was the authority of the other agencies. The conflict between England and the colonies, as we shall see, centered mainly on Parliament and the scope of its powers.

It was in the sphere of finance that the assemblies won their most important and decisive victory, and this proved to be the undoing of the British. Despite all of the theory repudiating the legal sovereignty of the colonial assemblies, these bodies in reality controlled the purse strings and in effect exercised a considerable amount of political sovereignty. The power to tax and spend rested in the hands of the colonial legislatures. Acting upon instructions from London, Royal governors repeatedly, but without success, demanded that the assemblies pass permanent revenue acts instead of annual appropriations. In New York, for example, the colonial assembly, patterning itself after the House of Commons, limited its appropriations to one year, stipulated in great detail how the money was to be spent, and refused to accept amendments to revenue bills. When Governor George Clinton tried to claim some authority over fiscal matters by the veto power, the assembly simply blocked all legislation and brought the Governor to his knees. Through the clever technique of appropriating the salaries of public officials by name and not by office, the colonial assemblies also effectively limited the governor's power of appointment and removal. Even the local militia were under the control of the assemblies. Similar incidents occurred in Pennsylvania, Massachusetts, and the Carolinas.

Between 1699 and 1766, the Virginia offices of treasurer and speaker of the House of Burgesses were always held by the same person, thereby giving the legislature not only control over fiscal policy but custody of the funds as well. In nearly all of the provinces money granted for special purposes, such as the payment of troops, was often lodged in the hands of commissioners named in an appropriation act. "He who pays the piper," according to an old English proverb, "can call the tune." The importance of local control of revenue and expenditures can hardly be overestimated. Governors were virtually helpless in many instances to support the royal prerogative or the wishes of the King's ministers in the face of colonial assemblies that could specify the expenditures of every cent and withhold funds from any governmental function they pleased. This situation contributed substantially to the growth of colonial independence and the gradual decline of British power in America.

In 1763, Patrick Henry defended the dominion of Virginia in an action at law called the Parson's Cause. The case arose when clergymen of the Church of England—which was Virginia's established church—brought suit against the commonwealth because Virginia's Assembly in 1758 had passed a statute that temporarily reduced the salaries paid to clergymen. In England, the Privy Council had declared the law to be unconstitutional; a parson therefore had to file suit to obtain the funds he had been denied. Although the jury in the Parson's Cause trial gave a verdict for the plaintiff, it awarded him only one penny in damages. The verdict was actually a victory, then, for the Assembly that had reduced the parsons' salaries. Patrick Henry, whose eloquence had won over the jury, argued in the case that the British Crown, as represented by the Privy Council in England, had no power to set aside an act of the Virginia Assembly. This argument was clearly close to declaring that Virginia was politically independent of Britain. Twelve years later, of course, Henry ended his famous speech to the Virginia Assembly with the cry, "Give me liberty, or give me death!" It was by such audacious men that colonial assemblies were persuaded by 1775 to cast off the authority of Crown and Parliament.

Local Government in the Colonies

If the representative assemblies in every colony were the most powerful feature of the colonial constitutions, the American institutions of local government still had nearly as much influence on the development of the American political system that culminated in 1787. English local government was far more vigorous and popular than local government in France or in most of the rest of Europe during the eighteenth century; but American local government was still more active than the British forms, and attracted heartier public support.

By 1763, the forms of American local government varied considerably from province to province, and even within provinces—or colonies. Along the wild western frontier, local government was democratic and informal, but highly effective—as it had need to be because of the frontier's perils and the need for prompt cooperation among neighbors. At the other extreme, some towns along the Atlantic seaboard held charters of incorporation that conferred great powers upon municipal governments, much like the privileges held by venerable European cities.

There were forms of county government throughout British North America, but the county system of local government was strongest in the South, and the "middle colonies" of New York and Pennsylvania. In Virginia, the political powers of the county were greater than they are today in any American county. Each Virginia county was controlled by a county court composed of the county's several Justices of the Peace. Even the colony's Assembly did not venture to interfere with the Justices' authority. New Justices of the Peace were selected by the Governor from a list submitted by the county court itself, so that the court became self-perpetuating. These Justices of the Peace were appointed from the class of landowners that was still specified in law as *gentlemen*. They were paid neither salaries nor fees, but served at their own expense. Virtually independent of both Williamsburg (then Virginia's capital) and London, these county courts amounted to a kind of federal system within Virginia, and also within other southern States that allocated large powers to counties. Thus county government became a preparation for the concept of federalism that triumphed in the Constitutional Convention of 1787.

In New England—and later, in those States to the west that were settled primarily by New Englanders—the "township" system of local government was more important than the county organization, even though
counties had their functions in New England, too. New England's town
meetings could be attended by almost anyone, although in 1763 not all
local residents were entitled to vote at these meetings. Township officers
were elected annually in those times, and that was another practice that
tended to make township government democratic. New England's town
meetings had begun as formal gatherings of men in good standing with
the Puritan or Congregational churches. By 1763, they had become civic
institutions and there was no religious test for participation.

Both county and township were political structures inherited from
centuries of English experience. Yet in America these institutions took
on a renewed vigor or were adapted to American circumstances. By the
1830s, for example, the French traveler Alexis de Tocqueville found the
system of American local government—especially the township—a major reason for the successes of the American democracy.

Earlier it was noted that representative government was Britain's most
important contribution to America's Constitution. The British succeeded
in conferring upon the colonies a truly representative system of provincial
and local government. This made possible the establishment of liberty,
order, and justice in the new nation. As Benjamin Franklin, John Dickinson, and a good many other leading men at the Constitutional Convention would recognize sadly even in 1787, it was a melancholy irony that
the political patrimony bequeathed to America by Britain should itself be
a major cause of Britain's loss of her North American empire.

Civil Liberties in the Colonies

Among the civil liberties that are enumerated in the Bill of Rights of the
American Constitution, those providing for the free exercise of religion,
freedom of speech, and freedom of the press are noteworthy. It is instructive to examine the status of these freedoms in the Thirteen Colonies on
the eve of the American Revolution.

First, the free exercise of religion. In the seventeenth century, America
was a refuge for fugitives from religious persecution, including Puritans,

Quakers, and Catholics. But the persecuted, when they have opportunity, sometimes persecute in turn, and so it was in North America until religious hostilities diminished in the eighteenth century on both sides of the Atlantic.

By 1763 the congeries of religious sects and denominations had learned tolerably well how to get along peaceably with one another. The Congregationalists of Massachusetts, for example, had found it necessary to permit Anglicans to settle among them in large numbers; the Quakers of Pennsylvania had come to terms with the Scotch-Irish Presbyterians of the western regions; Methodist preachers were evangelizing the backwoods and the frontier; the feeble Catholic minority in Maryland and New Jersey was tolerated; the handful of Jews were not even noticed; and the Deists, though as few in number as the Jews, had won over some eminent men, including Thomas Jefferson, Benjamin Franklin, and John Adams. Nine of the Thirteen Colonies had established churches in 1763: the Church of England in Virginia, Maryland, the Carolinas, Georgia, and the southern counties of New York; the Congregational Church in Connecticut, New Hampshire, and Massachusetts and its dependencies.

"Establishment" of a church meant that it was a "preferred" sect that might enjoy certain economic privileges; it did not mean that other churches were banned. For the colonial governments were far more tolerant of dissenting churches than were European governments. Sometimes religious minorities were exempted from paying tithes (church taxes enforced by the public authority); sometimes members of congregations were permitted to pay their tithes directly to the church of their choice. Such liberality on the part of the state was unknown in much of Europe at the time.

There was, nonetheless, discrimination against Roman Catholics, Jews, and even dissenting Protestants, particularly the Baptists, if they refused to comply with local laws that benefited a preferred sect. For example, colonial governors were instructed not to indulge Catholics in "liberty of conscience," because Catholics were regarded as potentially subversive of the established state and church. On the eve of the Revolution, only in Pennsylvania could Catholic masses be celebrated publicly. The British government's policies in 1763 that seemed to protect the French Catholics of Canada were especially frowned upon by New Englanders, New Yorkers, and other Americans who had hoped that British victory in the recent Seven Years' War (French and Indian) would result in the subjugation and possible suppression of Catholicism in Canada. Eleven years later, when Parliament passed the generous Quebec Act, patriots in America denounced the legislation as one of the "Intolerable Acts" because it guaranteed religious freedom to the Quebec Catholics. Sometimes the more ardent advocates of civil rights angrily draw the line at a proposal for the civil rights of *other* people.

All in all, though, Americans enjoyed the benefits of religious liberties—although some American leaders feared that fierce intolerance lay just beneath the surface of the religious calm. Nearly all Americans professed to be Christians, even if they sometimes were rather eccentric Christians. But not all Christians always observe the doctrine of brotherly love. Had it not been for the British Toleration Act of 1689, religious minorities in several of the Thirteen Colonies might have been driven away.

Second, what of "the freedom of speech, or of the press"? By 1763, a score of newspapers were published in the Thirteen Colonies, though sometimes eleven of a paper's twelve columns might be filled with advertisements. Two years after the British took Quebec from the French, there was little controversy within British North America. The only alarming news came from the region of the Great Lakes, where Chief Pontiac's Indians were attacking British garrisons. Freedom of the press and of speech seemed well established.

This had not been the case earlier in the eighteenth century, when printing and publication had required licenses from public authority in both Britain and America. In the early years of newspaper publication, before the average man had grown accustomed to newspapers, governments had feared (not without reason) the extent to which public opinion might be misled by libels and false reports printed in newspapers. But gradually controls upon the press on either side of the ocean had been relaxed, in part by court decisions, and, although some government power of licensing the press and of prior censorship remained in 1763, the American press was much freer than that of most of Europe. Freedom of speech was also protected by British statutes and by common law—short of speech that might encourage sedition, incite to riot, be slanderous, blasphemous, or obscene, or otherwise result in breaches of the peace. In 1763 there was no political dispute in America controversial enough to justify the breaking up of a public meeting by the guardians of the peace.

Only two years later, however, in 1765, this era of good feeling came to a most abrupt and disastrous end. The cause of disruption was the Stamp Act that the British imposed upon the colonies as a means of raising sixty thousand pounds in annual taxes to help defray the costs of the war with Pontiac's Indians on the northwestern frontier. (The British government expected to have to pay 350,000 pounds a year to maintain troops in North America.) Soon the famous cry "No taxation without representation" was heard from the Patriots. That the Stamp Act taxed newspapers and legal documents infuriated America's newspaper publishers and lawyers—and these were powerful classes to offend. One consequence was a concerted attack by most of the American newspapers upon both Parliament and King George III—and attacks by mobs upon the printing houses of the few Tory (or pro-British) newspapers.

Civil rights are sorely battered in time of war. Until the fighting ended in 1783, little freedom of speech or of the press was allowed, from New Hampshire to Georgia—except freedom of a sort for whichever side, Patriot or Loyalist, happened to be in control of a town or a region. Those two decades of violent interference with publication and public speaking were not forgotten when the first State constitutions were drafted.

The Movement Toward Independence

The Americans prospered, as we have seen, under more than a century of British rule. They enjoyed a great deal of personal freedom and independence. It would therefore be a gross mistake to view the colonists as living in a repressive state or to suggest they were brutalized by English tyrants. There were disagreements, to be sure, but none so fundamental as to provoke a public uprising threatening the existence of government.

Precisely how long this peaceful state of affairs might have lasted had the British continued to follow their "hands-off" policy toward the colonies is uncertain. In any event, 1763 marks an important turning point in Anglo-American relations, for this is the year when the mother country embarked upon a bold new course of action to increase revenue, tighten restrictions on colonial commerce, and require the Americans to assume a greater share of the imperial tax burden. In response to Parliament's abrupt change of colonial policy, the Americans began to question the constitutional basis of parliamentary statutes designed to impose a new economic relationship between the colonies and England. Reaffirming and at the same time reinterpreting their ancient rights and privileges, they turned in the final stages of resistance to thoughts about the nature of free government. In the end, they came reluctantly to the conclusion that secession was their only recourse.

It was thought in London that the new colonial policy was necessary because of economic conditions in England. British industry was rapidly advancing and manufacturers in the homeland were anxious to expand their markets and increase the flow of raw materials. Moreover, the Seven Years War between England and France, which ended in 1763, had left England in control of North America, but had also doubled the English national debt and greatly increased the tax burden of the English people. Already saddled with a system of monopoly that compelled them to purchase exclusively from England all the European articles they required, and to sell exclusively to England all their materials and productions, the Americans resisted these new reforms with increasing skill and determination. Their opposition laid the foundation for unification of the colonies, driving them reluctantly to the American War for Independence.

The responsibility for inaugurating the new colonial policy was placed in the hands of George Grenville, who became Prime Minister in the spring of 1763. Although the menace of the French and Indians on the western frontier had abated, Grenville persuaded Parliament to pass the Sugar Act (1764) and the Stamp Act (1765) for the announced purpose of "defending, protecting, and securing" the colonies. Complaints against the increased duties on sugar shipped to the colonies were mild compared to the commotion stirred up by the Stamp Act; for one of the underlying purposes of the Stamp Act was to establish the right of Parliament to tax the colonies. The actual revenue accruing from the purchase of stamps on newspapers, playing cards, legal documents, and various business instruments was relatively insignificant. What aroused the ire of the Americans was the imposition of a new and mischievous principle: that of raising a tax in the colonies for the treasury of England.

United in their opposition to the tax, the colonies, in their first effort at intercolonial union for resistance to British imperial authority, sent delegates to a Stamp Act Congress in New York which met on October 7, 1765. Representing nine colonies, the Congress drafted a bill of rights and a statement of colonial grievances based on the principle of "No Taxation Without Representation." The Americans argued that Parliament had exceeded its authority in passing the Stamp Act because the colonies, not being represented in Parliament, could be taxed only by their own assemblies.

Parliament wisely repealed the Stamp Act on March 17, 1766; but it refused to disavow its new claim to power, and with the repeal it appended a Declaratory Act affirming its right to legislate for the colonies in all matters. The Americans were so overjoyed by repeal that they overlooked the objectionable principle embodied in the Act. The British, as Americans soon realized, had changed their stance but not their position.

In 1767, upon the recommendation of Charles Townshend, the new Chancellor of the Exchequer, a stubborn Parliament counterattacked with another series of statutes designed to implement the new colonial policy. Relying upon the transparent argument that Parliament, by repealing the Stamp Act, had renounced a direct taxation on the colonies but had reserved the right of indirect taxation, the supporters of the new plan imposed a duty on glass, tea, lead, and paper imported into the colonies. The American response was predictably hostile. No less objectionable to many colonials was a provision of the act authorizing courts to grant writs of assistance to enable British officials to search any house or ship suspected of harboring smuggled goods (James Otis had publicly opposed such writs as early as 1761, contending that they were unconstitutional). Other objectionable Townshend Acts included the establishment of a board of custom officials and an act suspending the New York assembly because it had failed to make satisfactory arrangements for the quartering of British troops stationed in the colony.

The controversy over the Townshend Acts centered on questions of Parliament's constitutional powers. Chief among the American opponents was the able lawyer John Dickinson, who maintained in his widely circulated *Letters of a Farmer in Pennsylvania* that the Townshend Acts contravened established English constitutional principles. Resistance also took the form of a boycott by the merchants and some southern planters against the importation of British goods; and in Boston a clash between seven soldiers and a mob of townspeople, which resulted in the death of four citizens in the so-called Boston Massacre, aroused the people of Massachusetts to a fever of agitation.

Confronted with the fact that the Townshend Acts were a failure, both politically and economically, the ministry in London once again made a strategic withdrawal from the field of contention. The Townshend Duty Act was repealed in April 1770, except that the duty on tea was retained to save the principle that Parliament had the authority to tax the colonies. From that moment it was clear that the ministry, despite the folly of continuing the contest, was determined to subdue the colonies. Lord North, in fact, formally declared in Parliament that repeal of all the new taxes could not occur until the Americans were brought to the feet of Great Britain. By now the disposition to resistance had struck deep roots in every American colony. At first the Americans had only denied the right of Parliament to tax them; but the scope of their rebuttal had increased, by degrees. They began to question the authority of Parliament altogether.

The brief hiatus following the partial repeal of the Duty Act was broken in 1773 when Parliament enacted the Tea Act. The purpose of this ill-considered statute was to shore up the crumbling financial structure of the East India Company, and to establish a precedent to support England's right to tax the colonies. Neither objective was achieved. American resistance against the plan was immediate and strong, highlighted by the famous Boston Tea Party. Seemingly indifferent to the integrity of the Americans, who were waging a war of first principles and were not motivated simply by economic considerations, the English mistakenly believed that the colonials would acquiesce in the modest import duty under the Act because it permitted them to purchase tea at half the price paid in London.

This miscalculation was compounded by British reprisals characterized by the colonials as the "Intolerable Acts," which were passed by Parliament in 1774 to punish the obstreperous Bay Colony. The first of these, the Boston Port Act, closed the Boston harbor to nearly all trade until the citizens of Massachusetts paid the East India Company for the tea they had destroyed. The Massachusetts Government Act changed the colony's royal charter by transforming the upper house of the assembly from an elective into an appointive body, and by restricting the right of self-government in the towns. Under the Administration of Justice Act, the Crown's appointees in Massachusetts who were accused of capital offenses in the discharge of their official duties could be sent to England or other colonies for trial. A fourth measure, the Quartering of Troops Act, gave provincial governors the authority to requisition, with compensation to the owners, all inns, taverns, and unoccupied buildings needed for the proper housing of British troops stationed in the colonies. Not intended to be punitive, the Quebec Act, which among other things deprived Massachusetts, Connecticut, and Virginia of western land they claimed under the sea-to-sea clauses of their charters, was also regarded in America as one of the "Intolerable Acts."

In support of the Bostonians, the Virginia House of Burgesses passed a resolution designating June 1, 1774 (the day the Boston Port Act was scheduled to take effect) as a day of fasting and prayer. Governor John Dunmore viewed this as an act of defiance against the authority of the Crown and promptly dissolved the assembly. Earlier, in 1773, Virginia had taken the lead as the first colony to establish committees of correspondence on an intercolonial basis. These promoted cooperation among the colonies in a more continuous manner than had the Stamp Act Congress. The Virginia legislators now took the greatest step of all the colonies toward united action. Meeting on May 27, 1774, in a rump session at Raleigh Tavern in Williamsburg, the dismissed Burgesses issued a call to the other colonies to send delegates to a continental congress in order to consult upon the common grievance.

A congress of some fifty-five deputies, representing every colony except Georgia, met in September and October of 1774 at Philadelphia and devised a plan of united action against the English government. In essence, the delegates reaffirmed the longstanding principle that each colony was substantially autonomous within the British empire; and to achieve that end they declared economic war on the mother country. The delegates unanimously resolved that Congress request all merchants in the several colonies to withhold the shipment of goods to Great Britain, and further agreed that after December 1, 1774, there would be no importation of goods from Great Britain, Ireland, or the West Indies unless

Bostonians Tarring and Feathering a British Agent.

From a print published in London, 1774. (Courtesy of the Library of Congress.)

American grievances were redressed. To enforce the ban on all commerce with the mother country, the Congress established a continental association of local communities; but a proposal to establish a central government of united colonies was rejected.

The Declaration and Resolves of the First Continental Congress reveals the state of political thought of American colonial leaders at this stage of their quest for liberty. The Declaration was the product of the "Committee for States Rights, Grievances and Means of Redress" that was appointed on September 7, 1774, "to state the rights of the colonies in general, the several instances in which these rights are violated or infringed, and the means most proper to be pursued for obtaining a restoration of them." The committee consisted of two delegates from each colony (except Georgia), and included Richard Henry Lee of Virginia, John Jay of New York, John Rutledge of South Carolina, Edmund Pendleton of Virginia, William Livingston of New York, Roger Sherman of Connecticut, Joseph Galloway of Pennsylvania, and the two Adamses from Massachusetts.

A conciliatory tone of loyalty to the Crown, reflecting the conservatism of these reluctant rebels, pervades the document, despite the gravity of the charges it contains. Above all, the Declaration is a rudimentary statement of conflicting theories about the origin and nature of American freedom. In a single breath, the delegates affirmed their natural rights as men, their prescriptive rights as Englishmen, and their chartered rights as Americans. Thus they declared that, "by the immutable laws of nature, the principles of the English Constitution, and the several charters," the American people were "entitled to life, liberty and property . . . all the rights, liberties, and immunities of free and natural born subjects within the realm of England . . . [and] to the common law of England."

These sweeping assertions, it must be emphasized, are more the result of efforts by the committee to accommodate the opposing views of its members than of intellectual confusion. As John Adams later noted in one of his lively accounts of the first Congress, one of the major "Points which labored the most [was] whether We should recur to the Law of Nature, as well as to the British Constitution and our American Charters and Grants." Richard Henry Lee, for example, said he "Can't see why We should not lay our rights upon the broadest Bottom, the Ground of Nature." John Jay insisted that "It is necessary to recur to the Law of Nature." John Rutledge, on the other hand—joined by Joseph Galloway and James Duane of New York—argued that "Our Claims I think are well founded on the British Constitution, and not on the Law of Nature." Adams discloses that he "was very strenuous for retaining and insisting on it [the Law of Nature], as a resource to which We might be driven by Parliament," and this is the view that ultimately prevailed.

The rhetoric of the Declaration indicates that the members of the First Continental Congress earnestly believed that they were seeking merely a "restoration" of their established legal rights, and were not laying claim to new rights of a radical sort based on natural rights philosophy. Their assertion of rights based on the "law of nature," in other words, was written in anticipation of Parliament's rejection of their constitutional doctrines, more out of desperation than of solid conviction. Notwithstanding their reference to "the immutable laws of nature," the focal points of their brief against Parliament were their established rights under the English Constitution, the common law, and their colonial charters.

There were other fundamental issues, equally important in connection with American political and constitutional development, dividing the delegates. Adams recalled that a second point of major disagreement in the committee "was what authority we should concede to Parliament: Whether we should deny the Authority of Parliament in all Cases: Whether we should allow any Authority to it, in our internal Affairs: or whether we should allow it to regulate the trade of the Empire, with or without any restrictions." Rejecting the principle of legislative supremacy, they declared that the legislative authority of Parliament was limited by the higher law of the Constitution. The Intolerable Acts, the law establishing the board of commissioners, and the exercise of legislative power in the colonies by appointed councils, in violation of the principle "that the constituent branches of the legislature be independent of each other," were, said the delegates, "dangerous" and "unconstitutional." Proclaiming the "right of the people to participate in their legislative councils," the delegates finally agreed that Parliament could regulate the external commerce of the colonies but could not levy a tax on them.

The Declaration also reveals an early commitment not only to representative government and a broadly based system of civil liberties, but also to bicameralism and, most significantly, to the overarching principle of the American Constitution—namely, that a constitution is a higher law, and legislative enactments in conflict with it are "unconstitutional" and unenforceable. Here in embryo, then, was the distinctly American doctrine of judicial review, the rule of interpretation adopted by the Supreme Court in the landmark decision of *Marbury v. Madison* (1803).

The First Continental Congress, we may now observe, stands as an important milestone in American constitutional development. Here, for the first time, political leaders from throughout the colonies—many of whom would later serve in the Constitutional Convention of 1787—met for an extended period of time to discuss basic principles of constitutional government. For many, it was the first time they had met face-to-face, and it was the beginning of a long and close relationship among the Founding Fathers. In 1787 there were forty-one surviving members of the First Continental Congress. Ten were elected to the Constitutional Convention. Richard Henry Lee, Patrick Henry, and Richard Caswell refused to serve, but the remaining seven—John Dickinson, William Livingston, Thomas Mifflin, George Read, John Rutledge, Roger Sherman, and George Washington—signed the Constitution and supported its ratification. In addition, twenty of the surviving members of the First Congress were elected to the State ratifying conventions of 1787–1788; most of them supported adoption.

On May 10, 1775, three weeks after the battles of Lexington and Concord, the Second Continental Congress met in Philadelphia to consider "the state of America" and prepare the nation for armed rebellion. One of the first orders of business was the selection of a commander-in-chief for the Continental army. A number of New Englanders favored Artemus Ward, who was in command of troops around Boston, but the southerners, fearful of New England's imperial ambitions, successfully urged the unanimous election of George Washington. The Virginian reluctantly accepted, confiding to a friend that the "partiality of the Congress, added to some political motives, left me without choice."

While the delegates maneuvered to gain support for their States' "favorite sons" in the debate over the selection of Washington's generals, the bloody Battle of Bunker Hill was fought on June 17. News reached Philadelphia on June 22, the same day Congress elected eight brigadier generals and voted to issue $2 million in paper money. The next day Washington left to take command of the army in Massachusetts, and on June 23 a committee was appointed to draw up a declaration for Washington to read to

By the **LION** & **UNICORN**, Dieu & mon droit, *their Lieutenant-Generals, Governours, Vice Admirals, &c. &c. &c. &c.*

A H U E & C R Y.

WHEREAS I have been informed, from undoubted authority, that a certain **PATRICK HENRY**, of the county of Hanover, and a number of *deluded followers*, have taken up arms, chosen their officers, and, styling themselves an *independent company*, have marched out of their county, encamped, and put themselves in a posture of war; and have written and despatched letters to divers parts of the country, exciting the people to join in these *outrageous* and *rebellious* practices, to the *great terrour* of all his Majesty's *faithful* subjects, and in *open defiance* of *law* and *government* ; and have *committed other acts of violence*, particularly in *extorting* from his Majesty's *Receiver-General* the sum of 330 l. under *pretence* of *replacing the powder* I *thought proper* to order from the magazine; whence it undeniably appears, there is *no longer* the least security for the *life* or *property* of any man: Wherefore, I have *thought proper,* with the advice of his Majesty's *Council*, and in his Majesty's *name*, to issue this my proclamation, strictly charging *all persons*, upon their *allegiance*, not to *aid, abet*, or *give countenance* to the said **PATRICK HENRY**, or *any other persons* concerned in *such unwarrantable combinations;* but, on the contrary, to oppose *them*, and *their designs,* by *every means,* which designs must otherwise inevitably involve the *whole country* in the *most direful calamity*, as they will call for the *vengeance* of *offended Majesty*, and the *insulted laws*, to be *exerted here*, to vindicate the *constitutional* authority of government.

Given, &c. this 6th day of May, 1775.

D * * * *.

G * * d * * * the P * * * *.

Broadside Issued by Governor Dunmore of Virginia
against Patrick Henry, 1775.

When the Governor seized a large store of gunpowder in Williamsburg to prevent a rebellion, Henry and his followers marched on the capital and successfully demanded its return. Dunmore proclaimed Henry an outlaw, but was forced to flee a month later when Royal government collapsed in Virginia. (Courtesy of the Library of Congress.)

the troops at Cambridge. The Declaration of the Causes and Necessity of Taking up Arms of July 6, 1775, is the product of that committee.

Although probably all of the members of the Second Continental Congress were agreed that military resistance against Great Britain was necessary for the protection of American rights, they were far from unanimous with respect to the ends sought. One group of delegates, led by John Dickinson, favored reconciliation, still hoping that the Americans might remain in the British Empire. There were others, however, who agreed with the Lees of Virginia and the Adamses of Massachusetts that reconciliation was now hopeless. They too shied from the thought of independence, but favored a more aggressive stance against the mother country.

The committee, consisting of Benjamin Franklin, John Jay, Robert Livingston, Thomas Jefferson, John Dickinson, and Thomas Johnson of Maryland, reflected these differing attitudes. Two versions of the declaration were considered, one offered by Jefferson and the other, more conciliatory in tone, by Dickinson. Largely the work of these two men, the final draft served as a compromise between these factions of the Congress, while at the same time pointing the way toward the Declaration of Independence. Considering the nature and extent of this protracted struggle for liberty, with American blood already spilled on the battlefield and a large-scale military conflict in the offing, the Declaration of the Causes and Necessity of Taking up Arms is a tribute to American moderation and restraint in the revolutionary period.

Their quarrel was with Parliament, which, as they rightly complained, had ignored their earlier petitions. And instead of acting in a conciliatory manner, the Lords and Commoners seemed bent on "enslaving the colonies." Appealing to world opinion, the Americans listed their grievances, which included unlawful usurpations of power rightfully belonging to the colonial assemblies, violations of such basic liberties as trial by jury, and invasions by British troops who "have butchered our countrymen," committed arson, and "seized our ships." They denied, however, any intention "of separating from Great Britain and establishing separate States." In words written by Jefferson, they eloquently declared, "before God and the world," that "the arms we have been compelled by our enemies to assume, we will, in defiance of every hazard, with unabating firmness and perseverance, employ for the preservation of our liberties; being with one mind resolved to die freemen rather than to live slaves." As a stubborn Parliament was quick to learn, the Americans meant what they said.

The Declaration of Independence

Prodded by Thomas Paine's widely circulated pamphlet *Common Sense*, which passionately stated the case for permanent separation and convinced Americans at last that British officials were determined to subdue the colonies at any cost, the American people advanced step by step toward a final break. On July 4, 1776, they announced their decision to leave the empire. Although John Adams and Benjamin Franklin served on the committee that was charged with the responsibility of drafting a statement, the principal author of the Declaration of Independence was Thomas Jefferson.

The document is divided into two parts. The first offered a philosophical justification for secession, based on the theory that all men are entitled to certain basic rights, that the purpose of government is to protect those rights, and that the people have the right to abolish that government if it fails to fulfill its obligations. "We hold these truths to be self-evident," wrote Jefferson,

> that all men are created equal, that they are endowed by their Creator with certain unalienable Rights, that among these are life, liberty and the pursuit of Happiness. That to serve these rights, Governments are instituted among Men, deriving their just powers from the consent of the governed. That whenever any Form of Government becomes destructive of these ends, it is the right of the people to alter or abolish it.

In the second part of the document, Jefferson presented a long list of grievances against the King and Parliament, including those contained in the 1774 Declaration, to demonstrate the many ways in which the government had endeavored to establish "an absolute Tyranny over those States." The document ended with an appeal to God "for the rectitude of our intentions" and a solemn declaration that the thirteen colonies were now "Free and Independent States . . . absolved from all allegiance to the Crown." Fifty-six delegates signed the document, asserting that "we mutually pledge to each other our Lives, our Fortunes and our sacred Honor" to defend the country at any cost.

The Declaration of Independence is one of the most famous documents in the history of the world and from its inception has exerted a powerful influence on mankind. It has inspired revolutionary leaders abroad and has become such a basic ingredient of the American political tradition as to be regarded by some as almost part of the Constitution itself. Yet it has also been a source of profound disagreement, an object of

Thomas Jefferson (1743–1826).

continuing interest and debate, and in some respects an enigma. This may be attributed in large measure to the fact that the first part of the Declaration, the preamble, which has been the cause of these disputes, is obscured by vague and ambiguous language that is susceptible to different interpretations. As a result, there has always been some uncertainty about the exact origin and nature of the rights proclaimed. It is no small irony that Jefferson Davis, the President of the Confederacy, and Abraham Lincoln, President of the United States, both found support for their positions in the Declaration of Independence, Davis claiming that the Confederate States had a right to secede and declare their independence, and Lincoln asserting that slavery was incompatible with the principles of the Declaration.

As we noted in our examination of the Declaration and Resolves of 1774, the colonists experienced difficulty and disagreement in deciding whether to base their rights on the laws of nature, the common law and the English constitution, or their colonial charters. In the end, they opted to muddle their way through the problem by claiming that Parliament had abridged their natural rights, their common law rights, and their chartered or prescriptive rights. This confusion or inability to agree among themselves was carried over to the Declaration of Independence two years later. Thus in the preamble of the document Jefferson presented an argument for the right of revolution and secession based on the philosophy of natural rights; but when he turned to an enumeration of rights that had been abridged, he mentioned only constitutional, common law, and charter rights.

One right prominently mentioned, for example, is the right of trial by jury. This is a common law right, of course, that has never been regarded as universal in nature and is not even recognized under the Civil Law. Is the reference in the document to the "laws of nature" anything more than political rhetoric? What did the colonists mean when they asserted that "all men are created equal" and that they are endowed by their Creator with "certain" unalienable rights?

Puzzled by these anomalies, later generations called upon Jefferson after he had retired to Monticello to clarify the meaning of the document. Disclaiming any originality of thought, and seeing no inconsistencies, Jefferson told one correspondent in 1825 that the purpose of the Declaration was "not to find out new principles, or new arguments never before thought of . . . but to place before mankind the common sense of the subject." Jefferson was, in fact, accused of plagiarizing the views of others. The preamble of the Declaration of Independence bears a striking resemblance, for example, to the first part of the Virginia Bill of Rights, which George Mason wrote almost a month before the Declaration appeared. John Adams, who wrote the Declaration and Resolves of 1774, and the Resolution for Independence of May 1776, thought that the Declaration of Independence was founded on these two documents. On the other hand, Richard Henry Lee accused Jefferson of copying from Locke's *Second Treatise,* and another charged that he had simply lifted the wording from one of James Otis's pamphlets. Jefferson denied that he had relied on any single book or pamphlet, however, and insisted that the thoughts contained in the Declaration were derived from his general reading and knowledge of government and political philosophy. The Declaration of Independence, he said, "was intended to be an expression of the American mind. . . . All its authority rests then on the harmonizing sentiments of the day, whether expressed in conversations, in letters, printed essays or in the elementary books of public rights, as Aristotle, Cicero, Locke, Sidney &c."

But this explanation serves only to increase the confusion. Modern natural rights philosophy, as represented in the writings of Locke, is a rejection of classical political thought and the traditional natural law philosophy. Neither Aristotle nor Cicero subscribed to a natural rights theory, and Aristotle's teaching on the origin of government is contrary to Locke's *Second Treatise.*

To understand the natural rights philosophy of the Declaration of Independence, it is essential that we pause to compare and contrast it with the natural law philosophy. We begin with Aristotle. According to Aristotle, man is by nature a political animal. It is his nature to live with others and to establish the family unit. This gives rise to groups of families and household communities, which unite for mutual protection and to satisfy human wants and needs. These in turn join together to create the city-state. This is the origin of civil society. Government, then, is natural to man. The study of history and anthropology, we should note, confirms Aristotle's view. There is no evidence that mankind has ever lived in complete isolation. "A man alone," it is said, "is either a saint or a devil," and not of this world.

Aristotle was part of what is called the natural law tradition in Western thought, which began with the ancient Greeks. The idea of natural law stems from the belief that there is a higher law governing political rulers and the affairs of mankind which emanates from God. This higher law, said Aristotle, is knowable through reason. St. Thomas Aquinas, the thirteenth-century theologian who adapted Aristotle's teachings to Christian beliefs, wrote that revelation, that is, God's word as revealed through scripture, supplemented reason as a source of understanding the natural law.

What, in substance, is the natural law? By natural law we mean those principles which are inherent in man's nature as a rational, moral, and social being, and which cannot be casually ignored. The term is confusing at first because it suggests the laws of physical nature, such as the laws of chemistry or physics. Natural law refers, however, not to physical but to human nature. We mean by this term not law which has been enacted, but the law which has been, or may be, discovered by man's reason and experience. In essence, it is a system of ethics for governing the political and legal affairs of man. It insists that there are universal truths, such as justice, and that such truths are knowable through reason and revelation; and that to violate them is to contravene the natural law. In a famous passage in *De Republica,* Cicero described the natural law as "true law":

> True law is right reason in agreement with Nature; it is of universal application, unchanging and everlasting; it summons to duty by its commands, and averts from wrongdoing by its prohibitions. And it does not lay its commands or prohibitions upon good men in vain, though neither have any effect on the wicked. It is a sin to try to alter this law, nor is it allowable to attempt to repeal any part of it, and it is impossible to abolish it entirely. We cannot be freed from its obligations by the Senate or people, and we need not look outside ourselves for an expounder or interpreter of it. And there will not be different laws at Rome and at Athens, or different laws now and in the future, but one external and unchangeable law will be valid for all nations and for all times, and there

will be one master and one ruler, that is, God, over us all, for He is the author of this law, its promulgator, and its enforcing judge.

Constitutionalism, it should be observed, is a product of this natural law idea that there are certain unalterable truths, and that kings, parliaments, and judges as well as the citizens are and should be governed by them.

But if there is such a thing as a natural law of justice, what explains the fact that the meaning of justice is not exactly the same in all societies? Since the idea of liberty varies, in one degree or another, from one civilization to the next, how can there be only one objective standard of liberty? When the institution of slavery was debated in the United States in the early nineteenth century, some Americans argued that slavery was just and others insisted that it was unjust. Which view is correct? Philosophers have pondered these cultural diversities and differences of opinion for many years. Some have contended that such concepts as liberty and justice are illusory and mean whatever each society chooses to call them. A school of thought known as positivism, founded in the nineteenth century by a French philosopher named Auguste Comte, contended, for example, that the only truths were scientific truths, as determined by the scientific or empirical method. Since we cannot prove in a laboratory what liberty or justice means, suggested Comte, they have no meaning. Applying such assumptions to laws, the legal positivists asserted that the whole idea of natural law was a myth. A law is a law if it has passed the legislature, they said, because we can prove that it did or did not pass. But we cannot scientifically prove that the law protects liberty or justice because we don't have any way of knowing what these terms mean. Judges, therefore, should treat all laws the same, the only test of legitimacy being whether the law was formally enacted by the rules prescribed. "Who is to say," said the positivist, "whether a law is good or bad? Who is to say what is right or wrong? One man's opinion is as good as the next man's."

The natural law philosophers rejected this theory of knowledge. It is true, they conceded, that ideas about liberty and justice may vary. But the opinion of one, of many, or even the opinion of all, is not the test. A majority may even declare that a particular ruler, or law, or individual act, is just. But that does not make it so. Whole societies have committed murder and atrocity in the name of justice. What is legally just may not be what is naturally just. The test of truth, said the natural law thinkers, is not what people perceive it to be, or what they call it. There is, they insisted, a higher, more objective standard. Such qualities (or values) as honesty, integrity, courage, beauty, and of course liberty and justice, cannot be scientifically demonstrated; but this is not to say we are wholly incapable of understanding them and are totally ignorant of their meaning. Thus through reason and revelation, contended the natural law philosophers, it is possible for the human intellect to understand the natural law—if not in its entirety, then at least in part. At bottom, the doctrine of natural law is basically an assertion that the law is a part of ethics.

The idea that individuals uniformly possess certain "rights" against the state did not form a part of the natural law philosophy. There are certain aspects of human nature that are common to all; but no two individuals are exactly the same, and the differences among them are often considerable. It was Aristotle's view, for example, that entitlements differ from one individual to the next, according to each person's nature. Aristotle even maintained that slavery for some individuals is natural because some people are, by nature, incapable of being educated to virtue and are not suited to be masters. The notion that all men have "natural" or equal rights to life, liberty, and property (or to the pursuit of happiness) is foreign to Aristotle's teachings. The whole emphasis of traditional natural law, in fact, is not on rights, but on man's natural *duties* and obligations—to God and to his family, community, and country.

In the writings of John Locke and other natural rights thinkers, we encounter a different view of the origin and purpose of government. The true natural state of man, argued Locke in his *Second Treatise*, is not civil society, as Aristotle said, but the state of nature. There was a time, he suggested, when all men lived not in family units or villages but in a state of nature. Roaming the plains and forests at will, each man was free to come and go as he pleased, without restraint, and to enjoy "life, liberty and estate (property)." These were the rights, said Locke, that each man exercised in the state of nature, and these rights were therefore the "natural rights" of man.

But life in the state of nature was not idyllic. Thomas Hobbes, a seventeenth-century natural rights philosopher, in his work *Leviathan* (1651), reasoned that life in the state of nature must have been "nasty, brutish, and short." For Locke, it was more of an inconvenience than a state of misery. Whatever the condition of man in this state of nature, his natural rights were not secure, and he found it necessary, therefore, to leave this existence in order to protect these rights. According to both Hobbes and Locke (and later Rousseau), this was accomplished by means of a social contract—that is, man contracted out of the state of nature to create society. How this was accomplished, and how there could be an act of government before government was actually created, Locke did not say. Having now formed society by a social contract, the members then entered into a political contract with their rulers to establish a government. By the terms of this second contract, the subjects agreed to obey the government and the government in turn agreed to protect the natural rights of each individual. Should the government fail to provide this protection, the members of society had the right to replace the old government with a new one, thereby exercising their "right" of revolution. Locke's theory of natural law, in other words, was not a theory of natural law at all, but a theory of natural rights.

All of this "state of nature" business is pure fiction, of course, but there were some who talked glibly about "natural rights" in the founding period and believed they possessed them. Like most Americans of his day, Jefferson failed to grasp the inherent contradictions between natural law and natural rights doctrines, and he therefore saw no inconsistency between Aristotle and Locke. It would be the task of later generations to sort out the confusing and sometimes conflicting precedents that had laid the foundation of rights in America. There can be no doubt, however, that some Americans *thought* they had been endowed by their Creator with so-called natural rights and acted upon that assumption.

But how do we distinguish desires from rights? If there is any basis to the natural rights claim—and some contemporary scholars say there is—it is in spite of Locke's *Second Treatise*, not because of it. The argument has been made, for example, that individuals in all societies (but not all individuals in all societies) by nature and instinct desire at least some personal freedom. From this observation it might be concluded that freedom is a "natural right." But it would be "natural" because it conformed to the nature of man in organized society, not because it sprang from an anarchical and mythical state of nature.

The provision of the Declaration of Independence that has aroused the greatest controversy is Jefferson's statement "that all men are created equal." This was a poor choice of words, for it is obvious that the phrase does not mean what it says. Neither Jefferson nor any other member of the Continental Congress seriously believed that all people are equal. "In what are they created equal?" inquired a critical Englishman who read the Declaration. "Is it in size, strength, understanding, figure, moral or civil accomplishments, or situation of life?" The Americans, he asserted, "have introduced their self-evident truth, either through ignorance, or by design, with a self-evident falsehood, since I will defy any American rebel, or any of their patriotic retainers here in England, to point out to me any two men throughout the whole world of whom it may with truth be said, that they are equal."

Nor could Jefferson have possibly had in mind the type of "egalité" proclaimed by the French revolutionaries a decade later—that is, a radical leveling of society to a common stratum through government imposition of political, social, and economic equality. By the word "equal," the gentlemen freeholders who signed the Declaration of Independence did not mean a massive redistribution of the wealth, the eradication of all social distinctions, or universal suffrage. Moreover, the Americans could hardly boast that they had extended equal treatment to their fellow American Loyalists. "If the right of pursuing happiness be unalienable (not transferable)," argued John Lind, a London barrister, "how is it that so many others of their fellow-citizens are by the same injustice and violence made miserable, their fortunes ruined, their persons banished and driven from their friends and families?"

A more plausible interpretation of what the members of the Continental Congress intended by the assertion that "all men are created equal" would be to suggest that they meant the American people, as a nation, were entitled to the same rights as Englishmen. This is certainly what they believed, but the words do not very adequately convey this understanding either. If that is what they thought, why did they not declare simply that "all men are entitled to equal rights" or that "all English citizens are created equal"? We are left with the cryptic remark of Rufus Choate of Massachusetts, one of America's most eminent lawyers in the early nineteenth century, who dismissed the famous proclamation as a hodgepodge of "glittering and high-sounding generalities of natural right."

The Preamble of the Declaration of Independence, it would seem, embodies a theory of government that does not withstand the test of modern analysis. There is no denying that it contains sweeping propositions of doubtful validity. It must ever be remembered, however, that in politics what may seem true in theory is false in fact, and that the reverse is equally valid: political doctrines, though philosophically suspect, sometimes have a life of their own. A more generous reading of the Declaration of Independence would be to look upon it for what it was, what it became, and what its authors may or may not have intended: as a political manifesto, an impassional plea, or an overstatement, we might say, in defense of certain ideals. Had the colonists rested their case on the English Constitution, the common law, and their colonial charters alone, they would have made essentially the same claims in the preamble that they made in the body of the document. The weakness of their philosophical argument, in other words, should not be allowed to obscure or detract from the strength of their political and legal case against the British. They did not need to prove the validity of the natural rights theory in order to validate their claim that they were entitled to certain prescriptive rights they had inherited from their ancestors.

The rhetoric of the Declaration served to inspire Europeans battling privilege and autocratic government, and in due course the ideal of equal rights inherent in the Declaration made slavery increasingly objectionable in the United States. In the famous Lincoln-Douglas debates of 1858, Stephen Douglas stated his belief "that the Declaration of Independence, in the words 'all men are created equal,' was intended to allude only to the people of the United States, to men of European birth or descent, being white men, that they were created equal, and hence that Great Britain had no right to deprive them of their political and religious privileges; but the signers of that paper did not intend to include the Indian or the Negro in that declaration, for if they had would they not have been bound to abolish slavery in every State and colony from that day? Remember too that at the time the Declaration was put forth every one of the thirteen colonies were slaveholding colonies; every man who signed that Declaration represented slaveholding constituents."

Lincoln did not deny these facts. But he insisted nevertheless that all of the slaveholding communities "greatly deplored the evil." This is why "they placed a provision in the Constitution which they supposed would gradually remove the disease by cutting off its source. This was the abolition of the slave trade." Thus, said Lincoln, it may be asked: "if slavery had been a good thing, would the Fathers of the Republic have taken a step calculated to diminish its beneficent influences among themselves?" The Declaration, he contended, stands for the principle of equal justice, and if exceptions are made, "where will it stop?" It was meant by the Founders to serve as "a beacon to guide their children and their children's children" in the interminable struggle against special interests and privilege, in the hope that "their posterity might look up again to the Declaration of Independence and take courage to renew the battle which their fathers began—so that truth, and justice, and mercy, and all the humane and Christian virtues might not be extinguished from the land." In large measure, the commitment to equality that Lincoln found in the Declaration of Independence was essentially a moral equality, or the Christian doctrine that everyone is equal in the eyes of God. Lincoln's interpretation prevailed, and it was the preamble of the Declaration of Independence which elected him to the presidency and produced the Thirteenth Amendment.

In 1776, the slave trade was universally accepted by civilized as well as barbarous nations. Looking back, we see that the Americans, like their European counterparts, only gradually came to appreciate the evils of slavery. Despite the great outpouring of philosophical tracts in defense of liberty, few Enlightenment thinkers called for an immediate end to slavery, and some ignored it altogether. The name of John Locke and the doctrine of natural rights are commonly associated with the Declaration of Independence, as we have seen, and some have argued that his imprint is evident in the preamble of that great document. Yet it is a melancholy fact that Locke was an investor in the Royal African Company and clearly regarded Negro slavery as a justifiable institution. In his *Second Treatise*, he spoke of slavery as "vile and miserable," but as the author of the Fundamental Constitutions of Carolina, which were promulgated in 1669 for the governance of the Carolina colonies, Locke stipulated that "every freeman of Carolina shall have absolute power and authority over his negro slaves." Montesquieu attacked the traditional justifications for slavery, however, and Burke drafted an elaborate code to make both the African trade and colonial slavery more humane. The Quakers, followed by other Christian sects, came to the view that slaveholding was a sin against God, no matter how benevolent or charitable. Many leaders of both the American Revolution and the Abolitionist Movement, it is worthy of remarking, were members of the clergy.

The American Revolution probably served as a catalyst for anti-slavery sentiment by awakening a deeper appreciation of individual liberty. The debate with England produced a great body of literature on the meaning of freedom and the rights of Englishmen; and it stimulated interest in older works on political thought, history, and law that helped to justify the American cause. Above all, the case against the British rested on the thesis that Americans were entitled to the same rights as Englishmen at home. This demand for equal rights was the main thrust of the Declaration of Independence, which laid the foundation for the argument against slavery. Indeed, it was the Declaration of Independence, not the Constitution or the Bill of Rights, around which many opponents of slavery rallied for support in the nineteenth century. Beginning in the 1830s, some Abolitionist leaders condemned the Constitution as a "covenant with death" because, they said, it protected and perpetuated the slavery system. The Constitution, they charged, had subverted the ideals of the Declaration of Independence. At an anti-slavery rally in Massachusetts in 1854, the Abolitionist leader, William Lloyd Garrison, burned a copy of the Constitution before an angry crowd that had gathered to protest the capture of a fugitive slave. "An agreement with hell," he called it. "So perish all compromise with tyranny," he cried out as the document went up in flames. Other anti-slavery leaders contended that the alleged contradiction between the Declaration of Independence and the Constitution as depicted by some Abolitionists was actually a misreading of the documents. Slavery had already been abolished by the Declaration of Independence, they reasoned, and the Constitution was being manipulated by politicians to keep slavery in place.

If in their relations with Great Britain the Americans had a right to equal rights, it seemed to follow, said later generations, that in their relations with each other, all of the American people had a right to equal rights. Such, in fact, was the very basis of the principle of equality before the law—although in 1776 our understanding of this aspect of rule of law was rather muddled and confused. Even as the colonial patriots paraded through the streets of Boston, Philadelphia, and Charleston, however, and raised on high their proclamations of liberty, there was an inherent contradiction that suggested hypocrisy in the minds of some Tories. Here was a Declaration of Independence written by Thomas Jefferson, a slave owner. Here were thirteen colonies, all of them legally recognizing slavery, declaring their love of freedom. "How is it," quipped the great English writer Samuel Johnson, "that we hear the loudest *yelps* for liberty among the drivers of negroes?" That slaveholders should be fighting for their freedom in the name of the rights of man was indeed a paradox, and with each passing generation public awareness of the inconsistency between the American ideal of equal rights and the American practice of slavery became ever more pronounced. Yet the English were hardly any more intolerant of slavery than the Americans. Before the American Revolution, approximately one-third of the British merchant fleet was engaged in transporting fifty thousand Negroes a year to the New World. Parliament did not abolish slavery in the English colonies until 1833. It would be erroneous to conclude from this, however, that the English and the Americans, particularly those who participated in the writing and adoption of the Declaration of Independence, were insincere or hypocritical about their declarations of liberty. The growth of freedom in Anglo-America, it must be remembered, came about gradually. It began with the struggle between the King and the English nobility and trickled down to other classes, each claiming rights and privileges that were previously enjoyed only by the few. In 1776, this evolutionary process was still in its infancy, and the notion that all persons were entitled to the same rights was simply inconceivable to the average freeholder. The freemen saw their task as protecting *their* hard-fought rights, not creating new rights for others. Granting full rights of citizenship to women, to one's slaves and bonded servants, to Indians, to new immigrants speaking a foreign tongue, or to those without property was regarded as dangerous and contrary to the best interests of society. The democracy they practiced was limited to the ruling class, which included most white males, but it would be another century or more before all adults were part of that class and were participating freely in the democratic process.

It is interesting to note that the original Constitution of 1787 contained no provision guaranteeing equal rights. Nor did the Bill of Rights. To a degree, it is implicit in the Thirteenth Amendment abolishing slavery; but it appeared explicitly for the first time in the Equal Protection Clause of the Fourteenth Amendment. In a way, then, the Constitution has been amended by the Preamble of the Declaration of Independence.

There are different kinds of equality, as we have observed, however, and it is important to understand the distinctions among them from a constitutional standpoint. Some forms of equality are clearly compatible with individual liberty, equality before the law or equal rights being the most obvious. In this category we would also want to include equality of opportunity and the Judeo-Christian concept of moral equality based on the doctrine of original sin. These forms of equality are generally consistent with the ideal of individual liberty because they may be attained without coercion. No one is forced to act against his will, and no one is deprived of his earthly possessions, his earnings, his job and occupation, or his status in society, if the law is applied equally to all, and if all are given an opportunity to make their own way and carry out their own plans. Nor do these forms of equality conflict with any of the basic principles of the Constitution.

If an individual is free to participate in the political process by voting in an election or running for office, he possesses political liberty. If this freedom is exercised by all or most of the adult population, there is also political equality. This form of equality does not entail the use of government coercion. No one is forced to vote and the act of voting does not force others to act against their will. Political equality is therefore another form of equality that is compatible with individual liberty. *Political* liberty, to put it another way, is an important means to *individual* liberty, and the broader the franchise the greater the degree of political equality. There does not seem to be much support for political equality in the Declaration of Independence, however, in view of the widespread acceptance of a limited suffrage in 1776. Certainly less than half of the adult population enjoyed political liberty when the Declaration of Independence was written, and it would be inaccurate to interpret the document as a call for an expanded suffrage. The Americans demanded the same rights as Englishmen, not the right to vote. Between 1800 and 1860, virtually every State constitution adopted in 1776 was amended or revised to allow for an expanded electorate. The only exception to this general trend toward democratization was the abolition of voting privileges for free Negroes in Maryland, North Carolina, and Virginia as a result of increasing unrest over the slavery issue. This push for more democracy in the American political process, however, was largely independent of the anti-slavery movement that sprang from the Declaration of Independence. To the extent the Declaration affirmed the principle of political equality, it was a demand by the American people that they be given the same political rights collectively as other British citizens, not that each American be granted political liberty individually.

Social and economic equality, on the other hand, finds no support in the Constitution or in the political tradition that grew out of the Declaration of Independence. In 1776, as is true today, American society was very much diversified, and inequalities respecting wealth, property ownership, education, social status, and the like were part of the natural order. To reduce the entire American population to a single class of people, devoid of all social and economic distinctions, would have required massive and interminable coercion, resulting in a loss of individual liberty. Such drastic measures were never contemplated by those who wrote and approved the founding documents, and succeeding generations of Americans have traditionally rejected egalitarianism of this sort as basically inconsistent with personal freedom. By asserting that "all men are created equal," the Americans did not have in mind the French idea of making them equal by restructuring society, and the many differences and distinctions that existed in colonial society were essentially left intact after independence was achieved.

What, then, was the legacy of the Declaration of Independence, and in what ways did it contribute to the development of liberty, order, and justice under the Constitution? At the risk of oversimplification, we may conclude that the Declaration of Independence achieved two immediate goals. The first, as represented by the preamble, was a philosophical appeal resting on the claim of equal rights and the republican principle of government by consent. The second, as seen in the text of the Declaration, was a constitutional argument that Americans were entitled to the rights of Englishmen, and that those enumerated had been abridged by the King-in-Parliament. These included the right of trial by jury, the right of self-government, the right of taxation by consent, and the right against quartering troops in private households. These and other legally recognized rights asserted in the Declaration found expression in the first State constitutions and bills of rights and in the Federal Constitution and Bill of Rights.

As reinterpreted by the descendants of the Founding Fathers, the preamble of the Declaration became a two-edged sword. In the North it came to embody the ideal of equality before the law or equal rights for all Americans, whatever their race or color, and thus served as a springboard for the anti-slavery movement. In the South, however, the preamble was invoked to support secession, the theory being that the States in 1861, as in 1776, had a fundamental or natural right "to change their form of government and institute a new government, whenever necessary for their safety and happiness." With the military defeat of the confederacy, this ceased to play an important role in constitutional development. Beginning with the Thirteenth Amendment, the rhetoric of the preamble, seeming to affirm the principle of equal rights, became the dominant force, and over the years the Declaration of Independence has come to symbolize opposition to both slavery and racial discrimination. Beyond this, however, the influence of the Declaration from a constitutional standpoint is more difficult to ascertain. The Declaration offers little guidance on how or in what ways governments ought to be built and provides little insight into the workings of the American constitutional system. The Declaration, after all, was a proclamation calling for independence, stating the grounds for separation, not a manual or design for a new political system.

The Rights Proclaimed

The common theme of the various declarations issued by the Continental Congress between 1774 and 1776 was the claim of equal rights, the ar-

Slavery—A Southern View.

The defenders of the slave system often maintained, as this cartoon illustrates, that slavery was less oppressive than the drudgery of factory work in the industrialized areas of the North and England. "Is it possible," inquires a gentleman in the background of the upper picture, "that we of the North have been so deceived by false Reports? Why did we not visit the South before we caused this trouble between the North and South, and so much hard feelings amongst our friends at home?"

In the lower picture, the woman with the children proclaims: "Oh Dear! What wretched slaves this Factory Life makes me and my children." On the right, a barefooted man tells his companion that, "I am going to run away from the factory and go to the Coal Mines where they have to work only 14 hours a day instead of 17 as you do here." (Courtesy of the Library of Congress.)

gument being that Americans were entitled to the same rights as Englishmen. These rights, the Americans argued, were basically inherited rights, derived from the English Constitution and the great charters of liberty, the English common law, and colonial charters. Nature was another source of rights—"the right to life, liberty, and property"—but to suggest that Americans were motivated principally by a natural right theory is to overstate the importance of John Locke and natural rights doctrines. The controversy with Great Britain centered mainly on legally established constitutional rights, not abstract philosophical rights. As an authoritative source of rights, nature was mentioned either as an alternative source or as a rhetorical device.

The first official list of claimed rights appeared in Patrick Henry's famous Resolves, which the Virginia House of Burgesses adopted in 1765. They were passed in response to the Stamp Act and were repeated again and again in other State assemblies and in the Continental Congress down to the outbreak of the Revolution. Henry argued that the English had violated three rights. The first was the right of equality between the American and European subjects of George III. The colonists, said the Virginia Resolves, were entitled to "all the liberties, privileges, franchises, and immunities that have at any time been held, enjoyed, and possessed by the people of Great Britain." The second English right asserted was the right to be taxed only by representatives of one's choosing. And the third, closely related to the second, was government by consent: "the inestimable right of being governed by such laws, respecting their internal polity and taxation, as are derived from their own consent."

The most comprehensive statement of colonial privileges made during the revolutionary period appeared in the Declaration of Rights of 1774. Whereas Henry's resolves were concerned with the single issue of internal taxation, the Declaration of 1774 listed nearly all of the rights Americans had been claiming since the passage of the Stamp Act. Nine rights were identified: (1) the right to "life, liberty and property," which the colonists never "ceded to any sovereign power whatever"; (2) the right to equal rights; (3) the right of representation; (4) common law rights; (5) trial by jury; (6) rights under English statutes that were in force at the time of colonization; (7) the right to petition, the House of Commons having refused to receive colonial petitions; (8) the right to be free from standing armies unless legislative consent had been granted; and (9) the right to free government, which Parliament had abridged in several colonies by conferring legislative power on councils appointed by the Crown.

The Americans claimed other rights, of course, but many of these were seldom mentioned because they were not part of the dispute with England. Freedom of the press and the free exercise of religion, for example, did not enter into the debate, although these were rights much valued by the colonists. Although we no longer think of security as a "right," the colonists thought that security, especially security of property, was one of the most important guarantees of the English Constitution. "The absolute rights of Englishmen," wrote James Otis on behalf of the Massachusetts House of Representatives, "are the rights of personal security, personal liberty, and of private property." John Dickinson contended that "Men cannot be happy, without freedom; nor free, without security of property; nor so secure, unless the sole power to dispose of it be lodged in themselves."

In essence, however, the quarrels between Parliament and the American assemblies over the nature and scope of individual rights were symptomatic of a more fundamental disagreement: the meaning of the English Constitution and of constitutional government. The Constitution as the Americans understood it was the old English Constitution of customary powers, in which inherited and inherent rights were protected against the arbitrary capriciousness of government power. The Constitution as London viewed it was a modernized British Constitution—the emerging constitution of the nineteenth century—of sovereign command and unchecked parliamentary supremacy. The American dilemma was not simply that Parliament had denied certain rights, but Parliament's claim that it had the right to define them and impliedly to deny them at its pleasure. The real issue was sovereignty. "A paltry tax upon tea, a particular insult, a single act of violence or sedition," a member of the House of Lords wisely noted, "was not the true ground of the present dispute. It was not this tax, nor that Act, nor a redress of a particular grievance. The great question in issue is, the supremacy of this country and the subordinate dependence of America."

If Parliament was supreme, and free to revise the Constitution at will, how were American rights to be protected? Incredibly, only one member of Parliament ventured a solution during this great upheaval. "It was for liberty they fought, for liberty they died," said James Luttrell, a member of the House of Commons, in 1777. "An American Magna Charta is what they wisely contend for; not a Magna Charta to be taxed by strangers, a thousand leagues distant . . . but if constitutional freedom was secured to America every victory might then gain over some worthy friends to our cause." But Luttrell's proposal went unnoticed and was never debated. Perhaps it would not have resolved the problem anyway. Assuming that Parliament passed an American Magna Charta, what would have prevented a future Parliament from repealing it? Only fundamental law could guarantee the security of American rights; but a fundamental law is little more than an ordinary statute where a constitution is subject to parliamentary supremacy. As one constitutional historian put it, "American whigs began their resistance in 1765 in the belief that Parliament was acting unconstitutionally. They went to war in 1775 in the belief that they were fighting to defend the British Constitution, not rebelling against it; they were in fact doing both. They were defending the Constitution of limited government and of property in rights that had been the English Constitution. They were rebelling against the Constitution of arbitrary power that the British Constitution was about to become." In sum, the colonies had no choice but to declare independence and establish their own constitutions if they wished to secure the rights they had enjoyed under the old constitution they loved and cherished.

The First State Constitutions, 1776–1783

The year 1776 marks the birth of the American nation. It also signals the birth of constitutional government in the United States and in the world at large. For this was the first time in the world's history that a large group of communities—now thirteen independent and sovereign States—had begun the formation of their own governments under written constitutions. This was also the year in which the Articles of Confederation, our first national constitution of sorts, was written. Many of the colonial leaders who participated in the creation of these first constitutions—James

Madison, George Mason, John Rutledge, Charles Pinckney, John Dickinson, Robert Morris, Benjamin Franklin, Gouverneur Morris, and others—would later meet together in Philadelphia to draft the Constitution of the United States. In these respects, the writing of these constitutions was a dress rehearsal for the Federal Convention of 1787 and a valuable experience in the art of constitution-making.

To a large extent, the main pillars of the new governments were adaptations of the old colonial forms. Yet the task of writing the State constitutions was formidable. The participants were novices at drafting a body of fundamental laws, and most were unfamiliar with the mechanics of constitutional government. Added to this, the nation was at war, and many of the best minds were absorbed in the affairs of the Continental Congress and the war effort. Many of the State constitutions that emerged from the first phase of this endeavor (1776–1777) were thus seriously flawed, and all contained structural imperfections and awkward phraseology requiring subsequent revision. On the whole, however, it was a remarkable achievement, and a number of constitutions lasted longer than even their authors expected. No doubt the most important factor leading to the surprising success of this first effort was the rejection in all of the States of radical and visionary schemes of government and the general acceptance of established constitutional principles and inherited rights. There was little about these constitutions that was truly revolutionary, other than the fact they were written.

Because of the important role he played in the Philadelphia Convention of 1787 and in the first Congress of 1789, James Madison has sometimes been called the "Father of the Constitution" and also the "Father of the Bill of Rights." But to John Adams belongs the title "Father of American Constitutionalism." Deeply read in political and legal theory and ancient history, he was the most knowledgeable constitutional lawyer in all of New England and perhaps in all of the colonies. When the great Tory statesman and humanist Viscount Bolingbroke died in 1751, his reputation suffered a sharp decline, notwithstanding Alexander Pope's widely shared belief that Bolingbroke was one of the most brilliant thinkers England had ever known. "Who now reads Bolingbroke?" asked Burke. Jefferson read Bolingbroke and thought his style reached perfection. But John Adams could truthfully say he had read the works of Bolingbroke three times, especially *The Idea of a Patriot King* (1738). This was

John Adams (1735–1826).

Portrait by John Trumbull, 1793. (National Portrait Gallery, Smithsonian Institution.)

Bolingbroke's much neglected repudiation of Machiavelli's *The Prince*— in defense of political morality and limited constitutional government. Adams seems to have read every important work on government. His mastery of the great political classics was unequaled in the American colonies.

At a meeting in Philadelphia in the fall of 1775, Adams was persuaded by Richard Henry Lee of Virginia to put his constitutional ideas down on paper. Adams obliged his friend in the form of a letter outlining the main features for a constitution, and Lee carried it home to show others. It was soon widely read and distributed in Virginia. The scheme proposed by Adams was only a sketch, however, and he left the details for later consideration. He advocated the free choice of a House of Commons by the people, with the upper house chosen by the lower and the Governor appointed by both houses. The Governor's powers were to be extensive, including a veto and command of the military. Adams also suggested that, when peace came, then would be the opportune time to have the people elect both the Governor and the members of the upper chamber.

Later that same year, Adams gave a fuller expression to these ideas in a pamphlet entitled "Thoughts on Government," which was issued anonymously and widely distributed throughout the colonies. Adams's reputation as a constitutional expert spread rapidly, and in January 1776 the North Carolina delegates in Philadelphia were authorized to seek his advice on State government. On May 10, 1776, the Congress approved Adams's resolution calling upon all of the colonies that had not already done so to adopt new constitutions. Adams was also the driving force behind the constitution of his native State. Written in 1780 and largely the handiwork of Adams, the Massachusetts Constitution proved to be the best of the early State constitutions. It was the first to employ a true check and balance system.

Most of the early State constitutions were written under difficult conditions and in haste. This is especially true of the first two constitutions—those of New Hampshire and South Carolina. They were drafted in January and February respectively, six months before the Declaration of Independence was proclaimed, and were viewed at the time as temporary expedients that might later be withdrawn should England and the colonies reach an accord. Both constitutions lasted only a few years.

Virginia and New Jersey also drew up their constitutions before independence, but these constitutions were drafted under more favorable circumstances and were generally regarded at their inception as permanent instruments of government. Of the remaining nine States, Rhode Island and Connecticut decided to retain their charter governments, and Mas-

THOUGHTS

ON

GOVERNMENT:

APPLICABLE TO

THE PRESENT STATE

OF THE

AMERICAN COLONIES.

In a LETTER from a GENTLEMAN
To his FRIEND.

———

PHILADELPHIA, PRINTED;

BOSTON:
RE-PRINTED BY JOHN GILL, IN QUEEN-STREET.
M,DCC,LXXVI.

John Adams, *Thoughts on Government*, 1776.

This pamphlet was originally published in Philadelphia and reprinted several months later in Boston. Adams wrote the work partly in opposition to Thomas Paine's *Common Sense,* in which Paine had argued in favor of a unicameral legislature and against the separation of powers doctrine.

sachusetts elected to keep its charter temporarily. This left six States without a constitution: New York, Pennsylvania, Delaware, Maryland, North Carolina, and Georgia, all of which wrote their fundamental law after the Declaration of Independence. The whole process took sixteen months, beginning with New Hampshire's rudimentary instrument in early 1776 and ending with New York's more sophisticated product, which was adopted on April 20, 1777. That same year, Vermont drafted a Constitution, but the State was not admitted into the Union until 1790.

In no State was the new fundamental law the work of a specially elected constitutional convention; nor were any of these first State constitutions submitted to the people for approval. The first constitution submitted to a popular vote was the abortive Massachusetts Constitution of 1778, which was drafted by the legislature but later rejected by the people. The Massachusetts Constitution of 1780 became the first that was both prepared by the convention method and approved by the people. It thus stands out as the first written constitution resting on a thoroughly republican base, and in this respect it set the standard for the Federal and State constitutions that were to follow.

In the period between 1776 and 1783, four different procedures were followed for the creation of our first State constitutions:

(1) Constitutions framed by purely legislative bodies which had no express authority from the people to write a constitution and never submitted their handiwork to the people for approval. These were the constitutions of New Jersey, Virginia, and South Carolina, all of which were adopted in 1776. South Carolina adopted a second constitution in 1778.

(2) Constitutions framed by purely legislative bodies, but with express authority conferred upon them for this purpose by the people—without submission to the people for approval, however. These were the constitutions of New Hampshire, Delaware, Georgia, New York, and Vermont.

(3) Constitutions framed by purely legislative bodies but with express authority conferred upon them for this purpose by the people and formal or informal submission of the constitution to the people—Maryland, Pennsylvania, North Carolina, South Carolina (1778), and Massachusetts (1778). Among these, only Massachusetts *formally* submitted its constitution to the people.

(4) The framing of a constitution by a *convention* chosen for this pur-

pose only, with the subsequent submission of the Constitution to the people for approval. These were the States of Massachusetts (1779–1780) and New Hampshire (1779–1783) in their second attempts at establishing an acceptable fundamental law.

Some of these early constitutions made important contributions to the art of government which the Framers of the American Constitution later adopted. Maryland's constitution provided for the indirect election of the upper house. Here the electoral college, which Mason had suggested in Virginia, made its debut in American politics. The Constitution of New York was the first to provide for popular election of the Governor and to give the executive branch a reasonable degree of power and independence. Here was laid the foundation for the modern presidency under the American Constitution. And the Massachusetts Constitution of 1780, as we noted before, provided the model for a separation of powers based on a system of checks and balances. The Framers also incorporated this concept into the Constitution of 1787.

On the other hand, some of these first constitutions also contained major defects. In some ways, the Framers of the American Constitution profited as much from these mistakes as they did from the more successful efforts. No doubt the peculiar constitution of Pennsylvania was the worst of the lot and, above all, pointed out the risks of eccentricity and novelty. Two of the assembly's prominent leaders were mathematics professors. Dominated by radicals, "not one-sixth of whom," reported one observer, "has ever read a word upon constitutional topics," the assembly threw aside the advice of John Adams and ignored its colonial charter. Benjamin Franklin presided over the debacle. Franklin was a man of many talents, but it would seem that political science was not one of them. The constitution of unbalanced government that emerged from these proceedings reflected several of his questionable political ideas, including a unicameral legislature and a plural executive. The legislature was a single chamber. The executive consisted of a council of thirteen whose president and vice president were chosen by the council and the all-powerful legislature. They were mere figureheads presiding over a council that was virtually powerless. Thus, there was neither a Governor nor an upper house. The most bizarre feature of the Pennsylvania constitution, however, was the provision prohibiting any change for the first seven years. Thereafter, and at seven-year intervals, a council of censors was to be elected to review the operation of government and inquire whether the constitution had been violated. If the censors thought an amendment was needed, they had the power to call a State convention. The constitution met with a storm of protest and was soon an object of ridicule and jest among the State's more conservative citizens. Observers from other States shared these views and John Adams condemned the document as a sham. A member of Congress from North Carolina wrote home ridiculing the Pennsylvania Constitution as "a beast without a head." The constitution so convulsed the State that the government was barely able to function for more than a decade. Franklin, however, was so pleased with the constitution that he carried a copy of it to France to show to Turgot, Condorcet, and other admirers. In 1790, the French Constituent Assembly made the disastrous decision to adopt the Pennsylvania plan for a unicameral legislature. That same year, Pennsylvania unceremoniously abandoned its 1776 constitution in favor of a new one modeled after the other State constitutions, with a bicameral legislature and an independent Governor.

The defects in other State constitutions were numerous and varied, and in some cases fatal. Remarkably, four of these first constitutions lasted more than half a century. Although the North Carolina constitution gave the Governor too little power, it lasted the longest—seventy-five years. New Jersey's constitution—largely the work of two Presbyterian clergymen, Rev. Jacob Green and Dr. John Witherspoon, the noted theologian and President of Princeton college—remained in effect for sixty-eight years. Maryland's well-balanced constitution, perhaps the most conservative from the standpoint of property qualifications for holding office, was singled out by Hamilton in *Federalist* No. 63 as among the best, and it lasted for sixty-five years. Virginia's constitution, also generally regarded as one of the better achievements, lasted for fifty-four years. It was written by George Mason, who also drafted Virginia's famous Declaration of Rights. The Charter of Connecticut served as the State's constitution for forty-two years, and that of Rhode Island for no less than sixty-four. New York's constitution, unfortunately marred by two innovating devices (a Council of Revision and a Council of Appointment), nevertheless escaped unscathed from a convention in 1801 and, though burdened with many deficiencies, managed to survive for forty-five years. Its principal architect was John Jay. The Massachusetts Constitution of 1780, by far the most successful of all the State constitutions, has been subjected over the years to numerous amendments, mostly dealing with the suffrage. Still in force, it is the oldest in the land, and stands today as a fitting tribute to the political genius of John Adams.

In general, our first constitutions contained three major weaknesses, all of which were known and avoided in the Philadelphia Convention of 1787. First, they all failed to provide for an adequate system of separation of powers. Most of them established three separate and distinct branches of government, with no overlapping personnel; but the men who drafted them thought in terms of a "pure" separation and did not understand the need for checks and balances. As a result, political power tended to concentrate in the legislatures, which in turn often ruled in an arbitrary manner, tyrannizing over the other branches and oppressing the people, particularly disfavored minority groups. Jefferson addressed the problem in his own State in his *Notes on Virginia* (1784). This concentration of government power in the popular assembly, he charged, "is precisely the definition of despotic government. It will be no alleviation that these powers will be exercised by a plurality of hands, and not a single one. One hundred and seventy-three despots [the number of the Virginia legislators] would surely be as oppressive as one. Let those who doubt it turn their eyes on the republic of Venice—as little will it avail us that they are chosen by ourselves. An *elective despotism* was not the government we fought for, but one which should not only be founded on free principles, but in which the powers of the government should be so divided and balanced among several bodies of magistracy, as that no one could transcend their legal limits, without being effectually checked and restrained by the others."

Second, all of these first constitutions, with the exception of New York's, failed to establish an independent executive. In most cases, governors were appointed by and answerable to the legislatures, and their powers were severely restricted. Even those governors who enjoyed a semblance of authority found it difficult to protect their office because they lacked sufficient means by which to check legislative encroachments.

Third, all of these first constitutions lacked a provision establishing the constitution as the supreme law. One factor contributing greatly to the problem of legislative supremacy in the period between 1776 and 1787 was the common assumption that legislators were the sole judges of their own constitutional powers. Too few lawyers of the day believed that a State court had the right to declare a statute invalid on the ground that it violated the State constitution.

Finally, it is worth noting that the constitutions of four States—New York, New Jersey, Virginia, and North Carolina—contained no express provisions providing for their amendment. The assumption seemed to be that such provisions were unnecessary since the people were thought to have the sovereign right to change their form of government. How they were to exercise this right, and what the procedures would be, remained a mystery. In two States, Maryland and Georgia, changes in the constitution were expressly authorized through the legislature only. The constitutions of Delaware and South Carolina authorized two methods of amendment—through the legislature and by convention. Massachusetts and New Hampshire, on the other hand, specified the convention method only. The means by which the people might change their constitution thus varied from one State to the next, and in more than one State this basic ingredient of the republican principle was either neglected or compromised.

Not all of the earliest constitutions contained bills of rights, but the examples set by such States as Virginia, Pennsylvania, and Massachusetts set the trend for future constitutions. The Virginia Declaration of Rights, drafted by George Mason, was the most widely hailed and served as the favored model for the rest of the nation. The provisions of this Declaration (and the other bills of rights) may be traced to Magna Charta, the Petition of Right, and the English Bill of Rights. It set forth the usual requirements regarding trial by jury, cruel and unusual punishments, search warrants, freedom of the press, and the subordination of the military to civil government. Separation of Powers was also listed as a right of the people, and it was further stipulated that all men who could demonstrate that they had a permanent common interest with the community—that is, were property owners—should be given access to the ballot. Another important provision guaranteed freedom of religion. This was added at the insistence of Patrick Henry and James Madison.

Like the Declaration of Independence that Jefferson wrote shortly thereafter, the Virginia Declaration of Rights asserted that all authority is derived from the people, who have the inalienable right to reform the government if it fails to provide for their safety and happiness. As we noted earlier, however, "the people" of Virginia had not authorized the assembly to write either a new constitution or a declaration of rights, and the documents were not even submitted for popular approval. Moreover, the Virginia legislature represented the extreme opposite of the "one-person, one-vote" theory of representation. Following the English practice of geographical representation, Virginia allowed each county, whatever the size of its population, to send two members to the capital in Williamsburg, which gave the people in the aristocratic Tidewater section of the State a distinct political advantage over inhabitants in the western part of the State. Such sectional inequalities existed in other States as well, particularly Maryland and South Carolina.

By the words "the people," then, the Virginians meant the gentlemen freeholders, not the entire population equally apportioned. Indeed, a complete democracy on a grand scale was widely regarded throughout the colonies as a threat to law and order. The example of Pennsylvania, which abolished all property qualifications for voting and holding office and produced a document making a mockery of constitutional government in the eyes of some onlookers, confirmed the suspicions of many colonial leaders that an unrestrained democracy would drive good men out of public office and turn the affairs of state over to pettifoggers, bunglers, and demagogues. They wanted representation of brains, not bodies—and for a number of years the best minds in the country dominated American politics. Indeed, this probably worked to the advantage of the country in the long run, for it is questionable whether the entire public in 1776 was capable of exercising all of the responsibilities of self-government. No doubt the Virginia Constitution and Declaration of Rights, as well as the American Constitution of 1787, would have fallen even shorter of perfection had they been written by popularly chosen assemblies of untutored and inexperienced deputies of the people at large. "The voice of the people has been said to be the voice of God," said Alexander Hamilton in the Philadelphia Convention, "and however generally this maxim has been quoted and believed, it is not true to fact. The people are turbulent and changing, they seldom judge or determine right." It may therefore be doubted, he added when addressing the New York Ratifying Convention in 1788, whether they "possess the discernment and stability necessary for systematic government."

Certainly the antidemocratic sentiments expressed by many of the Founding Fathers strike the modern student of government as unenlightened. Perhaps they were. It must be remembered, however, that they were sailing on uncharted seas. They were not familiar with universal suffrage and mass democracy. Nor were many of their countrymen prepared for the duties that accompany political liberty. Besides, there was an abundance of historical evidence indicating that democracies tend toward mediocrity and tyranny of the majority. Cautiously but deliberately they nevertheless inched their way toward a more broadly based democracy, and with each passing decade their faith in the people grew stronger. There were many factors which propelled the nation in this direction, but none more important, as we shall see, than the establishment of a democratic republic under the Constitution of 1787.

The Articles of Confederation

The Articles of Confederation were written almost simultaneously with the Declaration of Independence. When Richard Henry Lee of Virginia introduced his resolution on June 7, 1776, proposing a formal dissolution of the colonial relationship with England, there was an accompanying resolution calling upon Congress to draft a constitution for the "united colonies." A committee was formed for this purpose under the chairmanship of John Dickinson, and on July 12 it reported a plan for a new government. The Dickinson draft was later revised in favor of strengthening the power of the States, however, and the Articles of Confederation were not agreed upon by Congress until November 15, 1777. Two days later they were submitted to the State legislatures for ratification, and every State except Maryland ratified within the next two years.

Maryland's refusal to join the confederation stemmed not from any objection to the Articles themselves, but from a concern about the status of trans-Allegheny land in the West. Virginia, New York, Massachusetts, and Connecticut all claimed western lands under their old charters, and there was considerable disagreement over rival claims of ownership by States and land companies. State jealousies also contributed to the dissention, for these vast expanses of territory were a potential source of great wealth and power. Maryland and four other small States—New Hampshire, Rhode Island, New Jersey, and Delaware—took the view that all western lands were or should be the common property of the nation. Fearing oppression by the large States, the small States were the last

The Issue of Sovereignty.

Lithograph by O. E. Woods. Published in Philadelphia, 1863. (Courtesy of the Library of Congress.)

to ratify the Articles, Delaware reluctantly assenting as late as May 1779. Maryland stood fast, however, and withheld her support until all western land claims were ceded to Congress. Virginia was equally stubborn and did not agree to abandon her claim until 1781. When Virginia at last renounced her right to all territory northwest of the Ohio River (the "old northwest"), Maryland representatives promptly signed the document. The Articles of Confederation did not officially take effect, therefore, until March 1, 1781.

The peaceful settlement of this protracted dispute permanently influenced the nature of the union and helped to lay the foundation for the federal system of government. Virginia contended that, under her sea-to-sea charter of 1609, her territory extended all the way to the "South Seas" (the Pacific Ocean). Had Virginia and the other States claiming western land refused to surrender their claims, it is doubtful whether the Articles of Confederation or any other scheme for a union of all the States would have succeeded. With virtually half of the continent under her sovereign jurisdiction, Virginia might well have become a nation unto herself, and North America might have become many countries instead of one. Ironically, it was Richard Henry Lee, a States' Rights man and a stalwart foe of centralization, who, more than any other Virginia leader, persuaded the State legislature to voluntarily limit the size of the State. Lee doubted the validity of Virginia's claim and believed that republican government would not succeed in a country so large as that contemplated by some Virginians. The cession of western territory by Virginia and other States thus served to unify the thirteen original States. It also made possible the creation of many new States in the future, resulting in the formation of a single federal union, under one flag, from the Atlantic to the Pacific.

The controversy over land was actually only one of many issues that divided the large States and the small States in 1776. Members of Congress also quarreled over the method of representation in the confederation Congress and the basis for determining how much each State should contribute to the national treasury to fund the government. The larger States favored proportional representation based on population, which would give them a larger delegation in Congress and more power. The smaller States wanted equal representation, which would give them a disproportionate share of power, particularly if they voted together as a bloc. Should the States pay an equal share into the Treasury or would it be preferable if the States were unequally taxed? These issues were debated throughout the summer of 1776, and the members finally agreed upon a compromise: each State would have one vote in Congress, thus securing the complete political equality of the States, but the expenses of the confederation government were to be supplied by the States in proportion to the value of land within each State. In other words, equality of the States was accepted as the basis of voting power in Congress, and inequality was accepted as the basis for State contributions to the Treasury.

At the heart of this debate was a fundamental problem that would return to haunt the delegates of the Philadelphia Convention in 1787. As Thomas Burke, a representative from North Carolina, put it, "The inequality of the States and yet the necessity of maintaining their separate independence, will occasion dilemmas almost inextricable." This was no exaggeration of the extent and depth of the difficulty. The Philadelphia Convention, as we shall see, nearly reached a permanent impasse trying to reconcile these conflicting interests. The solution that was finally agreed upon in 1787 was the creation of a bicameral legislature based on State equality in the upper chamber and proportional representation in the lower. From the standpoint of the larger States, this was actually an improvement, since the Congress established under the Articles was a unicameral legislature based on State equality alone. After the Constitution was adopted, this fear and antagonism between large and small States disappeared, only to be superseded by sectional conflicts between the northern and southern States.

Equally momentous in the summer of 1776 was the question of State sovereignty. The location of ultimate political authority was, in fact, the most important issue in the writing of the Articles. Should sovereignty reside in Congress or in the States? The issue was debated at length, but in the end the proponents of State sovereignty, many of whom were architects of the States' Rights school of thought in later years, ultimately prevailed. Not only did they secure the principle of State equality in the legislature, but they also incorporated language into Article II affirming that "Each State retains its sovereignty, freedom and independence." Like the Constitution of 1787, the Articles of Confederation rested on the premise that all legislative authority originated in the people of each State, and that the powers exercised by Congress were given or delegated to Congress by the people in the States. Those powers not delegated were reserved to the States or the people.

Article II further provided, however, that Congress was limited to those powers "expressly" delegated by the States. The intended effect of this wording was to prevent Congress from usurping the reserved powers of the States by claiming that it possessed not only delegated powers, but also certain additional powers that might be implied from those specifically granted. Significantly, no explicit references to State sovereignty were included in the Constitution of 1787. The word "expressly" was also omitted from the Tenth Amendment to the Constitution, which stated simply that, "The powers not delegated to the United States by the Constitution, nor prohibited by it to the States, are reserved to the States respectively, or to the people."

Underscoring the principle of State sovereignty, Article III described the confederacy formed under the Articles of Confederation as a "league of friendship." In essence, therefore, the Articles were ostensibly little more than a treaty among sovereign republics, comparable in this century to the League of Nations or its successor, the United Nations. The "league" was declared to be "perpetual," and like an international agreement, the Articles contained various provisions for mutual friendship and cooperation among the signatories.

Under traditional principles of international law and comity, for example, it is a common practice for one country to grant certain basic civil rights and privileges to foreigners traveling or residing within its borders that it grants to its own citizens. An American citizen visiting Italy, let us say, or almost any civilized nation of the free world, will find the same degree of protection to his person or property as is enjoyed by the citizens of those nations. He may, to cite just one example, file a lawsuit in the courts of a foreign country in order to assert a certain right. In recognition of this principle, Article IV of the Articles of Confederation provided that the "free inhabitants" of one State sojourning in another State were "entitled to all privileges and immunities of free citizens in the several States," to "free ingress and egress to and from any other State," and to "all the privileges of trade and commerce."

Article IV also provided for the extradition (surrender) of fugitives from justice. It sometimes occurs that a convicted felon or individual charged with a serious offense will escape to a foreign country. The country to which this person has fled is not obliged under the law of nations, however, to turn the individual over to the country from which he fled, even if requested. For this reason, arrangements between nations for the extradition of fugitives are made through treaties. Such is the manner in which this problem was handled under the Articles of Confederation, making extradition a legal obligation.

Finally, Article IV provided that "Full faith and credit shall be given in each of these States to the records, acts and judicial proceedings of the courts and magistrates of every other State." This meant that each State court was legally obligated to recognize the statutes and judicial decisions of other States, as is customary under what is called private international law or the "conflict of laws." Thus, in a case of contracts, the laws of a foreign country where the contract was made must govern. Article IV simply applied this principle of international law to the States of the confederacy.

All of these provisions, it should be noted, were carried over, in slightly different wording, to the Constitution of 1787. They were deemed essential because the several States were not legally obligated to recognize or enforce the rights protected. They assumed, in other words, that the States, in their quasi-international relationship with each other, were sovereign entities, and that it would be necessary, therefore, to establish these rights by agreement.

Although the several States, it may be seen, were treated under the Articles as sovereign powers, a heated debate would rage for nearly a century over the issue of whether the States, at the time they entered the confederacy, retained all the attributes of sovereignty. That they voluntarily surrendered certain powers to the confederate government is abundantly clear from a reading of the Articles, and there can be no question that in a real or practical sense they did not possess all of the sovereignty that is enjoyed by an independent nation. But did their voluntary renunciation of certain powers constitute a permanent transfer of power, thereby terminating or substantially reducing their *legal* sovereignty? This question became critical after the Constitution was adopted, for one of the major premises of the States' Rights theory of the nature of the union was that the States had always retained their sovereign right to secede from the confederacy or the Federal union. If the States were not sovereign *before* the Constitution was adopted, then they could hardly claim to possess sovereignty *after* adoption; but if they were sovereign before such adoption, then it would follow, at the very least, that they came to Philadelphia as sovereign States, which would serve as a point of departure for an argument in support of State sovereignty after 1787.

Statesmen, lawyers, and constitutional scholars have argued the question of State sovereignty almost from the inception of the Constitution. The answer, if there is one, depends in large measure on the definition of sovereignty we adopt, on the wording and text of the documents, and on the perceptions and understanding of the participants themselves. We need not venture a conclusion here to this complex question, however, except to point out that the Founding Fathers struggled mightily with the difficult question of sovereignty from the very beginning. By the very fact that they were taking the unprecedented step of creating a confederation and then a union of States, thereby dividing sovereignty between two levels of government, they necessarily introduced a new concept of sovereignty into political and constitutional theory. Their inability to address the issue of sovereignty directly and resolve it decisively one way or another proved to be a serious, though probably unavoidable, omission.

What kind of central government did the Articles of Confederation create amidst all this confusion over the location of sovereignty? In a way, the Articles created hardly any government at all. So rudimentary were its limited powers that some observers objected later to the description of the Articles as a "constitution," preferring instead to view the document as something less than fundamental law. The unicameral Congress established under the Articles possessed all of the powers of the confederate government, and these amounted to a paltry sum. Congress was given no more power than it was already exercising—to make war and peace, to send and receive ambassadors, to enter into treaties and alliances, to coin money, to regulate Indian affairs, and to establish a post office.

The powers of taxation and regulation of both foreign and domestic commerce, though essential to the government, were reserved to the

States. These were the powers that formed the basis of the dispute with England, and the States were therefore not of a mind to surrender them to another central government. Denied the power of tax, Congress was obliged to rely upon the system of State appropriations that had proved to be hopelessly inadequate in the colonial period. Many of the States failed to cooperate, as might be expected, and the Confederation was almost invariably in a chronic state of near bankruptcy.

Because the States retained their sovereignty, the Articles made no provision for an executive or judicial branch, and all of the functions of the confederation government were concentrated in one legislative body. A separation of powers was not deemed necessary since the confederation had so little power in the first place. The threat of legislative tyranny was indeed exceedingly remote. The executive function was therefore exercised by various committees of the Congress. At one point there were ninety-nine such committees, with overlapping jurisdiction and rival claims of authority. Consequently, there was no executive unity in the confederation, and not infrequently the government spoke in a babble of voices.

Having no judiciary of its own, the confederation authorized the Congress to settle a narrow range of disputes through *ad hoc* courts. If two or more States, for example, disagreed over a boundary line, any one of the parties to the dispute was free to appeal to Congress for relief. Congress settled some six disputes of this nature during the Confederation period. The Articles further provided that Congress could establish courts to try cases of piracy and felony committed on the high seas and to determine ownership of vessels and cargo in "cases of capture" or prize cases.

Otherwise, the Confederation relied upon the State judiciaries for the enforcement of national laws and treaties. Although certain provisions of the Articles seemed to indicate that they were to be accorded the status of law and "inviolably observed by every State," there was no provision comparable to the Supremacy Clause of the Constitution requiring the State courts to treat the Articles or any of the laws and treaties of the Confederation as the law of the land. This was perhaps the fatal weakness of the system. Answerable to the State legislatures that controlled their salaries and tenure, and often lacking any real independence because most of the early State constitutions were based upon legislative supremacy,

State judges were disinclined to defend Confederation enactments in the face of hostile State assemblymen. Thus the Treaty of Peace signed in 1783 with England, calling for the return of Tory property confiscated during the Revolution, was openly flouted by State legislatures and ignored by State courts. In their role as agents of the Confederation, State officials proved to be unreliable because their first loyalty was to the States they served. What the Confederation government needed and lacked was a system which, instead of going through the State governments, operated directly on individuals through its own agents. Not until the adoption of the Constitution was this serious deficiency corrected.

In light of these difficulties, it comes as no surprise that the Confederation fell woefully short of expectations. During the American Revolution, outbreaks of mutiny were a constant threat to General Washington and his officers because the army was hardly ever paid. In despair, the Continental Congress simply printed more money to finance the war effort, thereby devaluing the currency. In 1780 alone, more than $40 million of paper money, a considerable sum in those days (but "not worth a continental"), was issued by the legislature. Between 1778 and 1783, the United States borrowed several millions from the Dutch and French governments but was so financially destitute that it could not even pay the interest on these loans. After 1783, when the British agreed to vacate the trans-Allegheny territory, the Confederation also lacked the financial resources to garrison the West. As a result, British soldiers continued to occupy their forts in the Northwest, the Spanish intruded upon American soil in the southern regions and interfered with American navigation of the Mississippi, and the Indians roamed Kentucky and Tennessee at will, preying on settlers.

Not the least of the difficulties faced by the Confederation was the serious decline of commercial activity, which further impoverished the government. With impunity, a number of States erected trade barriers and imposed import duties to protect various State economic interests, thereby cutting off or delaying the flow of commerce among the States. Because the Congress had no means of enforcing trade agreements with foreign nations and could not guarantee that the States would comply with the terms, European powers refused to negotiate commercial treaties with the United States. England freely discriminated against American merchants in her home ports and even closed the West Indies to Yankee traders.

Often the States suffered as much from the helplessness of the Confederate government as they did from the excesses and turmoil of their own legislatures. According to the Articles of Confederation, the money power was lodged in Congress. In many of the States, however, radical factions supported by debtors, small farmers, mechanics, and other low-income groups gained control of the State legislatures and used their influence to pass laws fixing prices in paper money, fining merchants for their refusal to accept paper currency at face value, suspending the collection of debts, and forbidding courts to grant judgments for debt. In New England and in the middle Atlantic States, unruly mobs intimidated lawyers and judges, burned courthouses, and interfered with the administration of the law.

The most widely publicized event was Shays' Rebellion, which occurred in Massachusetts in 1786. Daniel Shays, leading an armed band of farmers and debtors, closed down the courts in the interior and western part of the State and threatened to march on Boston if the legislature did not pass inflationary legislation. Military force was required to put down the uprising. The Articles of Confederation were often blamed for these outbreaks of lawlessness, for the financial chaos of the country, and for the assaults on the rights of property. Shays' Rebellion probably quickened the pace toward constitutional reform. Those clauses in the Constitution prohibiting the States from coining money, emitting bills of credit, making anything but gold and silver legal tender in payment of debt, and impairing the obligation of contracts are directly attributable to these paper-money struggles in the 1780s.

Despite its many shortcomings, our nation's first instrument of national government was by no means a total failure. Under the Articles of Confederation, the United States fought to a successful conclusion a long war with one of the most powerful nations on earth, established a new government under a written constitution, and united a diverse population of some three million people scattered over thousands of miles of wilderness. No attempts were made to overthrow the government, and the regime actually achieved a fair degree of order and stability without trampling on the rights of people.

Some constitutional historians have speculated that the Articles of Confederation, had they remained in force, might have succeeded in the long
run, and that the government could have eventually evolved into a parliamentary system of some sort, with a cabinet made up of congressional
leaders exercising the executive function. This is an optimistic view of the
matter, however, and it may be doubted whether the Articles would have
long endured without substantial revision. The problem was that, even
when members of Congress were aware of the need for change, there was
little they could do about it. A major flaw in many of the first State constitutions was the failure of colonial draftsmen to include a provision allowing for amendments to correct errors in the founding document. In
some instances the State legislatures sidestepped this difficulty by simply
treating amendments as ordinary legislation, thereby assuming the right
to amend, as is customary under a parliamentary system. The Articles of
Confederation, however, presented a more serious obstacle. Simple legislation required the vote of nine States, making it relatively easy for a
minority of States, with a minority of the population, to block legislation.
Worse, the Articles specifically required the unanimous consent of all the
States for an amendment, making it possible for a single State to prevent
any change in the original compact. Thus in 1781 Rhode Island blocked
a proposed amendment that would have allowed the Confederation to
collect a five percent import duty. In effect, it was exceedingly difficult to
pass legislation and virtually impossible to pass an amendment. Indeed,
not a single amendment was adopted during the eight years in which the
Articles were in force, even though the need for a major overhaul of the
system was generally acknowledged by many of the members. Because
they could not in reality be changed much, if it all, the Articles of Confederation were doomed to extinction.

By 1786, the situation had become intolerable. The Treasury was empty.
The government was so weak and helpless that it could not even protect
its western frontier. The United States had become an object of ridicule
and jest in England and elsewhere in Europe, and the prospects for improvement and reform were bleak. In a final act of desperation, Charles
Pinckney of South Carolina forced the issue of a constitutional convention to a vote on the floor of Congress, only to be soundly rebuffed. Too
many members were more interested in their own positions and in the

parochial concerns of their individual States than in the general welfare of the country. The American nation was still thought of as a group of nation-States, and the members of Congress were reluctant to surrender their power voluntarily. The government was paralyzed.

If a movement for reform was to succeed, therefore, it would have to be launched outside of Congress. It began by chance in 1785, when Virginia and Maryland signed an agreement settling a longstanding dispute over conflicting commercial interests on the Potomac River. Enthused by this accomplishment, the Maryland legislature came up with the idea that it might be possible for a number of States, through interstate agreements, to improve their commercial relations. Accordingly, the Maryland assembly proposed a commercial convention to Virginia that would include the neighboring States of Pennsylvania and Delaware. Virginia responded by suggesting that the invitation be extended to all of the States, and that a convention be held to consider a general commercial agreement.

Maryland agreed, and in September 1786 a convention met in Annapolis. Only five States were represented, however, and no delegates from New England, the Carolinas, or Georgia made an appearance. Two important delegates to the Annapolis Convention were Alexander Hamilton and James Madison. Seizing an opportunity to organize a constitutional reform effort, they persuaded the delegates unanimously to adopt an address to the States, calling upon them to send delegates to a constitutional convention in Philadelphia the following May. But Congress refused to give its approval, and the proposal seemed headed for defeat.

In November 1786, however, the Virginia legislature broke the impasse with a resolution urging all of the States to send delegates to the Philadelphia Convention. Within a few days, New Jersey responded favorably, followed by North Carolina in January and Delaware in February of 1787. Perceiving the inevitable, a reluctant Congress adopted, without reference to the Annapolis recommendation, its own resolution providing for a convention to meet at the same time and place. All of the other States, with the exception of an intransigent Rhode Island, thereupon agreed to participate in the Philadelphia proceedings. The movement for constitutional reform now had the backing of the nation's leading statesmen. All the while the Federal Convention was in session in

Philadelphia in the summer of 1787, the Continental Congress remained in session in New York, helpless and acquiescent, a spectator, as it were, to its own demise.

The Constitution of the United States that was to emerge from these Philadelphia proceedings in September 1787, it is important to note, was initiated by the States, not by the people at large or by the Congress. Thus it was the States themselves that dissolved their own confederation. Never again would the States together initiate a constitutional change, although the Bill of Rights was the result of their recommendations. Since 1787, however, all of the amendments that have been added to the Constitution have originated in Congress.

SUGGESTED READING

Willi Paul Adams, *The First American Constitutions* (Chapel Hill: University of North Carolina Press, 1980).

Bernard Bailyn, *The Ideological Origins of the American Revolution* (Cambridge: Harvard University Press, 1967).

James Dealey, *Growth of American State Constitutions* (Boston: Ginn and Co., 1915).

Walter Fairleigh Dodd, *The Revision and Amendment of State Constitutions* (Baltimore: Johns Hopkins University Press, 1910).

John Fiske, *The Critical Period of American History, 1783–1789.* (Boston: Houghton Mifflin Co., 1888).

Charles Hyneman and Donald Lutz, *American Political Writing During the Founding Era, 1760–1805.* 2 vols. (Indianapolis: Liberty Fund, 1983).

Merrill Jensen, *The Articles of Confederation* (Madison: University of Wisconsin Press, 1959).

Marc W. Kruman, *Between Authority and Liberty: State Constitution Making in Revolutionary America* (Chapel Hill: University of North Carolina Press, 1997).

Leonard Woods Labaree, *Royal Government in America* (New Haven: Yale University Press, 1930).

Donald Lutz, *Colonial Origins of the American Constitution: A Documentary History* (Indianapolis: Liberty Fund, 1998).

Forrest McDonald, *E Pluribus Unum: The Formation of the American Republic, 1776–1790* (Indianapolis: Liberty Fund, 1979).

Allan Nevins, *The American States During and After the Revolution, 1775–1789.* (New York: Macmillan Co., 1924).

John Phillip Reid, *Constitutional History of the American Revolution.* 4 vols. (Madison: University of Wisconsin Press, 1986–1993).

C. Bradley Thompson, *John Adams and the Spirit of Liberty* (Lawrence: University Press of Kansas, 1998).

Gordon S. Wood, *The Creation of the American Republic, 1776–1787* (Chapel Hill: University of North Carolina Press, 1969).

The Mayflower Compact

IN THE NAME OF GOD, AMEN.

We, whose names are underwritten, the Loyal Subjects of our dread Sovereign Lord King *James*, by the Grace of God, of *Great Britain, France,* and *Ireland,* King, *Defender of the Faith,* &c. Having undertaken for the Glory of God, and Advancement of the Christian Faith, and the Honour of our King and Country, a Voyage to plant the first colony in the northern Parts of Virginia; Do by these Presents, solemnly and mutually in the Presence of God and one another, covenant and combine ourselves together into a civil Body Politick, for our better Ordering and Preservation, and Furtherance of the Ends aforesaid; And by Virtue hereof do enact, constitute, and frame, such just and equal Laws, Ordinances, Acts, Constitutions, and Offices, from time to time, as shall be thought most meet and convenient for the general Good of the Colony; unto which we promise all due Submission and Obedience. In WITNESS whereof we have hereunto subscribed our names at *Cape Cod* the eleventh of *November,* in the Reign of our Sovereign Lord King *James* of *England, France,* and *Ireland,* the eighteenth and of *Scotland,* the fifty-fourth. *Anno Domini,* 1620.

[41 signatures are appended to the document]

Fundamental Orders of Connecticut

January 14, 1639

Forasmuch as it hath pleased the Allmight God by the wise disposition of his divyne pruvidence so to Order and dispose of things that we the Inhabitants and Residents of Windsor, Harteford and Wethersfield are now cohabiting and dwelling in and uppon the River of Conectecotte and the Lands thereunto adioyneing; And well knowing where a people are gathered togather the word of God requires that to mayntayne the peace and union of such a people there should be an orderly and decent Government established according to God, to order and dispose of the affayres of the people at all seasons as occation shall require; doe therefore assotiate and conioyne our selves to be as one Publike State or Commonwelth; and doe, for our selves and our Successors and such as shall be adioyned to us att any tyme hereafter, enter into Combination and Confederation togather, to mayntayne and presearve the liberty and purity of the gospell of our Lord Jesus which we now professe, as also the disciplyne of the Churches, which according to the truth of the said gospell is now practised amongst us; As also is our Civell Affaires to be guided and governed according to such Lawes, Rules, Orders and decrees as shall be made, ordered & decreed, as followeth:—

1. It is Ordered . . . that there shall be yerely two generall Assemblies or Courts, the one the second thursday in September, following; the first shall be called the Courte of Election, wherein shall be yerely Chosen . . . soe many Magestrats and other publike Officers as shall be found requisitte: Whereof one to be chosen Governour for the yeare ensueing and untill another be chosen, and noe other Magestrate to be chosen for more than one yeare; provided allwayes there be six chosen besids the Governour; which being chosen and sworne according to an Oath recorded for that purpose shall have power to administer justice according to the

Lawes here established, and for want thereof according to the rule of the word of God; which choise shall be made by all that are admitted freemen and have taken the Oath of Fidellity, and doe cohabitte within this Jurisdiction, (having beene admitted Inhabitants by the major part of the Towne wherein they live,) or the major parte of such as shall be then present. . . .

4. It is Ordered . . . that noe person be chosen Governor above once in two yeares, and that the Governor be alwayes a member of some approved congregation, and formerly of the Magestracy within this Jurisdiction; and all the Magestrats Freemen of this Commonwelth: . . .

5. It is Ordered . . . that to the aforesaid Courte of Election the severall Townes shall send their deputyes, and when the Elections are ended they may proceed in any publike searvice as at other Courts. Also the other Generall Courte in September shall be for makeing of lawes, and any other publike occation, which conserns the good of the Commonwelth. . . .

7. It is Ordered . . . that after there are warrants given out for any of the said Generall Courts, the Constable . . . of ech Towne shall forthwith give notice distinctly to the inhabitants of the same, . . . that at a place and tyme by him or them lymited and sett, they meet and assemble them selves togather to elect and chuse certen deputyes to be att the Generall Courte then following to agitate the afayres of the commonwelth; which said Deputyes shall be chosen by all that are admitted Inhabitants in the severall Townes and have taken the oath of fidellity; provided that non be chosen a Deputy for any Generall Courte which is not a Freeman of this Commonwelth. . . .

8. It is Ordered . . . that Wyndsor, Harteford and Wethersfield shall have power, ech Towne, to send fower of their freemen as their deputyes to every Generall Courte; and whatsoever other Townes shall be hereafter added to this Jurisdiction, they shall send so many deputyes as the Courte shall judge meete, a reasonable proportion to the number of Freemen that are in the said Townes being to be attended therein; which deputyes shall have the power of the whole Towne to give their voats and allowance to all such lawes and orders as may be for the publike good, and unto which the said Townes are to be bownd.

9. It is ordered . . . that the deputyes thus chosen shall have power and liberty to appoynt a tyme and a place of meeting togather before any Gen-

erall Courte to advise and consult of all such things as may concerne the good of the publike, as also to examine their owne Elections. . . .

10. It is Ordered . . . that every Generall Courte . . . shall consist of the Governor, or some one chosen to moderate the Court, and 4 other Magestrats at lest, with the major parte of the deputyes of the severall Townes legally chosen; and in case the Freemen or major parte of them, through neglect or refusall of the Governor and major parte of the magestrate, shall call a Courte, it shall consist of the major parte of Freemen that are present or their deputyes, with a Moderator chosen by them: In which said Generall Courts shall consist the supreme power of the Commonwelth, and they only shall have power to make lawes or repeale them, to graunt levyes, to admitt of Freemen, dispose of lands undisposed of, to severall Townes or persons, and also shall have power to call ether Courte or Magestrate or any other person whatsoever into question for any misdemeanour, and may for just causes displace or deale otherwise according to the nature of the offence; and also may deale in any other matter that concerns the good of this commonwelth, excepte election of Magestrats, which shall be done by the whole boddy of Freemen.

In which Courte the Governour or Moderator shall have power to order the Courte to give liberty of spech, and silence unceasonable and disorderly speakeings, to put all things to voate, and in case the vote be equall to have the casting voice. But non of these Courts shall be adjorned or dissolved without the consent of the major parte of the Court.

11. It is ordered . . . that when any Generall Courte uppon the occations of the Commonwelth have agreed uppon any summe or sommes of mony to be levyed uppon the severall Townes within this Jurisdiction, that a Committee be chosen to sett out and appoynt what shall be the proportion of every Towne to pay of the said levy, provided the Committees be made up of an equall number out of each Towne.

Declaration and Resolves of the First Continental Congress

October 14, 1774

Whereas, since the close of the last war, the British parliament, claiming a power of right to bind the people of America by statute in all cases whatsoever, hath, in some acts expressly imposed taxes on them, and in others, under various pretenses, but in fact for the purpose of raising a revenue, hath imposed rates and duties payable in these colonies, established a board of commissioners with unconstitutional powers, and extended the jurisdiction of courts of Admiralty not only for collecting the said duties, but for the trial of causes merely arising within the body of a county.

And whereas, in consequence of other statutes, judges who before held only estates at will in their offices, have been made dependent on the Crown alone for their salaries, and standing armies kept in times of peace. And it has lately been resolved in Parliament, that by force of a statute made in the thirty-fifth year of the reign of King Henry the Eighth, colonists may be transported to England, and tried there upon accusations for treasons and misprisions, or concealments of treasons committed in the colonies; and by a late statute, such trials have been directed in cases therein mentioned:

And whereas, in the last session of Parliament, three statutes were made . . . [the Boston Port Act, the Massachusetts Government Act, the Administration of Justice Act], and another statute was then made [the Quebec Act] . . . All which statutes are impolitic, unjust, and cruel, as well as unconstitutional, and most dangerous and destructive of American rights.

And whereas, Assemblies have been frequently dissolved, contrary to the rights of the people, when they attempted to deliberate on grievances; and their dutiful, humble, loyal, & reasonable petitions to the crown for redress, have been repeatedly treated with contempt, by His Majesty's ministers of state:

The good people of the several Colonies of New-hampshire, Massachusetts-bay, Rhode-island and Providence plantations, Connecticut, New-York, New-Jersey, Pennsylvania, Newcastle, Kent and Sussex on Delaware, Maryland, Virginia, North-Carolina, and South-Carolina, justly alarmed at these arbitrary proceedings of parliament and administration, have severally elected, constituted, and appointed deputies to meet, and sit in general Congress, in the city of Philadelphia, in order to obtain such establishment, as that their religion, laws, and liberties, may not be subverted:

Whereupon the deputies so appointed being now assembled, in a full and free representation of these Colonies, taking into their most serious consideration the best means of attaining the ends aforesaid, do in the first place, as Englishmen their ancestors in like cases have usually done, for asserting and vindicating their rights and liberties, declare,

That the inhabitants of the English Colonies in North America, by the immutable laws of nature, the principles of the English constitution, and the several charters or compacts, have the following Rights:

Resolved, N. C. D.

1. That they are entitled to life, liberty, and property, & they have never ceded to any sovereign power whatever, a right to dispose of either without their consent.

2. That our ancestors, who first settled these colonies, were at the time of their emigration from the mother country, entitled to all the rights, liberties, and immunities of free and natural-born subjects within the realm of England.

3. That by such emigration they by no means forfeited, surrendered, or lost any of those rights, but that they were, and their descendants now are entitled to the exercise and enjoyment of all such of them, as their local and other circumstances enable them to exercise and enjoy.

4. That the foundation of English liberty, and of all free government, is a right in the people to participate in their legislative council: and as the English colonists are not represented, and from their local and other circumstances, cannot properly be represented in the British parliament,

they are entitled to a free and exclusive power of legislation in their several provincial legislatures, where their right of representation can alone be preserved, in all cases of taxation and internal polity, subject only to the negative of their sovereign, in such manner as has been heretofore used and accustomed. But, from the necessity of the case, and a regard to the mutual interest of both countries, we cheerfully consent to the operation of such acts of the British parliament, as are bona fide restrained to the regulation of our external commerce, for the purpose of securing the commercial advantages of the whole empire to the mother country, and the commercial benefits of its respective members excluding every idea of taxation, internal or external, for raising a revenue on the subjects in America without their consent.

5. That the respective colonies are entitled to the common law of England, and more especially to the great and inestimable privilege of being tried by their peers of the vicinage, according to the course of that law.

6. That they are entitled to the benefit of such of the English statutes, as existed at the time of their colonization; and which they have, by experience, respectively found to be applicable to their several local and other circumstances.

7. That these, his majesty's colonies, are likewise entitled to all the immunities and privileges granted and confirmed to them by royal charters, or secured by their several codes of provincial laws.

8. That they have a right peaceably to assemble, consider of their grievances, and petition the King; and that all prosecutions, prohibitory proclamations, and commitments for the same, are illegal.

9. That the keeping a Standing army in these colonies, in times of peace, without the consent of the legislature of that colony in which such army is kept, is against law.

10. It is indispensably necessary to good government, and rendered essential by the English constitution, that the constituent branches of the legislature be independent of each other; that, therefore, the exercise of legislative power in several colonies, by a council appointed during pleasure, by the crown, is unconstitutional, dangerous, and destructive to the freedom of American legislation.

All and each of which the aforesaid deputies, in behalf of themselves, and their constituents, do claim, demand, and insist on, as their indubitable rights and liberties; which cannot be legally taken from them, altered or abridged by any power whatever, without their own consent, by their representatives in their several provincial legislatures.

In the course of our inquiry, we find many infringements and violations of the foregoing rights, which, from an ardent desire that harmony and mutual intercourse of affection and interest may be restored, we pass over for the present, and proceed to state such acts and measures as have been adopted since the last war, which demonstrate a system formed to enslave America.

Resolved, That the following acts of Parliament are infringements and violations of the rights of the colonists; and that the repeal of them is essentially necessary, in order to restore harmony between Great Britain and the American colonies, . . . viz.:

The several Acts of 4 Geo. 3, ch. 15 & ch. 34, 5 Geo. 3, ch. 25; 6 Geo. 3, ch. 52; 7 Geo. 3, ch. 41 & 46; 8 Geo. 3, ch. 22; which impose duties for the purpose of raising a revenue in America, extend the powers of the admiralty courts beyond their ancient limits, deprive the American subject of trial by jury, authorize the judges' certificate to indemnify the prosecutor from damages that he might otherwise be liable to, requiring oppressive security from a claimant of ships and goods seized before he shall be allowed to defend his property; and are subversive of American rights.

Also the 12 Geo. 3, ch. 24, entitled "An act for the better preserving his Majesty's dockyards, magazines, ships, ammunition, and stores," which declares a new offense in America, and deprives the American subject of a constitutional trial by jury of the vicinage, by authorizing the trial of any person charged with the committing any offense described in the said act, out of the realm, to be indicted and tried for the same in any shire or county within the realm.

Also the three acts passed in the last session of parliament, for stopping the port and blocking up the harbour of Boston, for altering the charter & government of the Massachusetts-bay, and that which is entitled "An Act for the better administration of Justice," &c.

Also the act passed the same session for establishing the Roman Catholic Religion in the province of Quebec, abolishing the equitable system of English laws, and erecting a tyranny there, to the great danger, from so great a dissimilarity of Religion, law, and government, of the neighboring British colonies. . . .

Also the act passed the same session for the better providing suitable quarters for officers and soldiers in his Majesty's service in North America.

Also, that the keeping a standing army in several of these colonies, in time of peace, without the consent of the legislature of that colony in which the army is kept, is against law.

To these grievous acts and measures Americans cannot submit, but in hopes that their fellow subjects in Great-Britain will, on a revision of them, restore us to that state in which both countries found happiness and prosperity, we have for the present only resolved to pursue the following peaceable measures: 1st. To enter into a non-importation, non-consumption, and non-exportation agreement or association. 2. To prepare an address to the people of Great-Britain, and a memorial to the inhabitants of British America, & 3. To prepare a loyal address to his Majesty, agreeable to resolutions already entered into.

Declaration of the Causes and Necessity of Taking Up Arms

July 6, 1775

If it was possible for men, who exercise their reason to believe, that the divine Author of our existence intended a part of the human race to hold an absolute property in, and an unbounded power over others, marked out by his infinite goodness and wisdom, as the objects of a legal domination never rightfully resistible, however severe and oppressive, the inhabitants of these colonies might at least require from the parliament of Great-Britain some evidence, that this dreadful authority over them, has been granted to that body. But a reverence for our great Creator, principles of humanity, and the dictates of common sense, must convince all those who reflect upon the subject, that government was instituted to promote the welfare of mankind, and ought to be administered for the attainment of that end. The legislature of Great-Britain, however, stimulated by an inordinate passion for a power not only unjustifiable, but which they know to be peculiarly reprobated by the very constitution of that kingdom, and desperate of success in any mode of contest, where regard should be had to truth, law, or right, have at length, deserting those, attempted to effect their cruel and impolitic purpose of enslaving these colonies by violence, and have thereby rendered it necessary for us to close with their last appeal from reason to arms.—Yet, however blinded that assembly may be, by their intemperate rage for unlimited domination, so to slight justice and the opinion of mankind, we esteem ourselves bound by obligations of respect to the rest of the world, to make known the justice of our cause.

Our forefathers, inhabitants of the island of Great-Britain, left their native land, to seek on these shores a residence for civil and religious freedom. At the expense of their blood, at the hazard of their fortunes, without the least charge to the country from which they removed, by unceasing labor, and an unconquerable spirit, they effected settlements in the distant and inhospitable wilds of America, then filled with numerous and warlike nations of barbarians.—Societies or governments, vested with perfect legislatures, were formed under charters from the crown, and an harmonious intercourse was established between the colonies and the kingdom from which they derived their origin. The mutual benefits of this union became in a short time so extraordinary, as to excite astonishment. It is universally confessed, that the amazing increase of the wealth, strength, and navigation of the realm, arose from this source; and the minister, who so wisely and successfully directed the measures of Great-Britain in the late war, publicly declared, that these colonies enabled her to triumph over her enemies.—Towards the conclusion of that war, it pleased our sovereign to make a change in his counsels.—From that fatal moment, the affairs of the British empire began to fall into confusion, and gradually sliding from the summit of glorious prosperity, to which they had been advanced by the virtues and abilities of one man, are at length distracted by the convulsions, that now shake it to its deepest foundations.— The new ministry finding the brave foes of Britain, though frequently defeated, yet still contending, took up the unfortunate idea of granting them a hasty peace, and of then subduing her faithful friends.

These devoted colonies were judged to be in such a state, as to present victories without bloodshed, and all the easy emoluments of statutable plunder.—The uninterrupted tenor of their peaceable and respectful behavior from the beginning of colonization, their dutiful, zealous, and useful services during the war, though so recently and amply acknowledged in the most honorable manner by his majesty, by the late king, and by parliament, could not save them from the meditated innovations.— Parliament was influenced to adopt the pernicious project, and assuming a new power over them, have in the course of eleven years, given such decisive specimens of the spirit and consequences attending this power, as to leave no doubt concerning the effects of acquiescence under it. They have undertaken to give and grant our money without our consent, though we have ever exercised an exclusive right to dispose of our own property; statutes have been passed for extending the jurisdiction of courts of admiralty, and vice-admiralty beyond their ancient limits; for depriving us of the accustomed and inestimable privilege of trial by jury, in cases affecting both life and property; for suspending the legislature of one of the colonies; for interdicting all commerce to the capital of another; and for altering fundamentally the form of government established by charter, and secured by acts of its own legislature solemnly confirmed by the crown; for exempting the "murderers" of colonists from legal trial, and in effect, from punishment; for erecting in a neighboring province, ac-quired by the joint arms of Great-Britain and America, a despotism dan-gerous to our very existence; and for quartering soldiers upon the colo-nists in time of profound peace. It has also been resolved in parliament, that colonists charged with committing certain offenses, shall be trans-ported to England to be tried.

But why should we enumerate our injuries in detail? By one statute it is declared, that parliament can "of right make laws to bind us in all cases whatsoever." What is to defend us against so enormous, so unlimited a power? Not a single man of those who assume it, is chosen by us; or is subject to our control or influence; but, on the contrary, they are all of them exempt from the operation of such laws, and an American revenue, if not diverted from the ostensible purposes for which it is raised, would actually lighten their own burdens in proportion, as they increase ours. We saw the misery to which such despotism would reduce us. We for ten years incessantly and ineffectually besieged the throne as supplicants; we reasoned, we remonstrated with parliament, in the most mild and de-cent language. But administration sensible that we should regard these oppressive measures as freemen ought to do, sent over fleets and armies to enforce them. The indignation of the Americans was roused, it is true; but it was the indignation of a virtuous, loyal, and affectionate people. A Congress of delegates from the United Colonies was assembled at Phila-delphia, on the fifth day of last September. We resolved again to offer an humble and dutiful petition to the king, and also addressed our fellow-subjects of Great-Britain. We have pursued every temperate, every re-spectful measure: we have even proceeded to break off our commercial intercourse with our fellow-subjects, as the last peaceable admonition, that our attachment to no nation upon earth should supplant our attach-ment to liberty.—This, we flattered ourselves, was the ultimate step of the controversy: but subsequent events have shown, how vain was this hope of finding moderation in our enemies.

Several threatening expressions against the colonies were inserted in his majesty's speech; our petition, though we were told it was a decent one, and that his majesty had been pleased to receive it graciously, and to promise laying it before his parliament, was huddled into both houses among a bundle of American papers, and there neglected. The lords and commons in their address, in the month of February, said, that "a rebellion at that time actually existed within the province of Massachusetts-Bay; and that those concerned in it, had been countenanced and encouraged by unlawful combinations and engagements, entered into by his majesty's subjects in several of the other colonies; and therefore they besought his majesty, that he would take the most effectual measures to enforce due obedience to the laws and authority of the supreme legislature."—Soon after, the commercial intercourse of whole colonies, with foreign countries, and with each other, was cut off by an act of parliament; by another several of them were entirely prohibited from the fisheries in the seas near their coasts, on which they always depended for their sustenance; and large reinforcements of ships and troops were immediately sent over to General Gage.

Fruitless were all the entreaties, arguments, and eloquence of an illustrious band of the most distinguished peers, and commoners, who nobly and stren[u]ously asserted the justice of our cause, to stay, or even to mitigate the heedless fury with which these accumulated and unexampled outrages were hurried on. . . .

. . . General Gage, who in the course of the last year had taken possession of the town of Boston, in the province of Massachusetts-Bay, . . . on the 19th day of April, sent out from that place a large detachment of his army, who made an unprovoked assault on the inhabitants of the said province, at the town of Lexington, as appears by the affidavits of a great number of persons, some of whom were officers and soldiers of that detachment, murdered eight of the inhabitants, and wounded many others. From thence the troops proceeded in warlike array to the town of Concord, where they set upon another party of the inhabitants of the same province, killing several and wounding more, until compelled to retreat by the country people suddenly assembled to repel this cruel aggression. Hostilities, thus commenced by the British troops, have been since prosecuted by them without regard to faith or reputation.—The inhabitants of Boston being confined within that town by the general their governor, and having, in order to procure their dismission, entered into a treaty with him, it was stipulated that the said inhabitants having deposited their arms with their own magistrates, should have liberty to depart, taking with them their other effects. They accordingly delivered up their arms, but in open violation of honor, in defiance of the obligation of treaties, which even savage nations esteemed sacred, the governor ordered the arms deposited as aforesaid, that they might be preserved for their owners, to be seized by a body of soldiers; detained the greatest part of the inhabitants in the town , and compelled the few who were permitted to retire, to leave their most valuable effects behind. . . .

The General, further emulating his ministerial masters, by a proclamation bearing date on the 12th day of June, after venting the grossest falsehoods and calumnies against the good people of these colonies, proceeds to "declare them all, either by name or description, to be rebels and traitors, to supersede the course of the common law, and instead thereof to publish and order the use and exercise of the law martial."—His troops have butchered our countrymen, have wantonly burnt Charlestown, besides a considerable number of houses in other places; our ships and vessels are seized; the necessary supplies of provisions are intercepted, and he is exerting his utmost power to spread destruction and devastation around him.

We have received certain intelligence, that General Carleton, the Governor of Canada, is instigating the people of that province and the Indians to fall upon us; and we have but too much reason to apprehend, that schemes have been formed to excite domestic enemies against us. In brief, a part of these colonies now feel, and all of them are sure of feeling, as far as the vengeance of administration can inflict them, the complicated calamities of fire, sword, and famine. We are reduced to the alternative of choosing an unconditional submission to the tyranny of irritated ministers, or resistance by force.—The latter is our choice.—We have counted the cost of this contest, and find nothing so dreadful as voluntary slavery.—Honor, justice, and humanity, forbid us tamely to surrender that freedom which we received from our gallant ancestors, and which our innocent posterity have a right to receive from us. We cannot endure the infamy and guilt of resigning succeeding generations to that wretchedness which inevitably awaits them, if we basely entail heredi-tary bondage upon them.

Our cause is just. Our union is perfect. Our internal resources are great, and, if necessary, foreign assistance is undoubtedly attainable.—We gratefully acknowledge, as signal instances of the Divine favor to-wards us, that his Providence would not permit us to be called into this severe controversy, until we were grown up to our present strength, had been previously exercised in warlike operation, and possessed of the means of defending ourselves. With hearts fortified with these animating reflections, we most solemnly, before God and the world, declare, that, exerting the utmost energy of those powers, which our beneficent Crea-tor has graciously bestowed upon us, the arms we have been compelled by our enemies to assume, we will, in defiance of every hazard, with un-abating firmness and perseverance, employ for the preservation of our liberties; being with one mind resolved to die freemen rather than to live slaves.

Lest this declaration should disquiet the minds of our friends and fellow-subjects in any part of the empire, we assure them that we mean not to dissolve that union which has so long and so happily subsisted between us, and which we sincerely wish to see restored.—Necessity has not yet driven us into that desperate measure, or induced us to excite any other nation to war against them.—We have not raised armies with am-bitious designs of separating from Great-Britain, and establishing in-dependent states. We fight not for glory or for conquest. We exhibit to mankind the remarkable spectacle of a people attacked by unprovoked enemies, without any imputation or even suspicion of offense. They boast of their privileges and civilization, and yet proffer no milder con-ditions than servitude or death.

In our own native land, in defense of the freedom that is our birth-right, and which we ever enjoyed till the late violation of it—for the pro-tection of our property, acquired solely by the honest industry of our forefathers and ourselves, against violence actually offered, we have taken up arms. We shall lay them down when hostilities shall cease on the part of the aggressors, and all danger of their being renewed shall be removed, and not before.

With an humble confidence in the mercies of the supreme and impartial Judge and Ruler of the Universe, we most devoutly implore his divine goodness to protect us happily through this great conflict, to dispose our adversaries to reconciliation on reasonable terms, and thereby to relieve the empire from the calamities of civil war.

The Declaration of Independence (1776)

In Congress, July 4, 1776,

THE UNANIMOUS DECLARATION OF THE THIRTEEN
UNITED STATES OF AMERICA

When in the Course of human events, it becomes necessary for one people to dissolve the political bands which have connected them with another, and to assume among the powers of the earth, the separate and equal station to which the Laws of Nature and of Nature's God entitle them, a decent respect to the opinions of mankind requires that they should declare the causes which impel them to the separation.

We hold these truths to be self-evident, that all men are created equal, that they are endowed by their Creator with certain unalienable Rights, that among these are Life, Liberty and the pursuit of Happiness. That to secure these rights, Governments are instituted among Men, deriving their just powers from the consent of the governed. That whenever any Form of Government becomes destructive of these ends, it is the Right of the People to alter or to abolish it, and to institute new Government, laying its foundation on such principles and organizing its powers in such form, as to them shall seem most likely to effect their Safety and Happiness. Prudence, indeed, will dictate that Governments long established should not be changed for light and transient causes; and accordingly all experience hath shown, that mankind are more disposed to suffer, while evils are sufferable, than to right themselves by abolishing the forms to which they are accustomed. But when a long train of abuses and usurpations, pursuing invariably the same Object evinces a design to reduce them under absolute Despotism, it is their right, it is their duty, to throw off such Government, and to provide new Guards for their future security.—Such has been the patient sufferance of these Colonies; and such is now the necessity which constrains them to alter their former Systems of Government. The history of the present King of Great Britain is a history of repeated injuries and usurpations, all having in direct object the establishment of an absolute Tyranny over these States. To prove this, let Facts be submitted to a candid world.

He has refused his Assent to Laws, the most wholesome and necessary for the public good.

He has forbidden his Governors to pass Laws of immediate and pressing importance, unless suspended in their operation till his Assent should be obtained; and when so suspended, he has utterly neglected to attend to them.

He has refused to pass other Laws for the accommodation of large districts of people, unless those people would relinquish the right of Representation in the Legislature, a right inestimable to them and formidable to tyrants only.

He has called together legislative bodies at places unusual, uncomfortable, and distant from the depository of their Public Records, for the sole purpose of fatiguing them into compliance with his measures.

He has dissolved Representative Houses repeatedly, for opposing with manly firmness his invasions on the rights of the people.

He has refused for a long time, after such dissolutions, to cause others to be elected; whereby the Legislative Powers, incapable of Annihilation, have returned to the People at large for their exercise; the State remaining in the mean time exposed to all the dangers of invasion from without, and convulsions within.

He has endeavoured to prevent the population of these States; for that purpose obstructing the Laws of Naturalization of Foreigners; refusing to pass others to encourage their migration hither, and raising the conditions of new Appropriations of Lands.

He has obstructed the Administration of Justice, by refusing his Assent to Laws for establishing Judiciary Powers.

He has made Judges dependent on his Will alone, for the tenure of their offices, and the amount and payment of their salaries.

He has erected a multitude of New Offices, and sent hither swarms of Officers to harass our People, and eat out their substance.

He has kept among us, in times of peace, Standing Armies without the Consent of our legislatures.

He has affected to render the Military independent of and superior to the Civil power.

He has combined with others to subject us to a jurisdiction foreign to our constitution, and unacknowledged by our laws; giving his Assent to their acts of pretended Legislation:

For Quartering large bodies of armed troops among us:

For protecting them, by a mock Trial, from punishment for any Murders which they should commit on the Inhabitants of these States:

For cutting off our Trade with all parts of the world:

For imposing taxes on us without our Consent:

For depriving us in many cases, of the benefits of Trial by Jury:

For transporting us beyond Seas to be tried for pretended offenses:

For abolishing the free System of English Laws in a neighboring Province, establishing therein an Arbitrary government, and enlarging its Boundaries so as to render it at once an example and fit instrument for introducing the same absolute rule into these Colonies:

For taking away our Charters, abolishing our most valuable Laws, and altering fundamentally the Forms of our Governments:

For suspending our own Legislatures, and declaring themselves invested with power to legislate for us in all cases whatsoever.

He has abdicated Government here, by declaring us out of his Protection and waging War against us.

He has plundered our seas, ravaged our Coasts, burnt our towns, and destroyed the lives of our people.

He is at this time transporting large armies of foreign mercenaries to complete the works of death, desolation and tyranny, already begun with circumstances of Cruelty & perfidy scarcely paralleled in the most barbarous ages, and totally unworthy the Head of a civilized nation.

He has constrained our fellow Citizens taken Captive on the high Seas to bear Arms against their Country, to become the executioners of their friends and Brethren, or to fall themselves by their Hands.

He has excited domestic insurrections amongst us, and has endeavoured to bring on the inhabitants of our frontiers, the merciless Indian Savages, whose known rule of warfare, is an undistinguished destruction of all ages, sexes and conditions.

In every stage of these Oppressions We have Petitioned for Redress in the most humble terms: Our repeated petitions have been answered only by repeated injury. A Prince, whose character is thus marked by every act which may define a Tyrant, is unfit to be the ruler of a free people.

Nor have We been wanting in attention to our British brethren. We have warned them from time to time of attempts by their legislature to extend an unwarrantable jurisdiction over us. We have reminded them of the circumstances of our emigration and settlement here. We have appealed to their native justice and magnanimity, and we have conjured them by the ties of our common kindred to disavow these usurpations, which would inevitably interrupt our connections and correspondence. They too have been deaf to the voice of justice and of consanguinity. We must, therefore, acquiesce in the necessity, which denounces our Separation, and hold them, as we hold the rest of mankind, Enemies in War, in Peace Friends.

We, therefore, the Representatives of the United States of America, in General Congress Assembled, appealing to the Supreme Judge of the world for the rectitude of our intentions, do, in the Name and by Authority of the good People of these Colonies, solemnly publish and declare, That these United Colonies are, and of Right ought to be Free and Independent States; that they are Absolved from all Allegiance to the British Crown, and that all political connection between them and the State of Great Britain, is and ought to be totally dissolved; and that as Free and Independent States, they have full Power to levy War, conclude Peace, contract Alliances, establish Commerce, and to do all other Acts and Things which Independent States may of right do. And for the support of this Declaration, with a firm reliance on the protection of divine Providence, we mutually pledge to each other our Lives, our Fortunes and our sacred Honor.

John Hancock

Josiah Bartlett	Richd. Stockton	George Wythe
Wm. Whipple	Jno. Witherspoon	Richard Henry Lee
Matthew Thornton	Fras. Hopkinson	Th. Jefferson
	John Hart	Benja. Harrison
Saml. Adams	Abra. Clark	Ths. Nelson, Jr.
John Adams		Francis Lightfoot Lee
	Robt. Morris	Carter Braxton

Robt. Treat Paine
Elbridge Gerry

Step. Hopkins
William Ellery

Roger Sherman
Sam'el Huntington
Wm. Williams
Oliver Wolcott

Wm. Floyd
Phil. Livingston
Frans. Lewis
Lewis Morris

Benjamin Rush
Benja. Franklin
John Morton
Geo. Clymer
Jas. Smith
Geo. Taylor
James Wilson
Geo. Ross

Caesar Rodney
Geo. Read
Tho. M'Kean

Samuel Chase
Wm. Paca
Thos. Stone
Charles Carroll of Carrollton

Wm. Hooper
Joseph Hewes
John Penn

Edward Rutledge
Thos. Heyward, Junr.
Thomas Lynch, Junr.
Arthur Middleton

Button Gwinnett
Lyman Hall
Geo. Walton

APPENDIX F

Virginia Bill of Rights

A Declaration of Rights (June 12th, 1776)

Made by the Representatives of the good People of Virginia, assembled in full and free Convention, which rights to pertain to them and their posterity as the basis and foundation of government.

I. That all men are by nature equally free and independent, and have certain inherent rights, of which, when they enter into a state of society, they cannot by any compact, deprive or divest their posterity; namely, the enjoyment of life and liberty with the means of acquiring and possessing property, and pursuing and obtaining happiness and safety.

II. That all power is vested in, and consequently derived from, the people; that magistrates are their trustees and servants, and at all times amendable to them.

III. That government is, or ought to be, instituted for the common benefit, protection and security of the people, nation, or community; of all the various modes and forms of government, that is best which is capable of producing the greatest degree of happiness and safety, and is most effectually secured against the danger of maladministration; and that, when a government shall be found inadequate or contrary to these purposes, a majority of the community hath an indubitable, unalienable and indefeasible right to reform, alter or abolish it, in such manner as shall be judged most conducive to the public weal.

IV. That no man, or set of men, are entitled to exclusive or separate emoluments or privileges from the community but in consideration of public services, which not being descendible, neither ought the offices of magistrate, legislator, or judge to be hereditary.

V. That the legislative, executive and judicial powers should be separate and distinct; and that the members thereof may be restrained from oppression, by feeling and participating the burdens of the people, they should, at fixed periods, be reduced to a private station, return into that body from which they were originally taken, and the vacancies be supplied by frequent, certain and regular elections, in which all, or any part of the former members to be again eligible or ineligible, as the laws shall direct.

VI. That all elections ought to be free, and that all men having sufficient evidence of permanent common interest with, and attachment to the community have the right of suffrage, and cannot be taxed, or deprived of their property for public uses, without their own consent, or that of their representatives so elected, nor bound by any law to which they have not in like manner assented, for the public good.

VII. That all power of suspending laws, or the execution of laws, by any authority, without consent of the representatives of the people, is injurious to their rights, and ought not to be exercised.

VIII. That in all capital or criminal prosecutions, a man hath a right to demand the cause and nature of his accusation, to be confronted with the accusers and witnesses, to call for evidence in his favor, and to speedy trial by an impartial jury of twelve men of his vicinage, without whose unanimous consent he cannot be found guilty; nor can he be compelled to give evidence against himself; that no man be deprived of his liberty, except by the law of the land or the judgment of his peers.

IX. That excessive bail ought not to be required, nor excessive fines imposed, nor cruel and unusual punishments inflicted.

X. That general warrants, whereby an officer or messenger may be commanded to search suspected places without evidence of a fact committed, or to seize any person or persons not named, or whose offence is not particularly described and supported by evidence, are grievous and oppressive, and ought not to be granted.

XI. That in controversies respecting property, and in suits between man and man, the ancient trial by jury of twelve men is preferable to any other, and ought to be held sacred.

XII. That the freedom of the press is one of the great bulwarks of liberty, and can never be restrained but by despotic governments.

XIII. That a well regulated militia, composed of the body of the people, trained to arms, is the proper, natural, and safe defence of a free State; that standing armies in time of peace should be avoided as dangerous to liberty; and that in all cases the military should be under strict subordination to, and governed by, the civil power.

XIV. That the people have a right to uniform government; and therefore, that no government separate from or independent of the government of Virginia, ought to be erected or established within the limits thereof.

XV. That no free government, or the blessing of liberty, can be preserved to any people, but by a firm adherence to justice, moderation, temperance, frugality and virtue, and by a frequent recurrence to fundamental principles.

XVI. That religion, or the duty which we owe to our Creator, and the manner of discharging it, can be directed only by reason and conviction, not by force or violence; and therefore all men are equally entitled to the free exercise of religion, according to the dictates of conscience; and that it is the duty of all to practice Christian forbearance, love and charity towards each other.

Thoughts on Government

Boston, 1776

[By John Adams]

My dear Sir,

If I was equal to the task of forming a plan for the government of a colony, I should be flattered with your request, and very happy to comply with it; because, as the divine science of politics is the science of social happiness, and the blessings of society depend entirely on the constitutions of government, which are generally institutions that last for many generations, there can be no employment more agreeable to a benevolent mind than a research after the best.

Pope flattered tyrants too much when he said,

> "For forms of government let fools contest,
> That which is best administered is best."

Nothing can be more fallacious than this. But poets read history to collect flowers, not fruits; they attend to fanciful images, not the effects of social institutions. Nothing is more certain, from the history of nations and nature of man, than that some forms of government are better fitted for being well administered than others.

We ought to consider what is the end of government, before we determine which is the best form. Upon this point all speculative politicians will agree, that the happiness of society is the end of government, as all divines and moral philosophers will agree that the happiness of the individual is the end of man. From this principle it will follow, that the form of government which communicates ease, comfort, security, or, in one word, happiness, to the greatest number of persons, and in the greatest degree, is the best.

All sober inquirers after truth, ancient and modern, pagan and Christian, have declared that the happiness of man, as well as his dignity, consists in virtue. Confucius, Zoroaster, Socrates, Mahomet, not to mention authorities really sacred, have agreed in this.

If there is a form of government, then, whose principle and foundation is virtue, will not every sober man acknowledge it better calculated to promote the general happiness than any other form?

Fear is the foundation of most governments; but it is so sordid and brutal a passion, and renders men in whose breasts it predominates so stupid and miserable, that Americans will not be likely to approve of any political institution which is founded on it.

Honor is truly sacred, but holds a lower rank in the scale of moral excellence than virtue. Indeed, the former is but a part of the latter, and consequently has not equal pretensions to support a frame of government productive of human happiness.

The foundation of every government is some principle or passion in the minds of the people. The noblest principles and most generous affections in our nature, then, have the fairest chance to support the noblest and most generous models of government.

A man must be indifferent to the sneers of modern Englishmen, to mention in their company the names of Sidney, Harrington, Locke, Milton, Nedham, Neville, Burnet, and Hoadly. No small fortitude is necessary to confess that one has read them. The wretched condition of this country, however, for ten or fifteen years past, has frequently reminded me of their principles and reasonings. They will convince any candid mind, that there is no good government but what is republican. That the only valuable part of the British constitution is so; because the very definition of a republic is "an empire of laws, and not of men." That, as a republic is the best of governments, so that particular arrangement of the powers of society, or, in other words, that form of government which is best contrived to secure an impartial and exact execution of the laws, is the best of republics.

Of republics there is an inexhaustible variety, because the possible combinations of the powers of society are capable of innumerable variations.

As good government is an empire of laws, how shall your laws be made? In a large society, inhabiting an extensive country, it is impossible that the whole should assemble to make laws. The first necessary step, then, is to depute power from the many to a few of the most wise and good. But by what rules shall you choose your representatives? Agree upon the number and qualifications of persons who shall have the benefit of choosing, or annex this privilege to the inhabitants of a certain extent of ground.

The principal difficulty lies, and the greatest care should be employed, in constituting this representative assembly. It should be in miniature an exact portrait of the people at large. It should think, feel, reason and act like them. That it may be the interest of this assembly to do strict justice at all times, it should be an equal representation, or, in other words, equal interests among the people should have equal interests in it. Great care should be taken to effect this, and to prevent unfair, partial, and corrupt elections. Such regulations, however, may be better made in times of greater tranquillity than the present; and they will spring up themselves naturally, when all the powers of government come to be in the hands of the people's friends. At present, it will be safest to proceed in all established modes, to which the people have been familiarized by habit.

A representation of the people in one assembly being obtained, a question arises, whether all the powers of government, legislative, executive, and judicial, shall be left in this body? I think a people cannot be long free, nor ever happy, whose government is in one assembly. My reasons for this opinion are as follow:—

1. A single assembly is liable to all the vices, follies, and frailties of an individual; subject to fits of humor, starts of passion, flights of enthusiasm, partialities, or prejudice, and consequently productive of hasty results and absurd judgments. And all these errors ought to be corrected and defects supplied by some controlling power.

2. A single assembly is apt to be avaricious, and in time will not scruple to exempt itself from burdens, which it will lay, without compunction, on its constituents.

3. A single assembly is apt to grow ambitious, and after a time will not hesitate to vote itself perpetual. This was one fault of the Long Parliament; but more remarkably of Holland, whose assembly first voted themselves from annual to septennial, then for life, and after a course of

years, that all vacancies happening by death or otherwise, should be filled by themselves, without any application to constituents at all.

4. A representative assembly, although extremely well qualified, and absolutely necessary, as a branch of the legislative, is unfit to exercise the executive power, for want of two essential properties, secrecy and despatch.

5. A representative assembly is still less qualified for the judicial power, because it is too numerous, too slow, and too little skilled in the laws.

6. Because a single assembly, posed of all the powers of government, would make arbitrary laws for their own interest, execute all laws arbitrarily for their own interest, and adjudge all controversies in their own favor.

But shall the whole power of legislation rest in one assembly? Most of the foregoing reasons apply equally to prove that the legislative power ought to be more complex; to which we may add, that if the legislative power is wholly in one assembly, and the executive in another, or in a single person, these two powers will oppose and encroach upon each other, until the contest shall end in war, and the whole power, legislative and executive, be usurped by the strongest.

The judicial power, in such case, could not mediate, or hold the balance between the two contending powers, because the legislative would undermine it. And this shows the necessity, too, of giving the executive power a negative upon the legislative, otherwise this will be continually encroaching upon that.

To avoid these dangers, let a distinct assembly be constituted, as a mediator between the two extreme branches of the legislature, that which represents the people, and that which is vested with the executive power.

Let the representative assembly then elect by ballot, from among themselves or their constituents, or both, a distinct assembly, which, for the sake of perspicuity, we will call a council. It may consist of any number you please, say twenty or thirty, and should have a free and independent exercise of its judgment, and consequently a negative voice in the legislature.

These two bodies, thus constituted, and made integral parts of the legislature, let them unite, and by joint ballot choose a governor, who, after being stripped of most of those badges of domination, called prerogatives, should have a free and independent exercise of his judgment, and be made also an integral part of the legislature. This, I know, is liable to objections; and, if you please, you may make him only president of the council, as in Connecticut. But as the governor is to be invested with the executive power, with consent of council, I think he ought to have a negative upon the legislative. If he is annually elective, as he ought to be, he will always have so much reverence and affection for the people, their representatives and counsellors, that, although you give him an independent exercise of his judgment, he will seldom use it in opposition to the two houses, except in cases the public utility of which would be conspicuous; and some such cases would happen.

In the present exigency of American affairs, when, by an act of Parliament, we are put out of the royal protection, and consequently discharged from our allegiance, and it has become necessary to assume government for our immediate security, the governor, lieutenant-governor, secretary, treasurer, commissary, attorney-general, should be chosen by joint ballot of both houses. And these and all other elections, especially of representatives and counsellors, should be annual, there not being in the whole circle of the sciences a maxim more infallible than this, "where annual elections end, there slavery begins."

These great men, in this respect, should be, once a year,

> "Like bubbles on the sea of matter borne,
> They rise, they break, and to that sea return."

This will teach them the great political virtues of humility, patience, and moderation, without which every man in power becomes a ravenous beast of prey.

This mode of constituting the great offices of state will answer very well for the present; but if by experiment it should be found inconvenient, the legislature may, at its leisure, devise other methods of creating them, by elections of the people at large, as in Connecticut, or it may enlarge the term for which they shall be chosen to seven years, or three years, or for life, or make any other alterations which the society shall find productive of its ease, its safety, its freedom, or, in one word, its happiness.

A rotation of all offices, as well as of representatives and counsellors, has many advocates, and is contended for with many plausible arguments. It would be attended, no doubt, with many advantages; and if the society has a sufficient number of suitable characters to supply the great number of vacancies which would be made by such a rotation, I can see no objection to it. These persons may be allowed to serve for three years, and then be excluded three years, or for any longer or shorter term.

Any seven or nine of the legislative council may be made a quorum, for doing business as a privy council, to advise the governor in the exercise of the executive branch of power, and in all acts of state.

The governor should have the command of the militia and of all your armies. The power of pardons should be with the governor and council.

Judges, justices, and all other officers, civil and military, should be nominated and appointed by the governor, with the advice and consent of council, unless you choose to have a government more popular; if you do, all officers, civil and military, may be chosen by joint ballot of both houses; or, in order to preserve the independence and importance of each house, by ballot of one house, concurred in by the other. Sheriffs should be chosen by the freeholders of counties; so should registers of deeds and clerks of counties.

All officers should have commissions, under the hand of the governor and seal of the colony.

The dignity and stability of government in all its branches, the morals of the people, and every blessing of society depend so much upon an upright and skillful administration of justice, that the judicial power ought to be distinct from both the legislative and executive, and independent upon both, that so it may be a check upon both, as both should be checks upon that. The judges, therefore, should be always men of learning and experience in the laws, of exemplary morals, great patience, calmness, coolness, and attention. Their minds should not be distracted with jarring interests; they should not be dependent upon any man, or body of men. To these ends, they should hold estates for life in their offices; or, in other words, their commissions should be during good behavior, and their salaries ascertained and established by law. For misbehavior, the grand inquest of the colony, the house of representatives, should impeach them before the governor and council, where they should have time and opportunity to make their defence; but, if convicted, should be removed from their offices, and subjected to such other punishment as shall be proper.

A militia law, requiring all men, or with very few exceptions besides cases of conscience, to be provided with arms and ammunition, to be trained at certain seasons; and requiring counties, towns, or other small districts, to be provided with public stocks of ammunition and entrenching utensils, and with some settled plans for transporting provisions after the militia, when marched to defend their country against sudden invasions; and requiring certain districts to be provided with field-pieces, companies of matrosses, and perhaps some regiments of light-horse, is always a wise institution, and, in the present circumstances of our country, indispensable.

Laws for liberal education of youth, especially of the lower class of people, are so extremely wise and useful, that, to a humane and generous mind, no expense for this purpose would be thought extravagant.

The very mention of sumptuary laws will excite a smile. Whether our countrymen have wisdom and virtue enough to submit to them, I know not; but the happiness of the people might be greatly promoted by them, and a revenue saved sufficient to carry on this war forever. Frugality is a great revenue, besides curing us of vanities, levities, and fopperies, which are real antidotes to all great, manly, and warlike virtues.

But must not all commissions run in the name of a king? No. Why may they not as well run thus, "The colony of _____ to A.B. greeting," and be tested by the governor?

Why may not writs, instead of running in the name of the king, run thus, "The colony of _____ to the sheriff," &c., and be tested by the chief justice?

Why may not indictments conclude, "against the peace of the colony of _____ and the dignity of the same"?

A constitution founded on these principles introduces knowledge among the people, and inspires them with a conscious dignity becoming freemen; a general emulation takes place, which causes good humor, sociability, good manners, and good morals to be general. That elevation of sentiment inspired by such a government, makes the common people brave and enterprising. That ambition which is inspired by it makes them sober, industrious, and frugal. You will find among them some elegance, perhaps, but more solidity; a little pleasure, but a great deal of business; some politeness, but more civility. If you compare such a country with the regions of domination, whether monarchical or aristocratical, you will fancy yourself in Arcadia or Elysium.

If the colonies should assume governments separately, they should be left entirely to their own choice of the forms; and if a continental constitution should be formed, it should be a congress, containing a fair and adequate representation of the colonies, and its authority should sacredly be confined to those cases, namely, war, trade, disputes between colony and colony, the post-office, and the unappropriated lands of the crown, as they used to be called.

These colonies, under such forms of government, and in such a union, would be unconquerable by all the monarchies of Europe.

You and I, my dear friend, have been sent into life at a time when the greatest lawgivers of antiquity would have wished to live. How few of the human race have ever enjoyed an opportunity of making an election of government, more than of air, soil, or climate, for themselves or their children! When, before the present epocha, had three millions of people full power and a fair opportunity to form and establish the wisest and happiest government that human wisdom can contrive? I hope you will avail yourself and your country of that extensive learning and indefatigable industry which you possess, to assist her in the formation of the happiest governments and the best character of a great people. For myself, I must beg you to keep my name out of sight; for this feeble attempt, if it should be known to be mine, would oblige me to apply to myself those lines of the immortal John Milton, in one of his sonnets:—

> "I did not prompt the age to quit their clogs
> By the known rules of ancient liberty,
> When straight a barbarous noise environs me
> Of owls and cuckoos, asses, apes, and dogs."

Massachusetts Constitution of 1780

PREAMBLE

THE end of the institution, maintenance and administration of government, is to secure the existence of the body-politic; to protect it; and to furnish the individuals who compose it, with the power of enjoying, in safety and tranquility, their natural rights, and the blessings of life: And whenever these great objects are not obtained, the people have a right to alter the government, and to take measures necessary for their safety, prosperity and happiness.

THE body-politic is formed by a voluntary association of individuals: It is a social compact, by which the whole people covenants with each citizen, and each citizen with the whole people, that all shall be governed by certain laws for the common good. It is the duty of the people, therefore, in framing a Constitution of Government, to provide for an equitable mode of making laws, as well as for an impartial interpretation, and a faithful execution of them; that every man may, at all times, find his security in them.

WE, therefore, the people of Massachusetts, acknowledging, with grateful hearts, the goodness of the Great Legislator of the Universe, in affording us, in the course of His providence, an opportunity, deliberately and peaceably, without fraud, violence or surprise, of entering into an original, explicit, and solemn compact with each other; and of forming a new Constitution of Civil Government, for ourselves and posterity; and devoutly imploring His direction in so interesting a design, DO agree upon, ordain and establish, the following *Declaration of Rights, and Frame of Government,* as the CONSTITUTION of the COMMONWEALTH of MASSACHUSETTS.

PART THE FIRST

A Declaration of the Rights of the Inhabitants
of the Commonwealth of Massachusetts

ART. I. —ALL men are born free and equal, and have certain natural, essential, and unalienable rights; among which may be reckoned the right of enjoying and defending their lives and liberties; that of acquiring, possessing, and protecting property; in fine, that of seeking and obtaining their safety and happiness.

II.—IT is the right as well as the duty of all men in society, publicly, and at stated seasons, to worship the SUPREME BEING, the great creator and preserver of the universe. And no subject shall be hurt, molested, or restrained, in his person, liberty, or estate, for worshipping GOD in the manner and season most agreeable to the dictates of his own conscience; or for his religious profession or sentiments; provided he doth not disturb the public peace, or obstruct others in their religious worship.

III.—AS the happiness of a people, and the good order and preservation of civil government, essentially depend upon piety, religion and morality; and as these cannot be generally diffused through a community, but by the institution of the public worship of GOD, and of public instructions in piety, religion and morality: Therefore, to promote their happiness and to secure the good order and preservation of their government, the people of this Commonwealth have a right to invest their legislature with power to authorize and require, the several towns, parishes, precincts, and other bodies-politic, or religious societies, to make suitable provision, at their own expense, for the institution of the public worship of GOD, and for the support and maintenance of public protestant teachers of piety, religion and morality, in all cases where such provision shall not be made voluntarily.

AND the people of this Commonwealth have also a right to, and do, invest their legislature with authority to enjoin upon all the subjects an attendance upon the instructions of the public teachers aforesaid, at stated times and seasons, if there be any on whose instructions they can conscientiously and conveniently attend.

PROVIDED notwithstanding, that the several towns, parishes, precincts, and other bodies-politic, or religious societies, shall, at all times, have the exclusive right of electing their public teachers, and of contracting with them for their support and maintenance.

AND all monies paid by the subject to the support of public worship, and of the public teachers aforesaid, shall, if he require it, be uniformly applied to the support of the public teacher or teachers of his own religious sect of denomination, provided there be any on whose instructions he attends: otherwise it may be paid towards the support of the teacher or teachers of the parish or precinct in which the said monies are raised.

AND every denomination of christians, demeaning themselves peaceably, and as good subjects of the Commonwealth, shall be equally under the protection of the law: And no subordination of any one sect or denomination to another shall ever be established by law.

IV.—THE people of this Commonwealth have the sole and exclusive right of governing themselves as a free, sovereign, and independent state; and do, and forever hereafter shall, exercise and enjoy every power, jurisdiction, and right, which is not, or may not hereafter, be by them expressly delegated to the United States of America, in Congress assembled.

V.—ALL power residing originally in the people, and being derived from them, the several magistrates and officers of government, vested with authority, whether legislative, executive, or judicial, are their substitutes and agents, and are at all times accountable to them.

VI.—NO man, nor corporation, or association of men, have any other title to obtain advantages, or particular and exclusive privileges, distinct from those of the community, than what arises from the consideration of services rendered to the public; and this title being in nature neither hereditary, nor transmissible to children, or descendants, or relations by blood, the idea of a man born a magistrate, lawgiver, or judge, is absurd and unnatural.

VII.—GOVERNMENT is instituted for the common good; for the protection, safety, prosperity and happiness of the people; and not for the profit, honor, or private interest of any one man, family, or class of men: Therefore the people alone have an incontestible, unalienable, and indefeasible right to institute government; and to reform, alter, or totally change the same, when their protection, safety, prosperity and happiness require it.

VIII.—IN order to prevent those, who are vested with authority, from becoming oppressors, the people have a right, at such periods and in such manner as they shall establish by their frame of government, to cause their public officers to return to private life; and to fill up vacant places by certain and regular elections and appointments.

IX.—ALL elections ought to be free; and all the inhabitants of this Commonwealth, having such qualifications as they shall establish by their frame of government, have an equal right to elect officers, and to be elected, for public employments.

X.—EACH individual of the society has a right to be protected by it in the enjoyment of his life, liberty and prosperity, according to standing laws. He is obliged, consequently, to contribute his share to the expense of this protection; to give his personal service, or an equivalent, when necessary: But no part of the property of any individual, can, with justice, be taken from him, or applied to public uses without his own consent, or that of the representative body of the people: In fine, the people of this Commonwealth are not controllable by any other laws, than those to which their constitutional representative body have given their consent. And whenever the public exigencies require, that the property of any individual should be appropriated to public uses, he shall receive a reasonable compensation therefor.

XI.—EVERY subject of the Commonwealth ought to find a certain remedy, by having recourse to the laws, for all injuries or wrongs which he may receive in his person, property, or character. He ought to obtain right and justice freely, and without being obliged to purchase it; completely, and without any denial; promptly, and without delay; conformably to the laws.

XII.—NO subject shall be held to answer for any crime or offence, until the same is fully and plainly, substantially and formally, described to him; or be compelled to accuse, or furnish evidence against himself. And every subject shall have a right to produce all proofs, that may be favorable to him; to meet the witnesses against him face to face, and to be fully heard in his defence by himself, or his council, at his election. And no subject shall be arrested, imprisoned, despoiled, or deprived of his property, immunities, or privileges, put out of the protection of the law, exiled, or deprived of his life, liberty, or estate; but by the judgment of his peers, or the laws of the land.

AND the legislature shall not make any law, that shall subject any person to a capital or infamous punishment, excepting for the government of the army and navy, without trial by jury.

XIII.—IN criminal prosecution, the verification of facts in the vicinity where they happen, is one of the greatest securities of the life, liberty, and property of the citizen.

XIV.—EVERY subject has a right to be secure from all unreasonable searches, and seizures of his person, his houses, his papers, and all his possessions. All warrants, therefore, are contrary to this right, if the cause or foundation of them be not previously supported by oath or affirmation; and if the order in the warrant to a civil officer, to make search in suspected places, or to arrest one or more suspected persons, or to seize their property, be not accompanied with a special designation of the persons or objects of search, arrest, or seizure: and no warrant ought to be issued but in cases, and with the formalities, prescribed by the laws.

XV.—IN all controversies concerning property, and in all suits between two or more persons, except in cases in which it has heretofore been otherways used and practiced, the parties have a right to a trial by jury; and this method of procedure shall be held sacred, unless, in causes arising on the high-seas, and such as relate to mariners wages, the legislature shall hereafter find it necessary to alter it.

XVI.—THE liberty of the press is essential to the security of freedom in a state: it ought not, therefore, to be restrained in this Commonwealth.

XVII.—THE people have a right to keep and to bear arms for the common defence. And as in time of peace armies are dangerous to liberty, they ought not to be maintained without the consent of the legislature; and the military power shall always be held in an exact subordination to the civil authority, and be governed by it.

XVIII.—A FREQUENT recurrence to the fundamental principles of the constitution, and a constant adherence to those of piety, justice, moderation, temperance, industry, and frugality, are absolutely necessary to preserve the advantages of liberty, and to maintain a free government: The people ought, consequently, to have a particular attention to all those principles, in the choice of their officers and representatives: And they have a right to require of their law-givers and magistrates, an exact and constant observance of them, in the formation and execution of the laws necessary for the good administration of the Commonwealth.

XIX.—THE people have a right, in an orderly and peaceable manner, to assemble to consult upon the common good; give instructions to their representatives; and to request of the legislative body, by the way of addresses, petitions, or remonstrances, redress of the wrongs done them, and of the grievances they suffer.

XX.—THE power of suspending the laws, or the execution of the laws, ought never to be exercised but by the legislature, or by authority derived from it, to be exercised in such particular cases only as the legislature shall expressly provide for.

XXI.—THE freedom of deliberation, speech and debate, in either house of the legislature, is so essential to the rights of the people, that it cannot be the foundation of any accusation or prosecution, action or complaint, in any other court or place whatsoever.

XXII.—THE legislature ought frequently to assemble for the redress of grievances, for correcting, strengthening, and confirming the laws, and for making new laws, as the common good may require.

XXIII.—NO subsidy, charge, tax, impost, or duties, ought to be established, fixed, laid, or levied, under any pretext whatsoever, without the consent of the people, or their representatives in the legislature.

XXIV.—LAWS made to punish for actions done before the existence of such laws, and which have not been declared crimes by preceding laws, are unjust, oppressive, and inconsistent with the fundamental principles of a free government.

XXV.—NO subject ought, in any case, or in any time, to be declared guilty of treason or felony by the legislature.

XXVI.—NO magistrate or court of law shall demand excessive bail or sureties, impose excessive fines, or inflict cruel or unusual punishments.

XXVII.—IN time of peace no soldier ought to be quartered in any house without the consent of the owner; and in time of war such quarters ought not to be made but by the civil magistrate, in a manner ordained by the legislature.

XXVIII.—NO person can in any case be subjected to law-martial, or to any penalties or pains, by virtue of that law, except those employed in the army or navy, and except the militia in actual service, but by authority of the legislature.

XXIX.—IT is essential to the preservation of the rights of every individual, his life, liberty, property and character, that there be an impartial interpretation of the laws, and administration of justice. It is the right of every citizen to be tried by judges as free, impartial and independent as the lot of humanity will admit. It is therefore not only the best policy, but for the security of the rights of the people, and of every citizen, that the judges of the supreme judicial court should hold their offices as long as they behave themselves well; and that they should have honorable salaries ascertained and established by standing laws.

XXX.—IN the government of this Commonwealth, the legislative department shall never exercise the executive and judicial powers, or either of them: The executive shall never exercise the legislative and judicial powers, or either of them: The judicial shall never exercise the legislative and executive powers, or either of them: to the end it may be a government of laws and not of men.

PART THE SECOND

The Frame of Government

THE people, inhabiting the territory formerly called the Province of Massachusetts-Bay, do hereby solemnly and mutually agree with each other, to form themselves into a free, sovereign, and independent body-politic or state, by the name of THE COMMONWEALTH OF MASSACHUSETTS.

CHAPTER I

The Legislative Power

SECTION I

The General Court

ART. I.—THE department of legislation shall be formed by two branches, *a Senate* and *House of Representatives:* each of which shall have a negative on the other.

THE legislative body shall assemble every year, on the last Wednesday in May, and at such other times as they shall judge necessary; and shall dissolve and be dissolved on the day next preceding the said last Wednesday in May; and shall be styled, THE GENERAL COURT OF MASSACHUSETTS.

II.—NO bill or resolve of the Senate or House of Representatives shall become a law, and have force as such, until it shall have been laid before the Governor for his revisal: And if he, upon such revision, approve thereof, he shall signify his approbation by signing the same. But if he have any objection to the passing of such bill or resolve, he shall return the same, together with his objections thereto, in writing, to the Senate or House of Representatives, in which soever the same shall have originated; who shall enter the objections sent down by the Governor, at large, on their records, and proceed to reconsider the said bill or resolve: But if, after such reconsideration, two thirds of the said Senate or House of Representatives, shall, notwithstanding the said objections, agree to pass the same, it shall, together with the objections, be sent to the other branch of the legislature, where it shall also be reconsidered, and if approved by two thirds of the members present, shall have the force of a law: But in all such cases the votes of both houses shall be determined by yeas and nays; and the names of the persons voting for, or against, the said bill or resolve, shall be entered upon the public records of the Commonwealth.

AND in order to prevent unnecessary delays, if any bill or resolve shall not be returned by the Governor within five days after it shall have been presented, the same shall have the force of a law.

III.—THE General Court shall forever have full power and authority to erect and constitute judicatories and courts of record, or other courts, to be held in the name of the Commonwealth, for the hearing, trying, and determining of all manner of crimes, offenses, pleas, processes, plaints, actions, matters, causes and things, whatsoever, arising or happening within the Commonwealth, or between or concerning persons inhabiting, or residing, or brought within the same; whether the same be criminal or civil, or whether the said crimes be capital or not capital, and whether the said pleas be real, personal, or mixed; and for the awarding and making out of execution thereupon: To which courts and judicatories are hereby given and granted full power and authority, from time to time, to administer oaths or affirmations, for the better discovery of truth in any matter in controversy or depending before them.

IV.—AND further, full power and authority are hereby given and granted to the said General Court, from time to time, to make, ordain, and establish, all manner of wholesome and reasonable orders, laws, statutes, and ordinances, directions and instructions, either with penalties or without; so as the same be not repugnant or contrary to this Constitution, as they shall judge to be for the good and welfare of this Commonwealth, and for the government and ordering thereof, and of the subjects of the same, and for the necessary support and defence of the government thereof; and to name and settle annually, or provide by fixed laws, for the naming and settling all civil officers within the said Commonwealth, the election and constitution of whom are not hereafter in this Form of Government otherwise provided for; and to set forth the several duties, powers and limits of the several civil and military officers of this Commonwealth, and the forms of such oaths or affirmations as shall be respectively administered unto them for the execution of their several offices and places, so as the same be not repugnant or contrary to this Constitution; and to impose and levy proportional and reasonable assessments, rates, and taxes, upon all the inhabitants of, and persons resident, and estates lying, within the said Commonwealth; and also to impose, and levy reasonable duties and excises, upon any produce, goods, wares, merchandize, and commodities whatsoever, brought into, produced, manufactured, or being within the same; to be issued and disposed of by warrant, under the hand of the Governor of this Commonwealth for the time being, with the advice and consent of the Council, for the public service, in the necessary defence and support of the government of the said Commonwealth, and the protection and preservation of the subjects thereof, according to such acts as are or shall be in force within the same.

AND while the public charges of government, or any part thereof, shall be assessed on polls and estates, in the manner that has hitherto been practiced, in order that such assessments may be made with equality, there shall be a valuation of estates within the Commonwealth taken anew once in every ten years at least, and as much oftener as the General Court shall order.

CHAPTER I

SECTION II

Senate

ART. I—THERE shall be annually elected by the freeholders and other inhabitants of this Commonwealth, qualified as in this Constitution is provided, forty persons to be Counsellors and Senators for the year ensuing their election; to be chosen by the inhabitants of the districts, into which the Commonwealth may from time to time be divided by the General Court for that purpose: And the General Court, in assigning the numbers to be elected by the respective districts, shall govern themselves by the proportion of the public taxes paid by the said districts; and timely make known to the inhabitants of the Commonwealth, the limits of each district, and the number of Counsellors and Senators to be chosen therein; provided, that the number of such districts shall never be less than thirteen; and that no district be so large as to entitle the same to choose more than six Senators.

AND the several counties in this Commonwealth shall, until the General Court shall determine it necessary to alter the said districts, be districts for the choice of Counsellors and Senators, (except that the counties of Dukes County and Nantucket shall form one district for that purpose) and shall elect the following number for Counsellors and Senators, viz:

Suffolk	Six
Essex	Six
Middlesex	Five
Hampshire	Four
Plymouth	Three
Barnstable	One
Bristol	Three
York	Two
Dukes County and Nantucket	One
Worcester	Five
Cumberland	One
Lincoln	One
Berkshire	Two

II.—THE Senate shall be the first branch of the legislature; and the Senators shall be chosen in the following manner, viz: There shall be a meeting on the first Monday in April annually, forever, of the inhabitants of each town in the several counties of this Commonwealth; to be called by the Selectmen, and warned in due course of law, at least seven days before the first Monday in April, for the purpose of electing persons to be Senators and Counsellors. And at such meetings every male inhabitant of twenty-one years of age and upwards, having a freehold estate within the Commonwealth, of the annual income of three pounds, or any estate of the value of sixty pounds, shall have a right to give in his vote for the Senators for the district of which he is an inhabitant. And to remove all doubts concerning the meaning of the word "inhabitant" in this constitution, every person shall be considered as an inhabitant, for the purpose of electing and being elected into any office, or place within this State, in that town, district, or plantation, where he dwelleth, or hath his home.

THE Selectmen of the several towns shall preside at such meetings impartially; and shall receive the votes of all the inhabitants of such towns present and qualified to vote for Senators, and shall sort and count them in open town meeting, and in presence of the Town Clerk, who shall make a fair record in presence of the Selectmen, and in open town meeting, of the name of every person voted for, and of the number of votes against his name; and a fair copy of this record shall be attested by the Selectmen and the Town-Clerk, and shall be sealed up, directed to the Secretary of the Commonwealth for the time being, with a superscription, expressing the purport of the contents thereof, and delivered by the Town-Clerk of such towns, to the Sheriff of the county in which such town lies, thirty days at least before the last Wednesday in May annually; or it shall be delivered into the Secretary's office seventeen days at least before the said last Wednesday in May, and the Sheriff of each county shall deliver all such certifications by him received, in to the Secretary's office seventeen days before the said last Wednesday in May.

AND the inhabitants of plantations unincorporated, qualified as this Constitution provides, who are or shall be empowered and required to assess taxes upon themselves toward the support of government, shall have the same privilege of voting for Counsellors and Senators, in the plantations where they reside, as town inhabitants have in their respective towns; and the plantation-meetings for that purpose shall be held annually on the same first Monday in April, at such place in the planta-tions respectively, as the Assessors thereof shall direct; which Assessors shall have like authority for notifying the electors, collecting and returning the votes, as the Selectmen and Town-Clerks have in their several towns, by this Constitution. And all other persons living in places unincorporated (qualified as aforesaid) who shall be assessed to the support of govern-ment by the Assessors of an adjacent town, shall have the privilege of giv-ing in their votes for Counsellors and Senators, in the town where they shall be assessed, and be notified of the place of meeting by the Selectmen of the town where they shall be assessed, for that purpose, accordingly.

III.—AND that there may be a due convention of Senators on the last Wednesday in May annually, the Governor, with five of the Council, for the time being, shall, as soon as may be, examine the returned copies of such records; and fourteen days before the said day he shall issue his summons to such persons as shall appear to be chosen by a majority of voters, to attend on that day, and take their seats accordingly: Provided nevertheless, that for the first year the said returned copies shall be ex-amined by the President and five of the Council of the former Constitu-tion of Government; and the said President shall, in like manner, issue his summons to the persons so elected, that they may take their seats as aforesaid.

IV.—THE Senate shall be the final judge of the elections, returns and qualifications of their own members, as pointed out in the Constitution; and shall, on the said last Wednesday in May annually, determine and declare who are elected by each district, to be Senators, by a majority of votes: And in case there shall not appear to be the full number of Sena-tors returned elected by a majority of votes for any district, the defi-ciency shall be supplied in the following manner, viz. The members of the House of Representatives, and such Senators as shall be declared elected, shall take the names of such persons as shall be found to have the highest votes in each district, and not elected, amounting to twice the number of Senators wanting, if there be so many voted for; and, out of these, shall elect by ballot a number of Senators sufficient to fill up the vacancies in such district: And in this manner all such vacancies shall be filled up in every district of the Commonwealth; and in like manner all vacancies in the Senate, arising by death, removal out of the State, or otherwise, shall be supplied as soon as may be after such vacancies shall happen.

V.—PROVIDED nevertheless, that no person shall be capable of being elected as a Senator, who is not seized in his own right of a freehold within this Commonwealth, of the value of three hundred pounds at least, or of both to the amount of the same sum, and who has not been an inhabitant of this Commonwealth for the space of five years immediately preceding his election, and, at the time of his election, he shall be an inhabitant in the district, for which he shall be chosen.

VI.—THE Senate shall have power to adjourn themselves, provided such adjournments do not exceed two days at a time.

VII.—THE Senate shall choose its own President, appoint its own officers, and determine its own rules of proceeding.

VIII.—THE Senate shall be a court with full authority to hear and determine all impeachments made by the House of Representatives, against any officer or officers of the Commonwealth, for misconduct and maladministration in their offices. But, previous to the trial of every impeachment, the members of the Senate shall respectively be sworn, truly and impartially to try and determine the charge in question, according to evidence. Their judgment, however, shall not extend further than to removal from office and disqualification to hold or enjoy any place of honor, trust, or profit, under this Commonwealth: But the party, so convicted, shall be, nevertheless, liable to indictment, trial, judgment, and punishment, according to the laws of the land.

IX.—NOT less than sixteen members of the Senate shall constitute a quorum for doing business.

CHAPTER I

SECTION III

House of Representatives

ART. I—THERE shall be in the legislature of this Commonwealth, a representation of the people, annually elected, and founded upon the principle of equality.

II.—AND in order to provide for a representation of the citizens of this Commonwealth, founded upon the principle of equality, every corporate town, containing one hundred and fifty rateable polls, may elect one Representative: Every corporate town, containing three hundred and seventy-five rateable polls, may elect three Representatives; and proceeding in that manner, making two hundred and twenty-five rateable polls the mean increasing number for every additional Representative.

PROVIDED nevertheless, that each town incorporated, not having one hundred and fifty rateable polls, may elect one Representative: but no place shall hereafter be incorporated with the privilege of electing a Representative, unless there are within the same one hundred and fifty rateable polls.

AND the House of Representatives shall have power, from time to time, to impose fines upon such towns as shall neglect to choose and return members to the same, agreeably to this Constitution.

THE expenses of travelling to the General Assembly, and returning home, once in every session, and no more, shall be paid by the government, out of the public treasury, to every member who shall attend as seasonably as he can, in the judgment of the House, and does not depart without leave.

III.—EVERY member of the House of Representatives shall be chosen by written votes; and for one year at least next preceding his election shall have been an inhabitant of, and have been seized in his own right of a freehold of the value of one hundred pounds within the town he shall be chosen to represent, or any rateable estate to the value of two hundred pounds; and he shall cease to represent the said town immediately on his ceasing to be qualified as aforesaid.

IV.—EVERY male person, being twenty-one years of age, and resident in any particular town in this Commonwealth for the space of one year next preceding, having a freehold estate within the same town, of the annual income of three pounds, or any estate of the value of sixty pounds, shall have a right to vote in the choice of a Representative or Representatives for the said town.

V.—THE members of the House of Representatives shall be chosen annually in the month of May, ten days at least before the last Wednesday of that month.

VI.—THE House of Representatives shall be the Grand Inquest of this Commonwealth; and all impeachments made by them shall be heard and tried by the Senate.

VII.—ALL money-bills shall originate in the House of Representatives; but the Senate may propose or concur with amendments, as on other bills.

VIII.—THE House of Representatives shall have power to adjourn themselves; provided such adjournment shall not exceed two days at a time.

IX.—NOT less than sixty members of the House of Representatives shall constitute a quorum for doing business.

X.—THE House of Representatives shall be the judge of the returns, elections, and qualifications of its own members, as pointed out in the constitution; shall choose their own Speaker; appoint their own officers, and settle the rules and orders of proceeding in their own house: They shall have authority to punish by imprisonment, every person, not a member, who shall be guilty of disrespect to the House, by any disorderly, or contemptuous behavior, in its presence; or who, in the town where the General Court is sitting, and during the time of its sitting, shall threaten harm to the body or estate of any of its members, for any thing said or done in the House; or who shall assault any of them therefor; or who shall assault, or arrest, any witness, or other person, ordered to attend the House, in his way in going, or returning; or who shall rescue any person arrested by the order of the House.

No member of the House of Representatives shall be arrested, or held to bail on mean process, during his going unto, returning from, or his attending, the General Assembly.

XI.—THE Senate shall have the same powers in the like cases; and the Governor and Council shall have the same authority to punish in like cases. Provided, that no imprisonment on the warrant or order of the Governor, Council, Senate, or House of Representatives, for either of the above described offenses, be for a term exceeding thirty days.

AND the Senate and House of Representatives may try, and determine all cases where their rights and privileges are concerned, and which, by the Constitution, they have authority to try and determine, by committees of their own members, or in such other way as they may respectively think best.

CHAPTER II

Executive Power

SECTION I

Governor

ART. I.—THERE shall be a Supreme Executive Magistrate, who shall be styled, THE GOVERNOR OF THE COMMONWEALTH OF MASSACHUSETTS, and whose title shall be—HIS EXCELLENCY.

II.—THE Governor shall be chosen annually: And no person shall be eligible to this office, unless at the time of his election, he shall have been an inhabitant of this Commonwealth for seven years next preceding; and unless he shall, at the same time, be seized in his own right, of a freehold within the Commonwealth, of the value of one thousand pounds; and unless he shall declare himself to be of the christian religion.

III.—THOSE persons who shall be qualified to vote for Senators and Representatives within the several towns of this Commonwealth, shall, at a meeting, to be called for that purpose, on the first Monday of April annually, give in their votes for a Governor, to the Selectmen, who shall preside at such meetings; and the Town Clerk, in the presence and with the assistance of the Selectmen, shall, in open town meeting, sort and count the votes, and form a list of the persons voted for, with the number of votes for each person against his name; and shall make a fair record of the same in the town books, and a public declaration thereof in the said meeting; and shall, in the presence of the inhabitants, seal up copies of the said list, attested by him and the Selectmen, and transmit the same to the Sheriff of the county, thirty days at least before the last Wednesday in May; and the Sheriff shall transmit the same to the Secretary's office seventeen days at least before the said last Wednesday in May; or the Selectmen may cause returns of the same to be made to the office of the Secretary of the Commonwealth seventeen days at least before the said day;

and the Secretary shall lay the same before the Senate and the House of Representatives, on the last Wednesday in May, to be by them examined: And in case of an election by a majority of all the votes returned, the choice shall be by them declared and published: But if no person shall have a majority of votes, the House of Representatives shall, by ballot, elect two out of four persons who had the highest number of votes, if so many shall have been voted for; but, if otherwise, out of the number voted for; and make return to the Senate of the two persons so elected; on which, the Senate shall proceed, by ballot, to elect one, who shall be declared Governor.

IV.—THE Governor shall have authority, from time to time, at his discretion, to assemble and call together the Counsellors of this Commonwealth for the time being; and the Governor, with the said Counsellors, or five of them at least, shall, and may, from time to time, hold and keep a Council, for the ordering and directing the affairs of the Commonwealth, agreeably to the Constitution and the laws of the land.

V.—THE Governor, with advice of Council, shall have full power and authority, during the session of the General Court, to adjourn to prorogue the same to any time the two Houses shall desire; to dissolve the same on the day next preceding the last Wednesday in May; and, in the recess of the said Court, to prorogue the same from time to time, not exceeding ninety days in any one recess; and to call it together sooner than the time to which it may be adjourned or prorogued, if the welfare of the Commonwealth shall require the same: And in case of any infectious distemper prevailing in the place where the said Court is next at any time to convene, or any other cause happening whereby danger may arise to the health or lives of the members from their attendance, he may direct the session to be held at some other the most convenient place within the State.

AND the Governor shall dissolve the said General Court on the day next preceding the last Wednesday in May.

VI.—IN cases of disagreement between the two Houses, with regard to the necessity, expediency or time of adjournment, or prorogation, the Governor, with advice of the Council, shall have a right to adjourn or prorogue the General Court, not exceeding ninety days, as he shall determine the public good shall require.

VII.—THE Governor of this Commonwealth, for the time being, shall be the commander-in-chief of the army and navy, and of all the military forces of the State, by sea and land; and shall have full power, by himself, or by any commander, or other officer or officers, from time to time, to train, instruct, exercise and govern the militia and navy; and, for the special defense and safety of the Commonwealth, to assemble in martial array, and put in warlike posture, the inhabitants thereof, and to lead and conduct them, and with them, to encounter, repel, resist, expel and pursue, by force of arms, as well by sea as by land, within or without the limits of this Commonwealth, and also to kill, slay and destroy, if necessary, and conquer, by all fitting ways, enterprises and means whatsoever, all and every such person and persons as shall, at any time hereafter, in a hostile manner, attempt or enterprize the destruction, invasion, detriment, or annoyance of this Commonwealth; and to use and exercise, over the army and navy, and over the militia in actual service, the law martial, in time of war or invasion, and also in time of rebellion, declared by the legislature to exist, as occasion shall necessarily require; and to take and surprise by all ways and means whatsoever, all and every such person or persons, with their ships, arms, ammunition and other goods, as shall, in a hostile manner, invade, or attempt the invading, conquering, or annoyance of this Commonwealth; and that the Governor be intrusted with all these and other powers, incident to the offices of Captain-General and Commander-in-Chief, and Admiral, to be exercised agreeably to the rules and regulations of the Constitution, and the laws of the land, and not otherwise.

PROVIDED, that the said Governor shall not, at any time hereafter, by virtue of any power by this Constitution granted, or hereafter to be granted to him by the legislature, transport any of the inhabitants of this Commonwealth, or oblige them to march out of the limits of the same, without their free and voluntary consent, or the consent of the General Court; except so far as may be necessary to march or transport them by land or water, for the defence of such part of the State, to which they cannot otherwise conveniently have access.

VIII.—THE power of pardoning offenses, except such as persons may be convicted of before the Senate by an impeachment of the House, shall be in the Governor, by and with the advice of Council. But no charter of pardon, granted by the Governor, with advice of Council, before conviction, shall avail the party pleading the same, notwithstanding any general or particular expressions contained therein, descriptive of the offence, or offenses intended to be pardoned.

IX.—ALL judicial officers, the Attorney-General, the Solicitor-General, all Sheriffs, Coroners, and Registers of Probate, shall be nominated and appointed by the Governor, by and with the advice and consent of the Council; and every such nomination shall be made by the Governor, and made at least seven days prior to such appointment.

X.—THE Captains and subalterns of the militia shall be elected by the written votes of the train-band and alarm list of their respective companies, of twenty-one years of age and upwards: The field-officers of Regiments shall be elected by the written votes of the captains and subalterns of their respective regiments: The Brigadiers shall be elected in like manner, by the field officers of their respective brigades: And such officers, so elected, shall be commissioned by the Governor, who shall determine their rank.

THE Legislature shall, by standing laws, direct the time and manner of convening the electors, and of collecting votes, and of certifying to the Governor the officers elected.

THE Major-Generals shall be appointed by the Senate and House of Representatives, each having a negative upon the other; and be commissioned by the Governor.

AND if the electors of Brigadiers, field-officers, captains or subalterns, shall neglect or refuse to make such elections, after being duly notified, according to the laws for the time being, then the Governor, with advice of Council, shall appoint suitable persons to fill such offices.

AND no officer, duly commissioned to command in the militia, shall be removed from his office, but by the address of both houses to the Governor, or by fair trial in court martial, pursuant to the laws of the Commonwealth for the time being.

THE commanding officers of regiments shall appoint their Adjutants and Quarter-masters; the Brigadiers their Brigade-Majors; and the Major-Generals their Aids: and the Governor shall appoint the Adjutant General.

THE Governor, with advice of Council, shall appoint all officers of the continental army, whom by the confederation of the United States it is provided that this Commonwealth shall appoint,—as also all officers of forts and garrisons.

THE divisions of the militia into brigades, regiments and companies, made in pursuance of the militia laws now in force, shall be considered as the proper divisions of the militia of this Commonwealth, until the same shall be altered in pursuance of some future law.

XI.—NO monies shall be issued out of the treasury of this Commonwealth, and disposed of (except such sums as may be appropriated for the redemption of bills of credit of Treasurer's notes, or for the payment of interest arising thereon) but by warrant under the hand of the Governor for the time being, with the advice and consent of the Council, for the necessary defence and support of the Commonwealth; and for the protection and preservation of the inhabitants thereof, agreeably to the acts and resolves of the General Court.

XII.—ALL public boards, the Commissary-General, all superintending officers of public magazines and stores, belonging to this Commonwealth, and all commanding officers of forts and garrisons within the same, shall, once in every three months, officially and without requisition, and at other times, when required by the Governor, deliver to him an account of all goods, stores, provisions, ammunition, cannon with their appendages, and small arms with their accoutrements, and of all other public property whatever under their care respectively; distinguishing the quantity, number, quality and kind of each, as particularly as may be; together with the condition of such forts and garrisons: And the said commanding officer shall exhibit to the Governor, when required by him, true and exact plans of such forts, and of the land and sea, or harbours adjacent.

AND the said boards, and all public officers, shall communicate to the Governor, as soon as may be after receiving the same, all letters, dispatches, and intelligences of a public nature, which shall be directed to them respectively.

XIII.—AS the public good requires that the Governor should not be under the undue influence of any of the members of the General Court, by a dependence on them for his support—that he should, in all cases, act with freedom for the benefit of the public—that he should not have his attention necessarily diverted from that object to his private concerns—

and that he should maintain the dignity of the Commonwealth in the character of its chief magistrate—it is necessary that he should have an honorable stated salary, of a fixed and permanent value, amply sufficient for those purposes, and established by standing laws: And it shall be among the first acts of the General Court, after the Commencement of this Constitution, to establish such salary by law accordingly.

PERMANENT and honorable salaries shall also be established by law for the Justices of the Supreme Judicial Court.

AND if it shall be found, that any of the salaries aforesaid, so established, are insufficient, they shall, from time to time, be enlarged, as the General Court shall judge proper.

CHAPTER II

SECTION II

Lieutenant-Governor

ART. I.—THERE shall be annually elected a Lieutenant-Governor of the Commonwealth of Massachusetts, whose title shall be HIS HONOR—and who shall be qualified, in point of religion, property, and residence in the Commonwealth, in the same manner with the Governor: And the day and manner of his election, and the qualifications of the electors, shall be the same as are required in the election of a Governor. The return of the votes for this officer, and the declaration of his election, shall be in the same manner: And if no one person shall be found to have a majority of all the votes returned, the vacancy shall be filled by the Senate and House of Representatives, in the same manner as the Governor is to be elected, in case no one person shall have a majority of the votes of the people to be Governor.

II.—THE Governor, and in his absence the Lieutenant-Governor, shall be President of the Council, but shall have no vote in the Council: And the Lieutenant-Governor shall always be a member of the Council, except when the chair of the Governor shall be vacant.

III.—WHENEVER the chair of the Governor shall be vacant, by reason of his death, or absence from the Commonwealth, or otherwise, the

Lieutenant-Governor, for the time being, shall, during such vacancy, perform all the duties incumbent upon the Governor, and shall have and exercise all the powers and authorities, which by this Constitution the Governor is vested with, when personally present.

CHAPTER II

SECTION III

Council, and the Manner of Settling Elections by the Legislature

ART. I.—THERE shall be a Council for advising the Governor in the executive part of government, to consist of nine persons besides the Lieutenant-Governor, whom the Governor, for the time being, shall have full power and authority, from time to time, at his discretion, to assemble and call together. And the Governor, with the said Counsellors, or five of them at least, shall and may, from time to time, hold and keep a council, for the ordering and directing the affairs of the Commonwealth, according to the laws of the land.

II.—NINE Counsellors shall be annually chosen from among the persons returned for Counsellors and Senators, on the last Wednesday in May, by the joint ballot of the Senators and Representatives assembled in one room: And in case there shall not be found, upon the first choice, the whole number of nine persons who will accept a seat in the Council, the deficiency shall be made up by the electors aforesaid from among the people at large; and the number of Senators left shall constitute the Senate for the year. The seats of the persons thus elected from the Senate, and accepting the trust, shall be vacated in the Senate.

III.—THE Counsellors, in the civil arrangements of the Commonwealth, shall have rank next after the Lieutenant-Governor.

IV.—NOT more than two Counsellors shall be chosen out of any one district of this Commonwealth.

V.—THE resolutions and advice of the Council shall be recorded in a register, and signed by the members present; and this record may be called for at any time by either House of the Legislature; and any member of the Council may insert his opinion contrary to the resolution of the majority.

VI.—WHENEVER the office of the Governor and Lieutenant-Governor shall be vacant, by reason of death, absence, or otherwise, then the Council or the major part of them, shall, during such vacancy, have full power and authority, to do, and execute, all and every such acts, matters and things, as the Governor or the Lieutenant-Governor might or could, by virtue of this Constitution, do or execute, if they, or either of them, were personally present.

VII.—AND whereas the elections appointed to be made by this Constitution, on the last Wednesday in May annually, by the two Houses of the Legislature, may not be completed on that day, the said elections may be adjourned from day to day until the same shall be completed. And the order of elections shall be as follows; the vacancies in the Senate, if any, shall first be filled up; the Governor and Lieutenant-Governor shall then be elected, provided there should be no choice of them by the people: And afterwards the two Houses shall proceed to the election of the Council.

CHAPTER II

SECTION IV

Secretary, Treasurer, Commissary, etc.

ART. I.—THE Secretary, Treasurer and Receiver-General, and the Commissary-General, Notaries-Public, and Naval-Officers, shall be chosen annually, by joint ballot of the Senators and Representatives in one room. And that the citizens of this Commonwealth may be assured, from time to time, that the monies remaining in the public Treasury, upon the settlement and liquidation of the public accounts, are their property, no man shall be eligible as Treasurer and Receiver-General more than five years successively.

II.—THE records of the Commonwealth shall be kept in the office of the Secretary, who may appoint his Deputies, for whose conduct he shall be accountable, and he shall attend the Governor and Council, the Senate and House of Representatives, in person, or by his deputies, as they shall respectively require.

CHAPTER III

Judiciary Power

ART. I.—THE tenure that all commission officers shall by law have in their offices, shall be expressed in their respective commissions. All judicial officers, duly appointed, commissioned and sworn, shall hold their offices during good behavior, excepting such concerning whom there is different provision made in this Constitution: Provided, nevertheless, the Governor, with consent of the Council, may remove them upon the address of both Houses of the Legislature.

II.—EACH branch of the Legislature, as well as the Governor and Council, shall have authority to require the opinions of the Justices of the Supreme Judicial Court, upon important questions of law, and upon solemn occasion.

III.—IN order that the people may not suffer from the long continuance in place of any Justice of the Peace, who shall fail of discharging the important duties of his office with ability or fidelity, all commissions of Justice of the Peace shall expire and become void, in the term of seven years from their respective dates; and, upon the expiration of any commission, the same may, if necessary, be renewed, or another person appointed, as shall most conduce to the well being of the Commonwealth.

IV.—THE Judges of Probate of Wills, and for granting letters of administration, shall hold their courts at such place or places, on fixed days, as the convenience of the people shall require. And the Legislature shall, from time to time, hereafter appoint such times and places; until which appointments, the said Courts shall be holden at the times and places which the respective Judges shall direct.

V.—ALL causes of marriage, divorce and alimony, and all appeals from the Judges of Probate, shall be heard and determined by the Governor and Council until the Legislature shall, by law, make other provision.

CHAPTER IV

Delegates to Congress

THE delegates of this Commonwealth to the Congress of the United States, shall, sometime in the month of June annually, be elected by the joint ballot of the Senate and House of Representatives, assembled together in one room; to serve in Congress for one year, to commence on the first Monday in November then next ensuing. They shall have commissions under the hand of the Governor, and the great seal of the Commonwealth; but may be recalled at any time within the year, and others chosen and commissioned, in the same manner, in their stead.

CHAPTER V

The University at Cambridge, and Encouragement of Literature, etc.

SECTION I

The University

ART. I.—WHEREAS our wise and pious ancestors, so early as the year one thousand six hundred and thirty six, laid the foundation of Harvard-College, in which University many persons of great eminence have, by the blessing of GOD, been initiated in those arts and sciences, which qualified them for public employments, both in Church and State: And whereas the encouragement of Arts and Sciences, and all good literature, tends to the honor of GOD, the advantage of the christian religion, and the great benefit of this, and the other United States of America—It is declared, That the PRESIDENT AND FELLOWS OF HARVARD-COLLEGE, in their corporate capacity, and their successors in that capacity, their officers and servants, shall have, hold, use, exercise and enjoy, all the powers, authorities, rights, liberties, privileges, immunities and franchises, which they now have, or are entitled to have, hold, use, exercise and enjoy: And the same are hereby ratified and confirmed unto them, the said President and Fellows of Harvard-College, and to their successors, and to their officers and servants, respectively, forever.

II.—AND whereas there have been at sundry times, by divers persons, gifts, grants, devises of houses, lands, tenements, goods, chattels, legacies and conveyances, heretofore made, either to Harvard-College in Cambridge, in New-England, or to the President and Fellows of Harvard-College, or to the said College, by some other description, under several charters successively: IT IS DECLARED, That all the said gifts, grants, devises, legacies and conveyances, are hereby forever confirmed unto the President and Fellows of Harvard-College, and to their successors, in the capacity aforesaid, according to the true intent and meaning of the donor or donors, grantor or grantors, devisor or devisors.

III.—AND whereas by an act of the General Court of the Colony of Massachusetts-Bay, passed in the year one thousand six hundred and forty-two, the Governor and Deputy-Governor, for the time being, and all the magistrates of that jurisdiction, were, with the President, and a number of the clergy in the said act described, constituted the Overseers of Harvard-College: And it being necessary, in this new Constitution of Government, to ascertain who shall be deemed successors to the said Governor, Deputy-Governor and Magistrates: IT IS DECLARED, That the Governor, Lieutenant-Governor, Council and Senate of this Commonwealth, are, and shall be deemed, their successors; who, with the President of Harvard-College, for the time being, together with the ministers of the congregational churches in the towns of Cambridge, Watertown, Charlestown, Boston, Roxbury, and Dorchester, mentioned in the said act, shall be, and hereby are, vested with all the powers and authority belonging, or in any way appertaining to the Overseers of Harvard-College; PROVIDED, that nothing herein shall be construed to prevent the Legislature of this Commonwealth from making such alterations in the government of the said university, as shall be conducive to its advantage, and the interest of the republic of letters, in as full a manner as might have been done by the Legislature of the late Province of the Massachusetts-Bay.

CHAPTER V

SECTION II

The Encouragement of Literature, etc.

WISDOM, and knowledge, as well as virtue, diffused generally among the body of the people, being necessary for the preservation of their rights and liberties; and as these depend on spreading the opportunities and advantages of education in the various parts of the country, and among the different orders of the people, it shall be the duty of legislators and magistrates, in all future periods of this Commonwealth, to cherish the interests of literature and the sciences, and all seminaries of them; especially the university at Cambridge, public schools, and grammar schools in the towns; to encourage private societies and public institutions, rewards and immunities, for the promotion of agriculture, arts, sciences, commerce, trades, manufactures, and a natural history of the country; to countenance and inculcate the principles of humanity and general benevolence, public and private charity, industry and frugality, honesty and punctuality in their dealings; sincerity, good humour, and all social affections, and generous sentiments among the people.

CHAPTER VI

Oaths and Subscriptions; Incompatibility of an Exclusion from Offices; Pecuniary Qualifications; Commissions; Writs; Confirmation of Laws; Habeas Corpus; The Enacting Style; Continuance of Officers; Provision for a future Revisal of the Constitution, etc.

ART. I.—ANY person chosen Governor, Lieutenant-Governor, Counselor, Senator, or Representative, and accepting the trust, shall, before he proceed to execute the duties of his place or office, make and subscribe the following declaration, viz.—

"I, A. B. do declare, that I believe the christian religion, and have a firm persuasion of its truth; and that I am seized and possessed, in my own right, of the property required by the Constitution as one qualification for the office or place to which I am elected."

AND the Governor, Lieutenant-Governor, and Counsellors, shall make and subscribe the said declaration, in the presence of the two Houses of Assembly; and the Senators and Representatives first elected under this constitution, before the President and five of the Council of the former Constitution, and, forever afterwards, before the Governor and Council for the time being.

AND every person chosen to either of the places or offices aforesaid, as also any person appointed or commissioned to any judicial, executive, military, or other office under the government, shall, before he enters on the discharge of the business of his place or office, take and subscribe the following declaration, and oaths or affirmations, viz.—

"I, A. B. do truly and sincerely acknowledge, profess, testify and declare, that the Commonwealth of Massachusetts is, and of right ought to be, a free, sovereign and independent State; and I do swear, that I will bear true faith and allegiance to the said Commonwealth, and that I will defend the same against traitorous conspiracies and all hostile attempts whatsoever: And that I do renounce and adjure all allegiance, subjection and obedience to the King, Queen or Government of Great Britain, (as the case may be) and every other foreign power whatsoever: And that no foreign Prince, Person, Prelate, State or Potentate, hath, or ought to have, any jurisdiction, superiority, pre-eminence, authority, dispensing or other power, in any matter, civil, ecclesiastical or spiritual, within this Commonwealth; except the authority and power which is or may be vested by their Constituents in the Congress of the United States: And I do further testify and declare, that no man or body of men hath or can have any right to absolve or discharge me from the obligation of this oath, declaration or affirmation; and that I do make this acknowledgment, profession, testimony, declaration, denial, renunciation and abjuration, heartily and truly, according to the common meaning and acceptation of the foregoing words, without any equivocation, mental evasion, or secret reservation whatsoever. So help me GOD."

"I, A. B. do solemnly swear and affirm, that I will faithfully and impartially discharge and perform all the duties incumbent on me as according to the best of my abilities and understanding, agreeably to the rules and regulations of the Constitution, and the laws of this Commonwealth." "So help me GOD."

PROVIDED always, that when any person, chosen or appointed as aforesaid, shall be of the denomination of the people called Quakers, and shall decline taking the said oaths, he shall make his affirmation in the foregoing form, and subscribe the same, omitting the words "I do swear," "and adjure," "oath or," "and abjuration," in the first oath; and in the second oath, the words "swear and;" and in each of them the words "So help me GOD;" subjoining instead thereof, "This I do under the pains and penalties of perjury."

AND the said oaths or affirmations shall be taken and subscribed by the Governor, Lieutenant Governor, and Counsellors, before the President of the Senate, in the presence of the two Houses of Assembly; and by the Senators and Representatives first elected under this Constitution, before the President and five of the Council of the former Constitution; and forever afterwards before the Governor and Council for the time being: And by the residue of the officers aforesaid, before such persons and in such manner as from time to time shall be prescribed by the Legislature.

II.—No Governor, Lieutenant Governor, or Judge of the Supreme Judicial Court, shall hold any other office or place, under the authority of this Commonwealth, except such as by this Constitution they are admitted to hold, saving that the Judges of the said Court may hold the offices of Justices of the Peace through the State; nor shall they hold any other place or office, or receive any pension or salary from any other State or Government or Power whatever.

No person shall be capable of holding or exercising at the same time, within this State, more than one of the following offices, viz:—Judge of Probate—Sheriff—Register of Deeds—and never more than any two offices which are to be held by appointment of the Governor, or the Governor and Council, or the Senate, or the House of Representatives, or by the election of the people of the State at large, or of the people of any county, military offices and the offices of Justices of the Peace excepted, shall be held by one person.

No person holding the office of Judge of the Supreme Judicial Court—Secretary—Attorney General—Solicitor General—Treasurer or Receiver General—Judge of Probate—Commissionary General—President, Professor, or Instructor of Harvard College—Sheriff—Clerk of the House of Representatives—Register of Probate—Register of Deeds—Clerk of the Supreme Judicial Court—Clerk of the Inferior Court of Common Pleas—or Officer of the Customs, including in this description Naval Officers—shall at the same time have a seat in the Senate or House of Representatives; but their being chosen or appointed to, and accepting the same, shall operate as a resignation of their seat in the Senate or House of Representatives; and the place so vacated shall be filled up.

AND the same rule shall take place in case any judge of the said Supreme Judicial Court, or Judge of Probate, shall accept a seat in Council; or any Counsellor shall accept of either of those offices or places.

AND no person shall ever be admitted to hold a seat in the Legislature, or any office of trust or importance under the Government of this Commonwealth, who shall, in the due course of law, have been convicted of bribery or corruption in obtaining an election or appointment.

III.—IN all cases where sums of money are mentioned in this Constitution, the value thereof shall be computed in silver at six shillings and eight pence per ounce: And it shall be in the power of the Legislature from time to time to increase such qualifications, as to property, of the persons to be elected to offices, as the circumstances of the Commonwealth shall require.

IV.—ALL commissions shall be in the name of the Commonwealth of Massachusetts, signed by the Governor, and attested by the Secretary or his Deputy, and have the great seal of the Commonwealth affixed thereto.

V.—ALL writs, issuing out of the clerk's office in any of the Courts of law, shall be in the name of the Commonwealth of Massachusetts: They shall be under the seal of the Court from whence they issue: They shall bear test of the first Justice of the Court to which they shall be returnable, who is not a party, and be signed by the clerk of such court.

VI.—ALL the laws which have heretofore been adopted, used and approved in the Province, Colony or State of Massachusetts Bay, and usually practiced on in the Courts of law, shall still remain and be in full force, until altered or repealed by the Legislature; such parts only excepted as are repugnant to the rights and liberties contained in this Constitution.

VII.—THE privilege and benefit of the writ of *habeas corpus* shall be enjoyed in this Commonwealth in the most free, easy, cheap, expeditious and ample manner; and shall not be suspended by the Legislature, except upon the most urgent and pressing occasions, and for a limited time not exceeding twelve months.

VIII.—THE enacting style, in making and passing all acts, statutes and laws, shall be—"Be it enacted by the Senate and House of Representatives, in General Court assembled, and by the authority of the same."

IX.—TO the end there may be no failure of justice or danger arise to the Commonwealth from a change of the Form of Government—all officers, civil and military, holding commissions under the government and people of Massachusetts Bay in New-England, and all other officers of the said government and people, at the time this Constitution shall take effect, shall have, hold, use, exercise and enjoy all the powers and authority to them granted or committed, until other persons shall be appointed in their stead: And all courts of law shall proceed in the execution of the business of their respective departments; and all the executive and legislative officers, bodies and powers shall continue in full force, in the enjoyment and exercise of all their trusts, employments and authority; until the General Court and the supreme and executive officers under this Constitution are designated and invested with their respective trusts, powers and authority.

x.—IN order the more effectually to adhere to the principles of the Constitution, and to correct those violations which by any means may be made therein, as well as to form such alterations as from experience shall be found necessary—the General Court, which shall be in the year of our Lord one thousand seven hundred and ninety-five, shall issue precepts to the Selectmen of the several towns, and to the Assessors of the unincorporated plantations, directing them to convene the qualified voters of their respective towns and plantations for the purpose of collecting their sentiments on the necessity or expediency of revising the Constitution, in order to amendments.

AND if it shall appear by the returns made, that two thirds of the qualified voters throughout the State, who shall assemble and vote in consequence of the said precepts, are in favor of such revision or amendment, the General Court shall issue precepts, or direct them to be issued from the Secretary's office to the several towns, to elect Delegates to meet in Convention for the purpose aforesaid.

THE said Delegates to be chosen in the same manner and proportion as their Representatives in the second branch of the Legislature are by this Constitution to be chosen.

xi.—THIS form of government shall be enrolled on parchment, and deposited in the Secretary's office, and be a part of the laws of the land—and printed copies thereof shall be prefixed to the book containing the laws of this Commonwealth, in all future editions of the said laws.

Attest. SAMUEL BARRETT, *Secretary*   JAMES BOWDOIN, *President*

Articles of Confederation (1778)

To ALL TO WHOM these Presents shall come, we the undersigned Delegates of the States affixed to our names send greeting. Whereas the Delegates of the United States of America in Congress assembled did on the fifteenth day of November in the Year of our Lord One Thousand Seven Hundred and Seventy seven, and in the Second Year of the Independence of America agree to certain articles of Confederation and perpetual Union between the States of New Hampshire, Massachusetts-bay, Rhode Island and Providence Plantations, Connecticut, New York, New Jersey, Pennsylvania, Delaware, Maryland, Virginia, North-Carolina, South-Carolina, and Georgia in the Words following, viz. "Articles of Confederation and perpetual Union between the States of New Hampshire, Massachusetts-bay, Rhode Island and Providence Plantations, Connecticut, New-York, New-Jersey, Pennsylvania, Delaware, Maryland, Virginia, North-Carolina, South-Carolina and Georgia.

Art. I. The Stile of this confederacy shall be "The United States of America."

Art. II. Each State retains its sovereignty, freedom and independence, and every Power, Jurisdiction and right, which is not by this confederation expressly delegated to the United States, in Congress assembled.

Art. III. The said States hereby severally enter into a firm league of friendship with each other, for their common defence, the security of their Liberties, and their mutual and general welfare, binding themselves to assist each other, against all force offered to, or attacks made upon them, or any of them, on account of religion, sovereignty, trade, or any other pretence whatever.

Art. IV. The better to secure and perpetuate mutual friendship and intercourse among the people of the different States in this union, the free inhabitants of each of these States, paupers, vagabonds and fugitives from Justice excepted, shall be entitled to all privileges and immunities of free citizens in the several States; and the people of each State shall have free ingress and regress to and from any other State, and shall enjoy therein all the privileges of trade and commerce, subject to the same duties, impositions and restrictions as the inhabitants thereof respectively, provided that such restriction shall not extend so far as to prevent the removal of property imported into any State, to any other State of which the owner is an inhabitant; provided also that no imposition, duties or restriction shall be laid by any State, on the property of the United States, or either of them.

If any Person guilty of, or charged with treason, felony, or other high misdemeanor in any State, shall flee from Justice, and be found in any of the United States, he shall upon demand of the Governor or executive power, of the State from which he fled, be delivered up and removed to the State having jurisdiction of his offence.

Full faith and credit shall be given in each of these States to the records, acts and judicial proceedings of the courts and magistrates to every other State.

Art. V. For the more convenient management of the general interests of the United States, delegates shall be annually appointed in such manner as the legislature of each State shall direct, to meet in Congress on the first Monday in November, in every year, with a power reserved to each State, to recall its delegates, or any of them, at any time within the year, and to send others in their stead, for the remainder of the Year.

No State shall be represented in Congress by less than two, nor by more than seven Members; and no person shall be capable of being a delegate for more than three years in any term of six years; nor shall any person, being a delegate, be capable of holding any office under the United States, for which he, or another for his benefit receives any salary, fees or emolument of any kind.

Each State shall maintain its own delegates in a meeting of the States, and while they act as members of the committee of the States.

In determining questions in the United States, in Congress assembled, each State shall have one vote.

Freedom of speech and debate in Congress shall not be impeached or questioned in any Court, or place out of Congress, and the members of Congress shall be protected in their persons from arrests and imprisonments, during the time of their going to and from, and attendance of Congress, except for treason, felony, or breach of the peace.

Art. VI. No State without the consent of the United States in Congress assembled, shall send any embassy to, or receive any embassy from, or enter into any conference, agreement, or alliance or treaty with any King, Prince or State; nor shall any person holding any office of profit or trust under the United States, or any of them, accept of any present, emolument, office or title of any kind whatever from any King, Prince or foreign State; nor shall the United States in Congress assembled, or any of them, grant any title of nobility.

No two or more States shall enter into any treaty, confederation or alliance whatever between them, without the consent of the United States in Congress assembled, specifying accurately the purposes for which the same is to be entered into, and how long it shall continue.

No State shall lay any imposts or duties, which may interfere with any stipulations in treaties, entered into by the United States in Congress assembled, with any King, Prince or State, in pursuance of any treaties already proposed by Congress, to the courts of France and Spain.

No vessels of war shall be kept up in time of peace by any State, except such number only, as shall be deemed necessary by the United States in Congress assembled, for the defence of such State, or its trade; nor shall any body of forces be kept up by any State in time of peace, except such number only, as in the judgment of the United States, in Congress assembled, shall be deemed requisite to garrison the forts necessary for the defence of such State; but every State shall always keep up a well regulated and disciplined militia, sufficiently armed and accoutered, and shall provide and constantly have ready for use, in public stores, a due number of field pieces and tents, and a proper quantity of arms, ammunition and camp equipage.

No State shall engage in any war without the consent of the United States in Congress assembled, unless such State be actually invaded by enemies, or shall have received certain advice of a resolution being formed by some nation of Indians to invade such State, and the danger is so imminent as not to admit of a delay, till the United States in Congress assembled can be consulted: nor shall any State grant commissions to any ships or vessels of war, nor letters of marque or reprisal, except it be after a declaration of war by the United States in Congress assembled, and then only against the kingdom or State and the subjects thereof, against which war has been so declared, and under such regulations as shall be established by the United States in Congress assembled, unless such State be infested by pirates, in which case vessels of war may be fitted out for that occasion, and kept so long as the danger shall continue, or until the United States in Congress assembled shall determine otherwise.

Art. VII. When land-forces are raised by any State for the common defence, all officers of or under the rank of colonel, shall be appointed by the legislature of each State respectively by whom such forces shall be raised, or in such manner as such State shall direct, and all vacancies shall be filled up by the State which first made the appointment.

Art. VIII. All charges of war, and all other expenses that shall be incurred for the common defence or general welfare, and allowed by the United States in Congress assembled, shall be defrayed out of a common treasury, which shall be supplied by the several States, in proportion to the value of all land within each State, granted to or surveyed for any person, as such land and the buildings and improvements thereon shall be estimated according to such mode as the United States in Congress assembled, shall from time to time direct and appoint. The taxes for paying that proportion shall be laid and levied by the authority and direction of the legislatures of the several States within the time agreed upon by the United States in Congress assembled.

Art. IX. The United States in Congress assembled shall have the sole and exclusive right and power of determining on peace and war, except in the cases mentioned in the sixth article—of sending and receiving ambassadors—entering into treaties and alliances, provided that no treaty of commerce shall be made whereby the legislative power of the respective States shall be restrained from imposing such imposts and duties on foreigners, as their own people are subjected to, or from prohibiting the exportation or importation of any species of goods or commodities whatsoever—of establishing rules for deciding in all cases, what captures on land or water shall be legal, and in what manner prizes taken by land or naval forces in the service of the United States shall be divided or appropriated—of granting letters of marque and reprisal in times of peace—appointing courts for the trial of piracies and felonies committed on the high seas and establishing courts for receiving and determining finally appeals in all cases of captures, provided that no member of Congress shall be appointed a judge of any of the said courts.

The United States in congress assembled shall also be the last resort on appeal in all disputes and differences now subsisting or that hereafter may arise between two or more States concerning boundary, jurisdiction or any other cause whatever; which authority shall always be exercised in the manner following: Whenever the legislative or executive authority or lawful agent of any State in controversy with another shall present a petition to Congress, stating the matter in question and praying for a hearing, notice thereof shall be given by order of Congress to the legislative or executive authority of the other State in controversy, and a day assigned for the appearance of the parties by their lawful agents, who shall then be directed to appoint, by joint consent, commissioners or judges to constitute a court for hearing and determining the matter in question; but if they cannot agree, Congress shall name three persons out of each of the United States, and from the list of such persons each party shall alternately strike out one, the petitioners beginning, until the number shall be reduced to thirteen; and from that number not less than seven, nor more than nine names as Congress shall direct, shall in the presence of Congress be drawn out by lot, and the persons whose names shall be so drawn or any five of them, shall be commissioners or judges, to hear and finally determine the controversy, so always as a major part of the judges who shall hear the cause shall agree in the determination; and if either party shall neglect to attend at the day appointed, without showing reasons which Congress shall judge sufficient, or being present shall refuse to strike, the Congress shall proceed to nominate three persons out of each State, and the secretary of Congress shall strike in behalf of such party absent or refusing; and the judgment and sentence of the court to be appointed, in the manner before prescribed, shall be final and conclusive; and if any of the parties shall refuse to submit to the authority of such court, or to appear to defend their claim or cause, the court shall nevertheless proceed to pronounce sentence, or judgment, which shall in like manner be final and decisive, the judgment or sentence and other proceedings being in either case transmitted to Congress, and lodged among the Acts of Congress for the security of the parties concerned: provided that every commissioner, before he sits in judgment, shall take an oath to be administered by one of the judges of the supreme or superior court of the State, where the cause shall be tried, "well and truly to hear and determine the matter in question, according to the best of his judgment, without favor, affection or hope of reward": provided also that no State shall be deprived of territory for the benefit of the United States.

All controversies concerning the private right of soil claimed under different grants of two or more States, whose jurisdictions as they may respect such lands, and the States which passed such grants are adjusted, the said grants or either of them being at the same time claimed to have originated antecedent to such settlement of jurisdiction, shall on the petition of either party to the Congress of the United States, be finally determined as near as may be in the same manner as is before prescribed for deciding disputes respecting territorial jurisdiction between different States.

The United States in Congress assembled shall also have the sole and exclusive right and power of regulating the alloy and value of coin struck by their own authority, or by that of the respective States—fixing the standard of weights and measures throughout the United States.—regulating the trade and managing all affairs with the Indians, not members of any of the States, provided that the legislative right of any State within its own limits be not infringed or violated—establishing and regulating post-offices from one State to another, throughout all the United States, and exacting such postage on the papers passing thro' the same as may be requisite to defray the expenses of the said office—appointing all officers of the land forces, in the service of the United States, excepting regimental officers—appointing all the officers of the naval forces, and commissioning all officers whatever in the service of the United States—making rules for the government and regulation of the said land and naval forces, and directing their operations.

The United States in Congress assembled shall have authority to appoint a committee, to sit in the recess of Congress, to be denominated "A Committee of the States," and to consist of one delegate from each State;

and to appoint such other committees and civil officers as may be necessary for managing the general affairs of the United States under their direction—to appoint one of their number to preside, provided that no person be allowed to serve in the office of president more than one year in any term of three years; to ascertain the necessary sums of money to be raised for the service of the United States, and to appropriate and apply the same for defraying the public expenses—to borrow money, or emit bills on the credit of the United States, transmitting every half year to the respective States an account of the sums of money so borrowed or emitted—to build and equip a navy—to agree upon the number of land forces, and to make requisitions from each State for its quota, in proportion to the number of white inhabitants in such State; which requisition shall be binding, and thereupon the legislature of each State shall appoint the regimental officers, raise the men and cloath, arm and equip them in a soldier like manner, at the expense of the United States, and the officers and men so cloathed, armed and equipped shall march to the place appointed, and within the time agreed on by the United States in Congress assembled. But if the United States in Congress assembled shall, on consideration of circumstances, judge proper that any State should not raise men, or should raise a smaller number than its quota, and that any other State should raise a greater number of men than the quota thereof, such extra number shall be raised, officered, cloathed, armed and equipped in the same manner as the quota of such State, unless the legislature of such State shall judge that such extra number cannot be safely spared out of the same, in which case they shall raise officers, cloath, arm and equip as many of such extra number as they judge can be safely spared. And the officers and men so cloathed, armed and equipped, shall march to the place appointed, and within the time agreed on by the United States in Congress assembled.

The United States in Congress assembled shall never engage in a war, nor grant letters of marque and reprisal in time of peace, nor enter into any treaties or alliances, nor coin money, nor regulate the value thereof, nor ascertain the sums and expenses necessary for the defence and welfare of the United States, or any of them, nor emit bills, nor borrow money on the credit of the United States, nor appropriate money, nor agree upon the number of vessels of war, to be built or purchased, or the number of land or sea forces to be raised, nor appoint a commander in chief of the army or navy, unless nine States assent to the same; nor shall a question on any other point, except for adjourning from day to day be determined, unless by the votes of a majority of the United States in Congress assembled.

The Congress of the United States shall have power to adjourn to any time within the year, and to any place within the United States, so that no period of adjournment be for a longer duration than the space of six months, and shall publish the Journal of their proceedings monthly, except such parts thereof relating to treaties, alliances or military operations as in their judgment require secrecy; and the yeas and nays of the delegates of each State on any question shall be entered on the Journal, when it is desired by any delegate; and the delegates of a State, or any of them, at his or their request shall be furnished with a transcript of the said Journal, except such parts as are above excepted, to lay before the legislatures of the several States.

Art. X. The Committee of the States, or any nine of them, shall be authorized to execute, in the recess of Congress, such of the powers of Congress as the United States in Congress assembled, by the consent of nine States, shall from time to time think expedient to vest them with; provided that no power be delegated to the said committee, for the exercises of which, by the articles of confederation, the voice of nine States in the Congress of the United States assembled is requisite.

Art. XI. Canada acceding to this confederation, and joining in the measures of the United States, shall be admitted into, and entitled to all the advantages of this union; but no other colony shall be admitted into the same, unless such admission be agreed to by nine States.

Art. XII. All bills of credit emitted, monies borrowed and debts contracted by, or under the authority of Congress, before the assembling of the United States, in pursuance of the present confederation, shall be deemed and considered as a charge against the United States, for payment and satisfaction whereof the said United States, and the public faith are hereby solemnly pledged.

Art. XIII. Every State shall abide by the determinations of the United States in Congress assembled, on all questions which by this confederation are submitted to them. And the Articles of this confederation shall be inviolably observed by every State, and the union shall be perpetual; nor shall any alteration at any time hereafter be made in any of them; unless such alteration be agreed to in a Congress of the United States, and be afterwards confirmed by the legislatures of every State.

AND WHEREAS it hath pleased the Great Governor of the World to incline the hearts of the legislatures we respectively represent in Congress, to approve of, and to authorize us to ratify the said articles of confederation and perpetual union. KNOW YE that we the undersigned delegates, by virtue of the power and authority to us given for that purpose, do by these presents, in the name and in behalf of our respective constituents, fully and entirely ratify and confirm each and every of the said articles of confederation and perpetual union, and all and singular the matters and things therein contained. And we do further solemnly plight and engage the faith of our respective constituents, that they shall abide by the determinations of the United States in Congress assembled, on all questions, which by the said confederation are submitted to them. And that the articles thereof shall be inviolably observed by the States we respectively represent, and that the union shall be perpetual. In Witness whereof we have hereunto set our hands in Congress. Done at Philadelphia in the State of Pennsylvania the ninth Day of July in the Year of our Lord one Thousand seven Hundred and Seventy-eight, and in the third year of the independence of America.

It was a provision in the charters of the Virginia settlers granted by James I in 1606 and 1609, and in the charter to the colonists of Massachusetts in 1629; of the Province of Maine in 1639; of Connecticut in 1662; of Rhode Island in 1663; of Maryland in 1632; of Carolina in 1663; and of Georgia in 1732; that they and their posterity should enjoy the same rights and liberties which Englishmen were entitled to at home. Such privileges were implied by the law, without any express reservation.

James Kent, *Commentaries on American Law* (1826)

Formal declarations of rights, drawn from the common law, were incorporated in the earliest colonial legislation. Plymouth Colony, in the first of these, enumerated, among other privileges, that justice should be impartially and promptly administered, with trial by jury, and that no person should suffer in life, limb, liberty, good name, or estate, but by due process of law. Connecticut, in 1639, adopted an act closely similar. New York enacted, in 1691, that no freeman should be deprived of any rights, or liberties, or condemned, save by the judgment of his peers or the law of the land; that no tax should be levied except by act of the legislature in which the colonists were represented. . . . Massachusetts, in 1641, promulgated a Body of Liberties. . . . In like manner, declaration of rights was made by the legislature of Virginia in 1624 and 1676; by the legislature of Pennsylvania in 1682; of Maryland in 1639 and 1650; and of Rhode Island in 1663; and also by the proprietaries of Carolina in 1667, and of New Jersey in 1664, 1683, and at other dates. The assembly of Maryland of 1638–1639 declared Magna Carta to be the measure of their liberties.

C. Ellis Stevens, *Sources of the Constitution of the United States* (1927)

PART 3

The Achievement of the
Philadelphia Convention

⊶⇒ POINTS TO REMEMBER ⇐⊷

1. The initial task of the Constitutional Convention was to revise and improve the Articles of Confederation, not to write a new constitution.

2. The delegates were soon persuaded, however, that the Articles were fundamentally flawed and that a new constitution, based upon a separation of powers among three branches of the national government, and a division of powers between the national government and the States, was essential.

3. One of the major difficulties that the Framers confronted was reconciling the differences between the large States and the small States. This they accomplished by giving all of the States representation in the national government, while at the same time giving a substantial share of power to the large States.

4. The Framers of the Constitution were gentlemen of great learning and ability and religious conviction. The Convention was an unusual gathering of America's greatest leaders of the day. They resolved their differences by careful reasoning and thoughtful deliberation, not by force or violence.

5. The form of government which the Framers sought to create was a republic, or more specifically an extended republic that was both democratic and federal.

6. The Virginia Plan, the first proposal for a new political system debated at the Convention, favored a strong national government. The delegates who opposed this scheme and wished to reserve most political power to the States rallied around the New Jersey Plan.

7. Under the "Connecticut Compromise," the delegates satisfied the demands of both the small States and the large States on the crucial question of representation in Congress. The interests of the small States were protected by giving all of the States equal representation in the

Senate, and those of the large States by establishing representation in the House of Representatives on population.

8. The delegates wanted a strong Chief Executive who was independent and not chosen by or subservient to the legislature. They also desired a judiciary independent of the executive, but subject to some control by the legislature.

9. The delegates also reached an agreement on questions pertaining to slavery. They agreed to allow Congress to prohibit the importation of slaves after 1808. They also allowed the States to include three-fifths of their slave population for purposes of establishing representation in the House of Representatives. This came to be known as the "Three-Fifths Compromise." Under the fugitive slave clause, the new Constitution also provided that slaves who might escape from one State into another must be returned to their owners.

In the heart of Philadelphia stands a handsome two-story brick building with central tower, belfry, spire, and conspicuous exterior clocks. It was erected before 1735 as the State House of Pennsylvania. Today it is called Independence Hall.

Here, in 1776, the Declaration of Independence was signed. Here again, on May 25, 1787, twenty-nine gentlemen assembled to prepare a constitution for a nation. Some days later they were joined by twenty-six more delegates. Fifty-five delegates attended the Constitutional Convention in the summer of 1787, but for voting purposes the number of States represented during the Convention's four months of debate never rose above eleven at any one time. None ever arrived from Rhode Island.

Great empires have crashed since that day in May, but the Constitution framed in Independence Hall endures. Related here is the story of what happened at that Pennsylvania State House during the summer of 1787.

The Problems of the Convention

As noted earlier, the Articles of Confederation contained a number of flaws. How might the Articles be revised to remedy such defects? As matters soon turned out, the Convention delegates found it desirable to sweep away the Articles altogether and substitute an entirely new Constitution.

Whether under the old Articles or through some new instrument of government, the delegates to the Philadelphia Convention were expected to devise means for improving the operation of the Articles of Confederation. Fundamentally, the Convention was called to accomplish the following objectives:

(1) Put the general government on a sound financial footing.

(2) Remove trade barriers, both with foreign countries and among the several States, and improve the flow of commerce.

(3) Provide sound money for the country, and improve both public and private credit.

(4) Set up means for strengthening the United States in the conduct of foreign policy—including enforcement of Britain's obligations to the United States under the terms of the Peace of Paris, concluded in 1783 at the end of the War of Independence.

(5) Obtain a greater degree of cooperation among the thirteen States, and require the State legislatures to protect the rights of property owners.

(6) Maintain good order under a republican form of government by preventing rebellions and mob violence when the State governments might be incompetent for that important task.

(7) Give the whole country such advantages as uniform bankruptcy laws, copyrights and patents, a postal service, management of western territories and Indian relations, naturalization of immigrants, and in general provide important services that the State governments could not.

These tasks seemed sufficiently formidable, but as the Convention delved into its business, many delegates decided that they must do more than alleviate the weaknesses of the Articles of Confederation. In the short Preamble to the seven articles of the new Constitution, as the document took shape, the drafters of this new frame of government expressed their larger aims:

". . . to form a more perfect union . . ." That would require satisfying both the large States and the small States, and reassuring people who dreaded the powers of a central government. It meant, in short, effective federalism and a new relationship between the national government and the State governments.

"... establish justice ..." That meant a systematic Federal judiciary, Montesquieu's "depository of laws," with an independent Supreme Court.

"... insure domestic tranquillity ..." That implied adequate military force to maintain peace and order, and to avert organized violence.

"... provide for the common defense ..." That signified the need to give the general government the means by which to raise and support an army and a navy to defend the country.

"... promote the general welfare ..." Here the Framers had in mind one of their principal objectives: to establish a government that promoted the common good, and not just the interests of the few.

"... and secure the blessings of liberty to ourselves and our posterity ..." This reference to freedom meant that one of the major purposes of the Constitution was to protect individual liberty, not to sacrifice it for other goals.

In addition, the Convention delegates also had to resolve the following major difficulties if the Constitution was to be acceptable to the American people:

A. Political sovereignty—which certain philosophers believed to be indivisible—had to be divided between a Federal government and the several State governments, with jurisdiction over some public concerns assigned to the Federal government and over others reserved to the States. It would not be easy to persuade champions of State sovereignty—the people and their locally elected leaders—to surrender their States' independence.

B. Arrangements had to be made for separation of powers among the executive, legislative, and judicial branches of government. A system of checking and balancing power in order to avert the one extreme of tyranny and the other extreme of anarchy would also have to be designed.

C. A legislative branch of the Federal government which would truly represent the people of the nation and yet not deny adequate representation to the State governments had to be established. In doing so, the delegates would have to reconcile the claim of the smaller States to equality with the larger States, and also the claim of the richer and more populous States to greater representation.

D. An independent executive, a President able to act decisively, especially in diplomatic and military affairs, yet limited in power so as not to menace the legislative and judicial branches, had to be created.

E. A Federal judiciary had to be set up, one that would be firm and just, competent to rule on cases transcending State boundaries and able to guard the Constitution, while not usurping the functions of the State courts or of the other branches of the Federal government.

F. Important political and legal institutions inherited from the Confederation, colonial governments, and the English constitution had to be incorporated in the new constitution. In addition, the new constitution would have to recognize and preserve longstanding rights that Americans had enjoyed under English law, such as trial by jury in criminal cases.

G. The delegates had to come to grips with the fundamental problem of politics, which is how to reconcile the need for order with the need for freedom—or, to put the matter another way, the problem of how to provide for both the security of the commonwealth and the personal rights of the citizen.

H. The delegates had to write a constitution that would be a practical instrument of government, effectively limiting power, and not a mere declaration of abstract goals. They would have to try to make the written constitution permanent, yet subject to amendment when change might become necessary.

Few of the delegates to Philadelphia had clearly in mind all of these responsibilities when they were appointed to the Philadelphia Convention. But gradually most of them became aware of how much they had undertaken, and how much the Articles of Confederation would have to be altered. Then the question was raised among them, especially by delegates from Delaware and Maryland, as to whether their States had authorized them to write a new constitution.

Despite such doubts, however, the large majority of delegates moved rather swiftly away from a proposed revision of the Articles toward the framing of a new political system. This was one reason why they decided to keep their proceedings secret. Word that a handful of men were preparing a political structure to supplant the Articles of Confederation presumably would have alarmed a large part of the population of every State.

No subsequent constitutional convention, in any country on any continent, has enjoyed such success as America's in dealing with great difficulties. And yet the greatest difficulty facing the country was not surmounted when the Philadelphia Convention wound up its business in September of 1787. That difficulty was persuading the American public that the new Constitution offered them important advantages. The exercise of the art of persuasion would be undertaken by Hamilton, Madison, and Jay in *The Federalist*; by John Dickinson in his series of papers called *The Letters of Fabius*; and by the speeches and pamphlets of other notable delegates.

They were men of distinction, those gentlemen politicians, who could design such a lucid Constitution and persuade the skeptics of thirteen highly independent States to ratify it.

The Delegates to the Convention

The eighteenth-century gentlemen who drafted the Constitution did not outwardly resemble the members of Congress or the State legislatures today, because they wore knee breeches and long coats. Many of them also had short wigs on their heads. They looked very much like English gentlemen at a London assembly-room or in a London club, and very unlike the "tradesmen" or "mechanics" who thronged the narrow streets in the neighborhood of the old State House at Philadelphia. In addition, not many years earlier, some of these gentlemen politicians had worn swords at their sides.

Of the fifty-five delegates, twenty-one had fought in the Revolution (some as high officers), forty-six had served in colonial assemblies or State legislatures, twenty-four had been members of the Continental Congress, thirty-nine had served in the Congress under the Articles, ten had taken a hand in drafting State constitutions, six had signed the Declaration of Independence, and four had signed the Articles of Confederation. Twenty had been, were then, or later would be, governors of States, and twenty were at one time or another United States Senators.

Almost all were men of some property. A half-dozen were American aristocrats of great family and possessions, thirty-five were slaveholders, and some were prosperous merchants. Not all were rich. The two among them who in 1787 were the most prosperous, Robert Morris and James Wilson, would later die bankrupt, while the delegate of the smallest means, William Few, a Georgia frontiersman, ended his days as the well-to-do president of the City Bank in New York.

More than half the members of the Convention had been, or were, judges or lawyers. A good many Framers had been teachers at one time or another, and most were well educated. Many had studied at American colleges, at Oxford or Cambridge, or at the Scottish and Irish universities.

The spirit of religion and the spirit of a gentleman, an Irish statesman named Edmund Burke wrote in 1790, had sustained European manners and civilization. What, then, was the religion of these gentlemen-politicians meeting at Philadelphia? At least fifty of the Framers would have subscribed to the Apostles' Creed. Among them were some twenty-three Episcopalians, ten Presbyterians, seven Congregationalists, two Catholics, two Lutherans, two Quakers, and at least one Methodist. Two of the Framers professed a belief in the Almighty but did not belong to any religious sect.

Such were the common elements among the fifty-five Framers. In general, they got on uncommonly well with one another. Despite their differences on political questions, the Framers formed almost a club of gentlemen that was united to secure an enduring social order. The civility of the debates and the reasonable acceptance of compromises contrasts that Great Convention with all other grand attempts, ancient or modern, to form a new constitution. In an era of duelling, not one delegate "called out" any other delegate to an encounter with pistols—though two of them (Alexander Hamilton and Richard Dobbs Spaight) were in later years killed in duels with enemies.

The first article of the Constitution provided that the United States might grant no title of nobility, and that no office-holder should accept a foreign title without the consent of the Congress. But the men who framed that article were not opposed to the idea of a gentleman. What they opposed were hereditary titles and special privileges based on birth. Some of the Framers, especially the Episcopalians, had read Thomas Fuller's essays on the "True Gentleman" and the "Degenerous Gentleman," published in Fuller's big book, *The Holy State and the Profane State* (1642). "He is courteous and affable to his neighbors," Fuller wrote of the

True Gentleman. "As the sword of the best tempered metal is most flexible, so the truly generous are to their inferiors." The gentleman should be a man of honor who would not lie or cheat. He should be a man of valor who would serve the commonwealth as magistrate or member of an assembly, and a man of charity, both spiritual and material. No doubt a few of the Framers were what Fuller called Degenerous Gentlemen, that is, selfish and cunning opportunists. But most lived by gentlemen's rules as best they could. And some of them—Washington, George Mason, John Dickinson, Gouverneur Morris, Alexander Hamilton, C. C. Pinckney, Rufus King, John Rutledge, James Madison, Daniel Carroll, and others— fulfilled throughout their lives the gentleman's obligations of manners, honor, valor, duty, and charity.

The Constitutional Convention was therefore often more like a gathering of polite friends than an assemblage of angry political zealots. Under the influence of gentle manners, the Convention was conducted with a decorum not since encountered in these United States, as delegates of differing views observed with one another the old traditions of civility. Temperate speech led to moderation, and moderation made it possible for the Framers to resolve their differences peaceably and to achieve a lasting consensus.

Such was the general tone of things at Independence Hall in the summer of 1787. Of course in any legislative body, or large council or committee, most of the work is accomplished by a minority of the members. So it was at the Convention of 1787. A score at least of the delegates were very active, while the others, quiet enough, approved or disapproved developments. With that understanding let us examine the character and ideas of the Convention's leading men.

A Wide Range of Talents

George Washington, the most popular and most dignified of Americans, presided impartially over the Constitutional Convention. He was now first in peace as he had been first in war and represented both the American people as a whole and his native Virginia.

Edmund Randolph, Governor of Virginia, a man of great family and perfect manners, presented the Virginia Plan to the Convention. Eventually he decided not to sign the Constitution as it was drawn up at Philadelphia. Later still, however, he recommended its ratification by his State.

George Mason, of Gunston Hall in Virginia, author of the Virginia Bill of Rights and an accomplished debater, was a champion of the South and of the powers of the State governments. He was also a grand gentleman, admired for his integrity.

James Madison, a very learned man from Virginia, kept the most thorough notes on the Convention. More than anyone else he shaped the Constitution's principal provisions—though it is something of an exaggeration to call him "the Father of the Constitution." He saw the necessity for a strong national government, though he was the close friend of Thomas Jefferson. Jefferson also favored the Constitution but later became the leader of the Republicans, many of whom were former Anti-Federalists. In 1809, Madison was inaugurated as the fourth President of the United States.

William Paterson, of New Jersey, an Irish immigrant, had been a member of the Continental Congress and the Attorney-General of his State. A man of much knowledge, he presented the Convention with the "New Jersey Plan." In 1793 he became a Justice of the Supreme Court, as a Federalist.

Robert Morris, of Pennsylvania, the chief financier of the American Revolution and an authority on fiscal concerns, was a celebrated debater and a conservative who signed the Declaration of Independence, the Articles of Confederation, and the Constitution.

James Wilson, of Pennsylvania, a Scot with much learning in the law, professed his trust in the people, but was personally unpopular. A Philadelphia mob stormed his house in 1779, leaving many dead and wounded on both sides of the fight. A Carlisle crowd in Pennsylvania rioted against him and burned him in effigy in 1788. He would later write the first American treatise on the law and serve as a member of the Supreme Court of the United States.

Gouverneur Morris, of Pennsylvania, regarded by some as the most brilliant delegate, was a public man of high courage and great wealth. It was he who actually put down in writing the final draft of the Constitution. Never handicapped by his wooden leg and crippled arm, he later served as the United States Minister to Paris at the height of the French Revolution.

James Madison, 1751–1836.

Portrait by Chester Harding, ca. 1825–30. (National Portrait Gallery, Smithsonian Institution.)

John Dickinson, previously of Pennsylvania and now the leading delegate from Delaware, the smallest of the States, had been a chief leader of the Continental Congress and chairman of the committee that drafted the Articles of Confederation. Also, he was the composer of the young republic's most popular anthem, "The Song of the Farmer." He was cautious and persuasive, and many of his views were incorporated into the Constitution.

Alexander Hamilton, from New York, was born in the West Indies. He was a master of finance, a successful soldier, a considerable political thinker, and the close friend of George Washington. He later became the first Secretary of the Treasury under the Constitution, and died in a duel with Aaron Burr. He was not able to exert much influence at the Convention, but he later did much to obtain the Constitution's ratification in New York and elsewhere.

John Rutledge, of South Carolina. He was a man of great force of character whose approval would have been required for any new constitution—not merely in South Carolina, but nationally. He was insistent upon the security of private property in any social order.

Charles Cotesworth Pinckney, of South Carolina, had studied under the great English jurist Sir William Blackstone at Oxford University. He also studied botany, chemistry, and military science in France. He was convinced that the United States must develop military strength for national defense, and that the public debt must be drastically reduced through sound fiscal policies.

Elbridge Gerry, of Massachusetts, an astute politician, had also succeeded as a merchant. Like George Mason, he was suspicious of consolidation and centralized government. A powerful spokesman for States' Rights, he was elected Vice President of the United States on the ticket with James Madison in 1812.

Rufus King, of Massachusetts (later of New York), was one of the younger delegates. Very much a Yankee, he was rather hostile toward the South and the West. He was an outspoken opponent of slavery; he also advocated constitutional guarantees to prohibit the States from violating the sanctity of contracts.

William Samuel Johnson, a Connecticut lawyer originally trained for the church. He held degrees from Yale, Harvard, and Oxford, and was always addressed as Dr. Johnson. He had been neutral during the Revolution, though he was active in the earlier Stamp Act Congress. Johnson served as one of his State's first Senators under the new Constitution and as the first president of Columbia College.

Roger Sherman, of Connecticut, the mayor of New Haven, was a self-made man who began as a shoemaker. He spoke nearly a hundred and forty times at the convention—always effectively—and was a principal negotiator of its compromises.

Oliver Ellsworth, judge of the Supreme Court of Connecticut, was a defender of the small States and an advocate of the New Jersey Plan. He feared the possibility of intrusions by a federal government into the affairs of the several States.

Luther Martin, of Maryland, argued in favor of keeping most political power in the States, though he was willing to revise the Articles of Confederation. An immensely successful lawyer, he later fought the Federalists in courts during the first two decades of the nineteenth century.

Most of the delegates lived interesting lives. Anyone who studies the careers of all the fifty-five Framers must be surprised by the great energy that nearly all of them possessed. They came from a variety of backgrounds, including agriculture, trade, the law, the military, and political administration. Hugh Williamson of North Carolina, for example, had been Presbyterian preacher, professor of mathematics, physician, businessman, physical scientist (especially in astronomy), philosopher, political pamphleteer, Surgeon General of North Carolina, a member of the North Carolina legislature, and a member of the Continental Congress. He held more than seventy thousand acres of land on the frontier. Williamson put forth a variety of interesting and original proposals for the new Constitution, but few were accepted by his fellow-delegates.

Surprisingly, two of the more famous and talented of the delegates contributed little to the framing. One was Benjamin Franklin, because of his great age (though he remained witty and helpful), and the other was George Wythe, the great professor of law at William and Mary College. He had to depart early from Philadelphia because his wife was dying back at Williamsburg.

As noted earlier, the Framers in outward appearance did not much resemble the members of a twentieth-century American legislature. Neither did they much resemble today's politicians in their style as public speakers, nor in the sort of education they had obtained. For the men at Philadelphia in 1787 had studied formal rhetoric, and so spoke with care—and often with eloquence. The majority of them had attended colleges or universities during an era when intellectual disciplines were taken seriously. It was remarked, even then, that this was a gathering, as Jefferson put it, of "demigods." Yet some of America's most brilliant leaders were absent. Jefferson himself was in Paris and John Adams was in London, both representing the United States as foreign ministers. Patrick Henry and Richard Henry Lee of Virginia had refused to attend, and John Jay of New York had been refused an appointment.

Many of the Framers were intensely ambitious men who had great expectations for both the nation and themselves. They were acutely aware that at Philadelphia they had become involved in high concerns. That consciousness was reflected in their manner and speech. It has been remarked by many writers and political leaders that it would probably not be possible in the United States today to assemble a group of delegates equal in talent to the fifty-five men who met at Philadelphia two centuries ago. Qualified by personal experience, schooling, and character, and moved by their knowledge of America's necessities, the Framers of our Constitution acted with unusual wisdom.

Plans and Progress at Philadelphia

The more one reads about those delegates of 1787, the more one becomes aware that they came to Philadelphia with open minds—in the sense that few were committed in advance to any particular scheme for improving upon the Articles of Confederation. They believed strongly in certain political principles, but they did not advocate elaborately detailed political systems or master plans for the "perfect" commonwealth. The plans of government that were offered at the outset of the Convention were intended to serve merely as general guidelines.

Of course they took certain matters for granted. One was that the United States should remain a republic, as had been declared in 1776. By a republic, as we noted earlier, the Framers meant a state in which the sovereign power rests in the people as a whole but is exercised by representatives chosen by a popular vote. History furnishes examples of monarchic, aristocratic, and democratic republics. Sparta, Athens, and

Rome, for example, were called republics, but their limited franchise gave them an aristocratic character. Venice was styled a republic though absolute power was exercised by a small body of hereditary nobles. In the modern world, the term *republic* is so much abused that even despotic regimes apply it to their forms of government. Thus the Russians called their system the Union of Soviet Socialist Republics (USSR), implying that it was both federal and republican. In actuality it was a centralized form of government, governed by an elite cadre of Communist Party members who were neither chosen by, nor politically responsible to, the people.

James Madison, in *The Federalist*, stated that "The two points of difference between a democracy and a republic, are, first, the delegation of the government, in the latter to a number of citizens elected by the rest; secondly, the greater number of citizens and the greater sphere of country over which the latter may be extended." The American republic, according to Madison, then, was more precisely understood as a democratic and extended (or federal) republic, encompassing a broad geographical area and a large population. Thomas Jefferson, on the other hand, thought that "the first principle of republicanism" was simply rule by the majority. Perhaps the best definition is that offered by Judge Thomas Cooley of Michigan in his classic work, *Principles of Constitutional Law* (1890): "By a republican form of government is understood a government by representatives chosen by the people; and it contrasts on the one side with a democracy, in which the people or community as one organized whole wield the sovereign powers of government, and, on the other side, with the rule of one man, as king, emperor, czar, or sultan, or with that of one class of men, as an aristocracy."

A republic seemed to be the only possibility for the United States in 1787. The Americans had no royal family, no hereditary nobility; and few of the delegates were inclined toward the idea of a king, even if elected. Most of the delegates did see the need, however, for an executive head and a judiciary as well as a representative assembly—something lacking under the Articles. The word "democracy" was often used in the convention as a term of opprobrium and disgrace, because "democracy" was then understood to mean mob rule. Shays' Rebellion, fresh in the minds of the Framers and put down earlier that fateful year of 1787, was what "democracy" meant to the delegates. Not until the late 1820s did the term "democracy" become at all popular in America's practical politics.

In addition, the delegates were generally agreed, from the beginning, that the Articles of Confederation needed strengthening and improvement. This was true even of Luther Martin, George Mason, and other delegates who favored a weak central government. It was clear enough to everyone that somehow a means must be found by which the "general" government (that is, the existing government of the Articles) might improve the flow of commerce and raise revenue, because the economy was stagnant and national debt was becoming ruinous. It was clear, too, that at least in foreign affairs the general government must be enabled to act with greater firmness and authority.

But there were also points of disagreement among the delegates, the most significant being the question of whether the United States should remain a confederacy of sovereign States or whether a new form of national government should be undertaken. Allied to this dispute was the argument as to whether large and small States should remain equal in power under any new constitution, or whether representation in a new national government should be in accord with population and wealth, and so confer a heavy preponderance of political power upon the more populous, larger states. By the end of the Convention in September, all of these and most other differences were resolved.

The Meaning of "Federal"

In America today, the tendency is to contrast "federal government" with "state government"—almost as if to suggest "central government" versus "regional government." But that is not an adequate distinction.

Until nearly the end of the eighteenth century, the word "federal" was a synonym for the word "confederate." In politics, a *federation* was a league of states or cities. This had been the definition of such words from ancient times.

The member-states or member-cities of a "federation" or "confederation" did not acknowledge or create a central government. They remained independent, but were joined together loosely by a treaty or some other agreement by which the members pledged themselves to cooperate with each other under certain circumstances or for certain limited purposes—usually military action. A federal government scarcely was a government at all. It amounted to no more than a simple apparatus for enabling the members of the confederation to confer and cooperate.

Such federations were distinguished from a central government, which had always been understood to mean a political structure in which there is one central sovereign power that all lesser political units must obey. A centralized regime, sometimes called a consolidated or unitary system of government, is one in which most political power is vested in authorities located at a common center—usually a city. The growth of centralization means the transfer of power from the local level and its greater and greater concentration in the hands of central authorities. This power may be legislative, executive, or judicial, and is usually all three. In the modern world, France, Spain, and Italy are examples of centralized political systems, whereas Switzerland, Germany, and Austria have federal systems.

So the government of the United States under the Articles of Confederation from 1781 to 1789 was a "federal" government in the old sense of that term. The United States was a league of sovereign States, banded together for common advantages, but each retaining its independence. The coordinating body, chiefly the Congress, was called the government of the United States.

In the summer of 1787, the advocates of political reform, especially James Madison and Alexander Hamilton, were trying to bring into being a quite new form of general government—sometimes referred to as "national"—which would greatly reduce the powers of the States. Such plans were opposed by those delegates to the Great Convention who for a variety of reasons viewed with hostility any designs for centralizing power. The proponents of a strong national government first proposed what was called the Virginia or Randolph Plan. A second group of delegates, shocked by the nationalism of the Virginia Plan, put forward their New Jersey or Paterson Plan. Less detailed plans were proposed by Alexander Hamilton of New York and Charles Pinckney of South Carolina.

There emerged from this encounter a draft of a new constitution which was the result of a series of compromises among groups of delegates. It called for a constitution that would be neither a confederacy nor a centralized government. This new system would be a form of government that would forever change the meaning of the word "federal."

To understand how this novel proposal—our Constitution—took form, we first need to look at the rival plans laid before the Convention in its early weeks.

The Virginia Plan: A Supreme National Government

By May 29, the delegates had made their way through the preliminary stages of organization. The delegates from Virginia, then the most populous of the States, promptly presented to the Convention a bold design for abolishing the Articles of Confederation and substituting a national government.

Edmund Randolph, the Governor of Virginia, introduced the Virginia Plan. It consisted of fifteen resolutions that were drawn up primarily by James Madison. The first resolution criticized the operation of the Articles of Confederation. Then, in the succeeding resolutions, the Virginians proposed a new form of government for the whole nation.

They proposed three separate branches of government: legislative, executive, and judicial.

The legislative branch was to have two houses—a lower house (what we now call the House of Representatives) elected by the people of the several States, and an upper house (what we now call the Senate) whose members would be chosen by the first house from among persons nominated by the State legislatures.

For both houses of the national legislature, voting was to be in proportion to the amount of money contributed by each State to the national government, or in proportion to the number of free inhabitants of each State, or in proportion to both. This system of representation would give the large, populous States control of the legislature.

The legislature was to inherit the powers of the Congress of the Confederation, and be given additional powers. It would enact laws "in all cases to which the separate States are incompetent, or in which the harmony of the United States may be interrupted by the exercise of individual legislation." This new legislature would be empowered to wipe out all State laws contrary to the new articles of union. And it could use force against any State that disobeyed national policy.

As for the executive branch, the executive was to be chosen by the legislature. The Virginia resolutions did not indicate whether the executive was to consist of one person or of several persons, but it did specify that the executive could serve only one term. Also, the executive's salary could not be altered while the executive held office. (This was a protection against the executive being threatened by the legislature with loss of salary, as colonial assemblies had done to colonial governors.) The executive, together with "a convenient number of the national judiciary," could veto acts of the legislature. But the two houses of the legislature could overrule the executive's veto.

The judicial branch would consist of judges chosen by the Federal legislature. It was to have one or more supreme courts and also lesser Federal courts, and would try cases of maritime law, cases involving foreigners, and cases concerning "the collection of the national revenue, impeachments of any national officers, and questions which may involve the national peace and harmony."

Of the several other resolutions in the Virginia Plan, one required that all State officers swear to support the new constitution. Another required that the new constitution be ratified by State conventions chosen by popular vote.

The day after the Virginia Plan was introduced, Gouverneur Morris proposed that "a *national* Government ought to be established consisting of a *supreme* Legislative, Executive, and Judiciary." In adopting this resolution, the Convention in effect discarded the Articles of Confederation and embarked upon the task of drawing up a new constitution.

The details of the Virginia Plan remained to be debated, however, and very debatable they were. Opponents of centralization, together with delegates from the smaller States, were alarmed by the boldness and abruptness of the Virginia delegation's proposal. Many delegates had not even arrived at Philadelphia, and as they did, opposition to the Virginia Plan increased.

Had the Virginia Plan been adopted in its entirety, the smaller States would have been overshadowed by the larger States in the new government. The national legislature would have been supreme over the executive and judicial branches of the government. The several States would have been converted into little more than provinces directed by a central government.

Even if most Americans had been willing to accept such a centralized political structure—and they clearly were *not* willing in 1787 to do so—its operation would have been difficult. The United States encompassed an immense area and was growing rapidly westward. Communication among the States and even within the States was still chiefly by ship or boat. There was no body of civil servants to carry on the administration of a central government. That the Virginia Plan was even seriously considered by the delegates at Philadelphia was made possible only by the high reputation of George Washington, who was known to favor the Plan, and by the skillful management of James Madison.

Thus, the leading men of Virginia in 1787 were the most vigorous advocates of political centralization. By contrast, only twelve years later, the State of Virginia adopted the famous Virginia Resolutions protesting Federal usurpations of State powers under the Alien and Sedition Acts. And it was principally James Madison who wrote both the resolutions of the Virginia Plan in 1787 and the Virginia Resolutions of 1798. In 1787, however, it seemed as though Virginia would dominate national policies. The Virginia delegation to the Convention, except for George Mason, envisioned a powerful central government in which Virginia would play a dominant role.

Two weeks passed before opponents of the Virginia Plan were ready to offer an alternative design. Meanwhile, discussion of the Virginia Plan as the basis for a new constitution advanced. On June 15, William Paterson proposed the New Jersey Plan. He was supported by his own delegation and by the delegations from Connecticut, New York, and Delaware, and by one or two delegates from Maryland. Before debate on the alternative New Jersey Plan could commence, however, the young delegate from New York, Alexander Hamilton, proposed a third plan for a new governmental system.

Hamilton's Concept of a Unified America

For Hamilton, neither the New Jersey Plan nor the Virginia Plan went far enough. He made it clear that he desired for the United States a completely centralized government resembling that of England, one able to restrain "the amazing violence and turbulence of the democratic spirit." He hoped for an orderly America led by able men of property, and he expected the United States to become a great commercial and industrial power. The nation's government, he suggested, should be designed for such a future.

Therefore Hamilton proposed to give the national legislature "power to pass all laws whatsoever." His legislature would consist of two houses, of which the members of the upper house, a senate, would be chosen by electors—and those electors themselves were to be chosen by other electors whom the people would choose. The executive was also to be chosen by electors, who in turn would be chosen by other electors, and would be elected for life—as would be the members of the upper house. The executive would have an absolute veto over all legislation.

As for the States, they would be reduced to agencies of the central government, although they would retain their own legislatures. But each State's governor would be appointed by the central government, and would have power of the veto over all State legislation.

This scheme would never have been accepted by the public in 1787. Indeed, it was not accepted by any of Hamilton's colleagues at the Convention. Not long thereafter, Hamilton returned to New York. His real role in the development of American constitutionalism would soon be his masterful contribution to the essays of *The Federalist*, and his commanding role in President Washington's administration.

Hamilton did not propose to establish a monarchy, although some of his political adversaries accused him of intending to do just that. Though personally very courageous, Hamilton dreaded the power of mobs. There had been much unrest in several States after independence was secured, including the burning of court houses, confiscation of property, debasement of the currency, and Shays' Rebellion. Hamilton therefore sought as far as possible to remove political power from the control of the ignorant masses, and to place it in the hands of more responsible citizens. He believed that an all-powerful government was necessary to control lawless and unruly citizens. But his plan would have been even less acceptable to most Americans of that day than the one proposed by the Virginia delegates, and so nothing more was said about it at the Convention.

Alexander Hamilton (1755–1804).

Portrait by John Trumbull, 1804. (Andrew W. Mellon Collection. Photograph © Board of Trustees, National Gallery of Art, Washington, D.C.)

The New Jersey Plan:
Checks upon Central Power

If the delegations that united in mid-June behind the New Jersey Plan had brought forward their ideas at the beginning of the Convention, they might have prevailed over James Madison, James Wilson, and the large delegations from Virginia and Pennsylvania. For as William Paterson and his friends argued, their Plan much more nearly corresponded to the sentiments of the average American citizen than did the Virginia Plan. But as it is true in battle that the force which fires first ordinarily wins the fight, so in public discussions a great advantage is gained often by the side which speaks first and forcefully. By being introduced first, the Virginia Plan had become the basic design of the Convention before proponents of the New Jersey Plan spoke up. Put on the defensive, Paterson, Luther Martin, Oliver Ellsworth, and other critics of the Virginia Plan were able merely to modify the centralizing tendency of the Virginians' proposal.

Shorter than the Virginia Plan, the New Jersey Plan consisted of nine resolutions, intended to improve the Articles of Confederation rather than create a new constitutional instrument. It would have given the Congress authority to raise revenues through taxes on imports, stamp taxes, and postal charges. Power to regulate commerce among the States would have been conferred upon the Congress. If the Federal government still needed more money, it could requisition funds from the several States, proportionate to each State's population (counting three-fifths of the slaves as part of the population). Acts of Congress and treaties would have been declared the supreme law of the United States.

The New Jersey Plan would have included a Federal executive consisting of several persons (as was the Pennsylvania executive at that time), without a power of veto over acts of Congress. There would have been a United States Supreme Court, appointed by the executive, with original jurisdiction over cases of impeachment of Federal officers. The court would receive on appeal from State courts various cases affecting treaties, international and interstate trade, and collection of Federal taxes.

The New Jersey Plan would have preserved a strong influence for the smaller States in the Union, and in general tone would have made it clear that the several States were not being wholly subordinate to some central power. The Plan was supported by delegates who were alarmed at the lack of checks and balances in the Virginia design. As John Dickinson told Madison, "You see the consequences of pushing things too far."

On June 19, the Convention made its choice on whether to proceed with the Virginia Plan or the New Jersey Plan. The Virginia Plan won with votes from Massachusetts, Connecticut, Pennsylvania, Virginia, North Carolina, South Carolina, and Georgia. New York, New Jersey, and Delaware voted for the New Jersey Plan. The Maryland delegation was divided.

But the apparent defeat of the New Jersey faction was not total. The victorious supporters of the Virginia Plan now saw that if they wished the delegations from all States to sign a new Constitution, they must make important concessions to their colleagues, who feared centralization and who represented the smaller States. Even more importantly, the general public would have to be assured that the majority of men at the Convention did not mean to strike down the State governments by their new instrument of national government.

The Benefits of Compromise

In national politics, as in private life, it is sometimes wise to compromise one's goals on certain occasions. Not everybody can have everything he wants; and half a loaf is better than none. In every country there are competing interests, differing bodies of opinion, distinct classes, and other rival groups or factions. So from late June onward, the gentlemen politicians at the Convention endeavored to reconcile their differences.

Madison dropped from the Virginian proposals the word "national" because it offended the moderate delegates. Reference to the possible use of force against dissenting State governments also was eliminated. One faction of delegates wanted to elect members of the "first house" of the new legislature for three years, and another faction argued in favor of one-year terms. They finally agreed on a two-year term—and that became part of the draft of the new constitution. Agreements were also reached on a six-year term for the "second house" and on lesser concerns. Nonetheless, there remained a principal obstacle to consensus at the Convention.

The great stumbling block was the old issue of representation that had surfaced earlier under the Articles of Confederation. Proponents of the Virginia Plan wanted to base representation of each State on the State's population or its contribution to financial support of the Federal treasury. This was the position of most delegates from the larger and more wealthy States. By contrast, supporters of the New Jersey Plan wanted all the States to have equal representation in Congress—as they had enjoyed under the Articles of Confederation, with one State, one vote. This was the position of most delegates from the smaller States.

Presently a committee of one delegate from each State was chosen to arrange some compromise on this heated question. Dr. Benjamin Franklin appears to have worked out the committee's agreement, which in effect gave the small-State delegates more or less what they sought. The committee's report was hotly debated, and there were threats on either side that States might turn to violence if their cause was denied. More committees were therefore appointed, more concessions were made by either side, and at length the "Great Compromise" of the Convention was achieved. Five States voted for the Great Compromise, four against it, one was divided, and one State's delegation—New York's—went home in dismay. The result was a narrow margin of victory, but a victory that has nonetheless endured for two hundred years.

The concept of this Great Compromise was originally John Dickinson's. Other delegates adopted it. Madison opposed it. It is sometimes known as the "Connecticut Compromise" because Dr. William S. Johnson, Oliver Ellsworth, and Roger Sherman of Connecticut vigorously urged its adoption. By the provisions of this Great Compromise, each State would have an equal vote in the upper house of the Federal legislature. This meant, in effect, that each State—no matter how large or how small, nor how rich or how poor—would retain in the upper house (now the Senate) the power that it had enjoyed under the Confederation. This arrangement also satisfied the general desire of the delegates to keep the size of the Senate small for purposes of debate. If all thirteen States joined

the new union, the Senate would therefore consist of only 26 senators—
two from each state.

In the lower house (what is now the House of Representatives), the
number of members for the first Congress was specified for each of the
States. Thereafter, apportionment would be made by the Congress itself
on the basis of population, with three-fifths of the slaves being counted
in each State for purposes of representation. In other words, the upper
house (the Senate) would treat all States as equal, thus giving the small
States a strong voice in that body. Membership in the lower house (the
House of Representatives) would be based on population, thus giving an
obvious advantage to the more populous States.

Many other important details remained to be settled by the Convention. The Virginia Plan had become the basis of the Convention's work,
but much of that plan needed to be modified or clarified.

Of the many complicated issues confronting the members of the Philadelphia Convention, the nature of the presidency proved to be almost as
troublesome as the basis of representation in the legislature. In fact, in
some respects the creation of the executive office was more difficult, and
not until the closing days of the Convention were the delegates able to
come to a complete agreement. The Virginia Plan offered little more than
a general recommendation that "a national executive . . . chosen by the
national legislature be instituted," with the power to exercise "the executive rights" that had been vested in Congress under the Articles of Confederation. The Plan was silent on other specifics. Was the president to be
one person or a collection of individuals? Instead of being chosen by the
Congress, why not by the State governors, or by electors? Or should he
be chosen directly by the people in a national vote? How long should he
serve? Four years? Six? Seven? Eight? Eleven? Fifteen? For as long as
the executive displayed "good behavior"? Should he be eligible for re-
election? Should it be possible to impeach the chief executive, as members of the cabinet could be impeached by the House of Commons?

American precedents for a strong, independent executive under the
first State constitutions, as we noted previously, were sparse. Reacting
against the highhandedness of the royal governors, the framers of the
State constitutions had generally created weak executives and strong

Independence Hall, Philadelphia.

The Pennsylvania State House, later known as Independence Hall, where the Declaration of Independence was proclaimed and the Constitution was debated and written. (Courtesy of the Library of Congress.)

legislatures; and the Articles of Confederation had vested all executive power in a unicameral Congress. Experience had shown, however, that many of these State legislatures had acted without restraint and abused their power, and that certain executive functions should not be conferred on a legislative body. There was therefore considerable support for the establishment of a reasonably powerful executive to check the legislature.

The New York constitution offered a better guide than the Virginia Plan and served as a point of departure. It provided for the election of a governor by the people, who was thus independent of the legislature. His term was three years and he was indefinitely re-eligible. Except for his power to appoint and veto laws proposed by the legislature, he did not need the approval of another body to carry out the executive function. He was in charge of the militia, possessed the pardoning power, and was empowered to execute the laws. In *Federalist* No. 69, Hamilton later observed the similarities and differences between the President and the New York governor.

When the executive portion of the Virginia Plan was taken up on June 1, James Wilson of Pennsylvania moved that the executive should consist of a single person. He argued in favor of a strong executive— elected by the people, and free of dependence on the legislature as well as the States. Wilson also wanted an executive who was empowered to veto legislation (in concurrence with a council of revision) and was eligible for re-election indefinitely. The great requisites of the executive department, the delegates agreed, were "vigor, dispatch and responsibility," and Wilson's proposal met these requirements.

The vote on Wilson's motion was put over until the questions of method of selection, length of term, manner of removal, and powers of the office were determined. The Convention agreed that the executive should be independent of the legislature, but set its face against direct popular election of the executive, preferring instead an indirect method using State electors. "It would be as unnatural to refer the choice of a proper character for Chief Magistrate to the people," remarked Gouverneur Morris, "as it would to refer a trial of colors to a blind man." The term of office was set at four years, with indefinite re-eligibility, and the executive was armed with a veto power subject not to approval by a council of revision but to an override by a two-thirds vote of both houses of Congress. Given broad authority to exercise "the executive power" the Chief Executive was at the same time held in check by the people through presidential electors and subject to removal by Congress through the impeachment process. In general, then, Wilson was triumphant in attempting to lay the groundwork for the development of a strong independent executive, even though he was unsuccessful and virtually alone in advocating direct popular election of the President.

As for the judicial branch, the Virginia Plan suggested only "that a national judiciary be established" consisting of "one or more supreme tribunals, and of inferior tribunals to be chosen by the national legislature." The Plan further provided that the judges hold their offices "during good behavior," that their salaries be immune from legislative manipulation, and that their jurisdiction be limited to a narrow range of cases. The Plan thus envisaged a weak judiciary but one that was totally independent of the executive and partially removed from the influence of the legislature.

The members of the Convention were unanimously agreed that a national judiciary be established, but decided to strike the provision for inferior tribunals on the ground that they were not needed because State courts could deal with Federal cases at the trial stage. They ultimately decided, at the insistence of Wilson and Madison, that Congress be given the power to establish inferior courts as the need arose. As finally worked out in committee, the judicial power was increased well beyond the scope of the Virginia Plan.

At the apex of the national judiciary they established a Supreme Court headed by a chief justice. Before any Federal court could exercise the judicial power, however, it would first have to have jurisdiction over the case, meaning the authority to decide it. Placing primary responsibility for control of the courts in the hands of the legislature, the Framers gave Congress full authority not only to establish lower courts but to fix the size of the Supreme Court, regulate the jurisdiction of both the lower courts and the Supreme Court, set judicial salaries (but not reduce them), determine the time and place for sitting, and in general create and organize the whole judicial branch. As soon as the Constitution was ratified, Congress filled in these details in the Judiciary Act of 1789. The role of the President was limited to the appointment of the judges, subject to

Senate confirmation. There were other questions: how should the new constitution be presented to the States and the people? Should it be submitted to the State legislatures? Should it be submitted to special State conventions, popularly elected? Could it go into effect if ratified by less than all the States? Eager to establish the Constitution on a popular base, but to recognize as well the residual sovereignty of the States, the delegates decided to submit the Constitution to State ratifying conventions chosen by the people. The Constitution would go into effect as soon as nine States ratified it.

In reaching decisions and compromises on all these and many other important matters, the Convention relied heavily on key committees to resolve issues that were not addressed on the floor or had been left undecided, to hammer out the details, and to put the Constitution in writing. On July 26, the Convention adjourned until August 6 so the Committee of Detail could prepare a report. This committee consisted of five delegates: Rutledge of South Carolina, Randolph of Virginia, Gorham of Massachusetts, Wilson of Pennsylvania, and Ellsworth of Connecticut— all of whom had been active in the Convention debates. These delegates were expected to work out, in the space of ten days, all these difficult concerns. From August 6 to September 10, the Convention considered this report in detail. A Committee of Style, consisting of Johnson of Connecticut, Hamilton of New York, Gouverneur Morris of Pennsylvania, Madison of Virginia, and King of Massachusetts, was chosen on September 8 to put the new Constitution into final literary form.

Compromise and Consensus

With astonishing speed the Committee on Detail, headed by James Wilson, and the Committee on Style, headed by Gouverneur Morris, succeeded in putting together what we now know as the seven articles of the original Constitution of the United States. Wilson's committee arrived at acceptable agreements concerning the election of the executive (the President), the length of his term, impeachment, appointment of Federal judges and the jurisdiction of the Supreme Court, terms and functions of United States senators, and means of ratifying the proposed constitution.

Some subjects roused serious debate, particularly the matter of slavery, which greatly complicated questions concerning the basis of direct taxation and of representation. The system of requisitions—State contributions to the Federal treasury upon request—that prevailed under the Confederation might be continued, but how should those requisitions be allocated among the States? Oddly, there was no distinct recognition that the normal basis of representation ought to be persons, and that the normal basis of taxation ought to be wealth. It was finally decided, however, that both representatives and direct taxes should be apportioned among the several States according to population. The larger the population the greater the number of representatives. As a concession to the southern States, the population to be counted included three-fifths of the slave population, even though slaves were not entitled to vote.

The inclusion of three-fifths of the slaves constituted the so-called "Three-Fifths Compromise." There was some objection to it in the Convention, but the issue was not vigorously challenged there or in the State ratifying conventions. This adjustment, in fact, had already been suggested in the Confederation Congress, and it was not altogether strange or novel to the delegates.

Although the question of slavery would later bring about disunion and civil war, in 1787 it was overshadowed by other considerations. Of paramount concern to the delegates was the desperate need to reach a compromise on a great variety of issues and to develop a consensus sufficient to persuade the delegates and the State ratifying conventions to endorse the final draft of the Constitution. Far more troublesome than slavery was the jealousy between the large States and the small States—a jealousy that reached back to the Revolutionary War period and that, had it been aroused by a prohibition against slavery, would probably have made Union impossible.

This jealousy was based not on differences between free States and slave States, as would later be the case, but upon political, cultural, and economic factors. Among the delegates, there were slaveholders from the North as well as the South. We noted earlier, in fact, that nearly all of the States in 1787 had slaves, and that the opponents of slavery were not confined to any particular State. Some of the New England delegates—Rufus King of Massachusetts, in particular—objected to having the Constitution recognize slavery, but no less an opponent of this practice was George Mason of Virginia.

On the other hand, some of the delegates from the lower South—the Carolinas and Georgia—thought slavery was economically necessary. The people of those States looked forward to expanding into the western lands that now form Alabama, Mississippi, and Tennessee. They believed that only by employing slave labor could they carry on their rural plantation economy.

General Charles Cotesworth Pinckney, speaking for those three southern States, feared that Congress, under the new Constitution, could forbid the importation of slaves into the United States—as, indeed, King, Mason, and other delegates wished to do as soon as possible. Pinckney and his colleagues therefore warned that these States might refuse to join the Union if some protections of their economic interests were not included in the Constitution. One of the most passionate debates of the Convention was brought on by this conflict of convictions. The matter was finally settled by a compromise that was arranged in part by Oliver Ellsworth of Connecticut.

The antislavery delegates reluctantly agreed to a constitutional provision that would forbid Congress from interfering with the importation of slaves until the year 1808, and would permit a Federal tax on such importation of not more than ten dollars per slave. This compromise became part of Section 9 of Article I of the Constitution. Significantly, the exemption from Federal interference was limited to "the States now existing" and did not apply to territories or new States entering the Union. General Pinckney recognized that he could not obtain any better concession from the Convention but he had secured some time for the planters of North Carolina, South Carolina, and Georgia to adjust to the new restriction. As for the domestic slave trade, the new Constitution provided merely (Article IV, Section 2) that slaves who might escape from one State into another must be returned to their owners.

If it was possible to compromise on the slave trade, it was clearly possible to compromise on other questions. By September 17, 1787, therefore, the delegates were ready to publicize the Constitution they had written. Only thirty-nine of the original fifty-five delegates put their signatures to the document because several had gone home, including some in dissent. Three gentlemen who were present declined, for various reasons, to sign the Constitution. They were George Mason and Edmund Randolph of Virginia, and Elbridge Gerry of Massachusetts.

No signer of the Constitution considered the document to be perfect, but all were ready to explain it to citizens of the republic. In its final form, the Constitution gave far less power to the Federal government than James Madison had intended by his Virginia Plan. Indeed, the document that was presented for ratification followed moderate lines approved by that wise old man John Dickinson, even though Dickinson had not presented the Convention with a separate plan of his own.

As one looks back on these proceedings two hundred years later, it is easy to understand why historians have often referred to the Constitutional Convention as "the Miracle of Philadelphia." It seems incredible nowadays that such an event could actually occur, and even then it was viewed by the American people and foreign observers as an extraordinary affair. Here were fifty-five individuals, all prominent leaders of their States, many traveling long distances under primitive means of transportation, gathered in one room for four months to forge a new system of government such as the world had never seen. At considerable personal sacrifice—and many had already suffered severe losses during the Revolution—they were away from their homes, their families, their businesses, and their farms for an entire summer. A deep sense of civic pride and virtue, and a feeling of moral responsibility for the welfare of the American people and future generations, explain only in part what motivated these gentlemen. They were also driven by a profound intellectual and emotional attachment to individual liberty. What is truly remarkable is that they all realized at the time the historic significance of what they were seeking to accomplish. For never in recorded history had a society had the opportunity, under the direction of its natural leaders and best minds, to deliberate at such length on the best form of government, to write a fundamental law for a whole nation, and to establish a constitutional republic for liberty, order, and justice.

In Philadelphia, the American people said their final good-bye to the baleful influences of arbitrary and unrestricted government, feudalism, class privilege, and other stultifying and corrupting Old World influences. The great German thinker and poet Johann Wolfgang von Goethe

Assembly Room, Independence Hall in Philadelphia.

Birthplace of the Declaration of Independence and the Constitution. (Independence National Historical Park.)

spoke for many European onlookers when he congratulated the Americans on escaping the "ghosts" that had haunted Europe. The Framers had written not only a new Constitution but a new chapter in the history of mankind. The world would never be the same.

SUGGESTED READING

Catherine Drinker Bowen, *Miracle at Philadelphia* (Boston: Little, Brown & Co., 1966).

M. E. Bradford, *Founding Fathers: Brief Lives of the Framers of the United States Constitution* (Lawrence: University Press of Kansas, 1994).

Trevor Colbourn, ed., *Fame and the Founding Fathers. Essays by Douglas Adair* (Indianapolis: Liberty Fund, 1998).

Wesley Frank Craven, *The Legend of the Founding Fathers* (New York: New York University Press, 1956).

Max Farrand, *The Framing of the Constitution of the United States* (New Haven: Yale University Press, 1913).

Max Farrand, ed., *Records of the Federal Convention*. 4 vols. (New Haven: Yale University Press, 1937), and James H. Hutson, ed., *Supplement to the Records of the Federal Convention* (New Haven: Yale University Press, 1987).

Robert G. Ferris, *Signers of the Constitution* (Washington, D.C.: United States Department of the Interior, 1976).

James McClellan and M. E. Bradford, eds., *Jonathan Elliot's Debates in the Several State Conventions on the Adoption of the Federal Constitution. Vol. II. The Federal Convention of 1787* (Richmond: James River Press, 1991).

James McClellan and M. E. Bradford, eds., *Jonathan Elliot's Debates in the Several State Conventions . . . Vol. III. Debates in the Federal Convention of 1787 as Reported by James Madison* (Richmond: James River Press, 1989).

William M. Meigs, *The Growth of the Constitution in the Federal Convention of 1787* (Philadelphia: J. B. Lippincott Co., 1900).

Clinton Rossiter, *1787: The Grand Convention* (New York: W. W. Norton, 1966).

Jeffrey St. John, *Constitutional Journal: A Correspondent's Report from the Convention of 1787* (Ottawa, Ill.: Jameson Books, 1987).

David G. Smith, *The Convention and the Constitution* (New York: St. Martin's Press, 1965).

Carl Van Doren, *The Great Rehearsal: The Story of the Making and Ratifying of the Constitution of the United States* (New York: Viking Press, 1948).

Charles Warren, *The Making of the Constitution* (Boston: Little, Brown and Co., 1928).

Virginia Plan

1. Resolved, that the Articles of Confederation ought to be so corrected and enlarged as to accomplish the objects proposed by their institution, namely *common Defence, Security of Liberty* and *general welfare.*

2. Resolved therefore, that the rights of Suffrage in the National Legislature ought to be proportioned to the Quotas of contribution, or to the number of free inhabitants, as the one or the other rule may seem best in different cases.

3. Resolved, that the National Legislature ought to consist of *two branches.*

4. Resolved, that the Members of the first Branch of the National Legislature ought to be elected by the people of the several States every _____ for the term of _____ years, to be of the age of at least _____, to receive liberal stipends, by which they may be compensated for the devotion of their time to public service—to be ineligible to any office established by a particular State, or under the authority of the United States, (except those peculiarly belonging to the functions of the first Branch) during the term of service, and for the space _____ after its expiration; to be incapable of re-election for the space of _____ after the expiration of their term of service, and to be subject to recall.

5. Resolved, that the members of the second branch of the National Legislature ought to be elected by those of the first, out of a proper number of persons nominated by the individual Legislatures, to be of the age of _____ years at least; to hold their offices for a term sufficient to ensure their independency; to receive liberal Stipends by which they may be compensated for the devotion of their time to the public service; and to be in-eligible to any office established by a particular State, or under the authority of the United States (except those peculiarly belonging to the

functions of the second Branch) during the term of service, and for the space of _____ after the expiration thereof.

6. Resolved, that each Branch ought to possess the right of originating Acts, that the National Legislature ought to be empowered to enjoy, the *Legislative rights vested in Congress* by the Confederation, and moreover to Legislate in all cases to which the Separate States are incompetent; or in which the harmony of the United States may be interrupted, by the exercise of individual Legislation—to negative all Laws passed by the several States, contravening, in the opinion of the National Legislature, the articles of Union; and to call forth the force of the Union against any Member of the Union, failing to fulfil its duty under the articles thereof.

7. Resolved, that a National Executive be instituted; to be chosen by the National Legislature, for the term of _____ years—to receive punctually at stated times a fixed compensation for the services rendered, in which no increase or diminution shall be made so as to affect the Magistracy, existing at the time of such increase or diminution, and to be ineligible a second time; and that beside a general authority to execute the National laws, it ought to enjoy the Executive rights vested in Congress by the Confederation.

8. Resolved, that the Executive and a convenient number of the National Judiciary, ought to compose a *Council of revision,* with authority to examine every act of the National Legislature before it shall operate, and every act of a particular Legislature before a negative thereon shall be final; and that the dissent of the said council shall amount to a rejection, unless the act of the National Legislature be again passed, or that of a particular Legislature be again negatived by _____ of the Members of each Branch.

9. Resolved, that a National Judiciary be established to Consist of one or more supreme tribunals, and of inferior tribunals to be chosen by the National Legislature; to hold their Offices during good behavior, and to receive punctually at stated times fixed compensation for their services, in which no increase or diminution shall be made, so as to affect the persons actually in office at the time of such increase or diminution.

That the jurisdiction of the inferior Tribunals shall be to hear and determine in the first instance, and of the supreme tribunal to hear and determine in the dernier resort; all piracies and felonies on the high Seas, captures from an enemy; cases in which foreigners or citizens of other States applying to such jurisdictions may be interested, or which respect the collection of the National revenue; impeachments of any National officers and questions which may involve the national peace and harmony.

10. Resolved, that provision ought to be made for the *admission of States* lawfully arising within the limits of the United States, whether from a voluntary junction of Government and Territory or otherwise, with the consent of a number of voices in the National Legislatures less than the whole.

11. Resolved, that a Republican Government and the territory of each State (except in the instance of a voluntary junction of Government and Territory) ought to be guaranteed by the United States to each State.

12. Resolved, that provision ought to be made for the continuance of Congress and their authorities and privileges, until a given day after the reform of the Articles of Union shall be adopted, and for the completion of all their engagements.

13. Resolved, that provision ought to be made for the amendment of the Articles of Union whensoever it shall seem necessary (and that the assent of the National Legislature ought not to be required thereto).

14. Resolved, that the Legislative, Executive and Judiciary powers within the several States ought to be bound by oath to support the Articles of Union.

15. Resolved, that the amendments which shall be offered to the Confederation, by the Convention, ought at a proper time, or times, after the approbation of Congress, to be submitted to an assembly or assemblies of Representatives, recommended by the several Legislatures, to be expressly chosen by the people, to consider and decide thereon.

New Jersey Plan

1. Resolved, that the Articles of Confederation ought to be so revised, corrected, and enlarged as to render the federal Constitution adequate to the exigencies of Government, and the preservation of the Union.

2. Resolved, that in addition to the Powers vested in the United States in Congress by the present existing Articles of Confederation, they be authorized to pass Acts for raising a Revenue by levying a duty or duties on all goods or merchandise of foreign growth or manufacture, imported into any part of the United States,—by Stamps on Paper vellum or parchment,—and by a postage on all letters or packages passing through the general Post Office, to be applied to such federal purposes as they shall deem proper and expedient; to make rules and regulations for the collection thereof, and the same from time to time, to alter and amend in such manner as they shall think proper: to pass Acts for the regulation of trade and commerce, as well with foreign Nations, as with each other; provided that all punishments, fines, forfeitures and penalties to be incurred for contravening such acts, rules, and regulations shall be adjudged by the common Law Judiciarys of the State in which any offence contrary to the true intent and meaning of such acts and regulations shall have been committed or perpetrated; with liberty of commencing in the first instance all suits and prosecutions for that purpose in the superior Common Law Judiciary of such State, subject nevertheless, for the correction of all errors, both in law and fact, in rendering judgment, to an appeal to the Judiciary of the United States.

3. Resolved, that whenever requisitions shall be necessary, instead of the rule for making requisition mentioned in the Articles of Confederation, the United States in Congress be authorized to make such requisitions in proportion to the whole number of white and other free citizens

and Inhabitants of every age, sex and condition, including those bound to servitude for a term of years, and three fifths of all other persons not comprehended in the foregoing description—(except Indians not paying Taxes); that if such requisitions be not complied with, in the time to be specified therein, to direct the collection thereof in the non-complying States and for that purpose to devise and pass Acts directing and authorizing the same; provided that none of the powers hereby vested in the United States in congress shall be exercised without the consent of at least _____ States, and in that proportion, if the number of confederated States should be hereafter increased or diminished.

4. Resolved, that the United States in Congress be authorized to elect a federal Executive to consist of _____ persons, to continue in office for the Term of _____ years; to receive punctually at stated times a fixed compensation for their services in which no increase or diminution shall be made so as to affect the persons composing the Executive at the time of such increase or diminution; to be paid out of the Federal Treasury; to be incapable of holding any other office or appointment during their time of service, and for _____ years thereafter; to be ineligible a second time, and removable by Congress on application by a majority of the Executives of the several States; that the Executive, besides their general authority to execute the federal Acts, ought to appoint all federal officers not other wise provided for, and to direct all military operations; provided that none of the persons composing the federal Executive shall on any occasion take command of any troops so as personally to conduct any enterprise as General or in any other capacity.

5. Resolved, that a federal Judiciary be established, to consist of a supreme Tribunal, the Judges of which to be appointed by the Executive, and to hold their Offices during good behavior, to receive punctually at stated times a fixed compensation for their services, in which no increase or diminution shall be made so as to affect the persons actually in office at the time of such increase or diminution;—That the Judiciary so established shall have authority to hear and determine in the first instance on all impeachments of federal officers, and by way of appeal in the dernier resort in all cases touching the rights of Ambassadors, in all cases of captures from an enemy, in all cases of piracies and felonies on the high Seas, in all cases in which foreigners may be interested in the construction of

any treaty or treaties, or which may arise on any of the Acts for regulation of trade, or the collection of the federal Revenue: that none of the
Judiciary shall during the time they remain in Office be capable of receiving or holding any other Office or appointment during their time of service, or for _____ thereafter.

6. Resolved, that all Acts of the United States in Congress made by virtue and in pursuance of the powers hereby vested in them, and all Treaties made and ratified under the authority of the United States, shall be
the supreme law of the respective States, as far as those Acts or Treaties
shall relate to the said States or their Citizens, and that the Judiciary of
the several States shall be bound thereby in their decisions, anything in
the respective laws of the Individual States to the contrary notwithstanding; and that if any State, or any body of men in any State, shall oppose
or prevent the carrying into execution such acts or treaties, the federal
Executive shall be authorized to call forth the power of the Confederated
States, or so much thereof as may be necessary to enforce and compel an
obedience to such Acts, or an Observance of such Treaties.

7. Resolved, that provision be made for the admission of new States
into the Union.

8. Resolved, that the Rule for naturalization ought to be the same in
every State.

9. Resolved, that a Citizen of one State committing an offence in another State of the Union, shall be deemed guilty of the same offence, as if
it had been committed by a Citizen of the State in which the Offence was
committed.

Constitution of the United States of America (1787)

PREAMBLE

WE THE PEOPLE of the United States, in Order to form a more perfect Union, establish Justice, insure domestic Tranquility, provide for the common defence, promote the general Welfare, and secure the Blessings of Liberty to ourselves and our Posterity, do ordain and establish this CON-STITUTION for the United States of America.

ARTICLE. I.

SECTION. 1. All legislative Powers herein granted shall be vested in a Congress of the United States, which shall consist of a Senate and House of Representatives.

SECTION. 2. [Cl. 1.] The House of Representatives shall be composed of Members chosen every second Year by the People of the several States, and the Electors in each State shall have the Qualifications requisite for Electors of the most numerous Branch of the State Legislature.

[Cl. 2.] No Person shall be a Representative who shall not have attained to the Age of twenty-five Years, and been seven Years a Citizen of the United States, and who shall not, when elected, be an Inhabitant of that State in which he shall be chosen.

[Cl. 3.] Representatives and direct Taxes shall be apportioned among the several States which may be included within this Union, according to their respective Numbers, [which shall be determined by adding to the whole Number of free Persons, including those bound to Service for a Term of Years, and excluding Indians not taxed, three fifths of all other Persons.] The actual Enumeration shall be made within three Years after the first Meeting of the Congress of the United States, and within every subsequent Term of ten Years, in such Manner as they shall by Law direct. The Number of Representatives shall not exceed one for every thirty Thousand, but each State shall have at Least one Representative; and until such enumeration shall be made, the State of New Hampshire shall be entitled to choose three, Massachusetts eight, Rhode Island and Providence Plantations one, Connecticut five, New-York six, New Jersey four, Pennsylvania eight, Delaware one, Maryland six, Virginia ten, North Carolina five, South Carolina five, and Georgia three.]

[Cl. 4.] When vacancies happen in the Representation from any State, the Executive Authority thereof shall issue Writs of Election to fill such Vacancies.

[Cl. 5.] The House of Representatives shall choose their Speaker and other Officers; and shall have the sole Power of Impeachment.

SECTION. 3. [Cl. 1.] The Senate of the United States shall be composed of two Senators from each State chosen by the Legislature thereof, for six Years; and each Senator shall have one Vote.

[Cl. 2.] Immediately after they shall be assembled in Consequence of the first Election, they shall be divided as equally as may be into three Classes. The Seats of the Senators of the first Class shall be vacated at the Expiration of the second Year, of the second Class at the Expiration of the fourth Year, and of the third Class at the Expiration of the sixth Year, so that one third may be chosen every second Year; and if Vacancies happen by resignation, or otherwise, during the Recess of the Legislature of any State, the Executive thereof may make temporary Appointments until the next Meeting of the Legislature, which shall then fill such Vacancies.

[Cl. 3.] No Person shall be a Senator who shall not have attained to the Age of thirty Years, and been nine Years a citizen of the United States, and who shall not, when elected, be an Inhabitant of that State for which he shall be chosen.

[Cl. 4.] The Vice President of the United States shall be President of the Senate but shall have no Vote, unless they be equally divided.

[Cl. 5.] The Senate shall choose their other Officers, and also a President pro tempore, in the Absence of the Vice President, or when he shall exercise the Office of President of the United States.

[Cl. 6.] The Senate shall have the sole Power to try all impeachments. When sitting for that Purpose, they shall be on Oath or Affirmation. When the President of the United States is tried, the Chief Justice shall preside: And no Person shall be convicted without the Concurrence of two thirds of the Members present.

[Cl. 7.] Judgment in Cases of Impeachment shall not extend further than to removal from Office, and disqualification to hold and enjoy any Office of honor, Trust or Profit under the United States; but the Party convicted shall nevertheless be liable and subject to Indictment, Trial, Judgment and Punishment, according to Law.

SECTION. 4. [Cl. 1.] The Times, Places and Manner of holding Elections for Senators and Representatives, shall be prescribed in each State by the Legislature thereof; but the Congress may at any time by Law make or alter such Regulations, except as to the Places of choosing Senators.

[Cl. 2.] The Congress shall assemble at least once in every Year, and such Meeting shall be on the first Monday in December, unless they shall by Law appoint a different Day.

SECTION. 5. [Cl. 1.] Each House shall be the Judge of the Elections, Returns and Qualifications of its own Members, and a Majority of each shall constitute a Quorum to do Business; but a smaller Number may adjourn from day to day, and may be authorized to compel the attendance of absent Members, in such Manner, and under such Penalties as each House may provide.

[Cl. 2.] Each House may determine the Rules of its Proceedings, punish its Members for Disorderly Behavior, and, with the Concurrence of two thirds, expel a Member.

[Cl. 3.] Each House shall keep a Journal of its Proceedings, and from time to time publish the same, excepting such parts as may in their Judgment require Secrecy; and the Yeas and Nays of the Members of either House on any question shall, at the Desire of one fifth of those Present, be entered on the Journal.

[Cl. 4.] Neither House, during the Session of Congress, shall, without the Consent of the other, adjourn for more than three days, nor to any other Place than that in which the two Houses shall be sitting.

SECTION. 6. [Cl. 1.] The Senators and Representatives shall receive a Compensation for their Services, to be ascertained by Law, and paid out of the Treasury of the United States. They shall in all Cases, except Treason, Felony and Breach of the Peace, be privileged from Arrest during their Attendance at the Session of their respective Houses, and in going to and returning from the same; and for any Speech or Debate in either House, they shall not be questioned in any other Place.

[Cl. 2.] No Senator or Representative shall, during the Time for which he was elected, be appointed to any civil Office under the Authority of the United States, which shall have been created, or the Emoluments whereof shall have been increased during such time; and no person holding any Office under the United States, shall be a Member of either House during his Continuance in Office.

SECTION. 7. [Cl. 1.] All Bills for raising Revenue shall originate in the House of Representatives; but the Senate may propose or concur with Amendments as on other Bills.

[Cl. 2.] Every Bill which shall have passed the House of Representatives and the Senate, shall, before it becomes a Law, be presented to the President of the United States: If he approves, he shall sign it, but if not he shall return it, with his Objections to that House in which it shall have originated, who shall enter the Objections at large on their Journal, and proceed to reconsider it. If, after such Reconsideration two-thirds of that House shall agree to pass the Bill, it shall be sent, together with the Objections, to the other House, by which it shall likewise be reconsidered, and if approved by two-thirds of that House, it shall become a law. But in all such Cases the Votes of both Houses shall be determined by yeas and Nays, and the Names of the Persons voting for and against the Bill shall be entered on the Journal of each House respectively. If any Bill shall not be returned by the President within ten Days (Sundays excepted) after it shall have been presented to him, the same shall be a Law, in like Manner as if he had signed it, unless the Congress, by their Adjournment prevent its Return, in which Case it shall not be a Law.

[Cl. 3.] Every Order, Resolution, or Vote, to which the Concurrence of the Senate and House of Representatives may be necessary (except on a question of Adjournment) shall be presented to the President of the United States; and before the same shall take Effect, shall be approved by him, or being disapproved by him, shall be repassed by two thirds of the Senate and House of Representatives, according to the Rules and Limitations prescribed in the Case of a Bill.

SECTION. 8. The Congress shall have Power [Cl. 1.] To lay and collect Taxes, Duties, Imposts and Excises, to pay the Debts and provide for the common Defence and general Welfare of the United States; but all Duties, Imposts and Excises shall be uniform throughout the United States;

[Cl. 2.] To borrow Money on the credit of the United States;

[Cl. 3.] To regulate Commerce with foreign Nations, and among the several States, and with the Indian Tribes;

[Cl. 4.] To establish an uniform Rule of Naturalization, and uniform Laws on the subject of Bankruptcies throughout the United States;

[Cl. 5.] To coin Money, regulate the value thereof, and of foreign Coin, and fix the Standard of Weights and Measures;

[Cl. 6.] To provide for the Punishment of counterfeiting the Securities and current Coin of the United States;

[Cl. 7.] To establish Post Offices and post Roads;

[Cl. 8.] To promote the Progress of Science and useful Arts, by securing for limited Times to Authors and Inventors the exclusive Right to their respective Writings and Discoveries;

[Cl. 9.] To constitute Tribunals inferior to the supreme Court;

[Cl. 10.] To define and punish Piracies and Felonies committed on the high Seas, and Offenses against the Law of Nations;

[Cl. 11.] To declare War, grant Letters of Marque and Reprisal, and make Rules concerning Captures on Land and Water;

[Cl. 12.] To raise and support Armies, but no Appropriation of Money to that Use shall be for a longer Term than two Years;

[Cl. 13.] To provide and maintain a Navy;

[Cl. 14.] To make Rules for the Government and Regulation of the land and naval Forces;

[Cl. 15.] To provide for calling forth the Militia to execute the laws of the Union, suppress Insurrections, and repel Invasions;

[Cl. 16.] To provide for organizing, arming, and disciplining, the Militia, and for governing such Part of them as may be employed in the Service of the United States, reserving to the States respectively the Appointment of the Officers, and the Authority of training the Militia according to the discipline prescribed by Congress;

[Cl. 17.] To exercise exclusive Legislation in all Cases whatsoever, over such District (not exceeding ten Miles square) as may, by Cession of particular States, and the Acceptance of Congress, become the Seat of the Government of the United States, and to exercise like Authority over all

Places purchased by the Consent of the Legislature of the State in which the same shall be, for the Erection of Forts, Magazines, Arsenals, dock-Yards, and other needful Buildings;—And

[Cl. 18.] To make all Laws which shall be necessary and proper for carrying into Execution the foregoing Powers, and all other Powers vested by this Constitution in the Government of the United States, or in any Department or officer thereof.

SECTION. 9. [Cl. 1.] [The Migration or Importation of such Persons as any of the States now existing shall think proper to admit shall not be prohibited by the Congress prior to the Year one thousand eight hundred and eight, but a Tax or duty may be imposed on such Importation, not exceeding ten dollars for each Person.

[Cl. 2.] The privilege of the Writ of *Habeas Corpus* shall not be suspended, unless when in Cases of Rebellion or Invasion the public Safety may require it.

[Cl. 3.] No Bill of Attainder or *ex post facto* Law shall be passed.

[Cl. 4.] No Capitation, or other direct, Tax shall be laid, unless in Proportion to the Census or Enumeration herein before directed to be taken.

[Cl. 5.] No Tax or Duty shall be laid on Articles exported from any State.

[Cl. 6.] No Preference shall be given by any Regulation of Commerce or Revenue to the Ports of one State over those of another: nor shall Vessels bound to, or from, one State, be obliged to enter, clear, or pay Duties in another.

[Cl. 7.] No Money shall be drawn from the Treasury, but in Consequence of Appropriations made by Law; and a regular Statement and Account of the Receipts and Expenditures of all public Money shall be published from time to time.

[Cl. 8.] No Title of Nobility shall be granted by the United States: And no Person holding any Office of Profit or Trust under them shall, without the Consent of the Congress, accept of any present, Emolument, Office, or Title, of any kind what ever, from any King, Prince, or foreign State.

SECTION. 10. [Cl. 1.] No State shall enter into any Treaty, Alliance, or Confederation; grant Letters of Marque and Reprisal; coin Money; emit Bills of Credit; make any Thing but gold and silver Coin a Tender in payment of Debts; pass any Bill of Attainder, *ex post facto* Law, or Law impairing the Obligation of Contracts, or grant any Title of Nobility.

[Cl. 2.] No State shall, without the Consent of the Congress, lay any Imposts or Duties on Imports or Exports, except what may be absolutely necessary for executing its inspection Laws: and the net Produce of all Duties and Imposts, laid by any State on Imports or Exports, shall be for the Use of the Treasury of the United States; and all such Laws shall be subject to the Revision and Control of the Congress.

[Cl. 3.] No State shall, without the Consent of Congress, lay any Duty of Tonnage, keep Troops, or Ships of War in time of Peace, enter into any Agreement or Compact with another State, or with a foreign Power, or engage in War, unless actually invaded, or in such imminent Danger as will not admit of delay.

ARTICLE. II.

SECTION. I. [Cl. 1.] The executive Power shall be vested in a President of the United States of America. He shall hold his Office during the Term of four Years, and, together with the Vice President, chosen for the same Term, be elected, as follows:

[Cl. 2.] Each State shall appoint, in such Manner as the Legislature thereof may direct, a Number of Electors, equal to the whole number of Senators and Representatives to which the State may be entitled in the Congress: but no Senator or Representative, or Person holding an Office of Trust or Profit under the United States, shall be appointed an Elector.

[The Electors shall meet in their respective States, and vote by Ballot for two Persons, of whom one at least shall not be an Inhabitant of the same State with themselves. And they shall make a List of all the Persons voted for, and of the Number of Votes for each; which List they shall sign and certify, and transmit sealed to the Seat of the Government of the United States, directed to the President of the Senate. The President of the Senate shall, in the Presence of the Senate and House of Representatives, open all the Certificates, and the Votes shall then be counted. The Person having the greatest Number of Votes shall be the President, if such Number be a Majority of the whole Number of Electors appointed; and if there be more than one who have such Majority and have an equal Number of Votes, then the House of Representatives shall immediately choose by Ballot one of them for President; and if no Person have a Majority, then from the five highest on the list the said House shall in like Manner choose the President. But in choosing the President, the Votes shall be taken by States, the Representation from each State having one Vote; A quorum for this Purpose shall consist of a Member or Members from two-thirds of the States, and a Majority of all the States shall be necessary to a Choice. In every Case, after the Choice of the President, the Person having the greatest Number of Votes of the electors shall be the Vice President. But if there should remain two or more who have equal Votes, the Senate shall choose from them by Ballot the Vice President.]

[Cl. 3.] The Congress may determine the Time of choosing the Electors, and the Day on which they shall give their Votes; which Day shall be the same throughout the United States.

[Cl. 4.] No Person, except a natural-born Citizen, or a Citizen of the United States at the time of the Adoption of this Constitution, shall be eligible to that Office of President; neither shall any Person be eligible to that Office who shall not have attained to the Age of thirty-five Years, and been fourteen Years a Resident within the United States.

[Cl. 5.] In Case of the Removal of the President from Office, or of his Death, Resignation, or Inability to discharge the Powers and Duties of the said Office, the Same shall devolve on the Vice President, and the Congress may by Law provide for the Case of Removal, Death, Resignation, or Inability, both the President and Vice President, declaring what Officer shall then act as President, and such Officer shall act accordingly, until the Disability be removed, or a President shall be elected.

[Cl. 6.] The President shall, at stated Times, receive for his Services, a Compensation, which shall neither be increased nor diminished during the Period for which he shall have been elected, and he shall not receive within that Period any other Emolument from the United States, or any of them.

[Cl. 7.] Before he enter on the Execution of his Office, he shall take the following Oath or affirmation:—

"I do solemnly swear (or affirm) that I will faithfully execute the Office of President of the United States, and will, to the best of my Ability, preserve, protect, and defend the Constitution of the United States."

SECTION. 2. [Cl. 1.] The President shall be Commander in Chief of the Army and Navy of the United States, and of the Militia of the several States, when called into the actual Service of the United States; he may require the Opinion, in writing, of the principal Officer in each of the executive Departments, upon any Subject relating to the Duties of their respective Offices, and he shall have Power to grant Reprieves and Pardons for Offences against the United States, except in Cases of Impeachment.

[Cl. 2.] He shall have Power, by and with the Advice and Consent of the Senate, to make Treaties, provided two thirds of the Senators present concur; and he shall nominate, and by and with the Advice and Consent of the Senate, shall appoint, Ambassadors, other public Ministers, and Consuls, Judges of the supreme Court, and all other Officers of the United States, whose Appointments are not herein otherwise provided for, and which shall be established by Law: but the Congress may by Law vest the Appointment of such inferior Officers, as they think proper, in the President alone, in the Courts of Law, or in the Heads of Departments.

[Cl. 3.] The President shall have Power to fill up all Vacancies that may happen during the Recess of the Senate, by granting Commissions which shall expire at the End of their next Session.

SECTION. 3. He shall from time to time give to the Congress Information of the State of the Union, and recommend to their Consideration such Measures as he shall judge necessary and expedient; he may, on extraordinary Occasions, convene both Houses, or either of them, and in Case of Disagreement between them, with Respect to the Time of Adjournment, he may adjourn them to such Time as he shall think proper; he shall receive Ambassadors and other public Ministers; he shall take Care that the Laws be faithfully executed, and shall Commission all the Officers of the United States.

SECTION. 4. The President, Vice President and all civil Officers of the United States, shall be removed from Office on Impeachment for, and Conviction of, Treason, Bribery, or other high Crimes and Misdemeanors.

ARTICLE. III.

SECTION. 1. The judicial Power of the United States, shall be vested in one supreme Court, and in such inferior Courts as the Congress may from time to time ordain and establish. The Judges, both of the supreme and inferior Courts, shall hold their Offices during good Behavior, and shall, at stated Times, receive for their Services, a Compensation, which shall not be diminished during their Continuance in Office.

SECTION. 2. [Cl. 1.] The judicial Power shall extend to all Cases in Law and Equity, arising under this Constitution, the Laws of the United States, and Treaties made, or which shall be made, under their Authority;—to all Cases affecting Ambassadors, other public Ministers, and Consuls;—to all Cases of admiralty and maritime Jurisdiction;—to Controversies to which the United States shall be a Party;—to Controversies between two or more States;—between a State and Citizens of another State;—between Citizens of different States,—between Citizens of the same State claiming Lands under Grants of different States, and between a State, or the Citizens thereof, and foreign States, Citizens or Subjects.

[Cl. 2.] In all Cases affecting Ambassadors, other public Ministers, and Consuls, and those in which a State shall be Party, the supreme Court shall have original Jurisdiction. In all the other Cases before mentioned, the supreme Court shall have appellate Jurisdiction, both as to Law and Fact, with such Exceptions, and under such Regulations as the Congress shall make.

[Cl. 3.] The Trial of all Crimes, except in Cases of Impeachment, shall be by jury; and such Trial shall be held in the State where the said Crimes shall have been committed; but, when not committed within any State, the Trial shall be at such Place or Places as the Congress may by Law have directed.

SECTION. 3. [Cl. 1.] Treason against the United States, shall consist only in levying War against them, or in adhering to their Enemies, giving them Aid and Comfort. No Person shall be convicted of Treason unless on the Testimony of two witnesses to the same overt Act, or on Confession in open Court.

[Cl. 2.] The Congress shall have Power to declare the Punishment of Treason, but no Attainder of Treason shall work Corruption of Blood, or Forfeiture except during the Life of the Person attainted.

ARTICLE. IV.

SECTION. 1. Full Faith and Credit shall be given in each State to the public Acts, Records, and judicial Proceedings of every other State. And the Congress may by general Laws prescribe the Manner in which such Acts, Records and Proceedings shall be proved, and the Effect thereof.

SECTION. 2. [Cl. 1.] The Citizens of each State shall be entitled to all Privileges and Immunities of Citizens in the several States.

[Cl. 2.] A Person charged in any State with Treason, Felony, or other Crime, who shall flee from Justice, and be found in another State, shall on Demand of the executive Authority of the State from which he fled, be delivered up, to be removed to the State having Jurisdiction of the Crime.

[Cl. 3.] [No Person held to Service or Labor in one State, under the Laws thereof, escaping into another, shall, in consequence of any Law or Regulation therein, be discharged from such Service or Labor, but shall be delivered up on Claim of the Party to whom such Service or Labor may be due.]

SECTION. 3. [Cl. 1.] New States may be admitted by the Congress into this Union; but no new State shall be formed or erected within the Jurisdiction of any other State; nor any State be formed by the Junction of two or more States, or Parts of States, without the Consent of the Legislatures of the States concerned, as well as of the Congress.

[Cl. 2.] The Congress shall have Power to dispose of and make all needful Rules and Regulations respecting the Territory or other Property belonging to the United States; and nothing in this Constitution shall be so construed as to Prejudice any Claims of the United States, or of any particular State.

SECTION. 4. The United States shall guarantee to every State in this Union a Republican Form of Government, and shall protect each of them against Invasion; and on Application of the Legislature, or of the Executive (when the Legislature cannot be convened), against domestic Violence.

ARTICLE. V.

The Congress, whenever two thirds of both Houses shall deem it necessary, shall propose Amendments to this Constitution, or, on the Application of the Legislatures of two thirds of the several States, shall call a Convention for proposing Amendments, which, in either Case, shall be valid to all Intents and Purposes, as Part of this Constitution, when ratified by the Legislatures of three fourths of the several States, or by Conventions in three fourths thereof, as the one or the other Mode of Ratification may be proposed by the Congress; provided [that no Amendment which may be made prior to the Year One thousand eight hundred and eight shall in any Manner affect the first and fourth Clauses in the Ninth Section of the first Article; and] that no State, without its Consent, shall be deprived of its equal Suffrage in the Senate.

ARTICLE. VI.

[Cl. 1.] All Debts contracted and Engagements entered into, before the Adoption of this Constitution, shall be as valid against the United States under this Constitution, as under the Confederation.

[Cl. 2.] This Constitution, and the Laws of the United States which shall be made in Pursuance thereof; and all Treaties made, or which shall be made, under the Authority of the United States, shall be the supreme Law of the Land; and the Judges in every State shall be bound thereby, any Thing in the Constitution or Laws of any State to the Contrary notwithstanding.

[Cl. 3.] The Senators and Representatives before mentioned, and the Members of the several State Legislatures, and all executive and judicial Officers, both of the United States and of the several States, shall be bound by Oath or Affirmation to support this Constitution; but no religious Test shall ever be required as a Qualification to any Office or public Trust under the United States.

ARTICLE. VII.

The Ratification of the Conventions of nine States, shall be sufficient for the Establishment of this Constitution between the States so ratifying the Same.

Whatever may be the judgment pronounced on the competency of the architects of the Constitution, or whatever may be the destiny of the edifice prepared by them, I feel it a duty to express my profound and solemn conviction, derived from my intimate opportunity of observing and appreciating the views of the Convention, collectively and individually, that there never was an assembly of men, charged with a great and arduous trust, who were more pure in their motives or more exclusively or anxiously devoted to the object committed to them to . . . best secure the permanent liberty and happiness of their country.

James Madison, *Notes of the Debates in the Federal Convention* (1835)

PART 4

Basic Constitutional Concepts: Federalism, Separation of Powers, and Rule of Law

⋙ POINTS TO REMEMBER ⋘

1. The American system of federalism divides political power between two levels of government. Those powers not delegated to the Federal government are reserved to the States. Article I of the Constitution specifies the delegated and implied powers of Congress, and also enumerates those powers that are prohibited to both Congress and the States. Some powers of Congress are exclusive; and others are concurrent, meaning they are shared with another branch or with the States.

2. The States have certain obligations to the Federal government and to each other, and the Federal government has certain obligations to the States. Most of these obligations that each owes the other are framed in Article IV of the Constitution.

3. Formal changes of the constitutional structure must be approved by three-fourths of the States through the amendment process, which is provided by Article V of the Constitution. Every amendment that has been added to the Constitution was proposed by a two-thirds vote of Congress. The States may initiate amendments but have never exercised this power. Congress decides whether the amendment shall be ratified by the State legislatures or by the States meeting in convention. All but the 21st Amendment have been ratified by the State legislatures.

4. The American system of separation of powers is not a pure separation of powers. Although the officeholders in each branch are separate and distinct, the functions overlap. This overlapping of functions forms an elaborate check and balance system, allowing each branch to check the encroachments of another. In this way the separation of powers is actually maintained.

5. The American constitutional system is based on rule of law, the

Constitution itself being the supreme law. Thus in the United States, no man or government or branch of the government is above the law. If the Constitution is to be changed, only the people can change it—and then only by the amendment process.

6. Although the President is powerful and independent, and is charged with the duty of executing the laws, he is not above the law. Limitations on his power derive from the method by which he is elected by the electoral college and from the checks on his exercise of power by Congress and the Supreme Court.

THE CONSTITUTION OF THE UNITED STATES provides a framework of political and legal institutions. Within this framework are certain general concepts or ideas about freedom and political order. Although they are not explicitly stated in the Constitution, they nevertheless provide the theoretical structure upon which the seven articles of the original document are built. An understanding of these unwritten concepts is essential to an understanding of the meaning and purpose of the Constitution. The first of these is the concept of *federalism*. The American federal union is neither a centralized political structure nor a mere league of independent States. The federal system of government embodied in the Constitution is designed to limit power by dividing it.

The second is the concept of the *separation of powers*. This is intended to prevent a concentration and abuse of power by one branch over another. By separating the personnel and functions of government, the Constitution provides a mechanism that facilitates the achievement of Rule of Law.

The third is the concept of the *rule of law*. This is sometimes expressed as "a government of laws and not of men." All people who hold political authority are subject to the law of the land, and their public actions must conform to the Constitution and to certain principles of law.

All three of these concepts restrain the Federal government's powers. The Constitution, in short, set up a powerful general government; but it also established effective checks upon the exercise of power through a carefully designed system of constitutional devices.

A. Federalism

A federal system of government is one in which political authority is divided between a general or national government and regional (or "state") governments. The general government carries on the military and diplomatic functions of the country and deals with many other matters of national concern. The state or regional governments carry on the public activities that most directly affect the citizens, such as police and fire protection. In a federal political structure, the state governments are not mere provincial agencies of a central government. For under federalism, the state or regional governments have their own constitutional powers that the general government must recognize and respect. On the other hand, the state governments in a federal system have less independence than do states that are members of a confederation or league.

The governmental system of the United States is the earliest example of federalism in the modern sense of that word. Nowadays, when the word *federalism* is used throughout the world, it means a system like that of the United States, with political authority divided between two spheres of authority. The American federal system is an extremely complex pattern of interrelated processes simultaneously at work, a blend of independence and interdependence. Federalism may be defined as a system of government in which there are two levels of authority, national and state, operating side by side, with each level generally supreme within its sphere of power. K. C. Wheare, a noted British authority on federalism, defines the federal principle as a "method of dividing powers so that the general and regional governments are each, within a sphere, coordinate and independent," and further, "that each government should be limited to its own sphere and, within that sphere, should be independent of the other." To this we should add that federalism requires a written constitution. The reason is quite simple: there must be a fundamental law delineating the two spheres of authority, lest neither sphere will know the limit of its powers. If the central government acquires too much power, it may swallow up the weaker states, creating a unitary form of government. If, on the other hand, the state governments become too powerful, the union may be reduced to a league or confederation, or be abolished altogether.

Now the Framers of America's Constitution did not create a federal pattern of politics because they had read about something of the sort in an old book. No, American federalism resulted from circumstances in the United States in the year 1787 rather than an abstract theory. True, many of the Framers saw that a weak confederation, under the Articles, was an insufficient system of government. And they perceived that centralized or unitary government (then the pattern in nearly all European states) had its grave faults. But the primary reason why the Framers chose a federal system was that the federal arrangement was just what the American people wanted, and needed, in a very practical sense, in 1787. Federalism as a theory of government, in other words, emerged after the Framers wrote the Constitution.

One alternative to federalism was simply to continue the arrangement established under the Articles of Confederation, and a good many Americans might have been content enough to do so. But this feeble confederation had major economic disadvantages and scarcely could defend itself against foreign enemies.

The other alternative to federalism was a unitary, or centralized, form of government, with all real power concentrated in the nation's capital. Turgot, Condorcet, and other French political thinkers of the 1780s were surprised and almost indignant that the Americans had not formed such a political structure when they won their independence from Britain. But the American people, having thrown off the central power of the King-in-Parliament, were not disposed to establish some new central authority to tell them what to do. Besides, the great majority of American citizens were warmly attached to their State and local governments. They feared that consolidation would diminish their local and personal freedoms.

What the Framers agreed upon, then, was a satisfactory compromise between the people who desired a strong general government and the people who wanted to preserve State and local powers of decision. Under the federal arrangement—something new in human society, at least on so large a scale as in the United States—the several States were still called "sovereign," as if there were no higher political power above them. But through the federal arrangement, there was created a general government with vastly superior powers. The Constitution allocated some powers to the Federal government, and guaranteed that all other political powers would be reserved to the States or to the people in those States. This division of powers, or "dual sovereignty," though hotly debated during 1787–1788, was accepted by the States when they ratified the Constitution.

Powers Delegated to Congress

To understand the federal system of government set up by the Constitution, we must look first at Article I, Sections 8, 9, and 10 of that document. Sections 8 and 9 assign some powers to the general government, and deny that general government other powers; Section 10 denies certain powers to the State governments.

By these provisions, the Congress—that is, the Federal government—is authorized to "lay and collect taxes, duties, imposts, and excises, to pay the debts and provide for the common defense and general welfare of the United States; but all duties, imposts and excises shall be uniform throughout the United States." Thus the new Constitution gave the National Government money-raising power that the government of the Articles of Confederation never had enjoyed.

Many other powers were delegated by the States to Congress by the Constitution—powers that we now take for granted, but which in 1787 made many, and perhaps most, Americans very uneasy. As John Quincy Adams said in 1839, the Constitution "had been extorted from the grinding necessity of a reluctant nation." Independent of Britain for only a few years, the citizens of the new Republic did not relish the notion of surrendering State sovereignty, even some of it, to a national government. Indeed, even some villages and townships thought of themselves as sovereign, free from any higher political authority. They resented the interference of even State governments. So it is not surprising that the powers given to Congress by Article I of the Constitution alarmed some of the men who had been foremost in the struggle against British rule.

Section 8 of Article I also authorized the Congress to borrow money, regulate foreign and interstate trade, coin money, establish post offices and post roads, establish Federal courts, declare war, raise armies and build navies, put down rebellions, organize an armed militia within the States, and do all things "necessary and proper" to put into effect these and certain other specified powers. Today, nobody is surprised that the Federal government establishes rules for naturalization and bankruptcy, punishes counterfeiters, grants copyrights and patents. Yet until the Constitution was ratified in 1788, the government of the United States performed no such functions.

Powers Denied to Congress

These great grants of power to the Congress had to be balanced by certain strong restraints on federal authority if the people of the thirteen States were to be persuaded to ratify the Constitution. So Section 9 of Article I sets definite limits on what Congress may do.

The first-listed restraint, which seems odd to us today, is that Congress might not forbid the importation of slaves until 1808. This temporary provision is followed by guarantees of ancient rights and privileges derived from the British common law and constitution. The first of these is the privilege of *habeas corpus,* a Latin term meaning "you have the body." A writ of habeas corpus is an order issued by a court to an arresting officer, directing him to bring a prisoner before the court. If confinement was improper, the judge will order his release. The writ of habeas corpus, one of the most ancient liberties inherited from England, is wholly procedural in character and defines no rights. But it offers persons charged with a crime one of their most important protections against illegal arrest and confinement, and serves as an important check on the illegal usurpation of power by the executive. The writ has been used in England and the United States to test the legality of virtually any confinement, including detention by military authorities. Under the Constitution, Congress may suspend this privilege in times of rebellion or invasion. During the Civil War, President Lincoln suspended the writ without Congressional authorization, and was much criticized for his action.

The second guarantee is protection against bills of attainder. This is a legislative act designed to punish a particular individual without a jury trial. Congress can determine what conduct shall be considered a federal crime, but no one can be punished until after a jury trial. This guarantee is an important check on the illegal usurpation of power by the legislature. The prohibition was originally adopted in England to outlaw the practice of legislative punishment, whereby individuals could be condemned to death by a special act of Parliament. Legislative acts inflicting lesser punishments are called bills of "pains and penalties." As interpreted by the Supreme Court, the prohibition against bills of attainder extends to all legislative acts, "no matter what their form, that apply either to named individuals or to easily ascertainable members of a group in such a way as to inflict punishment on them without a judicial trial."

The third guarantee, which is also a check on the legislature inherited from English law, is protection against *ex post facto* laws. These are retrospective or retroactive laws which impose criminal penalties for acts that were not illegal when they were performed. Over the years, the Supreme Court has interpreted the prohibition to include any law which operates to the disadvantage of an individual accused of a crime committed before the law was passed. This includes laws that change the punishment and inflict a greater penalty than the one affixed to the crime when it was committed, and laws that alter the rules of evidence so as to permit less or different evidence for a conviction than was required at the time the crime was committed. The *ex post facto* clause was apparently intended by the Framers to apply to retrospective laws devaluing property rights, but very early in our history the Supreme Court held in *Calder v. Bull* (1798) that the restriction applies only to criminal laws.

Section 9 also forbids Congress to levy direct taxes unless in proportion to population; to tax exports; or to favor the ports or shipping of one State over the ports or shipping of another State. Federal officials are forbidden from drawing money from the Treasury except in accordance with Congress's appropriation of funds. Finally, Section 9 forbids Congress to grant titles of nobility. Nor can anyone connected with the Federal administration accept gifts, or titles, or other favors from foreign governments without Congressional consent.

Powers Denied to the States

The list of what State governments might not do under Section 10 was quite as specific as the longer list of prohibitions upon the Federal government. No State may make foreign alliances or treaties; license privately owned ships to prey upon enemy vessels (a power held under Section 8 by the Federal government); coin money or issue paper money, or otherwise impair the Federal government's monopoly of money-issuing; pass bills of attainder or *ex post facto* laws; interfere with contractual obligations; or grant titles of nobility.

Nor may any State's legislature—unless granted the consent of Congress—tax exports or imports, except for incidental expenses of inspection; and even should Congress permit such export-import taxes, the money collected must go into the Federal treasury. Neither may any State, without the express consent of Congress, maintain troops or naval vessels, enter into an agreement with any other State or with a foreign power, or go to war unless actually invaded and in imminent danger.

These limitations aside, the State governments could do much as they liked, so far as the Federal Constitution was concerned. It was up to the State constitutions to provide restraints upon political power at the State level, should the people of the States so choose.

The Division of Powers

These provisions of Article I promptly produced certain beneficial and practical effects. They gave the new general government essential powers that were sorely lacking in the old Confederation government; and they curtailed certain powers formerly asserted by the State governments that sometimes had endangered the Union itself.

Still more important, perhaps, in the long run, was Article I's creation of an enduring *federal* design of government. That federal system contrived in 1787 still is functioning in the United States—even though the powers of the Federal government have since grown at the expense of the State governments.

In effect, after 1788 the American nation would benefit from two coordinate governments, each with its own legislative, executive, and judicial branches. The general or Federal government would concern itself with matters of high national importance, chiefly diplomacy, the common defense, international and interstate commerce, issuing of money, management of the nation's western territories, ensuring a republican form of government in all States, and performing other public functions that no State could undertake adequately in isolation.

The State governments—thirteen of them to begin with, but soon several more—would carry on the administration of justice within their own boundaries, protecting people and property, maintaining the courts of law that dealt with most litigation, overseeing local governments, maintaining roads, transportation, and communications, and in general protecting the health, safety, and welfare of their citizens through the exercise of what is called "the state police powers."

Thus the State governments were in many ways independent of the Federal government. Ordinarily the actions of the Federal organization and the actions of the State governments would not conflict because they operated on different levels of public policy. Nevertheless, a good many American political leaders foresaw difficulties in the relationship between the national government and the States.

For most Americans in our early republic, the idea of a national capital in some remote city seemed alien. Their hearts did not warm to it. There were marked differences among the States, and also between North and South, East and West—contrasting patterns of culture, economic activity, social institutions, customs, manners, speech. So we ought not to be surprised that many Americans' first loyalty was to their State, rather than to the Federal union. The really surprising thing is that, despite this affection for one's State and one's local community, the people of the thirteen original States did assent, if reluctantly, to the federal structure set up by the new Constitution.

Their assent was reluctant because many of them could perceive that the autonomy, or self-government, of the States must be diminished in a federal system. This was because the Federal government was authorized by the Constitution to operate directly upon the citizens of every State, in a number of ways, whether or not a State government might agree with Federal policies. That is, the Federal power must prevail over State power when the Federal government is exercising one of the *enumerated* powers specified in the Constitution, usually in Article I.

Most enumerated powers are also called *delegated* powers because they originated in the States and were delegated or assigned by the States to the national government. In addition to enumerated powers, Congress also possesses under Article I, Section 8, by means of the "Necessary and Proper" Clause, certain *implied* powers. Article I, Section 8, Clause 18

The United States Capitol in 1846.

This is the first photograph of the structure known to exist; it was discovered only recently. The Capitol is pictured here with the old Bullfinch dome. The present dome was added during the Civil War. (Courtesy of the Library of Congress.)

provides that Congress shall have, in addition to the preceding enumerated powers, the power "to make all laws which shall be necessary and proper, for carrying into execution the foregoing powers, and all other powers vested by this Constitution in the Government of the United States, or in any Department or officer thereof." Congress was given, for example, the enumerated power to regulate commerce among the States. Through the Necessary and Proper Clause, Congress therefore might regulate the shipment of goods from one State to another, if it could be demonstrated that this was a necessary and proper exercise of its power to regulate interstate commerce generally. The Necessary and Proper Clause, it may thus be seen, expands the enumerated powers of Congress, and for that reason is also referred to as the "elastic clause."

But the clause does not give Congress the implied power to make laws for any purpose whatever—only for the purpose of executing its enumerated powers and "all other powers vested by this Constitution in the Government of the United States or in any department or officer thereof," meaning the President and the Federal courts. Congress' implied powers, therefore, are not limited to the execution of its own enumerated powers. By virtue of this "all other powers" provision, Congress has the implied power to share in the responsibilities of other departments. It is under the authority of this provision, for example, that Congress passes laws to implement treaty obligations of the United States and to organize the Federal judicial system. Accordingly, the Necessary and Proper Clause confers important and far-reaching powers on Congress; and by giving Congress a voice in the affairs of the other branches, it also plays a key role in the check and balance system that will be examined later.

It should also be noted that each house of Congress possesses additional powers that are not always clearly specified in the Constitution. These are powers inherited from the English Parliament and the early State legislatures, and thus are called "inherited" powers. Under certain circumstances, for example, each house can exclude persons from its membership. Other important inherited powers include the power to conduct investigations, to subpoena witnesses, and to judge the qualifications of members.

Taken together, the powers of Congress may be classified as: (1) *enumerated* or *delegated*, as seen in Article I, Section 8; (2) *implied*, as seen again in Article I, Section 8; (3) *prohibited*, as seen in Article I, Section 9; and (4) *inherited*, as seen in Article I, Section 5. These powers can be further subdivided as *exclusive* and *concurrent*. An example of an exclusive power of Congress is the power to declare war. Thus the President cannot, on his own authority, *declare* war against another country, though he can, as Commander-in-Chief of the armed forces, participate with Congress in *making* war against a foreign enemy. The war-making power is, in fact, a *concurrent* power, one that Congress shares with the President. Congress also shares certain powers with the States. Its power to levy an income tax, for example, is a concurrent power because the States can also levy such a tax.

All other powers are commonly called *reserved* or *residual* powers. These are the unspecified powers that the people or the States did not delegate or surrender to Congress or the general government, and reserved to themselves. This reservation of various powers to the States was reaffirmed in the Tenth Amendment to the Constitution, which provides that "The powers not delegated to the United States by the Constitution, nor prohibited by it to the States, are reserved to the States respectively, or the people." The Tenth Amendment is a rule of interpretation not only for the Federal courts, but also for Congress and the President. At one point in our history, the reserved powers were often regarded as the exclusive powers of the States. As such, they served to limit the powers of the Federal government. Article I, Section 8, for example, empowers Congress "to regulate commerce *among* the several States," suggesting, therefore, that local commerce, wholly *within* a single State, could not be regulated by the Federal government. The Supreme Court has rejected this interpretation, however, and the Tenth Amendment is no longer interpreted by the courts as a limitation on Federal power. Today, it usually makes no constitutional difference whether an act of Congress governs an institution or activity otherwise reserved to the States. For this reason, federalism has weakened over the years, and much power formerly controlled by the States has been shifted to the central government. This reallocation of power is known as the centralization or nationalization of power, a phenomenon that is praised by some and criticized by others.

The Supremacy Clause

In reviewing the relationship between the Federal and State governments, we should also note the significance of the "Supremacy Clause" of the Constitution. Article VI provides that,

> This Constitution, and the laws of the United States which shall be made in pursuance thereof; and all treaties made, or which shall be made, under the authority of the United States, shall be the supreme law of the land; and the judges in every State shall be bound thereby, any thing in the Constitution or laws of any State to the contrary notwithstanding.

This key provision, rarely found in other constitutions, establishes the supremacy of the *Constitution* over all Federal laws, State constitutions, and State laws. It also establishes the supremacy of *Federal laws* and *treaties* over State constitutions and State laws, so long as they are made in pursuance of (in conformity with) the Constitution and are therefore constitutional. If an act of Congress is constitutional, and conflicts with a State constitution or law, the Federal law prevails. Thus, a provision of a State constitution or law, even if it conforms to the United States Constitution, may nevertheless be set aside if it conflicts with an act of Congress or a treaty. Within the field of its powers, the powers of the national government are supreme, and the State courts are bound to uphold this supremacy.

Lodging so much power in the Federal government was viewed with suspicion by Samuel Adams of Massachusetts, by Patrick Henry of Virginia, and by many other American leaders. James Madison endeavored to assure such doubters that in truth the Constitution recognized and protected the sovereignty of the States in most matters. Writing in *Federalist* No. 45, while the States were debating ratification of the Constitution, Madison argued that the State governments would "enjoy an advantage" over the Federal government, commanding popular loyalty more than could Federal officials at the national capital. A State's power, Madison pointed out, "extends to all objects which, in the ordinary course of affairs, concern the lives, liberties, and properties of the people, and the internal order, improvements, and prosperity of the State." History has shown, however, that it is the Federal government, not the States, which dominates the American political system.

National and State Obligations

Up to this point, we have discussed only the *right* of the Federal government to govern the affairs of the nation, and the *right* of the States to govern their own affairs. Our examination of federalism would be incomplete, however, if we failed to include a discussion of their *obligations*. Under the Constitution, the Federal government incurs certain obligations to the States; and the States in turn have obligations both to the Federal government and to each other. Many of these obligations are contained in Article IV of the Constitution.

Obligations of the National Government to the States

This provision, sometimes known as "the federalism article," requires the national government to guarantee a republican form of government to every State, to protect the States against invasion, and, upon request, to protect them against domestic violence. The term "republican government" is not defined in the Constitution, but the Framers meant a representative form of government, as distinguished from a direct democracy or monarchy. This guarantee shows the high regard the Framers had for representative government and their concern, almost a decade after the Revolution, that the people might again wish to be governed by a monarch.

The Constitution of 1787 imposes no similar obligation on the States to establish a written constitution or a bill of rights, or to protect civil liberties, except those specified in Article I, Section 10. Federal involvement in civil liberties disputes between a State and its citizens did not commence until the adoption of the Thirteenth, Fourteenth, and Fifteenth Amendments (the "Reconstruction Amendments") after the Civil War. Even then, the extent of Federal activity was limited primarily to protecting economic rights and the rights of the newly freed slaves. Not until the mid-twentieth century did the Federal government, principally through the courts, become embroiled in civil liberties disputes between a State and its citizens involving such rights as freedom of speech and religion. Ironically, the Supreme Court has never interpreted the meaning of "republican government" and has taken the position that it is up to Congress to decide whether a particular State government is "republican" in character. Nor has Congress offered a definitive interpretation; and the Guarantee Clause, as it is known, is largely dormant.

Section 3 of Article IV places additional obligations upon the Federal government in the interest of State sovereignty. It provides that a new State cannot be created from a pre-existing State, from a combination of States, or from parts of States, unless the legislatures of the States concerned and also Congress give their consent. Five States—Vermont, Kentucky, Tennessee, Maine, and West Virginia—have been formed within the jurisdiction of other States and with the requisite consent. This provision also establishes what is called the "doctrine of equal footing," the principle being that Congress may not discriminate against one or more States and must treat all States as equals. Broadly speaking, every new State is entitled to exercise all the powers of government which belonged to the original States of the Union, and it must be admitted to the Union on an equal footing.

At the same time, Clause 2 of Section 3 makes it clear that Congress has the power to regulate or dispose of territories, public lands, or other property belonging to the United States government. No State can tax federally owned land within its borders, and Congress has full legislative power to govern the affairs of territories, including all subjects upon which a State legislature might act.

Obligations of the States to the National Government

The States' obligations to the national government are found in a number of constitutional provisions. Under Article I, Section 4, the States are obliged to hold elections for Senators and Representatives, and to prescribe the time, places, and manner for such elections. Congress can alter such regulations, however, except as to the places of choosing Senators. Article II, Section 1, which confers the executive power, requires the States to participate in the election of the President. The States are required to select presidential electors, but are free to choose them in any manner the State legislature sees fit. In the early history of the United States, electors were sometimes elected by the legislatures, by the voters in certain districts, by the voters in the entire State, or by a combination of these methods. Today, however, all presidential electors are elected by the voters on a statewide ticket. These electors cast their ballots in the States; the ballots are then transmitted to Congress, where they are counted.

Obligations of the States to Each Other

Obligations that the States have to each other, also specified in Article IV, are numerous, however. Section 1, applying especially to State court decisions, contains the Full Faith and Credit Clause. This provision requires each State to honor and enforce the Court judgments of other States. The requirement is not absolute, however, and under certain conditions, notably in cases involving divorce, a State can refuse to give full faith and credit to another State's court decree.

Under Section 2 of Article IV, the States are prohibited under certain circumstances from discriminating against out-of-state citizens. Although as a general rule they must extend the same privileges and immunities to other citizens that they extend to their own, this provision has been interpreted to mean that the States are not required to give them special privileges, particularly regarding the use and enjoyment of State property. Thus a State is free under this clause to charge out-of-state residents a higher fee than that paid by State residents for fishing and hunting licenses, or for tuition at a State university. On the other hand, a State is prohibited from denying out-of-state citizens access to its courts.

Section 2 of Article IV also provides for the extradition or return of fugitives. If a person commits a crime in one State and is caught in another, the State from which he fled may demand from the governor of the State which holds the fugitive that he be returned. In nearly all cases, escaped prisoners and fugitives charged with a crime are returned, but there is no judicial method of compelling extradition. State governors have on occasion refused to extradite on the ground that the fugitive might not receive a fair trial or has been rehabilitated. The other clause in Section 2 calling for the return of fugitive slaves was nullified by the Thirteenth Amendment, which abolished slavery.

The Role of the States in the Amendment Process

This brings us finally to Article V, which prescribes the method for amending the Constitution. Here the States play a crucial role because no *formal* change of the Constitution is possible without their assent. The States have the right under Article V to initiate amendments and approve their adoption. An amendment can be proposed by a two-thirds vote of *both* houses of Congress or by a national convention called by Congress at the request of the legislatures of two-thirds of the States. Every amendment added thus far to the Constitution, however, was proposed by Congress. The Constitution asserts that, in the event the States call for a convention, Congress "shall" do so. But there is no way to force Congress to act, and it would seem in this instance—as in many others—that the Framers relied upon the good faith of Congress for the observance of this requirement.

Once an amendment has been proposed, it must be ratified by the legislatures of three-fourths of the States or by a special convention of three-fourths of the States. Congress decides which method of ratification is to be used. Except for the Twenty-First Amendment, which repealed the Eighteenth, every amendment has been ratified by the State legislatures.

From the foregoing discussion, it may be seen that the States occupy a commanding position respecting the amendment process. They have the final say on whether the Constitution shall be amended. In this respect, they exercise sovereignty over the nation. This not only affords them an opportunity to protect their interests, but also serves as an ultimate check on the powers of the Federal government. Some amendments, in fact, have nullified decisions of the Supreme Court. For these reasons Article V of the Constitution is regarded as the arch of federalism—the provision that strengthens the States and protects them from being swallowed up by the Federal government. The American republic is a democratic republic because it is based on government by the people. But the people govern through their States, not *en masse*. In this sense they share sovereignty with the States. The American republic is therefore both a democratic republic and a federal republic.

The Federalism Factor

Upon close examination, it will be seen that the entire Constitution is actually honeycombed with provisions designed to protect the residual sovereignty and interests of the States and to give them influence in the decision-making process at the national level. To measure the federalism factor, it is necessary not only to analyze the powers specifically granted and denied to the national government, but to be mindful of those that are by implication reserved to the States—to "read between the lines," as the saying goes.

Article III of the Constitution defines the judicial power of the United States, which extends to nine classes of cases and controversies under Section 2 of that Article. Those classes of cases that are not specified are, by implication, left for resolution by the State tribunals. Section 2, for example, states that the judicial power shall extend to controversies between citizens of different States, but it does not declare that it shall also extend to controversies between citizens of the same State, except in those instances where they are claiming lands under grants of different States. Thus if two citizens of Utah have a contract dispute, it is clear from Article III of the Constitution that the Federal courts have no authority to settle the controversy because the judicial power does not extend to controversies between citizens of the same State in cases involving contracts. As a general rule, then, private disputes between citizens of the same State are settled in the State courts, even though the Constitution is silent on this question.

There are exceptions to this rule, one of the most notable being the Civil Rights Act of 1964. Under this major civil rights legislation, for example, a private dispute between the proprietor of a restaurant and a customer, involving the question of racial discrimination, may be taken to a Federal court because the Act prohibits "any restaurant" from denying a person "the full and equal enjoyment" of its "goods [and] services . . . on the ground of race, color, religion, or national origin." The Act is based on the power of Congress to regulate commerce among the States and presumes that all restaurants are engaged in interstate commerce. The dispute is treated not as a private dispute but as a controversy between the United States and the proprietor. It may be tried in a Federal court because the Act gives Federal district courts jurisdiction over the case. The Federal judicial power extends to "controversies to which the United States shall be a party."

Conceivably, if not in actuality, Congress can overshadow or circumvent the reserved powers of the States through its delegated and implied powers. It may thus be seen that if carried to extreme a broad interpretation of Congress's delegated powers could result in the virtual annihilation of the reserved powers of the States. Where the line separating Federal and State power should be drawn has been a source of constitutional controversy since the earliest days of the American Republic. This is because the powers of the Federal government are not spelled out in every particular and the powers of the States are not spelled out at all. For guidance in interpreting the constitutionality of Federal laws, members of the Supreme Court have understandably turned from time to time to the debates of the Federal and State ratifying conventions of 1787–1788, the essays in *The Federalist,* and other original sources in order to gain a better understanding of the Framers' intentions. Although most provisions of the Constitution are clear and precise, and may be interpreted from the text itself, the nebulous, unwritten reserved powers of the States constitute a gray area of constitutional law that has always been a source of disagreement and debate in American law and politics.

Article II of the Constitution, which establishes the office of the President and confers the executive power, represents another example of how the Framers wove federalism into the constitutional fabric. Although we do not ordinarily think of the executive branch as part of the federal design, it is nevertheless the case that the States play an important role in the election of the President. This is because of the Electoral College.

The manner in which the President shall be elected is stipulated in Section 2 of Article II. It provides that each State shall decide for itself how it shall choose electors, and that it is entitled to a number of electors that is equal to the number of Representatives and Senators it sends to Congress. The electors of each State then meet in their respective States to name two candidates for the presidency, one of whom must be from a different State. Then, when all of the nominations from all of the States have been tallied, the candidate with a majority of the electoral votes is declared President and the runner-up is chosen Vice-President. In the case of a tie, the House of Representatives elects one of the two candidates as President; and in case no candidate has a majority, then the House of Representatives shall select the President from a list of the five candidates who have received the highest number of votes. If the House is called upon to elect the President, the votes are taken not by the individual, but by the States, with each State receiving one vote.

This system lasted only until the election of 1800, when Thomas Jefferson and Aaron Burr each received the same number of electoral votes. It had been generally supposed that Burr really was a candidate for the vice presidency. But when he realized the possibility of being made President,

Burr seized the opportunity—and was defeated only with difficulty. After that, the Twelfth Amendment (1804) eliminated the possibility of such a situation by specifying that the electors "shall name in their ballots the person voted for as President, and in distinct ballots the person voted for as Vice President."

The Electoral College itself, surviving the Twelfth Amendment, has endured to the present day, and the President must be chosen by the vote of each State, rather than by a national popular vote. This means that each State continues to choose a number of electors equivalent to the number of U.S. Senators and Representatives that that particular State sends to Congress. Usually, though not in all presidential elections, the national popular vote for candidates and the vote of the Electoral College would have the same result; but it remains theoretically possible, under peculiar circumstances, for a candidate to be chosen President by receiving a majority of Electoral College votes though a minority of the popular vote.

Why so elaborate a scheme for choosing the President? Because the Framers desired to secure the *independence* of the President from both the Congress and the fickle mass of citizens. They wished to select for the presidency the ablest leader in the country—an individual who would not need to be subservient to the congressional majority in order to be elected, and at the same time would not need to be a demagogue, making extravagant promises to the voters in every State in order to get elected. The way to secure such an admirable President, they thought, was to have him chosen neither by Congress nor directly by the voters of the several States, but to select a few able and honest men in every State, make them electors, and have this small body of politically prudent people (the Electoral College) choose the best possible chief executive for the United States.

Why did this plan fail to work? Because in the several States the voters demanded that candidates who wished to be chosen electors commit to a certain individual for President. Thus the would-be electors felt compelled to name their choice for the presidency—and presently found themselves pledged to vote for that particular man. So the Electoral College has never worked precisely as it was supposed to, and the names of the electors do not even appear on the ballot in presidential elections. It remains true that an elector *could* cast his vote as a member of the Electoral College for a presidential candidate other than the one to whom he had nominally pledged himself; however, that rarely happens. Most American voters today are probably unaware that the Electoral College still exists.

From time to time, some members of Congress have argued that the Electoral College is outdated and should be abolished. Proposed amendments to the Constitution calling for the direct election of the President have repeatedly been rejected, however, and the Electoral College still enjoys wide support. Defenders of the Electoral College contend, in particular, that the present system strengthens federalism by making the States the crucial political units in the selection of the President. The direct-election proposals would change this by scuttling the nomination conventions that give State and local party leaders great influence in the nomination process, and by making State lines irrelevant in the general election. This in turn would encourage presidential candidates to ignore a broad cross-section of the country and the interests of States with small populations, and to direct their appeal to large industrial areas of the country—an invitation, the Electoral College defenders argue, to majority tyranny and a plebiscitary presidency unrestrained by the two-party system. Such arguments have been sufficiently persuasive to defeat the advocates of change, and the present consensus seems to be that the present system, though imperfect, is preferable to the proposed alternatives.

Perhaps the most important point to be remembered, as the foregoing discussion of federalism illustrates, is that there is more to the Constitution than meets the eye. A reading of the text and wording of the document is merely the first step toward a thorough understanding of its meaning and purpose. This is especially true when we stop to consider the influence of the unwritten and often obscure federalism ingredient of the Constitution. But, as we shall presently see, it is also true of other "silences of the Constitution," such as separation of powers and rule of law. It is impossible to understand the Constitution without first understanding the principles upon which it is built.

The Advantages of Federalism

What are the advantages of a federal system of government? Here are some that are commonly mentioned:

(1) Federalism enables States or peoples who differ a good deal from one another or have different backgrounds to join together for common benefits, without some of the States or groups being required to obey unquestioningly whatever the largest State or group orders. In this sense, federalism protects minority rights—the rights of communities or whole regions to maintain their customs, their diversity and individuality, their self-rule. It was so with the Federal union of 1787–1788: South Carolina was not required by the Constitution to model itself on Massachusetts, and in turn Massachusetts did not have to adopt the ways of South Carolina. Yet those two very different political communities found it possible to cooperate through the federal republic of the United States on many matters, most of the time, for the following sixty-four years, without resorting to force. Federalism, then, is associated with "States' Rights" and is regarded as an important means for the preservation of local self-government.

(2) Federalism provides that States or regions can manage their own affairs, rather than being directed by a central autocracy or bureaucracy. A federal structure is particularly necessary to modern representative democracy, especially one so large as the United States. For unless there are political units on a humane scale that are not too big for citizens to understand or share in, "democracy" becomes a mere phrase. Genuine democracy requires that a good many people should participate in public concerns and be governed by representatives chosen from and accountable to the local community. People enjoy a sense of personal safety and security when they are governed by representatives drawn from their own community, who share their values, customs, and mores, and are accessible for consultation, advice, and assistance. It is easier to control a native son, living in the community, than a stranger residing in a distant city. If the United States were a unitary system of government, with all decisions made in Washington, it would be impossible for many Americans to take any part in public affairs and it would be difficult for public officials to understand local needs or to be restrained by the local popula-

tion. The United States would then have, at best, what is called *plebiscitary democracy*—that is, rule by a single man or a narrow clique of administrators, endorsed perhaps by a national ballot at intervals, yet allowing the public no share in decisions beyond the opportunity to vote "yes" or "no" against the dominant regime. (And often, in such centralized systems, the voter is discouraged from voting anything but "yes.") To put all this another way, a federal structure provides means for representative democracy to operate in both regional (State) and national affairs. For this reason, federalism is an important feature of political liberty.

(3) In his famous work *On Liberty*, the nineteenth-century English political philosopher John Stuart Mill presented a powerful argument against centralized bureaucratic government that illustrates the advantages of federalism from another perspective. Federalism, he observed, encourages independence and self-reliance. Because of federalism,

> Americans are in every kind of civil business; let them be left without a government, every body of Americans is able to improvise one, and to carry on that or any other public business with a sufficient amount of intelligence, order, and decision. This is what every free people ought to be; and a people capable of this is certain to be free; it will never let itself be enslaved by any man or body of men because these are able to seize and pull the reins of the central administration. No bureaucracy can hope to make such a people as this do or undergo anything that they do not like. But where everything is done through bureaucracy, nothing to which the bureaucracy is really adverse can be done at all.

No less significant, he concluded, is the fact that decentralized government releases the creative force and genius of a free people. The absorption of all the nation's energy and ability into the central authority, said Mill, "is fatal, sooner or later, to the mental activity and progressiveness of the body itself." It destroys self-reliance. Government must aid and stimulate individual exertion and development or it will stultify and retard a society. "No great thing can really be accomplished" if there is a monolithic government which "substitutes its own activity for theirs; when, instead of informing, advising, and upon occasion, denouncing, it makes them work in fetters or bids them stand aside and does their work instead of them. The worth of a state, in the long run, is the worth of the individuals composing it."

(4) Federalism makes it difficult for an unjust dictator or fanatical political party to seize power nationally and rule the whole country arbitrarily, having first taken the national capital (a process which has occurred repeatedly in centralized countries, among them France most conspicuously). With a federal political structure, obedience to all orders from a national capital is not automatic, and State or regional leaders can resist political revolutions or *coups d'état* through political means or perhaps through State militia (as Thomas Jefferson thought Virginia's State militia might have occasion to resist the Federalist party in power at Washington). To gain dictatorial control over Germany in the 1930s, Adolf Hit-

Raising the Liberty Pole, 1776.

American revolutionaries frequently expressed their devotion to freedom by raising a liberty pole in the town square. The Tree of Liberty and the Liberty Cap were other favorite symbols. (Courtesy of the Library of Congress.)

ler had first to destroy the federal structure of the Weimar Republic. Total-itarianism cannot succeed where federalism thrives.

(5) Federalism allows States, regions, and localities to undertake re-forms and experiments in political, economic, and social concerns with-out involving the whole country and all its resources in some project that, after all, may turn out unsatisfactorily. If it is true that "variety is the spice of life," surely a nation is interesting and lively when it has some diversity and freedom of choice in its political methods. In America to-day, one State can plan some particular educational reform, another State can take a different approach to improving schools; and results can be compared and discussed. Or, different projects of unemployment relief, or experiments in making tax assessment more just, can be carried on in several States simultaneously and States can compete with one another in healthy fashion. In a unitary political structure, no place exists for in-novation or experiment except the bureaucratic central administration of modern nation-states. Commonly that central administration is compla-cent about its own policies.

Other good reasons for maintaining a federal political structure might be given readily enough. To some extent, the Framers of the Constitution were aware of these general or abstract reasons for preferring a federal plan to a central plan of national government. John Adams, Thomas Jef-ferson, James Madison, and James Monroe—who would become, re-spectively, the second, third, fourth, and fifth Presidents of the United States—all were champions of a federated pattern of politics, as against unitary power concentrated in a central administration. Such gentlemen—politicians who were acquainted with history and political theory—perceived the general arguments in favor of federalism.

Foreign commentators who have closely examined the American po-litical system have often shared these views, John Stuart Mill being only one of many examples. Alexis de Tocqueville, an astute French observer visiting the United States in the early 1830s, considered the American system of federalism unique and the greatest achievement of the Consti-tution. Yet he was a citizen of France, one of the most highly centralized countries of Europe. In his celebrated study of American government and society entitled *Democracy in America* (1832), Tocqueville came to the conclusion that the federal arrangement devised by the Framers was "the most favorable" form of government ever created to promote the "prosperity and freedom of man."

Half a century later, the distinguished British statesman and legal scholar James Bryce published *The American Commonwealth* (1888), a profound, comprehensive, and sympathetic analysis of American institutions that ranks with Tocqueville's work as one of the great American political classics. Like Tocqueville, Lord Bryce was favorably impressed by American federalism, notwithstanding his personal allegiance to the unitary system of Great Britain. He found federalism particularly well adapted to American soil because it united the States without extinguishing their governments and local traditions, and also supplied "the best means of developing a new and vast country." Moreover, he thought that the American system stimulated interest in local affairs, encouraged constructive experimentation in legislation and administration, and "relieved the national legislature of a part of that large mass of functions which might otherwise prove too heavy for it." Echoing Tocqueville, Bryce equated federalism with freedom and surmised that it had made a valuable contribution to the welfare of the American people by preventing the rise of "despotic central government" in the United States.

What was the secret of American federalism, and why had it succeeded while so many of man's earlier attempts at confederation had failed? On this question, Tocqueville and Bryce were of one mind. What particularly impressed Tocqueville was the fact that the general government of the United States operated directly on individuals rather than on the States. "This constitution," he explained,

> which may at first sight be confounded with the [con]federal constitutions which preceded it, rests upon a novel theory, which may be considered as a great invention in modern political science.

Continuing, Tocqueville pointed out that in all previous confederations, the allied States had agreed to obey the laws passed by the general government, but had reserved to themselves the right to enforce them. Under the arrangement drafted in 1787, however, the new Federal government would exercise both the law making and law enforcement functions, thereby avoiding one of the major problems experienced under the Articles of Confederation—the reluctance and even the inability or refusal of some member States to enforce the laws and treaties of the central government.

The durability of American federalism, according to Lord Bryce, should also be attributed to the fact that it tends to promote political stability. In framing a federal system, the architects of the Constitution faced an eternal dilemma: how to balance power between the central and state governments; or as Bryce put it colorfully in an astronomical metaphor: how "to keep the centrifugal and centripetal forces in equilibrium, so that neither the planet states shall fly off into space, nor the sun of the central government draw them into its consuming fires." The advantage of the constitutional edifice built by the Framers is that it solved the problem by giving the national government a direct authority over all citizens, irrespective of the State governments, thereby safely leaving broad powers in the hands of State authorities. "And by placing the Constitution above both the national and State governments," observed Bryce, "it has referred the arbitrament of disputes between them to an independent body [i.e., the Supreme Court], charged with the interpretation of the Constitution, a body which is to be deemed not so much a third authority in the government as a living voice of the Constitution, the unfolder of the mind of the people whose will stands expressed in that supreme instrument."

Tocqueville's and Bryce's praise of American federalism (and particularly of American local government) called the earnest attention of European and British scholars and public men to national federalism as an idea, a concept, a theory. And presently America's pattern of federalism was emulated in very different countries—sometimes with modest success, sometimes with no success at all. However that may be, and whether or not federalism is a pattern for good government everywhere, certainly it was the best design for the new American Republic that can be imagined.

The Future of Federalism

The practical operation of the principles of federalism and of separation of powers is diminished today from what most of the Framers desired. Because of the intense jealousy among the States, the deep emotional attachment of the people to their local communities and their States, and the popular belief that there could be no liberty without State sovereignty, it was thought by many Federalists in 1787 that the greatest threat to federalism was separatism, not consolidation. "It will always be far more easy for the State governments to encroach upon the national authorities," predicted Hamilton in *Federalist* No. 17, "than for the national government to encroach upon the State authorities." History, of course, has proved Hamilton wrong, and the trend since the early nineteenth century has been toward increased centralization, interrupted only by secession and the establishment of the Confederate States of America in the Civil War period from 1861 to 1865. Since the New Deal and the administration of President Franklin Roosevelt in the 1930s, the pace of centralization has quickened, more and more functions of government once reserved to the States have been assumed by Federal authorities, and both the States and their political subdivisions have lost considerable independence, power, and influence.

Federalism, as understood by the Framers, recognizes that the authority of the national government extends to a few enumerated powers only, and that all powers not delegated by the States to the national government, nor denied to the States by the Constitution, are reserved to the States. As Madison explained in *Federalist* No. 45,

> The powers delegated by the proposed Constitution to the Federal government are few and defined. Those which are to remain in the State governments are numerous and indefinite. The former will be exercised principally on external objects, as war, peace, negotiation, and foreign commerce. . . . The powers reserved to the several States will extend to all the objects which, in the ordinary course of affairs, concern the lives, liberties and properties of the people; and the internal order, improvement, and prosperity of the State.

This understanding of federalism was made explicit in the Constitution by the Tenth Amendment. Federalism, then, was viewed by the founding generation as a constitutionally based, structural theory of government designed to ensure political freedom and responsive, democratic government in a large and diverse society.

How and why federalism has declined is the subject of many studies. It may be explained in large part by the transformation of the relationship between the national government and the States that occurred in the 1930s, when Congress, under the leadership of President Roosevelt, decided it was necessary, in response to the Great Depression, to expand its commerce power to establish welfare and public work programs, and to regulate agricultural production, the labor force, transportation, and many other activities that had previously been under State control. The Supreme Court's new interpretation of Congress's power to regulate commerce among the States allowed the Federal government to gain control of virtually the entire commercial life of the nation, including many aspects of intrastate commerce wholly within one State, and a wide variety of other activities local in nature and only indirectly related to commerce, such as wildlife protection, flood and watershed projects, mountain streams, housing, even civil rights. After 1937, the Supreme Court, in a series of landmark decisions reversing many earlier cases, adopted the view that Congress was free to use its commerce power to regulate any activity that, in one way or another, might "affect" commerce. The Tenth Amendment, said the Court in *United States v. Darby* (1941), does not limit the commerce power and "states but a truism that all is retained which has not been surrendered." In only one case between 1937 and 1995 did the court strike down a Federal law under the commerce clause, and even that decision was subsequently overruled. In *Garcia v. San Antonio Metropolitan Transit Authority* (1985), the Supreme Court rejected the proposition that the Constitution places independent limits on Congress's commerce power, holding that participation by the States in the national political process is the only protection against Federal encroachments on their reserved powers. This may not be very reassuring to the States. Before the adoption of the Seventeenth Amendment, members of the Senate were elected by the State legislatures. Now they are elected directly by the people. The effect of this amendment has been to weaken the influence of the States in the national political process.

More recently, the Supreme Court has indicated that it may be moving away from the latitudinarian interpretation of the Commerce Clause it has followed during the last half century. Without reversing any earlier decisions, the Court ruled in *United States v. Lopez* (1995) that the power to regulate commerce among the States did not give Congress the authority to ban the mere possession of a firearm in a school zone. The Gun

Free School Zones Act of 1990 exceeded Congress's authority, said the Justices, because gun possession in itself did not necessarily affect inter-state commerce. The *Lopez* case is the first instance since 1937 in which the Supreme Court has overturned a Federal statute on the ground that Congress exceeded its powers under the Commerce Clause.

Similarly, in *Printz v. United States* (1997) the Court struck down a pro-vision of the Brady Gun Control Act which forced local law enforcement officials to conduct background checks on potential gun purchasers. Cit-ing *New York v. United States* (1992), which held that Congress cannot compel the States to enact or enforce a Federal regulatory program, the Court asserted that Congress may not circumvent that prohibition by en-listing State officials directly. "Our constitutional system of dual sover-eignty," said the Court, "is fundamentally incompatible with conscript-ing state and local officials to carry out federal programs."

Speaking for the majority of the judges, Justice Scalia agreed that, un-der the Supremacy and Full Faith and Credit clauses, State and local governments must comply with Federal laws, and that State judges are obliged to enforce Federal laws; but the Federal government may not co-erce State and local authorities into implementing, by legislation or ex-ecutive action, Federal regulatory programs. Scalia noted that, even un-der wartime conditions, President Woodrow Wilson was compelled to *request* the assistance of State governors in calling upon State officers to implement the militia draft in World War I. "The Framers," concluded Scalia, "explicitly chose a constitution that confers upon Congress the power to regulate individuals, not States." Whether the *Lopez* and *Printz* decisions represent the early stages of a constitutional revolution in Amer-ican federalism, or just a temporary lapse of faith in the wisdom of earlier judicial rulings, remains to be seen.

In addition, Congress's spending power under Article I, section 8 to "provide for the general welfare" has had a substantial impact on the federal system. Federal spending in the form of payments to individ-uals, such as old-age support under Social Security, conditional grants to States (as with education and welfare), and direct financing of Federal projects such as the Tennessee Valley Authority, has undermined local autonomy by allowing Federal instead of locally elected officials to de-

cide how money is to be spent. In some respects this has effectively trans-
formed State and local governments into administrative units of the national government, contributing to the gradual erosion of the State's
control over its own cities and other political subdivisions. The expansive use of the spending power by Congress—especially the practice of
conditioning eligibility for Federal grants on compliance with regulations having little or no relationship to the program being funded—has
led to a major expansion of Federal power over State budget priorities
and, in many instances, over State laws and constitutions. Litigation about
the scope of the spending power has been rare, and in those instances
where the Federal Judiciary has addressed the issue, the judges have generally declined to impose any constitutional limitations.

Civil rights legislation under the Commerce Clause and the enforcement clauses of the Thirteenth, Fourteenth, and Fifteenth amendments, in
conjunction with the "nationalization" of the Bill of Rights, has also contributed to the growth of Federal power at the expense of the States. As
originally drafted, the Bill of Rights restricted only Congress and the Federal government. By exempting the States, it gave them exclusive jurisdiction over disputes between a State and one of its citizens regarding such
matters as freedom of religion and the rights of the accused. These disputes were resolved in the State courts, in accordance with State laws and
State constitutions. In recent years, however, the Supreme Court has taken
command of these cases, holding that most provisions of the Bill of Rights
apply to the States as well as Congress, and that such disputes must now
be settled in Federal courts according to Federal standards. As a result of
this development in the courts, there has been a massive transfer of power
over civil liberties questions from the States to the general government.

These are only some of the examples that might be offered to explain
the decline of federalism. Technological advances making State regulation impractical, changing public attitudes about the proper role of the
Federal government, the incessant demand for public services and assistance: these and many other factors have also contributed to the growth
of "big government." The President, Congress, and the Courts have all
played significant roles in bringing about this state of affairs.

Some observers view this development favorably, arguing that much of it was necessary because the States were either unable or unwilling to adapt to technological advances requiring uniform regulation and control, or were indifferent and even hostile to the demands of minorities, especially in the field of civil rights. Critics, on the other hand, assert that centralization has produced bureaucratic inefficiency and waste, brought on deficit spending, undermined independence and self-government, contributed to the problem of political apathy, and encouraged judicial excesses that deny citizens a say in their own affairs. Perhaps the most frequently voiced complaint is the allegation that the Federal courts have excluded the people and their elected representatives from the decision-making process by dictating public policy on the scope and meaning of individual liberty, particularly as it relates to the apprehension and treatment of criminal offenders, control and supervision of neighborhoods and schools, religion and the family, abortion, pornography, and a wide assortment of other social concerns.

Whatever the merits of these arguments for and against the growth of centralization, federalism yet remains; and there seems to be no popular movement afoot to repudiate federalism, eradicate the States, or weaken the federal system further. Even in its weakened condition, federalism remains a basic principle of the American constitutional system.

Because the Constitution does not precisely draw a line to indicate where national power ends and State power begins, the issue of States' Rights will, it seems, continue to be a source of disagreement and debate in American public life. The difficulties associated with delineating two vaguely defined, overlapping spheres of power in the federal system are compounded by the fact that public figures are not always inclined to support the principles of federalism when they conflict with a desired program or policy; and by the tendency of the general public to favor or oppose particular policies without stopping to consider their constitutional impact on federalism. For this reason, the President, Congress, and the Courts, as well as the electorate, have not consistently supported federal principles. "Men of principle," with a consistent record on constitutional matters, and men who are willing to take unpopular stands in defense of federalism and the Constitution, are often unappreciated or misunderstood by the public. This is unfortunate, but it surely holds true in any constitutional democracy.

B. The Separation of Powers

Since ancient times, statesmen and political thinkers have struggled with a fundamental problem that is common to all civil societies: how to structure a government that is powerful enough to govern but itself is sufficiently controlled so that it does not become destructive of the values it was intended to promote. "In framing a government which is to be administered by men over men," observed Publius in *Federalist* No. 51, "the great difficulty lies in this: you must first enable the government to control the governed; and in the next place oblige it to control itself. A dependence on the people is, no doubt, the primary control of the government; but experience has taught mankind the necessity of auxiliary precautions."

The republican principle, in other words, should serve as the main pillar of the structure. A government based on consent, in which the people possess sufficient political liberty to control those who exercise political power, provides a barrier to despotism. Wise men that they were, the Framers understood, however, that we cannot rely solely and exclusively upon the people to control government or to protect the values of liberty, order, and justice. If we could, there would be no need for a constitution in the first place. Men are capable of both good and evil. This is because human beings are imperfect creatures, and it would be naive to think that all men are by nature good. "It may be a reflection on human nature," Publius agreed, "that such [auxiliary] devices should be necessary to control the abuse of government. But what is government itself, but the greatest of all reflections on human nature? If men were angels, no government would be necessary. If angels were to govern men, neither external nor internal controls of government would be necessary." From Christian teaching, the Framers had learned, then, that human nature is not to be trusted. Good laws and institutions are required to keep men from one another's throats.

Foremost among the "auxiliary precautions" Publius had in mind was the separation of powers. Whereas republicanism provides an external check on government, separation of powers supplies an internal or built-in form of restraint. Of all the theories of government that have been propounded to establish limited government, the doctrine of separation of powers has been the most influential and successful. It stands alongside that other great pillar of Western political thought—the concept of representative government—as the major support for constitutional government.

The American doctrine of separation of powers consists of four elements: (1) the idea of three separate and independent branches of government—the legislature, the executive, and the judiciary; (2) the realization that government performs different kinds of functions, and the belief that there are unique functions appropriate to each branch; (3) the belief that the personnel of the branches of government should be kept distinct, no one person being able to be a member of more than one branch of government at the same time; and (4) the belief that the legislature may not alter the distribution by delegating its powers to the executive or the judicial branch. A separation of powers is a necessary prerequisite to limited constitutional government because a concentration of political power is inherently dangerous and will sooner or later lead to the abuse of power and to oppressive government. "The accumulation of all powers, legislative, executive, and judiciary, in the same hands, whether of one, a few, or many, and whether hereditary, self-appointed, or elective, may justly be pronounced the very definition of tyranny," Publius wrote in *Federalist* No. 47.

The separation of powers doctrine is also closely associated with rule of law, and may be said to be an indispensable means for its attainment. If any one body had the power to interpret and enforce its own laws, there would be no force, other than good will, to counteract the temptation to use the powers of government to provide exemptions from the operation of the law and establish special privileges and immunities for the ruling class or governing faction.

The doctrine of the separation of powers may be traced back to the ancient world, where the concepts of governmental functions and theories of mixed and balanced government first appeared. Separation of powers, by itself, however, has never been a satisfactory safeguard against the usurpation and abuse of power, and even among the ancients it was realized that some form of checks and balances was necessary to prevent one branch from encroaching upon the powers of the others. The idea of internal checks, exercised by each branch over the others, first came to maturity in eighteenth-century England with the development of the "mixed and balanced" Constitution of Great Britain. The solution to the problem of political tyranny, thought the English, was to distribute the powers of government among monarchy (the crown), aristocracy (House of Lords), and democracy (House of Commons), so that each class would check the advances of the others, thereby producing a "mixed and balanced" government. The idea of a judicial power distinct from the executive, which complicated matters, was added to the equation and popularized by Montesquieu and Blackstone toward the end of the eighteenth century.

The American achievement was to substitute a functionally divided system for the "mixed" system, replacing a class-based structure with one in which all the branches of government drew their authority from the people. This was first achieved in the revolutionary State constitutions adopted in 1776, that of Virginia being an example: "The legislature, executive and judiciary departments shall be separate and distinct, so that neither exercise the powers properly belonging to the other." These first State constitutions also departed from the British model by requiring a complete separation of personnel as well as function, that of Virginia again being representative: "nor shall any person exercise the powers of more than one of them [branch] at the same time."

Working without any clear precedents or guidelines, and laboring under the erroneous assumption that an almost pure separation of powers would achieve the desired result of limited government, the framers of these first constitutions established powerful legislative bodies but failed to provide a check and balance system. It soon became apparent that this was a fatal omission. Throughout the country, the State legislatures became an embarrassment to republican government, not infrequently interfering with the operation of the courts, reducing governors to a condition of subservience, and violating the rights of property. Under the Virginia Constitution of 1776, "All the powers of government," complained Thomas Jefferson, "legislative, executive, and judiciary, result to the legislative body." His friend and colleague James Madison spoke for virtually the entire Federal Convention when he stated in *Federalist* No. 48: "a mere demarcation on parchment of the constitutional limits of the several departments is not a sufficient guard against those encroachments which lead to a tyrannical concentration of all the powers of gov-

He in a trice struck Lyon thrice   Who seiz'd the tongs to ease his wrongs,   Congress Hall,
Upon his head, enrag'd fir,   and Grifwold thus engag'd. fir.   in Philada Feb. 15.1798.
                                                                                                    S.H. Cor 6th & Chesnut f.

Congressional Pugilists.

Scene from a brawl between Representatives Mathew Lyon and Roger Griswold in the
Hall of Congress on February 15, 1798. Such behavior is rare, however, and Members
of Congress have traditionally conducted themselves in an orderly manner. In the
early days, as the cartoon correctly relates, members were permitted to bring their
hunting dogs into the chamber. (Courtesy of the Library of Congress.)

ernment in the same hands." Accordingly, the Framers enthusiastically
embraced the separation of powers doctrine but incorporated a check and
balance system into the machinery of government. This, together with the
distinctly American system of federalism, rendered the Constitution truly
unique. The credit for the checks and balances feature of the Constitution
probably goes to a group of astute Massachusetts lawyers, however, for it
was they, under the leadership of John Adams, who wrote the Massachusetts Constitution of 1780—the first to introduce the check and balance
concept that later became a part of the United States Constitution.

Checks and Balances

The check and balance system is probably the most ingenious and carefully crafted feature of the American Constitution. Like the principle of federalism, it permeates the document. Here is what the Framers did in order to reconcile the principle of separation with the urgent need for a vigorous new government that would exercise some self-control:

(1) They arranged that there should be some overlap of functions among the three major departments of government. In some ways, one department was allowed to touch upon the usual affairs of a different department. Montesquieu had written that no department should exercise "the *whole* power" of another department, but to exercise some part of the power of another department was permissible. There ought to be no insurmountable wall of separation shutting off executive and judicial branches from the legislative in every respect. Thus in the final version of the Constitution that was submitted for ratification, the President (executive branch) was given a part in the legislative process, through his power of veto and his power to make recommendations in "State of the Nation" addresses to the Congress. On the other hand, the legislative branch, through the Senate, was given some power over the executive branch, in that treaties and presidential appointments to major administrative posts and to the judiciary must be confirmed by the Senate. Likewise, the judiciary was given some executive power to manage its own internal affairs. By the power of judicial review, it might also overturn acts of the legislature deemed unconstitutional.

(2) They improved upon the State constitutions by arranging that the members of the three branches of government should be chosen in three different ways—so making the executive and judicial branches more independent from the legislative. (In the early State constitutions, usually the legislature had appointed and removed State executives and judges.) Under the new Constitution of the United States, members of the House of Representatives would be elected by the voters of geographic districts within the several States; Senators would be elected by their State legislatures; and Presidents would be elected by a College of Electors. Federal judges would be appointed by the President, subject to confirmation by the Senate, and would be appointed for life. By separating personnel as

well as functions, the authors of the Constitution sought to prevent the legislative branch from lording over a subordinate executive and a subordinate judiciary.

(3) The Framers provided each department with constitutional means for resisting attempts at domination by the other departments. The President's "qualified veto" over enactments of the Congress was a protection for the executive branch. Life tenure for judges was a protection for the judicial branch. As an additional device for strengthening the executive and judiciary against the legislature, the Framers arranged that members of the House and Senate would be chosen by different means, and in part at different times. The Congress, for its share, was given the constitutional power of impeaching the executive or members of the judiciary—a grim power inherited from the British Constitution.

(4) It may thus be seen that an elaborate system of *checks and balances* was woven into the Constitution. These checks and balances were intended to prevent any person or organ of government from interfering with constitutional freedoms or with the lawful functioning of another organ of government. They also help to *maintain* the separation of powers by arming each branch with a defensive power to resist encroachments from another branch.

These built-in checks upon the power of any person or office in the Federal government are still functioning two centuries after their invention.

To obtain a clearer notion of these several constitutional means for separating powers and providing checks and balances in the Constitution, study the following list of such provisions in the original seven Articles of the Constitution:

Checks upon the Congress

The Vice President (executive branch) presides over the Senate and can cast a tie-breaking vote (Article I, Section 3).

The President is empowered to call special sessions of the Congress, and to adjourn both houses if they cannot agree upon a time for adjournment (Article II, Section 3).

The President is given power to veto acts passed by the Congress (Article I, Section 7).

The Supreme Court has power to review enactments of the Congress for unconstitutionality (an unspecified power derived from Article III).

Checks upon the President

Congress has power to impeach and remove the President for high crimes and misdemeanors (Article II, Section 4).

Congress may override a presidential veto by a two-thirds majority (Article I, section 7).

Congress can assure civilian control of the military through its power to appropriate—or withhold—funds to support military and naval forces, to make regulations for those forces, to call forth the militia of the States, to suppress insurrections and to repel invasions, and to declare war (Article I, Section 8).

Congress has an inherent power to investigate actions of the executive branch concerning proper execution of the laws and proper expenditure of funds (Article I, Section 8).

Congress is empowered to appropriate the funds for operation of the executive branch (Article I, Section 8).

The Senate has power to approve, amend, or reject treaties. It may also attach reservations to the treaty, which may not alter the content but may qualify or limit the obligations assumed by the United States under the agreement (Article II, Section 2).

The Senate has power to confirm or reject presidential appointments to major posts (Article II, Section 2).

The Judiciary has power to review actions of the executive branch for their constitutionality (an unspecified power derived from Article III).

Checks upon the Judiciary

Congress has power to impeach and remove Federal judges for adequate cause (Article I, Section 3; Article II, Section 4; Article III, Section 1).

Congress has power to appropriate funds for operation of the judicial branch (Article I, Section 8).

Congress has power to determine the number of judges and the size of Federal courts (Article III, Section 1).

Congress has power to regulate the original jurisdiction of inferior Federal courts and the appellate jurisdiction of all Federal courts (Article III, Sections 1 and 22).

The President has power to appoint Federal judges (Article II, Section 2).

These checks upon the powers of all three major branches of the Federal government, if carried to extremes, might make it difficult to carry on government at all. This the Framers understood. So they checked or balanced the checks-and-balances system itself by adding to the Constitution provisions to protect each branch from interference with its operations by another branch, and to protect the members of each branch from threats and reprisals. Here are the major protective provisions:

The Independence of Congress

Congress is authorized to assemble annually, and the President may not dissolve a Congress (Article I, Section 4).

Both houses of Congress have the power to judge the elections, returns, and qualifications of their own members (Article I, Section 5).

Only the Congress can determine the rules for its proceedings, punish its members for disorderly behavior, and expel its members (Article I, Section 5).

Members of Congress are privileged from arrest while Congress is in session, except for cases of treason, felony, and breach of the peace (Article I, Section 6).

Members of Congress are exempt from arrest, prosecution, or lawsuit for what they may say on the floors of Congress or in committee—even if their remarks are slanderous or seditious (Article I, Section 6).

The Independence of the President

The President is chosen by electors, and is not appointed by the Congress (Article II, Section 1).

Congress may not raise or lower the President's salary while he is in office (Article II, Section 1).

Only the President may conduct diplomacy with foreign governments and extend diplomatic recognition (Article II, Section 3).

The President is given unrestricted power to remove all executive officers and Senate approval is not required (an unspecified power derived from Article II, Section 3).

The Independence of the Judiciary

Congress may not reduce the salary of a Federal judge while he holds office (Article III, Section 1).

Congress may not diminish the original jurisdiction of the Supreme Court (an unspecified restriction derived from Article III, Section 2).

Congress may not abolish the Supreme Court or the office of Chief Justice (Article III, Section 1; Article I, Section 3).

Summary and Review

All of this detail may seem somewhat confusing, so a summary and review of this information about the separation of powers and about checks and balances should be helpful.

The Framers understood, chiefly from the experience of the States and the general government under the Articles of Confederation, that only through a system of checks and balances might the separation of powers be maintained. So the Constitution contains the ingenious network of checks and protections previously described.

These checks and balances were devised to enable each branch to resist such invasions of their proper authority. They enabled each branch to exert some direct control over the other branches. This the Framers accomplished by *overlapping* some of the functions of the Federal government, so that each branch might play some part—though merely a limited part—in the exercise of the other branches' functions.

Thus the Congress was empowered to exercise a degree of executive and judicial power. The Senate, for example, actually exercises an executive function when it participates in the appointment and treaty-making processes; and both houses of Congress exercise a judicial power when they impeach and remove a judge or an executive official from office. A legislative check on the judiciary is established by the power of Congress to determine the size of the courts and to limit the appellate jurisdiction of both the Supreme Court and inferior Federal courts.

Similarly, the executive exercises some legislative powers. The presidential veto, for example, is a legislative power that permits the President to take part in the law-making process. The President exercises a judicial power, on the other hand, when he pardons a person convicted of a Federal crime.

The judiciary, in turn, possesses legislative power through judicial review, and enjoys some executive power through its authority to appoint clerks and other court personnel.

Each branch, it may be seen, is independent of the others, although the independence they possess is not absolute.

Such is the theory of the separation of powers as understood and applied in 1787. Madison and other Framers expected quarrels to break out from time to time between branches of government. Indeed, they counted on such quarrels. Why? Because jealousy and hostility among the chief divisions of the Federal government would prevent the three branches from combining in any scheme to infringe upon the powers of the several States or to diminish the liberties of citizens.

In other words, Madison and his colleagues meant to avert the rise of an oligarchy (the rule of a few rich and powerful men) or of a tyrant (an unlawful single ruler) by making it almost impossible for any man or faction to secure the simultaneous cooperation of the legislative, executive, and judicial branches. Thus the Constitution would be guarded against subversion by the ambition and the vanity of the men who respectively belonged to the legislature, the executive force, and the body of judges. "Ambition would counteract ambition," as Madison put it.

The principal men in Congress would tend to resent the power of the presidency and to assert the claims of Senate or House to national leadership. The President, for his part, would cherish his powers jealously and would vigorously repel attempts of the Congress to dictate executive policies. And the Supreme Court would maintain a stern defense of its prerogatives, rebuking both Congress and President from time to time.

Separation of Powers: A Critical Evaluation

Since 1789, when the First Congress convened, the executive branch has tended to grow in power, even during the administration of Presidents who professed to respect the legislative branch.

The judiciary, ever since John Marshall became Chief Justice in 1801, has tended to be much more assertive of its powers than the Framers had expected. (Alexander Hamilton, writing in *The Federalist*, assured his readers that the Supreme Court, "the weakest of the three branches," could take "no active resolution whatever.") Today, Federal courts examine and review Congressional enactments and presidential orders far more frequently than the Framers imagined.

Congress, though meddling little with the judiciary since the first decade of the nineteenth century, has bitterly attacked Presidents from time to time, often out of partisan motives. What is even more destructive of balanced government, Congress has delegated to a multitude of Federal regulatory commissions and administrative bodies major powers that, under separation of powers teaching, ought to be retained jealously within Congress. Indeed, some critics argue that it is chiefly from governmental commissions and agencies that the principal threat to citizens' rights comes today—not from old-fangled oligarchs and tyrants.

Over the years, certain misconceptions about the American doctrine of separation of powers, and criticisms of the system, have surfaced from time to time in writings on American politics. The assumption is often made, for example, that the Constitution established three "equal" or three "coordinate" branches of government. Such is not the case. As Madison observed in *Federalist* No. 51, "it is not possible to give to each department an equal power of self-defense. In republican government, the legislative authority necessarily predominates." Experience under the State constitutions had shown, he explained in *Federalist* No. 48, that "The legislative department is everywhere extending the sphere of its activity, and drawing all power into its impetuous vortex."

Moreover, the constitutional powers of Congress are "more extensive and less susceptible to precise limits," and Congress "can, with the greater facility, mask, under complicated and indirect measures, the encroachments which it makes on the coordinate departments." The executive power, on the other hand, is "restrained within a narrower compass," and the judiciary's powers are even more uncertain. "Projects of usurpation by either of these departments would immediately betray and defeat themselves." Not to be overlooked, added Madison, is the fact that "the legislative department alone has access to the pockets of the people," which gives it the power to reward and punish those who serve in the other branches.

In theory, at least, Congress has the constitutional authority to lord over the other branches. An angry House and Senate might, if it wished, reduce the entire Federal Judiciary down to one Supreme Court, with only the Chief Justice, exercising only limited, original jurisdiction. A legislative assault on the executive branch would be equally devastating, leaving the President with no cabinet, no departments, no army or navy, and no funds. All of this is possible because the other branches rely almost exclusively on Congressional statutes for their operation.

There are numerous examples of legislative encroachment, as witnessed, for example, by the impeachment of President Andrew Johnson. There have also been periods of legislative ascendancy, which Woodrow Wilson complained of in his book, *Congressional Government*. Throughout most of American history, however, Congress has probably exercised more restraint than the Framers anticipated. That an unruly Congress always has the potential of tyrannizing over other branches is a factor that should always be kept in mind, however; and it should also be emphasized that the main reason for the separation of powers and checks and balances system, as the Framers saw the problem, was to protect the executive and judicial branches against the legislative. This is not to say that the Framers overlooked the possibility that the President or the Supreme Court might also abuse their powers, but merely that in 1787 they seemed to lack the inclination and capacity.

It is true, of course, that all three branches have become far more powerful in the twentieth century than the Framers ever thought possible. The growth of Federal power, however, has been largely at the expense of the States, and the growth of presidential and judicial power has come about through the acquiescence or approval of Congress. The Congress is still the fountainhead of power, and the hub of the system. In the final analysis, there is practically no constitutional controversy or problem that Congress (and to a lesser extent the States through the initiation of amendments) cannot ultimately resolve, if it has the *will* to do it. Neither the President nor the courts can make this claim. Constitutionally speaking, therefore, Congress is the most powerful branch, but in practice it does not always assert itself and at times may even be overshadowed by the President or the Supreme Court.

Today, as in 1787, the separation of powers doctrine is venerated and praised as the mainstay of the Constitution. It has never been targeted for attack by any political reform movement and has traditionally enjoyed a broad consensus of support among the American people. But it has not been immune from criticism. From time to time there have been outcries of disappointment and frustration because the American political process does not always respond immediately to every call for action. Some critics have charged that separation of powers weakens the Federal government, and that the built-in tension and conflict among the branches produces political paralysis. In today's world, they argue, where the United States is embroiled in one global crisis after another in the seemingly endless struggle against terrorism and war, a more harmonious relationship between the President and Congress would allow the United States to act with greater certainty and dispatch.

It is true, of course, that the separation of powers slows the pace of government. More than once the United States Senate has blocked a treaty signed by the President. Congress and the President share the war and diplomatic powers and are not always of one mind on military and foreign policy. The Supreme Court has occasionally intervened, as in 1952, when the Justices ruled in the famous Steel Seizure Case that President Truman had exceeded his powers when he endeavored to prevent a nationwide strike in the steel industry by taking possession of the mills.

Speed, however, is not a virtue in the political process crafted by the Framers. The system is intended to promote careful deliberation, which is time-consuming, to be sure, but necessary to build a consensus so that the decision finally made has broad support. The Framers believed also that the deliberative process increases the likelihood that the policy finally adopted will be a wise one. Hasty decisions are often foolish decisions. Debate and negotiation have the salutary effect of cooling tempers and correcting mistaken views and false impressions. Compromise means

Andy Johnson, Tribune of the People.

Determined to resist the encroachments of Congress upon executive prerogatives and to protect the rights of the States after assuming the presidency in 1865, Andrew Johnson frequently clashed with the Radical Republicans over constitutional issues. This political cartoon by a Republican critic depicts "Andy Johnson, Tribune of the People," as a long-eared charlatan for having vetoed the Civil Rights Act of 1866. One of the coachmen compares Johnson with Mark Antony, who "was continually blowing before the People about his great love for the Constitution," all the while he was "conspiring with Caesar for the overthrow of the Republic." (Courtesy of the Library of Congress.)

that a variety of conflicting interests have some voice in public affairs; and without this complicated check and balance system, minorities of every description—property holders, rural folk, religious sects, racial and ethnic groups, certain occupations and professions, whole regions of the country—would be at the mercy of an unrestrained Congress, President, or Supreme Court. Separation of powers protects the American citizen against overbearing majorities as well as entrenched minorities.

The claim that separation of powers weakens government is equally unpersuasive. It is abundantly clear from an examination of the Constitution and a review of *The Federalist* that the national government was to be a strong government, with the power to fulfill the obligations placed upon it and the means to carry out those obligations. Separation of powers was designed not to emasculate the powers of government, but to give some assurance that they would not be exercised in an oppressive way. Preventing the aggrandizement, usurpation, and abuse of power is not the same as preventing the exercise of lawful power. There is no pattern of evidence that the separation of powers has prevented the United States from dealing with foreign aggression or domestic crises in a timely and efficient manner. Of the many examples that have been offered in defense of separation of powers, however, none is more convincing than the twentieth-century spectacle of totalist governments misruling more than half the world. The concentration of ruthless power in the hands of fanatical and half-mad rulers—often in the name of "liberation" or "people's democracy"—has resulted in a degree of human misery that even the worst government of the eighteenth century would have regarded with horror.

Separation of Powers at the Crossroads

The complex task of directing the affairs of a modern industrial state, with a large and growing population placing increased demands on government, has had a negative effect on separation of powers and the rule of law. So too has America's rise to power as the defender of the free world, which has changed the role of the President and what is expected of the office, and greatly enlarged his war and diplomatic powers.

Of the many factors which have contributed to the decline of separation of powers, however, the massive delegation of legislative powers by Congress to executive agencies and independent regulatory commissions has probably done the most to change the relationship among the branches and the law-making function of government. By delegation of powers is meant the transfer of the decision-making authority from one branch of the government to another. Independent regulatory commissions, such as the Federal Trade Commission, the Federal Communications Commission, or the Securities and Exchange Commission, are quasi-legislative, quasi-executive, and quasi-judicial bodies that lie outside the separation of powers system. The first such commission was the Interstate Commerce Commission, established in 1886; but most are primarily a phenomenon of the twentieth century. Many were created during the New Deal. They are independent in the sense that they are largely free of executive control. The President may appoint the members, but that is about the extent of his influence; and Congress may even prescribe and restrict the causes for which the President may remove them from office. These commissions are quasi-legislative in the sense that Congress has given them a portion of its own law-making authority so they can regulate certain activities, largely commercial in nature, such as the stock market, the licensing of radio and television broadcasting, and various trade practices. Regulations adopted by the commissions are treated as laws and enforced by the commissions. Independent regulatory commissions exercise a quasi-judicial function in the sense that affected parties may challenge their rulings in administrative proceedings, before administrative law judges, who conduct hearings much like a court of law. Administrative decisions are subject to review by the regular courts.

These independent boards, agencies, and commissions—and there are more than fifty today—are sometimes called "the headless fourth branch of government." The basic purpose in placing these hybrid organizations outside the regular executive departments was to keep them "out of politics," the idea being that they would perform the regulatory function in a more non-partisan manner, and would more likely be fair and reasonable, if they were free of presidential pressures and controls. But experience has shown that the commissions are not entirely independent of politics or immune from outside pressures. Special interest groups lobby the commissions just as they seek to influence public policy decisions in Congress and the executive branch. Thus corporations, manufacturers, labor organizations, and a variety of public interest groups, for example, all descend not only on the committees in Congress and the Department of Labor in order to advance their interests, but also on the National Labor Relations Board. Labor-related issues may also come before other commissions, legislative committees, and executive agencies. At the State level, there are fifty additional governments, all regulating through their own courts and departments of labor some aspect of labor-management relations, such as workers' compensation, while at the same time implementing Federal policies. It is an enormously complex affair, requiring considerable effort, expense, and expertise. The result is the establishment of an enormous bureaucracy.

As originally conceived, these independent regulatory commissions were thought to be necessary as a means of introducing order into a highly industrialized nation, providing uniform controls, eliminating monopolistic practices, and in general improving health, safety, and welfare. In a very emphatic way, they represented a rejection of the *laissez-faire* approach to economic activity, prevalent in the nineteenth century, which frowned on government interference in a free market economy and took the position that all members of society, and the nation at large, would enjoy greater prosperity and abundance if government refrained from meddling too much in the economy and allowed the laws of supply and demand to work naturally.

The wisdom of government regulation, and the extent to which the natural forces of the market should be controlled, are questions of great interest and debate. Our purpose here, however, is to evaluate the effect the creation of these independent commissions has had on the separation of powers system. The legislative powers of the Federal government, we recall, are delegated powers. They were originally in the possession of the States, which delegated them to Congress. An ancient maxim of the separation of powers doctrine holds that "that which has been delegated cannot be redelegated." A separation of powers would not long exist if Congress were free to transfer its delegated powers to another branch. Likewise, the system would not function properly if Congress could delegate its powers back to the States, or to the people at large. Although under some State constitutions the citizens may initiate legislation through what is called the "initiative," or repeal laws through "referendum," such practices circumventing the legislature are prohibited under the United States Constitution. They constitute an unconstitutional delegation of legislative power.

How, then, has it been possible for Congress to delegate its legislative powers to independent regulatory commissions (and executive agencies as well)? In addressing this issue, the courts have adopted the view that Congress may empower such commissions to issue rules and regulations as long as the authorizing statute provides guidelines for the regulators. The guidelines must be sufficiently explicit, however, so as to prevent the use of arbitrary discretion in the rule-making process. In general, the courts are satisfied that there has been no improper delegation if the regulation in question seems to reflect the will of Congress and the commission has merely "filled in the administrative details" for Congress.

In practice, the courts have tended to interpret these restrictions somewhat loosely by giving substantial leeway to the commissions to "fill in the details" of broadly stated congressional policies. Thus the commissions are, in effect, often making the law, even though the commissioners themselves are not elected to office and are not accountable for their actions to the electorate—or in many respects even to Congress.

The effect of all this on the American constitutional system is far-reaching. In the first place, it contributes to the decline of federalism, and has resulted in the transfer of vast amounts of State power to the Federal bureaucracy. The subject of labor relations is just one of many areas of public policy that could be cited to illustrate the problem. Among the delegated powers of Congress in Article I, Section 8 of the Constitution, there is no mention of labor, and throughout most of American history the power to deal with such issues as labor strikes, the right to organize unions, working conditions, wages and hours, and the problem of child labor was left to the States. Early in the twentieth century, however, Congress began claiming the right to regulate labor under the Commerce Clause. The Supreme Court at first resisted these claims on the ground that labor was not commerce as such and was therefore beyond the reach of Federal authority. During the New Deal period, however, the Court reversed its stand, and since that time the entire field of labor-management relations has been subject to Federal regulation and control.

Having taken command of the situation, the Congress quickly discovered that the subject was far too complex and time consuming for busy members of the House and Senate, and that it would be necessary, therefore, to turn the whole matter over to an independent regulatory commission. This commission would carry out the will of Congress through general statutes, but would be responsible for the day-to-day enforcement of the laws through the issuance of rules and regulations and the adjudication of disputes arising under them. Thus was born the National Labor Relations Board in 1935, which is actually neither the first nor the only commission dealing with labor problems. In large measure, however, the NLRB is now the repository of power that once belonged to the States.

In the second place, the creation of the NLRB and other such commissions, as previously noted, has tended to weaken separation of powers. It is simply humanly impossible for members of Congress to monitor the activities of all these commissions, which employ millions of people and issue thousands of highly technical regulations annually. Important policy decisions are thus actually made on a routine basis by Federal employees, many anonymous, who enjoy tenure under the Civil Service Act and cannot easily be removed from office or controlled by Congress.

The existence of so many independent commissions exercising so much power also frustrates the executive branch. The President has no say in their operation, yet is responsible for the general enforcement of the laws. Executive unity and uniformity of policy may also suffer if the President is pursuing one policy and a commission is moving in another direction. Since members of these commissions serve staggered terms, the President may even find that certain commissioners appointed by a previous President are actively working against him to undermine his programs.

Likewise, the courts have experienced difficulty in restraining overzealous regulators who may have exceeded their authority. Administrative decisions handed down by the commissions are subject to review by the regular courts. But only a small percentage are actually adjudicated because there are not enough judges or courts to handle the great volume of disputes. Much of what is actually decided in the commissions is never reviewed by the judges. Moreover, many of the rules and regulations in question are highly technical or scientific in nature, and beyond the range of judicial expertise. This further weakens the ability of the courts to superintend the commissions.

Critics argue that Congress, having decided it wants to regulate everything, actually regulates nothing, and has simply delegated enormous power to the bureaucracy. This is an overstatement, of course, but there is some truth to the charge. Keeping an eye on the commissions and holding them accountable is an enormous undertaking; and there is no question that at least in some respects these commissions are functioning as independent law-making bodies. With its limited time and limited resources, Congress does not even have the opportunity to debate many of the policies adopted by the commissions, let alone scrutinize them.

In response to these criticisms, it is argued nevertheless that the economic and technological complexities of modern America are so great that Americans have little choice but to accept these commissions as necessary and essential, lest there be chaos and disorder. No doubt there is some truth to this as well, suggesting that a strict separation of powers, as understood by the Framers, may not be altogether possible nowadays, and that the system can best be maintained by continually questioning the need for each commission, re-evaluating its authority and powers, and vigilantly guarding against excessive delegation of power.

Finally, it must always be borne in mind that the doctrine of the separation of powers is an integral part of the rule of law. When commissioners, agency heads, and their subordinates issue administrative rules and regulations that have the force of law, they are making laws and functioning as legislators. When they enforce these regulations, and, for example, take administrative action by denying disability benefits to a veteran whose injuries, in the judgment of the regulators, are not war-related, they are exercising an executive function. And when they adjudicate claims, as in the case of a trucking firm, challenging the Interstate Commerce Commission's refusal to grant a license, they are exercising a judicial function. In a sense, then, an independent regulatory commission is almost a government unto itself, performing all the functions of government in contravention of the separation of powers. Because it is impossible to fix the limits of administrative discretion and to spell out in detail all of the circumstances in which the regulators may exercise their individual judgment, there is the constant danger that rule of law may be supplanted by rule of men. Indeed, the separation of powers doctrine is based on the premise that rule of law cannot be attained if all of the functions of government are concentrated in the same hands.

Abuses in administrative discretion may be and frequently are brought to the attention of Congress, but the massive outpouring of regulations and all of the individual complaints far exceed the capacity of Congress for corrective action. In those rare instances where a legislator is able to focus on a particular case, there is often little that can be done to correct the problem from a practical standpoint. Congress, and certainly not an individual member, has no authority to remove an arrogant bureaucrat from office, and the President's limited power of removal is almost equally feeble, as demonstrated by the fact that only a small handful of commissioners have been forced out of office; and their subordinates are immune from reprisal or removal. Congress is always free, of course, to overturn administrative rulings by corrective legislation, but again, this is an arduous chore that seldom is attempted, and an option that is not usually available in the case of individual wrongdoings.

In the final analysis, it must also be admitted that the creation of so many independent regulatory commissions has also weakened the republican principle of representative government and the ideal of democratic government in which the decision-makers are held politically accountable to the voters for their actions. Judicial review of administrative decisions, which can address some of the worst abuses of power, offers the hope that *legal* accountability may nevertheless be upheld. "What is required under the rule of law," notes Friedrich A. Hayek in his great classic *The Constitution of Liberty*, "is that a court should have the power to decide whether the law [passed by Congress] provided for a particular action that an administrator has taken. In other words, in all instances where administrative action interferes with the private sphere of the individual, the courts must have the power to decide not only whether a particular action was [within the law], but whether the substance of the administrative decision was such as the law demanded. It is only if this is the case that administrative discretion is precluded."

C. The Rule of Law

The America of 1787 inherited from medieval England the concept of rule of law, sometimes expressed as "a government of laws, not of men."

One may trace the rise of this principle in English history all the way back to the signing of Magna Charta in the year 1215, when King John found it necessary to guarantee his obedience to English laws. For that matter, medieval English writers on law derived their understanding of the rule of law from ancient Roman jurisprudence.

"The king himself ought not to be under man but under God, and under the Law, because the Law makes the king. Therefore let the king render back to the Law what the Law gives him, namely, dominion and power; for there is no king where will, and not Law, wields dominion." So wrote Henry de Bracton, "the father of English law," about the year 1260, during the reign of Henry III. This teaching that law is superior to human rulers has run consistently through English politics and jurisprudence all the way down the centuries. It was rather belligerently asserted from time to time by the English colonies in North America.

This doctrine that no man is above the law applied not only to kings but also to legislative bodies and judges. Sir Edward Coke, we saw earlier, fiercely resisted not only attempts by King James I to interpret the law for himself but also Acts of Parliament that contravened the common law. Citing Bracton as an authority, he asserted that "the king must not be under any man, but under God and the law." In *Dr. Bonham's Case* (1610), Coke laid down the principle of judicial review, claiming that judges had a right, when interpreting Acts of Parliament, to declare them null and void if they conflicted with established principles of law and justice. "And it appears in our books," said Coke, "that in many cases, the common law will control Acts of Parliament, and sometimes adjudge them to be utterly void; for when an Act of Parliament is against common right and reason, or repugnant, or impossible to be performed, the common law will control it, and adjudge such an Act to be void."

That the English had turned their backs on their own tradition and respect for rule of law was the principal grievance of American colonial leaders. In his famous pamphlet *The Rights of the British Colonies Asserted and Proved* (1764), James Otis wrote:

> To say the Parliament is absolute and arbitrary, is a contradiction. The Parliament cannot make 2 and 2 [equal] 5. . . . Parliaments are in all cases to *declare* what is good for the whole; but it is not the *declaration* of parliament that makes it so. There must be in every instance a higher

> authority—God. Should an act of parliament be against any of *His* nat-
> ural laws, which are *immutably* true, *their* declaration would be contrary
> to eternal truth, equity and justice, and consequently void.

Similar arguments were made by the State supreme court judges after
1776. Their attempts to nullify legislative enactments through the power
of judicial review were largely unsuccessful, however, because most early
State constitutions, like the English Constitution, followed the doctrine of
legislative supremacy. Acts passed by the State legislatures were expected
to conform to the State constitutions. But there were no provisions calling
for the supremacy of the State's constitution over laws passed by the legislature should the judges decide that a law conflicted with the State's constitution. Thus, the absence of a supremacy clause in these State constitutions rendered the power of judicial review weak and ineffective.

The Federal Constitution of 1787 drastically changed the concept of
constitutional government by introducing the principle of constitutional
supremacy. Article VI declared that "This Constitution . . . Shall be the
supreme law of the land." Laws passed by Congress, though supreme
in relation to State constitutions and State laws, were ranked below the
Constitution. Indeed, Article VI explicitly stated that such laws must
conform to, and be made in pursuance of, the Constitution. Noting the
significance of the Supremacy Clause, Chief Justice John Marshall held in
the famous case of *Marbury v. Madison* (1803) that an Act of Congress contrary to the Constitution was not law:

> [I]n declaring what shall be the supreme law of the land, the Constitu-
> tion is first mentioned; and not the laws of the United States generally,
> but those only which shall be made in pursuance of the Constitution,
> have that rank.

It may thus be seen that the American Constitution and the power of
judicial review are an extension of rule of law. The Constitution is law,
the highest law, and the President, Congress, and the Federal Judiciary
are bound by its terms. A government of laws and not of men is, then,
the underlying principle of the American political and legal system.

This means that no person, however powerful or talented, can be allowed to act as if he were superior to the law of the land. Public decisions
must be made upon the basis of law, and the laws must be general rules

that everybody obeys, including those who make and enforce the law. A law that violates the Constitution is not a law and is not, therefore, enforced. This was the principle that Marshall followed in *Marbury v. Madison*. Likewise, rule of law means equality before the law. A law that singles out certain people for discriminatory treatment, or is so vague and uncertain that one cannot know what it requires, will not be treated as a law.

Rule of law, then, is not rule of *the* law, but a doctrine concerning what the law *ought* to be—a set of standards, in other words, to which the laws should conform. Merely because a tyrant refers to his commands and arbitrary rulings as "laws" does not make them so. The test is not what the rule is called, but whether the rule is general, known, and certain; and also whether it is prospective (applying to future conduct) and is applied equally. These are the essential attributes of good laws—laws that *restrain* but do not *coerce*, and give each individual sufficient room to be a thinking and valuing person, and to carry out his own plans and designs. This does not mean that the individual is free to do as he pleases; for liberty is not license. As the Framers knew well, absolute freedom would be the end of freedom, making it impossible for society to be orderly, safe from crime, secure from foreign attack, and effectively responsive to the physical, material, and spiritual needs of its members. Under God, said the exponents of the rule of law, the law governs us; it is not by mere men that we ought to be governed; we can appeal from the whims and vagaries of human rulers to the unchanging law.

Though this is a grand principle of justice, often it is difficult to apply in practice. Passion, prejudice, and special interest sometimes determine the decisions of courts of law; judges, after all, are fallible human beings. As the Virginia orator John Randolph of Roanoke remarked sardonically during the 1820s, to say "laws, not men," is rather like saying "marriage, not women": the two cannot well be separated.

Yet the Framers at Philadelphia aspired to create a Federal government in which rule of law would prevail and men in power would be so restrained that they might not ignore or flout the law of the land. The Supreme Court of the United States was intended to be a watchdog of the Constitution which might guard the purity of the law and forcefully point out evasions or violations of the law by the other branches of government or by men in public office.

The Framers knew, too, the need for ensuring that the President of the

United States, whose office they had established near the end of the Convention, would be under the law—not a law unto himself. The President's chief responsibility, in fact, is to enforce and uphold the law, and to "take care that the laws be faithfully executed." Whereas the members of Congress and the Federal Judiciary, and other Federal and State officials, all take an oath "to support this Constitution" (Article VI, Clause 3), the President—and the President alone—swears on the Bible (or affirms) that he will "preserve, protect and defend the Constitution" (Article II, Section 1, Clause 8).

Thus in the final analysis the nation looks to the President as the person ultimately responsible for upholding the rule of law and the supremacy of the Constitution. By making him Commander-in-Chief of the armed forces and by giving him the power to supervise the heads of the various departments of the executive branch, the Constitution also confers upon the President the means by which he may fulfill his law enforcement responsibilities.

By and large, America has enjoyed rule of law, not of men. No President of the United States has ever tried to make himself dictator or to extend his term of office unlawfully. Martial law—that is, a suspension of the law and the administration of justice by military authorities in times of war, rebellion, and disorder—has never been declared nationwide. No party or faction has ever seized control of the Federal government by force or violence. The Constitution of the United States has never been suspended or successfully defied on a large scale. Thus the rule of law has usually governed the country since 1787—a record true of very few other countries of the world.

The Basic Principles of the American Constitution

Federalism, separation of powers, and rule of law are the heart of the American Constitution. But there are other fundamental principles of the system as well, all of which contribute significantly toward the achievement of liberty, order, and justice. Viewing the Constitution as a whole, as the Framers perceived it, we observe that its essential features include the following:

First, the Constitution is based on the belief that the only legitimate

Daniel Webster Addressing the Senate, 1850.

One of the most remarkable debates ever staged in Congress occurred in March 1850 over the slavery question. This was the last joint appearance on the public stage of that great triumvirate, Henry Clay, Daniel Webster, and John C. Calhoun. Webster advocated compromise to save the Union, and his plea for moderation was heeded.

In this extraordinary picture, it is possible to identify each member because the artist used photographs to create an exact likeness. Webster is standing. To his left (front row, bottom right) is Stephen A. Douglas. Clay is directly behind Webster's uplifted hand, almost seeming to stare at the back of it. Calhoun is directly behind the fourth member (front row, left to right), and beside him, to his right, is Jefferson Davis. (Courtesy of the Library of Congress.)

constitution is that which originates with, and is controlled by, the people. Thus a constitution is more than a body of substantive rules and principles. As Thomas Paine wrote, "A constitution is not the act of a government, but of a *people* constituting a government, and a government without a constitution is power without right." This principle is declared in the Preamble of the Constitution, which proclaims that the Constitution is ordained and established not by the government, but by "We the People."

Second, the United States Constitution subscribes to the view that the government must in all respects be politically responsible both to the States and to the governed. This is achieved through the election and impeachment process, with only the members of the House of Representatives being directly accountable to the electorate. Though not directly represented, the States exercise some influence by virtue of the Electoral College, control of the franchise, and the amendment process. Prior to the adoption of the Seventeenth Amendment in 1913, the States were also able to protect their interests in some instances by virtue of the fact that members of the Senate were indirectly elected by State legislatures rather than directly by the people.

Third, the Constitution rested on the proposition that all constitutional government is by definition limited government. A constitution is a legal, not just a political limitation on government; it is considered by many the antithesis of arbitrary rule; its opposite is despotic government, the government of will instead of law. Parliamentary supremacy, identifying all law with legislation, is thus hostile to the American Constitution, which declares that the Constitution shall be the supreme law of the land.

Fourth, the Constitution embraced the view that in order to achieve limited government, the powers of government must be defined and distributed—that is, they must be enumerated, separated, and divided. A unitary and centralized government, or a government in which all the functions or functionaries were concentrated in a single office, was a government that invited despotism and would inevitably become tyrannical and corrupt. This tendency toward "tyranny in the head" might be prevented, or at least discouraged, through a separation of powers among the three branches of the Federal government, and a reservation to the

States of those powers that were not delegated to the Federal government.

Conversely, the Framers were also mindful that in order to be limited, it did not follow that government must also be weak. Too little power was as dangerous as too much, and if left unattended might produce "anarchy in the parts," or a state of disorder into which the man on the white horse would ride to forge tyranny out of chaos. The solution for avoiding these extremes of too much and too little power was to balance power and to balance liberty and order, allocating to the people and to each unit of government a share of the national sovereignty.

Fifth, the American Constitution was premised on the seemingly unassailable assumption that the rights and liberties of the people would be protected because the powers of government were limited, and that a separate declaration of rights would therefore be an unnecessary and superfluous statement of an obvious truth. Since the government of the United States was to be one of enumerated powers, it was not thought necessary by the Philadelphia delegates to include a bill of rights among the provisions of the Constitution. "If, among the powers conferred," explained Thomas Cooley in his famous treatise *Constitutional Limitations* (1871), "there was none which would authorize or empower the government to deprive the citizen of any of those fundamental rights which it is the object and duty of government to protect and defend, and to insure which is the sole purpose of a bill of rights, it was thought to be at least unimportant to insert negative clauses in that instrument, inhibiting the government from assuming any such powers, since the mere failure to confer them would leave all such powers beyond the sphere of its constitutional authority." In short, the Constitution itself was a bill of rights because it limited the power of the Federal government.

SUGGESTED READING

Herman V. Ames, ed., *State Documents on Federal Relations* (New York: Da Capo Press, 1970).

Walter H. Bennett, *American Theories of Federalism* (Tuscaloosa: University of Alabama Press, 1964).

Raoul Berger, *Federalism: The Founders' Design* (Norman: University of Oklahoma Press, 1987).

Joseph M. Bessette, ed., *Toward a More Perfect Union: Writings of Herbert J. Storing* (Washington, D.C.: The AEI Press, 1995).

Joseph M. Bessette and Jeffrey Tulis, *The Presidency in the Constitutional Order* (Baton Rouge: Louisiana State University Press, 1981).

James Bryce, *The American Commonwealth.* 2 vols. (Indianapolis: Liberty Fund, 1995).

George W. Carey, *In Defense of the Constitution* (Indianapolis: Liberty Fund, 1995).

George W. Carey, *The Federalist: Design for a Constitutional Republic* (Urbana: University of Illinois Press, 1989).

Edward S. Corwin, *The President: Office and Powers* (New York: New York University Press, 1957).

Martin Diamond, *The Founding of the Democratic Republic* (Itaska, Ill.: F. E. Peacock Publishers, 1981).

Robert A. Goldwin, ed., *A Nation of States. Essays on the American Federal System* (Chicago: Rand McNally, 1961).

Robert A. Goldwin and Art Kaufman, eds., *Separation of Powers: Does It Still Work?* (Washington, D.C.: American Enterprise Institute, 1986).

Alexander Hamilton, John Jay, and James Madison, *The Federalist*, ed. by George W. Carey and James McClellan (Dubuque, Iowa: Kendall-Hunt, 1989).

Alexander Hamilton and James Madison, *Letters of Pacificus and Helvidius.* Intro. by Richard Loss (Delmar, N.Y.: Scholars' Facsimiles and Reprints, 1976).

Friedrich A. Hayek, *The Constitution of Liberty* (Chicago: University of Chicago Press, 1960).

Eugene W. Hickok, Gary L. McDowell, and Philip Costopoulos, *Our Peculiar Security: The Written Constitution and Limited Government* (Lanham, Md.: Rowman & Littlefield, 1993).

Willmoore Kendall and George W. Carey, *The Basic Symbols of the American Political Tradition* (Baton Rouge: Louisiana State University Press, 1970).

Ralph Ketcham, *Framed for Posterity: The Enduring Philosophy of the Constitution* (Lawrence: University Press of Kansas, 1993).

Andrew C. McLaughlin, *The Foundations of American Constitutionalism* (New York: New York University Press, 1932).

Felix Morley, *Freedom and Federalism* (Indianapolis: Liberty Fund, 1981).

Ralph Rossum and Gary McDowell, *The American Founding* (Port Washington, N.Y.: Kennekat Press, 1981).

Ellis Sandoz, *A Government of Laws* (Baton Rouge: Louisiana State University Press, 1990).

William A. Schambra, ed., *As Far As Republican Principles Will Admit. Essays by Martin Diamond* (Washington, D.C.: The AEI Press, 1992).

Colleen A. Sheehan and Gary L. McDowell, eds., *Friends of the Constitution: Writings of the "Other" Federalists, 1787–1788* (Indianapolis: Liberty Fund, 1998).

Alexis de Tocqueville, *Democracy in America,* ed. by Phillips Bradley. 2 vols. (New York: Alfred A. Knopf, 1945).

M. J. C. Vile, *Constitutionalism and the Separation of Powers* (Indianapolis: Liberty Fund, 1998).

The Federalist No. 10

James Madison

November 22, 1787

To the People of the State of New York.

AMONG the numerous advantages promised by a well constructed Union, none deserves to be more accurately developed than its tendency to break and control the violence of faction. The friend of popular governments never finds himself so much alarmed for their character and fate as when he contemplates their propensity to this dangerous vice. He will not fail, therefore, to set a due value on any plan which, without violating the principles to which he is attached, provides a proper cure for it. The instability, injustice and confusion introduced into the public councils have, in truth, been the mortal diseases under which popular governments have every where perished, as they continue to be the favorite and fruitful topics from which the adversaries to liberty derive their most specious declamations. The valuable improvements made by the American Constitution on the popular models, both ancient and modern, cannot certainly be too much admired; but it would be an unwarrantable partiality to contend that they have as effectually obviated the danger on this side as was wished and expected. Complaints are every where heard from our most considerate and virtuous citizens, equally the friends of public and private faith, and of public and personal liberty, that our governments are too unstable, that the public good is disregarded in the conflicts of rival parties, and that measures are too often decided, not according to the rules of justice, and the rights of the minor party, but by the superior force of an interested and over-bearing majority. However anxiously we may wish that these complaints had no foundation, the evidence of known facts will not permit us to deny that they are in some degree true. It will be found indeed, on a candid review of our situation, that some of the distresses under which we labor have been erroneously charged on the operation of our governments; but it will be found, at the same time, that other causes will not alone account for many of our heaviest misfortunes; and particularly, for that prevailing and increasing distrust of public engagements, and alarm for private rights, which are echoed from one end of the continent to the other. These must be chiefly, if not wholly, effects of the unsteadiness and injustices, with which a factious spirit has tainted our public administration.

By a faction I understand a number of citizens, whether amounting to a majority or minority of the whole, who are united and actuated by some common impulse of passion, or of interest, adverse to the rights of other citizens, or to the permanent and aggregate interests of the community.

There are two methods of curing the mischiefs of faction: the one, by removing its causes; the other, by controlling its effects.

There are again two methods of removing the causes of faction: the one by destroying the liberty which is essential to its existence; the other, by giving to every citizen the same opinions, the same passions, and the same interests.

It could never be more truly said than of the first remedy that it is worse than the disease. Liberty is to faction what air is to fire, an aliment without which it instantly expires. But it could not be less folly to abolish liberty, which is essential to political life, because it nourishes faction, than it would be to wish the annihilation of air, which is essential to animal life, because it imparts to fire its destructive agency.

The second expedient is as impracticable, as the first would be unwise. As long as the reason of man continues fallible, and he is at liberty to exercise it, different opinions will be formed. As long as the connection subsists between his reason and his self-love, his opinions and his passions will have a reciprocal influence on each other; and the former will be objects to which the latter will attach themselves. The diversity in the faculties of men, from which the rights of property originate, is not less an insuperable obstacle to a uniformity of interests. The protection of these faculties is the first object of Government. From the protection of different and unequal faculties of acquiring property, the possession of different degrees and kinds of property immediately results: and from the influence of these on the sentiments and views of the respective proprietors ensues a division of the society into different interests and parties.

The latent causes of faction are thus sown in the nature of man; and we see them every where brought into different degrees of activity, according to the different circumstances of civil society. A zeal for different opinions concerning religion, concerning Government and many other points, as well of speculation as of practice; an attachment to different leaders ambitiously contending for pre-eminence and power; or to persons of other descriptions whose fortunes have been interesting to the human passions, have in turn divided mankind into parties, inflamed them with mutual animosity, and rendered them much more disposed to vex and oppress each other, than to co-operate for their common good. So strong is this propensity of mankind to fall into mutual animosities, that where no substantial occasion presents itself, the most frivolous and fanciful distinctions have been sufficient to kindle their unfriendly passions, and excite their most violent conflicts. But the most common and durable source of factions has been the various and unequal distribution of property. Those who hold, and those who are without property, have ever formed distinct interests in society. Those who are creditors, and those who are debtors, fall under a like discrimination. A landed interest, a manufacturing interest, a mercantile interest, a monied interest, with many lesser interests, grow up of necessity in civilized nations, and divide them into different classes, actuated by different sentiments and views. The regulation of these various and interfering interests forms the principal task of modern Legislation, and involves the spirit of party and faction in the necessary and ordinary operations of Government.

No man is allowed to be a judge in his own cause, because his interest would certainly bias his judgment, and, not improbably, corrupt his integrity. With equal, nay with greater reason, a body of men are unfit to be both judges and parties at the same time; yet, what are many of the most important acts of legislation but so many judicial determinations, not indeed concerning the rights of single persons, but concerning the rights of large bodies of citizens; and what are the different classes of legislators but advocates and parties to the causes which they determine? Is a law proposed concerning private debts? It is a question to which the creditors are parties on one side, and the debtors on the other. Justice ought to hold the balance between them. Yet the other parties are and must be themselves the judges; and the most numerous party, or, in other words, the most powerful faction, must be expected to prevail. Shall domestic manufactures be encouraged, and in what degree, by restrictions on foreign manufactures? are questions which would be differently decided by the landed and the manufacturing classes; and probably by neither, with a sole regard to justice and the public good. The apportionment of taxes on the various descriptions of property is an act which seems to require the most exact impartiality; yet, there is perhaps no legislative act in which greater opportunity and temptation are given to a predominant party, to trample on the rules of justice. Every shilling with which they overburden the inferior number is a shilling saved to their own pockets.

It is in vain to say that enlightened statesmen will be able to adjust these clashing interests and render them all subservient to the public good. Enlightened statesmen will not always be at the helm: Nor, in many cases, can such an adjustment be made at all, without taking into view indirect and remote considerations, which will rarely prevail over the immediate interest which one party may find in disregarding the rights of another, or the good of the whole.

The inference to which we are brought is that the *causes* of faction cannot be removed and that relief is only to be sought in the means of controlling its *effects*.

If a faction consists of less than a majority, relief is supplied by the republican principle, which enables the majority to defeat its sinister views by regular vote. It may clog the administration, it may convulse the society; but it will be unable to execute and mask its violence under the forms of the Constitution. When a majority is included in a faction, the form of popular government on the other hand enables it to sacrifice to its ruling passion or interest, both the public good and the rights of other citizens. To secure the public good, and private rights against the danger of such a faction, and at the same time to preserve the spirit and the form of popular government, is then the great object to which our enquiries are directed. Let me add that it is the great desideratum by which alone this form of government can be rescued from the opprobrium under which it has so long labored and be recommended to the esteem and adoption of mankind.

By what means is this object attainable? Evidently by one of two only. Either the existence of the same passion or interest in a majority at the same time must be prevented, or the majority, having such co-existent passion or interest, must be rendered, by their number and local situation, unable to concert and carry into effect schemes of oppression. If the impulse and the opportunity be suffered to coincide, we well know that neither moral nor religious motives can be relied on as an adequate control. They are not found to be such on the injustice and violence of individuals, and lose their efficacy in proportion to the number combined together, that is, in proportion as their efficacy becomes needful.

From this view of the subject, it may be concluded that a pure democracy, by which I mean, a society, consisting of a small number of citizens who assemble and administer the Government in person, can admit of no cure for the mischiefs of faction. A common passion or interest will, in almost every case, be felt by a majority of the whole; a communication and concert results from the form of Government itself; and there is nothing to check the inducements to sacrifice the weaker party, or an obnoxious individual. Hence it is, that such democracies have ever been spectacles of turbulence and contention; have ever been found incompatible with personal security, or the rights of property; and have in general been as short in their lives, as they have been violent in their deaths. Theoretic politicians, who have patronized this species of Government, have erroneously supposed, that by reducing mankind to a perfect equality in their political rights, they would, at the same time, be perfectly equalized and assimilated in their possessions, their opinions, and their passions.

A Republic, by which I mean a Government in which the scheme of representation takes place, opens a different prospect, and promises the cure for which we are seeking. Let us examine the points in which it varies from pure democracy, and we shall comprehend both the nature of the cure, and the efficacy which it must derive from the Union.

The two great points of difference between a Democracy and a Republic are: first, the delegation of the Government, in the latter, to a small number of citizens elected by the rest: secondly, the greater number of citizens and greater sphere of country over which the latter may be extended.

The effect of the first difference is, on the one hand, to refine and enlarge the public views by passing them through the medium of a chosen body of citizens, whose wisdom may best discern the true interest of their country and whose patriotism and love of justice will be least likely to sacrifice it to temporary or partial considerations. Under such a regulation, it may well happen that the public voice pronounced by the representatives of the people will be more consonant to the public good than if pronounced by the people themselves convened for the purpose. On the other hand, the effect may be inverted. Men of factious tempers, of local prejudices, or of sinister designs, may by intrigue, by corruption or by other means, first obtain the suffrages, and then betray the interests of the people. The question resulting is, whether small or extensive Republics are most favorable to the election of proper guardians of the public weal: and it is clearly decided in favor of the latter by two obvious considerations.

In the first place it is to be remarked that however small the Republic may be, the Representatives must be raised to a certain number in order to guard against the cabals of a few; and that however large it may be, they must be limited to a certain number in order to guard against the confusion of a multitude. Hence the number of Representatives in the two cases, not being in proportion to that of the Constituents, and being proportionally greatest in the small Republic, it follows, that if the proportion of fit characters be not less in the large than in the small Republic, the former will present a greater option, and consequently a greater probability of a fit choice.

In the next place, as each Representative will be chosen by a greater number of citizens in the large than in the small Republic, it will be more difficult for unworthy candidates to practice with success the vicious arts by which elections are too often carried; and the suffrages of the people being more free, will be more likely to center on men who possess the most attractive merit, and the most diffusive and established characters.

It must be confessed that in this, as in most other cases, there is a mean on both sides of which inconveniences will be found to lie. By enlarging too much the number of electors, you render the representative too little acquainted with all their local circumstances and lesser interests; as by reducing it too much, you render him unduly attached to these, and too little fit to comprehend and pursue great and national objects. The Federal Constitution forms a happy combination in this respect; the great and aggregate interests being referred to the national, the local and in particular to the State legislatures.

The other point of difference is the greater number of citizens and extent of territory which may be brought within the compass of Republican than of Democratic Government; and it is this circumstance principally which renders factious combinations less to be dreaded in the former than in the latter. The smaller the society, the fewer probably will be the distinct parties and interests composing it; the fewer the distinct parties and interests, the more frequently will a majority be found of the same party; and the smaller the number of individuals composing a majority, and the smaller the compass within which they are placed, the more easily will they concert and execute their plans of oppression. Extend the sphere, and you take in a greater variety of parties and interests; you make it less probable that a majority of the whole will have a common motive to invade the rights of other citizens; or if such a common motive exists, it will be more difficult for all who feel it to discover their own strength and to act in unison with each other. Besides other impediments, it may be remarked, that where there is a consciousness of unjust or dishonorable purposes, communication is always checked by distrust in proportion to the number whose concurrence is necessary.

Hence, it clearly appears that the same advantage which a Republic has over a Democracy in controlling the effects of faction is enjoyed by a large over a small Republic—is enjoyed by the Union over the States composing it. Does this advantage consist in the substitution of Representatives whose enlightened views and virtuous sentiments render them superior to local prejudices and to schemes of injustice? It will not be denied that the Representation of the Union will be most likely to possess these requisite endowments. Does it consist in the greater security afforded by a greater variety of parties, against the event of any one party being able to outnumber and oppress the rest? In an equal degree does the increased variety of parties comprised within the Union increase this security? Does it, in fine, consist in the greater obstacles opposed to the concert and accomplishment of the secret wishes of an unjust and interested majority? Here again the extent of the Union gives it the most palpable advantage.

The influence of factious leaders may kindle a flame within their particular States, but will be unable to spread a general conflagration through the other States. A religious sect may degenerate into a political faction in a part of the Confederacy; but the variety of sects dispersed over the entire face of it must secure the national Councils against any danger from that source. A rage for paper money, for an abolition of debts, for an equal division of property, or for any other improper or wicked project, will be less apt to pervade the whole body of the Union than a particular member of it, in the same proportion as such a malady is more likely to taint a particular county or district than an entire State.

In the extent and proper structure of the Union, therefore, we behold a Republican remedy for the diseases most incident to Republican Government. And according to the degree of pleasure and pride we feel in being Republicans ought to be our zeal in cherishing the spirit, and supporting the character of federalists.

PUBLIUS.

The Federalist No. 45

James Madison

January 26, 1788

To the People of the State of New York.

HAVING shown that no one of the powers transferred to the Federal Government is unnecessary or improper, the next question to be considered is whether the whole mass of them will be dangerous to the portion of authority left in the several States.

The adversaries to the plan of the Convention instead of considering in the first place what degree of power was absolutely necessary for the purposes of the Federal Government, have exhausted themselves in a secondary enquiry into the possible consequences of the proposed degree of power to the Governments of the particular States. But if the Union, as has been shown, be essential to the security of the people of America against foreign danger; if it be essential to their security against contentions and wars among the different States; if it be essential to guard them against those violent and oppressive factions which embitter the blessings of liberty, and against those military establishments which must gradually poison its very fountain; if, in a word the Union be essential to the happiness of the people of America, is it not preposterous to urge as an objection to a Government, without which the objects of the Union cannot be attained, that such a Government may derogate from the importance of the Governments of the individual States? Was, then, the American revolution effected, was the American confederacy formed, was the precious blood of thousands spilt, and the hard earned substance of millions lavished, not that the people of America should enjoy peace, liberty and safety, but that the Governments of the individual States, that particular municipal establishments, might enjoy a certain extent of power and be arrayed with certain dignities and attributes of sovereignty? We have heard of the impious doctrine in the old world that the people were made for kings, not kings for the people. Is the same doctrine to be revived in the new, in another shape—that the solid happiness of the people is to be sacrificed to the views of political institutions of a different form? It is too early for politicians to presume on our forgetting that the public good, the real welfare of the great body of the people, is the supreme object to be pursued; and that no form of Government whatever has any other value than as it may be fitted for the attainment of this object. Were the plan of the Convention adverse to the public happiness, my voice would be, Reject the plan. Were the Union itself inconsistent with the public happiness, it would be, Abolish the Union. In like manner, as far as the sovereignty of the States cannot be reconciled to the happiness of the people, the voice of every good citizen must be, Let the former be sacrificed to the latter. How far the sacrifice is necessary has been shown. How far the unsacrificed residue will be endangered is the question before us.

Several important considerations have been touched in the course of these papers, which discountenance the supposition that the operation of the Federal Government will by degrees prove fatal to the State Governments. The more I revolve the subject, the more fully I am persuaded that the balance is much more likely to be disturbed by the preponderancy of the last than of the first scale.

We have seen in all the examples of ancient and modern confederacies, the strongest tendency continually betraying itself in the members to despoil the general Government of its authorities, with a very ineffectual capacity in the latter to defend itself against the encroachments. Although in most of these examples the system has been so dissimilar from that under consideration as greatly to weaken any inference concerning the latter from the fate of the former, yet, as the States will retain under the proposed Constitution a very extensive portion of active sovereignty, the inference ought not to be wholly disregarded. In the Archæn league, it is probable that the federal head had a degree and species of power, which gave it a considerable likeness to the government framed by the Convention. The Lycian confederacy, as far as its principles and form are transmitted, must have borne a still greater analogy to it. Yet history does not inform us that either of them ever degenerated or tended to degenerate into one consolidated government. On the contrary, we know that the ruin of one of them proceeded from the incapacity of the federal authority to prevent the dissensions, and finally the disunion, of the subordinate authorities. These cases are the more worthy of our attention, as the external causes by which the component parts were pressed together, were much more numerous and powerful than in our case; and consequently, less powerful ligaments within would be sufficient to bind the members to the head, and to each other.

In the feudal system we have seen a similar propensity exemplified. Notwithstanding the want of proper sympathy in every instance between the local sovereigns and the people, and the sympathy in some instances between the general sovereign and the latter, it usually happened that the local sovereigns prevailed in the rivalship for encroachments. Had no external dangers enforced internal harmony and subordination, and particularly, had the local sovereigns possessed the affections of the people, the great kingdoms in Europe would at this time consist of as many independent princes as there were formerly feudatory barons.

The State Governments will have the advantage of the Federal Government, whether we compare them in respect to the immediate dependence of the one or the other; to the weight of personal influence which each side will possess; to the powers respectively vested in them; to the predilection and probable support of the people; to the disposition and faculty of resisting and frustrating the measures of each other.

The State Governments may be regarded as constituent and essential parts of the Federal Government; whilst the latter is nowise essential to the operation or organization of the former. Without the intervention of the State Legislatures, the President of the United States cannot be elected at all. They must in all cases have a great share in his appointment, and will perhaps in most cases of themselves determine it. The Senate will be elected absolutely and exclusively by the State Legislatures. Even the House of Representatives, though drawn immediately from the people, will be chosen very much under the influence of that class of men whose influence over the people obtains for themselves an election into the State Legislatures. Thus, each of the principal branches of the Federal Government will owe its existence more or less to the favor of the State Governments, and must consequently feel a dependence, which is much more likely to beget a disposition too obsequious than too overbearing towards them. On the other side, the component parts of the State Government will in no instance be indebted for their appointment to the direct agency of the Federal government, and very little, if at all, to the local influence of its members.

The number of individuals employed under the Constitution of the United States will be much smaller than the number employed under the particular States. There will consequently be less of personal influence on the side of the former than of the latter. The members of the legislative, executive and judiciary departments of thirteen and more States, the justices of the peace, officers of militia, ministerial officers of justice, with all the county, corporation, and town-officers, for three millions and more of people, intermixed and having particular acquaintance with every class and circle of people must exceed, beyond all proportion, both in number and influence, those of every description who will be employed in the administration of the federal system. Compare the members of the three great departments of the thirteen States, excluding from the judiciary department the justices of peace, with the members of the corresponding departments of the single Government of the Union; compare the militia officers of three millions of people with the military and marine officers of any establishment which is within the compass of probability, or, I may add, of possibility, and in this view alone, we may pronounce the advantage of the States to be decisive. If the Federal Government is to have collectors of revenue, the State Governments will have theirs also. And as those of the former will be principally on the sea-coast, and not very numerous, whilst those of the latter will be spread over the face of the country, and will be very numerous, the advantage in this view also lies on the same side. It is true that the Confederacy is to possess, and may exercise, the power of collecting internal as well as external taxes throughout the States; but it is probable that this power will not be resorted to, except for supplement purposes of revenue; that an option will then be given to the States to supply their quotas by previous collections of their own; and that the eventual collection under the immediate authority of the Union will generally be made by the officers, and according to the rules, appointed by the several States. Indeed it is extremely probable that in other instances, particularly in the organization of the judicial power, the officers of the States will be clothed with the correspondent authority of the Union. Should it happen, however, that separate collections of internal revenue should be appointed under the Federal Government, the influence of the whole number would not bear a comparison with that of the multitude of State officers in the opposite scale. Within every district to which a Federal collector would be allotted, there would not be less than thirty or forty, or even more, officers of different descriptions, and many of them persons of character and weight whose influence would lie on the side of the State.

The powers delegated by the proposed Constitution to the Federal Government are few and defined. Those which are to remain in the State Governments are numerous and indefinite. The former will be exercised principally on external objects, as war, peace, negotiation, and foreign commerce; with which last the power of taxation will, for the most part, be connected. The powers reserved to the several States will extend to all the objects which, in the ordinary course of affairs, concern the lives, liberties and properties of the people; and the internal order, improvement, and prosperity of the State.

The operations of the Federal Government will be most extensive and important in times of war and danger; those of the State Governments in times of peace and security. As the former periods will probably bear a small proportion to the latter, the State Governments will here enjoy another advantage over the Federal Government. The more adequate, indeed, the Federal powers may be rendered to the national defence, the less frequent will be those scenes of danger which might favor their ascendancy over the governments of the particular States.

If the new Constitution be examined with accuracy and candor, it will be found that the change which it proposes consists much less in the addition of NEW POWERS to the Union, than in the invigoration of its ORIGINAL POWERS. The regulation of commerce, it is true, is a new power; but that seems to be an addition which few oppose, and from which no apprehensions are entertained. The powers relating to war and peace, armies and fleets, treaties and finance, with the other more considerable powers, are all vested in the existing Congress by the Articles of Confederation. The proposed change does not enlarge these powers; it only substitutes a more effectual mode of administering them. The change relating to taxation may be regarded as the most important; and yet the present Congress have as complete authority to REQUIRE of the States indefinite supplies of money for the common defence and general welfare as the future Congress will have to require them of individual citizens; and the latter will be no more bound than the States themselves have been to pay the quotas respectively taxed on them. Had the States complied punctually with the Articles of Confederation, or could their compliance have been enforced by as peaceable means as may be used with success towards single persons, our past experience is very far from countenancing an opinion that the State Governments would have lost their constitutional powers, and have gradually undergone an entire consolidation. To maintain that such an event would have ensued would be to say at once that the existence of the State Governments is incompatible with any system whatever that accomplishes the essential purposes of the Union.

PUBLIUS.

The Federalist No. 47

James Madison

January 30, 1788

To the People of the State of New York.

HAVING reviewed the general form of the proposed government and the general mass of power allotted to it, I proceed to examine the particular structure of this government, and the distribution of this mass of power among its constituent parts.

One of the principal objections inculcated by the more respectable adversaries to the constitution is its supposed violation of the political maxim that the legislative, executive and judiciary departments ought to be separate and distinct. In the structure of the Federal government, no regard, it is said, seems to have been paid to this essential precaution in favor of liberty. The several departments of power are distributed and blended in such a manner as at once to destroy all symmetry and beauty of form, and to expose some of the essential parts of the edifice to the danger of being crushed by the disproportionate weight of other parts.

No political truth is certainly of greater intrinsic value or is stamped with the authority of more enlightened patrons of liberty than that on which the objection is founded. The accumulation of all powers legislative, executive and judiciary in the same hands, whether of one, a few or many, and whether hereditary, self appointed, or elective, may justly be pronounced the very definition of tyranny. Were the Federal Constitution therefore really chargeable with this accumulation of power or with a mixture of powers having a dangerous tendency to such an accumulation, no further arguments would be necessary to inspire a universal reprobation of the system. I persuade myself, however, that it will be made apparent to every one that the charge cannot be supported, and that the maxim on which it relies has been totally misconceived and misapplied. In order to form correct ideas on this important subject, it will be proper to investigate the sense in which the preservation of liberty requires that the three great departments of power should be separate and distinct.

The oracle who is always consulted and cited on this subject is the celebrated Montesquieu. If he be not the author of this invaluable precept in the science of politics, he has the merit at least of displaying and recommending it most effectually to the attention of mankind. Let us endeavour in the first place to ascertain his meaning on this point.

The British Constitution was to Montesquieu what Homer has been to the didactic writers on epic poetry. As the latter have considered the work of the immortal bard as the perfect model from which the principles and rules of the epic art were to be drawn, and by which all similar works were to be judged, so this great political critic appears to have viewed the constitution of England as the standard, or to use his own expression, as the mirror of political liberty; and to have delivered, in the form of elementary truths, the several characteristic principles of that particular system. That we may be sure, then, not to mistake his meaning in this case, let us recur to the source from which the maxim was drawn.

On the slightest view of the British Constitution we must perceive that the legislative, executive, and judiciary departments are by no means totally separate and distinct from each other. The executive magistrate forms an integral part of the legislative authority. He alone has the prerogative of making treaties with foreign sovereigns, which when made have, under certain limitations, the force of legislative acts. All the members of the judiciary department are appointed by him, can be removed by him on the address of the two Houses of Parliament, and form, when he pleases to consult them, one of his constitutional councils. One branch of the legislative department forms also a great constitutional council to the executive chief, as on another hand, it is the sole depository of judicial power in cases of impeachment, and is invested with the supreme appellate jurisdiction in all other cases. The judges, again, are so far connected with the legislative department as often to attend and participate in its deliberations, though not admitted to a legislative vote.

From these facts, by which Montesquieu was guided, it may clearly be inferred that in saying "there can be no liberty where the legislative and executive powers are united in the same person, or body of magistrates," or "if the power of judging be not separated from the legislative and executive powers," he did not mean that these departments ought to have no *partial agency* in, or no *control* over, the acts of each other. His meaning, as his own words import, and still more conclusively as illustrated by the example in his eye, can amount to no more than this, that where the *whole* power of one department is exercised by the same hands which possess the *whole* power of another department, the fundamental principles of a free constitution are subverted. This would have been the case in the constitution examined by him, if the King, who is the sole executive magistrate, had possessed also the complete legislative power, or the supreme administration of justice; or if the entire legislative body had possessed the supreme judiciary, or the supreme executive authority. This, however, is not among the vices of that constitution. The magistrate in whom the whole executive power resides cannot of himself make a law, though he can put a negative on every law, nor administer justice in person, though he has the appointment of those who do administer it. The judges can exercise no executive prerogative, though they are shoots from the executive stock; nor any legislature function, though they may be advised with by the legislative councils. The entire legislature can perform no judiciary act, though by the joint act of two of its branches, the judges may be removed from their offices, and though one of its branches is possessed of the judicial power in the last resort. The entire legislature, again, can exercise no executive prerogative, though one of its branches constitutes the supreme executive magistracy, and another, on the impeachment of a third, can try and condemn all the subordinate officers in the executive department.

The reasons on which Montesquieu grounds his maxim are a further demonstration of his meaning. "When the legislative and executive powers are united in the same person or body," says he, "there can be no liberty, because apprehensions may arise lest *the same* monarch or senate should *enact* tyrannical laws, to *execute* them in a tyrannical manner." Again, "Were the power of judging joined with the legislative, the life and liberty of the subject would be exposed to arbitrary control, for *the judge* would then be *the legislator.* Were it joined to the executive power, *the judge* might behave with all the violence of *an oppressor.*" Some of these reasons are more fully explained in other passages; but briefly stated as they are here, they sufficiently establish the meaning which we have put on this celebrated maxim of this celebrated author.

If we look into the constitutions of the several States we find that, notwithstanding the emphatical and, in some instances, the unqualified terms in which this axiom has been laid down, there is not a single instance in which the several departments of power have been kept absolutely separate and distinct. New Hampshire, whose constitution was the last formed, seems to have been fully aware of the impossibility and inexpediency of avoiding any mixture whatever of these departments, and has qualified the doctrine by declaring "that the legislative, executive and judiciary powers ought to be kept as separate from, and independent of each other *as the nature of a free government will admit; or as is consistent with that chain of connection, that binds the whole fabric of the constitution in one indissoluble bond of unity and amity.*" Her constitution accordingly mixes these departments in several respects. The Senate, which is a branch of the legislative department, is also a judicial tribunal for the trial of impeachments. The President, who is the head of the executive department, is the presiding member also of the Senate; and besides an equal vote in all cases, has a casting vote in case of a tie. The executive head is himself eventually elective every year by the legislative department; and his council is every year chosen by and from the members of the same department. Several of the officers of state are also appointed by the legislature. And the members of the judiciary department are appointed by the executive department.

The constitution of Massachusetts has observed a sufficient though less pointed caution in expressing this fundamental article of liberty. It declares "that the legislative department shall never exercise the executive and judicial powers, or either of them: The executive shall never exercise the legislative and judicial powers, or either of them: The judicial shall never exercise the legislative and executive powers, or either of them." This declaration corresponds precisely with the doctrine of Montesquieu, as it has been explained, and is not in a single point violated by the plan of the Convention. It goes no farther than to prohibit any one of the entire departments from exercising the powers of another department. In the very constitution to which it is prefixed, a partial mixture of powers has been admitted. The Executive Magistrate has a qualified negative on the legislative body; and the Senate, which is a part of the Legislature, is a court of impeachment for members both of the executive and judiciary departments. The members of the judiciary department, again, are appointable by the executive department, and removable by the same authority on the address of the two legislative branches. Lastly, a number of the officers of government are annually appointed by the legislative department. As the appointment to offices, particularly executive offices, is in its nature an executive function, the compilers of the Constitution have, in this last point at least, violated the rule established by themselves.

I pass over the constitutions of Rhode-Island and Connecticut, because they were formed prior to the revolution and even before the principle under examination had become an object of political attention.

The constitution of New-York contains no declaration on this subject, but appears very clearly to have been framed with an eye to the danger of improperly blending the different departments. It gives, nevertheless, to the executive magistrate a partial control over the legislative department, and what is more, gives a like control to the judiciary department, and even blends the executive and judiciary departments in the exercise of this control. In its council of appointment, members of the legislative are associated with the executive authority in the appointment of officers, both executive and judiciary. And its court for the trial of impeachments and correction of errors is to consist of one branch of the legislature and the principal members of the judiciary department.

The constitution of New-Jersey has blended the different powers of government more than any of the preceding. The governor, who is the executive magistrate, is appointed by the legislature; is chancellor and ordinary, or surrogate of the State; is a member of the Supreme Court of Appeals, and president, with a casting vote, of one of the legislative branches. The same legislative branch acts again as executive council to the governor, and with him constitutes the Court of Appeals. The members of the judiciary department are appointed by the legislative department, and removable by one branch of it, on the impeachment of the other.

According to the constitution of Pennsylvania, the president, who is head of the executive department, is annually elected by a vote in which the legislative department predominates. In conjunction with an executive council, he appoints the members of the judiciary department and forms a court of impeachments for trial of all officers, judiciary as well as executive. The judges of the Supreme Court and justices of the peace seem also to be removable by the legislature; and the executive power of pardoning, in certain cases, to be referred to the same department. The members of the executive council are made EX OFFICIO justices of peace throughout the State.

In Delaware, the chief executive magistrate is annually elected by the legislative department. The speakers of the two legislative branches are vice-presidents in the executive department. The executive chief, with six others, appointed three by each of the legislative branches, constitute the Supreme Court of Appeals; he is joined with the legislative department in the appointment of the other judges. Throughout the States it appears that the members of the legislature may at the same time be justices of the peace. In this State, the members of one branch of it are EX OFFICIO justices of peace; as are also the members of the executive council. The principal officers of the executive department are appointed by the legislative; and one branch of the latter forms a court of impeachments. All officers may be removed on address of the legislature.

Maryland has adopted the maxim in the most unqualified terms; declaring that the legislative, executive and judicial powers of government ought to be forever separate and distinct from each other. Her constitution, notwithstanding, makes the executive magistrate appointable by the legislative department; and the members of the judiciary by the executive department.

The language of Virginia is still more pointed on this subject. Her constitution declares "that the legislative, executive and judiciary departments, shall be separate and distinct; so that neither exercise the powers properly belonging to the other; nor shall any person exercise the powers of more than one of them at the same time; except that the justices of the county courts shall be eligible to either house of assembly." Yet we find not only this express exception, with respect to the members of the inferior courts, but that the chief magistrate with his executive council are appointable by the legislature; that two members of the latter are triennially displaced at the pleasure of the legislature; and that all the principal offices, both executive and judiciary, are filled by the same department. The executive prerogative of pardon, also, is in one case vested in the legislative department.

The constitution of North-Carolina, which declares "that the legislative, executive and supreme judicial powers of government ought to be forever separate and distinct from each other," refers at the same time to the legislative department, the appointment not only of the executive chief, but all the principal officers within both that and the judiciary department.

In South-Carolina, the constitution makes the executive magistracy eligible by the legislative department. It gives to the latter, also, the appointment of the members of the judiciary department, including even justices of the peace and sheriffs; and the appointment of officers in the executive department, down to captains in the army and navy of the State.

In the constitution of Georgia, where it is declared "that the legislative, executive and judiciary departments shall be separate and distinct, so that neither exercise the powers properly belonging to the other," we find that the executive department is to be filled by appointments of the legislature; and the executive prerogative of pardon to be finally exercised by the same authority. Even justices of the peace are to be appointed by the legislature.

In citing these cases in which the legislative, executive, and judiciary departments have not been kept totally separate and distinct, I wish not to be regarded as an advocate for the particular organizations of the several State governments. I am fully aware that among the many excellent principles which they exemplify, they carry strong marks of the haste, and still stronger of the inexperience, under which they were framed. It is but too obvious that in some instances the fundamental principle under consideration has been violated by too great a mixture, and even an actual consolidation of the different powers; and that in no instance has a competent provision been made for maintaining in practice the separation delineated on paper. What I have wished to evince is that the charge brought against the proposed Constitution of violating a sacred maxim of free government is warranted neither by the real meaning annexed to that maxim by its author, nor by the sense in which it has hitherto been understood in America. This interesting subject will be resumed in the ensuing paper.

                                                                  PUBLIUS.

The opinion of The Federalist *has always been considered as of great authority. It is a complete commentary on our Constitution, and is appealed to by all parties in the questions to which that instrument has given birth. Its intrinsic merit entitles it to this high rank, and the part two of its authors performed in framing the Constitution, put it very much in their power to explain the views with which it was framed.*

Chief Justice John Marshall, in *Cohens v. Virginia* (1821)

PART 5

Defending the Constitution: The Struggle over Ratification and the Bill of Rights

⊶⇒ POINTS TO REMEMBER ⇐⊷

1. After the Constitution was signed by the delegates to the Federal Convention in Philadelphia, it was submitted to the States for ratification. The approval of only nine States was needed to make the Constitution the supreme law of the land. The delegates to the State ratifying conventions were elected by the people, thereby placing the Constitution on a democratic foundation. The Americans were the first to establish popularly based constitutions.

2. The Anti-Federalists opposed the Constitution on a number of grounds, but their chief objection was that it gave too much power to the Federal government and encouraged consolidation.

3. The authors of *The Federalist* attempted to explain and defend the Constitution in a series of 85 essays that were published in New York newspapers and later distributed throughout the country. They agreed that the new government would be powerful, but denied that it would be too powerful or that it would be a threat to liberty and the independence of the States.

4. The federal system of government established by the new Constitution was a uniquely American contribution to the science of government. It was rooted not in abstract political theory but in compromise and the practical necessities of the time. It is unlikely that the Constitution would have been acceptable to the American people had the Framers stripped the States of their reserved powers and created a unitary form of government.

5. One of the major concerns expressed by the Anti-Federalists was the issue of local control of civil liberties. They insisted that the Federal government would be so powerful that it would trample on the rights

of the people and the rights of the States. To correct this problem, they demanded that a Bill of Rights be added to the Constitution. The Federalists, on the other hand, argued that a bill of rights was unnecessary because no power had been delegated to the Federal government to regulate such matters as freedom of the press and religion in the first place. A Bill of Rights was nevertheless added to the Constitution in 1791.

6. The addition of the Bill of Rights was the chief accomplishment of the Anti-Federalists. It strengthened and affirmed the federal principle of the Constitution. It not only assured the people that the Federal government was prohibited from abridging their liberties, but it also assured the States that they would retain jurisdiction and control over most civil liberties disputes between the States and their citizens.

7. The American Constitution seeks to prevent rule by tyrannical majorities as well as tyrannical minorities. But in a democratic republic the problem of majority factions is usually the more difficult to resolve. In *Federalist* No. 10, James Madison explained that by establishing an extended, commercial, federal and democratic republic, the Framers sought to reduce and possibly eliminate the threat of government by tyrannical majorities. The system of representation established by the Framers is the key to an understanding of how the Constitution deals with this basic problem of democratic government.

8. The Bill of Rights is not a complete catalogue of all the rights that are enjoyed by the American people and are protected by the Constitution. As provided by the Ninth and Tenth Amendments, the people and the States retain jurisdiction over additional rights under their State constitutions and bills of rights, which the Federal government may not touch.

Signed on September 17, 1787, by all the delegates who still remained at Philadelphia—except Gerry of Massachusetts and Randolph and Mason of Virginia—the text of the proposed Constitution was dispatched to New York City, where the last Congress under the Confederation was meeting. Then there commenced a struggle which would last for nearly a year to persuade the several States to accept the new Constitution. It would be a conflict with much shouting but no shooting.

The Great Convention, in submitting the proposed Constitution to the

Congress of the Confederation, had requested that Congress send copies to the State legislatures. Those legislatures, in turn, were asked to issue instructions for the election of delegates to a convention to be held in each State. At these State conventions, the new Constitution would be debated. Each State convention would then ratify or reject the document. If nine states ratified the Constitution, it would take effect as the country's organic law, supplanting the Articles of Confederation.

This method of adoption, it is important to remember, dates back to some of the State constitutions approved during the revolutionary period. It was intended to give the Constitution a popular base and to establish the new government on a firm democratic foundation. This foundation was lacking under the Articles of Confederation because our first national constitution was never submitted to the people for approval. Although Article VII of the new Constitution specified ratification by the States, the voters in each State elected the delegates who served in the State ratifying conventions. Hence the Constitution of 1787 was ratified by the people *and* by the States, or by "the people in the States" (rather than simply by the States or by the people at large). In sharp contrast, new constitutions and constitutional amendments in parliamentary systems of government are often written and approved by the parliament, and the consent of the electorate is not sought or required. The Americans were the first to establish popularly based constitutions.

From a legal standpoint, the American Constitution, at its inception, was a "revolutionary" document. It may be doubted whether the Constitution would have prevailed had it not been approved by the American people. The delegates to the Federal Convention, as we noted earlier, were representatives of the States and were acting in response to a call by the Congress of the Confederation. They were sent to Philadelphia not to write a new Constitution but to "revise" the Articles of Confederation. No change in the Articles was permitted unless *all thirteen* State *legislatures* agreed. Nevertheless, the delegates to the Federal Convention boldly exceeded their mandate by proposing an entirely new government that was to go into effect when only *nine* State *conventions* ratified the Constitution.

The two factions on opposite sides in this contest over the adoption of the Constitution are called the Federalists and the Anti-Federalists. These terms are mildly confusing, for at the time when the Great Convention's deliberations had begun, the men friendly to the Articles of Confederation thought of themselves as favoring a federal system of government; by comparison, the advocates of a new constitution who intended to create a stronger national union are often called "Nationalists" by historians of the period. A few years later, these two divisions of opinion would harden into regular political parties called, respectively, Federalists (friendly toward a strong central government) and Republicans or Democratic-Republicans (many of whom formerly were Anti-Federalists).

But by September 1787, the Nationalists were calling themselves Federalists. Like the Anti-Federalists, they sought to persuade the voters through speeches, pamphlets, newspaper articles, and personal correspondence. As we noted earlier, three of their leading men—James Madison, Alexander Hamilton, and John Jay—wrote eighty-five essays for New York newspapers under the pseudonym of "Publius." These essays, known as *The Federalist*, endeavored to explain and defend each provision of the Constitution and its underlying principles of government. To this day, *The Federalist* is regarded as one of the most insightful sources of understanding about the nature and purposes of the American political system. Anti-Federalist literature, previously uncollected and much ignored, is now available to the modern reader. Herbert Storing's *The Complete Anti-Federalist* (7 vols., 1981) is the most complete and up-to-date version.

Much knowledge about the Constitution is also to be gained by reading the debates in the several State ratifying Conventions. When the Philadelphia Convention adjourned on September 17, 1787, many of the delegates returned to their native States to defend the new Constitution and urge its adoption. Some, such as James Wilson of Pennsylvania, were elected to their State's convention and thus entered into a second round of deliberations on the Constitution. These ratification debates contain a rich source of both Federalist and Anti-Federalist thought on the Constitution. They were later collected and published as a four-volume work by Jonathan Elliot under the title of *The Debates in the Several State Conventions on the Adoption of the Federal Constitution* (1830). James Madison, it is interesting to note, was the last surviving member of the Federal Convention when he passed away in 1836. The comprehensive notes that he took at the Federal Convention were published after his death, and

Elliot added them as a fifth volume to his *Debates* in 1840. Taken together, these works—Madison's *Notes,* Elliot's *Debates, The Federalist,* and Storing's *The Complete Anti-Federalist,* represent the principal, though by no means the entire, source material of original documents on the framing and adoption of the United States Constitution.

A. THE ANTI-FEDERALIST PERSUASION

On the eve of the Federal Convention, the Anti-Federalists were basically in agreement with the Federalists that the Articles of Confederation needed to be changed. They admitted that the Articles were weak and that the powers of Congress, at least those respecting domestic and foreign commerce, needed to be strengthened. But they did not sense a need to abandon the Articles entirely and substitute a new system. Above all, the Anti-Federalists opposed any fundamental change in the existing relationship between the Confederation government and the States. They were strong advocates of States' Rights who believed that self-government, independence, and individual liberty were best protected at the local level. A distant and powerful central government over which they might exert little control or influence represented a threat to the values they cherished.

The Constitution Establishes a Consolidated Empire

Thus the Anti-Federalists' main objection to the proposed Constitution was that it created a central government that was too strong. "We drew the spirit of liberty from our British ancestors," Patrick Henry told the delegates of the Virginia ratifying convention, and "by that spirit we have triumphed over every difficulty. But now, Sir, the American spirit, assisted by the ropes and chains of consolidation, is about to convert this country to a powerful and mighty empire. If you make the citizens of this country agree to become the subjects of one great consolidated empire of America, your government will not have sufficient energy to keep them together. Such a government is incompatible with the genius of republicanism. There will be no checks, no real balances in this government." Like other Anti-Federalists, Henry saw no need for a powerful Federal government, preferring instead a loose-knit confederation that allowed the States to determine their own needs and interests. Why, asked Henry, should Virginia, a State with a large population, vast resources, and extensive territory, compromise its sovereignty and share power with smaller, less influential States? Given the great political, economic, cultural, and geographical differences among the States, was a powerful union either possible or desirable?

The Anti-Federalists did not think so. "Agrippa," the pseudonym of a Boston Anti-Federalist, warned the citizens of Massachusetts that the new Constitution was impractical and dangerous. "We find," he said,

> that the very great empires have always been despotic. . . . It is impossible for one code of laws to suit Georgia and Massachusetts. . . . This new system is, therefore, a consolidation of all the States into one larger mass, however diverse the parts may be of which it is composed. The idea of an uncompounded republic, on an average, one thousand miles in length, and eight hundred in breadth, and containing six million white inhabitants all reduced to the same standard of morals or habits, and of laws, is in itself an absurdity and contrary to the whole experience of mankind. The attempt made by Great Britain to introduce such a system struck us with horror, and when it was proposed by some theorist that we should be represented in Parliament, we uniformly declared that one legislature could not represent so many different interests for the purposes of legislation and taxation. This was the leading principle of the revolution.

The Constitution Establishes an Aristocracy

The size and diversity of the existing confederation, in other words, led the Anti-Federalists to believe that the union envisioned by the Framers should not even be attempted.

By republicanism, the Anti-Federalists meant democratic self-government, government close to the people, limited in scope, in which the representatives were held directly accountable through frequent elections. The problem with the new Constitution, they argued, was that it gave representatives too much power and independence. Once elected, representatives would be far from home, comfortable in their jobs, enjoying a big salary that they set themselves. They would be living in some distant, yet-to-be-built city far removed from the watchful eye of the people they represented. Under these circumstances, they surely would lose touch with their constituents. The system was an invitation to despotism.

These fears and suspicions were also confirmed by certain deficiencies in the Constitution itself. The Constitution, for example, made no provision for recalling elections; and rotation in office, argued the Anti-Federalists, was not frequent enough. A common theme in Anti-Federalist literature was the complaint, as "A Plebian" from New York wrote, that "the power of the general legislature to alter and regulate the time, place,

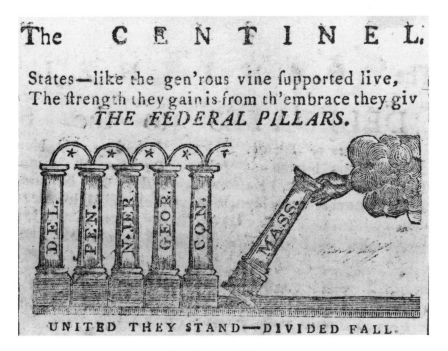

The Federal Pillars.

The *Massachusetts Centinel* published a number of allegorical illustrations in 1788 to mark the progress of each State's ratification of the proposed Constitution. This early one marked the pending ratification of Massachusetts and stressed the advantage of unity. (Courtesy of the Library of Congress.)

and manner of holding elections [Article I, Section 4] . . . will place in the hands of the general government the authority whenever they shall be disposed, and a favorable opportunity offers, to deprive the body of the people, in effect, of all share in the government."

Republicanism also meant rule by the majority. But the Constitution, insisted the Anti-Federalists, seemed to encourage government by minority factions and wealthy aristocrats. There would be too few members in the House of Representatives (only one for every 30,000 persons), and a mere handful of Senators—as few as eighteen if only nine States joined the Union—would be able to block legislation desired by a majority of the people. "Far from being a regular balanced government," complained "Centinel," a Pennsylvania Anti-Federalist, "it would be in practice a permanent aristocracy." Patrick Henry of Virginia echoed these sentiments, contending that the two-thirds requirement for proposing amendments and the three-fourths requirement for their adoption allowed entrenched minorities and "the most unworthy characters" to obstruct the will of the majority. It would be impossible, he argued, to pass an amendment by those difficult means:

> To suppose that so large a number as three-fourths of the States will concur is to suppose that they will possess genius, intelligence, and integrity approaching to miraculous. . . . For four of the smallest States that do not collectively contain one-tenth part of the population of the United States may obstruct the most salutary and necessary amendments. . . . A bare majority in these four States may hinder the adoption of amendments, so that we may fairly and justly conclude that one-twentieth part of the American people may prevent the removal of the most grievous inconveniences and oppression by refusing to accede to amendments. A trifling minority may reject the most salutary amendments. Is this an easy mode of securing the public liberty? It is, sir, a most fearful situation when the most contemptible minority can prevent the alteration of the most oppressive government. . . . Is this the spirit of republicanism?

Quoting from the Virginia Bill of Rights, Henry went on to assert that "a majority of the community have an indubitable, unalienable, and indefeasible right to reform, alter, or abolish" their government when it becomes inadequate. "This, sir, is the language of democracy: that a majority of the community have the right to alter their government when found to be oppressive. But how different is the genius of your new Constitution from this."

The Constitution Confers Too Much Power

No less disturbing to these critics of the Constitution were specific provisions which seemed to be inconsistent with the ideals of limited constitutional government. Elbridge Gerry, a delegate to the Federal Convention from Massachusetts who refused to sign the Constitution, spoke for most Anti-Federalists when he challenged the Constitution's broad delegations of power. In addition to the problems of representation and Congressional control of elections, "some of the powers of the Legislature are ambiguous, and others indefinite and dangerous." The President "is balanced with and will have undue influence over the Legislature." The Federal Judiciary "will be oppressive." And, Gerry argued, "the system is without the security of a bill of rights."

An Imperial Congress

Among the powers delegated to Congress, those authorizing the national legislature to provide for the general welfare, levy taxes, regulate the States' militia, regulate interstate commerce, and make all laws necessary and proper, gave the Anti-Federalists their deepest misgivings. "Brutus," writing in the *New York Journal*, offered one of the most perceptive and far-reaching examinations of Congressional power from the Anti-Federalist perspective. The "most natural and grammatical" construction of the General Welfare Clause in Article I, he observed, is that it authorizes the Congress "to do anything which in their judgment will tend to provide for the general welfare, and this amounts to the same thing as general and unlimited powers of legislation in all cases. . . ." The tax power is fundamentally unsound because "there is no limitation on this power" and Congress could levy any amount that it pleases, for any purpose, leaving the States no source of revenue. "This power therefore is neither more nor less than a power to lay and collect taxes, imposts, and excises, at their pleasure."

Likewise, the necessary and proper clause, wrote "Brutus," "is a power very comprehensive and . . . [may] be exercised in such manner as entirely to abolish the State legislatures." Taking the General Welfare, Tax, and Necessary and Proper clauses together, concluded "Brutus," "It is therefore evident that the legislature under this Constitution may pass any law which they may think proper."

There was also criticism of the Commerce Clause, mostly from the southern States. What is meant by the power to "regulate"? What, precisely, is "commerce"? The Constitution did not define these terms. Although vagueness and the possibility of an indefinite grant of power were considerations, the southern Anti-Federalists were especially concerned that northern States might use their superior numbers in the Congress to discriminate against southern commercial and economic interests.

It was Patrick Henry who opposed the Constitution because it impeded majority rule. On the question of commerce, however, the Anti-Federalists argued that majority rule was not enough: extraordinary or "super" majorities ought to be required for the enactment of commercial laws, in order to protect the agricultural interests of the South. Richard Henry Lee of Virginia thus complained that, "In this congressional legislature a bare majority of votes can enact commercial laws, so that the representatives of seven Northern States, as they will have a majority, can by law create the most oppressive monopoly upon the five Southern States." Opposition to the Constitution, it may thus be seen, stemmed not only from republican considerations and a general distrust of centralized power, but from other causes as well, including sectional differences and jealousies among the States.

An Elected Monarch

Nor was Anti-Federalist dissatisfaction with Federal power under the new Constitution limited to Congress. Patrick Henry alleged that the Constitution "has an awful squinting; it squints towards monarchy. . . . Your President may easily become king." A New York Anti-Federalist, writing under the name of "Cato," repeated the charge, asserting that the Constitution inclines toward an "odious aristocracy and monarchy." The President, he said, has so much power that his office "differs very immaterially from the establishment of monarchy in Great Britain."

An Omnipotent Judiciary

The Anti-Federalists were also generally agreed that the Federal Judiciary would swallow up the State courts under the new system of government. "Brutus" addressed the issue at considerable length, producing what are surely the most extensive analyses of judicial power written by an Anti-Federalist. His main concern was Article III, Section 2, which provides that "The judicial power shall extend to all cases in law and equity arising under this Constitution, the laws, and treaties made, or which shall be made, under their authority." This can only mean, said "Brutus," that Article III vests the judicial branch "with a power to resolve all questions that may arise in any case on the construction of the Constitution, either in law or in equity." By what principles of interpretation, he asked, is the Constitution to be construed?

Since the Federal courts were empowered to decide cases in equity as well as law, it appeared that the Federal judges were free to interpret the Constitution "according to the reasoning and spirit of it, without being confined to the words or letter." This was true, said "Brutus," because equity law gave the courts broad discretion. Equity law emerged not in the common law courts of England, which follow strict rules of construction, but in the courts of chancery, which follow virtually no principles of interpretation. The goal of equity jurisprudence is "natural justice"; it seeks to produce fairness, as the judges understand it, and to override the common law when it stands in the way of this objective. Quoting Hugo Grotius, the great scholar of international law, "Brutus" contended "That equity, thus depending essentially upon each individual case [rather than precedent], there can be no established rules and fixed principles of equity laid down, without destroying its very essence, and reducing it to a positive law."

It therefore followed, said Brutus, that "The judicial power will operate to effect in the most certain, but yet silent and imperceptible manner, what is evidently the tendency of the Constitution: an entire subversion of the legislative, executive, and judicial powers of the individual States." The inquiring citizen, he concluded, need only examine the Constitution itself, written "in general and indefinite terms, which are either equivocal, ambiguous, or which require long definitions," to appreciate the truth of these remarks. "I question whether the world ever saw, in any period of it, a court of justice invested with such immense powers."

In light of criticisms like these, the Anti-Federalists insisted that the Constitution must either be rejected or substantially amended. Their points of disagreement with the basic design of the system and its particular provisions varied from writer to writer, and they did not agree in all respects. Taken together, however, their writings demonstrated a remarkable uniformity when we consider the distances in time and location, and the limited means of communication from one State to the next in that era. And on one issue they were almost unanimously agreed: the Constitution, because it conferred so much power upon the Federal government, was a threat to personal freedom and States' Rights. They believed, therefore, that prohibiting the Federal government from abridging certain freedoms was absolutely essential. In the end, the Anti-Federalists were wholly unsuccessful in their effort to change the language of the Constitution and limit the power of the Federal government. They did succeed, however, in persuading the Federalists to add a bill of rights to the Constitution. This was their most important and lasting contribution to the making of the American Constitution.

B. THE FEDERALIST RESPONSE

Although the essays written by Hamilton, Madison, and Jay ("Publius") in *The Federalist* were by no means the only thoughtful response to Anti-Federalists' arguments, they were surely the most influential. Over the years they have come to be recognized as a primary source of understanding concerning the meaning and purpose of the Constitution. Indeed, no study of our political system and the ideas of the Framers is complete without a reading of this great American classic.

In defending the Constitution, the authors of *The Federalist* faced the difficult task of explaining and justifying a document that differed sharply from the Articles of Confederation. Although the Articles were unsatisfactory in a number of ways, they were nevertheless tolerable to a great many Americans. There had been no popular uprisings anywhere in the country demanding a new constitution, and many prominent political leaders—now Anti-Federalists—preferred a modest revision rather than abandonment of the Articles.

The Federalists thus found themselves in the awkward position of defending what appeared to be, at least on the surface, a radical and revolutionary change of government. Many though not all of the delegates to the Federal Convention had been instructed by their States to seek a modification of the Articles—not their wholesale elimination. These delegates were therefore highly vulnerable to the charge that they had violated the trust that had been placed in them, and had acted *ultra vires* (beyond the power vested in them). The Constitution itself, as the Anti-Federalists hotly contended, displayed all the characteristics of a novel experiment in government. The basic question was whether it strengthened and preserved freedom and independence, or whether it nullified the hard-fought gains of the American Revolution and promised to return America to the kind of tyranny it had known under George III.

The Constitution Limits and Distributes Power

The question was one of power, the Federalists arguing that the Articles of Confederation conferred too little power on the Federal government, and the Anti-Federalists asserting that the Constitution gave it too much. Conceding the point that the Constitution clearly increased the powers of the Federal government, the Federalists nonetheless insisted that the document had been carefully drafted to limit those powers. These limitations were sufficient, they contended, to allow for healthy and vigorous government, while at the same time preventing abuses of power. It was to be a powerful government, more powerful than the American people had known since the Revolution, the Federalists admitted. But it was not so powerful as to constitute a serious threat to liberty, and certainly not as powerful as the English monarchy.

This was true, said "Publius," because the Constitution disallowed concentrations of power. No single government, either Federal or State, possessed all the powers of government. Political power, in general, was *divided* between two levels of government under the principle of federalism. The national government was to be a government of limited and enumerated powers that were specifically laid out in the Constitution. Those powers not delegated to the national government remained with the States as "reserved" powers. The limited power that the national government possessed was further restricted because it was *separated* among three relatively independent branches—Congress, the President, and the Judiciary. This provided the machinery for the responsible exercise of power. The problem with the Articles of Confederation was that they did not provide for a proper distribution of power. Too much power had been concentrated in the States, making it difficult for the national government to deal effectively with foreign governments, interstate rivalries, insurrections, and military threats. And, what little power the national government did possess was concentrated in one branch—Congress. The government of the United States under the Articles thus suffered from "anarchy in the parts" rather than "tyranny in the head." It was so weak, the Federalists argued, that it could not promote economic prosperity or provide for the safety of the people. These were the bare essentials of government. The new Constitution, as the Preamble stated, promised to "establish justice, insure domestic tranquility, provide for the common defense, promote the general welfare, and secure the blessings of liberty. . . ."

The first step in gaining public support for the proposed Constitution was to explain and justify the redistribution of power crafted by the Framers. The American system of federalism, unprecedented in the history of nations, was a unique arrangement that seemed foreign to some and unworkable to others. What was the nature of this new union? If sovereignty was to be divided between the general or Federal government and the States, who had ultimate authority to govern? These were difficult questions, but the authors of *The Federalist* answered them with consummate skill.

The nature of the new union, explained Madison, was neither wholly national nor wholly federal, but contained both national and federal elements. Regarding the basic foundation of the government, it was federal because the Constitution must be ratified by the several States. With respect to the legislature, the new Union was partly national and partly federal, one house resting on a national and the other on a federal basis. The presidency was also partly national and partly federal, since the electoral vote was distributed partly in accordance with the principle of State equality, and partly according to population. Considering the operation of the government, it was seen as national rather than federal, inasmuch as it acted directly on individuals and not through the States. In the extent of its powers, however, the Union was federal because its jurisdiction was limited to specific objects, and all else was left to the States. Thus the government of the United States was to be neither a pure confederacy nor a "consolidated republic," but a new type of government, in a class by itself.

The States had not been reduced to provinces, the Federalists insisted, but remained in possession of "certain exclusive and very important portions of sovereign power." They still held "all the rights of sovereignty which were not . . . exclusively delegated to the United States." In a consolidated system, the local authorities are subject to control by the central government; but in the proposed Union the local authorities form distinct and independent portions of the supremacy, no more subject to the general authority than the general authority is to them within its own sphere." The States may not be completely sovereign, but they did have a residuary sovereignty.

Such was the nature of legal sovereignty under the Constitution. Real or political sovereignty rested, of course, not with the Federal or State governments, but with the "people." "The ultimate authority," concluded *The Federalist*, "resides in the people alone."

It therefore followed that the federal principle, woven into the entire fabric of the Constitution, would limit the power of both the Federal and State governments, while happily combining the best characteristics of both. The Anti-Federalists' claim that the Federal government would usurp the powers of the States, argued Madison in *Federalist* 45, was false. It was more likely that the States would continue to dominate the national government. They had the advantage with respect "to the weight of personal influence which each side will possess; to the powers respectively vested in them; to the predilection and probable support of the people; to the disposition and faculty of resisting and frustrating the measures of each other."

Virginia Ratifies the Constitution, June 25, 1788.

Based on the famous 1788 painting, *Watson and the Sharks*, by John Singleton Copley, this allegory of the Virginia ratification struggle by Kinuko Craft shows the Federalists and Anti-Federalists—James Madison, Patrick Henry, George Mason, Edmund Randolph, James Monroe—perceiving different dangers.

Painted originally for the Virginia Commission on the Bicentennial of the United States Constitution. (Courtesy of A. E. Dick Howard.)

Of paramount importance under the new scheme were the State legislatures. The President could not even be elected unless they acted. They played a key role in his election. Moreover, they elected the members of the Senate and would probably influence the election of members of the House of Representatives as well. Both the legislative and executive branches of the Federal government, in other words, owed their very existence to the State legislatures. Added to this, the States would exercise far more influence in public affairs because more people were employed under their authority than under that of the general government. "The members of the legislative, executive and judiciary departments of thirteen and more States; the justices of peace, officers of militia, ministerial officers of justice, with all the county corporation and town-officers, for three millions and more of people, intermixed and having particular acquaintance with every class and circle of people, must exceed beyond all proportion, both in number and influence, those of every description who will be employed in the administration of the federal system."

Accustomed to their own State constitutions, which except in Massachusetts and a few other States generally failed to provide for sufficient checks and balances, some Anti-Federalists also criticized the separation of powers system of the Constitution. There was too much "blending," they argued, and the departments ought to be kept wholly separate and distinct. Not all Anti-Federalists shared this view, however, and many accepted the argument of Madison in *Federalist* 47 that some overlapping of functions was necessary in order to prevent one branch from encroaching upon the functions of another. Hence the issue of separation of powers did not become a major bone of contention in the struggle over ratification of the Constitution. The Anti-Federalists were preoccupied with the question of States' Rights. This was the theme song of their campaign against the Constitution.

In response to the many complaints that the proposed Constitution not only redistributed power improperly but also failed to limit the powers that had now been shifted to the Federal government, the authors of *The Federalist* assured their adversaries that such fears were unfounded. "The powers delegated by the proposed Constitution to the Federal government," said Madison in *Federalist* 45, "are few and defined. Those

which are to remain in the State governments are numerous and indefinite." The scope of Federal power would be limited primarily to military
and foreign affairs, foreign commerce and taxation. The States, he continued, would retain full authority over matters pertaining to civil liberties
and the rights of property, the internal affairs of the States, and the administration of law and order.

Congress Is Not an Oligarchy

Turning to specific complaints lodged against the Constitution respecting the enumerated powers of Congress, Publius denied the allegation
that the "times, places and manner" provision, which gave Congress
concurrent authority to regulate the election of its own members, would
displace the State legislatures. The States would regulate Federal elections in the first instance, contended Alexander Hamilton in *Federalist* 59,
and Congress would not generally interfere except when "extraordinary
circumstances might render the interposition necessary to its safety." The
"times, places and manner" clause was simply a device to protect Congress from being placed at the mercy of the States. Without it, the States
might prevent the election of members of Congress altogether. It was justified by the general principle that "every government ought to contain
in itself the means of its own preservation."

Anti-Federalist arguments against the General Welfare, Tax, and Necessary and Proper clauses of Article I, and the Supremacy Clause of Article
VI, were also not justified, the Federalists countered. A proper interpretation of these provisions, said *The Federalist*, showed they were entirely consistent with the principles of limited government. The power "to lay and
collect taxes, duties, imposts and excises, to pay the debts and provide
for the common defense and general welfare" was not an "unlimited
commission to exercise every power which may be alleged to be necessary for the common defense or general welfare." Congress had not been
given a general power to legislate for the general welfare, because the
General Welfare Clause was tied inextricably to the power to tax and
spend. Congress, said Madison in *Federalist* 41, could tax and spend only
to carry out one of its enumerated powers. Any other interpretation

would render superfluous the specific enumeration of other Congressional powers.

It was true, of course, that the Framers had placed no limit on the amount that might be taxed. It would not be practical, the Federalists believed, to do so. In time of war and national emergencies, suggested Hamilton in *Federalist* 34, the situation might call for added revenue. "Constitutions of civil government are not to be framed upon a calculation of existing emergencies. . . . There ought to be a capacity to provide for future contingencies, as these may happen; and, as these are illimitable in their nature, it is impossible safely to limit that capacity." Given the various constitutional restraints on government and the system of popular control over members of Congress, abuses of the tax power thus seemed remote.

Similarly unwarranted, argued Publius, were Anti-Federalist assaults on the Necessary and Proper and Supremacy clauses. "These two clauses," observed Hamilton in *Federalist* 33, "have been sources of much virulent invective and petulant declamation. . . . [and] have been held up to the people, in all the exaggerated colors of misrepresentation, as the pernicious engines by which their local governments were to be destroyed and their liberties exterminated." Upon close examination, however, it was clear that both clauses were "perfectly harmless." Indeed, wrote Hamilton, "the constitutional operation of the intended government would be precisely the same, if these clauses were entirely obliterated. . . . They are only declaratory of a truth, which would have resulted by necessary and unavoidable implication from the very act of constituting a Federal government, and vesting it with certain specified powers." By this he meant that the Necessary and Proper clause was intended "to leave nothing to construction" and to remove all doubt that the delegation of certain powers to Congress carried with it the implied right to execute those powers by necessary and proper laws; and that the Supremacy Clause simply acknowledged the fact that "a law by the very meaning of the term includes supremacy." The supremacy of national laws "flows immediately and necessarily from the institution of a Federal government." The States were protected by language which "expressly confines this supremacy to laws made *pursuant to the Constitution.*"

The President Is Not a King

Anti-Federalist arguments that the President and the Federal courts also enjoyed excessive amounts of power under the proposed Constitution were also rebutted by Hamilton, principally in *Federalist* 69 and *Federalist* 78. Particularly weak was the charge that the President had been endowed with all of the rights and prerogatives of an English monarch. Astutely noting that the powers of the Chief Executive did not differ remarkably from those already being exercised by many State governors, Hamilton spelled out in exhaustive detail the differences between the President and the King of Great Britain: the President was elected by the people for four years, whereas the King is a perpetual hereditary prince; the President can be impeached and removed from office, whereas the person of the King is "sacred and inviolable"; the President has a qualified veto, whereas that of the King is absolute; the President is commander-in-chief of the armed forces, whereas the King not only raises and commands the military but may also declare war on his own authority; the President shares the treaty-making and appointment power with the legislature, whereas the King alone exercises these powers. These, and countless other differences, distinguished the two offices. "What answer," asked Hamilton, "shall we give to those who would persuade us that things so unlike resemble each other? The same that ought to be given to those who tell us, that a government, the whole power of which would be in the hands of the elective and periodical servants of the people, is an aristocracy, a monarchy, and a despotism."

The Judiciary Is the Least Dangerous Branch

On the question of Federal judicial power, however, Hamilton dismissed many of the Anti-Federalist objections out of hand, and never really came to grips with the issue. In *Federalist* 78, he argued persuasively for the principle of judicial independence, but the thought that Federal judges might usurp the powers of the State courts received only passing notice. The possibility that Federal judges might also encroach upon the powers of Congress or the President seemed equally remote. Historically, courts of law had served the interests of liberty as barriers to despotism. Because of the limited nature of their function—interpreting the law—they "will always be the least dangerous" branch. Under the Constitution, observed Hamilton, "The judiciary. . . . has no influence over either the sword or the purse, no direction either of the strength or of the wealth of society, and can take no active resolution whatever. It may truly be said to have neither Force nor Will, but merely judgment; and must ultimately depend upon the aid of the executive arm even for the efficacy of its judgments."

In sum, "the judiciary is beyond comparison the weakest of the three departments of power." "[T]he supposed danger of judiciary encroachments on the legislative authority," Hamilton surmised, "is in reality a phantom. Particular misconstructions and contraventions of the will of the legislature may now and then happen; but they can never be so extensive as to amount to an inconvenience, or in any sensible degree to affect the order of the political system."

Whether a Bill of Rights Was Necessary

On May 28, 1788, one year after the delegates to the Constitutional Convention had convened in Philadelphia to begin their deliberations, Alexander Hamilton published his reply to the Anti-Federalists on the question of a bill of rights. Not until the final hours of the Convention had the thought occurred to any delegate that a bill of rights ought to be included in the Constitution. It was then that George Mason of Virginia made the proposal, and Elbridge Gerry of Massachusetts moved to appoint a committee to draft a "declaration of rights." The motion was voted down unanimously (that is, by all of the States represented), because the general consensus was that a bill of rights was not necessary. This was essentially the same position taken by Hamilton in *Federalist* 84.

Opposition to a bill of rights did not stem from indifference or hostility toward civil rights, but from the widely held belief that a declaration of rights would be superfluous. The Federal government was to be a government of delegated and enumerated powers. It had no authority to interfere with such matters as speech and religion. A declaration that it had no such authority would merely make explicit what was already implicit in the Constitution, with excess verbiage that simply stated what was already obvious.

To this, Hamilton added other objections. First, the Constitution already contained specific guarantees of liberty. "The establishment of the writ of *habeas corpus*, the prohibition of *ex post facto* laws and of titles of nobility," he asserted, "are perhaps greater securities to liberty and republicanism" than any provided by his own Constitution of New York.

Second, a bill of rights does not properly belong in this kind of Constitution. Such bills of rights are ordinarily stipulations between kings and their subjects, "reservations of rights not surrendered to the prince"—as seen in the Magna Charta, the Petition of Right, and the English Bill of Rights of 1688. Hence, Hamilton argued,"they have no application to constitutions professedly founded upon the power of the people" because "in strictness, the people surrender nothing, and as they retain everything, they have no need of particular reservations." The Preamble of the Constitution, he believed, "is a better recognition of popular rights than volumes of those aphorisms which make the principal figure in several of our State bills of rights, and which would sound much better in a treatise of ethics than in a constitution of government."

Third, said Hamilton, a bill of rights might even be dangerous. By listing freedoms that the Federal government could not deny, the government, by implication, would be free to deny those rights that had not been included. A bill of rights, he reasoned, "would contain various exceptions to powers which are not granted; and on this very account, would afford a colorable pretext to claim more than was granted. For why declare that things shall not be done which there is no power to do? Why, for instance, should it be said, that the liberty of the press shall not be restrained, when no power is given by which restrictions may be imposed?"

Fourth, there was no clear understanding concerning the precise meaning of the liberties claimed, and the standards varied from State to State. "What signifies a declaration that 'the liberty of the press shall be inviolably preserved'? What is the liberty of the press? Who can give it any definition which would not leave the utmost latitude for evasion?" If freedom of the press is to be enjoyed, Hamilton argued, it will be because of public opinion and the spirit of the people, not because of "fine declarations."

Finally, a bill of rights was not needed, Hamilton maintained, because the Constitution was itself a bill of rights. What protects liberty and gives it meaning and substance is the structure of government—concrete limitations on power, not parchment declarations. If a constitution—and that of the United States is such a constitution—is properly designed to check abuses of power, the government upon which it rests will in the general course of events discourage political authorities from trampling on the liberties of the people. The privileges and immunities that might be proclaimed in such a bill of rights were already embodied in the original document.

In the end, Hamilton's view did not prevail. The ratification struggle began as soon as Congress submitted the Constitution to the States, and the Anti-Federalists steadfastly held their position that a bill of rights was essential. This issue overshadowed all others, including the issues of legislative power and representation. Although ratification was secured within nine months, the margin of victory in at least half of the States was narrow. Had the Federalists refused to budge on the bill of rights question, it is not unlikely that the proposed Constitution would have been defeated.

The Clash of Values

This brief review of the main points of contention between the Federalists and the Anti-Federalists shows that they were in disagreement on some very fundamental issues. To the Anti-Federalists, the new Constitution posed a threat to liberty, order, and justice, whereas the Federalists believed that it would secure these values.

Liberty depends on rule of law. Yet, as the Anti-Federalists repeatedly argued, the new system rested on a flagrant disregard of the forms of legality. The delegates to the Philadelphia Convention were sent to revise the Articles of Confederation, not to write a new Constitution. James Madison responded in *Federalist* 40 with the argument that even if the Framers had exceeded their powers (which he flatly denied), it was in the best interests of the country to substantially alter the system.

Such changes were legitimate, he suggested, if they were "calculated to accomplish the views and happiness of the people of America" and were approved by them.

Liberty also depended upon republicanism, said the Anti-Federalists, which in turn depended upon maintaining the primacy of the States. History and political theory persuaded the Anti-Federalists that free republican governments could extend only over small territories with homogeneous populations. Small republics were stable and orderly because they were public-spirited, enjoyed voluntary obedience to the laws, and were closely controlled by the people. Many Anti-Federalists preferred the simplicity of agrarian life to the complexity of a strife-ridden industrial society, and most agreed with Brutus that "in a republic, the manners, sentiments, and interests of the people should be similar. If this is not the case, there will be a constant clashing of opinions; and the representatives of one part will be continually striving against those of the other."

But the Federalists envisioned a different kind of America, and vigorously challenged this view. Homogeneous republics were possible only under the primitive conditions of pre-commercial society. "In every community whose industry is encouraged," said Hamilton, "there will be a division of it into the few and the many." And when this occurs, the innocence of agricultural life is lost. The Anti-Federalists criticized the man of commerce as rootless and greedy—"immersed in schemes of wealth" and "the last to take alarm when public liberty is threatened"; but they could not deny that America was already committed to a commercial order, and that the landed interests were fundamentally part of, and dependent upon, the commercial life of the nation. As Herbert Storing has observed, "The basic problem of the Anti-Federalists was that they accepted the need and desirability of the modern commercial world, while attempting to resist certain of its tendencies with rather half-hearted appeals to civic virtue. But such restraints, the Federalists replied, have never worked and will never work."

The solution, argued Madison in *Federalist* 10, was the extended commercial republic proposed by the Constitution. A loosely knit confederation of small republics was neither desirable nor possible. Small republics might even pose a threat to liberty because they were governed by single-minded majority factions that are difficult to control. Such factions

IN HONOUR of AMERICAN

BEER and CYDER,

It is hereby recorded, for the information of ftrangers and pofterity, that 17 000 people affembled on this green, on the 4th of July, 1788, to celebrate the eftablifhment of the conftitution of the United States, and that they feparated at an early hour, without intoxication, or a fingle quarrel.----They drank nothing but Beer and Cyder. Learn, reader, to prize thofe invaluable FEDERAL liquors, and to confider them as the companions of thofe virtues that can alone render our country free and refpectable.

Learn likewife to defpife

SPIRITOUS LIQUORS, as

Anti-federal, and to confider them as the companions of all thofe vices, that are calculated to difhonour and enflave our country.

A Sober Republic.

The joyous citizens of Philadelphia celebrated the Constitution (rather than the Declaration of Independence) on July 4, 1788, with a great parade and lavish ceremony. More than 17,000 people assembled on the green behind the State House to enjoy beer and cider, "those invaluable FEDERAL liquors." Broadside, reprinted in vol. 4 of *American Museum* (Philadelphia, 1788).

tend to be overbearing, and even tyrannical. They become intolerant of the rights of wealthy property owners, small religious sects, and other minority groups because they have few differences among themselves. The system of representation adopted by the Framers was preferable, said Madison, because it established a large commercial republic in which majority factions would represent diverse populations with different interests. Majority factions of this kind would be more moderate than small, homogeneous factions, since they would be forced to compromise many of their positions in order to function as a majority. The Federal government, in other words, would have a conservative, moderating influence on the affairs of the people, checking the radical elements in the States—like Daniel Shays.

Although the Federalists won the argument, we should not presume that the Anti-Federalists were wrong about any or all of these issues. The inquiring student, having examined the debates thoroughly and objectively, may well conclude that the Anti-Federalists were right about certain matters. For we must not lose sight of the fact that the debate over the Constitution was a political debate, and that both sides were seeking to persuade their fellow countrymen that their position was the correct one. In the course of the debate, both sides tended to exaggerate their claims, the Federalists playing down the fact that the Constitution did indeed confer great power on the Federal government, and the Anti-Federalists overstating the deficiencies of the Constitution.

Moreover, we should not over-inflate the effect and significance of the Anti-Federalists' victory in securing adoption of the Bill of Rights. For the Bill of Rights neither increased nor decreased the powers of the Federal government. The first ten amendments simply made explicit what was already implicit in the Constitution. Perhaps this is why the Federalists were only half-hearted in their opposition to a bill of rights, and in the end readily acceded to the demands of the Anti-Federalists.

Although no formal agreements were made, ratification in many States was conditioned on the understanding that the first order of business in the first Congress would be the preparation of a bill of rights for submission to the States. Toward that end, five of the States sent long lists of proposed amendments to Congress for consideration. These amendments, it should be borne in mind, were motivated as much by a desire to whittle down the powers of the Federal government as by a desire to protect civil liberties.

A review of the bill of rights proposals of the first three States to make them—Massachusetts, South Carolina, and New Hampshire—shows that the members of these conventions were much more concerned about the

The Progress of Ratification

		Vote on Ratification	
Order of Ratification	Date of Ratification	For	Against
1. Delaware	Dec. 7, 1787	Unanimous	
2. Pennsylvania	Dec. 12	46	23
3. New Jersey	Dec. 18	Unanimous	
4. Georgia	Jan. 2, 1788	Unanimous	
5. Connecticut	Jan. 9	128	40
6. Massachusetts	Feb. 7	187	168
7. Maryland	Apr. 28	63	11
8. South Carolina	May 23	149	73
9. New Hampshire	June 21	57	46
Total Vote of 9 States		*725*	*361*
10. Virginia	June 26	89	79
11. New York	July 26	30	27
Total Vote of 11 States		*844*	*467*
12. North Carolina	Nov. 21, 1789	195	77
13. Rhode Island	May 29, 1790	34	32
Total Vote		*1073*	*576*

Source: Winton U. Solberg, *The Federal Convention and the Formation of the Union*, p. 375

rights and powers of the States than about the rights of the people. Massachusetts proposed nine amendments, but only the sixth and seventh— referring, respectively, to indictment by grand jury and jury trials in civil disputes—dealt with individual liberty as such. The rest called for amendments declaring that: (1) all powers not expressly delegated were reserved to the States; (2) there shall be one representative for every thirty thousand persons until there are two hundred representatives; (3) Congress shall not exercise its "times, manner, and place" powers unless a State neglects or refuses to act or subverts the right of the people to free and equal representation; (4) Congress may not impose direct taxes unless there is insufficient money arising from imposts and excise taxes, and certain other conditions are met; (5) Congress may not create monopolies giving certain merchants an exclusive advantage; (6) The Supreme Court shall have no jurisdiction over disputes between citizens of different States unless the amount in contention is at least $3,000; (7) Congress shall never consent that a person holding office under the United States shall accept a title of nobility from a foreign state.

In one place the list proposed by South Carolina mentioned the "freedom of the people," but otherwise it dealt with the issue of "the sovereignty of the several States." Of the twelve proposed amendments offered by New Hampshire, less than half had a direct bearing on individual liberty. The many amendments proposed by Virginia and New York, which went into great detail, dealt in part with individual liberty and in part with proposed changes to increase the powers of the States.

Thus it may be seen that federalism was an important ingredient of the "Bill of Rights" as finally adopted. The Bill of Rights was, in fact, a concession to the Anti-Federalists and to the States' Rightists who feared Federal usurpation of State power, particularly in the sensitive area of civil liberties. By its terms, the Bill of Rights applied only to Congress (the Federal government) and exempted the States. Viewed in historical perspective, its purpose was two-fold: (1) to assure each *individual* that the Federal government would not encroach upon his civil liberties, and (2) to assure each *State* that the Federal government would not have jurisdiction over most civil liberties disputes between a State and its citizens. Each amendment was a guarantee to the individual *and* to the States, limiting the powers of the Federal government but not those of the States. On the question of freedom of the press, for example, Congress alone was prohibited by the First Amendment from abridging such freedom, thus leaving the States to establish their own standards of free press under their own constitutions and State bills of rights.

The task of drafting the Bill of Rights and submitting the amendments to the States for ratification fell on members of the First Congress in 1789. James Madison, who had been elected to the House of Representatives, was a member of the special committee that was responsible for sifting through the myriad amendments suggested by the States, and it was under his leadership that the Bill of Rights took shape.

The Bill of Rights as originally adopted by Congress and submitted to the States contained twelve amendments. The first two, proposing a new scale of representation for the House of Representatives and a limitation on increasing the salaries of members of Congress failed to gain ratification, and the last ten, known as the Bill of Rights, became part of the Constitution on December 15, 1791. What is now the First Amendment was originally the third. The amendment restricting changes of Congressional salaries was finally ratified in 1992, and it is now the 27th amendment to the Constitution. Not until the sesquicentennial year of 1941 did Connecticut, Georgia, and Massachusetts formally ratify the Bill of Rights.

C. THE BILL OF RIGHTS

The first ten amendments were proposed by Congress in 1789, at their first session; and, having received the ratification of the legislatures of three-fourths of the several States, they became a part of the Constitution December 15, 1791, and are known as the Bill of Rights.

[Amendment I.]
Congress shall make no law respecting an establishment of religion, or prohibiting the free exercise thereof; or abridging the freedom of speech or of the press; or the right of the people peaceably to assemble, and to petition the Government for a redress of grievances.

[Amendment II.]
A well regulated militia, being necessary to the security of a free State, the right of the people to keep and bear Arms, shall not be infringed.

[Amendment III.]
No Soldier shall, in time of peace, be quartered in any house, without the consent of the Owner, nor in time of war, but in a manner to be prescribed by law.

[Amendment IV.]
The right of the people to be secure in their persons, houses, papers, and effects, against unreasonable searches and seizures, shall not be violated, and no warrants shall issue, but upon probable cause, supported by oath or affirmation, and particularly describing the place to be searched, and the persons or things to be seized.

[Amendment V.]

No person shall be held to answer for a capital, or otherwise infamous crime, unless on a presentment or indictment of a grand jury, except in cases arising in the land or naval forces, or in the militia, when in actual service in time of war or public danger; nor shall any person be subject, for the same offense, to be twice put in jeopardy of life or limb; nor shall be compelled, in any criminal case, to be a witness against himself, nor be deprived of life, liberty, or property, without due process of law; nor shall private property be taken for public use, without just compensation.

[Amendment VI.]

In all criminal prosecutions the accused shall enjoy the right to a speedy and public trial, by an impartial jury of the State and district wherein the crime shall have been committed, which district shall have been previously ascertained by law, and to be informed of the nature and cause of the accusation; to be confronted with the witnesses against him; to have compulsory process for obtaining witnesses in his favor, and to have the Assistance of Counsel for his defence.

[Amendment VII.]

In suits at common law, where the value in controversy shall exceed twenty dollars, the right of trial by jury shall be preserved, and no fact tried by a jury shall be otherwise reexamined in any court of the United States, than according to the rules of the common law.

[Amendment VIII.]

Excessive bail shall not be required, nor excessive fines imposed, nor cruel and unusual punishments inflicted.

[Amendment IX.]

The enumeration in the Constitution, of certain rights, shall not be construed to deny or disparage others retained by the people.

[Amendment X.]
The powers not delegated to the United States by the Constitution, nor prohibited by it to the States, are reserved to the States respectively or to the people.

*   *   *   *   *

Some of the State constitutions drawn up during the Revolution included bills of rights. The most famous and influential of these was Virginia's Declaration of Rights, written by George Mason in 1776. (Mason also had a large hand in writing the Virginian Constitution at about the same time. Strictly speaking, the Declaration of Rights was not part of that constitution.) It is upon Mason's Declaration of Rights that much of the Bill of Rights of the Constitution is founded. The principal author of the Bill of Rights, however, was James Madison.

All early Americans with any serious interest in politics knew something about the English Bill (or Declaration) of Rights of 1688. But, as in many other matters, American leaders tended to be influenced more by recent or colonial American precedents and example than by those from British history. John Adams and Thomas Jefferson both earnestly supported the idea of a national bill of rights, and so did many other leading men.

We shall now examine those ten amendments, one by one, with a view to grasping their original purpose or meaning. For people of our time, the phrases of those amendments, like the phrases of the original Seven Articles of the Constitution, sometimes require interpretation. What did those words mean, as people used them near the end of the eighteenth century? One way to find out is to consult the first great dictionary of the English language, Samuel Johnson's, published at London in 1775; or, later, Noah Webster's *American Dictionary of the English Language* (1828). It is important to understand precisely, so far as possible, the meanings intended by the men (chiefly James Madison and George Mason) whose phrases are found in the Bill of Rights, because many important cases of constitutional law that affect millions of Americans are today decided on the presumed significance of certain phrases in the Bill of Rights. As the English jurist Sir James Fitzjames Stephen wrote in Victorian times,

Sources of the Bill of Rights

Amendment	Bill of Rights Guarantees	First Document Protecting	First American Guarantee	First Constitutional Guarantee
I	Establishment of religion	Rights of the Colonists (Boston)	Same	N.J. Constitution, Art. XIX
	Free exercise of religion	Md. Act Concerning Religion	Same	Va. Declaration of Rights, S. 16
	Free speech	Mass. Body of Liberties, S. 12	Same	Pa. Declaration of Rights, Art. XII
	Free press	Address to Inhabitants of Quebec	Same	Va. Declaration of Rights, S. 12
	Assembly	Declaration and Resolves, Continental Congress	Same	Pa. Declaration of Rights, Art. XVI
	Petition	Bill of Rights (1689)	Declaration of Rights and Grievances, (1765), S. XIII	Pa. Declaration of Rights, Art. XVI
II	Right to bear arms	Bill of Rights (1689)	Pa. Declaration of Rights, Art. XIII	Same
III	Quartering soldiers	N.Y. Charter of Liberties	Same	Del. Declaration of Rights, S. 21
IV	Searches	Rights of the Colonists (Boston)	Same	Va. Declaration of Rights, S. 10
	Seizures	Magna Carta, c. 39	Va. Declaration of Rights, S. 10	Same
V	Grand jury indictment	N.Y. Charter of Liberties	Same	N.C. Declaration of Rights, Art. VIII
	Double jeopardy	Mass. Body of Liberties, S. 42	Same	N.H. Bill of Rights, Art. XVI
	Self-incrimination	Va. Declaration of Rights, S. 8	Same	Same
	Due process	Magna Carta, c. 39	Md. Act for Liberties of the People	Va. Declaration of Rights, S. 8
	Just compensation	Mass. Body of Liberties, S. 8	Same	Vt. Declaration of Rights, Art. II

Sources of the Bill of Rights *Continued*

Amendment	Bill of Rights Guarantees	First Document Protecting	First American Guarantee	First Constitutional Guarantee
VI	Speedy trial	Va. Declaration of Rights, S. 8	Same	Same
	Public trial	West N.J. Concessions, c. XXIII	Same	Pa. Declaration of Rights, Art. IX
	Jury trial	Magna Carta, c. 39	Mass. Body of Liberties, S. 29	Va. Declaration of Rights, S. 8
	Cause and nature of accusation	Va. Declaration of Rights, S. 8	Same	Same
	Witnesses	Pa. Charter of Privileges, Art. V	Same	N.J. Constitution, Art. XVI
	Counsel	Mass. Body of Liberties, S. 29	Same	N.J. Constitution, Art. XVI
VII	Jury trial (civil)	Mass. Body of Liberties, S. 29	Same	Va. Declaration of Rights, S. 11
VIII	Bail	Mass. Body of Liberties, S. 18	Same	Va. Declaration of Rights, S. 9
	Fines	Pa. Frame of Government, S. XVIII	Same	Va. Declaration of Rights, S. 9
	Punishment	Mass. Body of Liberties, S. 43, 46	Same	Va. Declaration of Rights, S. 9
IX	Rights retained by people	Va. Convention, proposed amendment 17	Same	Ninth Amendment
X	Reserved Powers	Mass. Declaration of Rights, Art. IV	Same	Same

Source: Bernard Schwartz, *The Roots of the Bill of Rights*. Vol. 5 (New York: Chelsea House Publishers, 1980), 1204.

"Words are tools that break in the hand." We therefore need to define the concepts which lie behind the words of the Bill of Rights.

Another way to ascertain what the framers of the Bill of Rights intended by their amendments, and what the first Congress and the ratifying State legislatures understood by the amendments' language, is to consult Sir William Blackstone's *Commentaries on the Laws of England* (1765), and the early *Commentaries on the Constitution* (1833) and *Commentaries on American Law* (1826), written, respectively, by Joseph Story and James Kent. As eminent judges during the early decades of the Republic, both Story and Kent were more familiar with the constitutional controversies of the first five presidential administrations than any judge or professor of law near the close of the twentieth century can hope to be.

The comments on the Bill of Rights that follow are based on such sources of information, and also on the books, letters, and journals of political leaders and judges from 1776 to 1840.

It should be noted, moreover, that the Northwest Ordinance of 1787 also sheds light on the ideas and ideals of the generation that drafted the Constitution and the Bill of Rights. Passed by the Continental Congress on July 13, 1787, while the Federal Convention was meeting in Philadelphia, the Northwest Ordinance was later affirmed by the first Congress under the new Constitution. Its purpose was to provide a frame of government for the western territories that later became the States of Ohio, Indiana, Illinois, Michigan, and Wisconsin.

The Ordinance has been called our first national bill of rights, or "the Magna Charta of American Freedom." The great American statesman Daniel Webster said he doubted "whether one single law of any lawgiver, ancient or modern, has produced effects of more distinct, marked and lasting character than the Ordinance of 1787." In addition to protecting many civil liberties that later appeared in the Bill of Rights, the Northwest Ordinance also banned slavery in the Northwest Territory. The wording of the Thirteenth Amendment (1865) providing for the abolition of slavery in the United States was taken directly from the Northwest Ordinance. On the subject of religion, the ordinance provided that "No person, demeaning himself in a peaceable and orderly manner, shall ever be molested on account of his mode of worship or religious sentiments, in said Territory." The Ordinance also declared as a matter of public policy that because "Religion, morality, and knowledge, [are] necessary to good government and the happiness of mankind, schools and the means of education shall forever be encouraged."

The First Amendment: Religious Freedom, and Freedom to Speak, Print, Assemble, and Petition

We hear a good deal nowadays about "a wall of separation" between church and state in America. To some people's surprise, this phrase cannot be found in either the Constitution or the Declaration of Independence. Actually, the phrase occurs in a letter from Thomas Jefferson, as a candidate for office, to an assembly of Baptists in Connecticut.

The first clause of the First Amendment reads, "Congress shall make no law respecting an establishment of religion, or prohibiting the free exercise thereof." This clause is followed by guarantees of freedom of speech, of publication, of assembly, and of petitioning. These various aspects of liberty were lumped together in the First Amendment for the sake of convenience; Congress had originally intended to assign "establishment of religion" to a separate amendment because the relationships between state and church are considerably different from the civil liberties of speech, publication, assembly, and petitioning.

The purpose of the "Establishment Clause" was two-fold: (1) to prohibit Congress from imposing a national religion upon the people; and (2) to prohibit Congress (and the Federal government generally) from interfering with existing church-state relations in the several States. Thus the "Establishment Clause" is linked directly to the "Free Exercise Clause." It was designed to promote religious freedom by forbidding Congress to prefer one religious sect over other religious sects. It was also intended, however, to assure each State that its reserved powers included the power to decide for itself, under its own constitution or bill of rights, what kind of relationship it wanted with religious denominations in the State. Hence the importance of the word "respecting": Congress shall make no law "respecting," that is, touching or dealing with, the subject of religious establishment.

In effect, this "Establishment Clause" was a compromise between two eminent members of the first Congress—James Madison and Fisher

Morning Prayer, U.S. Senate, 1903.

(Courtesy of the Library of Congress.)

Ames. Representative Ames, from Massachusetts, was a Federalist. In his own State, and also in Connecticut, there still was an established church— the Congregational Church. By 1787–1791, an "established church" was one which was formally recognized by a State government as the publicly preferred form of religion. Such a church was entitled to certain taxes, called tithes, that were collected from the public by the State. Earlier, several other of Britain's colonies had recognized established churches, but those other establishments had vanished during the Revolution.

Now, if Congress had established a *national* church—and many countries, in the eighteenth century, had official national churches—probably it would have chosen to establish the Episcopal Church, related to the Church of England. For Episcopalians constituted the most numerous and influential Christian denomination in the United States. Had the Episcopal Church been so established nationally, the Congregational Church would have been disestablished in Massachusetts and Connecticut. Therefore, Fisher Ames and his Massachusetts constituents in 1789 were eager for a constitutional amendment that would not permit Congress to establish any national church or disestablish any State church.

The motive of James Madison for advocating the Establishment Clause of the First Amendment was somewhat different. Madison believed that for the Federal government to establish one church—the Episcopal Church, say—would vex the numerous Congregationalist, Presbyterian, Baptist, Methodist, Quaker, and other religious denominations. After all, it seemed hard enough to hold the United States together in those first months of the Constitution without stirring up religious controversies. So Madison, who was generally in favor of religious toleration, strongly advocated an Establishment Clause on the ground that it would avert disunity in the Republic.

In short, the Establishment Clause of the First Amendment was not intended as a declaration of governmental hostility toward religion, or even of governmental neutrality in the debate between believers and non-believers. It was simply a device for keeping religious passions out of American politics. The phrase "or prohibiting the free exercise thereof" was meant to keep the Congress from ever meddling in the disputes among religious bodies or interfering with the mode of worship.

During the nineteenth century, at least, State governments would have been free to establish State churches, had they desired to do so. The Establishment Clause restrained only Congress—not State legislatures. But the States were no more interested in establishing a particular church than was Congress, and the two New England States where Congregationalism was established eventually gave up their establishments— Connecticut in 1818, Massachusetts in 1833.

The remainder of the First Amendment is a guarantee of reasonable freedom of speech, publication, assembly, and petition. A key word in this declaration that the Congress must not abridge these freedoms is the article "the"—abridging *the* freedom of speech and press. For what the Congress had in mind, in 1789, was the civil freedom to which Americans already were accustomed, and which they had inherited from Britain. In effect, the clause means "that freedom of speech and press which prevails today." In 1789, this meant that Congress was prohibited from engaging in the practice of "prior censorship"—prohibiting a speech or publication without advance approval of an executive official. The courts today give a much broader interpretation to the clause. This does not mean, however, that the First Amendment guarantees any absolute or perfect freedom to shout whatever one wishes, print whatever one likes, assemble in a crowd wherever or whenever it suits a crowd's fancy, or present a petition to Congress or some other public body in a context of violence. Civil liberty as understood in the Constitution is ordered liberty, not license to indulge every impulse and certainly not license to overthrow the Constitution itself.

As one of the more famous of Supreme Court Justices, Oliver Wendell Holmes, put this matter, "The most stringent protection of free speech would not protect a man in falsely shouting fire in a theatre and causing a panic." Similarly, statutes that prohibit the publication of obscenities, libels, and calls to violence are generally held by the courts to conform to the First Amendment. For example, public assemblies can be forbidden or dispersed by local authorities when crowds threaten to turn into violent mobs. And even public petitions to the legislative or the executive branch of government must be presented in accordance with certain rules, or else they may be lawfully rejected.

The Constitution recognizes no "absolute" rights. A Justice of the Supreme Court observed years ago that "The Bill of Rights is not a suicide pact." Instead, the First Amendment is a reaffirmation of certain long-observed civil freedoms, and it is not a guarantee that citizens will go unpunished however outrageous their words, publications, street conduct, or mode of addressing public officials. The original, and in many ways the most important, purpose of freedom of speech and press is that it affords citizens an opportunity to criticize government—favorably and unfavorably—and to hold public officials accountable for their actions. It thus serves to keep the public informed and encourages the free exchange of ideas.

The Second Amendment: The Right to Bear Arms

This amendment consists of a single sentence: "A well regulated militia, being necessary to the security of a free State, the right of the people to keep and bear arms, shall not be infringed."

Although today we tend to think of the "militia" as the armed forces or national guard, the original meaning of the word was "the armed citizenry." One of the purposes of the Second Amendment was to prevent Congress from disarming the State militias. The phrasing of the Amendment was directly influenced by the American Revolutionary experience. During the initial phases of that conflict, Americans relied on the militia to confront the British regular army. The right of each State to maintain its own militia was thought by the founding generation to be a critical safeguard against "standing armies" and tyrants, both foreign and domestic.

The Second Amendment also affirms an individual's right to keep and bear arms. Since the Amendment limits only Congress, the States are free to regulate the possession and carrying of weapons in accordance with their own constitutions and bills of rights. "The right of the citizens to keep and bear arms," observed Justice Joseph Story of the Supreme Court in his *Commentaries on the Constitution* (1833), "has justly been considered as the palladium of the liberties of the republic, since it offers a strong moral check against the usurpation and arbitrary power of rulers, and will generally, even if these are successful in the first instance, enable the people to resist and triumph over them." Thus a disarmed population cannot easily resist or overthrow tyrannical government. The right is not absolute, of course, and the Federal courts have upheld Federal laws that limit the sale, possession, and transportation of certain kinds of weapons, such as machine guns and sawed-off shotguns. To what extent Congress can restrict the right is a matter of considerable uncertainty because the Federal courts have not attempted to define its limits.

The Third Amendment: Quartering Troops

Forbidding Congress to station soldiers in private houses without the householders' permission in time of peace, or without proper authorization in time of war, was bound up with memories of British soldiers who were quartered in American houses during the War of Independence. It is an indication of a desire, in 1789, to protect civilians from military bullying. This is the least-invoked provision of the Bill of Rights, and the Supreme Court has never had occasion to interpret or apply it.

The Fourth Amendment: Search and Seizure

This is a requirement for search warrants when the public authority decides to search individuals or their houses, or to seize their property in connection with some legal action or investigation. In general, any search without a warrant is unreasonable. Under certain conditions, however, no warrant is necessary—as when the search is incidental to a lawful arrest.

Before engaging in a search, the police must appear before a magistrate and, under oath, prove that they have good cause to believe that a search should be made. The warrant must specify the place to be searched and the property to be seized. This requirement is an American version of the old English principle that "Every man's house is his castle." In recent decades, courts have extended the protections of this amendment to require warrants for the search and seizure of intangible property, such as conversations recorded through electronic eavesdropping.

The Fifth Amendment: Rights of Persons

Here we have a complex of old rights at law that were intended to protect people from arbitrary treatment by the possessors of power, especially in actions at law. The common law assumes that a person is innocent until he is proven guilty. This amendment reasserts the ancient requirement that if a person is to be tried for a major crime, he must first be indicted by a grand jury. In addition, no person may be tried twice for the same offense. Also, an individual cannot be compelled in criminal cases to testify against himself, "nor be deprived of life, liberty, or property, without due process of law"; and the public authorities may not take private property without just compensation to the owner.

The immunity against being compelled to be a witness against one's self is often invoked in ordinary criminal trials and in trials for subversion or espionage. This right, like others in the Bill of Rights, is not absolute. A person who "takes the Fifth"—that is, refuses to answer questions in a court because his answers might incriminate him—thereby raises "a legitimate presumption" in the court that he has done something for which he might be punished by the law. If offered immunity from prosecution in return for giving testimony, either he must comply or else expect to be jailed, and kept in jail, for contempt of court. And, under certain circumstances, a judge or investigatory body such as a committee of Congress may refuse to accept a witness's contention that he would place himself in danger of criminal prosecution were he to answer any questions.

The Fifth Amendment's due process requirement was originally a procedural right that referred to methods of law enforcement. If a person was to be deprived of his life, liberty or property, such a deprivation had to conform to the common law standards of "due process." The Amendment required a procedure, as Daniel Webster once put it, that "hears before it condemns, proceeds upon inquiries, and renders judgment only after a trial" in which the basic principles of justice have been observed.

The prohibition against taking private property for public use without just compensation is a restriction on the Federal government's power of eminent domain. Federal courts have adopted a rule of interpretation that the "taking" must be "direct" and that private property owners are not entitled to compensation for indirect loss incidental to the exercise of governmental powers. Thus the courts have frequently held that rent-control measures, limiting the amount of rent which may be charged, are not a "taking," even though such measures may decrease the value of the property or deprive the owners of rental income. As a general rule, Federal courts have not since 1937 extended the same degree of protection to property rights as they have to other civil rights.

The Sixth Amendment: Rights of the Accused

Here again the Bill of Rights reaffirms venerable protections for persons accused of crimes. The Amendment guarantees jury trial in criminal cases; the right of the accused "to be informed of the nature and cause of the accusation"; also the rights to confront witnesses, to obtain witnesses through the arm of the law, and to have lawyers' help.

These are customs and privileges at law derived from long usage in

Britain and America. The recent enlargement of these rights by Federal courts has caused much controversy. The right of assistance of counsel, for example, has been extended backward from the time of trial to the time the defendant is first questioned as a suspect, and forward to the appeals stage of the process. Under the so-called "Miranda" rule, police must read to a suspect his "Miranda" rights before interrogation. Only if a suspect waives his rights may any statement or confession obtained be used against him in a trial. Otherwise the suspect is said to have been denied "assistance of counsel."

The Sixth Amendment also specifies that criminal trials must be "speedy." Because of the great backload of cases in our courts, this requirement is sometimes loosely applied today. Yet, as one jurist has put the matter, "Justice delayed is justice denied."

The Seventh Amendment: Trial by Jury in Civil Cases

This guarantee of jury trial in civil suits at common law "where the value in controversy shall exceed twenty dollars" (a much bigger sum of money in 1789 than now) was included in the Bill of Rights chiefly because several of the States' ratifying conventions had recommended it. It applies only to Federal cases, of course, and it may be waived. The primary purpose of the Amendment was to preserve the historic line separating the jury, which decides the facts, from the judge, who applies the law. It applies only to suits at common law, meaning "rights and remedies peculiarly legal in their nature." It does not apply to cases in equity or admiralty law, where juries are not used. In recent years, increasingly large monetary awards to plaintiffs by juries in civil cases have brought the jury system somewhat into disrepute.

The Eighth Amendment:
Bail and Cruel and Unusual Punishments

How much bail, fixed by a court as a requirement to assure that a defendant will appear in court at the assigned time, is "excessive"? What punishments are "cruel and unusual"? The monetary sums for bail have changed greatly over two centuries, and criminal punishments have grown less severe. Courts have applied the terms of this amendment differently over the years.

Courts are not required to release an accused person merely because he can supply bail bonds. The court may keep him imprisoned, for example, if the court fears that the accused person would become a danger to the community if released, or would flee the jurisdiction of the court. In such matters, much depends on the nature of the offense, the reputation of the alleged offender, and his ability to pay. Bail of a larger amount than is usually set for a particular crime must be justified by evidence.

As for cruel and unusual punishments, public whipping was not regarded as cruel and unusual in 1789, but it is probably so regarded today. In recent years, the Supreme Court has found that capital punishment is not forbidden by the Eighth Amendment, although the enforcement of capital punishment must be carried out so as not to permit jury discretion or to discriminate against any class of persons. Punishment may be declared cruel and unusual if it is out of all proportion to the offense.

The Ninth Amendment: Rights Retained by the People

Are all the rights to be enjoyed by citizens of the United States enumerated in the first eight amendments and in the Articles of the original Constitution? If so, might not the Federal government, at some future time, ignore a multitude of customs, privileges, and old usages cherished by American men and women, on the ground that these venerable ways were not rights at all? Does a civil right have to be written expressly into the Constitution in order to exist? The Seven Articles and the first eight amendments say nothing, for example, about a right to inherit property, or a right of marriage. Are, then, rights to inheritance and marriage wholly dependent on the will of Congress or the President at any one time?

The Federalists had made such objections to the very idea of a Bill of Rights being added to the Constitution. Indeed, it seemed quite possible to the first Congress under the Constitution that, by singling out and enumerating certain civil liberties, the Seven Articles and the Bill of Rights might seem to disparage or deny certain other prescriptive rights that are important but had not been written into the document.

The Stocks and Pillory at Williamsburg, Virginia.

(Courtesy of the Library of Congress.)

The Ninth Amendment was designed to quiet the fears of the Anti-Federalists who contended that, under the new Constitution, the Federal government would have the power to trample on the liberties of the people because it would have jurisdiction over any right that was not explicitly protected against Federal abridgment and reserved to the States. They argued in particular that there was an implied exclusion of trial by jury in *civil* cases because the Constitution made reference to it only in *criminal* cases.

Written to serve as a general principle of construction, the Ninth Amendment declares that "The enumeration in the Constitution of certain rights, shall not be *construed* to deny or disparage others retained by the people." The reasoning behind the amendment springs from Hamilton's 83rd and 84th essays in *The Federalist*. Madison introduced it simply to prevent a perverse application of the ancient legal maxim that a denial of power over a specified right does not imply an affirmative grant of power over an unnamed right.

This amendment is much misunderstood today, and it is sometimes thought to be a source of new rights, such as the "right of privacy," over which Federal courts may establish jurisdiction. It should be kept in mind, however, that the original purpose of this amendment was to *limit* the powers of the Federal government, not to expand them.

The Tenth Amendment: Rights Retained by the States

This last amendment in the Bill of Rights was probably the one most eagerly desired by the various State conventions and State legislatures that had demanded the addition of a bill of rights to the Constitution. Throughout the country, the basic uneasiness with the new Constitution was the dread that the Federal government would gradually enlarge its powers and suppress the States' governments. The Tenth Amendment was designed to lay such fears to rest.

This amendment was simply a declaration that "the powers not delegated to the United States by the Constitution, nor prohibited by it to the States, are reserved to the States respectively, or to the people." The Federalists maintained that the Framers at Philadelphia had meant from the first that all powers not specifically assigned to the Federal government were reserved to the States or the people of the States.

The amendment declares that powers are reserved "to the States respectively, or to the people," meaning they are to be left in their original state.

It should be noted that the Tenth Amendment does not say that powers not *expressly* delegated to the United States are reserved to the States. The authors of the Bill of Rights considered and specifically rejected such a statement. They believed that an amendment limiting the national government to its expressed powers would have seriously weakened it.

During much of our history, the Tenth Amendment was interpreted as a limitation of the delegated powers of Congress. Since 1937, however, the Supreme Court has largely rejected this view, and the Amendment no longer has the same operative meaning or effect that it once had.

Rights Versus Duties

Some Americans seem to fancy that the whole Constitution is a catalog of people's rights. But actually the major part of the Constitution—the Seven Articles—establishes a framework of national government and only incidentally deals with individuals' rights.

In any society, duties are often even more important than rights. For example, the duty of obeying good laws is more essential than the right to be exempted from the ordinary operation of the laws. As has been said, every right is married to some duty. Freedom involves individual responsibility.

With that statement in mind, let us look at some of the provisions of the Bill of Rights to see how those rights are joined to certain duties.

If one has a right to freedom of speech, one has a duty to speak decently and honestly, not inciting people to riot or to commit crimes.

If one has a right to freedom of the press (or, in our time, freedom of the "media"), one has the duty to publish the truth, temperately—not abusing this freedom for personal advantage or vengeance.

If one has a right to join other people in a public assembly, one has the duty to tolerate other people's similar gatherings and not to take the opportunity of converting a crowd into a mob.

If one enjoys an immunity from arbitrary search and seizure, one has the duty of not abusing these rights by unlawfully concealing things forbidden by law.

If one has a right not to be a witness against oneself in a criminal case, one has the duty not to pretend that he would be incriminated if he should testify: that is, to be an honest and candid witness, not taking advantage of the self-incrimination exemption unless otherwise one would really be in danger of successful prosecution.

If one has a right to trial by jury, one ought to be willing to serve on juries when so summoned by a court.

If one is entitled to rights, one has the duty to support the public authority that protects those rights.

For, unless a strong and just government exists, it is vain to talk about one's rights. Without liberty, order, and justice, sustained by good government, there is no place to which anyone can turn for enforcement of his claims to rights. This is because a "right," in law, is a claim upon somebody for something. If a man has a right to be paid for a day's work, for example, he asserts a claim upon his employer; but, if that employer refuses to pay him, the man must turn to a court of law for enforcement of his right. If no court of law exists, the "right" to payment becomes little better than an empty word. The unpaid man might try to take his pay by force, true; but when force rules instead of law, a society falls into anarchy and the world is dominated by the violent and the criminal.

Knowing these hard truths about duties, rights, and social order, the Framers endeavored to give us a Constitution that is more than mere words and slogans. Did they succeed? At the end of two centuries, the Constitution of the United States still functions adequately. Had Americans followed the French example of placing all their trust in a naked declaration of rights, without any supporting constitutional edifice to limit power and the claims of absolute liberty, it may be doubted whether liberty, order, or justice would have prevailed in the succeeding years. There cannot be better proof of the wisdom of the Framers than the endurance of the Constitution.

SUGGESTED READING

Walter Hartwell Bennett, ed., *Letters from the Federal Farmer to the Republican* (Tuscaloosa: University of Alabama Press, 1978).

M. E. Bradford, *Original Intentions: On the Making and Ratification of the United States Constitution* (Athens: University of Georgia Press, 1993).

Neil H. Cogan, ed., *The Complete Bill of Rights: The Drafts, Debates, Sources, and Origins* (New York: Oxford University Press, 1997).

Patrick T. Conley and John P. Kaminski, *The Constitution and the States: The Role of the Original Thirteen in the Framing and Adoption of the Federal Constitution* (Madison, Wis.: Madison House, 1988).

Saul Cornell, *Anti-Federalism and the Dissenting Tradition in America, 1788–1828* (Chapel Hill: University of North Carolina Press, 1999).

Jonathan Elliot, ed., *The Debates in the Several State Conventions on the Adoption of the Federal Constitution.* 5 vols. (Philadelphia: J. B. Lippincott, 1836–1840). See also James McClellan and M. E. Bradford, eds., *Elliot's Debates in the Several State Conventions . . . A New, Revised and Enlarged Edition.* 7 vols. (Richmond: James River Press, 1989–   ). In progress.

Paul Leicester Ford, ed., *Essays on the Constitution of the United States* (New York: Burt Franklin, 1970).

Paul Leicester Ford, *Pamphlets on the Constitution of the United States* (New York: Da Capo Press, 1968).

Michael Allen Gillespie and Michael Lienesch, eds., *Ratifying the Constitution* (Lawrence: University Press of Kansas, 1989).

Robert A. Goldwin, *From Parchment to Power: How James Madison Used the Bill of Rights to Save the Constitution* (Washington, D.C.: The AEI Press, 1997).

Eugene Hickok, ed., *The Bill of Rights: Original Meaning and Current Understanding* (Charlottesville: University of Virginia Press, 1991).

John Kaminski and Gaspare J. Saladino, eds., *The Documentary History of the Ratification of the Constitution.* 22 vols. (Madison: State Historical Society of Wisconsin, 1976–   ). In progress.

Philip B. Kurland and Ralph Lerner, eds., *The Founders' Constitution.* 5 vols. (Chicago: University of Chicago Press, 1987).

Leonard W. Levy and Dennis J. Mahoney, eds., *The Framing and Ratification of the Constitution* (New York: Macmillan Publishing Co., 1987).

Robert Rutland, *The Birth of the Bill of Rights* (Chapel Hill: University of North Carolina Press, 1955).

Robert Rutland, *The Ordeal of the Constitution: The Antifederalists and the Ratification Struggle of 1787–1788* (Norman: University of Oklahoma Press, 1966).

Jeffrey St. John, *A Child of Fortune: A Correspondent's Report on the Ratification of the U.S. Constitution and the Battle for a Bill of Rights* (Ottawa, Ill.: Jameson Books, 1990).

Jeffrey St. John, *Forge of Union, Anvil of Liberty: A Correspondent's Report on the First Federal Elections, the First Federal Congress, and the Creation of the Bill of Rights* (Ottawa, Ill.: Jameson Books, 1992).

Bernard Schwartz, ed., *The Roots of the Bill of Rights: An Illustrated Sourcebook of American Freedom.* 5 vols. (New York: Chelsea House Publishers, 1980).

Herbert Storing, ed., *The Complete Anti-Federalist.* 7 vols. (Chicago: University of Chicago Press, 1981).

John Taylor of Caroline, *New Views of the Constitution,* ed. by James McClellan (Washington, D.C.: Regnery Publishing Inc., 2000).

Helen Veit, Kenneth Bowling, and Charlene Bickford, eds., *Creating the Bill of Rights: The Documentary Record from the First Federal Congress* (Baltimore: Johns Hopkins University Press, 1991).

The Address and Reasons of Dissent of the Minority of the Convention of the State of Pennsylvania to Their Constituents

Anti-Federalist dissent from the proposed Constitution is adequately represented by this document presented to the Pennsylvania Convention on December 18, 1787, by the minority (Anti-Federalists). Similar protests against ratification were made by Patrick Henry in Virginia and by able opponents in other States.

It was not until after the termination of the late glorious contest, which made the people of the United States an independent nation, that any defect was discovered in the present confederation. It was formed by some of the ablest patriots in America. It carried us successfully through the war, and the virtue and patriotism of the people, with their disposition to promote the common cause, supplied the want of power in Congress.

The requisition of Congress for the five *per cent.* impost was made before the peace, so early as the first of February, 1781, but was prevented taking effect by the refusal of one State; yet it is probable every State in the Union would have agreed to this measure at that period, had it not been for the extravagant terms in which it was demanded. The requisition was new molded in the year 1783, and accompanied with an additional demand of certain supplementary funds for twenty-five years. Peace had now taken place, and the United States found themselves laboring under a considerable foreign and domestic debt, incurred during the war. The requisition of 1783 was commensurate with the interest of the debt, as it was then calculated; but it has been more accurately ascertained since that time. The domestic debt has been found to fall several millions of dollars short of the calculation, and it has lately been considerably diminished by large sales of the Western lands. The States have been called on by Congress annually for supplies until the general system of finance proposed in 1783 should take place.

It was at this time that the want of an efficient federal government was first complained of, and the powers vested in Congress were found to be inadequate to the procuring of the benefits that should result from the union. The impost was granted by most of the States, but many refused the supplementary funds; the annual requisitions were set at naught by some of the States, while others complied with them by legislative acts, but were tardy in their payments, and Congress found themselves incapable of complying with their engagements and supporting the federal government. It was found that our national character was sinking in the opinion of foreign nations. The Congress could make treaties of commerce, but could not enforce the observance of them. We were suffering from the restrictions of foreign nations, who had suckled our commerce while we were unable to retaliate, and all now agreed that it would be advantageous to the union to enlarge the powers of Congress, that they should be enabled in the amplest manner to regulate commerce and to lay and collect duties on the imports throughout the United States. With this view, a convention was first proposed by Virginia, and finally recommended by Congress for the different States to appoint deputies to meet in convention, "for the purposes of revising and amending the present articles of confederation, so as to make them adequate to the exigencies of the union." This recommendation the legislatures of twelve States complied with so hastily as not to consult their constituents on the subject; and though the different legislatures had no authority from their constituents for the purpose, they probably apprehended the necessity would justify the measure, and none of them extended their ideas at that time further than "revising and amending the present articles of confederation." Pennsylvania, by the act appointing deputies, expressly confined their powers to this object, and though it is probable that some of the members of the assembly of this State had at that time in contemplation to annihilate the present confederation, as well as the constitution of Pennsylvania, yet the plan was not sufficiently matured to communicate it to the public.

The majority of the legislature of this commonwealth were at that time under the influence of the members from the city of Philadelphia. They agreed that the deputies sent by them to convention should have no compensation for their services, which determination was calculated to prevent the election of any member who resided at a distance from the city. It was in vain for the minority to attempt electing delegates to the convention who understood the circumstances, and the feelings of the people, and had a common interest with them. They found a disposition in the leaders of the majority of the house to choose themselves and some of their dependents. The minority attempted to prevent this by agreeing to vote for some of the leading members, who they knew had influence enough to be appointed at any rate, in hopes of carrying with them some respectable citizens of Philadelphia, in whose principles and integrity they could have more confidence, but even in this they were disappointed, except in one member: the eighth member was added at a subsequent session of the assembly.

The Continental Convention met in the city of Philadelphia at the time appointed. It was composed of some men of excellent character; of others who were more remarkable for their ambition and cunning than their patriotism, and of some who had been opponents to the independence of the United States. The delegates from Pennsylvania were, six of them, uniform and decided opponents to the Constitution of this commonwealth. The convention sat upwards of four months. The doors were kept shut, and the members brought under the most solemn engagements of secrecy. Some of those who opposed their going so far beyond their powers, retired, hopeless, from the convention; others had the firmness to refuse signing the plan altogether; and many who did sign it, did it not as a system they wholly approved, but as the best that could be then obtained, and notwithstanding the time spent on this subject, it is agreed on all hands to be a work of haste and accommodation.

Whilst the gilded chains were forging in the secret conclave, the meaner instruments of the despotism without were busily employed in alarming the fears of the people with dangers which did not exist, and exciting their hopes of greater advantages from the expected plan than even the best government on earth could produce. The proposed plan had not many hours issued forth from the womb of suspicious secrecy, until such as were prepared for the purpose, were carrying about petitions for people to sign, signifying their approbation of the system, and requesting the legislature to call a convention. While every measure was taken to intimidate the people against opposing it, the public papers teemed with the most violent threats against those who should dare to think for themselves, and *tar and feathers* were liberally promised to all those who would not immediately join in supporting the proposed government, be it what it would. Under such circumstances petitions in favor of calling a Convention were signed by great numbers in and about the city, before they had leisure to read and examine the system, many of whom—now they are better acquainted with it, and have had time to investigate its principles—are heartily opposed to it. The petitions were speedily handed in to the legislature.

Affairs were in this situation, when on the 28th of September last, a resolution was proposed to the assembly by a member of the house, who had been also a member of the federal convention, for calling a State convention to be elected within *ten* days for the purpose of examining and adopting the proposed Constitution of the United States, though at this time the house had not received it from Congress. This attempt was opposed by a minority, who after offering every argument in their power to prevent the precipitate measure, without effect, absented themselves from the house as the only alternative left them, to prevent the measures taking place previous to their constituents being acquainted with the business. That violence and outrage which had been so often threatened was now practiced; some of the members were seized the next day by a mob collected for the purpose, and forcibly dragged to the house, and there detained by force whilst the quorum of the legislature *so formed,* completed their resolution. We shall dwell no longer on this subject: the people of Pennsylvania have been already acquainted therewith. We would only further observe that every member of the legislature, previously to taking his seat, by solemn oath or affirmation, declares "that he will not do or consent to any act or thing whatever, that will have a tendency to lessen or abridge their rights and privileges, as declared in the constitution of this State." And that constitution which they are so solemnly sworn to support, cannot legally be altered but by a recommendation of the council of censors, who alone are authorized to propose alterations and amendments, and even these must be published at least *six months* for the consideration of the people. The proposed system of government for the United States, if adopted, will alter and may annihilate the constitution of Pennsylvania; and therefore the legislature had no authority whatever to recommend the calling of a convention for that purpose. This proceeding could not be considered as binding on the people of this commonwealth. The house was formed by violence, some of the members composing it were detained there by force, which alone would have vitiated any proceedings to which they were otherwise competent; but had the legislature been legally formed, this business was absolutely without their power.

In this situation of affairs were the subscribers elected members of the Convention of Pennsylvania—a Convention called by a legislature in direct violation of their duty, and composed in part of members who were compelled to attend for the purpose, to consider a Constitution proposed by a Convention of the United States, who were not appointed for the purpose of framing a new form of government, but whose powers were expressly confined to altering and amending the present articles of confederation. Therefore the members of the continental Convention in proposing the plan acted as individuals, and not as deputies from Pennsylvania. The assembly who called the State Convention acted as individuals, and not as the legislature of Pennsylvania; nor could they or the Convention chosen on their recommendation have authority to do any act or thing that can alter or annihilate the Constitution of Pennsylvania (both of which will be done by the new Constitution), nor are their proceedings, in our opinion, at all binding on the people.

The election for members of the Convention was held at so early a period, and the want of information was so great, that some of us did not know of it until after it was over, and we have reason to believe that great numbers of the people of Pennsylvania have not yet had an opportunity of sufficiently examining the proposed Constitution. We apprehend that no change can take place that will affect the internal government or Constitution of this commonwealth, unless a majority of the people should evidence a wish for such a change; but on examining the number of votes given for members of the present State Convention, we find that of upwards of *seventy thousand* freemen who are entitled to vote in Pennsylvania, the whole convention has been elected by about *thirteen thousand* voters, and though *two-thirds* of the members of the Convention have thought proper to ratify the proposed Constitution, yet those *two-thirds* were elected by the votes of only *six thousand and eight hundred* freemen.

In the city of Philadelphia and some of the eastern counties there unto that took the lead in the business agreed to vote for none but such as would solemnly promise to adopt the system *in toto*, without exercising their judgment. In many of the counties the people did not attend the elections, as they had not an opportunity of judging of the plan. Others did not consider themselves bound by the call of a set of men who assembled at the State-house in Philadelphia and assumed the name of the legislature of Pennsylvania; and some were prevented from voting by the violence of the party who were determined at all events to force down the measure. To such lengths did the tools of despotism carry their outrage, that on the night of the election for members of convention, in the city of Philadelphia, several of the subscribers (being then in the city to transact your business) were grossly abused, ill-treated and insulted while they were quiet in their lodgings, though they did not interfere nor had anything to do with the said election, but, as they apprehend, because they were supposed to be adverse to the proposed constitution, and would not tamely surrender those sacred rights which you had committed to their charge.

The convention met, and the same disposition was soon manifested in considering the proposed constitution, that had been exhibited in every other stage of the business. We were prohibited by an express vote of the convention from taking any questions on the separate articles of the plan, and reduced to the necessity of adopting or rejecting *in toto*. 'Tis true the majority permitted us to debate on each article, but restrained us from proposing amendments. They also determined not to permit us to enter on the minutes our reasons of dissent against any of the articles, nor even on the final question our reasons of dissent against the whole. Thus situated we entered on the examination of the proposed system of government, and found it to be such as we could not adopt, without, as we conceived, surrendering up your dearest rights. We offered our objections to the convention, and opposed those parts of the plan which, in our opinion, would be injurious to you, in the best manner we were able; and closed our arguments by offering the following propositions to the convention.

1. The right of conscience shall be held inviolable; and neither the legislative, executive or judicial powers of the United States shall have authority to alter, abrogate or infringe any part of the constitution of the several States, which provide for the preservation of liberty in matters of religion.

2. That in controversies respecting property, and in suits between man and man, trial by jury shall remain as heretofore, as well in the Federal courts as in those of the several States.

3. That in all capital and criminal prosecutions, a man has a right to demand the cause and nature of his accusation, as well in the Federal courts as in those of the several States; to be heard by himself and his counsel; to be confronted with the accusers and witnesses; to call for evidence in his favor, and a speedy trial by an impartial jury of his vicinage, without whose unanimous consent he cannot be found guilty; nor can he be compelled to give evidence against himself; and, that no man be deprived of his liberty, except by the law of the land or the judgment of his peers.

4. That excessive bail ought not to be required, nor excessive fines imposed, nor cruel nor unusual punishments inflicted.

5. That warrants unsupported by evidence, whereby any officer or messenger may be commanded or required to search suspected places; or to seize any person or persons, his or their property not particularly described, are grievous and oppressive, and shall not be granted either by the magistrates of the Federal government or others.

6. That the people have a right to the freedom of speech, of writing and publishing their sentiments; therefore the freedom of the press shall not be restrained by any law of the United States.

7. That the people have a right to bear arms for the defence of themselves and their own State or the United States, or for the purpose of killing game; and no law shall be passed for disarming the people or any of them unless for crimes committed, or real danger of public injury from individuals; and as standing armies in the time of peace are dangerous to liberty, they ought not to be kept up; and that the military shall be kept under strict subordination to, and be governed by the civil powers.

8. The inhabitants of the several States shall have liberty to fowl and hunt in seasonable time on the lands they hold, and on all other lands in

the United States not inclosed, and in like manner to fish in all navigable waters, and others not private property, without being restrained therein by any laws to be passed by the legislature of the United States.

9. That no law shall be passed to restrain the legislatures of the several States from enacting laws for imposing taxes, except imposts and duties on goods imported or exported, and that no taxes, except imposts and duties upon goods imported and exported, and postage on letters, shall be levied by the authority of Congress.

10. That the House of Representatives be properly increased in number; that elections shall remain free; that the several States shall have power to regulate the elections for Senators and Representatives, without being controlled either directly or indirectly by any interference on the part of the Congress; and that the elections of Representatives be annual.

11. That the power of organizing, arming and disciplining the militia (the manner of disciplining the militia to be prescribed by Congress), remain with the individual States, and that Congress shall not have authority to call or march any of the militia out of their own State, without the consent of such State, and for such length of time only as such State shall agree.

That the sovereignty, freedom and independence of the several States shall be retained, and every power, jurisdiction and right which is not by this Constitution expressly delegated to the United States in Congress assembled.

12. That the legislative, executive and judicial powers be kept separate; and to this end that a constitutional council be appointed to advise and assist the President, who shall be responsible for the advice they give—hereby the Senators would be relieved from almost constant attendance; and also that the judges be made completely independent.

13. That no treaty which shall be directly opposed to the existing laws of the United States in Congress assembled, shall be valid until such laws shall be repealed or made conformable to such treaty; neither shall any treaties be valid which are in contradiction to the Constitution of the United States, or the constitution of the several States.

14. That the judiciary power of the United States shall be confined to cases affecting ambassadors, other public ministers and consuls, to cases

of admiralty and maritime jurisdiction; to controversies to which the United States shall be a party; to controversies between two or more States—between a State and citizens of different States—between citizens claiming lands under grants of different States, and between a State or the citizens thereof and foreign States; and in criminal cases to such only as are expressly enumerated in the Constitution; and that the United States in Congress assembled shall not have power to enact laws which shall alter the laws of descent and distribution of the effects of deceased persons, the titles of lands or goods, or the regulation of contracts in the individual States.

After reading these propositions, we declared our willingness to agree to the plan, provided it was so amended as to meet those propositions or something similar to them, and finally moved the convention to adjourn, to give the people of Pennsylvania time to consider the subject and determine for themselves; but these were all rejected and the final vote taken, when our duty to you induced us to vote against the proposed plan and to decline signing the ratification of the same.

During the discussion we met with many insults and some personal abuse. We were not even treated with decency, during the sitting of the convention, by the persons in the gallery of the house. However, we flatter ourselves that in contending for the preservation of those invaluable rights you have thought proper to commit to our charge, we acted with a spirit becoming freemen; and being desirous that you might know the principles which actuated our conduct, and being prohibited from inserting our reasons of dissent on the minutes of the convention, we have subjoined them for your consideration, as to you alone we are accountable. It remains with you whether you will think those inestimable privileges,which you have so ably contended for, should be sacrificed at the shrine of despotism, or whether you mean to contend for them with the same spirit that has so often baffled the attempts of an aristocratic faction to rivet the shackles of slavery on you and your unborn posterity.

Our objections are comprised under three general heads of dissent, viz.:

We dissent, first, because it is the opinion of the most celebrated writers on government, and confirmed by uniform experience, that a very extensive territory cannot be governed on the principles of freedom, otherwise than by a confederation of republics, possessing all the powers of internal government, but united in the management of their general and foreign concerns.

If any doubt could have been entertained of the truth of the foregoing principle, it has been fully removed by the concession of *Mr. Wilson,* one of the majority on this question, and who was one of the deputies in the late general convention. In justice to him, we will give his own words; they are as follows, viz.: "The extent of country for which the new Constitution was required, produced another difficulty in the business of the Federal Convention. It is the opinion of some celebrated writers, that to a small territory, the democratical; to a middling territory (as Montesquieu has termed it), the monarchical; and to an extensive territory, the despotic form of government is best adapted. Regarding then the wide and almost unbounded jurisdiction of the United States, at first view, the hand of despotism seemed necessary to control, connect and protect it; and hence the chief embarrassment rose. For we know that although our constituents would cheerfully submit to the legislative restraints of a free government, they would spurn at every attempt to shackle them with despotic power." And again, in another part of his speech, he continues: "Is it probable that the dissolution of the State governments, and the establishment of one *consolidated empire* would be eligible in its nature, and satisfactory to the people in its administration? I think not, as I have given reasons to show that so extensive a territory could not be governed, connected and preserved, but by the *supremacy of despotic power.* All the exertions of the most potent emperors of Rome were not capable of keeping that empire together, which in extent was far inferior to the dominion of America."

We dissent, secondly, because the powers vested in Congress by this Constitution must necessarily annihilate and absorb the legislative, executive, and judicial powers of the several States, and produce from their ruins one consolidated government, which from the nature of things will be *an iron handed despotism,* as nothing short of the supremacy of despotic sway could connect and govern these United States under one government.

As the truth of this position is of such decisive importance, it ought to be fully investigated, and if it is founded to be clearly ascertained; for, should it be demonstrated that the powers vested by this Constitution in Congress will have such an effect as necessarily to produce one consolidated government, the question then will be reduced to this short issue, *viz:* whether satiated with the blessings of liberty, whether repenting of the folly of so recently asserting their unalienable rights against foreign despots at the expense of so much blood and treasure, and such painful and arduous struggles, the people of America are now willing to resign every privilege of freemen, and submit to the dominion of an absolute government that will embrace all America in one chain of despotism; or whether they will, with virtuous indignation, spurn at the shackles prepared for them, and confirm their liberties by a conduct becoming freemen.

That the new government will not be a confederacy of States, as it ought, but one consolidated government, founded upon the destruction of the several governments of the States, we shall now show.

The powers of Congress under the new Constitution are complete and unlimited over the *purse* and the *sword,* and are perfectly independent of and supreme over the State governments, whose intervention in these great points is entirely destroyed. By virtue of their power of taxation, Congress may command the whole or any part of the property of the people. They may impose what imposts upon commerce, they may impose what land taxes, poll taxes, excises, duties on all written instruments and duties on every other article, that they may judge proper; in short, every species of taxation, whether of an external or internal nature, is comprised in section the eighth of article the first, *viz:*

"The Congress shall have power to lay and collect taxes, duties, imposts, and excises, to pay the debts, and provide for the common defence and general welfare of the United States."

As there is no one article of taxation reserved to the State governments, the Congress may monopolize every source of revenue, and thus indirectly demolish the State governments, for without funds they could not exist; the taxes, duties and excises imposed by Congress may be so high as to render it impracticable to levy farther sums on the same articles; but whether this should be the case or not, if the State governments should presume to impose taxes, duties or excises on the same articles with Congress, the latter may abrogate and repeal the laws whereby they are imposed, upon the allegation that they interfere with the due collection of their taxes, duties or excises, by virtue of the following clause, part of section eighth, article first, *viz.:*

"To make all laws which shall be necessary and proper for carrying into execution the foregoing powers, and all other powers vested by this constitution in the government of the United States, or in any department or officer thereof."

The Congress might gloss over this conduct by construing every purpose for which the State legislatures now lay taxes, to be for the *"general welfare,"* and therefore as of their jurisdiction.

And the supremacy of the laws of the United States is established by article sixth, viz.: "That this Constitution and the laws of the United States which shall be made in pursuance thereof, and *all treaties* made, or which shall be made under the authority of the United States, shall be the *supreme law* of the *land;* and *the judges in every State shall be bound thereby; anything in the constitution or laws of any State to the contrary notwithstanding."* It has been alleged that the words "pursuant to the Constitution," are a restriction upon the authority of Congress; but when it is considered that by other sections they are invested with every efficient power of government, and which may be exercised to the absolute destruction of the State governments, without any violation of even the forms of the Constitution, this seeming restriction, as well as every other restriction in it, appears to us to be nugatory and delusive; and only introduced as a blind upon the real nature of the government. In our opinion, "pursuant to the Constitution" will be co-extensive with the *will* and *pleasure* of Congress, which, indeed, will be the only limitation of their powers.

We apprehend that two co-ordinate sovereignties would be a solecism in politics; that, therefore, as there is no line of distinction drawn between the general and State governments, as the sphere of their jurisdiction is undefined, it would be contrary to the nature of things that both should exist together—one or the other would necessarily triumph in the fullness of dominion. However, the contest could not be of long continuance, as the State governments are divested of every means of defense, and will be obliged by "the supreme law of the land" *to yield at discretion.*

It has been objected to this total destruction of the State governments that the existence of their legislatures is made essential to the organization of Congress; that they must assemble for the appointment of the Senators and President-general of the United States. True, the State legislatures may be continued for some years, as boards of appointment merely, after they are divested of every other function; but the framers of the Constitution, foreseeing that the people will soon become disgusted with this solemn mockery of a government without power and usefulness, have made a provision for relieving them from the imposition in section fourth of article first, viz.: "The times, places and manner of holding elections for Senators and Representatives shall be prescribed in each State by the legislature thereof; *but the Congress may at any time by law make or alter such regulations, except as to the place of choosing Senators."*

As Congress have the control over the time of the appointment of the President-general, of the Senators and of the Representatives of the United States, they may prolong their existence in office for life by postponing the time of their election and appointment from period to period under various pretenses, such as an apprehension of invasion, the factious disposition of the people, or any other plausible pretence that the occasion may suggest; and having thus obtained life-estates in the government, they may fill up the vacancies themselves by their control over the mode of appointment; with this exception in regard to the Senators that as the place of appointment for them must, by the Constitution, be in the particular State, they may depute some body in the respective States, to fill up the vacancies in the Senate, occasioned by death, until they can venture to assume it themselves. In this manner may the only restriction in this clause be evaded. By virtue of the foregoing section, when the spirit of the people shall be gradually broken, when the general government shall be firmly established, and when a numerous standing army shall render opposition vain, the Congress may complete the system of despotism, in renouncing all dependence on the people by continuing themselves and children in the government.

The celebrated *Montesquieu,* in his Spirit of Laws, vol. i., page 12, says, "That in a democracy there can be no exercise of sovereignty, but by the suffrages of the people, which are their will; now the sovereign's will is the sovereign himself—the laws, therefore, which establish the right of suffrage, are fundamental to this government. In fact, it is as important to regulate in a republic in what manner, by whom, and concerning what suffrages are to be given, as it is in a monarchy to know who is the prince, and after what manner he ought to govern." The *time, mode* and *place* of the election of Representatives, Senators and President-general of the United States, ought not to be under the control of Congress, but fundamentally ascertained and established.

The new Constitution, consistently with the plan of consolidation, contains no reservation of the rights and privileges of the State governments, which was made in the confederation of the year 1778, by article the 2d, viz.: "That each State retains its sovereignty, freedom and independence, and every power, jurisdiction and right which is not by this confederation expressly delegated to the United States in Congress assembled."

The legislative power vested in Congress by the foregoing recited sections, is so unlimited in its nature, may be so comprehensive and boundless in its exercise, that this alone would be amply sufficient to annihilate the State governments, and swallow them up in the grand vortex of a general empire.

The judicial powers vested in Congress are also so various and extensive, that by legal ingenuity they may be extended to every case, and thus absorb the State judiciaries; and when we consider the decisive influence that a general judiciary would have over the civil polity of the several States, we do not hesitate to pronounce that this power, unaided by the legislative, would effect a consolidation of the States under one government.

The powers of a court of equity, vested by this Constitution in the tribunals of Congress—powers which do not exist in Pennsylvania, unless so far as they can be incorporated with jury trial—would, in this State, greatly contribute to this event. The rich and wealthy suitors would eagerly lay hold of the infinite mazes, perplexities and delays, which a court of chancery, with the appellate powers of the Supreme Court in fact as well as law would furnish him with, and thus the poor man being plunged in the bottomless pit of legal discussion, would drop his demand in despair.

In short, consolidation pervades the whole Constitution. It begins with an annunciation that such was the intention. The main pillars of the fabric correspond with it, and the concluding paragraph is a confirmation of it.

The preamble begins with the words, "We the people of the United States," which is the style of a compact between individuals entering into a state of society, and not that of a confederation of States. The other features of consolidation we have before noticed.

Thus we have fully established the position, that the powers vested by this constitution in Congress will effect a consolidation of the States under one government, which even the advocates of this Constitution admit could not be done without the sacrifice of all liberty.

We dissent, thirdly, because if it were practicable to govern so extensive a territory as these United States include, on the plan of a consolidated government, consistent with the principles of liberty and the happiness of the people, yet the construction of this Constitution is not calculated to attain the object; for independent of the nature of the case, it would of itself necessarily produce a despotism, and that not by the usual gradations, but with the celerity that has hitherto only attended revolutions effected by the sword.

To establish the truth of this position, a cursory investigation of the principles and form of this Constitution will suffice.

The first consideration that this review suggests, is the omission of a BILL OF RIGHTS ascertaining and fundamentally establishing those unalienable and personal rights of men, without the full, free and secure enjoyment of which there can be no liberty, and over which it is not necessary for a good government to have the control—the principal of which are the rights of conscience, personal liberty by the clear and unequivocal establishment of the writ of *habeas corpus*, jury trial in criminal and civil cases, by an impartial jury of the vicinage or county, with the common law proceedings for the safety of the accused in criminal prosecutions; and the liberty of the press, that scourge of tyrants, and the grand bulwark of every other liberty and privilege. The stipulations heretofore made in favor of them in the State constitutions, are entirely superseded by this Constitution.

The legislature of a free country should be so formed as to have a competent knowledge of its constituents, and enjoy their confidence. To produce these essential requisites, the representation ought to be fair, equal and sufficiently numerous to possess the same interests, feelings, opinions, and views which the people themselves would possess, were they

all assembled; and so numerous as to prevent bribery and undue influence, and so responsible to the people, by frequent and fair elections, as
to prevent their neglecting or sacrificing the views and interests of their
constituents to their own pursuits.

We will now bring the legislature under this Constitution to the test of
the foregoing principles, which will demonstrate that it is deficient in
every essential quality of a just and safe representation.

The House of Representatives is to consist of sixty-five members; that
is one for about every 50,000 inhabitants, to be chosen every two years.
Thirty-three members will form a quorum for doing business, and seventeen of these, being the majority, determine the sense of the house.

The Senate, the other constituent branch of the legislature, consists of
twenty-six members, being *two* from each State, appointed by their legislatures every six years; fourteen senators make a quorum—the majority of whom, eight, determines the sense of that body, except in judging
on impeachments, or in making treaties, or in expelling a member, when
two-thirds of the Senators present must concur.

The President is to have the control over the enacting of laws, so far as
to make the concurrence of two-thirds of the Representatives and Senators present necessary, if he should object to the laws.

Thus it appears that the liberties, happiness, interests, and great concerns of the whole United States, may be dependent upon the integrity,
virtue, wisdom, and knowledge of twenty-five or twenty-six men. How
inadequate and unsafe a representation! Inadequate, because the sense
and views of three or four millions of people, diffuse over so extensive a
territory, comprising such various climates, products, habits, interests,
and opinions, cannot be collected in so small a body; and besides, it is not
a fair and equal representation of the people even in proportion to its
number, for the smallest State has as much weight in the Senate as the
largest; and from the smallness of the number to be chosen for both
branches of the legislature, and from the mode of election and appointment, which is under the control of Congress, and from the nature of the
thing, men of the most elevated rank in life will alone be chosen. The
other orders in the society, such as farmers, traders, and mechanics, who
all ought to have a competent number of their best informed men in the
legislature, shall be totally unrepresented.

The representation is unsafe, because in the exercise of such great powers and trusts, it is so exposed to corruption and undue influence, by the gift of the numerous places of honor and emolument at the disposal of the executive, by the arts and address of the great and designing, and by direct bribery.

The representation is moreover inadequate and unsafe, because of the long terms for which it is appointed, and the mode of its appointment, by which Congress may not only control the choice of the people, but may so manage as to divest the people of this fundamental right, and become self-elected.

The number of members in the House of Representatives *may* be increased to one for every 30,000 inhabitants. But when we consider that this cannot be done without the consent of the Senate, who from their share in the legislative, in the executive, and judicial departments, and permanency of appointment, will be the great efficient body in this government, and whose weight and predominance would be abridged by an increase of the representatives, we are persuaded that this is a circumstance that cannot be expected. On the contrary, the number of representatives will probably be continued at sixty-five, although the population of the country may swell to treble what it now is, unless a revolution should effect a change.

We have before noticed the judicial power as it would affect a consolidation of the States into one government; we will now examine it as it would affect the liberties and welfare of the people, supposing such a government were practicable and proper.

The judicial power, under the proposed Constitution, is founded on well-known principles of the *civil law*, by which the judge determines both on law and fact, and appeals are allowed from the inferior tribunals to the superior, upon the whole question; so that *facts* as well as *law*, would be reexamined, and even new facts brought forward in the court of appeals; and to use the words of a very eminent civilian—"The cause is many times another thing before the court of appeals, than what it was at the time of the first sentence."

That this mode of proceeding is the one which must be adopted under this Constitution, is evident from the following circumstances: 1st. That the trial by jury, which is the grand characteristic of the common law, is secured by the Constitution only in criminal cases. 2d. That the appeal from both *law* and *fact* is expressly established, which is utterly inconsistent with the principles of the common law and trials by jury. The only mode in which an appeal from law and fact can be established, is by adopting the principles and practice of the civil law, unless the United States should be drawn into the absurdity of calling and swearing juries, merely for the purpose of contradicting their verdicts, which would render juries contemptible and worse than useless. 3d. That the courts to be established would decide on all cases *of law and equity,* which is a well-known characteristic of the civil law, and these courts would have cognizance not only of the laws of the United States, and of treaties, and of cases affecting ambassadors, but of all cases of *admiralty and maritime jurisdiction,* which last are matters belonging exclusively to the civil law, in every nation in Christendom.

Not to enlarge upon the loss of the invaluable right of trial by an unbiased jury, so dear to every friend of liberty, the monstrous expense and inconveniences of the mode of proceeding to be adopted, are such as will prove intolerable to the people of this country. The lengthy proceedings of the civil law courts in the chancery of England, and in the courts of Scotland and France, are such that few men of moderate fortune can endure the expense of them; the poor man must therefore submit to the wealthy. Length of purse will too often prevail against right and justice. For instance, we are told by the learned Judge *Blackstone,* that a question only on the property of an ox, of the value of three guineas, originating under the civil law proceedings in Scotland, after many interlocutory orders and sentences below, was carried at length from the court of sessions, the highest court in that part of Great Britain, by way of *appeal* to the House of Lords, where the question of law and fact was finally determined. He adds that no pique or spirit could in the Court of King's Bench or Common Pleas at Westminster have given continuance to such a cause for a tenth part of the time, nor have cost a twentieth part of the expense. Yet the costs in the Courts of King's Bench and Common Pleas in England are infinitely greater than those which the people of this country have ever experienced. We abhor the idea of losing the transcendent privilege of trial by jury, with the loss of which, it is remarked by the same learned author, that in Sweden, the liberties of the commons were extinguished by an aristocratic Senate; and that *trial by jury* and the liberty of the people went out together. At the same time we regret the intolerable delay, the enormous expense, and infinite vexation, to which the people of this country will be exposed from the voluminous proceedings of the courts of civil law, and especially from the appellate jurisdiction, by means of which a man may be drawn from the utmost boundaries of this extensive country to the seat of the Supreme Court of the nation to contend, perhaps, with a wealthy and powerful adversary. The consequence of this establishment will be an absolute confirmation of the power of aristocratical influence in the courts of justice; for the common people will not be able to contend or struggle against it.

Trial by jury in criminal cases may also be excluded by declaring that the libeller for instance shall be liable to an action of debt for a specified sum, thus evading the common law prosecution by indictment and trial by jury. And the common course of proceeding against a ship for breach of revenue laws by informal (which will be classed among civil causes) will at the civil law be within the resort of a court, where no jury intervenes. Besides, the benefit of jury trial, in cases of a criminal nature, which cannot be evaded, will be rendered of little value, by calling the accused to answer far from home; there being no provision that the trial be by a jury of the neighborhood or county. Thus an inhabitant of Pittsburgh, on a charge of crime committed on the banks of the Ohio, may be obliged to defend himself at the side of the Delaware, and so *vice versa.* To conclude this head: we observe that the judges of the courts of Congress would not be independent, as they are not debarred from holding other offices, during the pleasure of the President and Senate, and as they may derive their support in part from fees, alterable by the legislature.

The next consideration that the Constitution presents is the undue and dangerous mixture of the powers of government; the same body possessing legislative, executive and judicial powers. The Senate is a constituent branch of the legislature, it has judicial power in judging on impeachments, and in this case unites in some measure the characters of judge and party, as all the principal officers are appointed by the President-general, with the concurrence of the Senate, and therefore they derive their offices in part from the Senate. This may bias the judgments of the Senators, and tend to screen great delinquents from punishment. And the

Senate has, moreover, various and great executive powers, *viz.*, in concurrence with the President-general, they form treaties with foreign nations, that may control and abrogate the constitutions and laws of the several States. Indeed, there is no power, privilege or liberty of the State governments, or of the people, but what may be affected by virtue of this power. For all treaties, made by them, are to be the "supreme law of the land; anything in the constitution or laws of any State, to the contrary notwithstanding."

And this great power may be exercised by the President and ten Senators (being two-thirds of fourteen, which is a quorum of that body). What an inducement would this offer to the ministers of foreign powers to compass by bribery *such concessions* as could not otherwise be obtained. It is the unvaried usage of all free States, whenever treaties interfere with the positive laws of the land, to make the intervention of the legislature necessary to give them operation. This became necessary, and was afforded by the Parliament of Great Britain, in consequence of the late commercial treaty between that kingdom and France. As the Senate judges on impeachments, who is to try the members of the Senate for the abuse of this power! And none of the great appointments to office can be made without the consent of the Senate.

Such various, extensive, and important powers combined in one body of men, are inconsistent with all freedom; the celebrated Montesquieu tells us, that "when the legislative and executive powers are united in the same person, or in the same body of magistrates, there can be no liberty, because apprehensions may arise, lest the same monarch or *senate* should enact tyrannical laws, to execute them in a tyrannical manner."

"Again, there is no liberty, if the power of judging be not separated from the legislative and executive powers. Were it joined with the legislative, the life and liberty of the subject would be exposed to arbitrary control; for the judge would then be legislator. Were it joined to the executive power, the judge might behave with all the violence of an oppressor. There would be an end of everything, were the same man, or the same body of the nobles, or of the people, to exercise those three powers; that of enacting laws, that of executing the public resolutions, and that of judging the crimes or differences of individuals."

The President general is dangerously connected with the Senate; his coincidence with the views of the ruling junto in that body, is made essential to his weight and importance in the government, which will destroy all independence and purity in the executive department; and having the power of pardoning without the concurrence of a council, he may screen from punishment the most treasonable attempts that may be made on the liberties of the people, when instigated by his coadjutors in the Senate. Instead of this dangerous and improper mixture of the executive with the legislative and judicial, the supreme executive powers ought to have been placed in the President, with a small independent council, made personally responsible for every appointment to office or other act, by having their opinions recorded; and that without the concurrence of the majority of the quorum of this council, the President should not be capable of taking any step.

We have before considered internal taxation as it would effect the destruction of the State governments, and produce one consolidated government. We will now consider that subject as it affects the personal concerns of the people.

The power of direct taxation applies to every individual, as Congress, under this government, is expressly vested with the authority of laying a capitation or poll tax upon every person to any amount. This is a tax that, however oppressive in its nature, and unequal in its operation, is certain as to its produce and simple in its collection; it cannot be evaded like the objects of imposts or excise, and will be paid, because all that a man hath will he give for his head. This tax is so congenial to the nature of despotism, that it has ever been a favorite under such governments. Some of those who were in the late general convention from this State have labored to introduce a poll tax among us.

The power of direct taxation will further apply to every individual, as Congress may tax land, cattle, trades, occupations, etc., to any amount, and every object of internal taxation is of that nature; that however oppressive, the people will have but this alternative, either to pay the tax or let their property be taken, for all resistance will be vain. The standing army and select militia would enforce the collection.

For the moderate exercise of this power, there is no control left in the State governments, whose intervention is destroyed. No relief, or redress of grievances, can be extended as heretofore by them. There is not even a

declaration of RIGHTS to which the people may appeal for the vindica-
tion of their wrongs in the court of justice. They must, therefore, implicitly obey the most arbitrary laws, as the most of them will be pursuant to
the principles and form of the Constitution, and that strongest of all
checks upon the conduct of administration, *responsibility to the people*, will
not exist in this government. The permanency of the appointments of
Senators and Representatives, and the control the Congress have over
their election, will place them independent of the sentiments and resentment of the people, and the administration having a greater interest in
the government than in the community, there will be no consideration to
restrain them from oppression and tyranny. In the government of this
State, under the old confederation, the members of the legislature are
taken from among the people, and their interests and welfare are so in-
separably connected with those of their constituents, that they can derive
no advantage from oppressive laws and taxes; for they would suffer in
common with their fellow-citizens, would participate in the burdens they
impose on the community, as they must return to the common level, after
a short period; and notwithstanding every exertion of influence, every
means of corruption, a necessary rotation excludes them from permanency in the legislature.

This large State is to have but ten members in that Congress which is
to have the liberty, property and dearest concerns of every individual in
this vast country at absolute command, and even these ten persons, who
are to be our only guardians, who are to supersede the legislature of
Pennsylvania, will not be of the choice of the people, nor amenable to
them. From the mode of their election and appointment they will consist
of the lordly and high minded; of men who will have no congenial feelings with the people, but a perfect indifference for, and contempt of
them; they will consist of those harpies of power that prey upon the very
vitals, that riot on the miseries of the community. But we will suppose,
although in all probability it may never be realized in fact, that our deputies in Congress have the welfare of their constituents at heart, and will
exert themselves in their behalf, what security could even this afford?
What relief could they extend to their oppressed constituents? To attain
this, the majority of the deputies of the twelve other States in Congress
must be alike well disposed; must alike forego the sweets of power, and

relinquish the pursuits of ambition, which, from the nature of things, is not to be expected. If the people part with a responsible representation in the legislature, founded upon fair, certain and frequent elections, they have nothing left they can call their own. Miserable is the lot of that people whose every concern depends on the *will* and *pleasure* of their rulers. Our soldiers will become Janissaries, and our officers of government Bashaws; in short, the system of despotism will soon be completed.

From the foregoing investigation, it appears that the Congress under this Constitution will not possess the confidence of the people, which is an essential requisite in a good government; for unless the laws command the confidence and respect of the great body of the people, so as to induce them to support them when called on by the civil magistrate, they must be executed by the aid of a numerous standing army, which would be inconsistent with every idea of liberty; for the same force that may be employed to compel obedience to good laws, might and probably would be used to wrest from the people their constitutional liberties. The framers of this Constitution appear to have been aware of this great deficiency— to have been sensible that no dependence could be placed on the people for their support: but on the contrary, that the government must be executed by force. They have therefore made a provision for this purpose in a permanent *standing army* and a *militia* that may be objected to as strict discipline and government.

A standing army in the hands of a government placed so independent of the people may be made a fatal instrument to overturn the public liberties; it may be employed to enforce the collection of the most oppressive taxes, and to carry into execution the most arbitrary measures. An ambitious man who may have the army at his devotion, may step up into the throne, and seize upon absolute power.

The absolute unqualified command that Congress have over the militia may be made instrumental to the destruction of all liberty, both public and private; whether of a personal, civil or religious nature.

First, the personal liberty of every man, probably from sixteen to sixty years of age, may be destroyed by the power Congress have in organizing and governing of the militia. As militia they may be subjected to fines to any amount, levied in a military manner; they may be subjected to corporal punishments of the most disgraceful and humiliating kind; and to death itself, by the sentence of a court martial. To this our young men will be more immediately subjected, as a select militia, composed of them, will best answer the purposes of government.

Secondly, the rights of conscience may be violated, as there is no exemption of those persons who are conscientiously scrupulous of bearing arms. These compose a respectable proportion of the community in the State. This is the more remarkable, because even when the distresses of the late war, and the evident disaffection of many citizens of that description, inflamed our passions, and when every person who was obliged to risk his own life, must have been exasperated against such as on any account kept back from the common danger, yet even then, when outrage and violence might have been expected, the rights of conscience were held sacred.

At this momentous crisis, the framers of our State Constitution made the most express and decided declaration and stipulations in favor of the rights of conscience; but now, when no necessity exists, those dearest rights of men are left insecure.

Thirdly, the absolute command of Congress over the militia may be destructive of public liberty; for under the guidance of an arbitrary government, they may be made the unwilling instruments of tyranny. The militia of Pennsylvania may be marched to New England or Virginia to quell an insurrection occasioned by the most galling oppression, and aided by the standing army, they will no doubt be successful in subduing their liberty and independence; but in so doing, although the magnanimity of their minds will be extinguished, yet the meaner passions of resentment and revenge will be increased, and these in turn will be the ready and obedient instruments of despotism to enslave the others; and that with an irritated vengeance. Thus may the militia be made the instruments of crushing the last efforts of expiring liberty, of riveting the chains of despotism on their fellow-citizens, and on one another. This power can be exercised not only without violating the Constitution, but in strict conformity with it; it is calculated for this express purpose, and will doubtless be executed accordingly.

As this government will not enjoy the confidence of the people, but be executed by force, it will be a very expensive and burdensome government. The standing army must be numerous, and as a further support, it

will be the policy of this government to multiply officers in every department; judges, collectors, tax-gatherers, excisemen and the whole host
of revenue officers, will swarm over the land, devouring the hard earnings of the industrious—like the locusts of old, impoverishing and des-
olating all before them.

We have not noticed the smaller, nor many of the considerable blem-
ishes, but have confined our objections to the great and essential defects,
the main pillars of the Constitution; which we have shown to be inconsistent with the liberty and happiness of the people, as its establishment
will annihilate the State governments, and produce one consolidated government that will eventually and speedily issue in the supremacy of despotism.

In this investigation we have not confined our views to the interests or
welfare of this State, in preference to the others. We have overlooked all
local circumstances—we have considered this subject on the broad scale
of the general good; we have asserted the cause of the present and future
ages—the cause of liberty and mankind.

Northwest Ordinance (1787)

An ordinance for the Government of the Territory of the United States, north-west of the River Ohio be it ordained by the United States in Congress assembled, That the said territory, for the purposes of temporary government, be one district; subject, however, to be divided into two districts, as future circumstances may in the opinion of Congress, make it expedient.

Be it ordained by the authority aforesaid, That the estates, both of resident and non-resident proprietors in the said territory, dying intestate, shall descend to, and be distributed among their children, and the descendants of a deceased child in equal parts; the descendants of a deceased child or grandchild, to take the share of their deceased parent in equal parts among them: And where there shall be no children or descendants, then in equal parts to the next of kin, in equal degree; and among collaterals, the children of a deceased brother or sister of the intestate, shall have in equal parts among them, their deceased parents' share; and there shall in no case be a distinction between kindred of the whole and half blood; saving in all cases to the widow of the intestate, her third part of the real estate for life, and one third part of the personal estate; and this law relative to descents and dower, shall remain in full force until altered by the legislature of the district.—And until the governor and judges shall adopt laws as herein after mentioned, estates in the said territory may be devised or bequeathed by wills in writing, signed and sealed by him or her, in whom the estate may be (being of full age) and attested by three witnesses;—and real estates may be conveyed by lease and release, or bargain and sale, signed, sealed, and delivered by the person being of full age, in whom the estate may be, and attested by two witnesses, provided such wills be duly proved, and such conveyances be acknowledged, or the execution thereof duly proved, and be recorded within one year after proper magistrates, courts, and registers shall be appointed for that purpose; and personal property may be transferred by delivery; saving, however, to the French and Canadian inhabitants, and other settlers of the Kaskaskies, Saint Vincent's, and the neighboring villages, who have heretofore professed themselves citizens of Virginia, their laws and customs now in force among them, relative to the descent and conveyance of property.

Be it ordained by the authority aforesaid, That there shall be appointed from time to time, by Congress, a governor, whose commission shall continue in force for the term of three years, unless sooner revoked by Congress; he shall reside in the district, and have a freehold estate therein, in one thousand acres of land, while in the exercise of his office.

There shall be appointed from time to time, by Congress, a secretary, whose commission shall continue in force for four years, unless sooner revoked; he shall reside in the district, and have a freehold estate therein, in five hundred acres of land, while in the exercise of his office; it shall be his duty to keep and preserve the acts and laws passed by the legislature, and the public records of the district, and the proceedings of the governor in his executive department; and transmit authentic copies of such acts and proceedings, every six months, to the secretary of Congress. There shall also be appointed a court to consist of three judges, any two of whom to form a court, who shall have a common law jurisdiction, and reside in the district, and have each therein a freehold estate in five hundred acres of land, while in the exercise of their offices; and their commissions shall continue in force during good behavior.

The governor and judges, or a majority of them, shall adopt and publish in the district, such laws of the original States, criminal and civil, as may be necessary, and best suited to the circumstances of the district, and report them to Congress, from time to time; which laws shall be in force in the district until the organization of the General Assembly therein, unless disapproved of by Congress; but afterwards the Legislature shall have authority to alter them as they shall think fit.

The governor, for the time being, shall be commander-in-chief of the militia, appoint and commission all officers in the same below the rank of general officers; all general officers shall be appointed and commissioned by Congress.

Previous to the organization of the general assembly, the governor shall appoint such magistrates and other civil officers, in each county or township, as he shall find necessary for the preservation of the peace and good order in the same. After the general assembly shall be organized, the powers and duties of magistrates and other civil officers shall be regulated and defined by the said assembly; but all magistrates and other civil officers, not herein otherwise directed, shall, during the continuance of this temporary government, be appointed by the governor.

For the prevention of crimes and injuries, the laws to be adopted or made shall have force in all parts of the district, and for the execution of process, criminal and civil, the governor shall make proper divisions thereof—and he shall proceed from time to time, as circumstances may require, to lay out the parts of the district in which the Indian titles shall have been extinguished, into counties and townships, subject, however, to such alterations as may thereafter be made by the legislature.

So soon as there shall be five thousand free male inhabitants, of full age, in the district, upon giving proof thereof to the governor, they shall receive authority, with time and place, to elect representatives from their counties or townships, to represent them in the general assembly; *Provided*, That for every five hundred free male inhabitants, there shall be one representative, and so on progressively with the number of free male inhabitants shall the right of representation increase, until the number of representatives shall amount to twenty-five; after which, the number and proportion of representatives shall be regulated by the legislature: *Provided* that no person be eligible or qualified to act as a representative, unless he shall have been a citizen of one of the United States three years, and be a resident in the district, or unless he shall have resided in the district three years; and, in either case, shall likewise hold in his own right, in fee simple, two hundred acres of land within the same: *Provided* also, That a freehold in fifty acres of land in the district, having been a citizen of one of the States, and being resident in the district, or the like freehold and two years residence in the district shall be necessary to qualify a man as an elector of a representative.

The representatives thus elected shall serve for the term of two years; and in case of the death of a representative, or removal from office, the governor shall issue a writ to the county or township, for which he was a member, to elect another in his stead, to serve for the residue of the term.

The general assembly or legislature shall consist of the Governor, Legislative Council, and House of Representatives. The Legislative Council shall consist of five members, to continue in office five years, unless sooner removed by Congress; any three of whom to be a quorum: and the members of the Council shall be nominated and appointed in the following manner, to wit: As soon as representatives shall be elected, the Governor shall appoint a time and place for them to meet together, and, when met, they shall nominate ten persons, residents in the district, and each possessed of a freehold in five hundred acres of land, and return their names to Congress; five of whom Congress shall appoint and commission to serve as aforesaid; and, whenever a vacancy shall happen in the council, by death or removal from office, the House of Representatives shall nominate two persons, qualified as aforesaid, for each vacancy, and return their names to Congress; one of whom Congress shall appoint and commission for the residue of the term. And every five years, four months at least before the expiration of the time of service of the members of Council, the said House shall nominate ten persons, qualified as aforesaid, and return their names to Congress; five of whom Congress shall appoint and commission to serve as members of the Council five years, unless sooner removed. And the Governor, Legislative Council, and House of Representatives, shall have authority to make laws, in all cases, for the good government of the district, not repugnant to the principles and articles in this ordinance established and declared. And all bills having passed by a majority in the House, and by a majority in the Council, shall be referred to the Governor for his assent; but no bill, or legislative Act whatever, shall be of any force without his assent. The governor shall have power to convene, prorogue and dissolve the General Assembly, when, in his opinion, it shall be expedient.

The Governor, judges, Legislative Council, Secretary, and such other officers as Congress shall appoint in the district, shall take an oath or affirmation of fidelity, and of office; the Governor before the President of

Congress, and all other officers before the Governor. As soon as a legislature shall be formed in the district, the Council and House assembled, in one room, shall have authority, by joint ballot, to elect a delegate to Congress, who shall have a seat in Congress, with a right of debating, but not of voting during this temporary government.

And for extending the fundamental principles of civil and religious liberty, which form the basis whereon these republics, their laws and constitutions are erected; to fix and establish those principles as the basis of all laws, constitutions, and governments, which forever hereafter shall be formed in the said territory: to provide also for the establishment of States, and permanent government therein, and for their admission to a share in the federal councils on an equal footing with the original States, at as early periods as may be consistent with the general interest:

It is hereby ordained and declared by the authority aforesaid, That the following articles shall be considered as articles of compact between the original States, and the people and States in the said territory, and forever remain unalterable, unless by common consent, to wit:

Article the first. No person, demeaning himself in a peaceable and orderly manner, shall ever be molested on account of his mode of worship or religious sentiments, in the said territory.

Article the second. The inhabitants of the said territory, shall always be entitled to the benefits of the writ of *habeas corpus*, and of the trial by jury; of a proportionate representation of the people in the legislature; and of judicial proceedings according to the course of the common law. All persons shall be bailable, unless for capital offenses, where the proof shall be evident or the presumption great. All fines shall be moderate; and no cruel or unusual punishments shall be inflicted. No man shall be deprived of his liberty or property, but by the judgment of his peers, or the law of the land, and, should the public exigencies make it necessary, for the common preservation, to take any person's property, or to demand his particular services, full compensation shall be made for the same. And, in the just preservation of rights and property, it is understood and declared, that no law ought ever to be made, have force in the said territory, that shall, in any manner whatever, interfere with or affect private contracts or engagements, *bona fide,* and without fraud, previously formed.

Article the third. Religion, morality, and knowledge, being necessary to good government and the happiness of mankind, schools and the means of education shall forever be encouraged. The utmost good faith shall always be observed towards the Indians; their lands and property shall never be taken from them without their consent; and, in their property, rights, and liberty, they never shall be invaded or disturbed, unless in just and lawful wars authorized by Congress; but laws founded in justice and humanity shall from time to time be made for preventing wrongs being done to them, and for preserving peace and friendship with them.

Article the fourth. The said territory, and the States which may be formed therein, shall forever remain a part of this Confederacy of the United States of America, subject to the Articles of Confederation, and to such alterations therein as shall be constitutionally made; and to all the Acts and ordinances of the United States in Congress assembled, conformable thereto. The inhabitants and settlers in the said territory, shall be subject to pay a part of the federal debts contracted or to be contracted, and a proportional part of the expenses of government, to be appointed on them by Congress according to the same common rule and measure by which apportionments thereof shall be made on the other States; and the taxes for paying their proportion shall be laid and levied by the authority and direction of the legislatures of the district or districts, or new States, as in the original States, within the time agreed upon by the United States in Congress assembled. The legislatures of those districts or new States shall never interfere with the primary disposal of the soil by the United States in Congress assembled, nor with any regulations Congress may find necessary for securing the title in such soil to the *bona fide* purchasers. No tax shall be imposed on lands the property of the United States; and, in no case, shall non-resident proprietors be taxed higher than residents. The navigable waters leading into the Mississippi and St. Lawrence, and the carrying places between the same, shall be common highways and forever free, as well to the inhabitants of the said territory as to the citizens of the United States, and those of any other States that may be admitted into the confederacy, without any tax, impost, or duty therefor.

Article the fifth. There shall be formed in the said territory, not less than three, nor more than five States; and the boundaries of the States, as soon as Virginia shall alter her act of cession, and consent to the same, shall become fixed and established as follows, to wit: The western State in the said territory, shall be bounded by the Mississippi, the Ohio and Wabash rivers; a direct line drawn from the Wabash and Post Vincents due north to the territorial line between the United States and Canada; and by the said territorial line to the lake of the Woods and Mississippi. The middle State shall be bounded by the said direct line, the Wabash from Post Vincents to the Ohio; by the Ohio, by a direct line drawn due north from the mouth of the Great Miami, to the said territorial line, and by the said territorial line. The eastern States shall be bounded by the last mentioned direct line, the Ohio, Pennsylvania, and the said territorial line: *Provided* however, and it is further understood and declared, that the boundaries of these three States shall be subject so far to be altered, that if Congress shall hereafter find it expedient, they shall have authority to form one or two States in that part of the said territory which lies north of an east and west line drawn through the southerly bend or extreme of Lake Michigan. And whenever any of the said States shall have sixty thousand free inhabitants therein, such State shall be admitted, by its delegates, into the Congress of the United States, on an equal footing with the original States, in all respects whatever; and shall be at liberty to form a permanent constitution and State government: provided the constitution and government so to be formed, shall be republican, and in conformity with the principles contained in these articles; and so far as it can be consistent with the general interest of the confederacy, such admission shall be allowed at an earlier period, and when there may be a less number of free inhabitants in the State than sixty thousand.

Article the sixth. There shall be neither slavery nor involuntary servitude in the said territory, otherwise than in the punishment of crimes whereof the party shall have been duly convicted: *Provided, always,* That any person escaping into the same, from whom labor or service is lawfully claimed in any one of the original States, such fugitive may be lawfully reclaimed, and conveyed to the person claiming his or her labor or service as aforesaid.

Be it ordained by the authority aforesaid, That the resolutions of the 23rd of April, 1784, relative to the subject of this ordinance, be, and the same are hereby repealed and declared null and void.

Shall we imitate the example of those nations who have gone from a simple to a splendid Government? Are those nations more worthy of our imitation? What can make an adequate satisfaction to them for the loss they have suffered in obtaining such a Government —for the loss of their liberty? If we admit this Consolidated Government, it will be because we like a great splendid one. Some way or other we must be a great and mighty empire; we must have an army, and a navy, and a number of things: When the American spirit was in its youth, the language of America was different: Liberty, Sir, was then the primary object.

Patrick Henry, in the Virginia Ratifying Convention (1788)

Is there no virtue among us? If there be not, we are in a wretched situation. No theoretical checks, no form of government, can render us secure. To suppose that any form of government will secure liberty or happiness without any virtue in the people is a chimerical idea. If there be sufficient virtue and intelligence in the community, it will be exercised in the selection of these men; so that we do not depend on their virtue, or put confidence in our rulers, but in the people who are to choose them.

James Madison, in the Virginia Ratifying Convention (1788)

The Bill of Rights provides a fitting close to the parenthesis around the Constitution that the preamble opens. But the substance is a design of government with powers to act and a structure to make it act wisely and responsibly. It is in that design, not in its preamble or its epilogue, that the security of the American civil and political liberty lies.

Herbert J. Storing, "The Constitution and the Bill of Rights," in M. Judd Harmon, ed., *Essays on the Constitution* (1978)

PART 6

Interpreting and Preserving
the Constitution

1. Through self-imposed rules of interpretation, derived in part from ancient law, Roman law, and English law, American judges interpret the Constitution and all laws and treaties according to established principles of judicial construction.

2. The basic interpretive task is to determine the intent of the Constitution, laws, and treaties, and to construe all instruments according to the sense of the terms and the intentions of the parties.

3. In the interpretation of the Constitution, the first rule is to examine both the general structure and the component parts of the document, keeping in mind its overall objectives and scope of power.

4. The function of the judge is to interpret the law, not to ignore its provisions and make the law. Judges have a special duty to maintain the integrity of the American constitutional process, to see that the requirements of the law are uniformly followed, and to hold all public officials, including themselves, to the same standards.

5. The Supremacy Clause of the Constitution establishes a hierarchy of laws, with the Constitution itself standing at the apex of the system. All laws and treaties must conform to the Constitution, and those that do not may be declared null and void by the Supreme Court through the exercise of judicial review.

6. The Constitution embodies the constituent or "permanent will" of the American people, which gives it a republican basis. Through the proper exercise of judicial review, the Supreme Court preserves the Constitution and perpetuates the will of the people.

7. There are basically four types of judicial review: the power of the Supreme Court to declare unconstitutional an act of Congress, a State law or constitutional provision, or an executive action, and the power to overturn a State court decision that questioned the validity of a Fed-

eral law or treaty or rendered an interpretation of the Constitution that was challenged by one of the parties.

8. In practice, the Supreme Court is the *final* interpreter of the Constitution, unless the Court's interpretation is changed by the people and the States through the amendment process. Congress may also alter the Court's jurisdiction, thereby making the State courts and lower Federal courts the "court of last resort." In neither theory nor practice, however, is the court the *exclusive* interpreter of the Constitution.

9. Historically, the advocates of State's Rights have tended to favor a "strict" interpretation of the Constitution, and those favoring a more powerful, centralized regime have tended to support a "loose" construction of the Constitution.

10. Although Federal judges individually enjoy considerable independence, the independence of the judiciary itself is substantially limited by the separation of powers and checks and balances system.

11. The Federal judicial power is the power of a Federal court to decide and pronounce a judgment and carry it into effect between parties who bring a case before it. It is distinguishable from jurisdiction, which confers authority on a court to exercise the judicial power in a particular case.

12. The Constitution confers the judicial power on the Federal courts, but it is the Congress which confers jurisdiction; and without jurisdiction a Federal court cannot decide the case. The responsibility of limiting the power of the Federal judiciary and preventing abuses of the judicial power rests primarily with the Congress.

A CONSTITUTION," wrote Alexander Hamilton in *Federalist* No. 78, "is in fact, and must be, regarded by the judges as a fundamental law. It therefore belongs to them to ascertain its meaning as well as the meaning of any particular act proceeding from the legislative body." In carrying out this responsibility, what rules or principles of construction are the judges supposed to follow? The Constitution is silent on the question and thus offers no guidance. Congress is prohibited from imposing any rules of interpretation. It may regulate the jurisdiction of the Federal courts and tell the judges *when* they can decide a case, but it is prohibited by the separation of powers principle from instructing the judges on *how* they should interpret it; for the power to interpret the Constitution in a case or controversy is the essence of the judicial power, and thus beyond the reach of both Congress and President.

Accordingly, it is up to the judges themselves to develop and adopt their own rules of interpretation, just as members of Congress are free to adopt their own rules of legislative procedure (about which the Constitution is also silent).

It should not be concluded from this observation, however, that judges are given free rein under the Constitution to interpret it as they please. If this were the case, they might substitute their own intentions for those of the people, as expressed in the Constitution, and interpret the Constitution out of existence. A more accurate and reliable reading of the Constitution and the Convention debates suggests that the Framers assumed that the judges would interpret the Constitution according to established principles of Anglo-American law.

Principles of Statutory Construction

What are these established rules or principles of interpretation, and where might a judge turn for guidance? In 1789, when the Federal Judiciary was first organized, he would have first turned to the writings of the English jurists, especially Coke and Blackstone, and possibly also to the writings of the international law jurists of Europe, such as Jean Jacques Burlamaqui, Emerich Vattel, and Hugo Grotius. Over the centuries, the English jurists had developed coherent, well-defined principles of construction for interpreting acts of Parliament, and the international law jurists had likewise established rules for interpreting treaties among foreign nations. There was no body of legal literature to which American judges might turn for guidance for the interpretation of a constitution, however, because written constitutions were unprecedented. Hence the members of the new Federal judiciary, led by the Supreme Court, found it necessary to create their own rules of interpretation, based in part on principles adopted from the common law and the law of nations, and in part from the peculiar requirements of a popularly based written constitution that was declared to be the supreme law. In other words, it became readily apparent to them that certain principles useful for determining the meaning of a law or a treaty might also be applied for determining the meaning of a clause in the Constitution. In certain instances, however, new rules would have to be devised because a constitution is obviously different in many respects from a law or treaty and therefore raises unique interpretive problems.

A basic interpretive task common to all three is the task of determining *intent.* What was the intent of the lawmakers who made the law? Of the foreign ministers who drafted the treaty? Of the delegates who wrote the Constitution? In his *Commentaries on the Laws of England,* Blackstone noted that the first and fundamental rule in the interpretation of all instruments is to construe them according to the sense of the terms and the intention of the parties. "The fairest and most rational method to interpret the will of the legislator is by exploring his intentions at the time when the law was made," wrote Blackstone, "by *signs* the most natural and probable. And these signs are either the words, the context, the subject matter, the effects and consequence, or the spirit and reason of the law."

He went on to explain that words are generally to be understood according to their usual or popular usage. If they are ambiguous, then the next step is to try to establish their meaning from the context, or by comparing them with other words and sentences in the same instrument, or by comparing them with another law on the same subject. The law of England, for example, declares murder to be a felony "without benefit of clergy." To learn what the "benefit of clergy" means, it is necessary to turn for guidance to other laws employing this term.

Failing here, the judge may find the intent of the law by observing the subject matter or the purpose of the law. Blackstone cites as an example an English law forbidding members of the clergy from purchasing "provisions" in Rome. This does not mean they are prohibited from buying food and grain, but from securing nominations to ecclesiastical office, which were called "provisions." This is clearly what the statute intended because its purpose was to prevent the Pope in Rome from usurping the powers of the King, who is the head of the Church of England.

As for the effects and consequences, the rule, said Blackstone, is that where words seem to lead the court to absurd results, it is helpful to abandon their literal meaning and rely on common sense. A law, for example, stating that "whoever drew blood in the streets should be punished with the utmost severity" should "not extend to the surgeon who opened the vein of a person that fell down in the street with a fit."

Finally, wrote Blackstone, judges should consider the reason and spirit of the law when the words are dubious and the alternative means of construction have failed to uncover the intent of the lawmakers. To illustrate the point, he cited a case from the Roman law put by Cicero, the great statesman and orator. There was a law for ancient mariners providing that anyone who abandoned ship in a storm forfeited all of his personal property on board. Those who stayed with the ship were entitled to keep both the ship and its cargo. The intent of the law, obviously, was to encourage seamen to remain with a stricken vessel by offering them an economic incentive and to reduce the loss of valuable ships. A terrible storm arose, and every sailor except one who was too sick to move left the ship in question. The ship miraculously survived the storm, and when it reached port the sick man claimed ownership of the ship and its contents. The Roman judges properly rejected his claim because a reward to him, though technically correct, would defeat the intent of the law.

This method of interpreting the law according to its reason arises from what we call *equity*, which, as we saw earlier, is an interpretive device used by judges to correct a law which, because of its generality and universality, may be deficient when applied. But equity jurisprudence, as Blackstone further explained, is potentially dangerous to rule of law and must be applied with utmost caution. This is so because equity depends essentially upon the particular circumstances of each individual case, and the established rules are not as definite as in the law. Carried to extremes, it would make the judges a law unto themselves. "The liberty of considering all cases in an equitable light," he warned, "must not be indulged too far, lest thereby we destroy all law, and leave the decision of every question entirely in the breast of the judge. And law, without equity, though hard and disagreeable, is much more desirable for the public good than equity without law, which would make every judge a legislator, and introduce most infinite confusion; as there would be almost as many different rules of action laid down in our courts, as there are differences of capacity and sentiment in the human mind."

In 1803, the first American edition of Blackstone was published in Philadelphia by St. George Tucker, a professor of law at William and

Sir William Blackstone (1723–1780).

(Courtesy of the Library of Congress.)

Mary College in Virginia. Later, as American law developed under the new State and Federal constitutions, American lawyers began writing legal treatises and publishing their own reports of cases, so that American law, though English in origin, became increasingly distinguishable from its parent system.

The most prolific and influential of the early legal writers was Joseph Story, an Associate Justice of the Supreme Court from 1811 to 1845. Story, who also lectured at the Harvard Law School for many years and was widely acclaimed as America's foremost legal scholar, published nine major legal treatises while serving on the Court. The most famous of these was his three-volume classic, *Commentaries on the Constitution,* which was first published in 1833 but went through many subsequent editions. Included in the work was a complete analysis, based on *The Federalist* essays, of the origin, meaning, and purpose of every clause of the Constitution. This in itself was enormously helpful to judges and lawyers, who had little to go on except *The Federalist* and only limited access to the original founding documents that might be of assistance in determining the intent of particular provisions of the Constitution. James Madison's *Notes of the Debates in the Federal Convention of 1787* were not published until 1840. Jonathan Elliot did not publish his four-volume collection of *Debates in the Several State Conventions on the Adoption of the Federal Constitution* until 1830. In fact, debates in many State ratifying conventions were either fragmentary or nonexistent. Story's *Commentaries,* plus *The Federalist* and a few shorter and less comprehensive works, thus served as the principal guides for interpreting the Constitution in the founding era.

What was especially valuable to members of the bench and bar in Story's *Commentaries,* however, was the incorporation into the text of material on constitutional interpretation. Devoting a large portion of his treatise to "Rules of Interpretation," Justice Story endeavored to explain, step-by-step, the process to be followed for the proper interpretation of the Constitution. This is the first and only time a member of the Supreme Court has ever attempted to expound at length on the principles and mechanics of construing the American Constitution. It was an innovative and timely addition to the existing literature. When we stop to consider the influence of Story and his *Commentaries* on constitutional development, this was also a significant contribution to understanding the role of the judge in the American political system.

Borrowing heavily from Blackstone, but finding support as well from such noted authorities as Bacon and Vattel, Story affirmed Blackstone's first rule of interpretation: to construe the instrument "according to the sense of the terms and the intentions of the parties." Continuing, Story laid out the rule as follows:

> Mr. Justice Blackstone has remarked that the intention of a law is to be gathered from the words, the context, the subject matter, the effects and consequence, or the reason and spirit of the law. He goes on to justify the remark by stating, that words are generally to be understood in their usual and most known signification, not so much regarding the propriety of grammar as their general and popular use; that if words happen to be dubious, their meaning may be established by the context, or by comparing them with other words and sentences in the same instrument; that illustrations may be further derived from the subject matter, with reference to which the expressions are used; that the effect and consequence of a particular construction is to be examined because, if a literal meaning would involve a manifest absurdity, it ought not to be adopted; and that the reason and spirit of the law, or the causes which led to its enactment, are often the best exponents of the words, and limit their application.

From this it followed, said Story, that in many instances there is no problem of interpretation unless "there is some ambiguity or doubt" about the meaning of a particular word or phrase. "Where the words are plain and clear, and the sense distinct and perfect arising from them, there is generally no necessity to have recourse to other means of interpretation." In this situation, the instrument in question, whether it be a contract, a will, a statute, or the Constitution, is said to interpret itself, and the judge has only to acknowledge and declare the obvious intent of the parties.

Applying these principles to the interpretation of the Constitution, Story asserted that the first rule is to examine both the general structure and the component parts of the Constitution, keeping in mind its overall objectives and scope of power. "Where the words are plain, clear, and determinate, they require no interpretation." This is true of most provisions of the Constitution. Article I, Section 3, for example, states that "The Senate of the United States shall be composed of two Senators from each State." This seems clear enough. Each State is entitled to two Senators, no more, no less.

In some instances, however, "the words admit of two senses, each of which is conformable to common usage." In this situation, said Story, "that sense is to be adopted which, without departing from the literal import of the words, best harmonizes with the nature and objects, the scope and the design, of the instrument." A good example of this sort of difficulty would be Article II, Section 1, which provides that, "No person except a natural born citizen, or a citizen of the United States, at the time of the adoption of this Constitution, shall be eligible to the office of President." The clause making eligible persons who were citizens of the United States in 1787 was necessary, of course, since nobody old enough to become President in 1787, or for a long time afterward, was a "natural born" citizen of the United States. Every adult born in this country before 1776 had been born a British subject. (The first President born under the American flag was Martin Van Buren, who did not come into office until the elections of 1836.)

But what is a "natural born" citizen? An obvious interpretation of a "natural born" person would be a child born in the United States to American parents. Likewise, a "naturalized" citizen, that is a person born in a foreign country to foreign parents who later acquired American citizenship through naturalization, would not be eligible to serve as President because that person would not be a "natural born" citizen. What about a child born in a foreign country to American parents? This issue actually arose in 1967, when George Romney, Governor of Michigan, sought the presidency. Romney's American parents were living in Mexico when he was born. Was he eligible for the office of President?

As Judge Story suggests, the proper way in which to interpret the eligibility clause under the circumstances would be to look at its original purpose, and to adopt that interpretation which "best harmonizes with the nature and objects, the scope and design, of the instrument." Although the delegates to the Philadelphia Convention and the authors of *The Federalist* did not discuss at length the eligibility clause, we know from reason and experience, as Story explained, that "the great funda-

Justice Joseph Story (1779–1845).

From a crayon drawing by his son, William Wetmore Story, in *Life and Letters of Joseph Story* (Boston, 1851).

mental policy of all governments" is "to exclude foreign influence from their executive councils." This, he observed, "cuts off all chances for ambitious foreigners, who might otherwise be intriguing for the office; and interposes a barrier against those corrupt interferences of foreign governments in executive elections, which have inflicted the most serious evils upon the elective monarchies of Europe." It was thought dangerous, in other words, to make the presidency available to a person who might have just recently come to the United States and might still feel an allegiance to a king, a czar, or a foreign government. In light of these considerations, a ruling that George Romney, born of American parents, was a "natural born" citizen would seem to be consistent with the basic purpose of the eligibility clause.

A more troublesome interpretive problem arises when, even though the words are clear of doubt, the constitutional provision in which they appear is not entirely free of ambiguity. Consider, for example, Article II, Section 2, which provides that the President shall have the power to appoint ambassadors, other public ministers and consuls, Judges of the Supreme Court, and all other officers of the United States established by law. We know from Article III, Section 1 of the Constitution that judges of the Supreme Court shall hold their office "during good behavior," and cannot be removed from office by the President. But what about an ambassador or a department head? The Constitution is silent on the question of whether the President may remove one of these officials from office. Yet it would seem to follow, as a matter of common sense, that if the President has the power to appoint an ambassador that he also has the power to remove him, and that the removal power is therefore incidental to the appointment power. This is precisely how the Supreme Court has resolved the question. The removal power may be said to be, in effect, an implied power of the President, and one that is essential if the President is to be able to carry out the executive functions. It hardly makes sense to deny the President this power and at the same time expect him to administer the laws and conduct the foreign relations of the country. Otherwise the President would be at the mercy of his own cabinet and foreign ambassadors.

Granted, then, that the President may remove these officers, might the Senate nevertheless limit the President's removal power either by requiring its own consent or by specifying the causes for the removal? The Senate has in the past taken the position that, since the Senate must approve the appointment, it must also consent to the removal. It was precisely upon the basis of this claim that President Andrew Johnson was impeached and almost removed from office himself. Under the Tenure of Office Act of 1867, Congress prohibited the President from removing any department head without its consent. Judging the Act an unconstitutional interference with his executive powers, President Johnson ignored the statute and attempted to remove the Secretary of War on his own authority. The House of Representatives impeached Johnson, but the Senate failed to convict. Congress later repealed the statute and the issue was dropped.

In the famous case of *Meyers v. United States* (1926), the Supreme Court later ruled that the Senate may not restrict the power of the President to remove officers of the United States. In one of the longest and most elaborate opinions ever written for the Court, Chief Justice William Howard Taft, who had previously served as President, relied upon established practice and, more fundamentally, upon the separation of powers principle, in ruling that President Wilson had the right to remove a certain postmaster from office, notwithstanding an 1876 statute requiring senatorial approval. The President's unrestricted removal power, reasoned Taft, stemmed from "the executive power" and the "faithful execution of the laws" clause. The President must rely upon subordinates to execute the laws, said Taft, and he cannot perform this function, or be held accountable, if he cannot select administrative officers of his own choosing.

Chief Justice Taft's approach was essentially consistent with the rules of interpretation proposed by Judge Story almost a century earlier. When dealing with ambiguities of the Constitution, said Story, it is essential that all of the available sources of understanding be explored, including "the antecedent situation of the country and its institutions, the existence and operations of the State governments . . . contemporary history and contemporary interpretation. . . ." In the final analysis, he concluded, "the safest rule of interpretation after all will be found to be to look to the nature and objects of the particular powers, duties and rights, with all the lights and aids of contemporary history, and to give to the words of each just such operation and force, consistent with their legitimate meaning, as may fairly secure and attain the ends proposed."

These general principles of interpretation articulated by Story and derived in part from ancient law, Roman law, and English law, have been acknowledged as binding on courts since the earliest days of the American republic. Throughout American history, judges have subscribed to the ancient maxim of Sir Francis Bacon, who admonished the judges of England "to remember that their office is *jus dicere*, and not *jus dare*—to interpret law, and not to make law, or give law." This fundamental principle, as we noted earlier, is nowhere stated in the Constitution. Like federalism and separation of powers, it is nevertheless an implicit rule of the Constitution. It defines the judicial function, governs the behavior of judges, and is the essence of what is known as the doctrine of judicial self-restraint.

Because this rule is self-imposed and is not explicitly mandated by the Constitution, observance of it has not always been consistent. Judges, after all, are human beings, subject to the same temptations of power as any legislator or executive. Those who yield to such temptations are said to be judicial activists—judges who read their own bias into a law or the Constitution, in disregard of the lawmakers' or Framers' intent, in order to reach a decision they personally favor, or believe is convenient. The argument has even been made that judges have a special duty to promote "moral values" or that all citizens are entitled to certain undefined, philosophically based "natural rights," and that judges are therefore at liberty to render any interpretation they please in order to secure those "values" or "rights." Such practices may, however, produce judicial decisions that are in conflict with the Constitution. A judge, wrote Story in his *Commentaries*, should not "enlarge the construction of a given power beyond the fair scope of its terms merely because the restriction is inconvenient, impolitic, or even mischievous. If it be mischievous, the power of redressing the evil lies with the people by an exercise of the power of amendment. If they do not choose to apply the remedy, it may fairly be presumed that the mischief is less than what would arise from a further extension of the power, or that it is the least of two evils." Moreover, said Story, "it should not be lost sight of that the government of the United States is one of limited and enumerated powers, and that a departure from the true import and sense of its powers is *pro tanto* the establishment of a new constitution. It is doing for the people what they have not chosen to do for themselves. It is usurping the functions of a legislator and deserting those of an expounder of the law."

Judges, then, have a special duty to maintain the integrity of the American constitutional process, to see that the rules are uniformly followed, and to hold all public officials, including themselves, to the same standards. This has meant that American judges have been especially concerned about *procedure*. By following the same procedure in every case, whether it be in the conduct of a trial or in the interpretation of a statute or provision of the Constitution, a judge may rightfully claim that his personal preferences did not intrude upon the dispute. Certainty in the law—an essential attribute of rule of law—is undermined when judges repeatedly change the rules, overturn established precedents, and arbitrarily reverse themselves. This has been recognized since the dawn of Western civilization. Thus the ancient Code of Hammurabi, written by the Babylonians in 2100 B.C., declared that, "If a judge has tried a suit, given a decision, caused a sealed tablet to be executed, and thereafter varies his judgment . . . then they remove him from his place on the bench of judges in the assembly."

Such rigorous adherence to procedure has also meant that the actual outcome or result of a case might not be what the judge privately favored. But this is a small price to pay for rule of law. Strict adherence to procedure may even at times produce an unjust result, as occasionally occurs when an innocent person is judged guilty or a guilty person is judged innocent by an errant jury. But in the long run, it is generally believed, justice will usually prevail if the proper procedures are uniformly observed. Deliberate attempts by the judges to reach out for "justice" in each case, irrespective of established norms and procedures, have traditionally been viewed in American law as an abuse of office and the equity power. Such arbitrariness puts the law in a state of turmoil and uncertainty, invites political interference in the judicial process, and endangers the independence of the judiciary by encouraging legislative retaliation.

The Doctrine of Judicial Review

Having examined a statute to determine the intent of the legislature, an English judge's interpretive powers come to an end. He has only to apply the statute to the facts of the case and reach a decision. This is because the English courts, in spite of the claims once made by Lord Coke, do not have the power of judicial review. On rare occasions they may express an opinion on whether a particular act of Parliament conforms to the English Constitution, but Parliament is free to ignore it. In keeping with the principle of legislative supremacy, Parliament decides for itself whether its acts are constitutional. In fact, Great Britain does not even have a supreme court. The highest court of appeals in the British political system is actually the House of Lords, which, of course, is also the upper chamber of the legislature.

Under the American political system, a judicial inquiry into the legislature's intent is merely the first step of the judicial process. Once the meaning and intent of the statute have been determined, the judge must then decide whether it conforms to the Constitution. If it is a State law, he must take yet another step to determine whether the law conforms to Federal laws and treaties. All of this is necessary because of the Supremacy Clause of Article VI. As noted earlier, this is the most distinctive feature of the American Constitution. It is a key provision which, more than any other, distinguishes the American Constitution from the English— and most other constitutions of the world.

In essence, the Supremacy Clause establishes a hierarchy of laws, with the Constitution itself as the highest law, followed by Federal laws and treaties, descending finally to State constitutions, State laws, and local ordinances. Article VI declares that, "This Constitution, and the laws of the United States which shall be made in pursuance thereof; and all treaties made, or which shall be made, under the authority of the United States, shall be the supreme law of the land; and the judges in every State shall be bound thereby, any thing in the Constitution or laws of any State to the contrary notwithstanding."

It is important to study these words carefully. In the first place, there is no law higher than the Constitution. Political philosophers and even some judges have argued on occasion that there is a higher "natural law" governing American affairs, and that judges therefore have a higher duty not only to follow it, but to impose it if some provision of the Constitution or a law seems to conflict with it. Similar arguments have been made on behalf of "natural rights" and "moral values," as we noted earlier, and some have also maintained that the principle of equality embodied in the Declaration of Independence authorizes judges to reach beyond the Constitution in order to implement and protect it. In their struggle to end slavery, some abolitionists argued, for example, that the Constitution embraced the Declaration of Independence, and that slavery was therefore unconstitutional.

Such arguments are persuasive. It may well be that we are all governed by a higher, unwritten natural law, emanating from God; that certain rights are by nature indelibly impressed upon the hearts and minds of all mankind; and that the spirit of '76 is incorporated into our fundamental law. The problem is that these concepts, whatever their merit and value, are not provided for in the Constitution, and there is no evidence that the Framers ever intended them to be. This is not to say that the Framers rejected natural law ideas or that they opposed the principles of the Declaration of Independence—which they assuredly did not—but merely to state that the authors of the Constitution appreciated and understood the fact that any declaration to the effect that "The natural law" or "The natural rights of man" or "Moral values" or "The principles of the Declaration of Independence" of 1776 "shall be the supreme law of the land" would have produced not only widespread confusion, but the overthrow of the Constitution and the establishment of a judicial oligarchy as well. This is because there is considerable disagreement about the precise meaning of these concepts. Judges, after all, are trained in the law. They are not priests or philosopher kings, and no two judges are likely to agree on whether or why one right is "natural" and another is not. The practical effect of the Supremacy Clause, it should be kept in mind, is to expand the powers of the Supreme Court. It is the judges who must interpret the laws and decide whether they conform to the Constitution. To empower them also to decide whether the laws also conform to religious, moral, or philosophical doctrines would be an invitation to the exercise of arbitrary power. Taken to its logical conclusion, the assumption that there is a higher authority than the Constitution and that the judges may therefore invoke it at their pleasure would result in the death of the Constitution on the ground that perhaps it too violated some higher law.

In the second place, "the laws of the United States," that is, Federal laws passed by Congress, also enjoy supremacy—not over the Constitution, of course, but over State laws. Thus, if a Federal law conflicts with a State law, the latter is void and may not be enforced. Federal laws are not automatically treated as the supreme law, however, for the Supremacy Clause stipulates that they "shall be made in pursuance" of the Constitution. This means that they must conform to the Constitution. It is the duty of the courts to decide whether any law, State or Federal, meets this test. If it does, the courts are obliged to apply it to the case at hand, even if the judges think it unwise or are personally opposed to the policy it establishes. In this sense, the American Constitution establishes a qualified legislative supremacy in Congress, the only higher authority being the Constitution itself.

Third, the Supremacy Clause declares that treaties made "under the authority of the United States," shall also be supreme law of the land. Why, it may be asked, did the Framers not specify that treaties, like laws, must also be made "in pursuance of the Constitution"? Does this mean that treaties may ignore the Constitution? The wording of the clause seems uncertain on this point, and has aroused considerable debate over the years. The Framers were not careless draftsmen, however, and they chose their words carefully. Under the Articles of Confederation, the United States had entered into agreements with foreign powers, the Treaty of Peace of 1783 being a prime example. Had the Framers employed language that required all treaties to be made in pursuance of the Constitution, the legal status of such treaties would have been in doubt because the Constitution did not exist when they were made. By stating that all treaties would be regarded as the supreme law of the land if they were made "under the authority of the United States," however, these earlier agreements were left intact. Although the Supreme Court has never overturned a treaty on the ground that it violated the Constitution, the principle seems well established that treaties, like the laws of Congress, must be constitutionally acceptable. "There is nothing in this language," declared the Court in *Reid v. Covert* (1957), "which intimates that treaties do not have to comply with the provisions of the Constitution. Nor is there anything in the debates which accompanied the drafting and ratification of the Constitution which even suggests such a result."

The power of the Supreme Court to strike down an act of Congress on

the ground that it conflicts with the Constitution, it should be emphasized, is not explicitly provided for in the Constitution. There is no mention of the power of judicial review anywhere in the document, and its
legitimacy has therefore been questioned from time to time by some critics of the Court. Very early in our history, however, Chief Justice John
Marshall established the doctrine of judicial review in the celebrated case
of *Marbury v. Madison* (1803), and the Court has followed it ever since.

In *Federalist* Nos. 78 and 81, Alexander Hamilton probably spoke for
most of the Framers when he implied that judicial review was an inherent power of the Court under the new Constitution. "The interpretation
of the law," he wrote, "is the proper and peculiar province of the courts.
A Constitution is, in fact, and must be regarded by the judges, as a fundamental law. It therefore belongs to them to ascertain its meaning, as
well as the meaning of any particular act proceeding from the legislative
body. If there should happen to be an irreconcilable variance between the
two, that which has the superior obligation and validity ought, of course,
to be preferred; or, in other words, the Constitution ought to be preferred
to the statute, and the intention of the people to the intention of their
agents."

That "the intention of the people" should be preferred "to the intention of their agents" is a phrase that strikes the modern reader as peculiar. Do not elected representatives, the agents of the people, speak for the
people? Is not their intent the intent of the people? The founding generation did not equate the intent of the people with the intent of the legislature in every and all respects. Justice William Paterson, a delegate to the
Philadelphia Convention who later served on the Supreme Court, put it
this way in *Van Horne's Lessee v. Dorrance* (1795): the Constitution "is the
form of government delineated by the mighty hand of the people, in
which certain first principles of fundamental laws are established. . . . [I]t
contains the *permanent will of the people* and is the supreme law of the
land." It necessarily follows that there is nothing inherently undemocratic about judicial review in principle, in view of the magistrates' obligation to support and defend the permanent, or constituent, will of the
people, in preference to the temporary, or political, will of transient majorities. By "constituent" will, we mean the will of the people that is expressed when they create a government. The Framers understood the

difference, in other words, between *constituent* assemblies, such as those which frame and ratify a constitution, and *legislative* assemblies, which simply make the laws. Judicial review, it has been argued, is "undemocratic" because it permits unelected judges to nullify the decisions of elected representatives. This would be true only if the nullified statute was clearly constitutional. But to insist that the exercise of judicial review, as such, is undemocratic is to ignore the democratic foundation of the Constitution itself, which speaks in the name of "We the People" and is meant by the people—past as well as present and future generations—to be preferred to the wishes of their agents, who are but a fleeting reflection of current opinion and in many instances may be speaking only for themselves.

Thus understood, the true and permanent will of the American people is expressed in the Constitution. This is an unwritten assumption, applicable to each generation of Americans, until they deliberately and consciously cast it aside or amend it. It is an everlasting commitment by the people to self-restraint and to the restraint of government. By the word "people," then, Hamilton did not mean a collection of voters at any given time or place. He meant the American people in historical continuity. It is *their* will that they be governed by *their* Constitution which is written in *their* name and was adopted by *their* ancestors. This is not to say that they are to be ruled from the grave, but merely to observe that they have chosen to impose limitations on their autonomy, and to be governed ultimately not by politicians or judges, but by a higher law we call the Constitution of the United States of America. The practice of judicial review, it may thus be argued, runs counter to democratic principles when a judge ignores the Constitution or allows an unconstitutional statute to stand, not when he defends the Constitution against legislative assault.

In *Marbury v. Madison*, Chief Justice Marshall reasoned, in a brilliant display of deductive logic, that judicial review is a constitutional imperative. "The question, whether an act repugnant to the Constitution, can become the law of the land," he stated, "is a question deeply interesting to the United States." Marshall began by pointing out that certain fundamental principles of the constitutional system seem to warrant judicial review. The people had united to establish a government. They organized it into three departments and assigned certain powers to each, while at the same time setting limits to the exercise of those powers. These limits were expressed in a written constitution, which would be a useless document "if these limits may, at any time, be passed by those intended to be restrained." Because the Constitution is "a superior paramount law," it may not be changed by ordinary legislation. This means that "a legislative act contrary to the Constitution is not law."

The question, continued Marshall, thus presents itself: "If an act of the legislature, repugnant to the Constitution, is void, does it, notwithstanding its invalidity, bind the courts, and oblige them to give it effect?" The answer, said Marshall, is abundantly clear: No. The judges do not really have a choice in the matter. "It is emphatically the province and duty of the judicial department, to say what the law is." But judges do not interpret the law in the dark; they interpret it in the light of the Constitution, which provides the rule of interpretation. "If, then, the courts are to regard the Constitution, and the Constitution is superior to any ordinary act of the legislature, the Constitution, and not such ordinary act, must govern the case." To declare otherwise, Chief Justice Marshall asserted, would be to permit the legislature to surpass at will the limits imposed upon its powers by the Constitution. The very concept of a written constitution, in other words, justified judicial review.

But, Marshall further noted, the Framers did not leave the matter entirely to common sense and reason. They provided the Supremacy Clause, which gave the Constitution precedence over laws and treaties and specified that only laws "which shall be made in pursuance of the Constitution" are to be the supreme laws of the land. "Thus, the particular phraseology of the Constitution of the United States confirms and strengthens the principle, supposed to be essential to all written constitutions, that a law repugnant to the Constitution is void, and that *courts*, as well as other departments, are bound by that instrument."

The Supreme Court did not again render an act of Congress null and void through judicial review until 1857, when in the case of *Dred Scott v. Sandford* the Justices ruled that the Missouri Compromise of 1820, prohibiting slavery in the Territories, was unconstitutional. In general, the Court has been remarkably restrained in exercising judicial review over acts of Congress, and throughout much of American history has been rather reluctant to challenge the legislature. As indicated by the Court's reluctance to impose limits on the commerce power since 1937, the court has, in fact, virtually abandoned judicial review in many areas of the law.

Such a hands-off policy is most emphatically not the case with regard to the application of judicial review against the States. Between 1789 and 1860, the Supreme Court held a State constitutional provision, law, or ordinance unconstitutional in 36 instances. This number was quickly matched in the period from 1861 to 1873; and from 1861 to 1937, the number climbed to 515, about a 1,400 percent increase. The Supreme Court under Chief Justice Earl Warren held 166 State constitutional provisions, laws, or ordinances invalid, and under Chief Justice Warren Burger the number rose to 310. Altogether, the Supreme Court overturned more than 1,140 State laws, ordinances, and constitutional provisions between 1789 and 1989. Considerably more than half of these decisions have been delivered in the past fifty years.

The leading case in this area of judicial review is *Martin v. Hunter's Lessee* (1816). Under Section 25 of the Judiciary Act of 1789, Congress provided that final judgments in State supreme courts questioning the validity of any Federal law or treaty were subject to review by the Supreme Court. The Virginia high court challenged the constitutionality of this grant of power to the Supreme Court, however, arguing that it violated the reserved powers of the States. Conflicting views on the meaning of the Supremacy Clause and State sovereignty were at the heart of the controversy. The Virginia judges claimed that, while State judges were obliged under Article VI to obey the Constitution, laws, and treaties of the United States, they were not bound to obey the Supreme Court's *interpretations* of them. In their view, State and Federal judges were officers of two separate sovereignties, and neither was required to obey the decisions of the other. Congress therefore had no authority to enact a law subjecting State court decisions to review by the Federal Judiciary.

In an opinion by Justice Story, the Supreme Court rejected these arguments. Story denied the claim that State sovereignty equaled national sovereignty. The Constitution is "crowded with provisions which restrain or annul the sovereignty of the States," he pointed out, and the doctrine of absolute State sovereignty insisted upon by the Virginia judges ran counter to the whole theory of Federal supremacy.

Nowhere in the Constitution was it stated that the Supreme Court should exercise appellate jurisdiction over State courts. It did not follow from this, however, that the Supreme Court was prohibited from reviewing State court decisions. This is so, explained Story, because the appellate jurisdiction of the Supreme is not spelled out in the Constitution for any class of cases, and is left solely to the discretion of Congress. Article III of the Constitution provides that "the Supreme Court shall have appellate jurisdiction, both as to law and fact, with such exceptions, and under such regulations as the Congress shall make." The Constitution, in other words, gives Congress complete authority to establish and regulate the appellate jurisdiction of the Supreme Court. If the appellate power of the Supreme Court did not extend to cases decided in the State courts which were inconsistent with the Constitution or which challenged the validity of a Federal law or treaty, then Federal supremacy would be in jeopardy. It would also be impossible for the Supreme Court to carry out its function of protecting the supremacy of the Constitution and all Federal laws and treaties if it could not review these kinds of State court decisions. Accordingly, Section 25 of the Judiciary Act of 1789 was constitutional.

Very early in our history, it may thus be seen, judicial review of acts of Congress and judicial review of State court decisions became fixed principles of constitutional construction in the Supreme Court. Although the former rested on deductive reasoning and was understood as an inherent power implicit in the Constitution itself, and the latter was based on statute, both forms of judicial review drew their inspiration and legitimacy from the Supremacy Clause. That the Supreme Court also has the power to decide whether a State constitutional provision, law, or municipal ordinance conforms to the Constitution has never been seriously questioned. In *Fletcher v. Peck* (1810), the Supreme Court for the first time in its history held a State law void because it conflicted with a provision of the Constitution—the Contract Clause in Article I, Section 10. Previously, State laws had been held unconstitutional because they conflicted with Federal laws or treaties.

Under what is called the Doctrine of Preemption—a rule of interpretation that has been applied with increasing frequency in recent years and has been much criticized—the Court has also voided State laws not because they directly contravene a Federal law, but on the ground that

Congress has "preempted the field." As is often the case, especially in the matter of commerce, Federal statutes do not always specify whether all State and local regulations are suspended. The Court has adopted the rule of interpretation that in those instances where, in the opinion of the judges, the "scheme of Federal regulation is so pervasive as to reasonably infer that Congress has left no room for the States," or where the interest of the national government is "so dominant that it precludes State action," then the State law will be nullified even though it does not conflict with the Constitution or a Federal law.

Judicial review is thus an important power of the Supreme Court that comes in many forms. Basically, however, there are four types. The first is the power of the Supreme Court to declare acts of Congress unconstitutional. The second type is the power of the Court to declare invalid any State constitutional provision, State law, or other State action that infringes on the constitutional authority of the national government. A third type is the closely related power of the Court to overturn cases decided in State supreme courts where the validity of a Federal law or treaty was questioned or denied or where the construction of any clause in the Constitution was against a claim or right of either party. The fourth type is the power of the Court to review the actions of public officials exercising either delegated legislative or administrative powers, to determine whether they acted within their powers.

As a device for maintaining Federal supremacy, judicial review of State court decisions and State laws is the most frequently used and the most significant. *Martin v. Hunter's Lessee*, in the view of constitutional historian Charles Warren, is "the keystone of the whole arch of Federal judicial power." Justice Oliver Wendell Holmes, who served on the Court in the early part of the twentieth century, once remarked: "I do not think the United States would come to an end if we lost our power to declare an act of Congress void. I do think the Union would be imperilled if we could not make that declaration as to the laws of the several States." To be sure, it seems certain that the relationship between the Federal government and the States would be considerably different from what it is today if Section 25 of the Judiciary Act of 1789 had been overturned or later repealed.

The Supreme Court as Final Interpreter

In the United States, the opinions of the Supreme Court are routinely reported in the news by hundreds of journalists. Countless lawyers and judges, and regiments of local, State, and Federal officials examine the Court's rulings on a daily basis. Colleges, universities, and law schools devote many courses of study to constitutional law and constitution-related subjects. In no other country of the world is there such widespread interest in a nation's fundamental law. Probably more books and articles on the Constitution or the Supreme Court's interpretation of it are written in one year than all of the other countries of the world, writing about their constitutions, produce in a decade. We are indeed a constitution-minded people who take their constitution seriously.

This "constitutional colloquy" has persisted throughout our history and may be traced back to the founding period. It can almost be said that the debate in the Federal and State ratifying conventions of 1787–88 is a continuing debate. Much of this debate relates not only to disagreements over Supreme Court decisions, but more fundamentally over basic principles of the Constitution and its proper meaning and interpretation. But the word "interpretation," as we noted earlier, does not appear in the Constitution. The Constitution does not instruct the judges *how* they are to interpret the Constitution, and the separation of powers forbids Congress and the President from telling them how to interpret it. To complicate matters, the Constitution is also silent on the question of *who* is the final interpreter, or whether Congress, the President, or the States may also offer their interpretations. Although these questions have not been fully resolved, constitutional practice and experience over the years has apparently settled a number of issues.

It may be taken as a general rule that the Supreme Court of the United States is the final interpreter of the Constitution in a particular case that is brought before it and decided. But the finality of the Court's judgment is *conditional* because Congress, the several States, and the people thereof can take action to reverse the decision or render it inapplicable in future cases. Congress, for example, has the authority to withdraw the Court's appellate jurisdiction, and if it wished it could pass a law making it impossible for the Court to rule in the type of case previously determined.

Congress might even go further and remove the original jurisdiction of the lower Federal courts, thereby making the State supreme courts the final interpreters of the Constitution in those particular kinds of cases.

In examining this issue, it is important, however, to distinguish theory from practice. As a matter of constitutional theory, the Supreme Court is the final interpreter of the Constitution in a given situation because Congress permits it, not because it is required by the Constitution. As a matter of actual practice, Congress rarely exercises its power to restrict the Court's jurisdiction, and the Supreme Court is almost always the final interpreter of the Constitution.

A Supreme Court decision can also be reversed by a constitutional amendment, and this is precisely what has happened in a few instances. In this sense, it is the States and the people thereof who act as the final interpreter of the Constitution. Again, however, we must distinguish theory from practice and recognize the fact that only a handful of Supreme

The Supreme Court of the United States, 1888.

From a drawing by Carl J. Berger. Before 1935, the Supreme Court met in the U.S. Capitol. (Courtesy of the Library of Congress.)

Court decisions have been overturned by the amendment process. In other words, the Supreme Court is also the final interpreter because the States and the people thereof usually let the Court's decisions stand.

Being the final interpreter does not mean that the Supreme Court is the *exclusive* interpreter. Members of Congress and the President, who also take an oath of office to support the Constitution, must necessarily interpret its provisions in order to carry out their responsibilities. Congress does not debate in a constitutional vacuum. When a proposed bill is under consideration, the members must look beyond its desirability as a matter of public policy to the larger question of whether it conforms to the Constitution. Sometimes, in fact, they never reach the merits of legislation because of constitutional objections raised by its opponents. The constitutionality of laws is first tested in Congress, which means that members of the House of Representatives and the Senate ought to have an informed understanding of the Constitution in order to interpret and apply its provisions to proposed laws.

Likewise, the President is frequently called upon to interpret the Constitution in carrying out his executive duties. In the first place, he must decide whether to sign proposed legislation into law or whether to veto it and send it back to Congress. Here the laws of the land undergo a second constitutional test. If, in the judgment of the President, the law conflicts with the Constitution, he will often veto it strictly on constitutional grounds, without addressing its political, social, military, or economic policy objectives. In the second place, the President must execute and enforce the existing laws he has inherited from his predecessors. This involves more than a routine administration of the laws, for he must interpret the law for his subordinates and, as is often the case nowadays, direct them in drafting regulations for its enforcement. Congress does not always find it necessary or practical to include administrative details in its laws, and not infrequently allows executive agencies as well as independent regulatory commissions to "fill in the details" with administrative regulations. In performing this task, the President has the ultimate responsibility of making certain that these regulations do not violate the Constitution.

These are only a few examples to illustrate the interpretive roles played by Congress and the President. In the early Republic, when Congress was establishing a new government and sailing on uncharted seas, there was a great deal of constitutional debate in both houses. As time wore on and more and more issues were settled, the frequency and quality of constitutional debate declined somewhat. Still, the practice continues, as it must, and the discussion of constitutional issues as reported in the *Congressional Record* or in the committee reports of Congress can be highly instructive.

Presidential involvement in constitutional interpretation and debate is less extensive and frequent than congressional involvement, but not necessarily any less heated. Some Presidents, notably Thomas Jefferson, Andrew Jackson, Abraham Lincoln, and Franklin Roosevelt, and more recently Presidents Ronald Reagan and George Bush, have publicly and vigorously challenged Supreme Court interpretations of the Constitution, but no President has refused to enforce one of its decisions. Objecting to a decision of the Marshall Court involving the Cherokee Indians in Georgia, President Jackson was rumored to have said: "John Marshall has made his decision. Let *him* enforce it." There is no evidence that Jackson ever made that statement, however, or intended not to carry out the Court's ruling. Roger B. Taney, Jackson's Attorney General who later was appointed Chief Justice of the Supreme Court, explained Jackson's position in a letter that reflects a proper understanding of the President's interpretive powers:

> He [Jackson] has been charged with asserting that he, as an Executive Officer, had a right to judge for himself whether an act of Congress was constitutional or not, and was not bound to carry it into execution if he believed it to be unconstitutional, even if the Supreme Court decided otherwise; and this misrepresentation has been kept alive for particular purposes of personal ill-will, and has, I learn, been repeated in the Senate during its late session. Yet no intelligent man who reads the message can misunderstand the meaning of the President. He was speaking of his rights and duty, when acting as a part of the Legislative power, and not of his right or duty as an Executive officer. For when a bill is presented to him and he is to decide whether, by his approval, it shall become a law or not, his power or duty is as purely Legislative as that of a member of Congress, when he is called on to vote for or against a bill. If

he has firmly made up his mind that the proposed law is not within the powers of the general government, he may and he ought to vote against it, notwithstanding [that] an opinion to the contrary has been pronounced by the Supreme Court. It is true that he may very probably yield up his preconceived opinions in deference to that of the Court, because it is the tribunal especially constituted to decide the questions in all cases wherein it may arise, and from its organization and character is peculiarly fitted for such inquiries. But if a member of Congress, or the President, when acting in his Legislative capacity, has, upon mature consideration, made up his mind that the proposed law is a violation of the Constitution he has sworn to support, and that the Supreme Court had in that respect fallen into error, it is not only his right but his duty to refuse to aid in the passage of the proposed law. And this is all the President has said, and there was nothing new in this. For that principle was asserted and acted upon [by Jefferson] in relation to the memorable Sedition Law. That Law had been held to be constitutional by every Justice of the Supreme Court before whom it had come at circuit, and several persons had been punished by fine and imprisonment for offending against it. Yet a majority in Congress refused to continue the law, avowedly upon the ground that they believed it unconstitutional, notwithstanding the opinion previously pronounced by the judicial tribunals. But General Jackson never expressed a doubt as to the duty and the obligation upon him in his Executive character to carry into execution any Act of Congress regularly passed, whatever his own opinion might be of the constitutional question.

The States as Final Interpreters

Among the three branches of the Federal government, therefore, it is generally the case that the Supreme Court acts as final interpreter of the Constitution. Does the Court's dominance in constitutional interpretation apply with equal force of State supreme courts? To State legislatures? To State governors? These issues seem to be settled nowadays, but during the first one hundred years of constitutional government in the United States they were a continuing source of disagreement and debate. From

1787 down to the Civil War, the nation was preoccupied with questions of State sovereignty and the nature of the Union. State challenges to Federal power were the common order of the day, almost the theme song, it would seem, of American politics in the early Republic.

From a reading of the Convention documents, *The Federalist,* and the Constitution, it was by no means clear what kind of Union the Framers had designed. The Federalist party, favoring an expansive or nationalistic interpretation, pointed to the Preamble of the Constitution as proof that sovereignty resided in "We the People," not "We the States." The several States, said Federalist leaders such as John Marshall, had surrendered their sovereignty to the national government. The Jeffersonian Republican-Democrats, favoring a narrow or States' Rights interpretation, argued that the Union was a compact of States, each of which had retained the essential attributes of sovereignty. The Preamble refers to the "People" rather than the "States," they countered, because at the time of the Federal Convention it would have been premature to speak for all of the States. Rhode Island had not sent any delegates to the Convention, and there was considerable uncertainty at the time whether all of the States would ratify the Constitution. There were elements of truth to both sides of the argument, of course, because ultimate sovereignty had been reserved neither to the "people" as such nor to the States alone, but to those who ratified the Constitution—"the States *and* the people thereof."

The sentiment for State sovereignty and States' Rights was a powerful force throughout the Union, but as time wore on it became increasingly sectional—North against South. The "irrepressible conflict" over the issue of slavery contributed substantially to this polarization, but there were other differences—cultural and economic—which contributed significantly to sectional estrangement. The first major dispute actually involved freedom of speech and press when members of the Republican Party, led by Thomas Jefferson and James Madison, challenged the constitutionality of the Alien and Sedition Acts. Passed by a Federalist-controlled Congress in 1798, the Alien and Sedition Acts were designed to limit the influence of political radicals, particularly newspaper editors and pamphleteers, who were espousing French revolutionary doctrines and allegedly encouraging subversive activities. The Federalists, alarmed by the military aggression of revolutionary France and the atrocities committed in the name of "Liberty, Equality, and Fraternity," hoped through this legislation to prevent the spread of French radicalism to American shores.

Known collectively as the Alien and Sedition Acts, these measures consisted of four laws. The first three, directed in reality against French citizens, sought to limit the right of aliens to acquire U.S. citizenship. They authorized the President to expel aliens suspected of "treasonable or secret machinations against the government" and to apprehend them in case of war. The fourth law, outlawing seditious libel, made it a Federal crime to utter or print "false, scandalous or malicious" statements against the Federal government, either house of Congress, or the President, or to bring them into disrepute, stir up sedition, excite against them "the hatred of the good people of the United States," or encourage "any hostile designs of any foreign nation against the United States."

In response to the Alien and Sedition Acts, the States of Virginia and Kentucky passed resolutions declaring the Acts unconstitutional. The Virginia Resolutions of 1798 were drafted by James Madison and introduced in the Virginia legislature by John Taylor of Caroline. The Kentucky Resolutions, written by Thomas Jefferson (also of Virginia), were introduced in the Kentucky legislature by John Breckinridge.

Madison and Jefferson objected to the Alien and Sedition Acts on the grounds that they usurped the reserved powers of the States. Congress had no delegated power, they argued, over aliens residing under the jurisdiction and protection of State laws. By authorizing the President to expel such persons "without jury, without public trial, without confrontation of the witnesses against him, without having witnesses in his favor, without defense, [and] without counsel," this legislation also denied persons their liberty without due process of law and their procedural rights under the Fifth and Sixth Amendments.

Objections to the Sedition Act stemmed from the fact that the Congress had no authority under the First Amendment to regulate speech and press, and Federal tribunals therefore had no jurisdiction over cases involving "libels, falsehoods, [or] defamation." The authors of the Kentucky and Virginia Resolutions did not challenge the constitutionality of the statute because it limited freedom of speech and press, therefore, but because it invaded the reserved powers of the States. It was the right of the States to determine the scope and meaning of these freedoms. As the Tenth Amendment made clear, the States had retained "to themselves the right of judging how far the licentiousness of speech and of the press may be abridged without lessening their useful freedom. . . ."

Taken together, the Kentucky and Virginia Resolutions served as the well-spring for the development of the State sovereignty theory of the Union, a theory that became the point of reference for political and legal debate until 1865, when it was officially put to rest with the defeat of the Confederacy. The doctrines of Interposition, Nullification, and Secession that southern writers, lawyers, and politicians employed to justify resistance to Federal laws were derived from the Resolutions of '98.

The doctrine of Interposition, articulated by Madison in the Virginia Resolutions, suggested that State officials had the right to "interpose" themselves between the Federal government and the people to protect the latter, and that such interposition was necessary to prevent the enforcement of oppressive laws. "[I]n case of a deliberate, palpable, and dangerous exercise of other powers not granted by the said compact," wrote Madison, "the States, who are parties thereto, have the right and are in duty bound to interpose for arresting the progress of the evil."

Going a step further, Jefferson argued in the Kentucky Resolutions that nullification by the States was the proper remedy for unconstitutional acts of Congress. The Federal government, he said, cannot be the judge of its own powers. The States are "sovereign and independent," and for this reason "have the unquestionable right" to determine whether Federal laws are constitutional. The "rightful remedy," he concluded, is "a nullification . . . of all unauthorized acts done under the color" of the Constitution. Later generations, led by John C. Calhoun of South Carolina, took these arguments to the conclusion that any State could nullify Federal laws or secede from the Union if necessary, since the Union was a voluntary compact of States that had retained their individual sovereignty.

From time to time State legislatures may and do express their views on constitutional questions in the form of resolutions and petitions to Congress. Though strongly worded, the Kentucky and Virginia Resolutions amounted to no more than a formal protest, based on the claim that the States have a right to offer their own interpretations of the Constitution and Federal laws. Neither Kentucky nor Virginia interfered with the enforcement of the Alien and Sedition Acts. The Kentucky Resolution acknowledged, in fact, "That although this commonwealth, as a party to the Federal compact, will bow to the laws of the Union, yet it does at the same time declare, that it will not now, or ever hereafter, cease to oppose *in a constitutional manner,* every attempt . . . to violate that compact." Like Congress and the President, the Kentucky and Virginia legislatures, therefore, were merely claiming that they too had a right to interpret the Constitution, not that they had the right to be its *final* interpreter.

In one memorable instance, as we noted, a State supreme court did challenge the Supreme Court of the United States on a question of constitutional interpretation. This was the case of *Martin v. Hunter's Lessee* in which Spencer Roane, the Chief Justice of Virginia's highest court, argued that his court was not necessarily bound by Supreme Court precedents. Roane did not argue, however, that State courts were the final interpreters of the Constitution.

States' Rightists obeyed the decisions of the Supreme Court, but they continued to reject the Court's theory of the nature of the Union all the way down to the spring of 1865, when General Robert E. Lee, leader of the Confederate Army, surrendered at Appomattox, Virginia, to General Ulysses S. Grant, head of the Union forces. Thus in the final phase of this lengthy constitutional debate the issue was resolved on the battlefield, against the States. In *Texas v. White* (1869), the Supreme Court later declared that the States never possessed the right to secede from the Union, which is "indissoluble," and that the State of Texas, like the other States of the Confederacy, had, from a constitutional standpoint, never left the Union. Strictly speaking, concluded the Court, the Confederate States had been in a state of insurrection during the Civil War, and had not achieved sovereignty or independence in a legal sense.

Although the Interposition, Nullification, and Secessionist doctrines were southern in origin, it should not be overlooked that there were faithful adherents to these principles of interpretation throughout the Union. To be sure, the first serious political movement toward secession occurred in New England at the Hartford Convention of 1815. Prominent New England Federalists, representing Massachusetts, Connecticut, Rhode Island, Vermont, and New Hampshire, convened in the city of Hartford,

Connecticut, to air their grievances and consider remedial action. The Report and Resolutions adopted by the Convention reflected deep dissatisfaction with the policies of the Jeffersonian Republicans, the administration of President Madison and the War of 1812, and the dominant influence of the southern States in national affairs. The Hartford delegates complained about patronage, the Judiciary Act of 1801 abolishing certain Federal district courts, "the easy admission of naturalized foreigners to places of trust, honor and profit," the anti-British and pro-French stance of the Republican Party, and "the admission of new States into the Union . . . [that] has destroyed the balance of power which existed among the original States, and deeply affected their interest." Above all, they objected to the wartime commercial policies of the Republicans, which were injurious, they believed, to New England needs and interests.

To correct these problems, they proposed the adoption of seven constitutional amendments. Failing in that, they were prepared to consider more drastic action, and hinted at a possible withdrawal from the Union. If, said the Report, they were unsuccessful in getting the changes they wanted, "it will, in the opinion of this Convention, be expedient for the legislatures of the several States to appoint delegates to another Convention to meet in Boston." When commissioners of the Convention arrived in Washington to present their Resolutions, however, they decided to abandon their mission after learning that the War of 1812 was over. The Hartford Convention thus came to nothing, and the New England States thereafter became reconciled to the Union.

The several States, notwithstanding their claims, have thus never established themselves as final interpreters of the Constitution, even to the point of secession. Like Congress and the President, their primary interpretive role, once the Supreme Court has spoken on the issue, has been to offer their own interpretations as mere recommendations, objections, or expressions of opinion.

Strict Versus Loose Construction

In addition to arguing that the several States have a role to play in constitutional interpretation, many advocates of limited constitutional government have also insisted that there should be a rule of interpretation which favors the States in cases involving the scope of Federal power. Since the earliest days of the American republic, there has been considerable concern that the Federal government, through a broad interpretation of its powers, might swallow up the reserved powers of the States.

Many of the powers delegated by the States to Congress, for example, are expressed in general terms and are susceptible to conflicting interpretations, most especially when the implied or "necessary and proper" powers are added to expand the enumerated power. As we saw earlier, the power of Congress "to regulate commerce among the several States" is open to a wide variety of interpretations. Does the word "regulate" include the right to prohibit? Does the word "commerce" mean just the goods themselves, or does it include as well the environment in which commerce moves, such as waterways or the airspace above a State? Does "commerce" include manufacturing, mining, and other activities prior to the time the goods are shipped? Does it include agriculture before harvest? Does it include individuals traveling from one State to another to visit relatives? Is the commerce power an exclusive power, or may the States in the absence of Federal laws regulate commerce passing through their territory?

These are the kinds of difficult issues that have confronted the Supreme Court from the beginning, often requiring the judges to define the limits of power. If the powers are defined broadly, the Federal government tends to benefit. A narrow definition restricting the scope of a Federal power usually works to the advantage of the States. Very early in our history, States' Rightists in the Republican-Democratic Party, led by Thomas Jefferson, accused Chief Justice Marshall and many of the Associate Justices serving on the Court with him of a *federal* bias. They favored "strict" construction of the Constitution, whereas Marshall and other Federalists advocated a "loose" construction. The proper rule of interpretation, wrote St. George Tucker of Virginia in his American edition of Blackstone, was to interpret the Constitution strictly: "it is to be construed *strictly*, in all cases, where the antecedent rights of a State may be drawn into question." That is to say, although the Constitution should not necessarily be interpreted narrowly in all respects, it should be strictly construed in those instances where the rights of the States were at stake and a power previously exercised by the State governments was in danger of being usurped by the Federal government. His reasoning was that the Union was a compact or written agreement among the States. Like a contract between two or more parties, the Constitution established rights and obligations. The "loose" construction of its terms would defeat the intent of the parties and was inconsistent with State sovereignty.

Similarly, Thomas Jefferson laid down two rules for the interpretation of the Constitution. His first rule of interpretation was to reserve to the States authority over *all* matters that affected *only* their own citizens: "The capital and leading object of the Constitution was, to leave with the States all authorities which respected their own citizens only, and to transfer to the United States those which respected citizens of foreign or other States; to make us several to ourselves, but one as to all others. In the latter case, then, constructions should lean to the general jurisdiction, if the words will bear it; and in favor of the States in the former, if possible to be so construed."

The second rule of interpretation, said Jefferson, was to construe the Constitution as the Founding Fathers would have construed it: "On every question of construction, we should carry ourselves back to the time when the Constitution was adopted, recollect the spirit manifested in the debates, and instead of trying what meaning may be squeezed out of the text, or invented against it, conform to the probable one in which it was passed."

John Marshall and his brethren on the Supreme Court were in basic agreement with Jefferson that the original intent of the Framers ought to govern. What divided the "strict" constructionists from the "loose" constructionists, therefore, was not *whether* the original meaning of the Constitution should be followed, but *what* the Framers intended.

The "loose" constructionists, enjoying strong support on the Supreme Court through Marshall, Story, and other Justices, tended to prevail. In such major cases as *McCulloch v. Maryland* (1819) and *Gibbons v. Ogden* (1823), the Court broadly interpreted the powers of Congress. By 1835, when John Marshall was succeeded by Roger B. Taney as Chief Justice, the Court had built a strong array of judicial precedents that strengthened its own position in relation to the other two branches of the Federal government, and also laid the foundation for future expansions of national power.

It would be erroneous to conclude, however, that the nationalism of the Marshall Court reached into every nook and cranny of the Constitution, eclipsing the reserved powers of the States wherever it went. By today's practices, it was very limited. The principal gains of the national government were related to the commercial life of the young Republic, and the States continued to function as powerful, independent entities in public affairs. In the broad area of civil rights, for example, the Federal government had no major role to play—and would not for another century. In keeping with the original purpose and meaning of the Bill of Rights, a unanimous court, speaking through Chief Justice Marshall, held in *Barron v. Baltimore* (1833) that the Bill of Rights was designed to limit only the *Federal* government and did not apply to the *States*. Not until the adoption of the Thirteenth, Fourteenth, and Fifteenth amendments, otherwise known as the Civil War or Reconstruction Amendments, did the Federal government acquire much jurisdiction over civil rights disputes in the States. Even then, the main thrust of its involvement was the protection of the newly emancipated slaves in the post–Civil War era of Reconstruction and not such matters as freedom of speech and religion.

The States' Rightists, resisting the Marshall court, viewed judicial nationalism with great apprehension, fearing that the practice of loose construction would set dangerous precedents and weaken the States. Although States' Rights would later become a convenient peg upon which to defend the institution of slavery, the doctrine was rooted in the Federal Convention. And in the early days of the Republic, before slavery became a burning issue, States' Rights was a constitutional theory that cut across sectional lines between the North and South. One of the leading States' Rightists in the Federal Convention, we are reminded, was Elbridge Gerry of Massachusetts. The States' Rightist from Virginia, George Mason, spoke against slavery and vigorously opposed it. States' Rightists did not share the Federalists' vision of a great empire reaching from the Atlantic to the Pacific. They had strong attachments and loyalties to their States, and generally distrusted centralized political power. The constitutional theories they advanced in support of strict interpretation were almost fully developed by the time Thomas Jefferson was elected President.

These differing constitutional theories of interpretation between the

Nationalists and the States' Rightists dominated American politics during the first century of the Republic. The Civil War (or War Between the States, as the southerners preferred to call it) was the end result of this constitutional quarrel. To a very large extent, the great military conflict that erupted between the North and the South in 1861 was fought over this basic question: what is the correct interpretation of the Constitution respecting the powers of the States and the national government? The Civil War answered this question in part by laying to rest the doctrines of Nullification and Secession. But it did not put an end to federalism or change the rules of constitutional interpretation. The basic principle that the Constitution should be strictly construed to reflect the original meaning of the words and text has found considerable support on the Supreme Court since the Civil War, just as the principle that it should be loosely construed has also enjoyed considerable—if not majority—support.

In the final analysis, it must be remembered that the question of interpretation is inevitably affected by politics. Ideally, the Constitution should be given a consistent interpretation. But as the Founding Fathers understood well, the temptations of office are often too great to expect a uniform adherence to principle in all situations. Those who possess political power may be inclined to favor a broad interpretation of the Constitution in order to carry out their programs, whereas those who are out of power may be inclined to argue for a narrow interpretation in order to block those programs.

The task of the principled statesman and judge is to resist those temptations and consistently defend the proper interpretation of the Constitution—even when it results in the advancement of a particular social, economic, or political policy that he personally opposes. But perhaps too few public leaders are willing to put principle ahead of personal gain or partisanship. This is not to suggest that those who argue for a particular interpretation in any given situation may be insincere, but merely to put the student on notice that, in order to evaluate a constitutional interpretation fairly and honestly, he should judge it on its own merits and not by the policy it promotes. Principled constitutionalism is resisting the temptation to twist the meaning of the Constitution to suit a particular political goal, no matter how worthy, and letting the chips fall as they may.

Birth of the Monroe Doctrine.

James Monroe, our fifth President, was an American Revolutionary War hero who also served as a member of the Virginia Ratifying Convention in 1788. The Monroe Doctrine, embodied in his Annual Message to Congress in 1823, has been a corner-stone in American foreign policy for more than a century.

Its original purpose was to prevent European nations from extending their power and influence into the western hemisphere and to guarantee the sovereign indepen-dence of Latin American republics. John Quincy Adams, Monroe's Secretary of State, helped to formulate the policy. The Monroe Doctrine has become so deeply rooted in the American mind that it is commonly regarded as part of our unwritten Constitu-tion. (Courtesy of the Library of Congress.)

The Independence of the Judiciary

Although we do not ordinarily associate judicial interpretation with ju-dicial independence, the two practices are so closely related as to be made of the same cloth. The basic purpose of granting independence to any judicial body is to shield it from political interference and intrigue emanating from the legislative or the executive branch, so that it may reach a fair and impartial decision. By following intelligible, reasonable, and uniform rules of interpretation, the judiciary in turn assures the other branches that it is performing its function properly. To put it another way, there would be no justification for an independent judiciary if the judges habitually deferred to the legislature in every case or always bowed to the wishes of the executive.

Nor would their independence seem warranted if the judges ruled arbitrarily and continually fabricated new "rules" of interpretation to suit their personal policy preferences. If that were the case, they might just as well be elected to office and held directly accountable to the people for their actions. In many States today, judges are in fact elected to office. This practice of electing judges dates back to the Populist and Progressive movements of the late nineteenth and early twentieth centuries, when it was widely believed in certain States that too many judges had become corrupt, had ceased to be neutral administrators of justice, and had therefore forfeited the right to be independent. The practice of electing judges has not proved to be entirely satisfactory, however, owing to the fact judges running for office may be inclined to curry the favor of special interest groups in order to raise campaign funds, or may feel obliged to compromise principle and rule of law in order to satisfy a passionate majority and please the electorate.

Attempts to amend the Constitution to provide for the election of Federal judges have met with little or no success, and the independence of the Federal judiciary seems well established. It has not been immune from criticism, however, and throughout much of its history, especially in modern times, the Supreme Court has been accused of manipulating its own rules of interpretation and imposing upon the Constitution its own philosophy of government. This is the basis of allegations that the Court is engaged in "judicial activism," the assumption being that the Court should exercise "judicial restraint" and adhere more closely to fixed rules of interpretation and the original meaning of the Constitution.

A. ORIGINS OF JUDICIAL INDEPENDENCE

Although the judiciary was clearly a separate branch of government in England by the Middle Ages, it was not until the latter part of the seventeenth century that it achieved lasting independence. Much of the credit for the establishment of an independent judiciary (and Parliament) goes to Sir Edward Coke, or Lord Coke as he was known by his contemporaries. Coke, we will recall, was Queen Elizabeth's Attorney General and Chief Justice of both the Court of Common Pleas and the Court of King's Bench under James, first Stuart King of England.

A handsome country gentleman with considerable wealth, Coke was the personification of English law. On the courtroom floor, he could be raucous, witty, and ruthless. As Judge and as Speaker of the House of Commons, he risked his life for principles that are now embodied in our Constitution: a prisoner's right to public trial and the writ of habeas corpus, the right of the accused against self-incrimination in a court of law, and the right not to be jailed without cause shown. When Coke was seventy, James I imprisoned him in the Tower of London for championing these rights, complaining that "he had become an oracle amongst the people." In 1628, at the age of seventy-six, Coke led the fight in Parliament for the Petition of Right. "Sir Edward Coke never set foot on American soil," observed Catherine Drinker Bowen in her biography of this legal giant. "Yet no United States citizen can read his story without a sense of immediate recognition. In these parliamentary struggles, knights, citizens and burgesses fought not for themselves alone but for States as yet unformed: Pennsylvania, Virginia, California. In Westminster courtroom battles over procedure, jurisdiction, 'right reason and the common law,' constitutional government found its way to birth. When the time came we changed the face of this English constitution; amid the sound of guns we repudiated what we hated, adapted what we liked. Yet the heritage endured."

The famous *Case of Commendams*, a jurisdictional dispute involving the power of the King to grant ecclesiastical offices, illustrates the courage of Lord Coke in defending the principle of judicial independence. In June of 1616, King James I summoned the common law judges to his Whitehall palace (now the headquarters of the British bureaucracy). He was angry with them because, in defiance of his command to halt the proceedings of the case, the judges had refused. In a letter to the King, drafted by Coke, the judges had explained that their oaths of office compelled them to go ahead with the trial. They now stood before the King, trembling in fear of their lives. With a violent gesture, James ripped the letter in half. All twelve judges fell on their knees and begged humble pardon. The "form" of their letter, they confessed, had been wrong.

Sir Edward Coke (1552–1634).

(Courtesy of Corbis-Bettmann.)

504 Interpreting and Preserving the Constitution

But Chief Justice Coke remained true to his convictions. Still on his knees, he raised his face to the King. "The stay required by your Majesty," he said, "was a delay of justice and therefore contrary to law and the Judges' oath." "Mere sophistry," bellowed the King. As the Judges cowered at his feet, James asked each Judge what he would do if the King ever again told the Court to stay proceedings. Each replied that he would do "as His Majesty commanded."

When at last the King turned to Coke and asked him what he would do, the Chief Justice answered: "He would do that should be fit for a Judge to do." It was a statement never to be forgotten, and because of it, Coke was removed from office. It was ambiguous enough to save his head, however, and in time he was vindicated. By the end of the seventeenth century, the judges had achieved full independence, and the English Judiciary today, though considerably less powerful than its American counterpart, is no less independent.

It was often difficult for early American judges to retain their independence also, especially in the period immediately following the American Revolution. Violations of judicial independence occurred not at the national level, for there were no national courts under the Articles of Confederation. Rather, they occurred under the new State constitutions first adopted in 1776, which were influenced in varying degrees by the principle of legislative supremacy. What early State court judges often feared was not the encroachment of the executive branch, for the office of governor was usually weak. The principal threat to judicial independence was the powerful legislative assembly.

Ignoring the concept of separation of powers, State legislatures sometimes treated State courts as mere agencies of the legislature, as if they were personally accountable to the legislators. Committees of the legislature might summon judges and interrogate them. Occasionally, legislatures actually interfered with court proceedings, reversed court decisions, reduced the judges' salaries, and removed judges arbitrarily from office because of disagreement with their views. As late as 1808–1809, in Ohio, three supreme court justices, three presiding judges of the Court of Common Pleas, all of the associate justices of the courts of Common Pleas (more than 100 in number), and all of the justices of the peace were removed from their offices by a single resolution of the legislature.

Much of this was attributable to democratic excesses. The will of the people in many instances was considered omnipotent, and the legislature was simply carrying out the popular will. Hence, a number of early State legislatures did not hesitate to interfere with the traditional functions of the courts. During Shays' Rebellion in 1786, people in Massachusetts prevented the courts from functioning and demanded that all inferior courts be abolished. Similar notions were advanced in New Hampshire in the early Republic. In Vermont, courthouses were set afire; and in New Jersey debtors nailed up the doors of courthouses and irate mobs attacked lawyers and judges in the streets.

The Framers of the Federal Constitution, profoundly alarmed by these developments, endeavored to provide the nation with a truly independent judiciary at the Federal level. But we may ask: independent of whom? The answer is not as easy as it might appear, for the independence of the Federal courts is not absolute. The Federal Judiciary, like Congress and the President, is a part of our separation of powers and checks and balances system. Congress and the President not only have certain powers to "check" the Judiciary, but also share with the Supreme Court the right and the duty to interpret the Constitution. The arrangement carefully constructed by the Framers is a complicated one, often misunderstood and in need of careful examination if we are to understand the role of the courts in our political system.

In general, Federal judges are independent of Congress, the President, the States, and the people. Strictly speaking, however, their independence is limited. They are not self-appointed, and most of the power they exercise is conferred by Congress. Article II, Section 2 of the Constitution authorizes the President, by and with the consent of the Senate, to appoint "Judges of the Supreme Court and all other officers of the United States." Members of the Supreme Court and all Federal judges who sit on a lower Federal court that exercises the judicial power under Article III of the Constitution are thus classified as "Officers of the United States." They are informally known as "Article III" judges and the courts upon which they sit are called "constitutional" courts because they deal with issues arising under the Constitution.

These distinctions are necessary to avoid confusion with other kinds of Federal judges who serve on other kinds of Federal courts. Referring back to Article I, Section 8 of the Constitution, which enumerates the delegated powers of Congress, we note that Clause 9 authorizes Congress "To constitute Tribunals inferior to the Supreme Court." Congress has frequently exercised this power to create "legislative" courts, such as territorial courts and the U.S. Court of Military Appeals. The President appoints the judges to these courts, but Senate confirmation is not mandatory and the judges do not enjoy the same degree of independence as Article III judges. Instead of serving "during good behavior," for example, they serve for specified terms and then must leave office when their term expires. Their responsibility is to carry out the will of Congress, not to exercise the judicial power.

It may thus be seen that both the President and one branch of the legislature decide who shall sit on a constitutional court. Once the appointment has been agreed to by the Senate, however, the President ceases to have any direct control over the personnel of the Judiciary.

Whereas judicial independence of the executive is considerable, we find that the Federal Courts are potentially at the mercy of Congress. Primary control of the Judiciary rests with Congress, and its powers over the Courts are far-reaching. We noted earlier that if Congress had the *will* to do so, it could constitutionally reduce the entire Federal Judiciary down to one judge—the Chief Justice of the Supreme Court—leaving the Supreme Court virtually powerless. This has never happened, of course, but it should be borne in mind that the Framers of the Constitution gave Congress sufficient power to check an arrogant judiciary.

In the first place, it is Congress, not the Constitution, which creates the Federal Judiciary. Article III, Section 1 provides simply that "The Judicial power of the United States shall be vested in one Supreme Court, and in such inferior Courts as the Congress may from time to time ordain and establish." By these words, the Supreme Court is the only Federal Court that is required by the Constitution. Congress is free to create whatever lower Federal courts it pleases, and it may even abolish those already in existence. This first occurred in 1801, when the Jeffersonian Republicans abolished a number of Federal district courts that the administration of John Adams had established and packed with loyal Federalist party members.

Having once created the courts, Congress decides how many courts and judges there shall be, where they shall be located, what their salaries and administrative expenses shall be, what their duties shall be, and most importantly, what powers they shall exercise. Congress even has a voice in who shall be appointed to these courts and has sole authority in deciding who shall be removed.

With respect to the number of Federal judges we shall have, and what their qualifications shall be, the Constitution is silent. We know only that there must be a Supreme Court, because it is named in Article III, and that we must have a Chief Justice, because he is specifically mentioned in Article I, Section 3 as the officer who must preside over the impeachment trial of the President. During the course of American history, Congress has authorized as few as five and as many as ten Justices of the Supreme Court. For more than a century the number has remained constant at nine, including the Chief Justice. Today, the number of inferior Federal judges, also determined by statute, exceeds 700.

To protect the independence of the judges, Article III, Section 1 further provides that they shall serve during good behavior, and that Congress may not reduce their salaries while they are in office. The term "good behavior," inherited from the English Constitution, means—in practical terms—for life or as long as the judge wishes to serve since Federal judges have been removed from office only through the impeachment process. Although a number of inferior Federal judges have been impeached and convicted—the most recent being in 1986—no member of the Supreme Court has ever been removed by this method. Justice Samuel Chase was impeached in 1805, but the Senate failed to convict. However, at least one member of the Supreme Court—Justice Abe Fortas—resigned rather than face impeachment proceedings.

On what grounds may a Federal judge be impeached? The Constitution is not clear on this point. On the one hand, Article II, Section 4 states that "all civil officers" may be removed if they are impeached and convicted of treason, bribery, or other high crimes and misdemeanors. Since Federal judges are civil officers, it would seem to follow that the impeachment clause applies to them. The term "high crimes and misdemeanors" is also vague and undefined. In England, it comprehended criminal conduct as well as that not constituting an indictable offense, such as maladministration or abuse of office. The Senate apparently followed this interpretation during the trials of two Federal judges in this century who were convicted on articles of impeachment which charged them with misconduct that did not amount to a violation of a criminal statute. The argument has been made in other impeachment trials, however, that to be impeachable, the conduct complained of must constitute an indictable offense.

On the other hand, it has also been argued that Federal judges may be removed by means other than impeachment. They serve only during "good behavior," and it is therefore open to Congress to define "good behavior" and establish a mechanism by which judges may be removed. By this reasoning, Congress could remove Federal judges either by impeachment (for high crimes and misdemeanors) or by some other method (for "bad" behavior). Legislation has frequently been introduced to effect this idea since the 1930s, but it has never passed. All the same, Congress has adopted legislation which authorizes a judicial conference to discipline and incapacitate inferior Federal judges. The Supreme Court has declined to rule on the constitutionality of this procedure, which allegedly conflicts with the separation of powers. Whether Federal judges may be removed by a non-impeachment method is indeed a question of considerable interest that could ultimately place the Supreme Court in the awkward position of having to rule on its own tenure.

By prohibiting Congress from reducing the salaries of Federal judges, the Framers sought to protect them from retribution and revenge for handing down unpopular opinions, and to discourage legislative interference while a case was in progress. An angry Congress bent upon punishing a judge or group of judges financially can at best freeze the salaries of *all* the judges—an unsatisfactory and indiscriminate means of judicial control that has rarely been advocated. Designed to secure the independence of the judges, the prohibition against the diminution of judicial salaries has presented little controversy or litigation. Congress is also prohibited from reducing the salary of the President while he is in office, but unlike the Judiciary, Congress cannot increase it either.

B. THE JUDICIAL POWER

The independence of the Judiciary with respect to the *powers* it exercises is substantially limited, however, by federalism and the check and balance system of the Constitution. Section 1 of Article III states that the "judicial power" of the Federal government shall be vested in the Federal courts, and Section 2 of Article III lists the kinds of cases or controversies in which this power may be exercised. There are nine such classes of cases: (1) Cases arising under the Constitution, under a Federal law, or under a treaty; (2) cases affecting ambassadors, other public ministers, and consuls; (3) cases of admiralty and maritime jurisdiction; (4) controversies between two or more States; (5) controversies between a State and citizens of another State; (6) controversies between citizens of different States; (7) controversies between citizens of the same State claiming land under grants of different States; (8) controversies between a State and a foreign citizen; and (9) controversies between an American citizen and a foreign citizen. Taken literally, Section 2 would seem to say that the judicial power also extends to controversies between a State or citizen thereof and a foreign State. Under established principles of sovereignty and the law of nations, however, a foreign State cannot be sued without its consent. Thus, Mexico would be immune from a suit filed by the State of Texas or a citizen thereof. As a result of the Eleventh Amendment, which shall be examined later, this immunity also works in reverse, and the State of Texas would be immune from a suit filed by a citizen of Mexico.

Another way of understanding what kinds of cases the Federal courts are empowered to hear is to divide them into two categories: (1) *the nature of the dispute;* (2) *the parties to the dispute.* Under this first category fall cases arising under the Constitution, a Federal law or treaty, cases arising under admiralty and maritime jurisdiction, and cases involving title to land that is claimed because of land grants of two or more States. The second category, based on the parties to the dispute, covers cases in which the United States government is a party, cases in which a State is a party, cases in which the parties are citizens of different States, and cases that affect foreign ambassadors, ministers, and consuls.

The Constitution speaks of the "judicial power," but the term is nowhere defined. What did the Framers mean when they conferred the "judicial power" of the United States on the Federal courts? In answering this question, it is important to understand the difference between *authority* and *power.* In general, the authority to act is the *right* to act, whereas the power to act is the *capacity* to do so. Thus a policeman may have the power or capacity to conduct a search, but whether he has the authority or right to take such action often depends upon whether he has obtained a valid search warrant.

The judicial power, as explained by the Supreme Court, is "the power of a court to decide and pronounce a judgment and carry it into effect between persons and parties who bring a case before it for decision." It should not be confused with the "jurisdiction" of a court, which is the *authority* of a court to exercise "judicial power" in a particular case. If a court lacks jurisdiction over a case, then it cannot exercise judicial power and decide the case. In other words, the scope of the judicial power is limited by the jurisdictional requirement.

A careful reading of Article III of the Constitution reveals that the judicial power is limited in a number of ways. First, it is limited by *federalism.* The Federal judicial power can be exercised only in certain kinds of cases, not in every conceivable type of dispute that may come before a tribunal. If, for example, one citizen of Kentucky sues another citizen of Kentucky for wrongful injury (tort), the aggrieved party can bring an action to require the other party to pay damages. He would be required to sue in a Kentucky State court, however, because the Federal judicial power does not extend to controversies between citizens of the same State where the dispute involves negligent conduct. As a general rule, therefore, private disputes between citizens of the same State are reserved to the State courts. This is one reason why most cases are decided in the State rather than the Federal courts.

Bearing in mind that there were no national courts under the Articles of Confederation, the Framers were careful to extend the Federal judicial power only to those kinds of cases in which the national interest was at stake, or in those where the States had delegated their powers to the Federal government. These would include cases where a State court decision might interfere with a treaty or the conduct of foreign relations, where it might produce hostility or even armed conflict among the States and disrupt the Union, where uniform rules were needed to facilitate trade and commerce, where the States were unable to act, and where a Federal forum was needed for the convenience of the parties or a just resolution of the dispute. At the risk of oversimplification of these complex matters, it may be said that the judicial power reserved to the States under Article

III corresponds roughly to the power reserved to the States elsewhere in the Constitution, and that the Federal judicial power, which is designed to protect the national interest, is derived from and closely relates to the delegated powers of Congress and the powers of the President.

The principle of federalism also serves to limit the Federal judicial power in another way. The fact that the Constitution grants power to the Federal courts in certain types of cases does not, of itself, exclude State courts from exercising concurrent jurisdiction. Congress, as we shall see, is free to make the jurisdiction exclusive or concurrent. Under present law, for example, the Federal courts have exclusive jurisdiction in cases involving patent and copyright laws; but their jurisdiction is concurrent in cases where the parties are citizens of different States. We noted earlier that the State courts would have exclusive jurisdiction in a dispute be-tween two citizens of Kentucky over a case involving personal injury. What is the rule if one of the parties is a citizen of Kentucky and the other party is a citizen of Indiana, in light of the provision in Article III stating that the judicial power shall extend to cases in which the parties are citizens of *different* States? Congress has decided, by statute, that in diversity of citizenship cases, the case may be decided by the Federal courts or the State courts if the dispute involves more than $10,000, and that if the sum is less, it shall be tried in the State courts.

The power of Congress to regulate and control the Federal courts, it may thus be seen, is formidable. The judicial power is not self-executing and generally may not be exercised unless Congress has enacted a law authorizing Federal courts to take jurisdiction. The *Constitution* confers the *judicial power* on the Federal courts, but it is the *Congress* which con-fers *jurisdiction;* and without jurisdiction, a Federal court cannot decide the case. In brief, the responsibility of limiting the power of the Federal Judiciary under our checks and balances system rests primarily with the Congress; and this is accomplished by the second clause of Article III, Section 2, which authorizes Congress to regulate the jurisdiction of the Federal courts.

C. JURISDICTION

Whereas the first clause of Section 2 in Article III speaks of the *judicial power,* the second clause refers to *jurisdiction:* "In all cases affecting Ambassadors, other Public Ministers and Consuls, and those in which a State shall be a Party, the Supreme Court shall have *Original Jurisdiction.* In all other cases before mentioned, the Supreme Court shall have *Appellate Jurisdiction,* both as to law and fact, with such *Exceptions* and under such *Regulations* as the Congress shall make."

This is an important provision of the Constitution deserving careful study. It may be observed at the outset that the Supreme Court shall have two kinds of jurisdiction: original and appellate. Original jurisdiction is the power to hear and decide a case in the first instance. Unlike appellate jurisdiction, it flows directly from the Constitution, is self-executing, and does not depend upon an act of Congress. The Supreme Court's original jurisdiction is not significant. It applies to only two classes of cases, and it is not exclusive. Since 1789, inferior Federal courts have had concurrent jurisdiction in some instances under these two classes of cases. But Congress cannot increase or decrease the original jurisdiction of the Supreme Court.

The appellate jurisdiction of the Supreme Court, applying to the other classes of cases, authorizes the Court to hear cases on appeal. By statute, the Court has been authorized since 1789 to hear appeals from lower Federal courts and from the highest State courts. The Supreme Court's appellate jurisdiction is subject to "exceptions and regulations" prescribed by Congress. Noting that this power is complete and unqualified, the Supreme Court has always taken it for granted that Congress could, if it so desired, withhold all appellate jurisdiction, thereby making lower Federal courts or the State supreme courts the courts of last resort. "By the Constitution of the United States," said the Court in one opinion, "the Supreme Court possesses no appellate power in any case, unless conferred upon it by act of Congress." In order for a case to come within its appellate jurisdiction, the Court has stated, "two things must concur: the Constitution must give the capacity to take it, and an act of Congress must supply the requisite authority." Moreover, "it is for Congress to determine how far, within the limits of the capacity of this Court to take, appellate jurisdiction shall be given, and when conferred, it can be exercised only to the extent and in the manner prescribed by law. In these respects it is wholly the creature of legislation."

The power of Congress to regulate the appellate jurisdiction of the

Supreme Court is so broad that in one instance—the case of *Ex parte McCardle* (1868)—the Congress actually repealed the act which authorized the appeal in the case, thereby withdrawing jurisdiction while the case was being decided. Numerous restrictions on the Court's appellate jurisdiction have been upheld since the earliest days of the Republic. For a hundred years, for example, Congress refused to provide for a right of appeal to the Supreme Court in Federal criminal cases, except upon a certification of division by the circuit court. By and large, however, the Congress has been extremely reluctant to limit the Court's jurisdiction, and the general pattern of legislation over the years has reflected a desire to expand rather than decrease it.

Hence, much of the power presently enjoyed by the Supreme Court may be attributed to a friendly Congress. Efforts in Congress, particularly since the Second World War, to withdraw the Court's jurisdiction in cases involving such controversial issues as abortion and prayer in the public schools have failed to gain majority support. Though Congress has the power, therefore, to strip the Court of all of its appellate jurisdiction, it has never withdrawn a meaningful portion of it. The tendency has been to give the Court almost all of the appellate jurisdiction it can take, and to let the Court retain it once it has been granted. Congressional control of the Federal Judiciary, in other words, is more a question of theory than of practice.

This brings us finally to the jurisdiction of the lower Federal courts. The second clause of Article III, Section 2 refers to the original and appellate jurisdiction of the Supreme Court, but makes no mention of inferior Federal courts. What type of jurisdiction may they possess, and to what extent may Congress regulate their jurisdiction? The answer to these questions lies in the first clause of Article III, Section 2, which authorizes Congress to create such courts. The thought that it would not be necessary to create any inferior courts was expressed in the Philadelphia Convention. Since State judges were bound under Article VI to uphold the supremacy of the Constitution, Federal laws and treaties—irrespective of what their State constitutions might require—the possibility was raised of letting the State courts handle all Federal cases. The first Congress rejected this option, however, in the Judiciary Act of 1789. This legislation organizing the Federal Judiciary, it should be noted, is one of the most important statutes ever enacted by Congress, and provides to this day much of the basic organizational and procedural structure of the Federal judicial system.

The power to create includes the power to destroy, and Congress has always acted under the assumption that it therefore has the lesser power of shaping the jurisdiction of all inferior courts as it sees fit. The Supreme Court has generally sustained this view, and Congress may confer or withhold both original and appellate jurisdiction in the lower Federal courts at its discretion. As the Supreme Court explained in *Cary v. Curtis* (1845), "the judicial power of the United States, although it has its origin in the Constitution, is (except in enumerated instances applicable exclusively to this court) dependent for its distribution and organization, and for the modes of its exercise, entirely upon the action of Congress, which possesses sole power of creating tribunals (inferior to the Supreme Court), for the exercise of the judicial power, and of investing them with jurisdiction either limited, concurrent, or exclusive, and of withholding jurisdiction from them in the exact degrees and character which to Congress may seem proper for the public good."

Over the years, the Congress has determined the times and places for holding court (including the Supreme Court), times of adjournment, appointment of officers, issuance of writs and methods of appeal, and other matters relating to the administration of justice. Congress has also organized the nation into various judicial districts, or circuits as they are called, and today there are eleven such circuits, each encompassing a group of States in a particular region, plus the District of Columbia. Within these circuits are numerous Federal district courts. These are trial courts of original jurisdiction, where juries are used. An appellate court stands at the head of each circuit. Formerly called circuit courts, they are now known as U.S. Courts of Appeal. Most appeals to these courts come from the U.S. district courts. Most appeals to the Supreme Court emanate from the U.S. Courts of Appeal and the State supreme courts.

On the basis of the foregoing discussion, it would seem that the principle of judicial independence under the Constitution applies more to the individual judges than to the judicial branch as such. Members of the Federal bench, in terms of salary and tenure, are virtually immune from legislative or executive control; but the Judiciary itself is subject to far-reaching regulations of the Congress. Thus, the independence of the Judiciary, like the independence of the Congress and the independence of the President, is far from absolute and is generally understood to exist within the separation of powers and checks and balances framework.

In the final analysis, it may be seen that the idea of an independent judiciary went hand-in-hand with the idea of a written Constitution. Federal judges, sworn to uphold the supremacy of the Constitution rather than the supremacy of the legislature, would serve as guardians of the Constitution, protecting it from subversion by the political branches. This they would do through their inherent power, as judges, to interpret and apply laws adopted by Congress and the States. As interpreters, their task was simply to interpret the laws in the light of the Constitution. Although judicial precedents might later serve as a guide to correct interpretation, their ultimate standard, particularly in the early years, was the Constitution itself—its underlying principles, wording, and text.

By this mode of reasoning, Federal judges would have very little discretionary authority. It was not their responsibility to make the law, as that would be done by State and Federal legislatures. It was not their job to execute and enforce the law, for that function would be performed by the Chief Executive. Their sole task was to interpret the laws in cases or controversies presented to them for resolution, to determine the intent and meaning of the laws and weigh them against the intent and meaning of the governing constitutional provisions applicable to the situation. It was to be almost a mechanical function—to "discover" the law of the case, not to make it.

To do this fairly and objectively, it would be necessary to remove the judges from politics and give them independence of action. Through the judges, it was said, the voice of the people sober would speak to the warring factions drunk with power.

Such was the limited role of the Supreme Court envisioned by the Framers. Americans had little to fear, Hamilton assured the nation in *The Federalist*, from so weak an institution. The members of the Supreme Court would not be free, as the Anti-Federalists charged, to roam at will, invoking their personal biases and secret preferences in the name of some vaguely conceived "spirit" of the Constitution. Nor would they subvert the "common sense" of the Constitution by masking their interpretations in hypertechnicalities. "[T]he natural and obvious sense of its provisions, apart from any technical rules," said Hamilton, "is the true criterion of construction."

Writing in *Federalist No. 81*, Hamilton asserted that "there is not a syllable in the plan under consideration, which *directly* empowers the national courts to construe the laws according to the spirit of the Constitution, or which gives them any greater latitude in this respect, than may be claimed by courts of every State." It was clearly understood "that the Constitution ought to be the standard of construction for the laws, and that wherever there is an evident opposition, the laws ought to give place to the Constitution. But this doctrine is not deducible from any circumstance peculiar to the plan of the convention, but from the general theory of a limited constitution." It would thus seem, he concluded, "that the supposed danger of judiciary encroachments on the legislative authority, which has been upon many occasions reiterated, is in reality a phantom. Particular misconstructions and contraventions of the will of the legislature may now and then happen; but they can never be so extensive as to amount to an inconvenience, or in any sensible degree to affect the order of the political system." Should the judges get out of hand, there were ample means through the checks and balances system to restore constitutional government. In the first place, judges could be removed by "the important constitutional check" of impeachment. And in the second place, the Supreme Court's appellate jurisdiction was subject to legislative control, and "this will enable the government to modify it in such a manner as will best answer the ends of public justice and security."

SUGGESTED READING

Henry J. Abraham, *The Judicial Process* (New York: Oxford University Press, 1980).

Elizabeth K. Bauer, *Commentaries on the Constitution, 1790–1860* (New York: Russell and Russell, 1952).

Raoul Berger, *Government by Judiciary.* 2nd ed. (Indianapolis: Liberty Fund, 1997).

James E. Bond, *The Art of Judging* (New Brunswick, N. J.: Transaction Books, 1986).

Robert K. Faulkner, *The Jurisprudence of John Marshall* (Princeton: Princeton University Press, 1968).

Charles Hobson, *The Great Chief Justice: John Marshall and the Rule of Law* (Lawrence: University Press of Kansas, 1996).

Charles Hyneman, *The Supreme Court on Trial* (New York: Atherton Press, 1963).

Charles Hyneman and George W. Carey, *A Second Federalist: Congress Creates a Government* (Columbia: University of South Carolina Press, 1967).

David N. Mayer, *The Constitutional Thought of Thomas Jefferson* (Charlottesville: University of Virginia Press, 1994).

James McClellan, *Joseph Story and the American Constitution* (Norman: University of Oklahoma Press, 1971, 1990).

Gary McDowell, *The Constitution and Contemporary Constitutional Theory* (Cumberland, Va.: Center for Judicial Studies, 1985).

Gary McDowell, *Curbing the Courts* (Baton Rouge: Louisiana State University Press, 1988).

Gary McDowell, *Equity and the Constitution* (Chicago: University of Chicago Press, 1982).

James Madison, *The Virginia Report of 1799–1800* (New York: DaCapo Press, 1970).

R. Kent Newmyer, *Supreme Court Justice Joseph Story: Statesman of the Old Republic* (Chapel Hill: University of North Carolina Press, 1985).

Clinton Rossiter, *Alexander Hamilton and the Constitution* (New York: Harcourt, Brace & World, 1964).

Ralph Rossum, *Congressional Control of the Judiciary: The Article III Option* (Cumberland, Va.: Center for Judicial Studies, 1988).

Joseph Story, *Commentaries on the Constitution*. 3 vols. (Boston: Hilliard, Gray & Co., 1833). See also Story's one-volume abridgment of this work, designed for classroom use, entitled *A Familiar Exposition of the Constitution of the United States* (Washington, D.C.: Regnery Gateway, 1986).

John Taylor of Caroline, *Construction Construed and Constitutions Vindicated* (New York: DaCapo Press, 1970).

Abel P. Upshur, *A Brief Enquiry into the True Nature and Character of Our Federal Government* (New York: DaCapo Press, 1971).

Christopher Wolfe, *The Rise of Modern Judicial Review* (New York: Basic Books, 1986).

Marbury v. Madison

1 Cranch 137 (1803)

The elections of 1800 brought a defeat to the Federalists from which they never recovered. President Adams, however, did not leave office until March 1801. In a last-minute attempt to retain influence in the Judiciary after leaving office, the Federalists passed the Judiciary Act of February 13, 1801, which created six new circuit courts with 16 new judgeships. The Act also reduced the size of the Supreme Court from six to five in the hope that Thomas Jefferson, the incoming President, would be denied the opportunity to appoint a loyal Republican to the high bench. Two weeks later Congress passed another act to allow President Adams to appoint for the District of Columbia for five-year terms as many justices of the peace as he thought necessary.

Working right up until midnight of March 3, the day before Jefferson was to be inaugurated, Adams endeavored to fill the newly created vacancies before the clock struck twelve. Among the judicial appointments he made during the closing weeks of his administration was that of John Marshall to be Chief Justice of the United States. Marbury was one of those whom Adams had appointed to the office of justice of the peace, but time ran out before Marbury's commission could be delivered. The individual responsible for delivering the commission was John Marshall himself, who, notwithstanding the separation of powers principle, was still serving as Secretary of State (in spite of his judicial appointment).

Upon taking office, President Jefferson promptly took steps to gain the repeal of the Judiciary Act of 1801, which he accomplished on March 8, 1802. As for Marbury, Jefferson simply instructed his new Secretary of State, James Madison, to withhold Marbury's commission. Thereupon Marbury filed suit asking the Supreme Court, under its original jurisdiction, to issue a writ of mandamus (an order commanding performance of a specific duty) to compel Madison to give him his commission.

Mr. Chief Justice Marshall delivered the opinion of the Court, saying in part:

In the order in which the court has viewed this subject, the following questions have been considered and decided.

1st. Has the applicant a right to the commission he demands? ... [The Court finds that he has.]

2d. If he has a right, and that right has been violated, do the laws of his country afford him a remedy? ... [The Court finds that they do.]

3rd. If they do afford him a remedy, is it a mandamus issuing from this court? ...

This, then, is a plain case of a mandamus, either to deliver the commission, or a copy of it from the record; and it only remains to be inquired,

Whether it can issue from this court.

The act to establish the judicial courts of the United States authorizes the Supreme Court "to issue writs of mandamus in cases warranted by the principles and usages of law, to any courts appointed, or persons holding office, under the authority of the United States."

The Secretary of State, being a person holding an office under the authority of the United States, is precisely within the letter of the description, and if this court is not authorized to issue a writ of mandamus to such an officer, it must be because the law is unconstitutional, and therefore absolutely incapable of conferring the authority, and assigning the duties which its words purport to confer and assign.

The Constitution vests the whole judicial power of the United States in one Supreme Court, and such inferior courts as Congress shall, from time to time, ordain and establish. ...

In the distribution of this power it is declared that "the Supreme Court shall have original jurisdiction in all cases affecting ambassadors, other public ministers and consuls, and those in which a state shall be a party. In all other cases, the Supreme Court shall have appellate jurisdiction." ...

If it had been intended to leave it in the discretion of the legislature to apportion the judicial power between the supreme and inferior courts according to the will of that body, it would certainly have been useless to have proceeded further than to have defined the judicial power, and the tribunals in which it should be vested. The subsequent part of the section is mere surplusage, is entirely without meaning, . . . the distribution of jurisdiction, made in the Constitution, is form without substance. . . .

It cannot be presumed that any clause in the Constitution is intended to be without effect; and, therefore, such a construction is inadmissible, unless the words require it. . . .

To enable this court, then, to issue a mandamus, it must be shown to be an exercise of appellate jurisdiction, or to be necessary to enable them to exercise appellate jurisdiction. . . .

It is the essential criterion of appellate jurisdiction, that it revises and corrects the proceedings in a cause already instituted, and does not create that cause. Although, therefore, a mandamus may be directed to courts, yet to issue such a writ to an officer for the delivery of a paper, is in effect the same as to sustain an original action for that paper, and, therefore, seems not to belong to appellate, but to original jurisdiction. Neither is it necessary in such a case as this, to enable the court to exercise its appellate jurisdiction.

The authority, therefore, given to the Supreme Court, by the Act establishing the judicial courts of the United States, to issue writs of mandamus to public officers, appears not to be warranted by the Constitution; and it becomes necessary to inquire whether a jurisdiction so conferred can be exercised.

The question, whether an Act repugnant to the Constitution can become the law of the land, is a question deeply interesting to the United States; but, happily, not of an intricacy proportioned to its interest. It seems only necessary to recognize certain principles, supposed to have been long and well established, to decide it.

That the people have an original right to establish, for their future government, such principles as, in their opinion, shall most conduce to their own happiness, is the basis on which the whole American fabric has been erected. The exercise of this original right is a very great exertion; nor can it nor ought it to be frequently repeated. The principles, therefore, so established, are deemed fundamental. And as the authority from which they proceed is supreme, and can seldom act, they are designed to be permanent.

This original supreme will organizes the government, and assigns to different departments their respective powers. It may either stop here, or establish certain limits not to be transcended by those departments.

The government of the United States is of the latter description. The powers of the legislature are defined and limited; and that those limits may not be mistaken, or forgotten, the Constitution is written. To what purpose are powers limited, and to what purpose is that limitation committed to writing, if these limits may, at any time, be passed by those intended to be restrained? The distinction between a government with limited and unlimited powers is abolished, if those limits do not confine the persons on whom they are imposed, and if acts prohibited and acts allowed are of equal obligation. It is a proposition too plain to be contested, that the Constitution controls any legislative Act repugnant to it; or, that the legislature may alter the Constitution by an ordinary Act.

Between these alternatives there is no middle ground. The Constitution is either a superior paramount law, unchangeable by ordinary means, or it is on a level with ordinary legislative Acts, and, like other Acts, is alterable when the legislature shall please to alter it.

If the former part of the alternative be true, then a legislative Act contrary to the Constitution is not law; if the latter part be true, then written constitutions are absurd attempts, on the part of the people, to limit a power in its own nature illimitable.

Certainly all those who have framed written constitutions contemplate them as forming the fundamental and paramount law of the nation, and, consequently, the theory of every such government must be, that an Act of the Legislature, repugnant to the Constitution, is void.

This theory is essentially attached to a written Constitution, and, is consequently, to be considered, by this court, as one of the fundamental principles of our society. It is not therefore to be lost sight of in the further consideration of this subject.

If an Act of the Legislature, repugnant to the Constitution, is void, does it, notwithstanding its invalidity, bind the courts, and oblige them to give it effect? Or, in other words, though it be now law, does it constitute a rule as operative as if it was a law? This would be to overthrow in fact what was established in theory; and would seem, at first view, an absurdity too gross to be insisted on. It shall, however, receive a more attentive consideration.

It is emphatically the province and duty of the judicial department to say what the law is. Those who apply the rule to particular cases must of necessity expound and interpret that rule. If two laws conflict with each other, the courts must decide on the operation of each.

So if a law be in opposition to the Constitution; if both the law and the Constitution apply to a particular case, so that the court must either decide that case conformably to the law, disregarding the Constitution; or conformably to the Constitution, disregarding the law, the court must determine which of these conflicting rules governs the case. This is of the very essence of judicial duty.

If, then, the courts are to regard the Constitution, and the Constitution is superior to any ordinary Act of the Legislature, the Constitution, and not such ordinary Act, must govern the case to which they both apply.

Those, then, who controvert the principle that the Constitution is to be considered, in court, as a paramount law, are reduced to the necessity of maintaining that courts must close their eyes on the Constitution, and see only the law.

This doctrine would subvert the very foundation of all written constitutions. It would declare that an Act which, according to the principles and theory of our government, is entirely void, is yet, in practice, completely obligatory. It would declare that if the legislatures shall do what is expressly forbidden, such Act, notwithstanding the express prohibition, is in reality effectual. It would be giving to the legislature a practical and real omnipotence, with the same breath which professes to restrict their powers within narrow limits. It is prescribing limits, and declaring that those limits may be passed at pleasure.

That it thus reduces to nothing what we have deemed the greatest improvement on political institutions, a written constitution, would of itself be sufficient, in America, where written constitutions have been viewed with so much reverence, for rejecting the construction. But the peculiar expressions of the Constitution of the United States furnish additional arguments in favor of its rejection.

The judicial power of the United States is extended to all cases arising under the Constitution.

Could it be the intention of those who gave this power, to say that in using it the Constitution should not be looked into? That a case arising under the Constitution should be decided without examining the instrument under which it arises?

This is too extravagant to be maintained.

In some cases, then, the Constitution must be looked into by the judges. And if they can open it at all, what part of it are they forbidden to read or to obey?

There are many other parts of the Constitution which serve to illustrate this subject.

It is declared that "no tax or duty shall be laid on articles exported from any State." Suppose a duty on the export of cotton, of tobacco, or of flour; and a suit instituted to recover it. Ought judgment to be rendered in such a case? Ought the judges to close their eyes on the Constitution, and only see the law?

The Constitution declares "that no bill of attainder or ex post facto law shall be passed."

If, however, such a bill should be passed, and a person should be prosecuted under it, must the court condemn to death those victims whom the Constitution endeavors to preserve?

"No person," says the Constitution, "shall be convicted of treason unless on the testimony of two witnesses to the same overt act, or on confession in open court."

Here the language of the Constitution is addressed especially to the courts. It prescribes, directly for them, a rule of evidence not to be departed from. If the legislature should change that rule, and declare one witness, or a confession out of court, sufficient for conviction, must the constitutional principle yield to the legislative Act?

From these, and many other selections which might be made, it is apparent, that the framers of the Constitution contemplated that instrument as a rule for the government of courts, as well as of the legislature.

Why otherwise does it direct the judges to take an oath to support it? This oath certainly applies in an especial manner to their conduct in their official character. How immoral to impose it on them, if they were to be used as the instruments, and the knowing instruments, for violating what they swear to support!

The oath of office, too, imposed by the legislature, is completely demonstrative of the legislative opinion on this subject. It is in these words: "I do solemnly swear that I will administer justice without respect to persons, and do equal right to the poor and to the rich; and that I will faithfully and impartially discharge all the duties incumbent on me as—, according to the best of my abilities and understanding, agreeably to the Constitution and laws of the United States."

Why does a judge swear to discharge his duties agreeably to the Constitution of the United States, if that Constitution forms no rule for his government—if it is closed upon him, and cannot be inspected by him?

If such be the real state of things, this is worse than solemn mockery. To prescribe, or to take this oath, becomes equally a crime.

It is also not entirely unworthy of observation, that in declaring what shall be the supreme law of the land, the Constitution itself is first mentioned; and not the laws of the United States generally, but those only which shall be made in pursuance of the Constitution, have that rank.

Thus, the particular phraseology of the Constitution of the United States confirms and strengthens the principle, supposed to be essential to all written constitutions, that a law repugnant to the Constitution is void; and that courts, as well as other departments, are bound by that instrument.

The rule must be discharged.

Martin v. Hunter's Lessee

1 Wheaton 304 (1816)

Lord Fairfax, a Loyalist residing in Virginia who fled to England during the American Revolution, died in 1781. He willed a vast tract of land in northern Virginia to his nephew, Denny Martin, a British subject. Virginia confiscated the property under a special law passed after the death of Fairfax; and the common law of Virginia also forbade enemy aliens to inherit land.

Virginia thereupon sold part of the land to David Hunter in 1789. Litigation began in 1791 for the recovery of the property, and finally in 1810 the Virginia court of appeals sustained Hunter's title to the land. In 1813, however, the Supreme Court reviewed the case and held that, under the Treaty of 1794 with England, all British-owned property in the United States, including Denny Martin's, was protected from confiscation. In open defiance, the Virginia court of appeals declared that Section 25 of the Judiciary Act of 1789, which authorized the Supreme Court to review State court decisions, was unconstitutional.

Mr. Justice Story delivered the opinion of the Court, saying in part:

This is a writ of error from the Court of Appeals of Virginia, founded upon the refusal of that court to obey the mandate of this court, requiring the judgment rendered in this very cause, at February Term, 1813, to be carried into due execution. The following is the judgment of the Court of Appeals rendered on the mandate: "The court is unanimously of opinion, that the appellate power of the Supreme Court of the United States does not extend to this court, under a sound construction of the Constitution of the United States; that so much of the 25th section of the Act of Congress to establish the Judicial Courts of the United States, as extends the appellate jurisdiction of the Supreme Court to this court, is not in pursuance of the Constitution of the United States; that the writ of error in this cause was improvidently allowed under the authority of that Act; that the proceedings thereon in the Supreme Court were *coram non judice*, in relation to this court, and that obedience to its mandate be declined by the court."

The questions involved in this judgment are of great importance and delicacy. Perhaps it is not too much to affirm that, upon their right decision, rest some of the most solid principles which have hitherto been supposed to sustain and protect the Constitution itself. . . .

Before proceeding to the principal questions, it may not be unfit to dispose of some preliminary considerations which have grown out of the arguments at the Bar.

The Constitution of the United States was ordained and established, not by the States in their sovereign capacities, but emphatically, as the preamble of the Constitution declares, by "the people of the United States." There can be no doubt that it was competent to the people to invest the general government with all the powers which they might deem proper and necessary; to extend or restrain these powers according to their own good pleasure, and to give them a paramount and supreme authority. As little doubt can there be, that the people had a right to prohibit to the States the exercise of any powers which were, in their judgment, incompatible with the objects of the general compact; to make the powers of the State governments, in given cases, subordinate to those of the nation, or to reserve to themselves those sovereign authorities which they might not choose to delegate to either. The Constitution was not, therefore, necessarily carved out of existing State sovereignties, nor a surrender of powers already existing in State institutions, for the powers of the States depend upon their own constitutions; and the people of every State had the right to modify and restrain them, according to their own views of policy or principle. On the other hand, it is perfectly clear that the sovereign powers vested in the State governments, by their respective constitutions, remained unaltered and unimpaired, except so far as they were granted to the government of the United States.

These deductions do not rest upon general reasoning, plain and obvious as they seem to be. They have been positively recognized by one of the articles in amendment of the Constitution, which declares, that "the powers not delegated to the United States by the Constitution, nor prohibited by it to the States, are reserved to the States respectively, or to the people."

The government, then, of the United States, can claim no powers which are not granted to it by the Constitution, and the powers actually granted must be such as are expressly given, or given by necessary implication. On the other hand, this instrument, like every other grant, is to have a reasonable construction, according to the import of its terms; and where a power is expressly given in general terms, it is not to be restrained to particular cases, unless that construction grows out of the context expressly, or by necessary implication. The words are to be taken in their natural and obvious sense, and not in a sense unreasonably restricted or enlarged.

The Constitution, unavoidably, deals in general language. It did not suit the purposes of the people, in framing this great charter of our liberties, to provide for minute specifications of its powers, or to declare the means by which those powers should be carried into execution. It was foreseen that this would be a perilous and difficult, if not an impracticable, task. The instrument was not intended to provide merely for the exigencies of a few years, but was to endure through a long lapse of ages, the events of which were locked up in the inscrutable purposes of Providence. It could not be foreseen what new changes and modifications of power might be indispensable to effectuate the general objects of the charter; and restrictions and specifications, which at the present might seem salutary, might, in the end, prove the overthrow of the system itself. Hence its powers are expressed in general terms, leaving to the legislature, from time to time, to adopt its own means to effectuate legitimate objects, and to mould and model the exercise of its powers, as its own wisdom and the public interest should require.

With these principles in view, principles in respect to which no difference of opinion ought to be indulged, let us now proceed to the interpretation of the Constitution, so far as regards the great points in controversy.

The third article of the Constitution is that which must principally attract our attention. . . .

This leads us to the consideration of the great question as to the nature and extent of the appellate jurisdiction of the United States. We have already seen that appellate jurisdiction is given by the Constitution to the

Supreme Court in all cases where it has not original jurisdiction, subject, however, to such exceptions and regulations as Congress may prescribe. It is, therefore, capable of embracing every case enumerated in the Constitution, which is not exclusively to be decided by way of original jurisdiction. But the exercise of appellate jurisdiction is far from being limited by the terms of the Constitution, to the Supreme Court. There can be no doubt that Congress may create a succession of inferior tribunals, in each of which it may vest appellate as well as original jurisdiction. . . .

As, then, by the terms of the Constitution, the appellate jurisdiction is not limited as to the Supreme Court, and as to this court it may be exercised in all other cases than those of which it has original cognizance, what is there to restrain its exercise over State tribunals in the enumerated cases? The appellate power is not limited by the terms of the third article to any particular courts. The words are, "the judicial power (which includes appellate power) shall extend to all cases," &c., and "in all other cases before mentioned the Supreme Court shall have appellate jurisdiction." It is the case, then, and not the court, that gives the jurisdiction. If the judicial power extends to the case, it will be in vain to search in the letter of the Constitution for any qualification as to the tribunal where it depends. It is incumbent, then, upon those who assert such a qualification to show its existence by necessary implication. If the text be clear and distinct, no restriction upon its plain and obvious import ought to be admitted, unless the inference be irresistible. . . .

But it is plain that the framers of the Constitution did contemplate that cases within the judicial cognizance of the United States not only might but would arise in the State courts, in the exercise of their ordinary jurisdiction. With this view the sixth article declares, that "this Constitution, and the laws of the United States which shall be made in pursuance thereof, and all treaties made, or which shall be made, under the authority of the United States, shall be the supreme law of the land, and the judges in every State shall be bound thereby, anything in the Constitution, or laws of any State to the contrary notwithstanding." It is obvious, that this obligation is imperative upon the State judges in their official, and not merely in their private, capacities. From the very nature of their judicial duties they would be called upon to pronounce the law applicable to the case in judgment. They were not to decide merely according to the laws or Constitution of the State, but according to the Constitution, laws, and treaties of the United States, "the supreme law of the land." . . . .

It must, therefore, be conceded that the Constitution not only contemplated, but meant to provide for cases within the scope of the judicial power of the United States, which might yet depend before State tribunals. It was foreseen that in the exercise of their ordinary jurisdiction, State courts would incidentally take cognizance of cases arising under the Constitution, the laws and treaties of the United States. Yet to all these cases the judicial power, by the very terms of the Constitution, is to extend. It cannot extend by original jurisdiction if that was already rightfully and exclusively attached in the State courts, which (as has been already shown) may occur; it must therefore extend by appellate jurisdiction, or not at all. It would seem to follow that the appellate power of the United States must, in such cases, extend to State tribunals; and if in such cases, there is no reason why it should not equally attach upon all others within the purview of the Constitution.

It has been argued that such an appellate jurisdiction over State courts is inconsistent with the genius of our governments, and the spirit of the Constitution. That the latter was never designed to act upon State sovereignties, but only upon the people, and that, if the power exists, it will materially impair the sovereignty of the States, and the independence of their courts. We cannot yield to the force of this reasoning; it assumes principles which we cannot admit, and draws conclusions to which we do not yield our assent.

It is a mistake that the Constitution was not designed to operate upon States, in their corporate capacities. It is crowded with provisions which restrain or annul the sovereignty of the States in some of the highest branches of their prerogatives. The tenth section of the first article contains a long list of disabilities and prohibitions imposed upon the States. Surely, when such essential portions of State sovereignty are taken away, or prohibited to be exercised, it cannot be correctly asserted that the Constitution does not act upon the States. The language of the Constitution is also imperative upon the States, as to the performance of many duties. It is imperative upon the State legislatures to make laws prescribing the time, places, and manner of holding elections for Senators and Representatives, and for electors of President and Vice-President. And in these, as well as in some other cases, Congress have a right to revise, amend, or supersede the laws which may be passed by State legislatures. When, therefore, the States are stripped of some of the highest attributes of sovereignty, and the same are given to the United States; when the legislatures of the States are, in some respects, under the control of Congress, and in every case are, under the Constitution, bound by the paramount authority of the United States, it is certainly difficult to support the argument that the appellate power over the decisions of State courts is contrary to the genius of our institutions. The courts of the United States can, without question, revise the proceedings of the executive and legislative authorities of the States, and if they are found to be contrary to the Constitution, may declare them to be of no legal validity. Surely, the exercise of the same right over judicial tribunals is not a higher or more dangerous act of sovereign power.

Nor can such a right be deemed to impair the independence of State judges. It is assuming the very ground in controversy to assert that they possess an absolute independence of the United States. In respect to the powers granted to the United States, they are not independent; they are expressly bound to obedience by the letter of the Constitution; and if they should unintentionally transcend their authority, or misconstrue the Constitution, there is no more reason for giving their judgments an absolute and irresistible force, than for giving it to the acts of the other coordinate departments of State sovereignty.

The argument urged from the possibility of the abuse of the revising power, is equally unsatisfactory. It is always a doubtful course, to argue against the use or existence of a power, from the possibility of its abuse. It is still more difficult, by such an argument, to engraft upon a general power, a restriction which is not to be found in the terms in which it is given. From the very nature of things, the absolute right of decision, in the last resort, must rest somewhere—wherever it may be vested it is susceptible of abuse. In all questions of jurisdiction the inferior or appellate court must pronounce the final judgment; and common-sense, as well as legal reasoning, has conferred it upon the latter. . . .

This is not all. A motive of another kind, perfectly compatible with the most sincere respect for State tribunals, might induce the grant of appellate power over their decisions. That motive is the importance, and even necessity of uniformity of decisions throughout the whole United States, upon all subjects within the purview of the Constitution. Judges of equal learning and integrity, in different States, might differently interpret a statute, or a treaty of the United States, or even the Constitution itself. If there were no revising authority to control these jarring and discordant judgments, and harmonize them into uniformity, the laws, the treaties, and the Constitution of the United States would be different in different States, and might perhaps never have precisely the same construction, obligation, or efficacy, in any two States. The public mischiefs that would attend such a state of things would be truly deplorable; and it cannot be believed that they could have escaped the enlightened convention which formed the Constitution. What, indeed, might then have been only prophecy has now become fact; and the appellate jurisdiction must continue to be the only adequate remedy for such evils. . . .

It is the opinion of the whole court, that the judgment of the Court of Appeals of Virginia, rendered on the mandate in this cause, be reversed, and the judgment of the District Court, held at Winchester, be, and the same is hereby affirmed.

Mr. Justice Johnson delivered a concurring opinion.

Washington's Farewell Address (1796)

FRIENDS AND FELLOW-CITIZENS. The period for a new election of a citizen, to administer the executive government of the United States, being not far distant, and the time actually arrived, when your thoughts must be employed in designating the person who is to be clothed with that important trust, it appears to me proper, especially as it may conduce to a more distinct expression of the public voice, that I should now apprise you of the resolution I have formed, to decline being considered among the number of those out of whom a choice is to be made.

I beg you, at the same time, to do me the justice to be assured, that this resolution has not been taken without a strict regard to all the considerations appertaining to the relation which binds a dutiful citizen to his country; and that, in withdrawing the tender of service, which silence in my situation might imply, I am influenced by no diminution of zeal for your future interest; no deficiency of grateful respect for your past kindness; but am supported by a full conviction that the step is compatible with both.

The acceptance of, and continuance hitherto in, the office to which your suffrages have twice called me, have been a uniform sacrifice of inclination to the opinion of duty, and to a deference for what appeared to be your desire. I constantly hoped that it would have been much earlier in my power, consistently with motives which I was not at liberty to disregard, to return to that retirement from which I had been reluctantly drawn. The strength of my inclination to do this, previous to the last election, had even led to the preparation of an address to declare it to you; but mature reflection on the then perplexed and critical posture of our affairs with foreign nations, and the unanimous advice of persons entitled to my confidence, impelled me to abandon the idea.—

I rejoice that the state of your concerns, external as well as internal, no longer renders the pursuit of inclination incompatible with the sentiment of duty or propriety; and am persuaded, whatever partiality may be retained for my services, that, in the present circumstances of our country, you will not disapprove my determination to retire.

The impressions, with which I first undertook the arduous trust, were explained on the proper occasion. In the discharge of this trust, I will only say, that I have, with good intentions, contributed towards the organization and administration of the Government the best exertions of which a very fallible judgment was capable. Not unconscious, in the outset, of the inferiority of my qualifications, experience in my own eyes, perhaps still more in the eyes of others, has strengthened the motives to diffidence of myself; and every day the increasing weight of years admonishes me more and more, that the shade of retirement is as necessary to me as it will be welcome. Satisfied, that, if any circumstances have given peculiar value to my services, they were temporary, I have the consolation to believe that, while choice and prudence invite me to quit the political scene, patriotism does not forbid it.

In looking forward to the moment which is intended to terminate the career of my public life, my feelings do not permit me to suspend the deep acknowledgment of that debt of gratitude which I owe to my beloved country, for the many honors it has conferred upon me; still more for the steadfast confidence with which it has supported me; and for the opportunities I have thence enjoyed of manifesting my inviolable attachment, by services faithful and persevering, though in usefulness unequal to my zeal. If benefits have resulted to our country from these services, let it always be remembered to your praise, and as an instructive example in our annals, that under circumstances in which the passions, agitated in every direction, were liable to mislead, amidst appearances sometimes dubious, vicissitudes of fortune often discouraging, in situations in which not infrequently want of success has countenanced the spirit of criticism, the constancy of your support was the essential prop of the efforts, and a guarantee of the plans by which they were effected. Profoundly penetrated with this idea, I shall carry it with me to the grave, as a strong incitement to unceasing vows that Heaven may continue to you the choicest tokens of its beneficence; that your union and brotherly affection may be perpetual that the free constitution, which is the work of your hands, may be sacredly maintained that its administration in every department may be stamped with wisdom and virtue that, in fine, the happiness of the people of these States, under the auspices of liberty, may be made complete, by so careful a preservation and so prudent a use of this blessing as will acquire to them the glory of recommending it to the applause, the affection, and adoption of every nation which is yet a stranger to it.

Here, perhaps, I ought to stop. But a solicitude for your welfare, which cannot end but with my life, and the apprehension of danger, natural to that solicitude, urge me on an occasion like the present, to offer to your solemn contemplation, and to recommend to your frequent review, some sentiments, which are the result of much reflection, of no inconsiderable observation, and which appear to me all-important to the permanency of your felicity as a people. These will be offered to you with the more freedom, as you can only see in them the disinterested warnings of a parting friend, who can possibly have no personal motive to bias his counsel.— Nor can I forget, as an encouragement to it, your indulgent reception of my sentiments on a former and not dissimilar occasion.

Interwoven as is the love of liberty with every ligament of your hearts, no recommendation of mine is necessary to fortify or confirm the attachment.—

The unity of government, which constitutes you one people, is also now dear to you. It is justly so; for it is a main pillar in the edifice of your real independence, the support of your tranquility at home, your peace abroad; of your safety; of your prosperity; of that very liberty which you so highly prize. But as it is easy to foresee, that, from different causes and from different quarters, much pains will be taken, many artifices employed, to weaken in your minds the conviction of this truth; as this is the point in your political fortress against which the batteries of internal and external enemies will be most constantly and (though often covertly and insidiously) directed, it is of infinite moment that you should properly estimate the immense value of your national Union to your collective and individual happiness; that you should cherish a cordial, habitual, and immovable attachment to it; accustoming yourselves to think and speak of it as the palladium of your political safety and prosperity; watching for its preservation with jealous anxiety; discountenancing whatever may suggest even a suspicion that it can in any event be abandoned; and indignantly frowning upon the first dawning of every attempt to alienate any portion of our country from the rest, or to enfeeble the sacred ties which now link together the various parts.

For this you have every inducement of sympathy and interest. Citizens, by birth or choice, of a common country, that country has a right to concentrate your affections. The name of AMERICAN, which belongs to you, in your national capacity, must always exalt the just pride of patriotism, more than any appellation derived from local discriminations. With slight shades of difference you have the same religion, manners, habits, and political principles. You have in common cause fought and triumphed together; the independence and liberty you possess are the work of joint counsels and joint efforts, of common dangers, sufferings, and successes.

But these considerations, however powerfully they address themselves to your sensibility, are greatly outweighed by those, which apply more immediately to your interest. Here every portion of our country finds the most commanding motives for carefully guarding and preserving the union of the whole.

The *North*, in an unrestrained intercourse with the *South*, protected by the equal laws of a common Government, finds in the productions of the latter great additional resources of maritime and commercial enterprise and precious materials of manufacturing industry. The *South*, in the same intercourse, benefiting by the agency of the *North*, sees its agriculture grow and its commerce expand. Turning partly into its own channels the seamen of the *North*, it finds its particular navigation invigorated; and, while it contributes, in different ways, to nourish and increase the general mass of the national navigation, it looks forward to the protection of a maritime strength to which itself is unequally adapted. The *East*, in a like intercourse with the *West*, already finds, and in the progressive improvement of interior communications, by land and water, will more and more find, a valuable vent for the commodities which it brings from abroad, or manufactures at home. The *West* derives from the *East* supplies requisite to its growth and comfort, and, what is perhaps of still greater consequence, it must of necessity owe the *secure* enjoyment of indispensable *outlets* for its own productions to the weight, influence, and the future maritime strength of the Atlantic side of the Union, directed by an indissoluble community of interest as *one Nation.*—Any other tenure by which the *West* can hold this essential advantage, whether derived from its own separate strength, or from an apostate and unnatural connection with any foreign Power, must be intrinsically precarious.

While, then, every part of our country thus feels an immediate and particular interest in union, all the parts combined cannot fail to find in the united mass of means and efforts greater strength, greater resource, proportionably greater security from external danger, a less frequent interruption of their peace by foreign nations; and, what is of inestimable value, they must derive from union an exemption from those broils and wars between themselves, which so frequently afflict neighboring countries not tied together by the same governments, which their own rival ships alone would be sufficient to produce, but which opposite foreign alliances, attachments, and intrigues would stimulate and embitter. Hence, likewise, they will avoid the necessity of those overgrown military establishments, which, under any form of government, are inauspicious to liberty, and which are to be regarded as particularly hostile to Republican liberty. In this sense it is, that your union ought to be considered as a main prop of your liberty, and that the love of the one ought to endear to you the preservation of the other.

These considerations speak a persuasive language to every reflecting and virtuous mind, and exhibit the continuance of the UNION as a primary object of patriotic desire. Is there a doubt whether a common government can embrace so large a sphere? Let experience solve it. To listen to mere speculation in such a case were criminal. We are authorized to hope that a proper organization of the whole, with the auxiliary agency of governments for the respective subdivisions, will afford a happy issue to the experiment. 'Tis well worth a fair and full experiment.

With such powerful and obvious motives to union, affecting all parts of our country, while experience shall not have demonstrated its impracticability, there will always be reason to distrust the patriotism of those who in any quarter may endeavour to weaken its bands.

In contemplating the causes which may disturb our Union, it occurs as a matter of serious concern that any ground should have been furnished for characterizing parties by *geographical* discriminations, *North-*

ern and *Southern,* — *Atlantic* and *Western;* whence designing men may endeavour to excite a belief that there is a real difference of local interests and views. One of the expedients of party to acquire influence, within particular districts, is to misrepresent the opinions and aims of other districts. You cannot shield yourselves too much against the jealousies and heart-burnings which spring from these misrepresentations; they tend to render alien to each other those who ought to be bound together by fraternal affection. The inhabitants of our Western country have lately had a useful lesson on this head; they have seen, in the negotiation by the Executive, and in the unanimous ratification by the Senate, of the treaty with Spain, and in the universal satisfaction at that event throughout the United States, a decisive proof how unfounded were the suspicions propagated among them of a policy in the general government and in the Atlantic States unfriendly to their interests in regard to the MISSISSIPPI; they have been witnesses to the formation of two treaties, that with Great Britain and that with Spain, which secure to them everything they could desire, in respect to our foreign relations, towards confirming their prosperity. Will it not be their wisdom to rely for the preservation of theses advantages on the UNION by which they were procured? Will they not henceforth be deaf to those advisers, if such there are, who would sever them from their brethren and connect them with aliens?

To the efficacy and permanency of your union, a Government for the whole is indispensable. No alliances however strict between the parts can be an adequate substitute. They must inevitably experience the infractions and interruptions which all alliances in all times have experienced. Sensible of this momentous truth, you have improved upon your first essay, by the adoption of a Constitution of Government better calculated than your former for an intimate union, and for the efficacious management of your common concerns. This Government, the offspring of our own choice, uninfluenced and unawed, adopted upon full investigation and mature deliberation, completely free in its principles, in the distribution of its powers, uniting security with energy, and containing within itself a provision for its own amendment, has a just claim to your confidence and your support. Respect for its authority, compliance with its laws, acquiescence in its measures, are duties enjoined by the fundamental maxims of true liberty. The basis of our political systems is the right of the people to make and to alter their Constitutions of Government. But the Constitution which at any time exists, till changed by an explicit and authentic act of the whole people, is sacredly obligatory upon all. The very idea of the power and the right of the people to establish government presupposes the duty of every individual to obey the established Government.

All obstructions to the execution of the laws, all combinations and associations, under whatever plausible character, with the real design to direct, control, counteract, or awe the regular deliberation and action of the constituted authorities, are destructive of this fundamental principle, and of fatal tendency. They serve to organize faction, to give it an artificial and extraordinary force; to put in the place of the delegated will of the nation, the will of a party, often a small but artful and enterprising minority of the community; and, according to the alternate triumphs of different parties, to make the public administration the mirror of the ill-concerted and incongruous projects of fashion, rather than the organ of consistent and wholesome plans digested by common councils, and modified by mutual interests.

However combinations or associations of the above descriptions may now and then answer popular ends, they are likely, in the course of time and things, to become potent engines, by which cunning, ambitious, and unprincipled men will be enabled to subvert the power of the people, and to usurp for themselves the reins of government; destroying afterwards the very engines which have lifted them to unjust dominion.—

Toward the preservation of your Government, and the permanency of your present happy state, it is requisite, not only that you steadily discountenance irregular oppositions to its acknowledged authority, but also that you resist with care the spirit of innovation upon its principles, however specious the pretexts. One method of assault may be to effect, in the forms of the Constitution, alterations, which will impair the energy of the system, and thus to undermine what cannot be directly overthrown. In all the changes to which you may be invited, remember that time and habit are at least as necessary to fix the true character of governments as of other human institutions; that experience is the surest standard by which to test the real tendency of the existing Constitution of a country—that facility in changes, upon the credit of mere hypothesis and opinion, exposes to perpetual change, from the endless variety of hypothesis and opinion: and remember, especially, that for the efficient management of your common interests, in a country so extensive as ours, a government of as much vigor as is consistent with the perfect security of liberty is indispensable. Liberty itself will find in such a government, with powers properly distributed and adjusted, its surest guardian. It is, indeed, little else than a name, where the government is too feeble to withstand the enterprise of faction, to confine each member of the society within the limits prescribed by the laws, and to maintain all in the secure and tranquil enjoyment of the rights of person and property.

I have already intimated to you the danger of parties in the state, with particular reference to the founding of them on geographical discriminations. Let me now take a more comprehensive view, and warn you in the most solemn manner against the baneful effects of the spirit of party, generally.

This spirit, unfortunately, is inseparable from our nature, having its root in the strongest passions of the human mind. It exists under different shapes in all governments, more or less stifled, controlled, or repressed; but, in those of the popular form, it is seen in its greatest rankness, and is truly their worst enemy.—

The alternate domination of one faction over another, sharpened by the spirit of revenge natural to party dissension, which in different ages and countries has perpetrated the most horrid enormities, is itself a frightful despotism. But this leads at length to a more formal and permanent despotism. The disorders and miseries which result gradually incline the minds of men to seek security and repose in the absolute power of an individual; and sooner or later the chief of some prevailing faction, more able or more fortunate than his competitors, turns this disposition to the purposes of his own elevation, on the ruins of public liberty.

Without looking forward to an extremity of this kind (which nevertheless ought not to be entirely out of sight) the common and continual mischiefs of the spirit of party are sufficient to make it the interest and duty of a wise people to discourage and restrain it.

It serves always to distract the public councils, and enfeeble the public administration. It agitates the community with ill-founded jealousies and false alarms, kindles the animosity of one part against another, foments occasionally riot and insurrection. It opens the doors to foreign influence and corruption, which find a facilitated access to the Government itself through the channels of party passions. Thus the policy and the will of one country are subjected to the policy and will of another.

There is an opinion that parties in free countries are useful checks upon the administration of the Government, and serve to keep alive the spirit of liberty. This within certain limits is probably true; and in governments of a monarchical cast, patriotism may look with indulgence, if not with favor, upon the spirit of party. But in those of the popular character, in governments purely elective, it is a spirit not to be encouraged. From their natural tendency, it is certain there will always be enough of that spirit for every salutary purpose. And, there being constant danger of excess, the effort ought to be, by force of public opinion, to mitigate and assuage it. A fire not to be quenched, it demands a uniform vigilance to prevent its bursting into a flame, lest, instead of warming, it should consume.

It is important, likewise, that the habits of thinking in a free country should inspire caution in those entrusted with its administration, to confine themselves within their respective constitutional spheres, avoiding in the exercise of the powers of one department to encroach upon another. The spirit of encroachment tends to consolidate the powers of all the departments in one, and thus to create, whatever the form of government, a real despotism. A just estimate of that love of power, and proneness to abuse it, which predominates in the human heart, is sufficient to satisfy us of the truth of this position. The necessity of reciprocal checks in the exercise of political power, by dividing and distributing it into different depositories, and constituting each the guardian of the public weal against invasions by the others, has been evinced by experiments ancient and modern, some of them in our country and under our own eyes. To preserve them must be as necessary as to institute them. If, in the opinion of the people, the distribution or modification of the constitutional powers be in any particular wrong, let it be corrected by an amendment in the way which the Constitution designates. But let there be no change by usurpation; for, though this, in one instance, may be the instrument of good, it is the customary weapon by which free governments are destroyed. The precedent must always greatly overbalance in permanent evil any partial or transient benefit which the use can at any time yield.—

Of all the dispositions and habits which lead to political prosperity, religion and morality are indispensable supports. In vain would that man claim the tribute of patriotism who should labor to subvert these great pillars of human happiness, these firmest props of the duties of Men and Citizens. The mere politician, equally with the pious man, ought to respect and to cherish them. A volume could not trace all their connections with private and public felicity. Let it simply be asked: Where is the security for property, for reputation, for life, if the sense of religious obligation *desert* the oaths, which are the instruments of investigation in courts of justice? And let us with caution indulge the supposition, that morality can be maintained without religion. Whatever may be conceded to the influence of refined education on minds of peculiar structure, reason and experience both forbid us to expect that national morality can prevail in exclusion of religious principle.

It is substantially true, that virtue or morality is a necessary spring of popular government. The rule, indeed, extends with more or less force to every species of free government. Who, that is a sincere friend to it, can look with indifference upon attempts to shake the foundation of the fabric?

Promote, then, as an object of primary importance, institutions for the general diffusion of knowledge. In proportion as the structure of a government gives force to public opinion, it is essential that public opinion should be enlightened.

As a very important source of strength and security, cherish public credit. One method of preserving it is to use it as sparingly as possible; avoiding occasions of expense by cultivating peace, but remembering also that timely disbursements to prepare for danger frequently prevent much greater disbursements to repel it; avoiding likewise the accumulation of debt, not only by shunning occasions of expense, but by vigorous exertions in time of peace to discharge the debts, which unavoidable wars may have occasioned, not ungenerously throwing upon posterity the burden which we ourselves ought to bear. The execution of these maxims belongs to your representatives, but it is necessary that public opinion should cooperate. To facilitate to them the performance of their duty, it is essential that you should practically bear in mind, that towards the payment of debts there must be revenue; that to have revenue there must be taxes; that no taxes can be devised which are not more or less inconvenient and unpleasant; that the intrinsic embarrassment, inseparable from the selection of the proper objects (which is always a choice of difficulties), ought to be a decisive motive for a candid construction of the conduct of the Government in making it, and for a spirit of acquiescence in the measures for obtaining revenue which the public exigencies may at any time dictate.

Observe good faith and justice towards all nations; cultivate peace and harmony with all. Religion and morality enjoin this conduct; and can it be, that good policy does not equally enjoin it? It will be worthy of a free, enlightened, and, at no distant period, a great nation, to give to mankind the magnanimous and too novel example of a people always guided by an exalted justice and benevolence. Who can doubt, that, in the course of time and things, the fruits of such a plan would richly repay any temporary advantages, which might be lost by a steady adherence to it? Can it be, that Providence has not connected the permanent felicity of a nation with its virtue? The experiment, at least, is recommended by every sentiment which ennobles human nature. Alas! is it rendered impossible by its vices?

In the execution of such a plan, nothing is more essential than that permanent, inveterate antipathies against particular nations, and passionate attachments for others, should be excluded; and that, in place of them, just and amicable feelings towards all should be cultivated. The nation which indulges towards another an habitual hatred, or an habitual fondness, is in some degree a slave. It is a slave to its animosity or to its affection, either of which is sufficient to lead it astray from its duty and its interest. Antipathy in one nation against another disposes each more readily to offer insult and injury, to lay hold of slight causes of umbrage, and to be haughty and intractable, when accidental or trifling occasions of dispute occur. Hence, frequent collisions, obstinate, envenomed and bloody contests. The nation, prompted by ill-will and resentment, sometimes impels to war the Government, contrary to the best calculations of policy. The Government sometimes participates in the national propensity, and adopts through passion what reason would reject; at other times, it makes the animosity of the nation subservient to projects of hostility instigated by pride, ambition, and other sinister and pernicious motives. The peace often, sometimes perhaps the liberty, of nations has been the victim.—

So likewise, a passionate attachment of one nation for another produces a variety of evils. Sympathy for the favorite nation, facilitating the illusion of an imaginary common interest in cases where no real common interest exists, and infusing into one the enmities of the other, betrays the former into a participation in the quarrels and wars of the latter, without adequate inducement or justification. It leads also to concessions to the favorite nation of privileges denied to others, which is apt doubly to injure the nation making the concessions, by unnecessarily parting with what ought to have been retained, and by exciting jealousy, ill-will, and a disposition to retaliate in the parties from whom equal privileges are withheld. And it gives to ambitious, corrupted, or deluded citizens (who devote themselves to the favored nation), facility to betray or sacrifice the interests of their own country, without odium, sometimes even with popularity; gilding with the appearances of a virtuous sense of obligation, a commendable deference for public opinion, or a laudable zeal for public good, the base of foolish compliances of ambition, corruption, or infatuation.

As avenues to foreign influence in innumerable ways, such attachments are particularly alarming to the truly enlightened and independent patriot. How many opportunities do they afford to tamper with domestic factions, to practice the arts of seduction, to mislead public opinion, to influence or awe the public councils! Such an attachment of a small or weak, towards a great and powerful nation, dooms the former to be the satellite of the latter.

Against the insidious wiles of foreign influence (I conjure you to believe me, fellow-citizens) the jealousy of a free people ought to be *constantly* awake, since history and experience prove that foreign influence is one of the most baneful foes of Republican Government. But that jealousy, to be useful, must be impartial; else it becomes the instrument of the very influence to be avoided, instead of a defence against it. Excessive partiality for one foreign nation, and excessive dislike of another, cause those whom they actuate to see danger only on one side, and serve to veil and even second the arts of influence on the other. Real patriots, who may resist the intrigues of the favorite, are liable to become suspected and odious; while its tools and dupes usurp the applause and confidence of the people, to surrender their interests.

The great rule of conduct for us, in regard to foreign nations is, in extending our commercial relations, to have with them as little *political* connection as possible. So far as we have already formed engagements, let them be fulfilled with perfect good faith. Here let us stop.

Europe has a set of primary interests, which to us have none, or a very remote relation. Hence she must be engaged in frequent controversies, the causes of which are essentially foreign to our concerns. Hence, therefore, it must be unwise in us to implicate ourselves, by artificial ties in the ordinary vicissitudes of her politics, or the ordinary combinations and collisions of her friendships or enmities.

Our detached and distant situation invites and enables us to pursue a different course. If we remain one people, under an efficient government, the period is not far off, when we may defy material injury from external annoyance; when we may take such an attitude as will cause the neutrality we may at any time resolve upon, to be scrupulously respected; when belligerent nations, under the impossibility of making acquisitions upon us, will not likely hazard the giving us provocation; when we may choose peace or war, as our interest, guided by justice, shall counsel.

Why forego the advantages of so peculiar a situation? Why quit our own to stand upon foreign ground? Why, by interweaving our destiny with that of any part of Europe, entangle our peace and prosperity in the toils of European ambition, rivalship, interest, humor, or caprice?

It is our true policy to steer clear of permanent alliances with any portion of the foreign world; so far, I mean, as we are now at liberty to do it; for let me not be understood as capable of patronizing infidelity to existing engagements. I hold the maxim no less applicable to public than to private affairs, that honesty is always the best policy. I repeat it, therefore, let those engagements be observed in their genuine sense. But, in my opinion, it is unnecessary and would be unwise to extend them.

Taking care always to keep ourselves, by suitable establishments, on a respectable defensive posture, we may safely trust to temporary alliances for extraordinary emergencies.

Harmony, liberal intercourse with all nations, are recommended by policy, humanity, and interest. But even our commercial policy should hold an equal and impartial hand; neither seeking nor granting exclusive favors or preferences; consulting the natural course of things; diffusing and diversifying by gentle means the streams of commerce, but forcing nothing; establishing, with powers so disposed, in order to give trade a stable course, to define the rights of our merchants, and to enable the government to support them, conventional rules of intercourse, the best that present circumstances and mutual opinion will permit, but temporary, and liable to be from time to time abandoned or varied, as experience and circumstances shall dictate; constantly keeping in view, that it is folly in one nation to look for disinterested favors from another; that it must pay with a portion of its dependence for whatever it may accept under that character; that, by such acceptance, it may place itself in the condition of having given equivalents for nominal favors, and yet of being reproached with ingratitude for not giving more. There can be no greater error than to expect or calculate upon real favors from nation to nation. It is an illusion, which experience must cure, which a just pride ought to discard.

In offering to you, my countrymen, these counsels of an old and affectionate friend, I dare not hope they will make the strong and lasting impression I could wish; that they will control the usual current of the passions, or prevent our nation from running the course, which has hitherto marked the destiny of nations. But, if I may even flatter myself, that they may be productive of some partial benefit, some occasional good; that they may now and then recur to moderate the fury of party spirit, to warn against the mischiefs of foreign intrigue, to guard against the impostures of pretended patriotism; this hope will be a full recompense for the solicitude for your welfare, by which they have been dictated.

How far in the discharge of my official duties I have been guided by the principles which have been delineated, the public records and other evidences of my conduct must witness to you and to the world. To myself, the assurance of my own conscience is, that I have at least believed myself to be guided by them.

In relation to the still subsisting war in Europe, my Proclamation of the 22nd of April 1793 is the index to my plan. Sanctioned by your approving voice, and by that of your representatives in both Houses of Congress, the spirit of that measure has continually governed me, uninfluenced by any attempts to deter or divert me from it.

After deliberate examination, with the aid of the best lights I could obtain, I was well satisfied that our country, under all the circumstances of the case, had a right to take, and was bound in duty and interest to take, a neutral position. Having taken it, I determined, as far as should depend upon me, to maintain it, with moderation, perseverance, and firmness.

The considerations which respect the right to hold this conduct, it is not necessary on this occasion to detail. I will only observe, that, according to my understanding of the matter, that right, so far from being denied by any of the belligerent powers, has been virtually admitted by all.

The duty of holding a neutral conduct may be inferred, without anything more, from the obligation which justice and humanity impose on every nation, in cases in which it is free to act, to maintain inviolate the relations of peace and amity towards other nations.

The inducements of interest for observing that conduct will best be referred to your own reflections and experience. With me, a predominant motive has been to endeavour to gain time to our country to settle and mature its yet recent institutions, and to progress without interruption to that degree of strength and consistency which is necessary to give it, humanly speaking, the command of its own fortunes.

Though, in reviewing the incidents of my administration, I am unconscious of intentional error, I am nevertheless too sensible of my defects not to think it probable that I may have committed many errors. Whatever they may be, I fervently beseech the Almighty to avert or mitigate the evils to which they may tend. I shall also carry with me the hope, that my country will never cease to view them with indulgence; and that, after forty-five years of my life dedicated to its service with an upright zeal, the faults of incompetent abilities will be consigned to oblivion, as myself must soon be to the mansions of rest.

Relying on its kindness in this as in other things, and actuated by that fervent love towards it, which is so natural to a man who views in it the native soil of himself and his progenitors for several generations, I anticipate with pleasing expectation that retreat, in which I promise myself to realize, without alloy, the sweet enjoyment of partaking, in the midst of my fellow-citizens, the benign influence of good laws under a free government, the ever favorite object of my heart, and the happy reward, as I trust, of our mutual cares, labors, and dangers.

GEORGE WASHINGTON.

Gazette of the United States, September 17th, 1796.

We are bound to interpret the Constitution in the light of the law as it existed at the time it was adopted, not as reaching out for new guarantees of the rights of the citizen, but as securing to every individual such as he already possessed as a British subject — such as his ancestors had inherited and defended since the days of Magna Carta.

Justice Henry Brown of the Supreme Court,
in *Mattox v. U.S.* (1894)

Changing the Constitution —
Together with an Explanation of
the Amendments Added Since 1791

⤳ POINTS TO REMEMBER ⬳

1. The Constitution may be changed formally by amendment, but it also changes as a result of custom, practice, and judicial decisions.

2. Not all constitutional change has the same impact on the distribution of power. Some changes are supplementary in nature and merely refine or clarify a particular provision of the Constitution, while other changes are revisionary and truly alter the basic design of the system.

3. The difficulty of the amendment process assures evolutionary change; the extraordinary or "super majority" requirement assures democratic change that protects the States and sectional interests; the amendment procedure strengthens federalism by giving the States the final say as to whether an amendment should pass or fail. Ironically, most amendments added since 1791 have reduced the power of the States. One of the most far-reaching constitutional changes effected without a clearly authorizing amendment has been the nationalization of the Bill of Rights through the Doctrine of Incorporation.

4. The amendment process recognizes the sovereign right of the American people and the States to change their Constitution or even their form of government. A large share of the amendments that have been introduced over the years have sought to constitutionalize mere legislation and are otherwise inappropriate. There are many inherent limitations to the amendment power.

THOUGH ITS FLOW IS CONTINUOUS, the Mississippi River has often changed direction. Its main channel of movement has shifted at times.

Its current may be fast or sluggish. Precisely similar are the dynamics of the American Constitution. Throughout its history, the Constitution, as interpreted and applied by each generation, has changed almost without interruption. The Constitution today is different in many respects from the Constitution of 1787. A mere reading of the document itself, without consulting Supreme Court opinions, the history books, legal treatises, and other extrinsic aids, would give the student not only a meager understanding of what the Constitution meant in 1787 but in many ways a misunderstanding of what it means today.

Why, it may be asked, should the Constitution change at all? Does it not prescribe a *fixed* code of conduct for public officials? Does it not represent the "permanent will" of the American people? These questions may be answered in the affirmative, but our response requires some elaboration. It must be borne in mind that political societies, especially in advanced countries like the United States, are not static. Change is inevitable. Society must change—and slow change, we might add, is the means of its preservation, like the human body's perpetual renewal. If society changes, so too must its constitution, lest it fall by the wayside as an outmoded relic of the past. The Framers of the American Constitution understood this. That is why they wrote Article V into the Constitution, which sets forth the procedure to be followed for amending the Constitution.

Our Living Constitution

Formal amendments to the Constitution, however, are only one method of change. Constitutions may also change by subtle and informal means, as a result of changing political practices, new technology, and other forces. Most changes of this nature are *supplementary* rather than *revisionary*, and may be seen as additions to, or refinements of, a particular provision of the Constitution, not as alterations of the structure itself. Thus, as a result of political experience, presidential electors, as we saw earlier, no longer function as the Framers imagined they would; yet in other respects the Electoral College still functions as intended. Although the Constitution is silent on the qualifications for office of Supreme Court Justices, all members appointed to the Court have, by custom, been lawyers. Likewise, political parties were not anticipated by the Framers and no provision was made for them in the Constitution. Since the earliest days of the American republic, however, political parties have played a fundamental role in our political system, so fundamental, in fact, that it might be said they are an integral part of our constitutional system because it is through our party system that political power is organized, exercised, and transferred from one election to the next. The Constitution has nevertheless accommodated political parties without amendment. The same can be said of the President's cabinet, which is almost entirely the result of custom.

Similarly, the authors of the First Amendment did not foresee motion pictures, radio, or television. They knew only direct verbal communication and the printed word. The extension of the right of freedom of speech and press to a radio news broadcast has not altered the meaning of these freedoms, however, or required a revision of the First Amendment. It has merely changed the scope of the Amendment. The principle of free speech remains the same.

Legislation passed by Congress may also be of such a basic nature as to supplement the Constitution and give added meaning to its provisions. We have already noted the significance of the Judiciary Act of 1789, which has become virtually a permanent fixture of the American political system. The Constitution authorizes Congress to determine who shall be President in the event that both the President and the Vice President should be removed from office or be unable to serve because of death, incapacity, or resignation. By the Presidential Succession Act of 1947 Congress has provided that first the Speaker of the House, then the President Pro Tem of the Senate, and then cabinet heads should become President, in that order, if such a contingency should arise. Also, the Constitution nowhere prescribes the precise manner by which inferior officers are to be selected. Article II, Section 2 merely states that their appointment may be vested in the President alone, in the courts of law, or in the heads of departments. In 1883, however, Congress passed the Pendleton Act, which provided for the establishment of a Civil Service Commission and the recruitment and hiring of thousands of Federal employees on the basis of ratings derived from competitive examinations. That civil service system is still in place, influencing the manner in which the Federal government functions. But no amendment was needed to establish it.

Judicial opinions of the Supreme Court provide still another means for embellishing the original text of the Constitution—Article II, Section 3 provides, for example, that the President "shall take care that the laws be faithfully executed." Does this mean that the President's duty is limited to the enforcement of acts of Congress according to their express terms? The Supreme Court was called upon to provide an answer to this question in the bizarre case of *In Re Neagle* (1890). The case grew out of a dispute between Justice Stephen J. Field, a member of the Supreme Court, and David Terry, who had once been Chief Justice of the California Supreme Court. While presiding over a Federal circuit court in California in a suit involving Terry's wife, Justice Field criticized the lady's moral character during the course of the trial. Mrs. Terry began screaming insults, and Field ordered her removal from the courtroom. David Terry, her lawyer as well as her husband, became so enraged that he felled with one blow the deputy who was trying to carry out Field's order, knocking him unconscious.

Field later returned to Washington, and Terry began a campaign of vilification against Field, threatening to kill him. A headstrong southern gentleman who had once killed a friend of Field's in a duel over a question of honor, Terry had a reputation for violence. He often wore a six-shooter on his hip, and Mrs. Terry also frequently carried a pistol. Alarmed by these events, the Attorney General of the United States assigned a deputy marshal named David Neagle to protect Justice Field while out west on circuit duties. By coincidence, Field and Neagle ran into Terry in a railroad restaurant in a small town. Upon sight of Field, Terry leaped from his table and struck Field twice. Believing Terry was reaching for a gun, Neagle drew his own weapon and shot Terry dead. There was strong local sentiment for Terry, and Neagle was arrested by State authorities on a charge of murder.

A Federal circuit court issued a writ of habeas corpus for Neagle's release under a Federal statute which made the writ available to one "in custody for an act done or omitted in pursuance of a law of the United States." The problem was that Congress had not enacted any law authorizing the President or his Attorney General to assign marshals as bodyguards to Federal judges. The Supreme Court ruled nevertheless in favor of Neagle, arguing that no statute was necessary. "In the view we take of the Constitution," said the Court, "any obligation fairly and properly inferrible from that instrument, or any duty of the marshal to be derived from the general scope of his duties under the laws of the United States, is a 'law' within the meaning of this phrase." There is "a peace of the United States," the Court went on, and the President is necessarily the principal protector of the peace. His duty to see that the laws are faithfully executed is not limited to enforcing Congressional statutes and includes as well "the rights, duties and obligations growing out of the Constitution itself." The President's power to execute the laws, in other words, was a self-executing power to enforce the laws generally, and did not depend for its existence upon a specific act of Congress. The *Neagle* case, it may thus be seen, gave added meaning to the separation of powers and the President's law enforcement powers, without substantially altering them. Had the Court ruled against Neagle, the President's power would have been severely restricted and entirely at the mercy of Congress.

There are many Supreme Court decisions comparable to the *Neagle* case in which the Justices have found it necessary to add meaning to general provisions of the Constitution when applying them to specific facts. Ordinarily, such decisions arouse little controversy. The Constitution, after all, is based upon general principles as well as concrete rules, and it would be impossible for the judges to interpret and apply these principles without specifying their metes and bounds. Unlike the draftsmen of many tedious State constitutions that go on for pages and attempt to anticipate every possible contingency, the Framers wisely understood that a constitution is not an elaborate code of law and that it would soon be unwieldy and might go out of date if the principles of government embodied within it were burdened with countless details. A constitution must be adaptable to the changing needs and conditions of society. As Chief Justice John Marshall explained in the famous case of *McCulloch v. Maryland* (1819), in which the Court rendered a definitive interpretation of the Necessary and Proper Clause, "a constitution, to contain an accurate detail of all the subdivisions of which its great powers will admit, and of all the means by which they may be carried into execution, would partake of the prolixity of a legal code, and could scarcely be embraced by the human mind. It would probably never be understood by the public. Its nature, therefore, requires that only its great outlines should be marked, its important objects designated, and the minor ingredients which compose those objects be deduced from the nature of the objects themselves. . . . [I]t may with great reason be contended, that a government entrusted with such ample powers . . . must also be entrusted with ample *means* for their execution. The power being given, it is in the interest of the nation to facilitate its execution."

Our Changing Constitution

The accumulation of customs and usages that impinge upon the Constitution, and the actions of Congress, the President, and the Supreme Court that give meaning and substance to the powers that are granted and denied, form the basis of American constitutional law. In essence, such developments do not so much *change* the Constitution as they apply and *refine* it. The line between actual change and mere implementation cannot always be clearly drawn, of course, but we may take it as a general proposition that a grant of power carries with it, as Marshall contended, the means for its execution. Thus in *Gibbons v. Ogden* (1824), the great steamboat monopoly case involving the scope of the commerce power, Marshall argued persuasively that, inasmuch as Congress was authorized to regulate commerce, it followed that Congress must also be permitted to control the means, or the environment in which commerce moved, including navigation, "so far as that navigation may be, in any manner, connected with 'commerce with foreign nations, or among the several States, or with Indian tribes.' "

More troublesome and difficult to justify, however, are actions of the Federal and State governments that actually create power, alter the distribution or division of power, or otherwise redefine the general principles or specific provisions of the Constitution. Such changes, in the absence of an authorizing amendment to the Constitution, raise serious questions of legitimacy because they change the "rules of the game" and the basic structure of government. Because they also conflict with the "permanent will" of the American people, they play havoc with the underlying republican principle of the Constitution and the democratic foundation upon which it rests.

Examples of these substantive constitutional changes abound, and no branch of the Federal government is entirely innocent of the charge of over-reaching. Broad delegations of legislative power to executive agencies and independent regulatory commissions, as we previously saw, tend to undermine the separation of powers and democratic accountability. The unrestricted extension of the commerce clause into purely local affairs has changed the meaning of federalism. This is amply demonstrated by *U.S. v. Appalachian Electric Power Co.* (1940). In this case, the Supreme Court held that Congress's commerce power extended not only to navigable streams, but also to the whitewater rapids of the New River in West Virginia, on the theory that the river was navigable because it was capable of being made navigable at some future date. By means of this decision, much State power over local waterways, flood control, hydroelectric power, and watershed projects has been transferred to the Federal government. This represents an *expansion* of Federal power, not simply an application of a general power to regulate *commerce among* the States.

The expanded use of executive agreements since the 1930s, substantially increasing the power of the President in foreign affairs, represents yet another extension of power. Instead of making treaties, which require Senate approval, modern Presidents have relied increasingly on privately negotiated settlements with foreign governments, known as executive agreements. Although the Senate is bypassed and is thus denied an opportunity to fulfill its "advice and consent" obligations under Article II, Section 2, executive agreements are nevertheless regarded as having the same force of law as formal treaties. The conclusion seems unavoidable that the widespread use of these executive devices has resulted in a transformation of the Senate's role in foreign affairs.

Among the various constitutional changes that have occurred as a result of Supreme Court rulings, the Court's rule of interpretation known as the Doctrine of Incorporation has probably produced the most far-reaching reallocations of power. In our earlier discussion of the Bill of Rights, we noted that one of its principal objectives was to preserve intact State bills of rights under the new Constitution, and to protect the right of the States to define the scope and content of civil liberties in disputes between a State and its citizens. In *Barron v. Baltimore* (1833), a unanimous Supreme Court, speaking through Chief Justice Marshall, held that no provision of the Bill of Rights applied to the States.

Beginning in 1925 in the case of *Gitlow v. New York*, however, the Court initiated a series of decisions that resulted in the nationalization of the Bill of Rights. By 1947, every provision of the First Amendment had been made applicable to the States, and in the 1960s most provisions of the Bill of Rights protecting Federal criminal defendants were also applied to State proceedings. The vehicle used to accomplish this result was the Due Process Clause of the Fourteenth Amendment, which provides that, "No State shall deny any person life, liberty or property without due process of law." Focusing on the word "liberty" in the clause, the Supreme Court expanded it to include various provisions of the Bill of Rights, thereby making the restrictions against the Federal government in the Bill of Rights applicable to the States through the Fourteenth Amendment. In this way, for example, freedom of the press was incorporated into the word "liberty" of the Fourteenth Amendment, thereby giving the Federal judiciary the final say on the scope and meaning of this freedom at both the State and Federal level through its power of judicial review.

Aside from the fact that the Doctrine of Incorporation has considerably enhanced the power of the Supreme Court and brought about a significant shift of power from the State to the national courts, this interpretive device has also resulted in extensive changes of the liberties themselves. Thus before the Supreme Court first applied the Establishment Clause of the First Amendment to the States in the landmark case of *Everson v. Board of Education* (1947), it was a common practice in many States to encourage religion and promote religious morality. Since 1947, however, the Supreme Court has held that almost any aid of any kind to religion constitutes an unconstitutional establishment of religion. This includes voluntary, nondenominational prayers in the public schools, which have been outlawed since 1962 as a result of *Engel v. Vitale* (the New York Prayer Case).

Many constitutional scholars question whether the Framers and backers of the Fourteenth Amendment intended by its provisions to abolish the federalism of the Bill of Rights and overturn *Barron v. Baltimore,* and the Doctrine of Incorporation has therefore engendered widespread criticism, even among members of the Federal Judiciary. Whatever its merits, the

Doctrine of Incorporation represents a drastic transformation of power that serves to illustrate one of the ways in which the Constitution is changed without a clear mandate from the people and the States through the amendment process.

In his *Commentaries on the Constitution,* Joseph Story condemned judge-made law and cautioned against the use of interpretive techniques that change the meaning of the Constitution. The two greatest excesses of constitutional construction to be avoided, he advised, are excessively narrow and excessively broad interpretations, either of which can distort the intent of the Framers and rob the people of their Constitution. Taken to extremes, restrictions on the powers of government can make it difficult or impossible for government to function. Moreover, a power of government should not be restricted solely because it is susceptible of abuse. "Every power," he observed, "however limited, as well as broad, is in its own nature susceptible of abuse. No Constitution can provide safeguards against it. Confidence must be reposed somewhere, and in free governments the ordinary securities against abuse are found in the responsibility of the rulers to the people, and in the just exercise of their elective franchise, and ultimately in the sovereign power of change."

No less injurious to the public good are free and uninhibited interpretations in the name of expediency. Judges, wrote Story, should not "enlarge the construction of a given power beyond the fair scope of its terms merely because the restriction is inconvenient, impolitic, or even mischievous. If it be mischievous, the power of redressing the evil lies with the people by an exercise of the power of amendment. . . . Arguments drawn from impolicy or inconvenience ought here to have no weight. . . . Men on such subjects complexionally differ from each other. The same men differ from themselves at different times. Temporary delusions, prejudices, excitements, and objects have irresistible influence in mere questions of policy. And the policy of one age may ill suit the wishes or policy of another. The Constitution is not to be subject to such fluctuations. It is to have a fixed, uniform, permanent construction. It should be, so far at least as human infirmity will allow, not dependent upon the passions or parties of particular times, but the same yesterday, today, and forever."

That we have not fully lived up to these high standards and ideals of constitutional interpretation does not compel us to renounce them as un-

realistic or false, but to recognize the frailty of constitutional government, the need for constant vigilance, and the primacy of the amending
process as a device for protecting the constitution from unauthorized, il-
legitimate alterations of the basic design.

Amending the Constitution

"We must all obey the great law of change," declared Edmund Burke. "It
is the most powerful law of nature, and the means perhaps of its conser-
vation. All we can do, and that human wisdom can do, is to provide that
the change shall proceed by insensible degrees." Like Burke, the Framers
of the Constitution understood that not all change is reform. A constitution cannot long endure if it may be amended too easily or too swiftly.
Nor can it be expected to survive if it cannot be changed at all; for a constitution cannot be preserved if it cannot be altered to correct errors in the
document or meet the needs of society. The Articles of Confederation
were probably doomed from the start because they required the unanimous consent of the States before any change could be made.

The procedures to be followed for amending the Constitution, as we
noted in our discussion of federalism, are laid out in Article V. The Framers believed that the method adopted was a vast improvement over that
prescribed by the Articles because it achieved a balance between permanency and change and thus assured the continuity of the Constitution.
"The mode preferred by the convention," observed Publius in *Federalist*
No. 43, "seems to be stamped with every mark of propriety. It guards
equally against that extreme facility, which would render the Constitution too mutable; and that extreme difficulty, which might perpetuate its
discovered faults." Another virtue of the method selected, he added, is
that it "equally enables the general and the State governments to originate the amendment of errors, as they may be pointed out by experience
on one side, or on the other."

Both Congress and the States may initiate amendments, but only the
States may ratify them. An amendment can be proposed by a two-thirds
vote of both houses of Congress or by a national convention called by
Congress at the request of the legislatures of two-thirds of the States.
Once an amendment has been proposed, it must be ratified by the legis-

latures of three-fourths of the States or by a special convention of three-fourths of the States. Congress decides which method of ratification is to be followed and may specify the length of time in which the amendment must be ratified. Except for the Twenty-First Amendment, which repealed the Eighteenth, every amendment added to the Constitution has been ratified by the State legislatures. Now that there are fifty States in the Union, no amendment can take effect unless thirty-eight States approve it. The President, it should be emphasized, plays no role in the amendment process. He may not propose amendments, and those that Congress proposes are not submitted to the President for signature. This has not prevented certain Presidents, however, from persuading a member of Congress to introduce an amendment that reflects the President's wishes. In 1865, the proposed Thirteenth Amendment outlawing slavery was mistakenly submitted to President Lincoln and inadvertently signed by him.

The amendment process, as briefly outlined here, seems rather simple and straightforward. Upon closer inspection, however, we observe that it embraces a democratic theory of government and reaffirms basic principles of the American constitutional system.

First, it may be seen that the method of amendment reflects a certain philosophy of change. By requiring extraordinary rather than simple majorities, it prefers *evolutionary* to *revolutionary* change and establishes a cumbersome system that is intended to make the amendment process slow and difficult. The purpose is not to prevent change but to encourage careful deliberation, and to discourage hasty, ill-conceived, and sweeping alterations of the fundamental law by weak, impassioned, and transient majorities. In other words, it seeks to minimize the risks and uncertainties of change. Moreover, it guards against wholesale constitutional reform at breakneck speed that might so convulse the society as to produce turbulent disorder and revolutionary upheaval.

Second, the amendment process protects the States against each other and poses a barrier to sectional privilege and discrimination that might threaten the Union. Although some Anti-Federalists were critical of the extraordinary majority requirement on the ground that it was "undemocratic," the Framers understood that the two-thirds and three-fourths rules were necessary to prevent a simple majority of the States, with possibly only a minority of the population, from "ganging up" on a minority of the States, with possibly a majority of the population. The arrangement agreed upon offers some assurance that public support for change will be strong and deliberate, and that it will be based on a national rather than a regional consensus. In these respects, the method of amendment is analogous to the Electoral College system, which encourages presidential candidates to campaign nationally and construct a national consensus in the race for the presidency.

Third, the method for amending the Constitution acknowledges the sovereignty of the States and strengthens the principle of federalism. If there is to be a formal change of the system, the States play a commanding role. In fact, they have the last word and in this respect exercise sovereignty over the nation. If Congress chooses not to propose an amendment, the States may even initiate an amendment of their own by the convention method, ratify it on their own authority, and circumvent the Congress.

Every amendment that has been added thus far, however, was proposed by Congress, and the States have never taken advantage of the convention option. The Constitution asserts that, in the event the States call for a convention, Congress "shall" comply. But as a practical matter there is no way to force Congress to act, and it would seem in this instance—as in many others—that the Framers relied upon the good faith of Congress for the observance of this requirement. If Congress were to call a convention, it would be appropriate for Congress to enact legislation providing for the organization and procedure of a convention—a step the Congress has yet to take.

Because the Constitution sets forth no rules or standards for the conduct of such a convention, there is some uncertainty about its possible composition and scope of authority. Some observers wary of the convention method have argued that it is a risky alternative because such a convention, once called, might become a "runaway" assembly bent upon rewriting the entire Constitution. Others contend, however, that this is a phantom danger because Congress would insist upon instructing the delegates to limit their consideration to a single amendment proposal and would be free to reject other amendments that might arise from the convention. In other words, the chance of a "runaway" convention is slim or nonexistent, according to this view, because it could not succeed unless the Congress was equally supportive of a wholesale revision of the Constitution. This is highly unlikely, it is further argued, given the deep and abiding affection for the Constitution among the American people.

These matters aside, the convention method has also been advocated on the ground that it is an effective political tool of the States for pressuring Congress into proposing amendments, the assumption being that, once the requisite number of States had called for a convention, Congress would be inclined to step in to take control of the process. By proposing the amendment itself, Congress would thereby eliminate the need for a convention, and the question of a "runaway" convention would be moot. All of this is speculative, however, and the course of action that might be taken in the event a convention is called cannot be known with certainty until it happens.

Fourth, the method of amendment in Article V recognizes and confirms the republican principle upon which the Constitution is based. Although the States, in their sovereign capacity, make the final decision on whether to ratify or reject an amendment, they act not alone but through representatives of the people. It is, then, the people in the several States, speaking through their elected representatives (or their convention delegates), who possess the ultimate authority to amend the Constitution.

The Limits of the Amending Power

Moreover, the Constitution implicitly acknowledges the right of the people and the States to add whatever amendment they desire, the only exception being that they cannot amend the Constitution so as to deprive a State of equal representation in the Senate without its consent. Article V also banned amendments before 1808 dealing with the importation and taxation of slaves, but this exception has obviously expired. Although there are no other words of limitation in Article V concerning the nature and substance of an amendment, parties opposed to certain amendments over the years have argued that an amendment which subverts or destroys a basic principle of the Constitution is itself unconstitutional. The Nineteenth Amendment granting women the right to vote, for example,

The Washington Family, c. 1790–1796.

"If, in the opinion of the people," said President Washington in his famous Farewell Address, "the distribution or modification of the constitutional powers be in any particular wrong, let it be corrected by an amendment in the way which the Constitution designates. But let there be no change by usurpation; for, though this, in one instance, may be the instrument of good, it is the customary weapon by which free governments are destroyed." Portrait by Edward Savage. Andrew W. Mellon Collection. (Photograph © Board of Trustees, National Gallery of Art, Washington, D.C.)

was challenged on the ground that a State which had rejected the Amendment would be deprived of its equal suffrage in the Senate because its Senators would be persons not of its choosing—that is, persons chosen by the voters whom the State itself had not authorized to vote for senators. This was an ingenious argument, perhaps, but the Supreme Court was not persuaded. Strictly speaking, an amendment to the Constitution is part of the Constitution itself. It is therefore inherently incapable of being unconstitutional. An amendment may nevertheless violate the spirit of the Constitution, overthrow established principles of the system, and so drastically alter the structure as to create a new form of government. Thus an amendment abolishing the States or the separation of powers, though constitutional in a legal sense, would in reality be destructive of the American constitutional system as we know it. Even foolish amendments, however, are constitutional, and it is the prerogative of the American people under Article V to make fools of themselves and to abolish their form of government and replace it with a new system if that is their wish.

Fortunately, the Constitution has always enjoyed the overwhelming support of the American people, and such revolutionary amendments have never been seriously considered. A more direct and continuing threat to the Constitution is the frivolous amendment, that is, legislation presented in the guise of an amendment. Throughout American history, members of Congress have routinely offered amendments to the Constitution that are designed simply to implement a particular public policy. In the case of the Eighteenth Amendment, which outlawed the manufacture and sale of intoxicating liquor, they actually succeeded. The subsequent repeal of this amendment illustrates the wisdom of an old political maxim that is sometimes forgotten: when it is not necessary to amend the Constitution, it is necessary not to amend it. The distillation and distribution of spirituous beverages could have been prevented by ordinary legislation, and there was therefore no need for the amendment in the first place.

No less threatening to the integrity of the Constitution is the tendency of legislators to introduce formal amendments for the purpose of reversing a recent Supreme Court decision. The amendment process, however, was intended to correct errors in the original document and to adjust the Constitution to a changing world, not as a device for controlling the Court. Unless the Court's decision is a formidable one substantially altering the distribution of power and the bedrock principles of the system, an amendment to overturn a particular case may well be an abuse of the amendment process. Ordinary legislation, such as the withdrawal of jurisdiction, should be considered if it can accomplish the same objective as an amendment. Whether an undesirable judicial decision should be corrected by an amendment or by a statute depends, however, on the nature of the case and its constitutional impact. If the amendment is too narrowly drawn, there is the added difficulty that, even if adopted, it may fail to cure the cause of the problem. Constitutional amendments, in other words, should be viewed as a last resort, not as the only recourse; and certainly they should not be used for light or transient reasons. For once they become part of the Constitution, for better or for worse, they acquire permanency of a sort and cannot easily be corrected, improved, or removed.

The fact that the people in the several States have amended the Constitution only seventeen times since 1791, when the Bill of Rights was adopted, is testimony to the wisdom and genius of the Framers. Two of the seventeen amendments—the Eighteenth and the Twenty-First—cancel each other out because the latter repealed the former. This leaves only fifteen during a period of two centuries. At least half of these reduce the powers of the States. Half of them also expand the suffrage. By contrast, only one amendment—the Eleventh—reduces the powers of the Federal government, and only four—the Eleventh, Fourteenth, Sixteenth, and Twenty-Sixth—overturn a Supreme Court decision. The States, it would seem, have contributed noticeably to the growth of Federal power either by accepting amendments that reduce their powers or by abstaining from the practice of using their amendment powers to restore the rights of the States.

The Amended Constitution

The following summary of Amendments XI–XXVII completes this introduction to the constitutional principles of American government, bringing the reader up-to-date on formal changes of our political system that have been made since the founding period.

A. AMENDMENT XI (1798)

The Judicial power of the United States shall not be construed to extend to any suit in law or equity, commenced or prosecuted against one of the United States by Citizens of another State, or by Citizens or Subjects of any Foreign State.

Article III, Section 2 extends the judicial power to "cases or controversies between a State and citizens of another State." In *Chisholm v. Georgia* (1793), the Supreme Court turned a deaf ear to Georgia's claim of "sovereign immunity," and interpreted the clause literally to mean that a citizen of the State of South Carolina could sue the State of Georgia without its consent.

The Eleventh Amendment reversed that decision, thereby limiting Federal judicial power, at least in theory. In reality, it affords the States little protection against Federal courts. The Supreme Court has interpreted the Amendment to mean that any citizen can sue a State official if that official is allegedly acting in an illegal or unconstitutional manner. The Court has reasoned that a State officer who acts beyond the law ceases to be an official of his State. Congress also frequently gets around the Amendment by conditioning State participation in Federal programs on the States' willingness to waive immunity.

The Fourteenth Amendment, which prohibits the States from denying any person life, liberty, or property without due process of law or equal protection of the law, also blunts the effect of the Eleventh Amendment. The Supreme Court has held under this Amendment that Federal courts may stop State officials from enforcing a State law, even if its constitutionality has not yet been determined and has simply been challenged. The Court has also held that the Eleventh Amendment is limited by the Enforcement Clause of the Fourteenth Amendment, and that Congress may authorize persons to sue the States, cities, and counties directly, rather than State officers, to remedy denials of due process and equal protection.

B. AMENDMENT XII (1804)

The Electors shall meet in their respective States, and vote by ballot for President and Vice-President, one of whom, at least, shall not be an inhabitant of the same State with themselves; they shall name in their ballots the person voted for as President, and in distinct ballots the person voted for as Vice-President, and they shall make distinct lists of all persons voted for as President, and of all persons voted for as Vice-President, and of the number of votes for each, which lists they shall sign and certify, and transmit sealed to the seat of the government of the United States, directed to the President of the Senate; — The President of the Senate shall, in the presence of the Senate and House of Representatives, open all the certificates and the votes shall then be counted; — The person having the greatest number of votes for President, shall be the President, if such number be a majority of the whole number of Electors appointed; and if no person have such majority, then from the persons having the highest numbers not exceeding three on the list of those voted for as President, the House of Representatives shall choose immediately, by ballot, the President. But in choosing the President, the votes shall be taken by States, the representation from each State having one vote; a quorum for this purpose shall consist of a member or members from two-thirds of the States, and a majority of all the States shall be necessary to a choice. [And if the House of Representatives shall not choose a President whenever the right of choice shall devolve upon them, before the fourth day of March next following, then the Vice-President shall act as President, as in the case of the death or other constitutional disability of the President. —] The person having the greatest number of votes as Vice-President, shall be the Vice-President, if such number be a majority of the whole number of Electors appointed, and if no person have a majority, then from the two highest numbers on the list, the Senate shall choose the Vice-President; a quorum for the purpose shall consist of two-thirds of the whole number of Senators, and a majority of the whole number shall be necessary to a choice. But no person constitutionally ineligible to the office of President shall be eligible to that of Vice-President of the United States.

This Amendment is an example of how custom and usage have changed the Constitution. The Framers expected electors to be independent, distinguished citizens, but the rise of national political parties changed the character of the Electoral College.

By the election of 1800, Electors had come to be the party faithful, pledged to vote for their party's candidate. In this election, the Jeffersonian Republicans held a majority in the Electoral College. They voted without indicating their choice for President and Vice President, as Article II, Section 3 prescribed, but because they were voting along party lines, Thomas Jefferson and Aaron Burr received the same number of votes, even though Burr was the vice presidential candidate. The issue was settled by the House of Representatives, which gave the presidency to Jefferson.

The Twelfth Amendment was designed to prevent a recurrence of this situation by requiring Electors to cast separate votes for President and Vice President.

C. AMENDMENT XIII (1865)

SECTION 1. *Neither slavery nor involuntary servitude, except as a punishment for crime whereof the party shall have been duly convicted, shall exist within the United States, or any place subject to their jurisdiction.*
SECTION 2. *Congress shall have power to enforce this article by appropriate legislation.*

This is the first of the three Civil War or Reconstruction Amendments. Prior to its adoption, the States were free to decide for themselves whether to permit or prohibit slavery within their borders. The Thirteenth Amendment deprives both the State and Federal governments of this power, and forbids slavery and involuntary servitude. It does not prohibit compulsory labor and other forms of "involuntary servitude" associated with the punishment and treatment of criminals.

Prolonged angry debates over slavery, in the Congress and elsewhere, ended in violence—and in constitutional amendments that would produce striking political and social changes in America. By March 1861, when the southern States already had seceded from the Union and formed their Confederacy, Congress was considering a constitutional amendment which, if ratified, would have been the Thirteenth Amendment. (The Senate rejected this proposed amendment on March 2, just two days before the inauguration of Abraham Lincoln as President.) The text of this proposal, intended to conciliate the South and preserve the Union, ran as follows: "No amendment shall be made to the Constitution which will authorize or give to Congress the power to abolish or interfere within any State with the domestic institutions thereof including that of persons held to labor or service by the laws of said State."

This proposed but rejected Amendment XIII, in other words, would have forbidden the Federal government ever to interfere with slavery in States that desired to retain chattel slavery. But on April 12, 1861, Confederates fired on Fort Sumter, in Charleston harbor, and the Civil War began. Everyone forgot about the amendment that would have protected the "Peculiar Institution" of slavery.

By the end of 1862, it was uncertain whether the North or the South would win the terrible struggle. In December, Union armies suffered severe defeats in Virginia and Mississippi. Alarmed by the Confederates' successes, on January 1, 1863, President Lincoln issued the Emancipation Proclamation as an emergency measure, setting free all slaves within the "rebellious" states—that is, the Confederacy. This was a wartime device to damage the South's economy and produce disorder there. The Proclamation did not emancipate slaves in the "loyal slave states"—Delaware, Maryland, Kentucky, Missouri—nor did it guarantee that slavery might not be restored after the end of the war. Besides, many men in Congress believed the Emancipation Proclamation to be unconstitutional.

So a year later, in January 1864, there was introduced in Congress a proposal for a constitutional amendment that would forbid slavery anywhere in the Union. This joint resolution was passed by the Senate in April, but rejected by the House in June. Not until January 1865 did the House of Representatives approve the proposed amendment—and then by a narrow margin and after much persuasion. By that time the Confederacy clearly was losing the war. On December 18, 1865, enough States had ratified this new Thirteenth Amendment, and it became part of the Constitution—the first amendment since 1804.

In Section 2, we encounter for the first time in the Constitution an odd provision that will be repeated in the Fourteenth, Fifteenth, and later amendments. This is the Enforcement Clause, which seemingly confers a non-legislative power on Congress to *enforce* the Thirteenth Amendment by appropriate legislation.

D. AMENDMENT XIV (1868)

SECTION 1. *All persons born or naturalized in the United States, and subject to the jurisdiction thereof, are citizens of the United States and of the State wherein they reside. No State shall make or enforce any law which shall abridge the privileges or immunities of citizens of the United States; nor shall any State deprive any person of life, liberty, or property, without due process of law; nor deny to any person within its jurisdiction the equal protection of the laws.*

SECTION 2. *Representatives shall be apportioned among the several States according to their respective numbers, counting the whole number of persons in each State, excluding Indians not taxed. But when the right to vote at any election for the choice of electors for President and Vice President of the United States, Representatives in Congress, the Executive and Judicial officers of a*

State, or the members of the Legislature thereof, is denied to any of the male inhabitants of such State, being twenty-one years of age, and citizens of the United States, or in any way abridged, except for participation in rebellion, or other crime, the basis of representation therein shall be reduced in the proportion which the number of such male citizens shall bear to the whole number of male citizens twenty-one years of age in such State.

SECTION 3. *No person shall be a Senator or Representative in Congress, or elector of President and Vice President, or hold any office, civil or military, under the United States, or under any State, who, having previously taken an oath, as a member of Congress, or as an officer of the United States, or as a member of any State legislature, or as an executive or judicial officer of any State, to support the Constitution of the United States, shall have engaged in insurrection or rebellion against the same, or given aid or comfort to the enemies thereof. But Congress may by a vote of two-thirds of each House remove such disability.*

SECTION 4. *The validity of the public debt of the United States, authorized by law, including debts incurred for payment of pensions and bounties for services in suppressing insurrection or rebellion, shall not be questioned. But neither the United States nor any State shall assume or pay any debt or obligation incurred in aid of insurrection or rebellion against the United States, or any claim for the loss or emancipation of any slave; but all such debts, obligations and claims shall be held illegal and void.*

SECTION 5. *The Congress shall have power to enforce, by appropriate legislation, the provisions of this article.*

This second Civil War or Reconstruction Amendment accounts for more than half of all cases heard in the Supreme Court nowadays.

Divided into five parts, the Fourteenth Amendment's first section confers State and Federal citizenship on all persons born or naturalized in the United States, irrespective of race. It overturns the *Dred Scott Case,* which had held that blacks were not eligible for citizenship and therefore could not claim the privileges and immunities of American citizens.

Section 1 further provides that no State may abridge the privileges or immunities of United States citizens. The meaning of this confusing clause is obscured by the fact that it fails to define the nature and substance of these privileges and immunities. It should be distinguished from the privileges and immunities clause of Article IV of the Constitution, which requires the States to grant the same privileges and immunities (whatever the State determines them to be) to out-of-State citizens that it grants to its own citizens. The privileges and immunities of *State* citizens, in other words, vary from State to State. They are normally associated with such activities as the privilege of engaging in a trade or business, the use and enjoyment of State lands, and other *privileges* as opposed to basic fundamental *rights*.

In the *Slaughter-House Cases* (1873), the Supreme Court held that the privileges and immunities of United States, as opposed to State, citizens are not the same as the freedoms guaranteed by the Bill of Rights. Rather, they include privileges which owe their existence to the Constitution, Federal laws and treaties, such as the privilege to engage in interstate or foreign commerce, protection on the high seas and in foreign countries, and the privilege of voting in Federal elections. Thus limited, the privileges and immunities clause of the Fourteenth Amendment has never had much significance.

Section 1 of the Fourteenth Amendment also provides that no State shall deprive any person of life, liberty, or property without due process of law. This is the Due Process Clause that has become the primary source of civil rights litigation in today's Federal courts.

The clause does not forbid a State from taking one's life, liberty, or property. It provides merely that if these rights are to be denied, they must be denied according to the standards of due process. The concept of due process, we are reminded, dates back to Magna Charta (1215). As developed over time by the Anglo-American courts, the concept of due process came to mean that the individual, particularly in a criminal trial, was entitled to a fair trial. This meant that rich or poor, black or white, the defendant's trial would be conducted according to the same rules and requirements of evidence, testimony, and the make-up of the jury.

By the end of the nineteenth century, the Supreme Court had expanded the Due Process Clause of the Fourteenth Amendment in two ways: (1) By looking beyond procedure to substance or the actual *result* of the trial. In a series of cases involving alleged denials of economic liberty, the Court held that the determination of whether there had been a denial of due process did not depend upon procedure alone, but whether liberty had been abridged in the end result. This interpretation came to be known as "substantive due process." (2) The due process requirement, as originally conceived, was designed essentially to limit the courts and to make certain that they conducted fair trials. Under the doctrines of substantive due process, however, the standards of due process were applied to laws, not just trials, to limit the powers of the State legislatures and local governments.

Thus in a series of cases extending from the 1880s to 1937, the Supreme Court applied the concept of substantive or "economic" due process to strike down countless State laws that allegedly interfered with economic rights and had nothing to do with fair trials. In *Lockner v. New York* (1905), for example, the Court invalidated a State law limiting the working hours of bakery employees as a violation of "liberty of contract." In *West Coast Hotel v. Parrish* (1937), however, the Court suddenly abandoned this doctrine, taking a "hands-off" position that State legislatures should have broad discretion to regulate the conditions of employment as they saw fit.

Meanwhile, however, the Court began moving in yet another direction during this period with respect to non-economic freedoms. In *Gitlow v. New York* (1925), the Court applied its substantive due process rationale to the First Amendment. This Amendment, like the remaining portions of the Bill of Rights, applies *only* to the Federal government. The Court held in *Gitlow,* however, that the First Amendment also limited the States. The Court reasoned that the word "liberty" in the Due Process Clause of the Fourteenth Amendment, which prohibits a State from denying any person life, *liberty,* or property in a trial, also means liberty of speech and press. It is questionable whether the members of Congress who wrote the Fourteenth Amendment intended for it to be interpreted in this manner. This was the beginning of what has come to be known as the Supreme Court's doctrine of "incorporation," a rule of interpretation we have discussed before which holds that the various freedoms protected against Federal abridgment in the Bill of Rights may be "incorporated" or "absorbed" into the word "liberty" of the Due Process Clause of the Fourteenth Amendment to restrict the States.

The remaining provision of Section 1 of the Fourteenth Amendment prohibits the States from denying any person the equal protection of the laws. The Equal Protection Clause has been instrumental in striking down State laws that discriminate against racial minorities, religious minorities, and women. In the landmark case of *Brown v. Board of Education* (1954), the Supreme Court held that racial segregation in the public schools was discriminatory and therefore contrary to the equal protection of the laws. In this decision, the Court rejected its earlier holding in *Plessy v. Ferguson* (1896) which had maintained that "separate but equal" facilities for whites and blacks were not discriminatory.

The Equal Protection Clause, as interpreted by the Courts, does not demand a rigid equality in all respects. The basic test used by the Court is whether the distinction complained of is "reasonable." One way of deciding is to determine whether the group singled out favors or opposes the different treatment. If it tends to favor it, the group may be enjoying a particular privilege—as suggested, for example, by the military draft, which in the United States has always excluded women. If the group selected for unequal treatment tends to oppose it, however, the group may be experiencing unwarranted discrimination—as suggested by a law which arbitrarily excludes women or minorities from a certain profession.

Sections 2, 3, and 4 of the Fourteenth Amendment are largely of historical interest today. Section 2 modifies Article I, Section 2, Clause 3 of the Constitution, which provided that slaves should be counted at three-fifths of the number of free persons in apportioning representatives. Section 2 of the Fourteenth Amendment, taking account of the Thirteenth Amendment abolishing slavery, eliminates the three-fifths clause.

The other provision of this section authorizing Congress to reduce the number of representatives to which a State is entitled in the House of Representatives has never been enforced. It was intended to give Congress a retaliatory power against Confederate States which denied blacks the right to vote. It is also inconsistent with the Nineteenth Amendment, which extends the franchise to women, and the Twenty-Sixth Amendment, which lowers the voting age to eighteen.

Section 3 of the Fourteenth Amendment, designed by the triumphant Radical Republicans in Congress to punish the South and prevent any of its political or military leaders from assuming State or Federal office, rendered most former Confederate officials ineligible to serve in Congress, the Federal Judiciary, the executive branch of the United States government, the U.S. military, any State office, or in the Electoral College. Another objective of this section was to enhance the political power of "carpetbaggers" and "scalawags," who could be counted upon to support the policies of the Radical Republicans.

President Andrew Johnson opposed this provision on the ground that it improperly restricted his power to pardon the leaders of the Confederacy and restore their political and civil rights. Not until 1898 did Congress pass legislation removing the disability.

Inspired by the desire to remove all doubt concerning the validity of financial obligations incurred by the Federal government during the Civil War, Section 4 of the Fourteenth Amendment simply reaffirmed the debts of the Union and invalidated those of the Confederacy.

This Section forbids both Federal and State governments to pay any debts contracted by a State that belonged to the Confederacy, "or any claim for the loss or emancipation of any slave." (This latter prohibition of payment applied to slaves and slave owners in the "loyal free States," as well as to those in the "rebellious States"—in effect, denying the guarantee that no property shall be taken without just compensation.)

With the Fourteenth Amendment, the powers of the several States began to dwindle. For the defeated eleven States that had joined the Confederacy to be readmitted to the Union, they were required first to ratify this Fourteenth Amendment, much though the people of those eleven States might dislike its provisions. Also, there were loud complaints in most southern States that political trickery and intimidation had been employed to secure ratification of the Amendment. About Amendment XIV, then, hangs a cloud; and interpretation of that Amendment continues to be controversial in today's courts.

E. AMENDMENT XV (1870)

SECTION 1. *The right of citizens of the United States to vote shall not be denied or abridged by the United States or by any State on account of race, color, or previous condition of servitude.*

SECTION 2. *The Congress shall have power to enforce this article by appropriate legislation.*

This is the third and last Civil War or Reconstruction Amendment. Its original purpose was to extend the franchise to the newly emancipated

Women's Suffrage.

A delegation of "Suffragettes" appearing before the Judiciary Committee of the House of Representatives in 1871 to argue that the Fourteenth and Fifteenth amendments granted women the right to vote. (Courtesy of the Library of Congress.)

slaves. The Fifteenth Amendment does not technically give blacks the right to vote as such, but instead informs the States that race cannot be one of the factors it uses in determining voter qualifications. In effect, however, the Amendment as interpreted by the Supreme Court confers a right to vote upon all blacks who otherwise meet a State's eligibility standards regarding such matters as age and residency. The Supreme Court has also held that the right extends beyond the general election to primary elections.

Section 2 of the Fifteenth Amendment repeats the Enforcement Clause language of the Thirteenth and Fourteenth amendments. Congress rarely used this power before it enacted the Voting Rights Act of 1965 and its ensuing amendments. Under this Act, Congress abolished literacy tests and racial gerrymandering, thereby prohibiting the States and their political subdivisions from intentionally "watering down" the black vote by drawing up electoral districts that reduce the impact of the black vote or reduce the chances of electing a black candidate to office. The Act also restricts the States in those instances where the drawing of electoral districts simply *results* in a dilution of black voting strength, whether by accident or design.

F. AMENDMENT XVI (1913)

The Congress shall have power to lay and collect taxes on incomes, from whatever source derived, without apportionment among the several States, and without regard to any census or enumeration.

In *Pollack v. Farmer's Loan & Trust* (1895), the Supreme Court held unconstitutional an Act of Congress establishing an income tax derived from property. An income tax, said the Court, is a "direct" tax, and Article I, Section 2, Clause 3 and Article I, Section 9, Clause 4 of the Constitution specify that direct taxes must be apportioned according to population. Such apportionment might be possible under a uniform capitation tax, but not under an income tax based on property.

The Sixteenth Amendment overturned the *Pollock* case, authorizing Congress to levy a tax on income, whatever its source, without apportionment. This Amendment strengthens the tax power of Congress, but necessarily reduces the power of States by reducing their tax base. In other words, there is less tax revenue available to the States as a result of this Amendment because there is less to collect after the Federal government has levied its tax. In this respect, the Sixteenth Amendment vitally affects the institution of federalism.

The Sixteenth Amendment, then, altered the relationships between the Federal government and the State governments. For Washington now enjoyed means for raising money more efficient than the means most States possessed. Beginning in the era of Franklin Roosevelt, the Congress found it expedient to secure cooperation from State legislatures by offering the States grants of money for purposes approved by the Federal government. Often the State could obtain the "grant-in-aid" by matching the Federal contribution; sometimes Washington required that the States contribute only a small percentage of the total costs, or perhaps nothing at all.

Thus increasingly, since the Second World War, the Federal government has paid the bills for large public projects and induced or compelled State governments to adopt and administer Federal programs. Federal funds are awarded for compliance or withheld for lack of cooperation from a State. States that do not comply "lose" Federal money given to other States. The result of this policy has been to diminish greatly the power of the State governments to make their own decisions, so shifting the political structure of the United States toward centralization, and toward policy-making by an elite of central administrators, rather than through the established processes of a democratic republic.

A recent example of how Federal grants may be used to "bribe" or compel State governments to obey Congress's will—or perhaps the will of lobbyists in Washington who bring pressure to bear upon members of Congress—is the requirement that State governments must make the use of seat-belts in all automobiles compulsory, on pain of losing Federal funds for highway-building if a State fails to comply. In the past, States have also run the risk of losing Federal highway funds if they refused—as did California—to require motorcyclists to wear helmets. Such concerns formerly were regarded as falling wholly within the established police powers of the States. When many such decisions no longer can be made statewide or locally, but are determined in Washington by Congress, executive administrators, or interest groups—then it would seem the original federal plan of government has given way, for the most part, to a centralized political scheme not contemplated by the Constitution. But for the Income Tax Amendment, Congress would not have the financial resources that make these intrusions into the domain of State power possible.

G. AMENDMENT XVII (1913)

The Senate of the United States shall be composed of two Senators from each State, elected by the people thereof, for six years; and each Senator shall have one vote. The electors in each State shall have the qualifications requisite for electors of the most numerous branch of the State legislatures.

When vacancies happen in the representation of any State in the Senate, the executive authority of such State shall issue writs of election to fill such vacancies; Provided, That the legislature of any State may empower the executive thereof to make temporary appointments until the people fill the vacancies by election as the legislature may direct.

This amendment shall not be so construed as to affect the election or term of any Senator chosen before it becomes valid as part of the Constitution.

The Framers of the Constitution specified in Article I, Section 3 that United States Senators should be chosen by each State legislature, two for each State, while members of the House of Representatives should be chosen by popular election from congressional districts. The main purpose of this method of indirect election of Senators was to give each State, no matter how small its population, a voice in the Congress.

In effect, each State's two Senators thus represented the State itself, rather than the voters in particular districts; and they represented their State in the sense that each State was a sovereign political body, not simply an aggregation of voters. Senator Daniel Webster represented Massachusetts as a commonwealth with a culture of its own and interests of its own. Senator John C. Calhoun represented the proud State of South Carolina in Washington—not merely a constituency of rural voters. Sometimes it may be necessary for a public man to sacrifice himself *for* the people, Calhoun said on one occasion, but never *to* the people. Senators were delegates or symbols of their States, so to speak; and often the State legislatures, aware of senatorial dignity, chose some remarkable men as their United States Senators—at least for the first half-century of the Republic.

Senators, it was thought, would exercise a moderating influence on the popularly based House of Representatives. The Framers expected State legislatures, made up for the most part of experienced politicians, to be able to choose distinguished Senators better than could average citizens. Presumably the legislatures of the several States would tend to select senatorial candidates of superior mind, character, and education; often the Senators so chosen would also be men of some wealth—which the Framers considered all to the good. And in truth, especially in the early Republic, the Senate at Washington was a gathering of men of unusual talent and strength of character, somewhat comparable to the body of men who had been delegates to the Great Convention of 1787.

But societies change. As the franchise was enlarged in every State, the American people looked with increasing suspicion upon the indirect election of Senators. Gradually, in many States, the legislatures yielded to popular pressure, and members of those bodies pledged themselves at the time of their own election, or on some other occasion, to vote for some particular candidate for the United States Senate when the State legislature chose the next Senator. This was the process that had converted the Electors of the Electoral College into mere registrars of the popular choice for the Presidency. In theory, then, United States Senators still were chosen by legislatures. But in reality, State legislators voted for senatorial candidates quite as their constituents told them to vote. When the Senate finally capitulated in 1912, the voters in some twenty-nine States had already obtained the right to indicate their preferences for Senator in the party primaries—and State legislatures invariably followed the wishes of the voters.

Like the Sixteenth Amendment, the Seventeenth grew out of the Populist and Progressive revolt of the late nineteenth and early twentieth centuries. Generally favoring more democracy in every aspect of political life, State as well as Federal, the Populists and Progressives launched major political reform efforts, particularly in the Deep South and west of the Mississippi River, to reduce the political and economic power of America's burgeoning class of plutocrats—men of humble origin, often, who had become wealthy almost overnight as a result of the industrial revolution and exerted a powerful influence in State governments.

In the legendary stories of Horatio Alger, they were America's heroes, symbols of the American success story—immigrants, perhaps, who through self-sacrifice and hard work had risen to the top. To the Populists and Progressives, however, they were often the proverbial business tycoons—greedy capitalists, they charged, who engaged in monopolistic practices to maximize their wealth and used their wealth to buy votes in legislative bodies, courts of law, and governors' mansions. The restructuring of State Constitutions throughout the country at this time—for the purpose of circumventing State legislatures through the initiative and referendum devices, and controlling the courts through the election or recall of judges—was the fruit of their labor.

Whereas the Sixteenth Amendment promised to limit the wealth and economic power of these millionaire industrialists, the Seventeenth was premised on the assumption that the direct election of Senators would limit their political influence. Many Senators were millionaires themselves, and many more, it was generally believed, were obligated to special economic interests. The wealthy might bribe State legislators but they could not bribe the entire electorate. The direct election of Senators, thought the Populists and Progressives, would cure the evils of Big Business, giant trusts, and corporate monopolies. Buttressed by the Sixteenth Amendment, the Seventeenth might then prepare the way for breaking up great concentrations of wealth and, hoped some of the more radical Populists, lead to a redistribution of wealth. But some argue that no conspicuous improvement in the talents and character of members of the Senate seems to have been the result of this Amendment.

One prominent public leader of recent decades, Eugene McCarthy—United States Senator from Minnesota for two terms—remarks in his book *Frontiers of American Democracy* that the Seventeenth Amendment did harm to the quality of the United States Senate. A principal reason for this is the fact that although a Representative in the House has to please only his constituents in his district, a United States Senator must campaign statewide—and wander about his State fairly frequently, if he wishes to remain in office. Much of his time is wasted in perpetual campaigning. Besides, the campaign expenditures of a senatorial candidate, both in the primary and in the regular election, usually are gigantic; this money must be found somewhere; so either a candidate's family must be very wealthy, and have wealthy friends, or else the candidate may find it necessary to make promises to special interests, or voting blocs that he cannot fulfill or ought not to fulfill. It is noteworthy that most Senators today are very well-to-do, and many are multimillionaires. The task of courting an immense State-wide electorate may invite as much corruption as courting a small body of State legislators ever did.

However that may be, nowadays the principal distinction between members of the House of Representatives and members of the Senate is that Senators hold office for six years, and Representatives for merely two. The longer term tends to give Senators greater independence of decision, at least during the earlier years of the six-year term, so enabling them to be something better than mere delegates to Washington.

The Seventeenth Amendment supersedes Article I, Section 3 of the Constitution. As a result, members of the United States Senate have ceased to speak for, represent, or be responsible to the State legislatures. That the change enlarged the influence of the voters and weakened that of federalism is abundantly clear.

H. AMENDMENT XVIII (1919)

SECTION 1. *After one year from the ratification of this article the manufacture, sale, or transportation of intoxicating liquors within, the importation thereof into, or the exportation thereof from the United States and all territory subject to the jurisdiction thereof for beverage purposes is hereby prohibited.*
SECTION 2. *The Congress and the several States shall have concurrent power to enforce this article by appropriate legislation.*
SECTION 3. *This article shall be inoperative unless it shall have been ratified as an amendment to the Constitution by the legislatures of the several States, as provided in the Constitution, within seven years from the date of the submission hereof to the States by the Congress.*

Known as the Prohibition Amendment, this short-lived amendment prohibited the manufacture, sale, or transportation of intoxicating liquors throughout the United States. Although the Amendment was enthusiastically ratified by every State in the Union except Connecticut and Rhode Island, the "noble experiment" proved to be largely unenforceable. Just fourteen years after its adoption, it was repealed.

The colossal failure of the Eighteenth Amendment demonstrates the folly of using the amendment process for purposes for which it was not intended. National Prohibition was a specific public policy that could have easily been achieved by a simple Act of Congress. It would also seem that the issue should have been left for resolution by the States, as was the case prior to its adoption. The Constitution is not served well when the amendment process is used to implement specific policies that might otherwise be accomplished by a statute. Such, it would seem, is the lesson to be learned from this well-intentioned but unwise amendment. One of the more unfortunate results of this amendment is that it fostered the growth of bootleggers, which in turn gave rise to organized crime, from which the United States has not yet recovered.

I. AMENDMENT XIX (1920)

The right of citizens of the United States to vote shall not be denied or abridged by the United States or by any State on account of sex.

Congress shall have power to enforce this article by appropriate legislation.

This Amendment establishing women's suffrage is the culmination of a political reform effort that began in the 1840s. When the Amendment was first adopted, it was argued that the Amendment enlarged the electorate without a State's consent, destroyed its autonomy, and therefore exceeded the amending power. Pointing to the Fifteenth Amendment as precedent, the Supreme Court rejected this view, and has seldom had occasion to interpret the Amendment since.

J. AMENDMENT XX (1933)

SECTION 1. *The terms of the President and Vice President shall end at noon on the 20th day of January, and the terms of Senators and Representatives at noon on the 3d day of January, of the years in which such terms would have ended if this article had not been ratified; and the terms of their successors shall then begin.*

SECTION 2. *The Congress shall assemble at least once in every year, and such meeting shall begin at noon on the 3d day of January, unless they shall by law appoint a different day.*

SECTION 3. *If, at the time fixed for the beginning of the term of the President, the President elect shall have died, the Vice President elect shall become President. If a President shall not have been chosen before the time fixed for the beginning of his term, or if the President elect shall have failed to qualify, then the Vice President elect shall act as President until a President shall have qualified; and the Congress may by law provide for the case wherein neither a President elect nor a Vice President elect shall have qualified, declaring who shall then act as President, or the manner in which one who is to act shall be selected, and such person shall act accordingly until a President or Vice President shall have qualified.*

SECTION 4. *The Congress may by law provide for the case of the death of any of the persons from whom the House of Representatives may choose a President whenever the right of choice shall have devolved upon them, and for the case of the death of any of the persons from whom the Senate may choose a Vice President whenever the right of choice shall have devolved upon them.*

SECTION 5. *Sections 1 and 2 shall take effect on the 15th day of October following the ratification of this article.*

SECTION 6. *This article shall be inoperative unless it shall have been ratified as an amendment to the Constitution by the legislatures of three-fourths of the several States within seven years from the date of its submission.*

This is the so-called Lame Duck Amendment. It supersedes Article I, Section 4, Clause 2 of the Constitution, which called for Congress to begin each session on the first Monday in December. Members of Congress now convene on January 3. The Amendment also changes the date when the terms of President and Vice President shall begin—from March 4 to January 20.

The Constitution does not specify a date when the terms of Senators and Representatives shall begin. It does provide, however, that one-third of the Senate and all of the Representatives shall be elected every two years. Nor does the Constitution indicate when the terms of the President and Vice President shall commence. The First Congress resolved the issue in 1789 by passing a statute providing that the terms of President and Vice President and of Senators and Representatives shall begin on March 4.

What this meant, however, was that Congress had a short session every other year. In the "off year," when there were no elections, Congress convened on the first Monday of December and remained in session throughout much of the next year. But in the following election year, Congress was required to hold a short session because of the November elections. After convening in December, Congress had to end the session in March, when the terms expired for those Senators and Representatives defeated in the previous November elections.

These short sessions came to be known as "lame duck" sessions because they allowed members of Congress who had been defeated in the November elections ("lame ducks") to remain in office until March of the following year, when their terms expired. It also meant that individuals elected in November had to wait for five months before taking office, and could not really begin their work until the following December—thirteen months after their election. Not the least of the difficulties solved by the

Twentieth Amendment was the democratic problem of having defeated members of Congress, accountable to no one, representing their constituents for almost half a year.

An obvious question is why the Amendment was necessary since the original date of March 4 was set by statute. The answer is that the changes to January 3 and January 20 shortened the terms of those in office, and these changes would therefore have been unconstitutional if accomplished through the legislative rather than the amendment process.

Congress has fulfilled its obligations under Section 3 of the Twentieth Amendment by enacting legislation from time to time dealing with presidential succession. The Presidential Succession Act of 1947, for example, deals with the problem that would arise if both the President and Vice President died or were otherwise unable to qualify for office on or before January 20.

K. AMENDMENT XXI (1933)

SECTION 1. *The eighteenth article of amendment to the Constitution of the United States is hereby repealed.*

SECTION 2. *The transportation or importation into any State, Territory, or possession of the United States for delivery or use therein of intoxicating liquors, in violation of the laws thereof, is hereby prohibited.*

SECTION 3. *This article shall be inoperative unless it shall have been ratified as an amendment to the Constitution by conventions in the several States, as provided in the Constitution, within seven years from the date of the submission hereof to the States by the Congress.*

This Amendment simply repeals the Eighteenth Amendment and restores to the States the power to regulate the manufacture, sale, and consumption of alcoholic beverages. State regulations may nevertheless be set aside by Congress under its commerce power or if they violate the Export-Import Clause.

L. AMENDMENT XXII (1951)

SECTION 1. *No person shall be elected to the office of the President more than twice, and no person who has held the office of President, or acted as President,*

for more than two years of a term to which some other person was elected Pres-
ident shall be elected to the office of the President more than once. But this Ar-
ticle shall not apply to any person holding the office of President when this Ar-
ticle was proposed by the Congress, and shall not prevent any person who may
be holding the office of President, or acting as President, during the term within
which this Article becomes operative from holding the office of President or act-
ing as President during the remainder of such term.

SECTION 2. *This article shall be inoperative unless it shall have been ratified as*
an amendment to the Constitution by the legislatures of three-fourths of the
several States within seven years from the date of its submission to the States
by the Congress.

This Amendment arose out of resentment or uneasiness at President
Franklin D. Roosevelt's defiance of the "no third-term" tradition established by George Washington. Might not some man more charismatic
even than Roosevelt succeed in getting elected for his whole life term—
as if he were a king?

The maximum period that a person can now serve as President is ten
years—two years by elevation to the office because of the death, disability, or resignation of the elected President and two elected terms of four
years each. Otherwise, a person can serve no more than eight years or
two terms as President as a result of the Twenty-Second Amendment.

Critics of the Amendment contend that an able and popular President,
in many circumstances, is more of a treasure than a danger, and ought
not to be absolutely forbidden election to a third term. In addition, this
Amendment necessarily reduces the influence of a President during his
second term because members of Congress have less incentive to support
his policies if they know he will be retiring and cannot punish or reward
them for their actions in the next administration.

M. AMENDMENT XXIII (1961)

SECTION 1. *The District constituting the seat of Government of the United*
States shall appoint in such manner as the Congress may direct:

A number of electors of President and Vice President equal to the whole
number of Senators and Representatives in Congress to which the District

would be entitled if it were a State, but in no event more than the least populous
State; they shall be in addition to those appointed by the States, but they shall
be considered, for the purposes of the election of President and Vice President,
to be electors appointed by a State; and they shall meet in the District and per-
form such duties as provided by the twelfth article of amendment.
SECTION 2. *The Congress shall have power to enforce this article by appropriate*
legislation.

The purpose of this Amendment is to give residents of the District of Columbia the right to vote in presidential elections. Washington, D.C., receives three electoral votes under the Amendment since that is all that
"the least populous State"—Alaska—is assigned.

N. AMENDMENT XXIV (1964)

SECTION 1. *The right of citizens of the United States to vote in any primary or*
other election for President or Vice President, for electors for President or Vice
President, or for Senator or Representative in Congress, shall not be denied or
abridged by the United States or any State by reason of failure to pay any poll
tax or other tax.
SECTION 2. *The Congress shall have power to enforce this article by appropriate*
legislation.

Known as the Poll Tax Amendment, the Twenty-Fourth Amendment eliminates the poll tax in all *Federal* elections. Two years after its adoption, an
impatient Supreme Court curiously ruled in *Harper v. Virginia Board of Elec-*
tors that the Equal Protection Clause of the Fourteenth Amendment forbids a poll tax in all *State* elections.

O. AMENDMENT XXV (1967)

SECTION 1. *In case of the removal of the President from office or of his death or*
resignation, the Vice President shall become President.
SECTION 2. *Whenever there is a vacancy in the office of the Vice President, the*
President shall nominate a Vice President who shall take office upon confirma-
tion by a majority vote of both Houses of Congress.
SECTION 3. *Whenever the President transmits to the President pro tempore of*

the Senate and the Speaker of the House of Representatives his written decla-
ration that he is unable to discharge the powers and duties of his office, and un-
til he transmits to them a written declaration to the contrary, such powers and
duties shall be discharged by the Vice President as Acting President.

SECTION 4. *Whenever the Vice President and a majority of either the principal*
officers of the executive departments or of such other body as Congress may by
law provide, transmit to the President pro tempore of the Senate and the Speaker
of the House of Representatives their written declaration that the President is un-
able to discharge the powers and duties of his office, the Vice President shall im-
mediately assume the powers and duties of the office as Acting President.

Thereafter, when the President transmits to the President pro tempore of the
Senate and the Speaker of the House of Representatives his written declaration
that no inability exists, he shall resume the powers and duties of his office un-
less the Vice President and a majority of either the principal officers of the ex-
ecutive department or of such other body as Congress may by law provide,
transmit within four days to the President pro tempore of the Senate and the
Speaker of the House of Representatives their written declaration that the Presi-
dent is unable to discharge the powers and duties of his office. Thereupon Con-
gress shall decide the issue, assembling within forty-eight hours for that purpose
if not in session. If the Congress, within twenty-one days after receipt of the latter
written declaration, or, if Congress is not in session, within twenty-one days after
Congress is required to assemble, determines by two-thirds vote of both Houses
that the President is unable to discharge the powers and duties of his office, the
Vice President shall continue to discharge the same as Acting President; other-
wise, the President shall resume the powers and duties of his office.

In retrospect, it seems that the Framers of the Constitution overlooked
the problem that arises when a President is no longer able to fulfill the
duties of his office because he has become physically or mentally dis-
abled. The Twenty-Fifth Amendment attempts to resolve this problem,
which became a critical one on a number of occasions in this century. Two
Presidents—Wilson and Eisenhower—lay gravely ill while in office.
Franklin Roosevelt was apparently senile in his last days, and Ronald
Reagan was struck down by an assassin's bullet that could have left him
in a coma, as was the case when President Garfield lay unconscious for
eighty days before he died. The Twenty-Fifth Amendment also deals

with the contingency that arises when a President resigns from office—
something that had never before happened but then occurred only seven
years after the Amendment was adopted when Richard Nixon resigned
to avoid removal from office.

Most of the Amendment is self-explanatory. Section 1 provides that
the Vice President shall become President if the President dies in office,
is removed, or resigns. Section 2 provides that the President shall nominate a Vice President when there is a vacancy in the office, and that *both*
houses shall confirm the appointment. This provision was later implemented when Vice President Spiro Agnew resigned in 1973. President
Nixon then nominated Gerald Ford for Vice President, who was promptly
confirmed. When President Nixon resigned, the office of Vice President
again became vacant because Ford was elevated to the presidency. President Ford in turn nominated Nelson Rockefeller to be Vice President, who
served out Agnew's term and then died shortly after leaving office.

Section 3 states the procedures that are to be followed in the event the
President decides that he cannot discharge his responsibilities. When the
written declaration stating that he is unable to discharge his duties is
sent, the Vice President serves as Acting President until the President is
able to resume his responsibilities.

Continuing, Section 4 states the procedures that are to be followed
when the President is personally unable to inform the Congress that he can
no longer meet his responsibilities. In this instance, the Vice President becomes Acting President whenever he and a majority of the President's cabinet send a written declaration to Congress that the President is unable to
continue. If there is a disagreement between the President on the one hand
and Vice President and a cabinet majority on the other, Congress must decide whether the President is fit to resume his responsibilities. The presumption is in favor of the President, because a two-thirds vote in both
houses is required to retain the Vice President as Acting President.

P. AMENDMENT XXVI (1971)

SECTION 1. *The right of citizens of the United States, who are eighteen years of
age or older, to vote shall not be denied or abridged by the United States or by
any State on account of age.*

SECTION 2. *The Congress shall have power to enforce this article by appropriate legislation.*

Our Twenty-Sixth Amendment confers the right to vote on all persons who are eighteen years of age or older. The Amendment applies to State as well as national elections.

Q. AMENDMENT XXVII (1992)

No law, varying the compensation for the services of the Senators and Representatives, shall take effect, until an election of Representatives shall have intervened.

The Bill of Rights, as originally proposed in 1789 by the First Congress, contained twelve rather than ten amendments. The amendments were arranged by James Madison, then a member of the House of Representatives, not in order of importance or preference, but according to the order of the provisions of the Constitution they were intended to modify; for Madison's original plan, soon to be rejected by the House, was to incorporate the amendments into the constitutional text.

Roger Sherman of Connecticut, who had served with Madison as a delegate to the Philadelphia Convention, led the opposition to Madison's plan. Incorporation of the amendments, he argued, would destroy the integrity of the document, necessitating a new draft of the Constitution every time a new amendment was added. "We ought not to interweave our propositions into the work itself," he said, "because it will be destructive of the whole fabric." The basic principles of legal draftmanship applicable to statutory law, he reasoned, apply as well to the fundamental law: "when an alteration is made in an act, it is done by way of supplement." Moreover, continued Sherman, Madison's plan was not consistent with the democratic theory of the Constitution. "The Constitution is an act of the people," he reminded his colleagues, "and ought to remain entire. But amendments will be the act of the State governments." The House agreed and adopted Sherman's principle of construction. This vote set the precedent for all future exercises of the amending power.

Of the twelve amendments proposed, the first two dealt with Congress rather than with individual rights. The first, a reapportionment amendment, would have altered Article I, Section 2 by tying the size of the House of Representatives to increases in population. The amendment provided that there should be one Representative for every 30,000 people until the size of the House reached 100 members, after which there would be one Representative for every 40,000 people until the House had 200 members. Congress would then set a new ratio that allowed for no more than one representative for every 50,000 people.

The scheme was hardly realistic, however, and grossly underestimated the future growth of the nation. The population of the United States at this writing, at the turn of the century, is more than 250 million people. Had this amendment been approved, it would be necessary to increase the membership of the House of Representatives from 435 (as currently set by statute) to 5,000 members! Such a large assembly obviously could not function as a legislative body. Fortunately, the proposed Reapportionment Amendment was ratified by only ten States and thus failed to be approved by the necessary three-fourths of the States, as provided by Article V of the Constitution.

The second proposed amendment, sometimes referred to as "the Congressional Pay," "Pay Raise," "Compensation," or "Madison" Amendment, stipulated that no law changing the compensation of members of the House of Representatives and Senate could go into effect until after an election to the House had taken place. The purpose of this amendment was to force Representatives to go before the voters, and Senators before the State legislatures, and seek approval for salary increases before they went into effect. If a Representative or Senator was then elected after voting to increase his or her own salary, the increase was presumably acceptable to a majority of the electorate, and the legislator would receive the pay raise when he was returned to office. The broader purpose of the amendment, however, was to discourage the election of self-serving opportunists who might use public office for personal financial gain.

Madison's "Congressional Pay Amendment" did not fare much better than the abortive Reapportionment Amendment. By 1791, only six States had ratified the proposal, and it soon fell into obscurity. With the exception of Ohio's isolated ratification in 1873, as part of a protest against massive salary increases throughout the Federal government, and Wyoming's ratification in 1978 to protest a 1977 Congressional pay increase, Madison's proposal was virtually forgotten for nearly two centuries.

Beginning in 1982, an extraordinary series of events revived public interest in the moribund amendment, largely because of the diligence and perseverance of a young college student. While looking for a research topic, Gregory D. Watson, an undergraduate economics major at the University of Texas at Austin, stumbled upon the Congressional Pay Amendment. He discovered that the two unratified proposals in the original Bill of Rights contained no internal time limits for ratification, and concluded not only that the Congressional Pay Amendment was a worthy proposal, but that it was also still viable. In his research paper, he described the origin, meaning, and history of the Amendment, and argued in favor of its adoption. Theoretically, he reasoned, a proposed amendment remains valid for ratification indefinitely, unless Congress has placed a time limit upon it.

But Watson's college instructor was unpersuaded. He gave Watson a grade of C on his paper, informing him that the Amendment was defunct and would never become a part of the Constitution. Ten years later, Watson proved his teacher wrong, as well as members of Congress, legal scholars, and historians, when the Archivist of the United States certified in 1992, after the thirty-eighth State (Michigan) had approved the measure, that the Congressional Pay Amendment had been duly ratified by three-fourths of the States. Originally the second amendment, it was now officially declared to be the Twenty-Seventh Amendment to the Constitution.

Watson's personal triumph was unparalleled in the history of the amendment process, for the ratification of this Amendment was mainly the result of one individual's prophetic vision, indomitable spirit, and hard labor. After leaving the University, Gregory Watson became an aide in the Texas legislature. During his free time he waged a lonely ten-year battle to generate support for the Amendment. Truly a one-man lobbying firm, Watson encouraged State legislators throughout the Union to support the Amendment. One by one, first Maine in 1983, then Colorado in 1984, the States rallied to the cause.

No doubt much of Watson's success may be attributed to increasing

Father of the Twenty-Seventh Amendment.

Gregory D. Watson, Administrative Assistant, Texas House of Representatives, in front of the Texas State Capitol in Austin, Texas.

public resentment at this time against various legislative devices Congress had concocted to enable members to raise their own salaries without registering a vote. One such device was the creation in 1967 of the President's Commission on Executive, Legislative, and Judicial Salaries. The Commission's recommendations would take effect automatically unless members of Congress registered a negative vote. Thus by merely doing nothing Federal legislators routinely enjoyed generous salary increases. The Twenty-Seventh Amendment put an end to this charade, and members of Congress are now held accountable for their salary increases.

Conclusion

At the close of the twentieth century, American society is very different from what it was at the close of the eighteenth century. Yet the Constitution ratified in 1788 still functions vigorously enough in a nation vastly increased in territory and population, vastly altered in its economy and technology. It seems worthwhile to take inventory of the Constitution's enduring advantages.

(1) The Federal Union, held together by the Constitution, makes the United States the greatest power in the world, well prepared for national defense, able to muster immense resources in time of need, virtually invulnerable to attack until the development of long-distance nuclear weapons.

(2) The huge internal free-trade area of the United States, and the constitutional protections afforded to private property, commerce, and industry, have produced remarkable and enduring material prosperity—all directly related to the organic law of the United States, the Constitution.

(3) The division of political powers and functions between Federal and State governments gives the country energetic national policy, and yet leaves many important concerns in the hands of States and localities.

(4) An elaborate system of courts of law, both Federal and State, keeps the peace for Americans and maintains the rule of law far better than in most of the rest of the world.

(5) Civil rights for all citizens are jealously guarded by the Constitution, and effective measures are taken to make sure that no one will suffer

solely because of his race, sex, or religion. In no country does there exist a higher degree of personal freedom.

(6) Participation in public affairs and decision-making is open to everyone interested, through the constitutional institutions of representative government. From local school boards and township offices to the Congress and the presidency, it is possible for an American to make his opinions known and his vote sought.

(7) No person, however rich or well known, exerts arbitrary power in America. Checks upon power, and balances of power, still function in the national and the State governments. Nor does any class or social group enjoy special privileges at law.

(8) Individual freedom of choice in many things, personal privacy, and opportunity for success in many walks of life are made possible by a political system that takes heed of the dignity of the human person and looks upon the state as designed for the advancement and protection of that person.

(9) Freedom of religious belief and practice is secure in the United States, and fanatic ideologies have not thrust aside the American habit of thinking for one's self.

(10) Freedom of speech and of the press and other media of communication are virtually unlimited; opportunities for education, training, and self-improvement are greater than in any other country.

All these ten large advantages, and a good many more, are bound up with our constitutional system and the customs and traditions that have been nurtured by the Constitution. But also the Constitution of the United States encounters real difficulties nowadays. Can it endure for another two centuries? Listed below are some of the problems that must be confronted by Americans who know that liberty, order, and justice do not endure if they are left unattended.

(1) Any political order, including that of the United States, rests upon a moral order—a body of common convictions about good and evil, about duties and rights. The Constitution was drawn up by men who shared certain realistic and healthy assumptions about human nature and society. But nowadays in this country, as generally in the modern world, signs of widespread moral decay are obvious enough. Good laws are not upheld by corrupt men and women. The Framers of the Constitution spoke often

of *virtue,* meaning by that word both personal courage and integrity, and
a general willingness to sacrifice one's own interests, if need be, for the
common good. Are the American people, most of them, still aware of
moral obligations and prepared to uphold the Constitution in an hour of
need?

(2) The Congress and the State legislatures often seem to be lacking
in able leadership, frequently timid, and too easily influenced by pressure groups and special interests. Too few Senators and Representatives
take long views. Too many look upon politics merely as a means to personal advancement. The American democracy cannot endure a great
while without a leadership that retains some aristocratic qualities—
particularly a sense of honor, of duty, and of country.

(3) More and more power is concentrated in the legislative and executive branches of the Federal government. Congress, with an immense new
bureaucracy of its own, continues to create new executive departments
and regulatory agencies and appropriate increasingly huge amounts of
money for thousands of Federal programs. Matters previously subject to
the jurisdiction of the States, in ever increasing degrees, are pulled into the
orbit of Congressional supremacy, often by an unrestricted use of the commerce power, the welfare and spending power, and the enforcement
powers of the Fourteenth and Fifteenth amendments. The administrative
details, requiring the constant exercise of discretion and broad decision-
making authority, are then turned over to a massive Federal bureaucracy.
Congress has so many programs, infinitely complex, varied, and demanding, that the members are no longer able to debate the measures they propose in an intelligent and thorough manner.

The executive department also grows larger, and the powers of the
President expand as new agencies and programs are added by Congress.
Immense new responsibilities around the world greatly amplify the President's diplomatic and military powers. Many major public decisions are
actually made by the President's army of advisors and personal staff—a
body of persons whose names are virtually unknown outside of the White
House. The people expect more and more of the President; but any man,
however able, has but twenty-four hours in his day, and is not infallible.

(4) With each passing term, the Supreme Court and lower Federal
courts handle more and more cases and resolve more and more disputes

that were once considered to be within the exclusive domain of the State judiciaries. Both Federal and State courts are immensely overburdened by their case loads, principally because they have more laws to interpret. More judges are also willing to take cases that augment the judicial power. Months, often years, go by before cases are settled; and truly justice delayed is justice denied.

Americans, it is feared, have become a litigious people, always filing lawsuits—many of them seeking to extract material advantages from wealthy individuals and corporations. Judges are made arrogant by the power that they have themselves amassed or has been thrust into their hands by legislatures. Some, instead of exercising self-restraint and confining their duties to the interpretation of the law, stretch the meaning of words in order to reach desired results, becoming law- and policy-makers. And jurisprudence—the philosophy and history of law—is neglected in nearly all the law schools. When the legal system decays, however, the organic law called the Constitution becomes infected, threatening the life of the nation.

(5) The fifty States of the Union have given up to Washington many of their proper responsibilities, and frequently look to that national capital for direction. For many of their functions they have become dependent upon funds from the national treasury. If this decay of State and local energy and resources and imagination continues much longer, America will cease to have a federal system of government except in name, and instead will have stumbled into a centralized structure in which the States have been converted into obedient provinces. But the United States is too big in extent and too populous for a centralized political system to function tolerably well. The American democracy, too, has its roots in local and State government. Under large-scale centralization, real democracy would wither.

(6) America's cities, nearly all of them, have decayed in all respects over the past half-century. Most Americans cannot remember a time when "inner cities" were good places to live. Jefferson feared that cities would be to the Republic what sores are to the body. We seem to be justifying his fears at the end of the twentieth century. The word *civilization* is derived from the Latin word for city; and a country in which cities become dreary and crime-ridden presently ceases to have a decent civilization. The most

fundamental of civil rights is the right to walk the streets in safety. If the cities become places of ugliness, drug abuse, and terror, is not talk about extending the rights of the accused absurd?

(7) Over the past half-century there has grown in the United States, with alarming speed, that class of people the old Romans (and the modern Marxists) called a *proletariat*: that is, people who perform no duties, give nothing to the community but their children, and exist at public expense. America's leading men of 1787 saw a good many people who were poor enough, but they did not have to deal with a true proletariat. Such a class, apathetic but potentially dangerous, has been produced, ironically enough, by America's technological and economic triumph. The hope of the Framers of the Constitution was that a vigorous and conscientious American people would cherish and refresh that Constitution. A nation of proletarians would require a very different sort of constitution, far less free. Has America today sufficient imagination and intelligence to redeem "the lonely crowd" from proletarian life?

(8) The generation of Americans that framed the Constitution were humanely schooled in classical literature and English literature, history, the sciences of the time, political theory, and religion. It was understood in the early republic that a principal aim of formal education was the building of good character. But today's public instruction neglects moral knowledge, actually forbids religious teaching, reduces historical studies to a minimum, discards great books in favor of "current awareness," and shrinks from the task of forming a philosophical habit of mind. From kindergarten up through graduate school, American education nowadays is weighed in the balance and found wanting, by official commissions and foundations' studies. Study of the Constitution, for one thing, has been shabbily neglected in the typical school, public or private. A people whose schooling has been reduced to a vague familiarity with current events or the mastering of money-making skills may not understand how to keep a good constitution, or even understand its benefits. Can our democratic republic survive if our educational system fails to encourage such values as an informed and virtuous citizenry and an understanding and appreciation of the American constitutional system?

(9) A grim destructive power in the modern world is *ideology*, or political fanaticism, bent upon the destruction of all existing political, social,

and economic institutions and venerable traditions and beliefs. Whether Communist, or Nazi, or ferocious revolutionary of some other persuasion, the ideologue always has a master plan or utopian scheme, based on "scientific" reasoning, to remake the world. He detests constitutional order and aspires to erect a domination of his own party upon the ruins of "bourgeois culture" or "reactionary imperialist powers"—the United States in particular. Ideology is what Edmund Burke called "armed doctrine"—false ideas promoted by weapons.

The Framers of the Constitution were no ideologues, but realistic men keenly aware of the lessons of the past and the limitations of human nature. The political structure they put together was quite free of ideological illusions. Have the Americans of our era enough sound sense to detect the fallacies in such an ideology as Marxism? Would they, like the Americans of 1776, venture their lives, their fortunes, and their sacred honor in defense of their inheritance of liberty, order, and justice? Hard choices lie ahead, even into the twenty-first century.

(10) To sustain a good constitutional order, it is necessary for many people in a society to participate intelligently and voluntarily, with real energy, often at expense to themselves, in public affairs at every level. The Framers took for granted this price that must be paid for the preservation of the commonwealth. What proportion of the American population today takes any active part in practical politics—counting as political activity any action beyond the mere act of voting? Making a small contribution to a campaign fund, attending a local political meeting, giving a friend a ride to an election booth—all of these acts count toward being politically active.

Well, what percentage of registered voters are politically active? In California, the state with the highest level of political activity, about five percent are politically active.

Americans generally have not been political fanatics, and one hopes that they may never be. But to preserve and renew America's constitutional order, more than five percent of the American people must take some interest in the Constitution of the United States, and make at least some gesture toward active participation in public responsibilities.

The preceding ten problems of American society have been outlined succinctly not to dishearten young men and women, but to suggest the ways in which all of us can help to keep American life worth living. The recognition of difficulties ought not to make us despair.

For the American republic is only two centuries old—young for a nation. The old Roman civilization endured for a thousand years; the Byzantine civilization, centered at Constantinople, for another thousand. English civilization is nine centuries old, at least; Italian and French and Spanish and Germanic civilization, older still.

So there is good reason to expect that the American Republic will endure for many more centuries—supposing enough of us are willing to confront our national difficulties and work intelligently at renewal of our civilization. In Shakespeare's line, we must "take arms against a sea of troubles, and by opposing end them."

How do we commence this work of renewal and reinvigoration? One of the better ways is to light what Patrick Henry called "the lamp of experience," to peer into the future by the light of the past. America's political past is best apprehended by tracing the development of the Constitution of the United States, from its roots in the ancient world and British institutions, all the way to the constitutional controversies that are so lively today.

What we have offered you in this book is the basic structure of America's constitutional order. It is up to you to preserve and improve that structure; and you have a lifetime in which to work at it.

SUGGESTED READING

American Bar Association, *Amendment of the Constitution by the Convention Method Under Article V* (Chicago: ABA, 1974).

Herman V. Ames, *Proposed Amendments to the Constitution of the United States During the First Century of Its History* (New York: Burt Franklin, 1970).

Richard Bernstein, with Jerome Agel, *Amending America* (New York: Random House, 1993).

Judith Best, *The Case Against Direct Election of the President: A Defense of the Electoral College* (Ithaca, N.Y.: Cornell University Press, 1971).

Russell L. Caplan, *Constitutional Brinkmanship: Amending the Constitution by National Convention* (New York: Oxford University Press, 1988).

Edward S. Corwin, *The Constitution and What It Means Today* (Princeton: Princeton University Press, 1978).

Walter Fairleigh Dodd, *The Revision and Amendment of State Constitutions* (Baltimore: Johns Hopkins University Press, 1910).

Orrin G. Hatch, *The Equal Rights Amendment: Myth and Reality* (Provo, Utah: Savant Press, 1983).

Roger Sherman Hoar, *Constitutional Conventions: Their Natural Powers and Limitations* (Boston: Little, Brown, 1919).

John A. Jamerson, *A Treatise on Constitutional Conventions: Their History, Powers and Modes of Proceeding* (New York: Da Capo Press, 1972).

David E. Kyvig, *Explicit and Authentic Acts: Amending the U.S. Constitution, 1776–1995* (Lawrence: University Press of Kansas, 1997).

Lester Bernhardt Orfield, *The Amending of the Federal Constitution* (Ann Arbor: University of Michigan Press, 1942).

Paul J. Weber and Barbara A. Perry, *Unfounded Fears: Myths and Realities of a Constitutional Convention* (New York: Praeger, 1989).

Palatino was designed in 1948 by Hermann Zapf, a prolific type designer and notable writer on type. Palatino Roman was first cut by hand and cast in metal at the Stempel Foundry, then adapted by Zapf for the Linotype machine. Palatino is based on Renaissance forms and is a superbly balanced, powerful, and graceful font.

This book is printed on paper that is acid-free and meets the requirements of the American National Standard for Permanence of Paper for Printed Library Materials, z39.48-1992. ∞

Book design by Louise OFarrell,
Gainesville, Florida

Typography by Impressions Book and Journal Services, Inc.,
Madison, Wisconsin

Printed and bound by Worzalla Publishing Company,
Stevens Point, Wisconsin